THE HARE KRISHNA MOVEMENT

The
Hare Krishna
Movement

THE POSTCHARISMATIC FATE
OF A RELIGIOUS TRANSPLANT

EDITED BY

Edwin F. Bryant and Maria L. Ekstrand

COLUMBIA UNIVERSITY PRESS
NEW YORK

Columbia University Press
Publishers Since 1893
New York Chichester, West Sussex
Copyright © 2004 Columbia University Press
All rights reserved
Library of Congress Cataloging-in-Publication Data
The Hare Krishna movement : the postcharismatic fate of a religious
transplant / edited by Edwin F. Bryant and Maria L. Ekstrand.
p. cm.
Includes bibliographical references and index.
ISBN 0–231–12256–X (cloth)
1. International Society for Krishna Consciousness—History. I. Bryant,
Edwin. II. Ekstrand, Maria.
BL1285.83.H37 2004
294.5'512—dc22 2003055557

Columbia University Press books are printed on permanent
and durable acid-free paper.
Printed in the United States of America
c 10 9 8 7 6 5 4 3 2 1

Designed by Lisa Hamm

CONTENTS

PART 6   Reevaluations 391

CONTRIBUTORS

ANUTTAMA DAS ADHIKARI is the current Director of Communications for ISKCON and was appointed to the Governing Body Commission in 1999. He is editor of the *Hare Krishna Report*, a bimonthly media newsletter. He is a trustee of the ISKCON Foundation and a board member of Children of Krishna. He is the president of the Washington, DC chapter of the Religion Communicator's Council and a member of that interfaith group's national Board of Governors.

SUNIL AWATRAMANI (ADRIDHARAN DAS) was until recently the president of ISKCON Calcutta and is now chairman of the ISKCON Reform Movement (IRM). He is co-author of *The Final Order* (available online at <http://www.iskconirm.com/tfo.htm>) and *No Change in ISKCON* (available online at <http://www.iskconirm.com/no_change_in_iskcon.paradigm.htm>).

GUY L. BECK received his Ph.D. in South Asian religion and his M.A. in musicology from Syracuse University and is currently an assistant professor at Tulane University in New Orleans. He is the author of *Sonic Theology: Hinduism and Sacred Sound* (University of South Carolina Press, 1993) and performs on his CD, *Sacred Raga*.

SWAMI BHAKTI BHAVANA VISHNU is the "*co-acharya*" of Shri Narasingha Chaitanya Matha, a Gaudiya Vaishnava mission headquartered in Shri Rangapatna, Karnataka. He is the author of numerous articles and the book *Our Affectionate Guardians: A Historical Perspective* (New Delhi: Gaudiya Vaishnava Society, 1996; available online at <http://www.gosai.com/tattva/>).

EDWIN F. BRYANT received his Ph.D. in Indology from Columbia University in 1997 and is currently an associate professor at Rutgers University, where he teaches Hinduism. His publications include *The Quest for the Origins of Vedic Culture: The Indo-Aryan Migration Debate* (New York: Oxford University Press, 2001) and *Krishna, the Beautiful Legend of God: Srimad Bhagavatam Purana Book X* (London: Penguin, 2003); he is the editor of the forthcoming

Sources of the Krishna Tradition (New York: Oxford University Press, forthcoming).

JAN BRZEZINSKI has a Ph.D. in Sanskrit from the University of London (SOAS). His most recent publication is *Mystic Poetry*, a translation of Rupa Goswami's messenger poems, *Hamsaduta* and *Uddhava-sandesa* (San Francisco: Mandala Media, 1999). He works as a Sanskrit translator in Laval, Quebec.

IRVIN H. COLLINS received a B.A. in sociology and psychology from the University of California-Berkeley in 1999. He was a full-time member of ISKCON for two decades and is now associated with the organization of Narayana Maharaja. He currently works as an elementary school teacher in the San Francisco Bay area.

GABRIEL DEADWYLER (YUDHISTHIRA DAS) was born in ISKCON and attended *gurukulas* in Dallas, Pennsylvania, and Vrindavan. He holds an undergraduate degree in Diplomatic History from the University of Pennsylvania and is currently pursuing further studies in music and intellectual history.

WILLIAM H. DEADWYLER (RAVINDRA SVARUPA DAS) received his Ph.D. in religion from Temple University. He has been a member of ISKCON's Governing Body Commission since 1987 and is the president of ISKCON Philadelphia and an initiating guru. He has written extensively on Vaishnava philosophy and ISKCON reform and is the author of *Encounter with the Lord of the Universe: Collected Essays 1978–1983* (Washington, DC: Gita Nagari Press, 1984).

NEAL DELMONICO received his Ph.D. in South Asian Languages and Civilizations from the University of Chicago in 1990. He has taught in the Religious Studies Program at Iowa State University and in philosophy and religious studies at Truman State University. He is the author of *First Steps in Vedanta* (New york: FID Global Scholarly Publications, 2003) and is collaborating on an online text repository for Sanskrit and Bengali texts at <www:granthamandira.org>.

MARIA L. EKSTRAND received her Ph.D. in clinical psychology from Auburn University in 1986. She has counseled devotees for more than twenty years and has been active in ISKCON's child protection efforts. She currently is assistant professor in the Department of Medicine at the University of California, San Francisco, conducting AIDS prevention studies, primarily in Mumbai and Bangalore, India, and teaching at the School of Public Health at UC Berkeley.

STEVEN J. GELBERG has an M.A. in comparative religion from Harvard. He was a staff writer for the Bhaktivedanta Book Trust, the publishing arm of ISKCON. He is the author of *Hare Krishna, Hare Krishna: Five Distinguished Scholars on the Krishna Movement in the West* (New York: Grove Press, 1983).

MICHAEL GRANT (MUKUNDA GOSWAMI) joined ISKCON in 1966 and served on the Governing Body Commission from 1984 to 1999 as the ISKCON Minister of Communication. He accepted the renounced order of *sannyasa* in 1982. He is the author of *Coming Back: The Science of Reincarnation* (Los Angeles: Bhaktivedanta Book Trust, 1982) and the co-author of *Divine Nature* (Los Angeles: Bhaktivedanta Book Trust, 1995) and *Inside the Hare Krishna Movement* (Badger, CA: Torchlight, 2001).

THOMAS HERZIG (TAMAL KRISHNA GOSWAMI) joined ISKCON in 1968 and served on its Governing Body Commission from its inception in 1970 until his death in March 2002. He accepted the renounced order of *sannyasa*, and at the time of his death, he was enrolled in the doctoral studies program at Cambridge University, England. His publications include *Reason and Belief: Problem Solving in the Philosophy of Religion* (Dallas: Pundits Press, 1997); *Science of Yoga: The Story of Li Kuang Shi* (Los Angeles, California: Bhaktivedanta Book Trust, 1989); *Prabhupada Antya-lila: The Final Pastimes of Srila Prabhupada* (Washington, DC: Institute for Vaishnava Studies, 1998); *Jagannatha-Priya Natakam: The Drama of Lord Jagannatha* (Cambridge, MA: Bhaktivedanta Institute of Religion and Culture, 1985); and *Servant of the Servant* (Los Angeles: Bhaktivedanta Book Trust, 1984).

CONRAD JOSEPH (KUNDALI DAS) was affiliated with ISKCON for twenty-three years before severing ties with its management structure in 1996. He has written numerous books on the social dynamics of ISKCON, including the four-volume series *Our Mission*, published by Abhaya (New Delhi: Rakha Printers Pvt. Ltd., 1997 [part 2], 1999 [part 3]). Available online at <http://saragrahi.org/kundalidasa/index.htm>.

KIM KNOTT is a professor of religious studies at the University of Leeds, England. She is the author of *My Sweet Lord: The Hare Krishna Movement* (San Bernardino, CA: Borgo Press, 1990) and *Hinduism: A Very Short Introduction* (New York: Oxford University Press, 1998). She has published extensively on questions of religion and identity among religious minorities and the relationship of religion and ethnicity in Britain.

KRISHNAKANT DESAI received his B.A. and M.A. from Cambridge University, where he studied computer science. He serves as full-time advisor to the ISKCON Reform Movement and is a member of its executive committee. He is the primary author of the tract *The Final Order* (available online at <http://www.iskconirm.com/tfo.htm>) and *False Dawn of Guru Reform* (available online at <http://www.iskconirm.com/False_Dawn.htm>).

EKKEHARD LORENZ is a student of Indology with focus on medieval and ancient Sanskrit at the Institute for Oriental Languages at the University of Stockholm, Sweden. He was an editorial advisor at ISKCON's North European Bhaktivedanta Book Trust (BBT), specializing in assisting BBT translators in understanding Bhaktivedanta Swami's English translations of original Sanskrit texts.

MADHU PANDIT DAS is the president of ISKCON Bangalore, which is the world headquarters of the ISKCON Reform Movement (IRM). He is secretary of the IRM and co-author of *The Final Order* (available online at <http://www.iskconirm.com/tfo.htm>) and *No Change in ISKCON* (available online at <http://www.iskconirm.com/no_change_in_iskcon.paradigm.htm>).

NORI J. MUSTER received an M.S. in interdisciplinary studies from Western Oregon State College in 1992 and is the author of *Betrayal of the Spirit* (Urbana: University of Illinois Press, 1997). She worked as associate editor of the *ISKCON World Review*, the movement's in-house newspaper, from 1981 to 1989.

HOWARD RESNICK (HRIDAYANANDA DAS GOSWAMI) joined ISKCON in 1969 and received the renounced order of *sannyasa* in 1972. He received his Ph.D. in Sanskrit and Indian studies from Harvard University in 1997. He is the author of numerous studies on Vaishnava philosophy and is currently translating the *Mahabharata* epic. He has been a member of ISKCON's Governing Body Commission since 1972.

E. BURKE ROCHFORD JR. is a professor of sociology and religion at Middlebury College in Vermont. He has been studying the Hare Krishna movement for more than twenty-five years. In addition to his book *Hare Krishna in America* (New Brunswick: Rutgers University Press, 1985), he has published numerous articles and book chapters on the movement.

STEVEN J. ROSEN (SATYARAJA DAS) is the author of fifteen books on East Indian spirituality, including two hagiographic volumes on Shri Chaitanya. His most recent books are *Gita on the Green: The Mystical Tradition Behind Bagger Vance* (Continuum International, 2001) and *Holy War: Violence and the Bhagavad Gita* (Deepak Heritage Books, 2002). He is the senior editor of *The Journal of Vaishnava Studies* and is co-editing *The Encyclopedia of Hinduism*, an eighteen-volume compendium of Indian thought.

GRAHAM M. SCHWEIG earned his Ph.D. in comparative religion from Harvard in 1998. He is currently Associate Professor of Religious Studies, Department of Philosophy and Religious Studies, Christopher Newport University, Virginia. Schweig is an editor of *The Journal of Vaishnava Studies* and the author of two forthcoming books, *The Bhakti Sutra: Concise Teachings of Nara-*

da on the Nature of Devotional Love and *Dance of Divine Love: The Rasa Lila of Krishna and the Cowherd Maidens of Vraj from the* Bhagavata Purana (Princeton, forthcoming) and *The* Bhakti Sutra: *Concise Teachings of Narada on Devotional Love* (Columbia, forthcoming).

PAUL H. SHERBOW served as Bhaktivedanta Swami's senior Sanskrit editor from 1968 to 1977, assisting in the production of his translations of the *Bhagavata Purana, Chaitanya Charitamrita*, and other works published by the Bhaktivedanta Book Trust. He studied Sanskrit at Ohio State University (1968–69) and Harvard University (1970–71). He holds a B.A. in Middle Eastern Studies from Columbia University (1991).

LARRY D. SHINN is president of Berea College, Kentucky. He received his Ph.D. in the history of religion from Princeton University in 1972. He is the author of *Dark Lord: Cult Images and the Hare Krishnas in America* (Philadelphia: Westminster Press, 1987).

SHUKAVAK N. DASA was a disciple of Bhaktivedanta Swami and is the founder of the Sanskrit Religions Institute (SRI). He received his Ph.D. from the University of Chicago and is the author of *Hindu Encounter with Modernity: Kedarnath Datta Bhaktivinoda, Vaisnava Theologian* (Los Angeles: SRI, 1997).

KENNETH VALPEY (KRISHNA KSHETRA DAS) holds a Ph.D. from the University of Oxford and is a researcher at the Oxford Centre for Vaishnava and Hindu Studies. As a member of ISKCON since 1972, he participates in the society's development in central Europe and pursues research in Chaitanya Vaishnava temple worship traditions.

DAVID WOLF holds a Ph.D. in social work from Florida State University. He has published a book, *Krsna, Israel, and the Druze—An Interreligious Odyssey* (Badger, CA: Torchlight, 2003), and several articles on Vedic mental health and social sciences. Dr. Wolf serves as a Social Work Services Program Consultant for the State of Florida Department of Health, and as director of the Association for the Protection of Vaishnava Children, an international child protection organization affiliated with ISKCON.

FOREWORD

C AN A CONSERVATIVE, devotional (*bhakti*) Hindu religious tradition from India successfully transplant its faith and culture in America and the West? If so, who will be its converts and leaders? How much accommodation must it make to be successful in its new cultural locations? Simply put, can a truly faithful Hindu devotional missionary movement ever be more than a marginalized minority institution in America and other western societies? These are some of the large questions facing the Hare Krishnas (formally known as the International Society for Krishna Consciousness or ISKCON) in their fourth decade in America, and it is questions like these that provide the subtext and undercurrent of analysis in the essays of this remarkable volume. Furthermore, the variety of voices that the editors have included provides diverse answers.

It is common for scholars to write about religious traditions that are not their own and to bring various disciplinary perspectives to bear in analyzing such groups as the Hare Krishnas. My religious studies approach to ISKCON in America, *The Dark Lord: Cult Images and the Hare Krishnas in America* (1987), is one example, and Malory Nye's recent sociological analysis of ISKCON in Britain, *Multiculturalism and Minority Religions in Britain: Krishna Consciousness, Religious Freedom, and the Politics of Location* (2001), is another. It is also not uncommon for a disillusioned former Krishna devotee to do an exposé or "former insider's story" on ISKCON that does not pretend to be scholarly but does have the benefit of lived experiences that tell an important part of the society's story. An example is Nori J. Muster's *Betrayal of the Spirit: My Life Behind the Headlines of the Hare Krishna Movement* (1997, 2001). Then, of course, there are the current "insiders" who remain committed to its faith and ideals and who are grappling with the numerous institutional and developmental challenges of a thirty-seven-year-old missionary movement in the West, while seeking their salvation and life's meaning from their devotion to Krishna. Current ISKCON publications like *Back to Godhead* and the numerous translated books of the founder A.C. Bhaktivedanta Swami Prabhupada are but a few examples of insider accounts. The genius of this collection of essays is that it includes all three kinds of voices.

Many scholars of the Hare Krishnas in its early years dealt with ISKCON as a New Religious Movement (NRM), and critics saw it as a dangerous cult. The 1960s and 1970s in America were days of heightened religious ferment and experimentation. Indian gurus like Rajneesh or Guru Maharaj-ji brought watered-down versions of their Indian faiths, engaged in practices that got them expelled from their own Indian ashrams, and attracted much negative attention in their new home in America. The Moonies, the Scientologists, The [Christian] Family, and other such groups helped spawn the anticult and deprogramming industries and galvanized much of the media and public opinion in America against marginal and "foreign" evangelical religious groups. It was during the anti-Vietnam War and countercultural days in the mid-1960s that a sixty-nine-year-old Indian guru named A.C. Bhaktivedanta Swami Prabhupada attempted to transmit to American youth his very traditional, devotional Krishna faith. His missionary movement derived its basic form from the sixteenth-century revitalization movement of Chaitanya in Bengal and its contemporary missionary expression from Prabhupada's Indian guru, Swami Bhaktisiddhanta. Certainly not a "new" religious movement or cult, ISKCON is better described as a devotional Hindu missionary movement from India, transmitted to America when Prabhupada arrived in New York City in the fall of 1965, bringing his pious faith in Krishna to a western world that was "absorbed in material life." I made this distinction in my 1987 book.

One of the continuing attractions of ISKCON is its ancient Sanskrit texts and traditional yet lively religious practice. Its guru could trace his lineage back to Krishna himself, and the Sanskrit texts that were read, translated, and expounded upon represented an Asian "wisdom tradition" for many young American converts who sought to escape the material life in which they had been raised. Yet the world around them lumped their "new" religion with all of the other "cults" of the day and provided a hostile context for their effort to practice their "ancient" faith. As you read the essays in this book, be aware of the tension in ISKCON between insiders' claims that they are recipients of an ancient faith and that they represent the vanguard of a new Vedic cultural community on foreign soil. As with many missionary movements around the world, ISKCON has had enthusiastic converts who encountered hostile and defensive native traditions and cultural assumptions. It has never been left to ISKCON alone to determine the full range of issues and challenges it must address or the cultural norms and traditions to which it must adjust. Such issues of accommodation in a new culture have always been foremost in determining whether or not a new missionary movement succeeds. And even when such movements succeed, they often remain marginalized minority religious traditions. This has been the case with ISKCON in the West.

It can be argued that it was precisely because Prabhupada's devotional Hindu tradition was faithful to its Indian and Hindu roots that it has had difficulties accommodating itself to America and the West. Numerous tensions that have arisen throughout ISKCON's four-decade history here can be attributed, at least in part, to its Indianness, its Hinduness, and its adherence to its Krishna devotional (*bhakti*) roots in Chaitanya's Bengali reform movement. These three factors are intertwined as they represent ever-tighter circles of meaning and behavior. On the most general level, ISKCON's Indian assumptions of time, space, and material existence are in tension with competing western assumptions. In the West, religious conceptions of time and space are linear (i.e., both natural and personal histories have a single beginning and an end) and teleological (i.e., have a divine purpose and end). Time and space in India are viewed as cyclical (*samsara*), devolve over time (four *yugas*), and then repeat another cycle. In western religions, the individual has one lifetime on earth and then either ceases to exist or spends eternity in an afterlife in heaven or hell (viewed differently by various traditions of Judaism, Christianity, and Islam). In Indian religions, individuals are born and reborn in life after life (popularly called reincarnation) according to their birth duties (*dharma*) and deeds (*karma*). Thus ISKCON (as well as Buddhism and other Indian religions) brought an alternative Indian worldview to America and the West that confronted basic assumptions about time, the self, and material existence.

A second tension ISKCON has had with its new western home is its Hindu assumptions and religious institutions. For example, complete submission to the guru as the living representative of God, the channel of salvation, and the supreme authority is very understandable in Hindu traditions, but not comfortable for many westerners, who usually assume that an individual's independence applies to his or her own reason in the exercise of his or her faith. Likewise, the Hindu emphasis on liberation from additional rebirths (*moksha*) stands in strong contrast to western notions of the afterlife as the reward of a lifetime's faithfulness. In addition, Hindu notions of world renunciation make little sense in a materialistic western world that is created by God and is "good." Very tellingly, ISKCON's promotion of "Vedic Culture" as a religious social model led to monastic (and pejorative) views of women, laity, and worldly life that stood at odds, for the most part, with American and western religious traditions. Those Hindu gurus like Maharish Mahesh Yogi (of Transcendental Meditation fame) who adapted quickly to western norms and values were much less threatening, but also tended to be absorbed into "New Age" culture. Prabhupada's Indian and Hindu assumptions were not set aside when he came to America in 1965, but rather were fully a part of his devotion to Krishna, the third source of tension with the traditions of his new home.

Perhaps Prabhupada's piousness centering upon his deep faith in Krishna was both his greatest strength and the source of ISKCON's most consistent tension in America. As an *acharya* or teacher of the Krishna scriptures and devotional faith, Prabhupada was a "holy man," a guru whose translations of the Sanskrit scripture of the *Bhagavata Purana*, the *Bhagavad Gita*, and of Chaitanya's teachings were the center of his own devotional life and of his education of his new American devotees. His insistence on the infallibility of the Krishna scriptures and his interpretation of them continues to be a source of unrest within ISKCON, and certainly between ISKCON and its surrounding culture. Likewise, the particular form of Krishna worship that was spawned by Chaitanya in the sixteenth century included public chanting and dancing (*sankirtana*), worship (*puja*) before images (*archa*) of Krishna or his "perfect devotees," and devotional repetition of Krishna's name (*nama japa*). These religious practices that are so faithful to Chaitanya's sixteenth-century Krishna faith (and, therefore, quite traditional in India) have also been the source of much conflict with western religious sensibilities and practices.

In one respect, it was the authenticity of Prabhupada's Krishna faith and practice that enticed new converts to ISKCON and also caused the society to stand out in contrast, and even opposition, to western religious and cultural values. It is therefore not surprising that a devotional Krishna tradition from India that adhered closely to literal interpretations of Hindu scriptures by a guru whose views were not to be questioned had difficulty adapting to an American context where religious fundamentalism of any kind is often viewed as archaic and/or uneducated behavior. Likewise, it is not surprising that a Hindu religious tradition that imported Indian views of the subordination of women to men came into conflict with a more egalitarian American culture. Finally, a devotional Hindu tradition that taught all devotees that their salvation was dependent upon themselves and the guru who guided them of course had difficulty maintaining its cohesive center when that spiritual leader died in 1977.

In the pages of this volume and in the diverse voices it presents, the reader will find echoes of the above tensions I have briefly outlined. Certainly, ISKCON shares with all missionary movements the challenges that arise in establishing an ongoing institutional form. Likewise, certain excesses of behavior mark the enthusiastic adoption of a new faith when previous ethical norms are abandoned and new ones have not yet been fully appropriated. Still, I wonder if the very Indianness, Hinduness, and foreignness of Chaitanya's public devotional displays have engendered the fundamental tensions between ISKCON and its adopted culture in the West—and will ultimately ensure its continuation as a marginal but accepted religious tradition in America. ISKCON's authenticity as a devotional Hindu tradition has led many devotees to find a satisfying religious path where they least expected it. Such devotees of Krishna continue their spiritual quest in ISKCON in spite of its institutional crises, and have attracted immigrant Indian Hindus in America and the West to Krishna temples in such diverse cities as Los Angeles, Dallas, Philadelphia, and London. And such "dancing white elephants" from America and Europe conduct daily worship (*puja*) for thousands of native Indian devotees of Krishna in Bombay, Vrindavan, and Mayapur, India. As you listen to the different voices in this volume, listen also for the continuity of centuries of Indian devotion to Krishna that has offended some, attracted some, and become the path to salvation for others. For many in the West and in India, Prabhupada's pious devotion to Krishna lives on in their imperfect devotional lives. That too is Prabhupada's legacy that frames the diverse perspectives presented here.

Dr. Larry D. Shinn
Berea College
April 2, 2002

THE HARE KRISHNA MOVEMENT

INTRODUCTION

EDWIN F. BRYANT AND MARIA L. EKSTRAND

THE HARE KRISHNA MOVEMENT, registered as the International Society for Krishna Consciousness (ISKCON), was the most visible face of the eastern religions exported to the West during the 1960s and 1970s, and did much to define popular representations of Hinduism during that period. Although less visible nowadays in the West than in their heyday, Krishna devotees with their shaved heads and saffron robes are still seen chanting and dancing in many urban centers all over the world. This volume traces the theology, history, and social legacy of the Krishna Consciousness movement, with attention to its postcharismatic phase in the West—the period since its founder passed away almost a quarter of a century ago—a time of particularly dramatic and consequential turmoil.

The Hare Krishna movement is a branch of what is traditionally known as Gaudiya or Chaitanya Vaishnavism (both terms are used interchangeably throughout this book), a movement inaugurated by the charismatic saint Chaitanya Mahaprabhu in the sixteenth century, in what was formally known as the land of Gauda, East India. Chaitanya established a religious system featuring the chanting of Krishna's names and dancing in public places that is still practiced by the various branches of the lineage in East India as well as in the Mathura–Vrindavan area near Delhi in the northwest of the subcontinent. Krishna is considered to be God, the absolute supreme Being, by the Gaudiya Vaishnava school, rather than a derivative incarnation of Vishnu, who is held to be the original godhead and ultimate source of all other incarnations by the older Vaishnava schools.[1]

A further distinctive feature of the Chaitanya school is the belief that Chaitanya himself is actually Krishna incarnated again in the present age, partly in order to spread the particular process of *bhakti* yoga, devotion to God, distinctive of this school of Vaishnavism. Since the name of Krishna is considered to be nondifferent from Krishna himself, Chaitanya traveled around India engaging in the ecstatic chanting and propagation of the Krishna mantra: *Hare Krishna, Hare Krishna, Krishna, Krishna, Hare Hare, Hare Rama, Hare Rama, Rama, Rama, Hare Hare.* This chanting and hearing of the names of Krishna is the primary feature of the yoga practiced by this school, and it is bolstered by immersing the mind in hearing, reciting, and remembering the stories about Krishna from the *Bhagavata Purana*, the principal scriptural text for Krishna-centered theology; worshipping the deity form of Krishna in the temple; visiting the places of pilgrimage associated with Krishna; and other devotional activities.

Chaitanya's disciples, the six Gosvamis, who resided in Vrindavan near Krishna's birthplace, were sophisticated men of letters who wrote numerous volumes formulating and articulating the theology of the sect, which they grafted onto various established branches of thought and theories of literary aesthetics current in their time.[2] Philosophically, Gaudiya Vaishnavism is a monotheistic tradition that has its roots in the theistic schools of Vedanta stemming from the great Vaishnava theologians Madhva in the thirteenth century and Ramanuja in the twelfth,[3] which in turn have their roots in the Upanishads, the earliest philosophical texts of India. The Chaitanya tradition remained centered in East India and the Vrindavan region until the early twentieth century, when a follower of Chaitanya from Bengal, Bhaktisiddhanta Saraswati, established a missionary wing called the Gaudiya Math, which attempted to propagate the teachings of Chaitanya and the chanting of the Hare Krishna mantra around India and even sent some missionaries to the West.[4]

Although, for all intents and purposes, the Gaudiya Math disintegrated as a viable unified missionary movement after Bhaktisiddhanta Saraswati passed away, his disciple, Bhaktivedanta Swami, arrived in New York City in 1965 as a representative of the Gaudiya lineage. Alone and penniless, he sat in Tompkins Square Park and began to chant the Hare Krishna mantra, and soon became a fixture in the hippie culture of the East Village. Although the first few months were difficult for the seventy-year-old swami, or Prabhupada, as he was to be called by his disciples, he soon began to attract a small but devoted following, and the Hare Krishna movement was born (see W. Deadwyler's and Sherbow's essays for descriptions of this early period).

Although the movement's strict requirements—no meat, fish, or eggs; no intoxication; no sex except for procreation; and no gambling—contrasted sharply with the bohemian lifestyle of New York's Lower East Side counter-culture, the teachings imparted by Bhaktivedanta gave meaning and purpose to many disaffected youths. A center was established in a storefront, and the newly registered International Society for Krishna Consciousness (ISKCON) soon spread to other major cities of America, and subsequently sprang up across Europe and on other continents. Young converts, prepared to sacrifice everything for Lord Krishna and his representative, Bhaktivedanta Swami, re-nounced their families, gave up all their possessions, and moved into the tem-ples that were rapidly being opened in these urban centers. They applied sa-cred sectarian clay markings to their foreheads and adopted traditional Hindu attire, the males shaving their heads and donning traditional robes and the fe-males wearing their hair in long braids and garbing themselves in *saris*. They rose at 4:00 A.M. and participated in a four- or five-hour regimen of devotion-al chanting and dancing, mantra meditation, and theological discussions be-fore spending the rest of the day in "service" to Krishna. Such service typical-ly included preaching work, book production and distribution, *sankirtana* (public chanting and dancing), *prasadam* (sanctified food) distribution, and activities in the society's rapidly expanding temples, schools, farms, and restaurants. The almost overnight worldwide propagation of the movement caused devotees to feel they were the first generation of a tradition carrying spiritual truths all but unknown outside of India that they believed would transform the religious and social landscape of the world. The idealism of the time can be sensed in the various hagiographical accounts of Bhaktivedanta Swami and his disciples.[5]

As the essays in this book elaborate upon in detail, the carefree devotional spontaneity of the early days was not to last. Although Bhaktivedanta was heir to a respectable and sophisticated Indian devotional tradition (see the first sec-tion of this volume), problems plagued the movement during his lifetime (see Mukunda and Anuttama's essay), due in part to its rapid expansion and the im-maturity of the young hippies Bhaktivedanta attracted, who found themselves suddenly managing a rapidly growing international organization. Anxious to avoid the pitfalls that led to the collapse of his own guru's institution (see Brzezinski's essay), Bhaktivedanta Swami established a Governing Body Com-mission (GBC) comprised of his senior disciples to act as the managerial au-thority for all affairs of the society. Young men (primarily, although, as Knott outlines, a few women had some positions of responsibility in the very early days) fresh off the hedonistic streets of San Francisco and New York, despite their previous anti-establishment and anti-authoritarian orientations, found themselves running an institution organized very much on corporate lines (see W. Deadwyler). The GBC was bolstered by a hierarchy of regional secretaries, temple presidents and vice presidents, and temple commanders who directed an ever-expanding army of new recruits inspired to propagate Bhaktivedanta Swami's mission in exchange for the barest minimal necessities of life.

Institutionalization brought its price: preaching gave way to revenue production (see Burke), gender equality to celibate male hierarchy (see Knott), devotional camaraderie to bureaucratic stratification (see Herzig and Valpey), and, inevitably, scandals and corruption flourished along with the institutional growth of the society (see Mukunda and Anuttama). Questionable fundraising tactics, confrontational attitudes to mainstream authorities, and an isolationist mentality, coupled with the excesses of neophyte proselytizing zeal, brought public disapproval and, by the late 1960s and '70s, the movement was a prime target of the anticult crusades of the period. Internally, the early inspiration, vision, and hope that Bhaktivedanta succeeded in imparting to his disciples gave way to large-scale disillusionment and disaffection among rank-and-file ISKCON members, particularly in the postcharismatic period (see Gelberg and Rochford).

Nonetheless, by the time Bhaktivedanta Swami passed away in 1977, he had achieved an impressive array of accomplishments: ISKCON had well over a hundred temples, and dozens of farm communities, restaurants, and *gurukula* (boarding) schools for the society's children. In India, in particular, the opulence and lavish worship services of ISKCON temples all over the subcontinent have caused them to be highly frequented. Bhaktivedanta Swami was also a prolific author, and translated and published most of the multivolume *Bhagavata Purana*, describing the life and activities of Krishna and other incarnations of Vishnu; the entire multivolume *Chaitanya Charitamrita*, depicting the life of Chaitanya; and dozens of other books on the practice of Krishna devotion, which he pressed his disciples to translate into all the major languages of the world and to distribute profusely.[6] Exact figures are impossible to come by, but, by now, certainly hundreds of millions of Bhaktivedanta Swami's books and booklets have been distributed worldwide.[7]

The postcharismatic phase of the Krishna Consciousness movement in the West has been a period of particularly dramatic turmoil and has presented the movement with new sets of problems. Bhaktivedanta Swami did not clearly specify how the lineage was to continue after his demise in terms of the initiation of new members, and when he passed away, eleven of his most senior disciples monopolized the function of guru for the sect. The world was divided into eleven preaching "zones," and each guru had the exclusive right to initiate new recruits to the movement within his respective zone. This led to the first major schism within the movement, and a significant number of Bhaktivedanta Swami's other disciples defected to another branch of ISKCON's parent organization, the Gaudiya Math (see Swami B.B. Vishnu).

In time, most of these eleven gurus became embroiled in various dramatic scandals and the system came under increasing attack from other members of the movement headed by William Deadwyler, whose essay in this volume outlines the entire history of this crisis. Even after what came to be known as the "zonal *acharya* (guru)" system had been dismantled and the authority of initiation extended to any of Bhaktivedanta's disciples in good standing, scandals connected to the new gurus continued to erupt regularly, most involving deviations from the vows of celibacy. Frustration with this state of affairs developed into an ongoing (but now excommunicated) reform position known as "*ritvik*." According to this view, represented here by one of its most outspoken proponents, Adridharan Das and his associates, all incoming second-generation members of ISKCON should be considered Bhaktivedanta's direct disciples even after the founder's death, rather than disciples of his disciples.

As a result of such crises of leadership, the movement has splintered into a variety of independent expressions and is undergoing further schisms centered on issues of transmission of authority. A majority of its members have disaffiliated themselves from the institution, and there has been a widespread exodus of large numbers to other representatives of the Chaitanya lineage in India, the most recent and divisive being Narayana Maharaja, whose confrontation with ISKCON is discussed by Collins in this volume. The splintering has spawned various debates over dogma, particularly in instances where Bhaktivedanta's teachings conflicted with previous authorities in the lineage, resulting in the formation of an orthodoxy and the excommunication of heretics—Conrad Joseph is perhaps the most outspoken such "heretic," who presents here his firsthand version of events. The society is experiencing the stirrings of a suffragette movement reacting against the historical disempowerment and denigration of women, who have long been denied access to prominent roles as a result of the *sannyasi* (male, lifelong renunciant) culture and ethos that developed in ISKCON in the 1970s (see Knott and Muster). This resulted in the (fiercely contested but historic) appointment of one woman to ISKCON's Governing Board Commission (GBC) in 1998. Most seriously, at the time of writing, ISKCON is settling a multimillion-dollar child abuse case sponsored by more than a hundred alumni of its *gurukula*s, private religious boarding schools (which have for all intents and purposes since become defunct in the West; see Wolf). Such problems have shaken even the movement's most loyal followers and threaten the very survival of the institutional aspect of the tradition.

The movement must also face other serious issues that will determine its relevance in the religious landscape of the modern world. Its scriptural literalism and subscription to *varnashram*, the social system of ancient and medieval India, bring it into conflict with the dominant intellectual and social currents of our times. But, as Mukunda and Anuttama argue, some individuals within ISKCON have matured and made efforts to redress the excesses of the past. They have opened themselves to dialogue with, and influence from, the academic, social, legal, and other mainstream institutions of the greater society. As with any more-established religious tradition, there is an inevitable tension between a fundamentalist, literalist element and a more liberal, progressive one. Ultimately, the very fact that there is now a wide spectrum of participatory possibilities outside the jurisdiction of ISKCON suggests that the tradition of Gaudiya Vaishnavism may be taking some broader roots in the West.

All in all, the postcharismatic phase of the Hare Krishna movement provides a rare glimpse of the formative stages of a religious tradition. This volume attempts to capture and record some of these ongoing developments. It also serves as a resource for scholars interested in researching the transplantation of this tradition—the bibliographies and references provide a compilation of much of the published scholarship, as well as of unpublished in-house material, much of it now available on the Internet. Represented herein are the voices of some of the most senior and prominent devotees loyal to ISKCON, who critically scrutinize their involvement with the Hare Krishna movement, portraying insider vantage points on essential issues; academic scholars who have studied the movement over the decades from various disciplinary approaches (to the extent that scholars with such research interests exist) and offer outsider perspectives on key aspects; and former ISKCON members, who have been the most vocal critics of the institutional aspect of the Krishna tradition and/or have established reformist or alternative expressions of Chaitanya Vaishnavism. This multidisciplinary collection thus contributes to the insider vs. outsider dialectic in the study of religion and navigates between such boundaries and polarities as apologetic or confessional vs. academic or critical by presenting a wide range of voices and perspectives on ISKCON and its offshoots from different participatory contexts and analytical disciplines.

We have attempted to include a spectrum of the subjects and issues most relevant to the postcharismatic history of the Krishna tradition in the West, all of which are indispensable to a comprehensive anthology on this topic, and the contributors are authorities on the particular areas assigned to them. At least two sets of essays (14 and 15, and 22 and 23) represent opposing views on two important issues, and those in part 3 are different developments ensuing from the same, and what proved to be the most seminal, crisis faced by the movement—the perpetuation of the function of guru after Bhaktivedanta Swami's demise. Since this volume is aimed at the academic community, our initial intention was to include only contributions from insiders who had graduate-level academic training. However, due to lack of alternatives, we found ourselves soliciting essays on schismatic developments that were of immense import to the trajectory of the Krishna movement from authors who, although without such backgrounds, were catalysts or players in each of these developments. It soon became evident to us that this very interplay, between detached analysis and passionate advocacy, is what brings the volume to life and constitutes its strength. These essays capture the individual reactions of the various parties and make the book authentic in a way that a collection of exclusively academic discussions could not (see the contributors list for an introduction to the authors).

In addition to these, we have included four autobiographical essays that we have subtitled "Personal Story" I, II, III, and IV. What these may lack in terms of critical distance, they make up for by providing firsthand, and in places quite poignant, narratives of different experiences in and reactions to the Hare Krishna movement by both present and former members. The volume thus attempts to capture some of the sense of hope, disillusionment, commitment, rejection, determination, and bitterness that motivated the participants in these events. This real-life history is often lacking in academic treatments. The collection, as a result, is a very privileged look at some of the people and issues shaping ISKCON's recent and ongoing development, which has significant general relevance for the study of emerging religious traditions, including early Christianity.

The book has been divided into six sections, according to subject. Part 1 situates important aspects of the theology and praxis of Krishna Consciousness in the historical context of Hindu thought and practice. The first essay, by Schweig, introduces Krishna himself, and the particular way in which he is understood by the Gaudiya or Chaitanya Vaishnava school. The second, by Delmonico, is a short comment on the history of Hindu monotheism prior to its manifestation in Chaitanya's theology, and on the challenges the historical study of a tradition poses for modern followers of Gaudiya Vaishnavism. In the third essay, Beck situates the chanting of the Hare Krishna mantra within the context of the history of sacred sound in Indic traditions. In the fourth, Valpey traces ISKCON's deity worship of Krishna from within the larger historical context of related practices in India.

Part 2 of the volume examines important aspects of the lineage of the Hare Krishna movement as a branch of the Chaitanya or Gaudiya Vaishnava tradition. Steven Rosen presents a synopsis of the hagiography of Chaitanya, the inaugurator of the Krishna movement in the sixteenth century. Brzezinski examines the developments following the passing away of two previous charismatics in the Chaitanya lineage: Chaitanya himself, and Bhaktivedanta's own guru, Bhaktisiddhanta Saraswati, the founder of the Gaudiya Math in the early twentieth century. Shukavak Das then introduces another prominent figure in ISKCON's lineage, namely the father of Bhaktisiddhanta Saraswati, Bhaktivinoda Thakur, in the nineteenth century, and considers whether he provides a role model for present-day Krishna devotees struggling to reconcile a traditional faith system with modern rational thought. Lorenz considers the extent to which certain of Bhaktivedanta Swami's particularly conspicuous and polemical views are representative of previous authorities in the lineage. In the final essay, Sherbow examines some of the philosophical aspects of Bhaktivedanta Swami's doctrines in the light of those of his predecessors.

Part 3 examines controversies over lineage and initiation, presenting differing views on what constitutes authority in, and legitimate expressions of, post-Bhaktivedanta Chaitanya Vaishnavism. The first essay, by William Deadwyler, documents perhaps the most devastating postcharismatic crisis undergone by ISKCON as a result of the implementation of the zonal guru system mentioned earlier; this sets the backdrop for the rest of the section. Swami B.B. Vishnu traces how this system led to the first major schism within ISKCON after the passing away of its founder, as a result of a major exodus of its members to the organization of Bhaktivedanta Swami's godbrother, Shridhara Swami. Adridharan, Madhu Pandit, and Krishnakant's essay then offers a very different response to the zonal guru system and an account of the causes of ISKCON's travails, presenting the merits of the schismatic *ritvik* reform position noted earlier. The last paper in this section, by Collins, describes the historical development of events leading to yet another challenge posed by charismatic figures of the Chaitanya lineage outside of ISKCON, in the person of Narayana Maharaja, who is presently traveling around the world recruiting and reinitiating many disgruntled and disenfranchised ISKCON members.

Part 4 examines the emergence of the categories of orthodoxy and heresy in the Krishna movement. These two essays focus on a major theological point of contention concerning the origin of the *jiva*, or soul. Conrad Joseph's paper analyzes the mechanics behind the reaction to his methods of resolving this issue, deemed heretical by ISKCON's orthodoxy, and the implications this has for critical thinking and rational inquiry. Resnick responds on behalf of ISKCON and its reaction to this controversy.

The main focus of part 5 is the sociocultural issues related to interactions between ISKCON and the greater society, as well as individual and interpersonal dynamics within the institution. The first essay, by Rochford, addresses the fund-raising techniques that were developed by the movement in its early days and their consequences for both external relations between ISKCON and the greater society and internal interactions among its own membership. Knott then gives a historical overview of the status of women in ISKCON from the early days under Bhaktivedanta Swami's tutelage to the jurisdiction of a male renunciant ethos in the postcharismatic period. This is followed by Nori Muster's poignant account of a woman's personal ordeal as a new devotee in the ISKCON Los Angeles temple. The next essay, by Wolf, outlines the history of child abuse in the ISKCON system of boarding school education (*gurukulas*), from the heyday of these schools in the 1970s to their almost complete demise in the 1990s. Gabriel Deadwyler provides a personal perspective on *gurukula* life. In the concluding essay, Lorenz seeks insights into the devastating social problems that have plagued ISKCON, by compiling Bhaktivedanta Swami's own views on *varnashram*, the social system of ancient and medieval India, which he encouraged his disciples to re-create in the fledgling organization he founded.

The final part, 6, deals with issues pertaining to reform, revision, and reevaluation. The first two essays are simple confessional pieces, counterpodes to each other. Gelberg, an ex-devotee, presents his reasons for leaving ISKCON, thus providing a wide-ranging critique of the society's social, moral, and spiritual failings. Mukunda and Anuttama present two insiders' view of what might motivate followers to remain within an institution that has been subject to so much scandal and controversy. Finally, Herzig and Valpey's essay offers a blueprint for ISKCON's reform by mining the tradition itself for resources that might redress the errors of the past as well as address the modern context of Chaitanya Vaishnavism.

We must note, in conclusion, that there are by now multiple Chaitanya Vaishnavisms, and any one anthology such as this can do no more than offer a glimpse of some of them. This volume has documented institutional developments of the tradition in the West, but has left unexplored the rapid expansion of Chaitanya Vaishnavism in the former Soviet Union over the last decade (following a period of state persecution); the constraints and conditions of pursuing and propagating Krishna Consciousness in other environments hostile to religious plurality and the freedom to proselytize in regions such as China and the Middle East; the changing dynamic between western temples and the Hindu diaspora; and the very well-connected and highly visible face of the movement across India, where massive, multimillion-dollar marble ISKCON temples continue to spring up in major urban centers and holy places. There are by now many facets of the Hare Krishna movement and its offshoots, and this volume can only attempt to reflect a few. Nonetheless, whatever may be the ultimate destiny of Chaitanya Vaishnavism in the West, we hope that this book offers sociologists and historians of religion a view of the germinating stages of a distinctive religious tradition attempting to put down roots in foreign soil, and of some of the major issues it has had to confront in the process of transplantation.

NOTES

1. "Vaishnavism" refers to a complex of religious traditions, the older schools of which hold Vishnu to be the supreme Godhead who incarnates into the world in times of strife by assuming various forms, such as that of Krishna. Gaudiya Vaishnavism reverses this relationship, considering Vishnu to be a derivative manifestation of Krishna.

2. For the history of Gaudiya aesthetics see David Haberman, *Acting as a Way to Salvation* (New York: Oxford University Press, 1988); for the early history of the sect see S. K. De, *The Early History of the Vaishnava Faith and Movement in Bengal* (Calcutta: Firma K.L. Muukhopadyay, 1961); for an exposition of Gaudiya philosophy and theology see O. B. L. Kapoor, *The Philosophy and Religion of Sri Chaitanya* (Delhi: Munshiram Manoharlal, 1977).

3. The Vedanta is the most influential of the six schools of orthodox Hindu philosophy (for comparative glances between Gaudiya philosophy and theology and that of other Vaishnava schools see Kapoor, previous citation).

4. See, for example, Tridandi Swami B. H. Bon, *My First Year in England* (London: n.p., 1934).

5. See, for example, Satsvarupa Dasa Goswami, *Srila Prabhupada Lilamrta*, vols. 1–7 (Los Angeles: Bhaktivedanta Book Trust, 1980); Hari Sauri Dasa, *A Transcendental Diary*, vols. 1–4 (San Diego: HS Books, 1992); Howard Wheeler, *Vrindavan Days* (n.p.: Palace, 1990); Mahanidhi Swami, *Prabhupada at Radha Damodara* (n.p.: n.p.,1990). For an anthropologist's perception of the period see Francine Jeanne Daner, *The American Children of Krsna* (Stanford: Stanford University Press, Case Studies in Anthropology, 1992). The most important study of this period is J. Stillson Judah, *Hare Krishna and the Counterculture* (New York: Wiley, 1974).

6. These books are published by the Bhaktivedanta Book Trust, which has headquarters in Los Angeles and branches in various regions of the world.

7. According to a former devotee who worked in the Northern European BBT (there are a number of BBTs around the world), at least 50 million books of various sizes were distributed in Northern Europe and the former Soviet bloc alone between 1988 and 1998. In 1994, the best year, 10 million books were distributed in this area.

PART I
Krishna Consciousness in the Context of Hindu Theology

[1]

KRISHNA

The Intimate Deity

GRAHAM M. SCHWEIG

THE RISE OF KRISHNA'S NAME IN THE WEST

The name Krishna[1] became widely recognized throughout America only in the second half of the past century. The deity Krishna received unprecedented attention in America in the 1960s when two synchronistic events occurred. Western scholars began to focus their studies on Krishna, discovering how popular he had been throughout India and Indian history. During the same period, an elderly Indian monk brought Krishna directly to the West, discovering the magnetism that the philosophy and worship would enjoy outside the boundaries of India, specifically, in America and Europe. Indeed, 1966, the year that Bhaktivedanta Swami formed the worldwide society in New York, was the year of the seminal publication of several scholars' work on the social practices, literature, and history of the Krishna movement in India: *Krishna: Myths, Rites, and Attitudes*.[2] The movement begun by Bhaktivedanta Swami was established as the International Society for Krishna Consciousness (ISKCON).[3]

By the end of the 1960s, then, the exposure of the name and image of Krishna was rapidly growing in North America and Western Europe. Bhaktivedanta Swami's disciples created various artistic renderings of the deity, and widely distributed books and magazines, authored and translated by Bhaktivedanta Swami, describing the divine personage. Western young men and women could be seen on the streets of major cities, dressed in traditional Indian religious garb, reenacting the ecstatic chanting of the divine names of God in the form of the *mahamantra* (the greatest mantra for deliverance):[4]

Hare Krishna, Hare Krishna, Krishna Krishna, Hare Hare
Hare Rama, Hare Rama, Rama Rama, Hare Hare

George Harrison of the Beatles produced several songs related to Krishna, including a top hit, "My Sweet Lord," in which the *mahamantra* was repeatedly sung. Due to all these occurrences during this period, the name Krishna became known in the West in unprecedented ways.

THEOLOGICAL ORIGINS OF THE KRISHNA MOVEMENT

The rise of the Krishna movement in the western world introduced an established, traditional form of religion from India based on a special type of theism that could perhaps be best characterized as "theistic intimacy," or just "intimism."[5] The word implies, drawing from its Latin origins, a vision of God that presents his "innermost" relations within the godhead, his "nearest" or "closest" relationships of love. Typically, in traditions of theistic intimism, the love between the soul and God is expressed through various loving, intimate relationships that resemble those of this world, such as the adoring love of a parent for a child or the love shared between two friends. However, it is the love that resembles the passionate feelings between lover and beloved that is common to most traditions of intimacy, as those found in certain forms of Jewish, Christian, and Islamic mysticism. The Chaitanyaite tradition is also absorbed in the erotic vision of God, Krishna, as the lover, along with his beloved consort Radha, as the most worshipable forms of the intimate deity. The passionate vision of Krishna with his divine counterpart is not metaphorical, as it easily becomes in other traditions. Rather, intimistic revelations of the deity, described in rich poetic Sanskrit verse, are understood as spiritually tangible, as very real narrations of the supreme play (*lila*) and activities of God. This developed form of theistic intimism was introduced and established outside of India when Bhaktivedanta Swami founded the Krishna movement.

In this chapter, I present key theological tenets that Bhaktivedanta Swami transmitted from the Chaitanyaite tradition to the West. I demonstrate that this tradition, whose practice and vision is centered upon love relations with the ultimate deity, presents an elaborate intimistic theography, or "images of the divine," perhaps the most of any extant religion. One can observe the intimistic practices of the tradition through elaborately decorated hand-carved statues, most often of Krishna with his feminine counterpart, the Goddess Radha, which are the focal point of daily worship in virtually every temple that Bhaktivedanta Swami established. This practice of worshipping sacred images in the temple is a continuation of a pan-Indian, ancient, and highly personalistic ritual known as *puja*, which includes the offering of personal articles, such as incense and fire lamps, flowers, fans, foodstuffs, etc. Such worship becomes very intimate when performed for the pleasure of the supreme lover and his supreme beloved.

The movement's particular conception of the deity Krishna originated with the Bengali saint and medieval revivalist Krishna Chaitanya, through whose mystical visions and ecstatic experiences, witnessed by his closest associates, can be understood the vision of God for this tradition. Here it is important to point out that the immediate followers of Chaitanya, as well as their disciples, were the theologians and philosophers of the tradition out of which the Krishna movement of modern times has arisen.[6] Their vision of Krishna is derived primarily from one of India's most adored sacred texts, the *Bhagavata Purana* (BhP),[7] along with the famous biography of Chaitanya, *Chaitanya Charitamrita* (CC),[8] for which Bhaktivedanta Swami provided English translations and commentaries. Below, I will explore aspects of the intimistic theology of the tradition.

VAISHNAVA THEISM

A personal form of the deity is always associated with those Hindu traditions for whom *bhakti*[9] is a means, and thus such a tradition has the appearance of a theism. When a loving relationship with the deity in *bhakti* is not merely a means but the goal of a religious tradition, that tradition sustains a theism in the fullest sense. Those Hindu traditions that can claim *bhakti* as both a means and an end are called Vaishnava, while others retain the curtain of impersonalism and monism behind their devotional and theistic practices and thinking.[10] In this way Vaishnavism could be said to be the most strictly theistic among traditions within the Hindu complex.

The several theistic devotional traditions dedicated to the worship of Vishnu—who is known by the names of Krishna, Govinda, and many others—are broadly referred to as "Vaishnavism" (Vishnu-ism). Vishnu is verily the *sa-guna brahman* (the supreme being possessing personal attributes), which is considered to be prior to and higher than the *nir-guna brahman* (the monistic or impersonal supreme spirit without any personal qualities).[11] Vishnu, *the* supreme personal being from whom *brahman* comes, fills the cosmos with a stratified government of minor divinities working under his direction. He is often recognized as part of the triune cosmic godly powers: Brahma, the god of creation; Vishnu, the god of sustenance; and Shiva, the god of destruction. From the Vaishnava theological perspective, Brahma and Shiva, although extraordinarily powerful minor divinities within the complex cosmic government, are not on an equal level with Vishnu.

Divine Forms of Vishnu

Vishnu is acknowledged as having various cosmic or divine forms in his transcendent spiritual realms. He is also understood to appear in this world in varying manifestations, known as *avataras* (divine descents).[12] When Vishnu descends to this world, it is understood that he comes in his own spiritual and immortal form. Therefore, he is not incarnate; rather, he becomes a divine descent of his own form.

There are many such *avatara* forms of Vishnu honored and celebrated by Vaishnavas. The most famous, as A. L. Basham states, are those of Rama and Krishna. Basham characterizes the *avatara* Rama as a deity of loyalty and righteousness in the following words:

> Rama and his faithful wife Sita combine the ideals of heroism, long suffering, righteousness, loyalty, and justice in a story so full of exciting incident that it has become part of the tradition not only of India, but also of most of South-East Asia. . . . He figures as the divinity of countless minor shrines throughout the length and breadth of India, and is the personification of the strong arm of the Lord, ever ready to help the righteous in the hour of need.[13]

The source most known for describing the deeds of Rama is the scriptural text *Ramayana* by Valmiki.

By comparison, the deity of Krishna shares more personal and passionately loving relationships with his worshippers. A. L. Basham confirms this in the following quick portrait of Krishna's personality:

> Krishna, probably even more popular than Rama, is a divinity of a rare completeness and catholicity, meeting almost every human need. As the

divine child, he satisfies the warm maternal drives of Indian womanhood. As the divine lover, he provides romantic wish fulfillment in a society still tightly controlled by ancient norms of behaviour which give little scope for freedom of expression in sexual relations. As charioteer of the hero Arjuna on the battlefield of Kurukshetra, he is the helper of all those who turn to him, even saving the sinner from evil rebirths, if he has sufficient faith in the Lord.[14]

Here, Basham presents what I have termed the "intimate deity" of Krishna. This intimate deity is elaborately described in the great classical texts of India, especially in the *Mahabharata,* from which the famed *Bhagavad Gita* comes, and in the *Bhagavata Purana,* particularly its tenth book, in which Krishna's activities as a child, a youthful cowherd boy, and divine lover are narrated.

Generally speaking, throughout the Indic traditions, Krishna is identified as another *avatara* form of Vishnu. However, within those Vaishnava traditions for whom the form of Krishna is considered the supreme and ultimate form of the divinity, he is both an *avatara* and the *adi-purusha devata* (the original person of the godhead). He is the supremely intimate deity from whom the more powerful and cosmic forms emanate.

These intimate activities are not attached exclusively to the *avatara* form; rather, they are a manifestation, according to certain Vaishnava sects, of the ultimate and intimate deity and his or her activities from within the very center of the godhead. In other words, the deity's activities are going on in the spiritual realm and are manifest by the deity here in this world simultaneously. This is explained further in the next section.

Three Manifestations of Divinity

The commonly held Hindu belief is that Krishna is limited to the *avatara* form originating from the cosmic Vishnu. The Chaitanya school agrees with the popular conception that when Krishna comes to this world as the manifest deity, he does so as an *avatara* of Vishnu. However, the Chaitanyaites consider Krishna as the ultimate transcendent Lord at the very center of the godhead from whom the majestic and powerful cosmic Vishnu emanates. Krishna is known as the *purnavatara*, "full descent of the deity." Thus, the school not only views Krishna as the ultimate source of all manifestations of the divine; it also regards him as descending to earth through the power of his Vishnu form. These three levels of divinity can be schematized as follows:

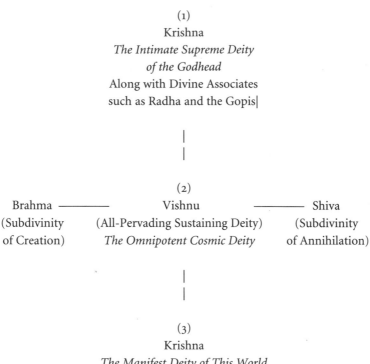

(1)

Krishna

The Intimate Supreme Deity
of the Godhead

Along with Divine Associates
such as Radha and the Gopis|

|

|

(2)

Brahma —————— Vishnu —————— Shiva

(Subdivinity   (All-Pervading Sustaining Deity)   (Subdivinity

of Creation)   *The Omnipotent Cosmic Deity*   of Annihilation)

|

|

(3)

Krishna

The Manifest Deity of This World
The divine descent of the *purnavatara*, the intimate form
of the deity, as well as all other *avataras.*

For the Chaitanya school, the most intimate form of God is the most personal, ultimate form, which I have termed in the above scheme "The Intimate
Supreme Deity of the Godhead." From this foundational level of the deity
comes "The Omnipotent Cosmic Deity," who is Vishnu, the manifestation of
God's sustaining power and almightiness, including Brahma (creator) and
Shiva (annihilator). It is Vishnu who is the source of the deity of this world—
the manifest deity, Krishna—as well as other *avatara* manifestations.

Polymorphic Theism and Bi-Monotheism

Vaishnavism is indeed a theistic tradition, but could be further characterized
as a polymorphic monotheism, i.e, a theology that recognizes many forms
(*ananta rupa*) of the one, single unitary divinity. The power of God is expressed in this Vaishnava metaphysics as the capacity to be in many places and
appear in a variety of forms at the same time, without being diminished in any

way. Polymorphic monotheism (too often characterized simplistically and incorrectly as "polytheism") has been characterized as belief in a single unitary deity who takes many forms and manifests at different levels of reality, and from whom come many minor divinities.

Another aspect of this theology pushes our characterization closer to a polymorphic *bi*-monotheism, or many forms of the dual-gendered divinity. In the Gaudiya Vaishnava tradition in Bengal and the surrounding region of Vraja in northern India, the area sacred to Krishna and his intimate *lilas*, one can observe *devi* or goddess worship, worship of the supreme feminine, incorporated. The godhead is essentially androgynous, comprised of both supreme masculine and feminine aspects. Indeed, many devotees of Krishna, especially the Chaitanyaite Vaishnavas, worship Krishna with Radha as the highest level of divine intimacy within the godhead; thus polymorphic bi-monotheism comes into play.[15]

Three Aspects of Divinity   The *adi-purusha*, the "original supreme person,"[16] identified as Krishna, is understood to be the source of all manifestations. His nature is comprised of three principal aspects of divinity identified as *brahman*, "supreme spirit,"[17] *paramatman*, "the supreme soul,"[18] and *bhagavan*, "the one in whom all excellences exist."[19] The *brahman* aspect is understood as the all-pervading and impersonal energy, the foundation for all spiritual and material existences. The *paramatman* aspect is the all-pervading personal form of God, located at the center of all universes and in the hearts of all living beings.[20] And the *bhagavan* aspect is considered the very highest existence within the godhead from whom all other aspects and manifestations come: "all of these manifestations are but a mere part of the [supreme] person; for, indeed, Krishna is Bhagavan himself."[21] This highest and most powerful aspect is paradoxically his most intimate *madhurya* form: "In his original form (*svayam-rupa*) dressed as a cowherd boy, he thinks of himself as a *gopa* (cowherd boy)."[22]

Identity of Radha and the Gopis   These three aspects of Krishna are understood as originating from three essential attributes of Krishna's form, i.e., "eternal existence" or *sat*, related to the *brahman* aspect; "knowledge" or *chit*, to the *paramatman*; and "bliss" or *ananda*, to *bhagavan*. There are three energies or potencies that pervade Krishna's spiritual realm, corresponding to these three personal attributes.[23] Most relevant here is *ananda*, referring to the "pleasure potency," *hladini*,[24] of which Radha is considered the full embodiment.[25] In Radha are found all the Gopis, and all other goddesses as well; indeed, she is understood to be the supreme Goddess, the embodiment of all divine women.[26] Krishnadasa further identifies Radha as the special Gopi who is the supreme *shakti* of Krishna:

Radha and Krishna are of one soul,
although they bear two bodies.
So they can enjoy the experience
of *rasa*[27] with each other.[28]

(CC 1.4.56)

Krishnadasa states that Krishna (*bhagavat*) with the Gopis (*shaktis*) is confounded by the level of enjoyment that his *shaktis* experience from being loved by him. Indeed, their enjoyment is ever-increasing. Since Krishna loves his devotees supremely, they receive an unsurpassable bliss that even he longs to experience.[29]

Rasa: Intimate Relationship with God

Krishna has intimate family members and dear friends with whom he interacts in loving ways. Krishna is considered the best of the Vrishnis, born to Queen Devaki in the dynasty of the Satavatas. He is fathered by the cowherd Nanda, and acts like a mischievous boy with his foster mother Yashoda. Krishna and his older brother, Balarama, herd the cows of Vraja together with their cowherd friends. The Gopis, the cowherd maidens of Vraja, many of whom have husbands, are also recognized as the spiritual wives of Krishna. Krishna, in his cosmic form of Vishnu, is the husband or Lord of the goddess Rama, or Shri. The Gopis praise him, saying: "Certainly you are the most dear supreme beloved of all living beings, and you are the most intimate relation."[30]

The teachers of the Chaitanya school, specifically Rupa, Jiva, and Krishnadasa Kaviraja Gosvamins, define and describe these types of relationships with God as *rasa*. The word *rasa*, a term originally used in Sanskrit dramaturgy and poetics, means literally, "taste."[31] It can mean, connotatively and more generally, "spiritual experience," or more specifically, a particular "relationship" with God. The Chaitanyaite Vaishnavas interpret it as meaning the "disposition of the heart or mind;" the general connotative meaning being the directly experienced intimate relationship with God.

The Chaitanya school describes five essential types of *rasa*, which are progressively more intimate and intense, up to the fifth and highest *rasa*.

Shanta Rasa The word *shanta* means "peace." This *rasa* is the passive love of awe and reverence for a great and powerful person. The devotee experiences the majesty or greatness of God, either in his direct personal presence or in his presence throughout everything. The connection or attachment (*asakti*) to God at this first stage is described as appreciation of his greatness (*guna ma-*

hatmya), attachment to his beauty (*rupa*), and attachment to the remembrance of God (*smarana*). The experience of pantheism and God's omnipresence is found at this level. *Shanta* is a passive and contemplative relationship with God, unlike the more active and dynamic forms of love that follow.

Dasya Rasa The word *dasya* means "servitude." This *rasa* is the active love of a devotee expressed through devotional acts. The experience is that of a subordinate with a superior, and the attachment of the devoted soul is one of obedient, loving service. This stage can perhaps be compared to that of the divine "Father," the "King" of the universe, or the divine "Mother" found in various religious traditions.[32] The great distance between the soul and God experienced in *shanta rasa* is lessened through dynamic service in *dasya rasa*.[33]

Sakhya Rasa The word *sakhya* means "friendship." The dynamic at this level of *bhakti* is one of equality, demonstrated in the reciprocal love between dear and intimate friends. This *rasa* constitutes a greater level of intimacy with the divine, since God's superior position is no longer emphasized. At this stage, majesty or formality is replaced by intimate exchanges on an equal level of close comradery.

Vatsalya Rasa The word *vatsalya* means "parental love." At this level the intensity of intimacy has increased so much that the devotee possesses feelings of caring for God, the way an affectionate parent feels toward a dependent child. God plays the part of a child and allows the devotee to protect and nurture him. Here, the power and magnificent glory of the *shanta* and *dasya* relationships is replaced, not by feelings of friendship as in the *sakhya rasa*, but rather by all-consuming paternal and maternal feelings for the Lord.

Shringara/Madhurya Rasa The word *shringara* means "erotic sentiment," and *madhurya* or "sweetness" connotatively refers to amorous love. This highest and most intense form of intimacy with the divine is characterized as the feelings that lovers have for each other (*kanta*). In this *rasa*, attachment to God is demonstrated in the total self-surrender of love (*atma nivedana*), overwhelming the lover with affectionate feelings for the beloved. At this most advanced level of intimacy, the devotee becomes a confidential lover of God.

Vishvanatha points out that *rasa*, as in *Rasalila*, refers to the sum of all *rasas*, or all intimate experiences with the supreme.[34] These five *rasas* are to be viewed, according to Krishnadasa, as progressively greater levels of intimacy. He states that while each of the first four *rasas* is a perfection,[35] the fifth, or *shringara rasa* has the greatest intimacy of all. The Chaitanya school views the *madhurya* of the Gopis as the superlative example of devotion, even among all other perfect relationships with God.

Rasa Lila Reveals the Intimate Krishna For the Chaitanya school, the conception of divine love of God is most ideally expressed in the *Bhagavata Purana*, especially in the tenth book describing the personal episodes of Krishna as a cowherd boy. Within this book, the Rasa Lila is treasured as the highest and most sacred revelation of God's love. The story describes the amorous love of the young cowherd maidens, known as the Gopis, for their beloved Lord, Krishna, the beautiful cowherd boy who plays the flute. Krishna, though God himself, is overtaken by the power of love, and the Gopis are irresistibly drawn to the forest by his enchanting flute music. After they meet and play in the forest, Krishna suddenly disappears and the Gopis search fervently for him. In the final chapter of the story, Krishna reappears and they unite in "the dance of divine love" (*Rasa Lila*), under the full autumn moon in the paradisial forest of Vraja.

In the *lila* or play of Krishna's Rasa dance with the Gopis, Krishna duplicates himself from the center of the encircling maidens by virtue of his mystic power, in order to become the sole male partner for each and every Gopi. While remaining in the center of the Rasa *mandala*, or "circle of the Rasa dance," Krishna stands with his most favored Gopi, who is understood to be the supremely loving Goddess Radha. As the Gopis move in the circular dance, each experiencing the exclusive attention of Krishna, they sing songs of love in harmony with him.

The Portraiture of Krishna

Since the Rasa Lila is the *lila* of all *lilas*, as the school claims, it should not be surprising that the episode engages many of the most important dimensions of Krishna theology in its portraiture of Krishna, briefly presented here.

Three Dimensions of Krishna's Divinity The complex character of Krishna can be divided into three general dimensions, described by the teachers of the Chaitanya school: *aishvarya*, the dimension of divine majesty and supremacy; *madhurya*, the dimension of divine tenderness and intimacy; and *karunya*, the dimension of compassion and protection.[36] The *aishvarya* has to do with the majesty of God, and the various ways in which he manifests himself and exercises power, whereas the *madhurya* has to do with Krishna's Vraja *lilas*, including his birth, childhood and youth as a cowherd, and his activities as a member of the warrior class. The school favors the *madhurya* activities and attributes, and claims that God himself prefers his intimate devotee:

The whole world is furnished with awareness
of God's supreme divinity (*aishvarya*).
[The Lord would say,] "I am not pleased by love (*prema*)
weakened by this [awareness] of my supreme power (*aishvarya*)."

(CC 1.4.17)

According to Jiva, one who is devoted to God in his *aishvarya* aspect does not experience a love for God as exalted as that of one who is devoted to God in his *madhurya* aspect. Jiva states, however, that realization of both the *aishvarya* and *madhurya* manifestations of God increases devotion to him.[37] In fact, he claims that manifestations of the *aishvarya* assist in the realization of Krishna's *madhurya* aspects.[38]

Heroic acts of Krishna, such as the killing of many demons,[39] are not placed in either category, *aishvarya* or *madhurya*, most likely because they engage Krishna's superhuman powers to protect the residents of Vraja, yet are performed by the intimate cowherd himself. Therefore, the teachers of the school add a third category called *karunya*, the "compassionate" dimension of God.[40] Krishna extends himself to everyone, including the demonic. His heroic acts of killing demons are compassionate, not only because he is protecting his devotees but also because whomever he kills attains liberation.[41] Thus, Krishna is understood as the "true friend of all souls."[42]

Beauty of the Divine Form   The beauty of Krishna's form is elaborately described throughout the Bhagavata text, and especially in the Rasa Lila. He is depicted as "exquisitely brilliant,"[43] the "exclusive reservoir of beauty in all the three worlds."[44] His hair is a deep dark-blue color and his face, along with other bodily attributes, is often compared to the beautiful lotus flower. Krishna, "whose unique luster is like that of unlimited numbers of love gods,"[45] is famous for having an effulgent deep-bluish hue, comparable to a fresh monsoon cloud.

Krishna's feet are distinguishable by the unique signs appearing on their soles.[46] His feet are especially desired by gods, goddesses, mystics, and lovers alike, because, along with other beneficial effects, they dispel sins.[47] They also relieve suffering, as well as "grant the highest satisfaction."[48] Indeed, the Gopis describe Krishna's feet as worshipable, "the ornament of the earth."[49]

Always dressed and decorated in pleasing ways, Krishna wears silken yellow garments, and on his head is an ornament adorned with a peacock feather. His garland is made of colored forest flowers and leaves, and he often carries a herding stick and buffalo horn. Perhaps one of the most outstanding features of this divine cowherd is that he usually holds a bamboo flute, from which he produces divine music.[50] Indeed, the Gaudiya school states that the special symbol of the intimate deity of Krishna—as compared with the numerous four-armed forms of Vishnu, who hold various arrangements of the disc, conch, club, and lotus in their hands—is his two arms holding the flute up to his mouth.

The Flute Player Bilvamangala, in his work of Sanskrit poetic verse known as the *Krishna Karnamrita*, demonstrates the significant place that the flute has as a symbol of Krishna's identity, and the importance of the flute music in attracting souls to him. It is especially worth noting a particular verse that describes this music not only in terms of the *madhurya* activities of Krishna but also as it is connected to *aishvarya* as well as ontological dimensions:

> All hail to the child's flute notes coming forth so
>   that *Om* might sound.
> The flute notes cause the worlds to exult, the Vedas to
>   sound, trees to rejoice,
> mountains to fly, deer to be tame, cows blissful,
> and cowherds bewildered; ascetics' flesh to
>   rise and the seven basic notes to sound.[51]
>   (*KRISHNAKARNAMRITA*, II.110)

In the *bhakti* tradition, appreciation for God's beauty becomes paramount, and the flute symbolizes this, as the following passage from the *Brahma Samhita* expresses:

> The one who plays the flute,
>   whose eyes blossom like lotus petals,
> With a peacock's feather adorning his head,
>   whose beautiful form is the hue of dark rainclouds,
> Whose unique luster is like that
>   of countless love gods,
> Who is Govinda, the original person—
>   it is he whom I worship.
>
>   (5.30)

This is a distinguishing feature of *bhakti*: the enchanting beauty of God ever drawing souls back to him, by means of his divine flute playing.

Krishna as the God of Love It is perhaps the greatest expression of the intimate deity of Krishna that he allows himself in various ways to come under the control of love. In the first verse of the Rasa Lila episode, Krishna submits himself fully to a power that makes arrangements for love, Yogamaya:

Even the Beloved Lord,
  seeing those nights
  in autumn filled with
  blooming jasmine flowers,
Turned his mind toward
  love's delights,
  fully taking refuge in
  Yogamaya's[52] illusive powers.[53]

(BHP 10.29.1)

What is important to note here is that Krishna places himself in a dependent position in order to enjoy love with the cowherd maidens, the Gopis. Vishvanatha claims that the Lord enjoys this, although he has no need to since he is already completely fulfilled.

Two verses later, we are informed that the music emanating from Krishna's flute is an expression of his being moved by love, and thus is a kind of divine love call:

Seeing lotus flowers bloom
  and the perfect circle of the moon,
Beaming like the face of the Goddess Rama[54]
  reddish as fresh saffron *kumkuma*,[55]
Then seeing the forest colored
  by the moon's gentle rays,
He began to make sweet music,
  melting the hearts of fair maidens
  with beautiful eyes.

(BHP 10.29.3)

Krishna, inspired toward love by the paradisal beauty of Vraja, makes enticing music to enchant the Gopis, causing them spontaneously to rush off to join him in the forest.[56]

CONCLUDING REMARKS

Whatever controversies and challenges have occurred within or beyond the boundaries of the modern Krishna movement, it is important to note that it represents a faithful continuation of the ancient practices and worship of Vaishnava traditions centered upon the deity of Krishna. Perhaps Bhaktivedanta Swami's greatest theological contribution to the West was the deliverance of a tradition that revels in the unlimited forms, or omnimorphism, of the supreme deity. The Chaitanyaite tradition regards Krishna not only as the personal deity with whom the devotee can experience a variety of intimate relationships but also as the fountainhead of so many *avataras,* all descending from his cosmic form of Vishnu, who are celebrated and worshipped on numerous holy days throughout the year.

The form of intimism that Bhaktivedanta Swami introduced to the West, as we have seen, is hardly a metaphorical or allegorical presentation of the deity; rather, for practitioners, it is verily a window into the intimate world of the highest deity of the godhead. This iconocentric conception of the deity, unexpectedly appearing several decades ago, sharply contrasts with our own western iconophobic and iconoclastic conceptions of God from the Abrahamic traditions.

Every religious tradition speaks in its own terms of the supreme unlimited, which is perceived, worshipped, etc., by practitioners, through what may appear to nonpractitioners as too limiting a form, whether it be sacred images, divine revelation, etc. This apparently limited form, however, is not perceived by practitioners as limited; on the contrary, it is often seen as an act of grace and transcendent power,[57] through which the supreme unlimited can be intimately accessed. In other words, the supreme unlimited is so unlimited in its power that it can enter into a limited form, yet not be restricted by it. The supreme unlimited can exist powerfully however it may choose.

This is not just a metaphysical vision but also a vision of love. It is natural that practitioners would desire intimate manifestations of their beloved deity, just as any person would have pictures or belongings of a beloved spouse or child as "limited forms" extending the presence of the one who is absent. The desire to create these limited forms of beloved beings, human or divine, expresses the eternal longings within the human heart.

The Chaitanyaite school as a theistic tradition sharply contrasts with Abrahamic traditions, even in their more rarified mystical forms such as Kabbalism, the bridal mysticism of Catholicism, and Sufism, in its uninhibited desire to celebrate and honor the boundless capacity of the supreme unlimited to take apparently limited forms.[58] Indeed, the Krishna movement that Bhaktivedanta Swami established has introduced to the West this type of elaborate intimism found in the Chaitanyaite tradition.

NOTES

1. It is important to note that the name Krishna is found in either an English phonetic spelling, as is the case here, or a Sanskrit transliteration spelling of Krsna (with dots appearing under the "r," "s," and "n"), as it appears in Bhaktivedanta Swami's books discussed below.

2. Edited by Milton Singer (Chicago: University of Chicago Press, 1966), with a foreword by Daniel H. H. Ingalls. This work on Krishna is an anthology of nine schol-

ars, including Edward C. Dimock Jr., who in the same year published *The Place of the Hidden Moon: Erotic Mysticism in the Vaisnava-sahajiya Cult of Bengal* (Chicago: University of Chicago Press, 1966). Other works with the prominent theme of Krishna followed. Klaus Klostermaier wrote *In the Paradise of Krishna: Hindu and Christian Seekers* (Philadelphia: Westminster Press, 1969). Other scholars, such as Charlotte Vaudeville, Norvin Hein, Charles S. J. White, Thomas J. Hopkins, et al. focused on the theme of Krishna beginning in the mid-1960s. A steady swell of interest is evident in the following three decades and continues in the present. In addition to these works, Bhaktivedanta Swami published *KRSNA: The Supreme Personality of Godhead,* with a foreword by George Harrison (Los Angeles: Bhaktivedanta Book Trust, 1970).

3. See *Srila Prabhupada-lilamrta,* the multivolume work on Bhaktivedanta Swami's life and mission, by Satsvarupa dasa Goswami (Los Angeles: Bhaktivedanta Book Trust, 1980–86).

4. The *mahamantra* is considered by the Chaitanya tradition to be the most powerful among numerous mantras (sacred Sanskrit word phrases or sounds) employed by Indian traditions, and thus is called *maha-,* meaning "the great" mantra. This mantra is a special ordering and repetition of proper names of God in the vocative case, whereas most mantras contain, along with the name of a specific deity, words of supplication and homage. The words in the *mahamantra* do not form a complete sentence; rather, the *mahamantra* consists of a series of repeated names of God. Such repetition within a single mantra also distinguishes it. Moreover, the *mahamantra* does not possess any type of *bija* (seed) sound syllables, such as *om,* often placed at the beginning of a mantra phrase for its power of invoking the presence of the deity. The names in the mantra that invoke "the supreme loving, devotional and feminine power of the Lord" (*hara*), "the supremely attractive Lord" (*krishna*), and "the supremely delighted Lord" (*rama*) are understood as extraordinarily efficacious and sufficient for invoking the presence of God.

5. The word "intimism" has been used in the history of art to refer to the stylistic period in early twentieth-century French painting that engaged familiar subject matter or intimate scenes from everyday life. That dimension, present among many historico-religious complexes, involving a religious experience that could be characterized as the familiar or intimate scenes or occasions from God's everyday life, is herein referred to as theistic "intimism."

6. The history and identity of Chaitanya are covered in Rosen's chapter in this volume.

7. The evolution of the development of Krishna's divine biography has been traced in *The Divinity of Krishna* by Noel Sheth (Delhi: Manshiram Manoharlal, 1984), by comparing Krishna's life stories found in the *Harivamsha, Vishnu,* and *Bhagavata Puranas.* Sheth observes that while Krishna's divinity is recognized and expressed in the *Harivamsha,* it is far more developed in the *Vishnu Purana* and finds its most sophisticated form in the *Bhagavata Purana.*

8. The Krishna movement publishes a translation and commentary of the *Chaitanya Charitamrita* by Bhaktivedanta Swami Prabhupada, an edition that has the advantage of providing the full Bengali text (Los Angeles: Bhaktivedanta Book Trust, [1975] 1996). A new introduction to and translation of the CC is published by Harvard Oriental Series, by Edward C. Dimock (Cambridge: Harvard University Press, 1999). It is important to note that the verse numbering systems are different between the two editions, even though the texts are almost identical. The numbering system of the former edition of the CC is used in this chapter.

9. The word *bhakti* denotes devotional love and affectionate self-surrender offered to the personal deity, as well as God's transforming grace for the worshipper of Krishna, known as the *bhakta*, or "devotee." It is to be contrasted to other *margas* or paths, or other *yogas* (means for achieving union with God), such as *karma* (the way of action), or *jnana* (the way of knowledge). While *bhakti* is a pan-Indian/Hindu phenomenon, it was primarily the Vaishnava traditions all around India that developed it into sophisticated theologies and practices, especially during the *bhakti* renaissance of the medieval period, from the eleventh through the sixteenth centuries.

10. In this matter, Rudolf Otto states, "the special problems of the doctrine of grace have been developed more acutely and in greater detail among the Vishnu *bhaktas* than among those of Shiva" (*India's Religion of Grace and Christianity Compared and Contrasted*, trans. Frank Hugh Foster [New York: Macmillan, 1930], 27). In spite of the evolved forms of *bhakti* in the Shaivaite tradition, especially in the Shaiva Siddhanta of South India, in my estimation, an ultimate veil of monism or impersonalism seems to eclipse a fully developed *bhakti* theism of the sort found in Vaishnava sects.

11. In Christianity, these types of distinctions are made with the terms *via positiva* (or *via affirmativa*) and *via negativa*, or cataphatic and apophatic distinctions, respectively, by theologians.

12. The word *avatara* is very often translated by the English word "incarnation," which possesses certain unavoidable Christian senses that are not present in the word it attempts to translate. These different senses can be seen even etymologically. The word "incarnation" means "the act of coming into a body," and *avatara* means a "con-(-*tara* = to cross) -descent (*ava-* = down)."

13. A. L. Basham, ed., *A Cultural History of India* (Delhi: Oxford University Press, 1997), 80–81.

14. Ibid., 81. While Basham observes correctly Krishna's popularity and completeness as a divinity, it is interesting to note his explanation of Krishna's role as the divine lover. India, the culture that produced the famed *Kama Sutra*, the manual of passionate love and explicit sexual formulations, certainly does not seem to be lacking in its own type of freedom of expression within sexual relations.

15. The Gaudiya school will at times espouse a tri-monotheism in which Chaitanya himself is seen as the *avatara* personification of the love that is shared between Radha and Krishna. This will be discussed in Rosen's essay in this volume.

16. BhP (*Bhagavata Purana*) 10.29.31, 41. *Dance of Divine Love: The Rasa Lila of Krishna and the Gopis from the Bhagavata Purana*, trans. Graham M. Schweig (Princeton: Princeton University Press, forthcoming).

17. BhP 10.29.12.

18. BhP 10.29.11, 10.30.24.

19. "Those who are learned in the truth describe this truth as nondual [or absolute] knowledge, which is also known as *brahman, paramatman*, and *bhagavan*" (BhP 1.2.11 or CC 2.20.158). This verse, from the first book of the *Bhagavata*, is relied upon by the school to establish these three ultimate dimensions.

20. Vishnu, in the *paramatman* aspect, is the one "whose seat is arranged within the most interior hearts of all as the supreme mystic" (*yogeshvarantar-hridi kalpitasanah*, BhP 10.32.14).

21. *ete chamsha-kalah pumshah krishnas tu bhagavan svayam* (BhP 1.3.28). Demonstrating the significance of this verse to the early teachers, Krishnadas quotes from

this BhP verse in the following verses: CC 1.2.67, 1.5.79; 2.9.143, 2.20.156, 2.23.67, and 2.25.134.

22. *svayam-rupera gopa-veshga, gopa-abhimana* (CC 2.20.177).

23. CC 1.4.61.

24. CC 1.4.62–68. Other discussions of these potencies are CC 2.8.155–56, 2.18.114, and 3.5.127.

25. CC 1.4.59 and 60.

26. See my article, "Radha and the Rasalila: The Esoteric Vision of Chaitanyaite Vaishnavism" (*Journal of Vaishnava Studies* 8 [2] [spring 2000]), for an explanation of the relationship between Radha and the Gopis.

27. "Divine relationship" or "loving encounter" is a possible translation for the word *rasa*. This important term is reviewed in the next section below.

28. *radha-krishna eka atma, dui deha dhari'*
    anyonye vilase rasa asvadana kari'
    Unless otherwise indicated, translations of Sanskrit and Bengali texts in this chapter are my own.

29. For the discussion on the Gopis' unending and ever-increasing bliss in loving Krishna, see CC 1.4.185–221.

30. BhP 10.29.32.

31. The word *rasa* means literally "the sap or juice of plants," "the juice of fruit," "the best or finest or prime part of anything," and "essence." It also means "flavor," and can mean "love," "affection," or "desire" (*Sanskrit-English Dictionary*, by M. Monier-Williams [Oxford: Oxford University Press, 1899]) (hereafter, SD).

32. If the relationships of divine "Father" or "Mother" possess the greater intimacy of family affections, then they could be characterized more accurately by the fourth *vatsalya rasa*, discussed below.

33. It should be noted that within the *dasya rasa* (and the other *rasas* as well), there are different degrees of intimacy found in the variety of possible relationships. For example, it is safe to say that the relationship between child and parent is potentially more intimate than that between servant and master or subject and king.

34. SD 5.2.

35. CC 1.4.42–43. The first of the *rasas, shanta rasa,* is often not considered a perfection in the ways in which the upper four *rasas* are, since technically the former excludes active reciprocal interactions. There are, however, exceptions to this in Krishna's most intimate region of Vraja.

36. Jiva presents these three divisions in his Priti Sandarbha (PrS) (*Bhagavat-sandarbha: Bhakti-Priti Sandarbhas* [Sanskrit text in Bengali script, critical notes by Haridas Sarman] [Vrindaban: Puridas, 1952], translation mine), section 275, and Krishnadasa presents these in CC 2.24.42.

37. PrS 175.

38. PrS 187.

39. These various heroic acts of Krishna are recalled by the Gopis, first in BhP verses 10.30.14–22, and then again in verse 10.31.3.

40. See CC 2.24.42.

41. There are numerous examples of various demons Krishna kills throughout the tenth book of the BhP.

42. BhP 10.32.13.

43. BhP 10.32.10.

44. BhP 10.32.14.

45. *Shri Brahma-samhita* (BS), with commentary of Shrila Jiva Goswami (with Sanskrit texts), trans. Bhakti Siddhanta Saraswati Goswami (Calcutta: Saraswat Press, 1985), vs. 30. Translation mine.

46. "This is discernable by anyone because of the flag, lotus, thunderbolt, elephant goad, and barley seed, along with all other signs" (BhP 10.20.25).

47. See BhP 10.30.29 and BhP 10.31.7.

48. BhP 10.31.13.

49. BhP 10.31.13.

50. There are many statements from the *Bhagavata* text in which a description of Krishna with his flute is given. The earliest is BhP 3.2.29, and a more full description is BhP 10.14.1.

51. Taken from *The Love of Krishna: Krsnakarnamrta of Lilasuka Bilvamanagala*, trans. Frances Wilson (Philadelphia: University of Pennsylvania Press, 1975).

52. Yogamaya is both a force and the embodiment of the force that makes arrangements for God and the soul to experience intimate loving encounters. A literal translation of the name can be, "the divine power (*maya*) of intimate connections (*yoga*)" or simply "uniting powers."

53. This verse and the next from the Rasalila chapters of the *Bhagavata Purana* are my translations. For a complete presentation of this important tract of epic poetry and story along with the Chaitanyaite commentarial vision of it, see my *Dance of Divine Love: The Rasalila of Krishna and the Cowherd Maidens of Vraja,* with introduction, transliteration, translation and commentary (Princeton: Princeton University Press, forthcoming).

54. Rama is the goddess Lakshmi, the divine consort of Vishnu or Narayana.

55. *Kumkuma* is vermilion, a deep reddish powder.

56. BhP 10.29.4.

57. For the more extreme monistic traditions of India, even limited forms of the supreme are delusional, but often still seen as a necessary step in order to get beyond them. In this scenario, the forms are not limiting the supreme because they lead to the supreme unlimited.

58. Of course, this tradition is without the profoundly intense prohibition against graven images such as that declared in the Hebrew Bible.

[2]

THE HISTORY OF INDIC MONOTHEISM AND MODERN CHAITANYA VAISHNAVISM

Some Reflections[1]

NEAL DELMONICO

A N ACADEMIC STUDY of the development of monotheism leading to the theology of Sri Chaitanya in the sixteenth century C.E. must be based on a historical and critical analysis of that theology's antecedents in Indic religious phenomena. Monotheism in India, which is unlike that of the Middle Eastern religions, developed slowly over thousands of years in the rich environment provided by a continuous and multifaceted civilization. One must be prepared to sift through over three thousand years of religious and intellectual history, with a huge and rich textual tradition, in order to trace the development of Indic monotheism into the specific forms it took in the sixteenth century. The roots of Indic monotheism can be followed back to the ancient Rig-Vedic vision of creation from the sacrifice of a giant, divine being (*purusha*) found in a famous hymn called the *Purusha-shukta* (10.90). That hymn, one of the latest of the Veda, is usually dated to around 1000 B.C.E. This idea of the primordial, dismembered giant gradually developed and transformed into the infinitely divisible, multipersonalitied conception of deity dominant in Hinduism today. A great many other lines of thought have contributed as well to the monotheism of Chaitanya's tradition: the Nyaya school's defense of theism from the Buddhist challenges, Kashmiri Shaivism's early development of the implications of tantric practice and thought, and the theistic explorations of the Shaiva Siddhanta tradition, to name just a few. A complete understanding would require a detailed examination not only of the main line of interpretation but also of those less direct lines of influence.

The academic way of looking at Indic theism is problematic for modern members of the Gaudiya Vaishnava tradition who wish to see their deity, Krishna, and their scriptures, particularly the *Bhagavata Purana*, as eternal and unchanging. How can one bridge the gulf between these two points of view? There may be no easy solution for this problem. Nevertheless, it is certain that modern members of the Chaitanya tradition, both within ISKCON and beyond it, must resolve the challenge somehow if they wish to engage today's intelligent and educated people in any kind of meaningful dialogue. The first step in the process is to articulate the distinctive Indic meaning of "monotheism."

Of course, it is always risky to apply terms developed and used in one set of religious traditions to another set with its own insights, history, and way of thinking and talking about religious matters. Such risk attaches especially to the use of the word "monotheism" in connection with the religious traditions of India. There is no comparable word or conception in any of the Indic languages. The idea of there being one and only one god would seem strange and even perverse to people nurtured in the rich, diverse, and densely populated religious world that has flourished in India for thousands of years. Even the terms that are used for the supreme god indicate a sense of the plurality of cosmic powers: God of gods (*deva-deva*), Lord of gods (*devesha*), master of the moving (*jagannatha*), the fortunate one (*bhagavan*), etc. Each of these indicates the singling out of one god from among many.

Thus on the surface Indic theism has more of the feel of the old biblical monolatry—the worship of one god among many as supreme—than of anything like monotheism. Nevertheless, the theism that developed in India is not a form of monolatry; nor does it fit the henotheism—the worship of one god at a time as supreme—that Max Muller invented to describe the early Vedic kind of theistic worship.[2] For Hindu theologians do not see all the various gods as separate and independent, but as different aspects or expansions of one supreme god. The best term for what happens to theism in India, therefore, *is* monotheism as long as one is willing to allow it enough plasticity to be molded by the Indic tradition into a form of monotheism unlike any other in the history of religions.

The extreme conservatism of the Indic traditions has continually sent Hindus back in times of challenge and change to their roots, which, because of the continuity of the civilization, have always been available to them. Although new influences have often exerted themselves during this long history, they were shaped and adapted to fit into the patterns of those ancient visions. Thus it is that an ancient vision of deity like that found in the *purusha* hymn could provide the fundamental structure on which the later forms of theistic belief and practice were built. The image of the primordial giant who was sacrificed to become the world and all beings in it was refracted in a number of ways to form the various types of religious belief found in India today. At one end of the spectrum are the monistic forms of belief represented by the nondualistic forms of Vedanta, in which all living beings are seen as digits of the one supreme, impersonal being called Brahman. Any sense of distinction among them is the result of ignorance. At the other extreme are the monotheistic forms of Vedanta, in which all beings are seen as tiny, separate offshoots of the supreme being—in this case, Vishnu—similar in nature but not in power, like so many tiny sparks shooting out of a fire. As that fire is capable of unlimited reduplication, so is the deity capable of expanding into unlimited forms each equal to the others. Somewhere in the middle of the spectrum rests the theo-monism of Kashmiri Shaivism, which attributes an identity or personality to the deity—in this case, Shiva—but understands all living beings as projections or instances of that deity. All of these different adumbrations of the primordial giant have interesting histories. Some aspects of the *purusha* presented in that revelatory text of the Veda dropped out of the tradition over time—the sacrificial dismemberment, for instance—while others have survived intact or have been transformed into something new—the "three-quarters beyond," for example, or the meaning of the "thousand heads, eyes, and feet." One can trace these developments through the Upanishads, the Epics, the Puranas, and then as they split off into the various sectarian literatures. Nevertheless, the long development of monotheism in India can be seen as originating in the old mysterious *purusha*.

The problem for modern members of the Chaitanya tradition remains, however. How does one bridge the gulf between a historical-critical understanding of the primordial giant as mythopoetic and subject to long and gradual transformations into the deities of modern Hinduism, and the understanding of the Chaitanya devotee in which godhead—that is, Krishna specifically—and sacred text are eternal? One of the main challenges modern devotees must confront is that, from an academic perspective, the normative historical analysis of Indic traditions does not find a deity called Krishna anywhere in the oldest corpus of Vedic texts—the four Vedas, the Brahmanas, the Aranyakas, and the Upanishads.[3] And when Krishna finally fully emerges in the Puranic and Epic textual genre of the post-Vedic period, he is not the only being who pronounces himself the supreme absolute God; Shiva, Vishnu, and eventually Devi, the Goddess, also lay claim to this status in unambiguous terms in the texts associated with each of them.[4]

On the basis of the above comments about the Indian tradition in general, one might suggest that the modern Krishna devotee follow the lead of his or her predecessors in the tradition and return to traditional sources. Once there, he or she may well find resources already in existence that might help resolve many of the modern questions and challenges, at least to the satisfaction of a person of faith. Modern devotees might find a useful line of thought, for instance, among the philosophers of Mimamsa, who argue that the Veda is eternal and yet was still revealed to certain sages at certain historically definable times. Just as a word is not created anew every time it is spoken, but exists as part of the language before and after its physical enunciation, so the Vedas are not created every time they are enunciated. Rather, they are merely manifested. This thesis is called the eternity of word thesis (*shabda-nityata-vada*) and rests on drawing a distinction between word (*shabda*) and sound (*dhvani*). Sound is only the means by which word is revealed. Word itself, revealed or unrevealed, is eternal. In the same way, one might argue that Krishna precedes and supersedes the particular, historically defined texts that act only as the vehicles of his self-revelation. In ways such as this, a historical reading of a tradition need not cripple a religious one. Be that as it may, it remains to be seen what strategies are adopted to confront the academic challenges outlined above, since engagement with the historical and text-critical methods of western scholarship still awaits most of the modern followers of Chaitanya Vaishnavism.

NOTES

1. Editors' note: Delmonico's original paper for this volume was an elaborate and comprehensive history of Indic monotheism with comparative glances at the Abrahamic traditions. Due to the considerable size and primary focus of that paper, however, and the constraints of this volume in these regards, Delmonico kindly agreed to withdraw that essay and submit in its stead this brief comment for this volume. The reader is referred to his Web site (www.bhajankutir.net) for the original essay containing a much more detailed discussion of Indic monotheism.

2. Muller coined the term "henotheism" to represent the religious attitudes he felt were exhibited in the *Rig-Veda*, where one god was worshipped as the supreme god of all for the duration of a hymn or rite, but then another god would be lauded as the supreme in another hymn or rite.

3. The possible exception to this is the reference in the *Chandogya Upanishad* (3.17.6) to Krishna, the son of Devaki, who is indeed Krishna's mother in the *Bhagavata Purana*. However, since this Krishna is connected with both a sage and esoteric practices not associated with the Krishna of the Puranas, there have been differences of opinions among scholars as to whether or not they refer to the same personality.

4. Moreover, in all other texts apart from the *Bhagavata Purana* and the *Bhagavad Gita* (and, at least according to some academic as well as traditional scholars from other sects, even in these most quintessential of Krishna-centered texts), Krishna is depicted as an incarnation of Vishnu, and thus a secondary or derivative manifestation of godhead, rather than the absolute source being.

[3]

HARE KRISHNA *MAHAMANTRA*

Gaudiya Vaiṣhnava Practice and the Hindu Tradition of Sacred Sound

GUY L. BECK

THE CHANTING OF THE HARE KRISHNA *mahamantra* (great mantra), *Hare Krishna, Hare Krishna, Krishna Krishna, Hare Hare, Hare Rama, Hare Rama, Rama Rama, Hare Hare,* is most readily associated with the Hare Krishna movement, or ISKCON (The International Society for Krishna Consciousness), founded in America by His Divine Grace A.C. Bhaktivedanta Swami Prabhupada in 1966. Besides a requirement for formal initiation, it is a precondition for achieving the society's spiritual goals, namely the bliss of devotion to Lord Krishna and ultimate communion with him in the Kingdom of God. These are also the aims of Gaudiya Vaishnavism, of which ISKCON is the largest and, arguably, most important branch.

In a small book published by the Bhaktivedanta Book Trust, *Chant and Be Happy: The Story of the Hare Krishna Mantra (Based on the Teachings of A.C. Bhaktivedanta Swami Prabhupada),* the Hare Krishna *mahamantra* is described as a "pleasure principle that operates beyond the limits of time and space and emanates from the very innermost part of our being," and a genuine "transcendental vibration" that is "the sublime method for reviving our transcendental consciousness."[1] Such consciousness is believed to be attained through both hearing and chanting the mantra: "When we hear this transcendental vibration, this consciousness is revived," and "By practical experience also, one can perceive that by chanting this *mahamantra*, or the 'great chanting for deliverance,' one can at once feel a transcendental ecstasy coming through from the spiritual stratum."[2]

Accordingly, members engage in congregational chanting and singing (*kirtana*) as well as private chanting on rosary beads (*japa*), said to be the single most important religious duty: "It is the duty of each initiated ISKCON devotee to chant sixteen rounds each day on the 108-bead rosary that he or she is given in initiation. There is, in ISKCON, no religious practice that supersedes the chanting of the Krishna *mantra*, or prayer formula."[3] As the mantra is comprised of names of God believed to contain transcendental potencies that bestow benedictions upon both practitioners and listeners, it is also set to music and sung congregationally in temples and in public arenas, accompanied by musical instruments.

Many people who today chant the Hare Krishna *mahamantra* are content with the simple and uncomplicated explanations given by the literature of the society, for, as nicely phrased by former Beatle and patron George Harrison, "The proof of the pudding is in the eating—All You Need is Love (Krishna)."[4] Certainly, advanced expertise in Hindu theology, linguistics, or music is not required to obtain the anticipated ecstasies or other spiritual benefits of chanting or hearing. It is not even required that one intellectually comprehend the chant or the process of chanting, as Srila Prabhupada himself states in an essay entitled, "On Chanting the Hare Krsna *mantra*": "There is no need . . . to understand the language of the *mantra*, nor is there any need of any mental speculation or intellectual adjustment for chanting this *mahamantra*. It springs automatically from the spiritual platform, and thus anyone can take part in the chanting without any previous qualification and dance in ecstasy."[5]

On the other hand, there are rich intellectual traditions within Hindu "sonic theology" that serve to illuminate the theoretical and historical background of the phenomenon of sacred sound in Gaudiya Vaishnavism, along with the practices associated with chanting, that are not commonly understood and provide rewards of their own.[6] Moreover, the most renowned saints, *acharyas*, and scholars throughout Indian history have applied considerable attention to the philosophical issues surrounding the divine nature and origin of sound and the "spiritual mechanics" of chanting. This chapter will outline some key points and issues that provide a positive step toward understanding the Hare Krishna *mahamantra*, and Shrila Prabhupada's statements about it, in the broader context of the traditions of sacred sound and theistic Hinduism.

The chanting of mantras in Indian religion has a long and complex history that transcends sectarian affiliation. The practice of formal recitation and chanting of sacred utterances is traceable back to the Vedic period (ca. 4000–1000 B.C.E.) when the sections of the *Rig-Veda* that were recited by priests during fire sacrifices were referred to as mantras. In fact, the entire *Rig-Veda* has been classified as "Mantra," in distinction from the later Brahmana, Aranyaka, and Upanishad additions.

Sacred sound during the Vedic period was bound up with the Vedic sacrifice. The chanted word was recognized by all the schools of Vedic brahmins and pandits as a powerful means to interact with the cosmos and to obtain spiritual merit. Selected verses of the *Rig-Veda* were arranged according to ritual format and chanted in three simple musical tones said to possess magical properties.[7] As such, the chanted mantras were believed to have the capacity to support and petition the deities that controlled the forces of the universe, to consecrate the ritual offerings to them, and to obtain unseen merit (*adrishta*), which led to a heavenly afterlife for the practitioner. *Vak*, the power of speech in the ancient rites, was personified as the Goddess of Speech and integrated into the rather intricate ritual detail outlined in the Vedic texts. Since the theoretical concept of *vak* as "powerful speech" was inherent in the pronunciation and metrical structure of the mantras, they were thought to be more powerful than the gods, who were ultimately dependent on the sacrificial offerings. Gradually the natural metaphors and mystical powers associated with *vak* became compacted into the seed syllable *om* and the metaphysical concept of *shabda brahman.*

The terms *vak*, *shabda brahman*, and *om* were soon used interchangeably in the Vedic tradition as concepts for sacred sound. In the principal Upanishads, the syllable *om* generally displayed three divisions (*matra*)—A, U, M—but sometimes added a fourth stage as "no stage" (*amatra*) or "empty." Interpreted as pointing toward the formless beyond form, the soundless beyond sound, this analysis gradually became the standard model for the monistic philosophical tradition known as *advaita*-Vedanta, but was ultimately rejected by the dualistic traditions associated with theism.

The developing theistic religious traditions preferred other explanations found in the Upanishads, such as where *om* is referred to as a "friction-stick" that invokes God or Brahman within the heart prior to seeing the deity. Furthermore, the three-stage analysis of *om* was soon modified by the yogic, tantric, and theistic traditions so that the previously "empty" fourth stage was replaced by a substantive fourth degree (*turiya*) comprised of the female *nada*, symbolized by the half moon, and the male *bindu*, symbolized by the dot, as in the Sanskrit *anusvara*. There were also rudimentary discussions of *nada* in early phonetic texts attached to the Veda, alluding to the "voiced sound" produced by the combination of internal fire and air in the human body. The yogic and tantric traditions enlarged upon this, combining it with the concepts of *om* and *shabda brahman* found in the Upanishads, and established the term *nada brahman*, which soon became important in all theistic traditions as well as in the musicological texts, and which also more clearly allowed for a dualistic interpretation of a supreme being and a divine energy.

Consequently, *nada brahman* gradually eclipsed *shabda brahman* as the chief cosmological and psychological characterization of sacred sound within Hindu theistic traditions connected to Shiva, Vishnu, or the Goddess. As it included both linguistic sound (sound with semantic meaning, i.e., language or *shabda*) and nonlinguistic sound (sound without semantic meaning, i.e., musical tone or *svara*), it was also suitable for indicating the notion of a primal undifferentiated sound said to be "heard" by yogis and saintly musicians like Tyagaraja, the great South Indian musician and devotee of Rama, also known as a *nada yogi*.

Nada yoga is the type of yoga aimed at transcendental awareness of *nada brahman*, and its sonic techniques along with the accompanying theories have influenced many Hindu traditions, including Vaishnavism. The philosophical tradition of yoga, including Patanjali's *Yoga Sutra* and the commentaries by Vyasa, Vachaspati, and Vijnana Bhiksu, endorsed the theory and practice of *om* meditation and provided a solid orthodoxy for the development of *nada yoga*, such that several Yoga Upanishads, including especially the *Nadabindu Upanishad*, as well as the three major *hatha yoga* texts in the Gorakhnath tradition, *Shiva Samhita*, *Gheranda Samhita*, and *Hatha Yoga Pradipika*, recommend the practical application of *nada yoga* disciplines.

Within the field of Sanskrit linguistics, two rival schools emerged that claimed a basis in Vedic tradition and that proved significant regarding the issue of chanting mantras. The Vedic sacrificial philosophy known as Mimamsa, headed by Jaimini, stressed that the divine potencies of language were present only in the eternal Vedic texts and particularly in the individual syllables of those texts. This view of language was called *varnavada*. The opposing view, taught by the Sanskrit grammarians headed by Bhartrihari, was known as *sphotavada*. *Sphotavada* insisted that the potencies of all language were found in the overall sentence meanings and not in the individual syllables, implying that all speech that was semantically coherent had meaning and power, including ordinary language. The implication of the Mimamsa view was that Vedic language was automatically powerful or "spiritual" with or without the cognitive component as long as the pronunciation was correct, and that it was not mandatory for the practitioner to "understand" the meaning as it was for the *sphotavada*. This view is supported by the fact that for centuries many brahmin priests have memorized and chanted the Vedas without full knowledge of the literal meaning of the texts.

Theistic Hindu traditions, whether Vaishnava, Shaiva, or Shakta, preferred the *varnavada* position on language since it was the only logical explanation for the special sacred power of the Vedic texts, as well as their own mantras, which were viewed as distinct from ordinary language and hence "Vedic." This allowed for the use of apparently "meaningless" mantras and syllables. It was, however, stipulated by the theists that the potencies in the particular syllables of the revealed mantras and scriptures were delegated directly by a supreme being for the purpose of bringing about salvation for human beings in the present age of *kali yuga*. This initiative was known as grace or *anugraha*, especially present in theistic mantras: "All *mantra*s are manifestations of god in his pristine glory as saviour . . . *mantra*s are god's forms assumed out of grace, embodiments of that grace (*anugraha murti*)."[8] In the case of Shaivism, "There can be no doubt that these *mantra*s can be traced back to nothing but the decree of Shiva himself . . . for the salvation of men."[9] And most theistic mantras contain revealed names of God: "In order to be effective, [chanting] must be undertaken with a name that God himself has revealed in the Scriptures. God is identical with such a self-revealed name."[10]

For Shaivism, the Shaiva Agamas contained theories of *om* as well as speculations on *nada* and *bindu* in terms of Shiva and his Shakti, influencing Shaiva Siddhanta, the groups reflected in the *Shiva Purana*, and monistic Kashmiri Shaivism, which offered theories of *para vak* (*para nada*) and *spanda* or cosmic vibration. The connection of Shiva with *nada*, *bindu*, or *om* is found throughout Shaivism, which also preferred the *varnavada* position.

The worship of the Goddess as supreme is the basis of Shakta tantra. The *Sharada Tilaka Tantra* is the key text for the study of *nada brahman* in most Shakta traditions and is accepted as authoritative by Shaiva and Vaishnava groups. Most Shakta texts discuss mantra, *bija*, and *nada* in the theory and practice of Shakta worship, identifying the Goddess with *nada*, and prefer the *varnavada* position on language. The tantric notions of *bija* (seed) and *matrika* (little mother) within each letter or syllable indicate gender polarization, and reflect the form of *om* as the embodiment of Shiva and Shakti, or Vishnu and Lakshmi in Vaishnavism. The internalization of the alphabet as *nada shakti* or *nada brahman* throughout the chakra centers in the human body form the substance of *kundalini yoga*, also present in Shaiva and Vaishnava practices, but especially in Shakta tantra.

Vaishnavism, the largest and most pervasive among the Hindu theistic groups, incorporated the same theology and practice of sacred sound found in Shaivism and Shakta tantra. Parallels among the three groups are prominent in the Pancharatra tradition, the *Bhagavata Purana*, and the literature of the major Vaishnava *sampradayas*. The Pancharatra texts are the authoritative foundation for nearly all Vaishnava theory and practice, and teach the worship of Vishnu in order to attain his divine abode. Pancharatra soteriology strongly emphasizes the path of mantra meditation, referring to its own scriptures as "*mantra-shastra*."

Like the Shaiva Agamas, the Pancharatra texts are divided into four parts: *jnana*, knowledge; *yoga*, concentration; *kriya*, making; and *charya*, doing. The major Pancharatra texts display significant attention to sacred sound as *nada brahman*. The concepts of *nada* and *nada brahman* appear already in the *Jayakhya Samhita* and the *Sattvata Samhita*, two of the earliest (ca. 500 C.E.) and most canonical, while the later *Ahirbudhnya Samhita* contains the fullest elaboration of *nada brahman*. The *Jayakhya Samhita* also refers to the practice of *japa* with the rosary (*aksha mala*), earlier than Islamic or Christian allusions.

The *Sattvata Samhita*, one of the most respected Pancharatra works, describes the letters of the Sanskrit alphabet as born from *nada*, the *shakti* of Vishnu or Narayana, while the *Paushkara Samhita* (ca. 450 C.E.) contains a long digression on mantra yoga. Exploration of the states of being at the climax of *nada* (*nadanta*) occur in the *Sesha Samhita*, which has an analysis of the nine components of *om*: A, U, M, *bindu*, *nada*, *nadanta*, *nadatita* (beyond *nada*), *nadatitanta* (the end beyond *nada*), and *nadatitantantara* (within the end beyond *nada*), with their corresponding Vaishnava meanings, including a list of names for Vishnu or his incarnations, such as Narasimha, Narayana, Ramachandra, Kesava, Vasudeva, Purushottama, and Bhagavan Hari.

The *Lakshmi Tantra* (ca. 900–1300 C.E.) displays many Shakta elements, yet is a Pancharatra text due to association of Lakshmi with Vishnu as his *Shakti*, discussion of the four *vyuha* expansions, and a large number of citations from other Pancharatra works. Lakshmi identifies herself as the "Mother of all Sound," and explains her presence in the syllable *om*. The linguistic cosmogony in this text contains the elements of *nada* and *bindu*.

In league with Mimamsa and *varnavada*, the Pancharatra tradition perceives the essential potency of language in the syllables and letters, which are both named and empowered by Lakshmi. As in most Hindu theistic traditions, except for some of the Upanishads and Advaita Vedanta, *om* is divided into four substantive degrees in Pancharatra, including *nada* and *bindu* counted as fourth, which are linked to the four *vyuha*s or emanations of Vishnu: A for Aniruddha, U for Pradyumna, M for Samkarshana, and the fourth Vasudeva and his consort Lakshmi.

The *Bhagavata Purana* (ca. 600–900 C.E.), a large Purana that reflects the devotional milieu of South India as well as the blending of Vedic, Agamic, yogic, and philosophical sources, is crucial for understanding sacred sound in Vaishnavism after 1000 C.E. The text reveals its own syncretism, wherein Vishnu, the original "speaker," agrees to receive both Vedic and tantric modes of worship.[11] The activities of hearing and chanting mantras are given high status among the nine methods of devotional service or *bhakti*.

The importance of sacred sound in the *Bhagavata Purana* is found in the last canto (12.6.37–44), with a detailed description of its own sonic origin, including the theologies of *nada brahman*. Suta Goswami, the narrator, replies to an inquiry about the source of the text with an explanation of the origin of *om*, the Vedas, and the Sanskrit alphabet.[12] The importance of *om* here is self-evident: it is the first linguistic manifestation of *nada brahman* and the source of the Vedas, language, and consciousness. Brahma the Creator is said to have begun the Vaishnava tradition of initiation (*diksha*) whereby mantras (*om*, Gopala *mantra*, Hare Krishna *mahamantra*) were first received from Krishna, and then passed down to succeeding gurus.

Krishna reveals his personal appearance as sacred sound in the *Bhagavata Purana* (11.12.18) using the Upanishad metaphor of a "friction-stick."[13] Krishna is also depicted (11.12.17) as manifesting *nada brahman* within the human body in terms of the chakras of tantric yoga.[14] Gaudiya Vaishnava commentator Vishvanatha Chakravarti has elaborated on the mystical nature of this verse.[15] The subtle form of Krishna is to be perceived within the body at the very culmination of *nada*, according to the *Bhagavata Purana* (11.27.23–24): "In his own body . . . the worshipper should contemplate on My highest form, atomic in size, located in the heart lotus, which the perfected meditate upon as being beyond the '*nada*' [*nadante*, literally "at the end of *nada*"]."[16] Shridhara Swami, a medieval commentator on this text, stated that the syllable *om* has four to five parts, as in the Shaiva and Shakta ideologies: "*Pranava*, or *omkara*, has five parts; A, U, M, the nasal *bindu* and the reverberation (*nada*). Liberated souls meditate upon the Lord at the end of that vibration."[17] The *Bhagavata Purana* (11.15.16) had already blended Vishnu into the fourth "degree" of *om*.[18]

The major Vaishnava *sampradayas* (lineages) were formed by Ramanuja, Madhva, Nimbarka, Vallabha, and Chaitanya. Parallel with the *Bhagavata Purana*, these traditions recognized *nada brahman* as the energy of Vishnu or Krishna. First Ramanuja (1050–1137 C.E.) discussed *om* in many of his writings and advocated the chanting of the Shri Vaishnava mantra, *om namo Narayanaya*. Madhva (thirteenth century C.E.), the formulator of Dvaita Vedanta and the founder of the Madhva *sampradaya*, discussed *om* in his *Rig-Bhashya*, and chanting in his *Tantra Sara Sangraha*, *Sadachara Smriti*, and *Krishnamrita Maharnava*. Ramanuja and Madhva both accepted *varnavada* as the only possible explanation for the eternal power of mantras and refuted *sphotavada*. Nimbarka (ca. 1120–1200 C.E.) taught a version of Vedanta known as *dvaitadvaita*, and advocated a personal devotion to Krishna or Gopala and his consort Radha by chanting of the Gopala mantra, *Klim Krishnaya Govindaya Gopijana-Vallabhaya Svaha*, which gained currency in Gaudiya Vaishnavism. Conforming to *varnavada*, the followers of Nimbarka also chant their own Krishna *mahamantra*: *Radhe Krishna, Radhe Krishna, Krishna Krishna, Radhe Radhe, Radhe Shyama, Radhe Shyama, Shyama Shyama, Radhe Radhe*. According to tradition, Vallabha (1479–1533 C.E.), founder of the Pushtimarga *sampradaya*, received his principal initiatory mantra, *Shri Krishnah sharanam mama*, "Krishna is my refuge," directly from Krishna. The highest liberation of the Vallabhites is to participate in the eternal *rasalila* with Krishna by constant repetition of this mantra.

Gaudiya Vaishnavism, which began historically as an organized movement with Chaitanya Mahaprabhu (1486–1533 C.E.), is theologically linked to the Madhva *sampradaya* and influenced by Shridhara Swami. Like Ramanuja and Madhva before him, Shridhara Swami rejected the Grammarian theory of *sphotavada* and favored the Mimamsa theory.[19] And like Madhva and Shridhara, Jiva Goswami (1513–1598 C.E.), among the most prolific Gaudiya Vaishnava writers, rejected the *sphotavada* doctrine and adhered to the Mimamsa position of *varnavada*.[20]

Considering the eminence of specific mantras in each of the Vaishnava lineages, the Hare Krishna *mahamantra* appears most unique to Gaudiya Vaishnavism. The *Kali Santarana Upanishad* (ca. before 1500 C.E.) probably contains the earliest reference to this now world-famous mantra: "*Hare Rama, Hare Rama, Rama Rama, Hare Hare, Hare Krishna, Hare Krishna, Krishna Krishna, Hare Hare* [O Hari, O Rama, O Krishna, etc.]—This collection of sixteen names is destructive of the baneful influences of Kali [*kali yuga*, the age of *kali*]. . . . Beyond this there is no other better means to be found in all the Vedas."[21] While the biographies of Chaitanya only mention a ten-syllable mantra, the *mahamantra* is believed to be the same one Chaitanya received at his initiation in Gaya, and which he propounded as the true means of deliverance in the present age of *kali yuga*. According to Vaishnava etymology, the expression "Hare" is the vocative form of "Hara," a name for Radha or the Shakti of Krishna (*nada shakti*), and betrays the presence of the Shakti or energy of God in the mantra itself: "Now the name 'Hare' means 'O Hara,' 'O Stealer.' Hara is she who steals the mind of Krishna; she is Radha. The eight 'Hare's in the *mahamantra* call out to Radha in the eight phases of her love for Krishna."[22]

Gaudiya Vaishnavism places strong emphasis on the audible chanting or singing of the Hare Krishna *mahamantra*. Whereas some other groups may hold that silent or low-volume "muttering" is equally efficacious, Chaitanya and his followers proclaimed that the loud chanting of God's name(s) was most effective in obtaining salvation, since it purifies the heart of both chanter and listener, and is most conducive to achieving love of God. This at least is the interpretation given to Rupa Goswami's *Prathama Chaitanyashtaka* (5), which states that Chaitanya himself had chanted "the *mahamantra* in a loud voice" (*Hare Krishnety uccaih*).[23]

Consequently, there is a distinct emphasis on "transcendental sound" by modern Gaudiya Vaishnavas, including Shrila Bhaktisiddhanta Saraswati (1874–1937), founder of the Gaudiya Math, who stated in 1931: "We should always be hearing the Absolute through the transcendental Sound . . . [which] comes here to designate God-head. The transcendental Sound is the Name of God-head."[24] And for Gaudiya Vaishnavas, including ISKCON, the Hare Krishna *mahamantra* also qualifies as "transcendental sound" because it is overpowering by nature (empowered by Krishna) and may not be fully ascertained or experienced in silence or at low volume. That is, it seems that only by audible exclamation are the full potencies of the *mantra* revealed and the sinful propensities in the heart removed, fostering "true" *bhakti* sentiments.

In conclusion, the theory and practice of sacred sound in Gaudiya Vaishnavism conform to the patterns that are observed throughout Hindu theism, including the philosophy of *nada brahman*, the idea of *nada* as the *shakti* of a supreme deity, *varnavada* linguistics, sonic cosmogonies, and the use of names of God chanted on a rosary. Echoing back to the Vedic use of mantra in ritual, the soteriological modus operandi of chanting the Hare Krishna *mahamantra* may be conceived as the guru's creation of an interior sonic world or "battery" in the body of the disciple that is sustained and augmented by regular mantra recitation and chanting until the accumulated sonic merit or "charge" secures awards in the afterlife. And yet, unlike the Vedic and Mimamsa viewpoints, theistic Vaishnavism also strives to cultivate the appropriate moods and emotional states associated with the *bhakti* tradition, and hence anticipates not only release from the material suffering of rebirth but an eternal life of bliss and devotion to Krishna.

NOTES

1. *Chant and Be Happy: The Story of the Hare Krishna Mantra* (Los Angeles: Bhaktivedanta Book Trust, 1982), vii–viii.
2. Ibid., xii.
3. Larry D. Shinn, *The Dark Lord: Cult Images and the Hare Krishnas in America* (Westminster: John Knox Press, 1987), 101.
4. *Chant and Be Happy*, i.
5. Srila Prabhupada, "On Chanting the Hare Krishna Mantra," in *On Chanting Hare Krishna* (Los Angeles: Bhaktivedanta Book Trust International, 1999), 13.
6. The interested reader is advised to consult the author's book.
7. These initial three tones were expanded into seven for singing the Sama-Veda, forming the basis of Indian music.
8. Sanjukta Gupta, "The Pancharatra Attitude to Mantra," in *Understanding Mantras*, ed. Harvey P. Alper (Albany: SUNY Press, 1989), 243.
9. Gerhard Oberhammer, "The Use of Mantra in Yogic Meditation: The Testimony of the Pasupata," in Alper, ed., *Understanding Mantras*, 220.
10. Klaus K. Klostermaier, *A Survey of Hinduism* (Albany: SUNY Press, 1989), 216.
11. N. Raghunathan, trans., *Srimad-Bhagavatam* (Madras: Vighnesvara Press, 1976), II:628.
12. Ibid., 668.

13. Ibid. 566.

14. Ibid., 566.

15. Quoted in Bhaktivedanta Swami, trans., *Srimad-Bhagavatam* (New York and Los Angeles: Bhaktivedanta Book Trust, 1982), Eleventh Canto, Part Three, 145.

16. Raghunathan, trans., II:629.

17. Quoted in Bhaktivedanta Swami, trans., Eleventh Canto, Part Five (1984), 577.

18. Raghunathan, trans., II:577.

19. Prabhatchandra Chakravarti, *The Philosophy of Sanskrit Grammar* (Calcutta: Calcutta University, 1930), 121.

20. Stuart M. Elkman, *Jiva Goswami's Tattra-Sandarbha* (Delhi: Motilal Banarsidass, 1986), 75.

21. T. R. Srinivasa Ayyangar, trans., *The Vaisnava Upanishads* (Madras: Adyar, 1953), 19.

22. Basanti Choudhury, "Love Sentiment and Its Spiritual Implications in Gaudiya Vaisnavism," in *Bengal Vaisnavism, Orientalism, Society and the Arts*, ed. Joseph T. O'Connell (East Lansing, MI: Asian Studies Center, Michigan State University, 1985), 4.

23. Rupa Vilasa Dasa (Robert D. MacNaughton), *A Ray of Vishnu* (Washington, MS: New Jaipur Press, 1988), 22.

24. Bhaktisiddhanta Saraswati Goswami Maharaj, *Shri Chaitanya's Teachings* (Madras: Sree Gaudiya Math, 1967), 419–20.

[4]

KRISHNA IN *MLECCHA DESH*

ISKCON Temple Worship in Historical Perspective

KENNETH VALPEY (KRISHNA KSHETRA DAS)

BHAKTIVEDANTA SWAMI PRABHUPADA'S final visit to England in September 1977 included a brief stop at the Bury Place Radha-Krishna Temple in downtown London. Prabhupada sat silently before the deities of Krishna and Radha, "Sri Sri Radha-London-ishvara,"[1] as he had named the half-lifesized marble images in 1969. Devotees present at the time felt that he was saying good-bye to the brightly dressed, smiling figures for whom he had always shown great affection, perhaps offering a prayerful, silent appeal similar to one he had uttered before the Radha-Krishna deities he had consecrated in Sydney, Australia, in 1971: "I am leaving You here in this *mleccha desh*.[2] Now, these devotees, they have come to You, kindly give them intelligence so that they can serve You nicely. This is my prayer" (K. Dasa 415–16).

Indeed, the continual devotional worship of Krishna by the traditional Vaishnava formal ritual system (*archanam*) would be a great challenge for Prabhupada's followers. They were handicapped not only by non-Vaishnava, non-Indian, nonbrahmanical backgrounds but also by the fact that they were as much products of modernity as any twentieth- and twenty-first-century westerners. However charged they might have been with enthusiasm by their guru's vision and conviction, it was not clear that they would be able to bypass their cultural shadows by adhering to a Vaishnava devotional regimen. Nor was it clear that they would be able to pass on the same, barely transplanted sprout of Krishna *bhakti* to the next generation. The test would be whether they could carry on the strict demands of temple deity worship, "keeping Krishna in the center" of their lives despite all contrary influences and inclinations.

Initially these devotees met the challenge in grand American can-do fashion. Service for the deities in a style fit for kings was the pace-setting standard established by Prabhupada in the Los Angeles temple in 1969 and the early 1970s, and the devotees' competitive spirit, which they considered spiritually wholesome since it was based on desire to please their preceptor, soon produced similarly ambitious temple worship programs elsewhere.[3] In ISKCON temples scattered across the United States and Canada—and soon thereafter in Europe, India, and South America—a daily schedule from four in the morning until ten at night kept a sizeable detachment of cooks and *pujaris* (priests) constantly occupied with offering the best of comforts to Krishna in his various deity forms.[4]

But ISKCON devotees' fierce dedication to a life of high ritual density (Bell 173) was not motivated merely by pious showmanship and eagerness for spiritual novelty. The logic of devotional life aimed at self-realization and dedicated to Krishna's service, as they understood from Prabhupada's teachings in his books and lectures, pointed to the necessity for adherence to the practice of *sadhana*.[5] And this practice directs Krishna devotees to render daily service (*seva*) to Krishna in the form of his three-dimensional image according to elaborate prescriptions provided by Sanskrit texts held to be authoritative by Krishna devotees, or more specifically, followers of Shri Chaitanya (1486–1533). Prabhupada, seeing himself as a faithful deliverer of these texts unaltered, insisted that he had not invented the process of "devotional service;"[6] rather, he intended to transmit a tradition long established in sacred scriptures and temples that revered and followed those scriptures.

In this article I will sketch some features of this tradition of deity worship in India as the background for deity worship in ISKCON. This will be in the spirit of "*Wirkungsgeschichte*," as opposed to "*Entstehungsgeschichte*,"[7] with an eye to indications of continuity and innovation. It is apparent that Prabhupada, aware of the odds against his purposes of transplantation, felt that nevertheless the tradition possessed the vitality and resilience necessary to realize his goal. Therefore, within the brief period of his remaining few years of life he strove to introduce a self-contained culture of spirituality that would thrive well beyond the duration of his personal presence. This was accomplished largely by encouraging devotional spontaneity (centered on reciting and singing the

Hare Krishna *mahamantra*). But of almost equal importance for the survival of his mission would be the introduction of rule-governed devotional practices (centered on deity worship) enjoined in scripture and followed in Indian temples. I focus here on this second factor. I will sketch the scriptural background to ISKCON deity worship practices and look at some important Indian temple models immediately influencing them, then offer some observations on present-day ISKCON deity worship in the context of the scriptural and temple backgrounds and in light of Prabhupada's missionary intentions.

THE SCRIPTURAL AND TEMPLE BACKGROUND

Prabhupada's overarching scheme for transplanting "Krishna-conscious" culture emphasized printed books as conveyors of sacred knowledge. Books would also, he hoped, communicate the practical means by which this knowledge could be applied in people's lives. Thus he considered an important component in the corpus of his writings to be his "summary study" of a sixteenth-century Sanskrit work, *Bhakti-rasamrita-sindhu* (The Ocean of the Nectar of Devotional Relish), authored by a preeminent Vaishnava theologian, Rupa Goswami.[8] In the beginning chapters of this text, Rupa outlines the principles and practices of *vaidhi bhakti sadhana*, regulated devotional practice. While his discussion on this topic is relatively brief, it is clearly in concert with *Hari-bhakti-vilasa* (The Charm of Devotion to Hari), a much more detailed treatment of *vaidhi bhakti sadhana* by two of Rupa's colleagues, Gopala Bhatta and Sanatana.[9] This latter work (compiled probably slightly prior to the writing of *Bhakti-rasamrita-sindhu*) leads quickly into the rich fabric of textual sources of Vaishnava deity worship, as it contains among its nine thousand Sanskrit verse couplets quotations from more than two hundred other Sanskrit works. These references are largely from two major genres, Agama and Purana, both of which emphasize image worship as important means for cultivating devotional piety.

Within the broad category of Agama texts (some of which are said to predate Buddhism),[10] a major textual source and authority for all Vaishnava image worship practices up to the present day is the collection known as Vaishnava Samhitas, also known as Pancharatra Agamas or simply Pancharatra (Beck 173).[11] Traditionally numbering 108 *samhitas* (Schrader 4), the approximately sixty extant texts offer a system of worship in marked contrast to earlier Vedic and Upanishadic styles. Some common features of the Pancaratric texts are: a clear focus on the worship of Vishnu, also known as Narayana, with the purpose of attaining some form of union or communion with him (or attaining his eternal association and residence in his transcendent abode); explication of the *vyuha* theology of the divine and cosmic replication and descent of various forms of God (*avataras*); and an emphasis on mantra meditation and recitation as the center of *sadhana,* or disciplined practice (Beck 173–4, Gonda 49). Pancharatra literature has this last element in common with Shaiva Agama; the same is true of its relation to Shakta tantra:[12]

> Pancharatra has a great deal in common with other Tantric sects, and this holds also for its attitude to mantra. Like the other sects, Pancharatra refers to its own scriptures as Mantra-shastra and regards them as teaching mantras, meditation on those mantras, and the ritual accompanying that meditation; the whole constituting the means (*sadhana*) to salvation (*mukti*). (Gupta 228–29)

A further characteristic of Pancharatra, linked to its understanding of mantra, is the importance placed on the power of Vishnu, namely *shakti,* identified as the divine Word—*vak, nada brahman,* or *shabda brahman*—and understood to be Vishnu's consort Lakshmi or Shri. As the energy of Vishnu, Lakshmi becomes the essential *via medium* between the *sadhaka,* or practitioner, and the supreme Lord, Vishnu. As such she is identified as the conveyor of divine grace, theologically crucial for the flourishing of the Vaishnava *bhakti* movement[13] and particularly important later as a theoretical basis for the worship of Radha together with Krishna in the Chaitanya Vaishnava tradition. This emphasis on *shakti* combines with the theology of replication and descent of the supreme divinity into the world to highlight Vishnu or Krishna.

Divine accessibility, in turn, becomes crucial to the theology of *archanam* (ritual worship) elaborated by later Vaishnava writers. Divine descent combines with the logic of divine sentience to give the *sadhaka* entrance into transcendent relationship with a distinct and personal God by service with his or her own physical senses. *Bhakti,* the devotional attitude of service to Vishnu or Krishna, preempting *mukti,* or liberation, as the highest goal for these theologians, is the means by which physical sense activity becomes sanctified. As above, so below: the *sadhaka* engaged in *archana* practice anticipates life beyond this life as a continuation and perfection of present devotional activities, minus the inebriety characteristic of this-world sense activity. Yet, by holding fast to the goal of satisfying the object of worship perpetually, Vaishnavas are distinguished from practitioners of those strains of Indian religiosity (often found in the worship of Shiva or Shakti) that aim for some type of perfection involving equivalence or erasure of difference with the object of worship. Vaishnavism celebrates divine differentiation to such an extent that the *archa murti,* or deity, to all appearances made of earthly substance and showing humanlike attributes, is considered no less the Deity than the Lord who exists eternally in a form beyond the ken of mortal senses.[14] By elaborate consecration procedures prescribed in Agama literature, and on the basis of devotional desire held by a qualified person, the Lord is understood to accept the particular deity form (fashioned according to iconographic stipulations also found in Agama texts) as his very form.[15]

The *Hari-bhakti-vilasa* also quotes liberally from Puranic literature—a genre that both incorporates elements of and complements Agama texts. More so than is the case with the Agamas, the Puranas display a rich narrative dimension that serves to extol one or another divine personage and to celebrate the virtues of devotional dedication to the deity's service. Among Vaishnava Puranas, the *Bhagavata Purana* is most prized by the Chaitanya Vaishnavas,[16] and is quoted more than any other Purana in the *Hari-bhakti-vilasa*. As a treatise on Vishnu or Krishna *bhakti*, the *Bhagavata Purana* provides the basis and patterns for the devotional attitudes, which the rules of regulated deity worship cultivate, according to Chaitanya Vaishnavism. Far less concerned with technical details of deity worship ritual than the Agamas, the *Bhagavata Purana* elaborates on the theology of *bhakti* that Jiva Goswami, the nephew of Rupa Goswami, developed systematically in his *Sat sandarbha* (Six Treatises).

Although the Bhagavata upholds a substantial degree of social orthodoxy, as, for example, in Narada's descriptions of *varna* and *ashram* duties (7.11–15), the principle of devotion is invariably propounded wherein material/social disqualification is superseded by devotional qualification.[17] Thus, for example, Prahlada, "although born in a demonic family" (Bhag. 7.9.8) is favored before all the gods to offer prayers to the Nrisimha (man-lion) *avatara* of Vishnu. This and similar statements in the *Bhagavata Purana* (and later, in the *Chaitanya Charitamrita* of Krishnadas Kaviraja[18]) served as important sources for Prabhupada's conviction that westerners—people outside brahmanical, and even Indian, culture—may become qualified to practice devotional service, including the activities of *archanam*, or ritual worship of deities in temples, provided they carefully adhere to the regulative regimens enjoined in the above-mentioned sacred texts.

The extant Puranic literature displays a marked focus on physical, iconic images as objects of worship, especially as located in particular sacred places, usually *tirthas* (lit: "crossings") in India. Temple worship, with its emphasis on *darshan* (vision, sight, but also insight, philosophy) as an essential means of accessing the deity, thus became a major feature of the Indian religious landscape from the early centuries of the Common Era.[19] The visible deity, housed in a palatial construction modeled after the *purusha* "cosmic Man" (Gonda 27), became accessible to a much broader social spectrum than the invisible recipients of sacrificial oblations characteristic of Vedic worship.

Within the three Indian geographical loci of Chaitanya Vaishnavism—Puri (in Orissa), Vrindavan (between Delhi and Agra), and Navadvipa (north of Calcutta)—Puri's early medieval Jagannatha temple can be best termed "palatial" in size and in grandeur of worship rituals. As the place where Shri Chaitanya is reported to have spent hours daily during the latter half of his life, the temple of Jagannatha ("Lord of the universe," considered to be a form of Krishna) is of special importance to Chaitanya Vaishnavas. At present, however, accessibility of this deity is restricted: temple management forbids entry to all "non-Hindus," which, in their eyes, includes western Vaishnavas.[20] This has not prevented ISKCON devotees from establishing Jagannatha worship in the West and performing Jagannatha Rathayatra[21] in several cities worldwide. However, it has ensured that ISKCON worship of Jagannatha remains quite simple in comparison with both the daily and festival procedures in Puri, where a complex caste structure is sustained largely on the basis of identification with specific temple services.[22]

An important concentration of Vaishnava temples styled as *havelis*, or large residences, is found in and around Vrindavan as a result of Vaishnava clerical promotion and royal/mercantile patronage. One such temple important to many of Prabhupada's followers is that of Gopala Bhatta's Krishna deity, Radharamana. Among the original Krishna deities worshipped by Chaitanya's principle disciples in Vrindavan headed by Rupa, Radharamana is the only one that was not removed to places considered safe from Moghul iconoclastic destruction during the seventeenth century. Toward the end of British rule in the 1930s Bhaktisiddhanta Saraswati, Prabhupada's guru, encountered strong opposition from Vrindavan temple leaders for his practice of giving brahmanical initiation to those not born in Brahmin families (Brooks 87; R. V. Dasa 115, 116). This conservative attitude is retained today by some, but not all, of the Radharamana Gosvamis; others show considerable hospitality to western Vaishnavas.[23] Hence, with Prabhupada's approval, many ISKCON members frequent this temple and observe its well-conducted ceremonies, appreciating its ethos of care and attention to the delicate form of Krishna.[24] From the Radharamana priests a few ISKCON devotees have also learned ritual details, many of which were stipulated in *Hari-bhakti-vilasa* by the temple's founder, Gopala Bhatta.[25]

The third locus of Chaitanya Vaishnavism is the area of Navadvipa—Chaitanya's birthplace—in present-day West Bengal. Temples in this area have been generally modest in size, and it seems (from Chaitanya's early biographers) that Chaitanya and his associates were satisfied to worship small images of Krishna or Vishnu (and, after Chaitanya's demise, images of Chaitanya and Nityananda) in their homes.[26] But in more recent times, Bhaktisiddhanta Saraswati began his Chaitanya Vaishnava mission in Navadvipa, overseeing several missionary centers (Gaudiya Maths) with ashrams for celibate preachers surrounding a central shrine housing fairly large images of Radha-Krishna and Chaitanya. The larger deities (certainly not unique to his mission) would suggest both confidence in the indifference of a secular government and perhaps a somewhat defiant attitude toward nineteenth- and early twentieth-century Hindu reformers who had altogether rejected deity worship as an embarrassment.

Yet with Bhaktisiddhanta's emphasis on missionary activity, Gaudiya Math temple worship was given a somewhat secondary role in ashram life, which was nevertheless to be strictly regulated by a small manual, *Archana paddhati* (Procedures for Worship).[27] As the immediate institutional forerunners of Prabhupada's mission in the West, the Gaudiya Math establishments served in some respects as models for ISKCON practices—especially in deity worship procedures. Hence this text was followed by ISKCON temples, as was the Gaudiya Math sequence of devotional songs to be sung at prescribed times as well as the lecture style of morning and evening scriptural readings. Even the style of cooking favored by Prabhupada—the Bengali vegetarian fare he knew from childhood[28]—was essentially the same as that familiar to Gaudiya Math ashramites and was the style he hoped would prevail in his western temples.

Indeed, food was to become a major vehicle for missionary activity in ISKCON. Through vegetarian food offerings to the temple deities that were then distributed to the public, deity worship was strongly linked to propagation. With good-tasting Krishna *prasadam* (food ritually offered to the deity), elaborate dress and ornamentation of the deities, and much attention to cleanliness and punctuality, the more esoteric details of worship procedures described in *Hari-bhakti-vilasa* (and followed in such temples as Radharamana) could be either dispensed with or set aside for later inculcation. Perceiving ISKCON as a revival of flagging Gaudiya Math missionary spirit, Prabhupada emphasized what he considered the essentials of deity worship: a system supportive of the primary devotional activities centered on the recitation of the Hare Krishna mantra and the regular reading of the *Bhagavata Purana*.

RECORDED TRADITION

Yet already under Prabhupada's direct guidance ISKCON had its own distinctive style and mood of temple worship. In 1970 Prabhupada requested that a recently recorded musical rendering of the "Govindam Prayers" be played in all ISKCON temples at the time of the daily morning "greeting of the deities" or *darshan arati*.[29] This three- or four-minute-long recording, arranged by George Harrison (of Beatles fame) and sung by London devotees, encapsulates Prabhupada's reshaping of traditional Krishna deity worship in a western context. It consists of two Sanskrit verses selected from a text revered by Chaitanya Vaishnavas, sung in choral style, accompanied by both acoustic and electric instruments. Rhythm is provided by a subdued rock band-style drum set.

The Sanskrit prayers (left untranslated, which poetically describe Krishna's beauty and the transcendent nature of his form, are faithful to scriptural tradition. The use of an electronic recording for this high point of the ritual day is innovative. The "Govindam Prayers" are an embellishment or prelude for the singing and playing of traditional musical instruments by temple community members at the principal daily deity *darshan* (viewing).

That the lead singer of the recording is a woman is also significant. Such would have been unthinkable in the Gaudiya Math temples. Indeed, a notable difference between Indian temples and ISKCON temples outside India is the participation of women as temple priests. From early on, as the Hare Krishna movement attracted women as well as men, Prabhupada awarded brahmanical initiation to both, authorizing and particularly encouraging his women disciples to perform deity worship in ISKCON temples.[30] ISKCON temples within India, in deference to public expectations, exclude women from service directly in the deity room, though they participate in other services related to deity worship, including cooking.[31]

The "Govindam Prayers" recording also points to Prabhupada's emphasis on rules and regulations related to deity worship that define the practice as *vaidhi bhakti sadhana*. The song was to be played daily, without exception, and to begin punctually—to the minute—at 7:15 each morning with the opening of the altar curtain to allow viewing of the freshly dressed and decorated deities. Punctuality became a symbol for both self-discipline and regenerated missionary vigor.

Such steps toward "routinization," instituted by the founder of ISKCON himself,[32] reflect the notion of regulated practice, or *sadhana*, common to a wide spectrum of Indian religion. Yet within the Gaudiya Vaishnava tradition, already at the time of Rupa Gosvami, there is evidence of awareness that regulation can deviate as much as it can navigate. In one of his shortest works, *Upadeshamritam* (The Nectar of Instruction or Nectarean Instructions), Rupa warns aspiring practitioners of *bhakti* to avoid *niyamagraha*—either "nonacceptance of regulation" or "indiscriminate acceptance of regulation." His call for moderation anticipates modern-day ISKCON devotees' struggle to maintain a balance they feel Prabhupada expertly demonstrated in his own behavior. The challenge is to avoid extremes: on the one hand, of making a virtue of rule-following with little attention to how it relates to the spiritual goal of spontaneous devotion, and, on the other, of expecting high spiritual accomplishment to be rapidly achieved despite minimal attention to regulations.

Many ISKCON devotees view strictness in *vaidhi sadhana* positively as a cornerstone of the tradition they seek to perpetuate, the cruchial anchor for maintaining present temple standards, and the basis for overcoming personal disqualifications for devotional spirituality. They would say that adherence to regulations has not only been the basis for individual devotees to develop tangible spiritual progress in their lives but also ensured the continued functioning of temple worship programs. Indeed, as a quarter century passes since Prabhupada's demise, deity worship remains a distinctive, visible feature and "central tenet"[33] of "Krishna consciousness" in ISKCON temple life. This can be felt in the temples where regular deity worship is conducted. In a small number, worship continues with impressive opulence and painstaking adherence to regulations and standards set by Prabhupada. There are generally substantial numbers of visitors, attracted largely by the well-conducted deity worship. These visitors often seek help from ISKCON priests for ceremonial functions or spiritual guidance, indicating that the priests are viewed as competent in their duties.

On the other hand, some ISKCON devotees would argue that *over*emphasis on *sadhana* regulations has contributed to the exodus from many ISKCON temples, which are now almost empty on weekdays, and where one is likely to see imported Eastern European devotees of varying competence maintaining the daily worship schedule.[34] A larger number of temples with moderate programs of worship have been radically reconfigured, evolving from semimonastic to congregational institutions, with an emphasis on Sunday and occasional festivities. Some of these establishments struggle financially, and it is not unknown that a temple closes and its deities are removed to a devotee's home to receive much-reduced service and numbers of visitors. Emphasis on rules and regulations does not, these devotees say, compensate for the lack of inspired leadership giving personal example in the performance of deity worship practices. Nor does it compensate for the tendency to emphasize mission at the cost of spiritual nourishment of committed members—attention to "externals" at the cost of "internal" needs. ISKCON is spread far and wide, but also thinly—making the few leaders who *do* give inspired example in deity worship rarely, if at all, accessible to remote temple communities.

Both parties would agree that Krishna worship is not to be contained within the walls of a few temples. Rather, as congregations expand, Krishna becomes domesticated as the Lord of the Home, where institutional regulation is less felt. Some congregation members (whether Indian or western) take formal initiation from an ISKCON guru who, following tradition, instructs disciples individually in the practices of deity worship.[35] Others do not take formal initiation but nevertheless become customers in an expanding business of Radha-Krishna or Gaura-Nitai images readily available in temple shops and Vrindavan's Loi Bazaar. In such circumstances, though there is more room for innovation in worship practices,[36] as often as not, congregation members endeavor to learn the *archanam* procedures from a worship manual recently published by ISKCON,[37] from temple devotees, or from an active Internet list within ISKCON's internal communication system.[38]

Prabhupada praying to the deity of Krishna to "give intelligence" to his followers; his followers showing enthusiastic, if not always steady, efforts to uphold scriptural injunctions for *archanam*; scriptures broadening the social franchise for devotional (including *archanam*) practices; and present-day Indian temples giving greater or lesser access to western Krishna devotees—all share a common theme, namely the quite ancient Indian concern about *adhikara*, or competence.[39] But in the context of a contemporary world mission to spread "Krishna consciousness," the frame of the discourse has radically changed from that which preoccupied ancient, or even precolonial, Indian thinkers. Charles Brooks has carefully explored the dynamics of this discourse in contemporary Vrindavan, where western ISKCON devotees have taken up extended residence, "shar[ing] primary resources of cultural knowledge" with Indians (Brooks 14). Vrindavan remains one of three important spiritual centers for ISKCON in India; but as the mission has moved geographically outward, the same "resources of cultural knowledge" are shared in quite different and varied circumstances than those found in a pilgrimage center dedicated almost exclusively to Krishna devotion. Service to a deity of Krishna in a rented building in Sofia, Bulgaria, or on a farm near Mendoza, Argentina, is not directly supported by any components of the Vrindavan, Puri, or Navadvipa cultural matrices.

In the quarter century since the demise of ISKCON's founder, there has been a wide spectrum of perspectives expressed about the institution's present condition and future hope. Some current or erstwhile participants are convinced that ISKCON is a sinking ship; others are just as confident that it is a troubled but essentially healthy adolescent enduring a full share of growing pains. But whatever the condition of the formal institution, all those who either observe or participate in Krishna devotional practices would certainly agree that the worship of Krishna in deity form is in the West to stay. And, closely allied to the practice of *archanam* in the West, the discourse over *adhikara* will surely continue—both in the narrower sense of who is qualified to perform worship and guide others in worship, and in the broader sense of how the practice of *archanam* fits into the spiritual development of both individual practitioners and collective spiritual life. Even more generally, this discourse will necessarily deepen to address numerous related issues that western culture forces upon it, leaving no intellectual stone unturned concerning the place of Krishna *bhakti* and its practices in a pluralistic world.[40]

One hopes that the followers of Krishna *bhakti* practices will not shy away from such discourse but rather see it as opportunity for enriching the tradition, developing deity and temple culture into the vital aspect of *sadhana bhakti* as experienced by Rupa and the other Goswamis of Vrindavan. This means there will be an ongoing need for thoughtful interpretation of the accepted scriptures in response to issues perhaps unanticipated either by them or by earlier preceptors. Perhaps for this purpose western devotees do well to take seriously the hopes of their founding preceptor that Krishna will "give intelligence" to them such that they may understand how to achieve their goal of pure-hearted Krishna *bhakti*.

All such reflection and thoughtfulness is not to ignore that deity worship is about active service with one's body and senses. Many ISKCON devotees recognize increasingly that for the practice of *archanam* to thrive as a vital aspect of the devotional process, it will be necessary for those claiming spiritual leadership, as recipients of Prabhupada's spiritual legacy, to show themselves at least competent in this basic form of devotion in practice, *vaidhi bhakti sadhana*. At present, such exemplariness is wanting as other institutional priorities persist. The hope and prayer of devotees concerned about developing the *archanam* tradition is that Krishna, in his seemingly silent deity form, will adjust the imbalances so that Krishna *bhakti* may thrive unimpeded in its new western home.

NOTES

1. "Radha and the Lord of London." Vaishnavas place the name of Krishna's consort prior to Krishna's when referring to them together. I use the term "deity" where one might use "image," since it is the term preferred in (English-speaking) ISKCON.
2. *Mleccha-desh*—"land of the uncivilized." Apologies to Sanskritists and knowers of Bengali: diacritics have been dropped from this article to accommodate a wider readership, and some words/names have been phoneticized.
3. Consequent rising maintenance overhead for temples with elaborate worship programs became one impetus for the development of aggressive collection methods in the 1970s.
4. The standard full altar configuration in ISKCON temples consists of Radha-Krishna, Gaura-Nitai (Chaitanya and Nityananda), and Jagannatha-Subhadra-Baladeva. Daily worship services consist of several routines of ritual hospitality, including bathing, offering (vegetarian) meals and snacks, and offering *aratika* (ceremonial waving of select items before the hosted personage)—all accompanied by mantras and prayers. In form, they follow patterns common to most worship of images throughout India.
5. See Joseph O'Connell, "Sadhana Bhakti," in *Vaisnavism: Contemporary Scholars Discuss the Gaudiya Tradition*, ed. Steven J. Rosen (New York: FOLK Books, 1992) for a discussion on the Chaitanya Vaishnava understanding of *sadhana*. "*Sadhana*

is a program, if you will, in which the Vaishnava uses not only his or her mind but the physical senses also—eyes, ears, voice—to develop the underlying capacity for devotion into a more perfect culmination of it."

6. See Schweig (1998) on Prabhupada's use of this term.

7. *Wirkungsgeschichte*: "a history of effects, understood as the tradition of successive interpretations of particular symbolic complexes in the core texts of the traditions." *Entstehungsgeschichte*: "a history of origins and cause-effect relations" (Holdrege 79).

8. Prabhupada referred to his book, entitled *The Nectar of Devotion*, first published in 1970, as a "summary study" of the *Bhakti-rasamra-sindhu.*

9. Contending claims that one or the other authored this work are perhaps resolved by assuming that they collaborated on its composition.

10. "The early agama and Tantric traditions predate Buddhism and possibly inform it: 'The agamic (Tantric) texts, as we know them today, had for the most part preceded Buddhism'" (Beck 150, quoting M. Arunachalam, *The Saivagamas* [1983], 3). F. Otto Schrader more cautiously says that Pancharatra possibly existed before the Narayaniya section of the *Mahabharata*. He proposes the eighth century c.e. as the *terminus ad quem* for Vaishnava-Agama composition (Schrader 17, 22).

11. Beck cites H. Daniel Smith, "The 'Three Gems' of the Pancharatragama Canon—An Appraisal," *Vimarsa* 1 (1) (1972): 45–51.

12. Harvey Alper notes, "In dealing with the literature of the Pancharatra—and the same point holds true for virtually all Indian religious traditions: Vaishnava, Saiva, Sakta, or even 'non-Hindu'—one should not fall into the trap of making hard and fast sectarian distinctions. Distinctions are there, but they are regional, communal, familial, and preceptorial" (367).

13. See Gonda 59–61 on the important position of Lakshmi in the Pancharatra system. "It is Laksmi, mythologically God's wife, and always intent on delivering, by her favour and compassion (*anugraha*), the incarnated souls out of the misery of mundane existence, who, identified with Visnu's highest location or manifestation . . . is the highest goal of the devotees—whose souls are parts or rather 'contractions' of the Goddess" (60).

14. See John Carman, *Majesty and Meekness: A Comparative Study of Contrast and Harmony in the Concept of God* (Grand Rapids, Mich.: Eerdmans, 1994) for an excellent discussion on the notion of accessibility of God, especially in the Shri Vaishnava tradition. For elaboration on Vaishnava theology of the divine image, see Vasudha Narayanan, "Arcavatara: On Earth as He is in Heaven," in *Gods of Flesh, Gods of Stone: The Embodiment of Divinity in India*, ed. J. P. Waghorne and N. Cutler (New York: Columbia University Press, 1996). For an ISKCON devotee's perspective on this theology, see (in the same volume) William H. Deadwyler III, "The Devotee and the Deity: Living a Personalistic Theology."

15. Again, the theology of divine replication allows for a simultaneous unrestricted multiplicity of *arca* forms, whereby the deity is equally present in any number of forms as well as in the divine abode, Vaikuntha.

16. See Schweig, this volume.

17. Still, aside from the Vraja setting in the Tenth Book wherein Krishna's worshippers—the *gopas* and *gopis*—are *vaishyas* (the third *varna*), the *Bhagavata Purana* primarily presents *kshatriyas* or Brahmins as exemplary worshippers or devotees of Vishnu. Notable exceptions are Narada (in his previous life as the son of a maidservant) and Vidura, the *shudra* half-brother of Dhritarastra.

18. *Chaitanya Charitamrita* was probably completed in the late sixteenth to early seventeenth centuries.

19. There is no empirical evidence of temple worship in India during the period of Vedic sacrifice; however, it is possible or even probable that worship centered around a sacred fire in homes was performed, a practice suggesting Indo-Iranian origins wherein offerings to a personal deity were given through fire. Whereas most historians postulate a succession from *yajna* to *puja*, or worship of iconic images, an alternative view is offered by Natalia Lidova that both types of worship were practiced concurrently, considering the presence, however scarce, of the word *puja* in the *Rig-Veda*, the *Grihyasutras*, and *Chandogya Upanishad* (Lidova ch. 3). See also Kane II:705–14 and V:34–37 for discussion on theories of image worship origins in India.

20. The present king of Puri, ritually considered Jagannatha's living incarnation (Marglin 134), himself a life member of ISKCON, is in strong disagreement with this policy (personal conversations with Gajapati Maharaja Dibyasingha Deb in 1997).

21. Rathayatra, or the "Car Festival," is the annual occasion when the Jagannatha deity is brought out of the temple, together with Subhadra and Baladeva, and they are paraded on three huge wooden chariots to a nearby temple and back.

22. See Marglin 131–74 for an interesting analysis of these caste relationships in relation to the worship of Jagannatha.

23. This openness suggests, if not outright acceptance of all western Vaishnavas as regular Brahmins, at least acceptance of them as Vaishnavas, some of whom prove themselves through training as Brahmins by qualification. See Brooks 155–70 on attitudes about Brahmin status in Vrindavan, and about growing acceptance of ISKCON devotees as Brahmins.

24. For a description of day-to-day and special worship in this temple, see Case (2000:82–97).

25. The deity is said to have "self-manifested" (i.e. not been fashioned by human hands) to Gopala Bhatta in 1542 (Case 75). This would probably have been *after* completion of *Hari-bhakti-vilasa.*

26. Modest-size images may well have been a response to Muslim rule; private worship in homes would not bring undue attention from government authorities.

27. Essentially extracted from *Hari-bhakti-vilasa*, one notable variation in this manual is in the style of *aratrika* (or *arati*), which reflects Bengali styles of worship, especially worship of Durga. *Hari-bhakti-vilasa* mentions only lights followed by water offered in a conch to be waved before the deity in *aratrika*, whereas Gaudiya Math, as well as ISKCON temples, add incense, cloth, and flowers, as well as whisk and fan (the latter two mentioned in *Hari-bhakti-vilasa* as features of special, kingly service).

28. Prabhupada was revered by all his followers, especially his earliest ones who tasted his cooking, as an excellent cook—an art he learned from his mother, whose cooking was of the special style practiced in the Mullik clan to which the family belonged.

29. This recording has since then been remastered on CD: *The Radha Krishna Temple.* CD-6. (Sandy Ridge, NC: Bhaktivedanta Archives, 1991).

30. One exception to ISKCON inclusion of women in deity worship was, until 1998, at the Radha-Madanmohan/Nrisimha temple near Passau, Germany. Although this temple had a negligible number of Indian visitors, the former (German) head

priest sought as far as possible to model it after the Radharamana temple. For him this meant also excluding women from direct worship "on the altar," though not from the kitchen. Some pressure from increasingly vocal German ISKCON women, combined with a shortage of men qualified to perform the daily services, led to inclusion of women in 1998.

31. I am informed that Radharamana temple, for one, has only Brahmin men cook for the deity; I suspect this is the case in most public Vaishnava temples in India, though it is a matter for research.

32. One recalls Max Weber's observation that routinization can occur in a religious organization both during the charismatic founder's presence and after his departure (60).

33. Selengut lists deity worship along with reincarnation, vegetarianism, and celibacy as "central tenets of Krsna consciousness" thought by followers of Prabhupada to show the path to higher spirituality (57).

34. Yet these temples continue to be regarded by congregation members as vital spiritual centers largely due to the presence and continued regular worship of the presiding deities. Scattered among ISKCON temples are a few devotees who have proven themselves exceptional by their steady service to temple deities, sometimes for twenty to twenty-five years or more; they command high respect within their communities for steadiness in a service that can be physically and mentally demanding.

35. Although somewhat overgeneralizing perhaps, Charles Brooks writes, "In the Indian context, the practice of *bhakti* is highly individualized, structured primarily by an intimate personal relationship between devotee and guru. Subsequently, standardization is minimal; each individual develops his own style of practice over time" (183). While individual style is certainly pervasive, one cannot ignore the existence of standardizing forces, in the form of *puja* manuals adopted by temples, to be followed by all priests. Pancharatra texts have served this purpose for centuries, and continue to do so; hence ISKCON can be seen as conforming to tradition in regard to providing standards for worship in its temples.

36. One sort of "innovation" is a more varied representation of deities of preference. Some congregation members—especially Indians—have affinity for Rama from their own family tradition more than for Krishna; some, whether Indian or western, are inclined to worship "Laddu Gopala"—a form of Krishna as a child favored by followers of the Vallabhacharya Vaishnavas. Western devotees have shown great affinity for the "half-man, half-lion" Nrisimha *avatara* of Vishnu.

37. *Pancharatra-Pradipa: Nitya-seva—Daily Worship—The Process of Deity Worship for the International Society for Krishna Consciousness* (Mayapur, India: ISKCON-GBC Press, 1995). I was the compiler/editor of this volume.

38. This list, I am told, presently has several hundred members, with daily postings on a range of topics related to deity worship. Occasionally controversies arise and discussions can become heated. A recent issue was whether it is proper, according to the tradition, for women to blow a conch shell (as is done before and at the end of *aratrika* ceremonies); an earlier controversy that had some devotees fearing a major split in the society centered on whether deities of Chaitanya should or should not be ornamented with a peacock feather on the crown (a standard insignia of Krishna). A handful of ISKCON pandits who have undertaken to make themselves knowledgeable from textual sources and temple traditions try to serve this audience with their learning.

39. See Wilhelm Halbfass, *Tradition and Reflection: Explorations in Indian Thought* (Albany: State University of New York Press, 1991), 66–74, for a discussion on the concept of *adhikara* in Indian religious discourse.

40. Space constraints prevent me from elaborating on this point. The notion of "idolatry" is an obvious issue directly related to—challenging—the entire notion of deity worship. This is a particularly western concern that can be seen as generative of the constructed polarity "primitivism" versus "modernism" (Taylor 1). Moreover, a Krishna devotee in the twenty-first-century West claiming that "the Lord is fully present in the form of the deity" certainly must anticipate and address the misgivings that modernity will bring forth in response.

REFERENCES

Alper, Harvey P., ed. *Understanding Mantras.* Albany: State University of New York Press, 1989.

Beck, Guy L. *Sonic Theology: Hinduism and Sacred Sound.* Delhi: Motilal Banarsidass, 1995.

Bell, Catherine. *Ritual: Perspectives and Dimensions.* Oxford: Oxford University Press, 1997.

Bhaktivedanta Swami Prabhupada, A.C. *The Beginning: The 1966 New York Journal.* Los Angeles: Bhaktivedanta Book Trust, 1996.

——. *Complete Works.* Bhaktivedanta Vedabase CD-ROM. Sandy Ridge, NC: The Bhaktivedanta Archives, 1998.

Brooks, Charles R. *The Hare Krishnas in India.* Princeton: Princeton University Press, 1989.

Case, Margaret H. *Seeing Krishna: The Religious World of a Brahman Family in Vrindaban.* New York: Oxford University Press, 2000.

Dasa, Kurma. *The Great Transcendental Adventure: Pastimes of His Divine Grace A.C. Bhaktivedanta Swami Prabhupada in Australia and New Zealand.* Botany, Australia: Chakra Press, 1999.

Dasa, Rupa Vilasa (Robert D. MacNaughton). *A Ray of Vishnu: The Biography of a Saktyavesa Avatara.* Washington, Mo.: New Jaipur Press, 1988.

Gonda, J. *Vishnuism and Saivism: A Comparison.* London: Athlone Press, 1970.

Gupta, Sanjukta. "The Pancharatra Attitude to Mantra." In Harvey P. Alper, ed., *Understanding Mantras.* Albany: State University of New York Press, 1989.

Holdrege, Barbara A. "What's Beyond the Post?—Comparative Analysis as Critical Method." In Barbara A. Holdrege, ed., *A Magic Still Dwells: Comparative Religion in the Postmodern Age.* Berkeley: University of California Press, 2000.

Kane, Dr. Pandurang Vaman. *History of Dharmashastra (Ancient and Medieval Religious and Civil Law).* 8 vols. Government Oriental Series. Poona: Bhandarkar Oriental Research Institute, 1974.

Lidova, Natalia. *Drama and Ritual of Early Hinduism.* Performing Arts Series, Vol. IV, gen. ed. Farley P. Richmond. Delhi: Motilal Banarsidass, 1994.

Marglin, Frederique. "The Famous Ratha Jatra Festival of Puri." *Journal of Vaisnava Studies* 7 (2) (spring 1999).

O'Connell, Joseph T. "Sadhana Bhakti." In Steven J. Rosen, ed., *Vaisnavism: Contemporary Scholars Discuss the Gaudiya Tradition.* New York: FOLK Books, 1992.

Schrader, F. Otto. *Introduction to the Pancharatra and the Ahirbudhnya Samhita.* Adyar, India: The Adyar Library and Research Centre, 1973.

Schweig, Graham M. "Universal and Confidential Love of God: Two Essential Themes in Prabhupada's Theology of Bhakti." *Journal of Vaisnava Studies* 6 (2) (spring 1998): 93–123.

Selengut, Charles. "Charisma and Religious Innovation: Prabhupada and the Founding of ISKCON." *ISKCON Communications Journal* 4 (2) (n.d. [1996?]): 51–63.

Taylor, Mark C., ed. *Critical Terms for Religious Studies.* Chicago: University of Chicago Press, 1998.

Weber, Max. *The Sociology of Religion.* 1922; reprint, Boston: Beacon Press, 1993.

PART 2
Bhaktivedanta Swami and His Predecessors

[5]

WHO IS SHRI CHAITANYA MAHAPRABHU?

STEVEN J. ROSEN (SATYARAJA DAS)

INTRODUCTION

The modern-day Hare Krishna movement traces its roots to the personality of Shri Chaitanya (1486–1533), though it participates in the older Vedic tradition. Shri Chaitanya and his accomplishments are viewed in various ways by scholars and devotees alike. Edward Dimock asserts that "the intense and unprecedented revival of the Vaishnava faith in Bengal" was due to "the leadership and inspiration of Chaitanya."[1] A. K. Majumdar lauds Chaitanya as "the founder of the last great Vaishnava sect."[2] S. K. De describes his contribution as "Vaishnavism par excellence."[3]

In the traditional hagiographies, of which seven are most prominent,[4] Chaitanya is viewed as Vishnu, the Oversoul, at least in the earliest texts. Gradually, the tradition shifted its perception, claiming that he was "more than Vishnu or one of many *avatara*s." Rather, he was a combined manifestation of Radha and Krishna, a unique dual incarnation of God in the mood of his own devotee. This is the view found in the final major Bengali work on Chaitanya's life, the

Chaitanya Charitamrita, showing that the hagiographical texts changed their emphasis, from Shri Chaitanya as "the aspect of God that evokes awe and reverence" (*aishvarya*) to "the aspect that instigates love" (*madhurya*).[5]

Unlike many "Godmen" or "*avataras*" of India, Chaitanya was not "divinized" subsequent to his life on earth. Rather, his earliest biographers—who knew him in the flesh—proclaim his Godhood. Svarupa Damodara and Kavi Karnapura are primary examples. They are among the first to devise the doctrine of the *pancha tattva*, wherein Chaitanya is seen as God.[6] Rupa and Sanatana also refer to his divinity, as do many of his early followers. As O'-Connell writes, "During Chaitanya's own lifetime, it became axiomatic among his closer devotees that he was in some fashion Hari/Krishna (even Krishna with the feelings and complexion of Radha) descended in human form."[7] A virtual storehouse of voluminous literature, in Bengali and Sanskrit, was written about Chaitanya and his religion, both in his lifetime and soon thereafter. All of these works elaborate upon the mystery of his divinity.

CHAITANYA'S LIFE IN THE ENGLISH LANGUAGE

Although Chaitanya comes out of the Indic Bengali tradition, there have been many studies of his identity and life in English. Among the earliest is no doubt the work of Kedarnath Dutta (Bhaktivinoda Thakura), specifically his *Sri Chaitanya: His Life and Precepts*, which was published for the first time toward the end of the nineteenth century. Although written from a devotional perspective, Dutta's work included hitherto untranslated facts about Chaitanya's life and was thus appreciated by the scholarly community.

Soon after, in the first couple of decades of the twentieth century, D. C. Sen published a series of books on Chaitanya, including *Chaitanya and His Companions* (Calcutta University Press, 1917) and *Chaitanya and His Age* (Calcutta University Press, 1924), both of which have become classics in English scholarship. M. T. Kennedy's important work, *The Chaitanya Movement: A Study of Vaishnavism in Bengal* (Calcutta: Association Press, 1925), was released soon thereafter, contributing the perceptions of a Christian missionary. At this point, the devotional/scholarly contingent of the Chaitanya Vaishnava community produced valuable English studies of their own, beginning with Nisikanta Sanyal's *Sree Krishna Chaitanya, Vol. 1* (Madras: Gaudiya Math, 1933) and Sambidananda Das's Ph.D. dissertation (1935) for Calcutta University, "The History and Literature of Gaudiya Vaishnavas and Their Relation to Medieval Vaishnava Schools," which included newly discovered details of Chaitanya's life.

In the 1940s, the thorough scholarship of S. K. De offered the English-speaking world elaborate insights into Chaitanya and his age, and B. P. Tirtha Swami's *Sri Chaitanya Mahaprabhu* (Calcutta: Gaudiya Mission, 1947) finally presented a full account of Chaitanya's life in English. In the modern era, there have been many important works, both scholarly and devotional, on Chaitanya's life and teachings. A few of the more significant studies should be mentioned: A. K. Majumdar, *Chaitanya: His Life and Doctrine* (Bombay: Bharatiya Vidya Bhavan, 1969); A. C. Bhaktivedanta Swami Prabhupada, *The Teachings of Lord Chaitanya: The Golden Avatara* (Los Angeles: Bhaktivedanta Book Trust, 1974); A. N. Chatterjee, *Srikrsna Chaitanya* (New Delhi: Associated Publishing, 1983); Swami B. R. Sridhara, *The Golden Volcano of Divine Love* (San Jose, Calif.: Guardian of Devotion Press, 1984); O. B. L. Kapoor, *Lord Chaitanya* (Mathura: Saraswati Jayasri Classics, 1997); and, finally, Edward C. Dimock Jr. (with Tony Stewart), *Chaitanya-Charitamrita* (Cambridge: Harvard University Press, 1999).

This latter work is important on a number of levels. Ed Dimock is often considered the doyen of Chaitanyaite Vaishnava studies in the West, and *Chaitanya Charitamrita* is seen by the tradition itself as the most important of Chaitanya's biographies. Although there have been many partial translations, the *Chaitanya Charitamrita* has been translated into English in its entirety only three times; Dimock's is the fourth. The first of these appeared in the early part of the twentieth century. It was called *Sree Chaitanya Charitamrita of Sree Sree Krisnadas Kaviraj Goswami*, translated into English by Sanjib Kumar Chawdhury (Faridabad, Dacca: Nagendra Kumar Roy, n.d.); soon after this, Nagendra Kumar Roy published his own translation, which is essentially the same as Sanjib's. Perhaps, since he was Sanjib's publisher, he later decided to claim the scholar's work as his own. No one really knows. In the 1970s, A. C. Bhaktivedanta Swami Prabhupada published his seventeen-volume *Chaitanya Charitamrita* (Los Angeles: Bhaktivedanta Book Trust, 1974–75), complete with original Bengali and Sanskrit text, word-for-word transliteration, English translation, commentary, and full-color plates. And now we have the work again, this time by Edward C. Dimock Jr. and Tony Stewart.

WHO IS SHRI CHAITANYA?

Why all this literature on one personality? Just who is Shri Chaitanya, and what do existing records tell us about his actual life and doctrine? According to all traditional accounts, Chaitanya Mahaprabhu was born on Friday, February 18, 1486. His birth name was Vishvambara Mishra, and he was later known as Nimai Pandita, and still later (after becoming a renunciant) as Chaitanya Mahaprabhu. His place of birth was the simple village of Navadvipa, also known as Mayapura, West Bengal.

According to the traditional hagiographies, Navadvipa was, at that time, a center for sensual pleasure. Although it was a seat of Sanskrit learning—a well-known university town—its inhabitants were deeply engaged in what, according to Vaishnavas, was base, materialistic behavior.

Haridasa Thakura and Advaita Acharya, two senior and well-respected religious personalities from the local area, prayed for the descent of the *Yugavatara*, someone who could put an end to the evil that had become centralized in Navadvipa. In answer to their prayers, the tradition tells us, Shri Chaitanya came to this world to inaugurate the *sankirtana* movement—the religious movement centered around the congregational chanting of the holy name. But this, says the tradition, was only the external reason for his appearance.

The internal reason is theologically elaborate. Put simply, in the descent of Chaitanya, God desired to taste the love of his topmost devotees. This love was so intense that he wished to directly experience it from their unique perspective. For this reason, he appeared in this world as his own perfect devotee—as Chaitanya Mahaprabhu—in order to fully taste this divine love, the most cherished goal of the Vaishnavas.

His Childhood and Youth

The summer that followed his winter birth was a happy one for his parents, Jagannatha Mishra and Shachidevi. They had suffered through the deaths of their first eight children, all girls. But the birth of Vishvarupa, Mahaprabhu's elder brother, signaled a change in their lives. And then Mahaprabhu was born.

In approximately 1494, when he was about eight years of age, he began school under the tutelage of Gangadasa Pandita. Two years later, in 1496, when he was ten, he developed renown as a child prodigy, a scholar, having mastered several languages, logic, rhetoric, hermeneutics, and philosophy. It was in this year, too, that his elder brother, Vishvarupa, took *sannyasa*, or the renounced order of life, and became a traveling mendicant. This had deep influence on little Nimai.

Four years later, in the year 1500, he married Lakshmipriya. He was fourteen years old. In 1502, now sixteen and happily married, he opened his own *tol* (school) and began teaching language and syntax. It was during this period, in fact, that he wrote his own commentary on an intricate Sanskrit grammar, which, regrettably, is no longer extant. All things considered, this could have been a fulfilling and prosperous time. However, biographers and historians inform us that it was a difficult period for him.

While Mahaprabhu was visiting his ancestral village on business, deep in East Bengal (now Bangladesh), his wife died after being bitten by a poisonous snake. The reverential biographers say that it was "the poisonous snake of separation" that took her life. Whatever the case, at his mother's request, he quickly remarried. The new bride was Vishnupriya, a dedicated young ascetic who eventually became one of the most important female devotees in the Gaudiya (Chaitanyaite) Vaishnava community.

Shri Chaitanya's father passed away that same year, and so, as was the custom, early the next year (in 1503), Mahaprabhu traveled to Gaya, in Bihar province, to perform the funeral rites. There he met Ishvara Puri, a renunciant of the Madhva lineage. He had met this man once before in Navadvipa, but took initiation from him at their second meeting. Thus, when Mahaprabhu was about seventeen years of age, he was given the ten-syllable Gopala mantra, a confidential incantation that translates, "Salutations to the beloved of the *gopis* (i.e., Krishna)."

Along with this mantra, Shri Chaitanya also began to chant the Hare Krishna *mahamantra* (*Hare Krishna, Hare Krishna, Krishna Krishna, Hare Hare, Hare Rama, Hare Rama, Rama Rama, Hare Hare*). A. C. Bhaktivedanta Swami Prabhupada, the founder of the modern-day Hare Krishna movement, translates this as follows, "O Lord! O Energy of the Lord! Please engage me in Your causeless service." By chanting these mantras under the direction of a spiritual master—Ishvara Puri—Shri Chaitanya soon became God-intoxicated. This, according to Vaishnava scriptures, is the open secret of true transcendental meditation: spiritual sound virtually comes to life when it is bestowed upon a disciple by a genuine spiritual preceptor. This would eventually become the basis of Mahaprabhu's central doctrine, simple but profound: one can come into direct contact with the Absolute by vibrating His name, both silently (*japa*) and loudly (*kirtana*). The effect, Chaitanya taught, is enhanced further still by chanting loudly in a congregational format (*sankirtana*). When it is taken into the street (*nagara sankirtana*), it reaches its fullest potency. Chaitanya favored this last form of *kirtana* and often practiced it with his followers. The modern-day Hare Krishna movement has brought this kind of Chaitanyaite meditation to every town and village of the world.

His Transformation

Chaitanya's biographers tell us that just after his initiation, a vital transformation took place. Divine love started to emanate from his very being. The *Pandita* (scholarship) gave way to *Prema* (love of God). Dialectics moved aside, and devotion reigned supreme. His followers are quick to point out that Chaitanya's apparent transformation was only *lila*, or divine play, for he eternally partakes of divine nature—he does not transform; he is constantly and unchangeably supreme. The *lila*, they say, is meant to show the transformative power of the holy name.

The hagiographical texts tell us that for the next six years the transformed Nimai, Chaitanya Mahaprabhu, was like a live wire, charging everyone he met with ecstatic love. Now twenty-three years old, he had long since closed his school so he could devote all his time to his religion of ecstasy. He more fully organized his massive *sankirtana* movement, centered around the congregational chanting of the holy name of Krishna. As a result, he attracted not only the pious and the learned but also notorious criminals of the time, such as Jagai and Madhai. The most erudite scholars, like Keshava Kashmiri, were eventually humbled by Chaitanya and his message. Even powerful political leaders in the Islamic government, such as Chand Kazi, were soon overtaken by his current of divine love. All of Navadvipa was inundated with Chaitanya's mood of sweet divinity.

The Renounced Order of Life

When Shri Chaitanya was twenty-four, at the beginning of 1510, he traveled to nearby Katwa and was initiated into the renounced order of life (*sannyasa*) by Keshava Bharati. The devotees did not like seeing him adopt the life of a mendicant. Their love for him was intense, beyond words, and so with great trepidation they contemplated the fact that he would have to perform severe austerities, as a *sannyasi* does. Madhu, the barber who was to cut his raven locks, wept pitifully as he did his duty. Devoted onlookers, such as Prabhu Nityananda (whom the Chaitanya school sees as an incarnation of Balarama), Acharyaratna, and Mukunda Datta—others were there as well—watched the dreaded ceremony in disbelief. Nonetheless, to set an example and to win the respect of the religious men of his time (who had deep regard for *sannyasis*), Chaitanya accepted the austere renounced order of life in the winter of 1510. He wanted the respect of his peers so that he might influence them with his message.

After *sannyasa*, he wanted to visit Vrindavan, the land of Krishna. For three days and nights he wandered in a trancelike state along the roads of Radhadesha, which is now called Bardhamana. Nityananda Prabhu convinced him, however, to go to Shantipur instead, where he was once again reunited with his Navadvipa followers, including his mother, who asked him to establish nearby Jagannatha Puri as his central headquarters. In this way she would regularly hear of his activities.

Pilgrimage to the South

By March 1510, Mahaprabhu arrived in Puri and soon met Sarvabhauma Bhattacharya, a great monistic philosopher of the period. Mahaprabhu succeeded in converting Bhattacharya to his intensely theistic conclusion, and this was seen as a great conquest for the Vaishnava movement. By April, Mahaprabhu began a tour of South India.

Soon after he began his journey, he met Ramananda Raya in Madras on the banks of the Godavari River. This was an important meeting, for here, to his intimate associate, Mahaprabhu revealed his identity as a dual manifestation of Radha and Krishna. This episode is eloquently preserved by Kaviraja Goswami, in the *madhya lila* portion of his book *Chaitanya Charitamrita*. More importantly, a dialogue of deep spiritual magnitude ensued between Ramananda and Shri Chaitanya. These conversations engendered the most complex theological truths of the Gaudiya Vaishnava tradition. They are also recorded in the middle section of the *Chaitanya Charitamrita*.

That summer—roughly from August to November of 1510—Shri Chaitanya spent his time at the famous temple of Ranga Swami, at Rangakshetra (also called Shrirangam). There he met the three pious brothers, Vyenkata Bhatta, Tirumalla Bhatta, and the famous Prabodhananda Saraswati. And he also spent time with Vyenkata's little boy, Gopala Bhatta, who, in later years, came to be one of Mahaprabhu's most important theologians: Gopala Bhatta Goswami, one of the famous six Goswamis of Vrindavan.

Then, after continuing his travels throughout South India—which took a total of about two years—he returned to Jagannatha Puri. It was the summer of 1511 and he was twenty-six years of age. At this time, he attended the Rathayatra festival. By now, he was well known—a celebrity—throughout the subcontinent. Because of this, guests were coming to Puri from all over India. Some say he met Guru Nanak, the founder of Sikhism, at this time, and that they danced together at Ratha-yatra. Most of the well-known biographies seem to doubt the veracity of this incident. But Ishvara Dasa, an Oriyan follower in the generation of devotees immediately following Chaitanya's time, wrote about it at length in his *Chaitanya Bhagavata* (not to be confused with Vrindavandasa's work of the same name).

Rupa and Sanatana Goswamis

By fall 1514, when Mahaprabhu was twenty-eight, he decided once again to go to Shri Krishna's land of Vrindavan. On the way he hoped to meet Dabir Khash and Shakara Malik, two important and learned officials in the Islamic government of North India. They were writing him lengthy letters, expressing their dissatisfaction with the state of the country and political life in general. They wanted to participate in his *sankirtana* movement but felt that their entanglement in mundane affairs was overwhelming, stopping them from pursuing spiritual life with the commitment that it warranted.

Thus, Mahaprabhu stopped in their town, Ramakeli, on his way to Vrindavan. He met them and accepted them as his disciples. They came to be known as Rupa and Sanatana Goswamis, the chief followers of Shri Chaitanya. Once again, he did not consummate his trip to Vrindavan.

By that summer he was back in Puri, having decided for various reasons that he should postpone his visit to Krishna's holy land. However, after a few months, he decided that life without Vrindavan is not worth living. So, by June 1515, when Mahaprabhu was twenty-nine years old, he went to Vrindavan and, it is said, basked in the spiritual ecstasy of being in close proximity to the *lila* (divine play) of Krishna.

After visiting all of the holy forests where Krishna is said to have engaged in his divine pastimes some 4,500 years earlier, bathing in the holy rivers, identifying certain holy places, and associating with the various devotees of Vrindavan, Mahaprabhu decided to return to Puri. So, by January 1516, he left Vrindavan via Allahabad, which was then called Prayag. There he spent months with Rupa Goswami, instructing him in the esoterica of *rasa tattva*, or the minutiae of man's relationship with God. He then sent Rupa to Vrindavan (to unearth long-lost holy places and to build temples) and left for Benares on the road to Puri. At Benares he instructed Sanatana Goswami in the philosophy of *avataras*, explaining how God descends to this world and why He does so. After explaining these things to his disciple at length, he asked him to go to Vrindavan (to work with Rupa). While in Benares, too, Mahaprabhu converted one of India's most famous monists, Prakashananda Saraswati. When this particular ascetic was swayed by Mahaprabhu's perspective, he and his tens of thousands of disciples surrendered to the Master.

His Final *Lila*

Having just turned thirty, in the year 1516, Mahaprabhu settled in Puri, never to leave again. He was being more and more overtaken by *Radha bhava*, the ecstasy associated with Radharani's essence. In the last few years of his stay in this world, he experienced profound ecstatic symptoms. For example, his bodily limbs would periodically recede into his body and then expand again, like a turtle's limbs into its shell, as he cried uncontrollably in love for Krishna. According to Gaudiya taxonomy, such symptoms only manifest in the twelfth stage of *mahabhava*—an exalted level of devotion, rarely achieved. He thus spent the final eighteen years of his life in Puri, after which he left this world, at age forty-eight.

There are various theories of his passing. Most devotee-biographers did not write about it, so painful was the idea. However, several theories emerged among his later followers, the most prominent of which was his mystical merging into the Totha Gopinatha Deity. Tony Stewart has thoroughly analyzed the various stories of Chaitanya's death in his excellent essay, "When Biographical Narratives Disagree: The Death of Krsna Chaitanya," which appeared in *Numen* 38 (2) (1991): 231–60.

CONCLUSION

It should be reiterated that by the time of Chaitanya's demise, he was accepted as a divinity by the mass of people and even by King Prataparudra, who had influence not only in Orissa but also in much of the subcontinent. Great, learned *panditas* and scholars came to visit and even surrendered to the *sankirtana* mission. At this juncture in history, Puri was a center for spiritual seekers and lovers of God, who came to see and learn from Shri Chaitanya's immediate followers.

Chaitanya inspired hundreds of thousands in his own lifetime, and many millions more after that. Christian theologian John Moffitt wrote of him in glowing terms:

If I were asked to choose one man in Indian religious history who best represents the pure spirit of devotional self-giving, I would choose the Vaishnavite saint Chaitanya, whose full name in religion was Krishna-Chaitanya, or "Krishna consciousness." Of all the saints in recorded history, East or West, he seems to me the supreme example of a soul carried away on a tide of ecstatic love of God. This extraordinary man, who belongs to the rich period beginning with the end of the fourteenth century, represents the culmination of the devotional schools that grew up around Krishna. .. . Chaitanya delighted intensely in nature. It is said that, like St. Francis of Assisi, he had a miraculous power over wild beasts. His life in the holy town of Puri is the story of a man in a state of almost continuous spiritual intoxication. Illuminating discourses, deep contemplation, moods of loving communion with God, were daily occurrences. (129, 135–36)[8]

Again we ask, Who is Shri Chaitanya? Bhaktivinoda Thakura, an influential saint in Chaitanya's own lineage, points out that Shri Chaitanya's divinity is not the real point. It is the love that is witnessed in his activities, and his teachings, that are the real jewels of Gaudiya Vaishnavism:

We leave it to our readers to decide how to deal with Mahaprabhu. The Vaishnavas have accepted Him as the great Lord, Shri Krishna Himself. Those who are not prepared to accept this perspective may think of Lord Chaitanya as a noble and holy teacher. That is all we want our readers to believe. We make no objection if the reader does not believe His miracles, as miracles alone never demonstrate Godhead. Demons like Ravana and others have also worked miracles and these do not prove that they were gods. It is unlimited love and its overwhelming influence that would be seen in God Himself. (60–61)[9]

NOTES

1. Edward C. Dimock Jr., *The Place of the Hidden Moon* (Chicago: University of Chicago Press, 1966), 25.
2. A. K. Majumdar, *Chaitanya: His Life and Doctrine* (Bombay: Bharatiya Vidya Bhavan, 1969), 1.
3. S. K. De, *Early History of the Vaisnava Faith and Movement in Bengal* (Calcutta: General Printers & Publishers, 1942), i.
4. These works, in chronological order, are (1) Murari Gupta's Sanskrit diary; (2) Kavi Karnapura's Sanskrit *Mahakavya*; (3) Vrindavandas Thakur's *Chaitanya-bhagavata* (the first vernacular biography, in Bengali); (4 and 5), the two *Chaitanya-mangalas*, by Lochandas and Jayananda, respectively, both in Bengali; (6) Kavi Karnapura's later Sanskrit play about Chaitanya's life, the *Chaitanya-chandrodaya-nataka*; and (7) Krishnadas Kaviraja's Bengali *Chaitanya Charitamrita*. I have summarized these biographies in my *India's Spiritual Renaissance: The Life and Times of Lord Chaitanya* (New York: Folk Books, 1986).
5. This gradual shift in emphasis regarding Chaitanya's divinity is elaborately explained by Tony K. Stewart in his unpublished Ph.D. thesis, "The Biographical Images of Krsna-Chaitanya: A Study in the Perception of Divinity" (University of Chicago, 1985). For an interesting summarization of Stewart's perception on Chaitanya's divinity, see "One Text From Many: The *Chaitanya Charitamrita* as 'Classic' and 'Commentary,'" in *According to Tradition: Hagiographical Writing in India*, ed. Winand M. Callewaert and Rupert Snell (Wiesbaden: Harrassowitz Verlag, 1994), 229–56.
6. Tony K. Stewart, "On Changing the Perception of Chaitanya's Divinity," in *Bengal Vaisnavism, Orientalism, Society, and the Arts*, ed. Joseph T. O'Connell (Michigan State University, 1985), 38. For an excellent essay on Chaitanya's birth, see Stewart's "When Rahu Devours the Moon: The Myth of the Birth of Krsna Chaitanya," *The International Journal of Hindu Studies* 1 (2) (August 1997): 221–64.
7. Joseph T. O'Connell, "Historicity in the Biographies of Chaitanya," *The Journal of Vaishnava Studies* 1 (2) (winter 1993): 110.
8. John Moffitt, *Journey to Gorakhpur: An Encounter with Christ Beyond Christianity* (New York: Holt, Rinehart and Winston, 1972), 129, 135–36.
9. Bhaktivinode Thakur, *Shri Chaitanya Mahaprabhu: His Life and Precepts* (1896; reprint, Madras: Sree Gaudiya Math, 1984), 60–61.

[6]

CHARISMATIC RENEWAL AND INSTITUTIONALIZATION IN THE HISTORY OF GAUDIYA VAISHNAVISM AND THE GAUDIYA MATH

JAN BRZEZINSKI

"History is the biographies of great men." —Thomas Carlyle

I F TRADITIONAL INDIA could be said to subscribe to a theory of history, it would be the "great man theory," which holds that history moves by the actions of great men upon it. Perhaps the best known of the *Bhagavad Gita*'s 700 verses is the one in which Krishna promises to appear in the world whenever there is irreligious practice or rampant injustice in human society.[1] However different this belief may be from the Shi'a belief in the Mahdi or the Jewish expectation of a messiah, its influence has been equally pervasive in Hindu society. It has led not only to messianic hopes for a savior but also to the conviction that wherever or whenever greatness appears in human society, it is a manifestation of the divine.[2] Though such an idea can naturally be exploited for political ends and to buttress the status quo, it has also played a role in the religious sphere as a means of legitimizing change. It thus seems that almost every prominent spiritual leader who makes a mark on Hindu society sooner or later claims to be an *avatara*, or becomes, as the Indian media disparagingly love to call them, "a God-man."

This belief is present in almost every branch of Hinduism, whether Vaishnava, Shakta, or Shaiva, though its expression may take different forms. Vaishnavas, who resist the temptation to identify themselves with God as the last snare of illusion, still understand the spiritual master in this way, though this identity is based on his being God's "dearmost" or "most intimate servant."[3] Even so, there is a hierarchization within this category also, and particularly powerful individuals may be identified with some mythological figure, a divine being or "eternal companion" of Vishnu or Krishna. Thus Ramanuja is thought to be an incarnation of Ramachandra's brother Lakshman, while Madhva is taken by his disciples to be an incarnation of the wind god Vayu. In some cases, the powerful individual may be an ordinary person (or *jiva*) in whom God has invested his potency. The technical name Gaudiya Vaishnavas give such individuals is *shaktyavesh* avatar.[4]

Thus, though the scriptures prescribe the indifferent equation of all spiritual masters with God, a *de facto* distinction exists between the specially gifted individuals who influence the course of religious history by promoting new understandings and others who act to maintain these new traditions with a more limited charisma based on tradition or legislated rights. The very injunction of the scriptures to see the spiritual master as God needs to be enforced in the postcharismatic phase of a religious movement; in the presence of a genuinely charismatic individual, such an attitude comes naturally.

The history of Gaudiya Vaishnavism may also be analyzed according to the "great man" model. This is facilitated by the sociological categories defined by Max Weber, to whom the "great man" is the charismatic prophet, who breaks with tradition to proclaim a radical new message. Though this volume is primarily concerned with an examination of the postcharismatic phase of the branch of Vaishnavism that spread outside of India and took shape as the International Society for Krishna Consciousness under the leadership of its founder, A.C. Bhaktivedanta Swami, the purpose of this article is to examine two previous charismatic phases of the Gaudiya Vaishnava religion, the first one brought about by Chaitanya himself, the second coming in the twentieth century with the creation of the Gaudiya Math, which was founded by Bhaktisiddhanta Saraswati, the spiritual master of the above-mentioned Bhaktivedanta Swami. I will compare the critique of society and religion that these two charismatic leaders undertook, the methods they employed to legitimize their leadership, and the institutional models they left in place to routinize their own charisma and legitimize their succession. To conclude, I will briefly examine whether these findings have any implications for understanding the various directions Gaudiya Vaishnavism is likely to take in the twenty-first century. I will try to do all this succinctly, at the risk of making sweeping generalizations without sufficient documentation.

KRISHNA CHAITANYA

Much has been written about the social conditions into which Chaitanya was born that made an enthusiastic revival of Vaishnavism possible. I would hold that the primary factor was the strong presence of Islam, not necessarily as a direct threat, but for the effect it exerted on Brahminical society, and by extension, the rest of Hinduism. The Brahmins had become inward looking, obsessed with purity and ritualism while holding on to social forms that had ceased to have meaning in the changed context; they had no influence on polity and a diminished hold on the rest of society. Though they continued to claim an exclusive monopoly on religious life and practice (ritual, study of scripture, etc.), a large portion of the Brahmin community found such religion sterile. Some among them also recognized that all members of society had a spiritual need that extended beyond the orthodox principle of Varnashram Dharma, which declared that everyone "attains perfection through the performance of his prescribed duty," even though it would take future lifetimes for one to become a Brahmin and attain direct spiritual experience. The alienated Brahmins, many of whom had already gravitated toward Vaishnavism, were looking for a savior.

Krishna Chaitanya was a young teacher in Nabadwip, the cultural capital of Hindu Bengal at the time. He had shown no particular talent for leadership or religion until he suddenly underwent a conversion experience following his initiation into Vaishnavism. Through his remarkable ecstasies while engaging in *sankirtana*, or congregational chanting, he quickly established his authority as a leader of the nascent Vaishnava movement in his hometown. Within a very short period of time—only thirteen months separated the beginning of his ecstatic experiences and his leaving Nabadwip to live in Puri—the basis of a religious movement that washed over Bengali society was firmly established. This was due in part to his own leadership, but also to a great extent to two other figures, Advaita Acharya and Nityananda Avadhuta, who shared in his charisma and recognized his value as a powerful symbol.

It is said that when Advaita Acharya, a prominent Brahmin and leader of the Vaishnava community, saw the desperate condition of society, he prayed for an incarnation of the Lord. When Chaitanya began publicly going into trance states and claiming to be an incarnation of Krishna, it was Advaita who confirmed his claims and worshipped him with the *namo brahmanya-devaya* mantra ("I bow to you, the god of Brahminical society"). According to Vrindavandas, Advaita was also the source of the socially liberal religious ethic of the movement.[5]

Chaitanya was soon identified as the *yuga* avatar, the incarnation of Krishna who had come to spread the religious teaching of the age, the chanting of his own names. The success of his mission was accepted as confirmation of his divine status, as Krishna Das wrote in the *Chaitanya Charitamrita*:

> In the Age of Kali, the religious practice of the age is the chanting of Krishna's names. It cannot be spread successfully by anyone unless empowered by Krishna himself. Since you have successfully set the sankirtan movement into motion, you must therefore possess Krishna's powers. You have spread the chanting of the holy names throughout the world and anyone who sees you immediately experiences love of God. Love for God is never manifest without the power of Krishna, for Krishna alone is capable of giving love for himself.[6]

Though it is now an article of faith in Gaudiya Vaishnava circles to connect Chaitanya to the Madhva *sampradaya*, it is important to note that Chaitanya did not derive the legitimacy he enjoyed among his followers from Madhva, though he may have derived a portion of it from his connection to his spiritual master Ishwar Puri, and through him, to Madhavendra Puri, many of whose disciples, including Advaita, became a part of his entourage.[7] The consensus in scholarly circles is that a Krishna devotional movement originating in South India made its way north through a Vaishnava-oriented group of Shankarite *sannyasis* of the Puri and Bharati orders, including Madhavendra Puri. Their principal authority seems to have been Shridhara Swami, who lived in Jagannatha Puri, which was also the home base of these particular *sannyasi* orders. Despite Chaitanya's connection with these lines (to the Puris by initiation and the Bharatis by *sannyasa*), however, his followers quickly identified him as an incarnation of Krishna. By so doing, they placed him in a category outside previously established traditions that allowed him to claim an authority that was *sui generis*.

The Post-Chaitanya Period

Though Chaitanya's personality was the source of the efflorescence of the religious enthusiasm of the Bengali Vaishnavas, he never exercised any kind of administrative direction. He lived an increasingly reclusive life, and his direct input into the society that developed around him was limited. He did not himself give initiation to anyone.[8] He never appointed any individual "successor"; nor was there in his lifetime or ever after a central executive body as such. It is often pointed out that Chaitanya left little in the way of written instruction, though Krishna Das Kaviraj has taken pains to establish him as the source of the teachings found in the writings of Rupa and Sanatana Goswamis, the principal authors of the Gaudiya Vaishnava canon. He also could and did offer advice and act as a final authority on cruchial matters. On the whole, however, he served primarily as an inspiration, a divine example and symbolic rallying point; the nuts and bolts of the movement were left in the hands of others to whom he delegated certain responsibilities.

Of these delegated responsibilities, two are particularly important historically. One was the responsibility to preach, especially among the lower strata of Bengali society, which he gave to Nityananda Avadhuta in Jagannatha Puri in 1513.[9] The other mission was given to Rupa and Sanatana Goswami, to lead exemplary lives of spiritual dedication, to develop Vrindavan (Vraja) as a pilgrimage center, and to write texts on various aspects of Vaishnava theology and practice.

This instruction to write ultimately had the greatest influence on the history of the *sampradaya* as it, more than anything, legitimized and unified the movement by taking it beyond the enthusiastic effusions of a purely popular phenomenon to one that possessed an innovative and thorough theology and also participated more clearly in the pan-Indian Vaishnava tradition.

Three epicenters of Gaudiya Vaishnavism thus grew: the principal one in Bengal, which would always be the main source of converts; Vrindavan, which remained the ideal spiritual center or ultimate destination for retirement and monastic dedication; and Jagannatha Puri, which, though it lost considerable influence in Bengal after Chaitanya's death, remained the main center of Chaitanya (Gaudiya) Vaishnavism in Orissa, and had considerable influence on the religious life of that region. Three distinct institutional patterns thrived in each of these places. In Nabadvipa and Gauda (Bengal), householder guru or Goswami dynasties dominated; in Vrindavan, the eremetic style of asceticism became the dominant model; and in Puri, it was cenobytic monasticism, or the "*math.*"

Perhaps predictably, the early period of the fledgling Vaishnava movement in post-Chaitanya times was not without a certain amount of turmoil, particularly in its homeland of Gauda. The principal reasons for this were the conflicting visions of who Chaitanya himself was and of the nature of his teaching, as well as a certain amount of jostling for supremacy among the followers of his leading associates, particularly Advaita and Nityananda.

It was only when the influence of the Vrindavan school, carried east by Narottama, Shyamananda, and Shrinivasa Acharya, was brought to bear in the last third of the sixteenth century that the Gaudiya Vaishnava world was consolidated and took on the characteristics that held it in good stead for several hundred years. The writing of the *Chaitanya Charitamrita* by Krishna Das in 1612, which reproduced the principal ideas of the Vrindavan school in the Bengali language, may be said to mark the completion of the consolidation process, but the festival at Kheturi in the early 1570s was its defining moment.[10]

Along with the theology of Radha and Krishna as the supreme form of the godhead, the Vrindavan doctrine emphasized the idea that Chaitanya was something more than a *yuga avatara*—he was the combined form of Radha and Krishna. This strengthened the basis for the legitimacy of the entire movement by adding layers of meaning to the Chaitanya symbol; the need for him to be legitimized by any external agent thereby became even less important. Thus, though certain passages in the scriptures were reinterpreted—and others invented—to support Chaitanya's claims to incarnation, these played a secondary role in creating faith in his followers and inspiring new converts to the movement.

Expanded liturgical norms were also established at Kheturi, in particular that of *lila kirtana*, devotional chanting about Krishna's pastimes. The songs of Jnana Das and Govinda Das in particular, who were both more profoundly influenced by the poetic writings of Rupa Goswami than by the *Bhagavata* itself, the avowed ultimate scriptural authority of the school, had a tremendous impact on the Bengali popular culture of the time.

Besides firmly establishing the Vrindavan theology, which presented a clear hierarchical understanding of religious experience, culminating in service to Radha and Krishna in the *madhura rasa,* devotion to God in the mood of lover, the principal doctrine with practical effects established at Kheturi was that of the *pancha tattva*.[11] This doctrine confirmed the status of Nityananda and Advaita as incarnations of the deity in their own right, gave specific prominence to Gadadhar as the incarnation of Krishna's *shakti* energy, i.e., Radha, and identified all of Chaitanya's other associates as descents of Krishna's eternal companions in the spiritual world.[12] This had the effect of confirming the descendants of these now-deceased members of the movement's first generation as participants in their charisma. It is notable that the *Gauraganoddesha-dipika* even identifies Nityananda's wife, Jahnava, as Radha's sister Ananga Manjari, and Virabhadra, his son, as a form of Vishnu, even though neither of them ever met Chaitanya.

It also seems likely that the particular esoteric practices of identifying as a participant in Krishna's pastimes became a part of the Gaudiya Vaishnava culture of *raganuga bhakti* at this time (*siddha pranali*).[13] This concept first appeared textually in the writings of Gopal Guru and Dhyana Chandra Goswami, the monks responsible for the prestigious Radha Kanta Math, which stood on the grounds of Chaitanya's residence in Puri. Jahnava, an important organizer of the Kheturi festival, was a major force in the sixteenth century, who changed the orientation of the Nityananda group from the devotional mood of friendship with God, *sakhya rasa*, to that of *madhura rasa*.

Brahmins and *Kula* Gurus

Despite the stresses on Hindu society in the sixteenth century, the existing social system was based on long-established principles that the Vaishnavas could and did opt into, despite their philosophical recognition of its limitations. The

Vaishnava religion was not a radical departure from the *sanatana dharma* social system, but a particular interpretation of it. As such, it shared in the respect for birth in accordance with the karma theory. It was thus accepted that by birth one participated in the charisma of one's forefathers and that this could be transmitted to others by initiation. With this understanding, the already existing system of hereditary *kula* gurus serving client families for generation after generation fit perfectly into the operative worldview of the time. Sanatana Goswami, in his commentary to *Hari-bhakti-vilasa* 4.41, fairly clearly approves of householder gurus; on the other hand, there appear to be clear injunctions against those in the renounced order of *sannyasa* taking on disciples.[14] The *dashnami sannyasa* tradition, which had always been confined to Brahmins only and to which Chaitanya and his spiritual masters had belonged, was categorically rejected, along with its saffron-colored cloth.

Though other types of orthodox renunciates avoided giving initiation, they gained respect for their exemplary spiritual practice. Renunciation, which came to be known simply as *bhekh,* or "taking the cloth" (in reference to the simple white cloth adopted by such renunciates), was open to all castes, and in some cases even became a refuge for lower castes. The *babajis,* as these renunciates came to be called, could gain a certain amount of social prestige by refusing any claim to social power, i.e., by refusing marriage. If they did get married, any claim to social authority was usually lost and they became marginalized. On the whole, attempts to establish patterns of renounced authority failed in Bengal and tended to collapse into deviant lines or *apasampradaya*s and Jati Vaishnavism.[15]

Advantages and Disadvantages of the Established Institutions

Thus, even without the creation of a "hard institution" with a single center, the Chaitanya Vaishnava movement established itself in Bengal as a single identifiable religion with a strong symbol system and a loose network of "intermediate" institutions of disciplic successions traced to the original associates of Chaitanya.[16] Festivals like the one at Kheturi provided informal settings for *sadhu sanga,* community bonding or hashing out controversial theological or policy questions. The noncoercive nature of the school permitted a wide degree of variability of value orientation within the broad standards of Chaitanya Vaishnava, and there thus existed variations in theology, practice, and social ethos among the main branches of hereditary and nonhereditary guru *shishya* lines in Bengal. Joseph O'Connell comments on the capacity of these traditional lines to faithfully preserve traditions:

A standard criticism of the hereditary guru-*shishya* system is that genuine devotion, moral probity and other qualities suitable for spiritual direction cannot be assured by heredity. On the other hand, traditional India seems to have had a rather good record of passing down from one generation to the next the particular expertise and style of performance upon which the reputation and livelihood of such families depend. . . . Though lacking a centralized mechanism for insuring standards of performance, the Chaitanya Vaishnavas have had subtle ways of exerting peer pressure and influencing reputation within the community as whole. The Vaishnava understanding of guru-*shishya* relations does allow for abandoning a guru known to be positively bad; and, in the case of an initiating or *diksha* guru of limited abilities, a disciple may, preferably with the initiating guru's approval, go to one or more others as instructional or *siksha* gurus.[17]

Liberal Bengali social historians have long lamented the transformation of Bengal Vaishnavism from an egalitarian movement that broke through caste barriers, as epitomized by Nityananda, to one that returned to Brahminical domination as a result of the Sanskrit writings of the Goswamis, such as the *Hari-bhakti-vilasa*. According to Hitesranjan Sanyal, "The Goswamis of Vrindavan derived their spiritual inspiration from Chaitanya, but did not seem to have the strong social commitment of the Master."[18] Some cynics even argue that Advaita Acharya appropriated the mystic Chaitanya to restore Brahminical influence over a disintegrating Hindu society. The Brahmin Vaishnavas made some cosmetic adjustments to their social doctrine, as powerful elites are wont to do. Some concessions had to be, and were, made to the lower castes, but real control of the movement remained in the hands of the Brahmins. The fact that over 75 percent of Chaitanya's associates were Brahmins may be taken as evidence.[19] Whatever advances the lower castes made in Chaitanya's movement, the general feeling is that it simply maintained the status quo.

> But the mechanism for social and spiritual relief to the underprivileged and oppressed sections of society developed by the Gaudiya Vaishnavas was overlaid with orthodox ritualism which suppressed the remnants of the spirit of freedom in respect of actual social action. In effect, the dichotomy of Gaudiya Vaishnavism became an effective medium for diffusing social tension growing from the rise of people from the lowest strata into importance and thus for maintaining the status quo. (Sanyal 1981:64)[20]

It is quite true that Bengal Vaishnavism did not change the social system as found in Bengal; rather, it made use of it. There are positive ways at looking at the preservation of the so-called "status quo." Joseph O'Connell, for instance, argues that Chaitanya Vaishnava values helped defuse Muslim–Hindu tensions and also preserved social peace within Hindu society, a benefit that accrued to all, not only the Brahmins.[21]

Whatever successes the system may have had, there were certain failures; the criticisms are not altogether without merit. Thus even though Chaitanya Vaishnavas universally affirmed that Krishna *bhakti* is available for all, including women, *shudras*, and sinners, certain lineages retained an abhorrence of contact with lower castes and refused to give initiation to them. In some cases, they may have authorized non-Brahmin disciples to carry out this function among outcastes. The inevitable consequences of this are explained by R. K. Chakravarti:

> The assertion of Brahminical dominance in a religious movement that was rooted in mysticism, and which was anti-caste and anti-intellectual, inevitably led to the growth of deviant orders. If a Brahmin guru tried to initiate persons belonging to castes lower than the Shudra caste, the motive behind such initiation was questioned and the orthodox elements gave him the bad name of a Sahajiya and expelled him from the Gaudiya Vaishnava order.[22]

Thus the Hindu tendency to enforce social rigidity rather than correct dogma emerged in the world of Gaudiya Vaishnava orthodoxy.

BHAKTISIDDHANTA SARASWATI

Our second "great man," Bhaktisiddhanta Saraswati, was a charismatic figure who acted as a reformer of the Gaudiya Vaishnava tradition and, according to some, broke with it. Though the extent of his influence on Bengali society as a whole was nowhere near that of Chaitanya Mahaprabhu, he must nevertheless be included among the many Bengali reformers in the nineteenth and early twentieth centuries who contributed to the revitalization of Hindu pride in its own traditions. His role in inspiring others to carry the Chaitanya Vaishnava message beyond Bengali society alone makes him worthy of examination.

Unlike Chaitanya, Bhaktisiddhanta Saraswati was not an ecstatic but an ascetic and intellectual, who was driven by a vision of the potential glory of Chaitanya Vaishnavism and by the desire to overcome the restraints placed on it by contemporary conditions. He saw himself as continuing his father Bhaktivinoda Thakur's attempts to rationalize Gaudiya Vaishnavism and bring it into the modern age. Ironically, in view of his later preaching, part of Bhaktisiddhanta Saraswati's charisma came from being the son of this leading Vaishnava. Born in 1874 in Jagannatha Puri (the hagiographers say, as the answer to Thakur's prayer for a "ray of Vishnu"), Bhaktisiddhanta Saraswati was both materially and spiritually advantaged as Bhaktivinoda Thakur's son. He participated with his father in the publication of books and periodicals; on several occasions, he took extended trips with his father to important sites connected with Gaudiya Vaishnava history and accompanied him to Puri in 1901 after his retirement, where the two intended to live a life of devotional dedication together.

Nevertheless, whereas Bhaktivinoda Thakur, though possessing strong opinions about the needs for reform in Gaudiya Vaishnava society, stayed within the traditional structures of the Chaitanya Vaishnava lineage and dealt with it in a conciliatory manner, Bhaktisiddhanta Saraswati took a more directly confrontational approach. As a reformer, he broke with the traditional authority structures in the Gaudiya Vaishnava world. This, coupled with the desire to make use of modern institutions to preach Gaudiya Vaishnavism, resulted in the creation of the Gaudiya Math in 1920.

Much has been made of the perceived illegitimacy of Bhaktisiddhanta Saraswati's initiation. Nitai Das, for example, catalogues the various differences between the Gaudiya Math and contemporaneous Gaudiya Vaishnava disciplic lines, some of which are major, others minor.[23] I look into some of the most fundamental of his innovations here.

Bhaktisiddhanta Saraswati's Social Philosophy

In his brief mention of the Gaudiya Math (or Gaudiya Mission), Ramakanta Chakravarti states that it "ostensibly had no social aim. It did not pretend that it was an organization with a social mission. But it set up schools, libraries, research centers, and free hospitals. These, however, had only secondary importance. Its primary object was to preach mysticism."[24] Though Bhaktisiddhanta Saraswati's ultimate purpose may indeed have been mystical, it is a serious error to underestimate the social concerns that underlay the creation of the Gaudiya Math. Bhaktisiddhanta Saraswati's interest in the sociology of Gaudiya Vaishnavism were no doubt inspired by his father's articles on the subject in *Sajjana-toshani*,[25] which presented a wide-ranging critique of the social structures in Bengal, and in particular within the Vaishnava world. In 1900, Bhaktisiddhanta Saraswati published a book, *Bange samajikata* (Social Relationships in Bengal), that indicates a preoccupation with the subject.[26] In a letter written in 1910, Bhaktivinoda Thakur told him to "establish the *daivi varnashram dharma*—something you have already started doing."[27] What exactly Bhaktivinoda Thakur was referring to is not clear, but evidently it was an acknowledgment that Bhaktisiddhanta Saraswati was already active in some kind of social reform program based on Vaishnava principles. Bhaktisiddhanta Saraswati's researches into the Shri *sampradaya* of Vaishnavism based in

South India also seem to have informed his thinking about reforming social structures, if not in Bengal as a whole, at least in Bengal Vaishnavism.[28]

A defining moment of Bhaktisiddhanta Saraswati's career came on September 8, 1911, when he participated in an assembly in Balighai, Midnapore, where Vaishnavas from all over Bengal were summoned to debate aspects of the recurring Brahmin and Vaishnava controversy. The probable points of discussion were whether those belonging to non-Brahmin castes were authorized to worship Shalagram Shila, the stone sacred to Vaishnavas as a form of Vishnu or Krishna, after receiving Vaishnava initiation, or to act as *acharyas* by giving initiation in the mantras.[29] Bhaktisiddhanta Saraswati's arguments presented on that occasion were later published as a booklet, *Brahmana o Vaishnava taratamya vishayaka siddhanta* (Ascertaining the Relative Positions of Brahmins and Vaishnavas). This is one of the earliest available expressions of Bhaktisiddhanta Saraswati's ideas that led to the eventual creation of his separate branch of Gaudiya Vaishnavism, and is therefore an important document to which I will refer often.[30]

From the point of view of European culture, the arguments presented by Bhaktivinoda Thakur and Bhaktisiddhanta Saraswati appear self-evident. Indeed, the general democratic thinking that had arisen in the European Enlightenment was not without influence on the English-educated new aristocracy of Bengal, from which the Brahmo Samaj, an organization representing the first wave of Hindu modernization, had sprung and to which Bhaktivinoda Thakur himself belonged. The educated classes saw India through the eyes of their British rulers and deeply felt the need to make changes. In the later nineteenth century, with the rise of the Ramakrishna Mission, reform and revival joined hands and there was a general recrudescence of pride in Hindu culture. Bhaktivinoda and Bhaktisiddhanta were a part of this movement. Their feeling was that the Vaishnava culture was in no way inferior to any other religious system; indeed, it was superior. Nevertheless, they admitted the need for certain societal reforms. Bhaktivinoda Thakur's principal criticisms concerned the deteriorating morality in the Vaishnava world. He saw no harm in maintaining the institutions that had served Gaudiya Vaishnavism for three centuries, as long as everyone did what they were supposed to. Vaishnava gurus should lead exemplary lives of religious leadership, while renunciates were to either maintain their vows of chastity and poverty or take up a respectable householder life.

Bhaktivinoda Thakur wrote that a man's caste should never be determined by birth alone, but according to his actual qualities or nature. Thus a son's caste might be quite different from that of his parents. It should not be considered at all before one attained the age of fifteen and, once fixed, should be preserved and protected from the assaults of so-called *samaja patis*, zamindars, or government.[31]

Bhaktivinoda Thakur also proposed a solution for the so-called Jati Vaish-navas, considered untouchable by the higher castes. He asked them to give up begging and practices deviating from the Vaishnava orthodoxy and make an honest living from cottage industries.

In *Brahmana o Vaishnava*, Bhaktisiddhanta Saraswati furthers the cause by presenting arguments for the existence of caste mobility in ancient times, citing the *Mahabharata*, Puranas, and even the Smritis and Dharma Shastras. He also points out how Bengali social customs had deviated in other ways from the pristine Vedic model.[32] When Bhaktisiddhanta Saraswati began taking disciples, as an aspect of his effort to establish *daivi varnashram*, he would give the sacred thread and Gayatri mantra to them, no matter what their caste, thus appointing them as Brahmins, or what he hoped would be an exemplary class of spiritual leaders. This was a controversial move, though by no means his most controversial.

In 1918, Bhaktisiddhanta Saraswati took another major step in his plan for *daivi varnashram*, an ideology combining social organization with devotion to Krishna, by initiating himself in a new order of *sannyasa* that had a form quite distinct from the existing Vaishnava tradition of *bhekh*. He took the reviled saffron cloth, seen by Vaishnavas as representative of the "Mayavada" sects of Hinduism, and the triple staff (*tridanda*), reviving a tradition that, though mentioned in the Puranas, never had much currency in any of the Vaishnava lines.[33] Bhaktisiddhanta Saraswati's objective here was twofold: to criticize the existing system of renunciation, which he felt brought the institution established by Rupa Goswami into disrepute, and to create a committed preaching brotherhood of impeccable character. The Gaudiya Math *sannyasi*, though fully committed to his spiritual practice, was to be a part of society, not divorced from it. The essence of this attitude of renunciation was to be *yukta vairagya*, mentioned by Rupa Goswami in *Bhakti-rasamrita-sindhu*, which seems to give license for a "this-worldly asceticism."[34]

Bhaktisiddhanta Saraswati's Initiation (*Bhagavati Diksha*)

Just as Bhaktisiddhanta Saraswati rejected Brahminical status by birthright, he rejected the idea of automatic accession to guru status by the same means. This is one of the linchpins of the Gaudiya Math and requires some detailed analysis, especially since legitimacy in Gaudiya Vaishnavism (even in some of the deviant lines) customarily required initation in a recognized line leading back to one of Chaitanya's associates. Bhaktisiddhanta Saraswati claimed to be initiated by Gaura Kishor Das Babaji, but contrary to custom, placed no importance on the line of disciplic succession in which his guru himself had taken initiation and never communicated this line to his own disciples.[35] Rather, he invented something called the *bhagavata parampara*. Furthermore, Bhaktisiddhanta Saraswati clearly marked his separation from the rest of Gaudiya Vaishnavism by giving initiation to Vaishnavas who had already received the mantra from a family guru (*kula guru*).[36]

Though some point to the fact that Bhaktisiddhanta Saraswati "did not have high regard for Bipin Bihari Goswami" (his father's spiritual master),[37] it seems that his quarrel was not with an individual but with the entire existing system. Bhaktisiddhanta Saraswati claimed that the Gaudiya Vaishnava tradition had been infected by a kind of ritualistic approach to religion, styled as *vidhi marga*, in opposition to the spontaneous devotional spirit of the *bhagavata* school of Vaishnavism that had existed at the origins of Chaitanya's movement.

Bhaktisiddhanta Saraswati took initiation from Gaura Kishor Das Babaji in January 1901. Legend has it that he had to ask his master three times before being accepted, as the humble hermit of lower-caste background at first doubted the sincerity of the well-to-do scholar. There are differing ideas about the type of initiation Bhaktisiddhanta Saraswati received: according to some biographers he was given mantra, according to others it was a *bhagavati diksha*.[38] Not surprisingly, *bhagavati diksha* is a concept unfamiliar to most people, even those within the Gaudiya Math, as the only kind of initiation current in Vaishnava circles has always been of the *pancharatrika* type, which consists of standard initiatory rituals. The result is that many have wasted much time and effort unnecessarily trying to establish that Bhaktisiddhanta Saraswati received *pancharatrika*-type mantra initiation from Gaura Kishor Das.

We get an idea of what Bhaktisiddhanta Saraswati meant by *bhagavati diksha* from his *Brahmana o Vaishnava* essays, where he cites the example of Hari Das Thakur, a Muslim convert, who likely never received *pancharatrika* initiation. Hari Das Thakur says:

> I have been initiated into a vow to perform a great sacrifice by chanting the holy name a certain number of times every day. As long as the vow to chant is unfulfilled, I do not desire anything else. When I finish my chanting, my vow comes to an end (*dikshara vishrama*). . . . I have vowed to chant ten million names in a month. I have taken this vow (*diksha*), but it is now nearing its end.[39]

Bhaktisiddhanta Saraswati continues, "Unless one becomes qualified as a sacrificial Brahmin in the sacrifice of chanting the holy names, the name of Krishna does not manifest. Although Hari Das was not a seminal or Vedic Brahmin, he had attained the position of a qualified initiated (*daiksha*) Brahmin."[40] In other words, the simple commitment to regularly chant the holy names a certain number of times constitutes *bhagavati diksha*.

Bhaktisiddhanta Saraswati then goes on to distinguish between the Bhaga-vata and Pancharatra schools of Vaishnavism. According to his analysis, al-though there were originally many categories of Vaishnava, all but two had been lost. These were the Bhagavatas, whom he associates broadly with *bhava marga*, or the path of emotion (*raganuga bhakti*), and the Pancharatras, who are associated with the ritualistic path of deity worship (*vidhi marga*). The for-mer followed the ecstatic path of chanting the Holy Name, the religious pro-cedure meant for the age of Kali, while the latter followed a path that had been prescribed in a previous age.[41]

Bhaktisiddhanta Saraswati divides the four principal Vaishnava *acharyas* ac-cording to these two categories, assimilating Madhvacharya and Nimbaditya to *bhagavata marga* and Ramanujacharya and Vishnuswami to *pancharatrika marga*. Nevertheless, to a greater or lesser extent, he admits there had been an intermingling of the two broad groups of Vaishnavas, with the elements of the Bhagavata culture based on hearing and chanting being accepted by the Pan-charatrikas, and the Bhagavatas accepting the need for ritualistic deity worship at the lower stages of practice (*kanishtha adhikara*).[42]

According to Bhaktisiddhanta Saraswati, though Madhva strictly speaking followed the *bhagavata marga* and Madhavendra Puri had accepted initiation in his line, neither Madhavendra nor Chaitanya accepted his doctrines, which had in time been infiltrated by Pancharatrika ideas. In fact, Bhaktisiddhanta Saraswati even equates Madhva's philosophical exposition, "Tattva-vada," with Pancharatra. Bhaktisiddhanta Saraswati cites Baladeva Vidyabhushan who, though considered by many to be wholly responsible for the Gaudiya claims of connection to the Madhvas, pointed out four teachings in the Mad-hva line to be particularly unacceptable to Gaudiya Vaishnavas.[43] Thus, Bhak-tisiddhanta Saraswati says, "This Tattva-vada, or Pancharatrika system, is not acceptable in the opinion of Sri Chaitanya Mahaprabhu. Rather, He taught the path of *bhagavata-marga*."[44]

Bhaktisiddhanta Saraswati further goes on to associate everything connect-ed to the *vidhi marga* with Pancharatra, and all connected to the *raga marga* to Bhagavata. This is particularly significant, especially in view of the claims of traditional Gaudiyas to be faithfully following the *raganuga* process and to whom initiation and the practice of *raganuga* are integrally linked. He writes,

The regulated worshipers on the Pancharatrika path serve their wor-shipable Lord Narayan here under the shelter of two and half rasas—*shanta*, *dasya*, and *sakhya* with awe and reverence. Above Vaikuntha is Goloka Vrindavan, where Sri Krishna Chandra, the perfect object for all five rasas, is eternally worshiped by His devotees who are the repositories of love. . . . The worshipable Lord of the Pancharatrika Vaishnavas resides in Vaikuntha, and the worshipable Lord of the Bhagavata Vaishnavas resides in Goloka. (121–22)

Bhaktisiddhanta Saraswati then directly criticizes the situation in the contemporary Gaudiya Vaishnava world:

> The Pancharatrika Vaishnava principles of medieval South India have to some extent entered the current practices of the Gaudiya Vaishnavas. Descendants of the Gaudiya Vaishnava acharyas became more or less attached to the path of *archan*, like the followers of the Pancharatras, and spread subordination to Sriman Mahaprabhu [Chaitanya], sometimes in its pure form but more often in a perverted form. Like the householder acharyas of the Ramanuja sampradaya who are addressed as Swamis, Gaudiya householder acharyas have similarly accepted the title of Goswami. While preaching the pure path of *bhava* [spontaneous love of God] explained in the *Srimad Bhagavatam*, Sriman Mahaprabhu distinguished it from mundane formalities, but in due course of time His teachings have become distorted into a branch of the Pancharatrika system. This, however, is not the purpose of Sriman Mahaprabhu's pure preaching. (98–99)

He extended this criticism to the hereditary gurus of the Gaudiya Vaishnava *sampradaya*, accusing them of further distortions:

> some immature Pancharatrika mantra traders are presenting imaginary material names and forms as the goal of life and the path of perfection (*siddha pranali*); in this way they gratify the minds of their disciples as well as disclose their own foolishness and ignorance of the Vaishnava literatures.[45]

Followers of the Gaudiya Math hold that the *siddha pranali* tradition is not to be found in the earliest texts of the school. They have a very different idea of the practice of *raganuga bhakti*. The spiritual identity is something that comes out of one's inner being as a result of purification through spiritual practice and not through formal instruction. This implication is present in the following statement by Shridhara Maharaja:

> To get the mantra from a *sat guru*, a genuine guru, means to get the internal good will or real conception about the Lord. The seed of a banyan tree may be a small seed, but the great big banyan tree will come out of that seed. The will with which the particular sound is given by the guru to the disciple is all-important. We may not trace that at present, but in

time, if a favorable environment is there, it will express itself and develop into something great.[46]

To summarize, it would appear that Bhaktisiddhanta Saraswati went beyond simply criticizing the deterioration of morality in the *sampradaya* to attack its very foundations as established at the Kheturi festival.

Bhaktisiddhanta Saraswati and the "Hard Institution"

According to one legend, Gaura Kishor gave Bhaktisiddhanta Saraswati the traditional instruction for renunciates to keep away from Calcutta, which he called Calcutta *kalira brahmanda*, "Maya's universe," and avoid taking disciples. According to Bhaktisiddhanta Saraswati's biographers, he had a vision in 1915 in which Gaura Kishor and many other great saints of the disciplic succession enjoined him to preach widely. This vision confirmed his intuition and gave him the determination to take the *tridandi sannyasa* system and establish the Gaudiya Math.

In view of the attempts made by Bhaktisiddhanta Saraswati to establish the Gaudiya Math as an institution, and of its evident successes, it is rather surprising to find in his writings a very pessimistic attitude to institutional religion as such. Perhaps this derived from the inevitable jostling for power among his disciples while he was still alive, or from a deep-seated philosophical conviction. In 1932, he wrote:

> The idea of an organized church in an intelligible form, indeed, marks the close of the living spiritual movement. The great ecclesiastical establishments are the dikes and the dams to retain the current that cannot be held by any such contrivances. They, indeed, indicate a desire on the part of the masses to exploit a spiritual movement for their own purpose. They also unmistakably indicate the end of the absolute and unconventional guidance of the bona-fide spiritual teacher.[47]

In view of the above vision of organized religion, and of Bhaktisiddhanta Saraswati's view of the bona fide spiritual teacher as an outsider and prophet, it is perhaps not surprising that there was a disruption in the organization of the movement after Bhaktisiddhanta Saraswati's death. It is not altogether clear how he intended the charismatic center of the movement to be preserved, or how the principle of *bhagavata parampara* was meant to be continued. The *bhagavata parampara* idea had never stopped Bhaktisiddhanta Saraswati from initiating disciples according to a Pancharatrika model. On the other hand, his ideas about unconventional leadership may have prevented him from designating a successor, in the expectation that a true spiritual leader would emerge from the ranks of his disciples. His principal instruction on his deathbed appears to have been for everyone to "work together to preach the message of Rupa and Raghunath."[48]

Bhaktisiddhanta Saraswati left a council of three governors to handle the affairs of the Gaudiya Math—Ananta Vasudeva, Paramananda,and Kunjabihari—without designating any of them as *acharya*. All three were *brahmacharis*, and with the presence of a sizable contingent of *sannyasis*, it does not seem that he intended that they should form anything other than an ad hoc group to handle the management of the properties and continued publication of Vaishnava literature. Nevertheless, Kunjabihari (who, upon taking *sannyasa* in 1948, became Bhaktivilas Tirtha) and Ananta Vasudeva (who in 1941 became Bhaktiprasad Puri) each had their individual charisma and their own group of dedicated followers, and there were no doubt others who saw themselves as playing the traditional guru role.

The Ramakrishna Mission had survived the untimely passing of its founder by the election of a single successor, and there was little protest when the leaders among Bhaktisiddhanta Saraswati's disciples chose Ananta Vasudeva to act as *acharya*. Unfortunately, this did not sit well with Kunjabihari, nor with his followers, who familiarly called Kunjabihari *guru preshtha* ("most dear to the guru"). Lawsuits and even violence followed, and the disciples of Bhaktisiddhanta Saraswati either fell into the camp of one of these two individuals or left in disgust. Shridhara Maharaj, Keshava Maharaj, Goswami Maharaj, Bharati Maharaj, and others all founded their own independent *maths* in the 1940s and 1950s.

Puri Maharaj, or Puri Das as he later called himself, and his close associate Sundarananda Vidyavinoda, both of whom had been intellectual pillars of the Gaudiya Math, took up a spirited regimen of scholarly criticism of their own movement. They abandoned secondary literature and concentrated on the primary works of the six Goswamis of Vrindavan. Puri Das was particularly unhappy about the proselytizing work of the Gaudiya Math, which he considered to have been overly zealous, ill informed, and offensive to the true spirit of Vaishnavism. To a great extent these two leaders of the organization were disillusioned by the rapaciousness of Puri Maharaj's opponents in the succession battles, which they came to attribute to the very nature of the *math* institution itself. *Yukta vairagya*, complete renunciation, was a difficult discipline indeed; the vices associated with wealth, reputation, and power were not the monopoly of any religious school or institutional system.

Puri Das and Sundarananda eventually came to accept the necessity for initiation in an accredited disciplic line and advised all Bhaktisiddhanta Saraswati's disciples to also seek *diksha* from such gurus.[49] The position formulated on the basis of early writings of Chaitanya's followers was expounded in Sundarananda's treatise, "The Characteristics of the Guru According to Vaishnava Theology" (*Vaishnava-siddhante shri-guru-svarupa*),[50] in which he gives an exhaustive critique of Gaudiya Math deviations from the traditional Gaudiya Vaishnava position.

Despite the extremely damaging defection of Puri Das and Sundarananda, the Gaudiya Math survived, but lost much of the momentum it had had during the life of its founder. One of the strongest critics of the situation was Bhaktivedanta Swami who, as a householder, had been a relative outsider in the Gaudiya Math's heyday. In the 1950s, Bhaktivedanta wrote several articles appealing for a return to the previous institutional unity, but to no avail. With the loss of the strong, centralized "hard" institution, the institutional model of the Gaudiya Math appears to have reverted to one not so radically different from what existed in the Gaudiya Vaishnava world.

First of all, the Gaudiya Math has its "soft" institutions or symbol system, and despite sharing much with the greater Gaudiya Vaishnava *sampradaya*, it is sufficiently different to be a distinct species. For example, the liturgical corpus or hymnology is almost entirely based on the writings of Bhaktivinoda Thakur and the great authorities of the post-Chaitanya effervesence—Govinda Das, Jnana Das, and others—and most of the books of the six Goswamis that are not purely philosophical or theological in content have been almost entirely purged from the religious practices of members of the Gaudiya Math. Moreover, the practice of *lila kirtana*, the *nama yajna*, and other staple practices of the greater Gaudiya Vaishnava community are consipicuously absent, and the *siddha pranali* aspect of the traditional *raganuga* practice[51] has been entirely jettisoned. As a result, the identification of Bhaktivinoda Thakur and Bhaktisiddhanta Saraswati as associates of Radha and Krishna (as the *gopis* Kamala Manjari and Nayanamani Manjari) is considered a special sign of their eternally perfect status rather than a routine aspect of the Gaudiya Vaishnava culture, even though in at least Bhaktivinoda's case, it was received in precisely the traditional manner.

Though the Gaudiya Math was born as a "hard" institution, the current situation is closer to the kind of loose collection of disciplic lines that existed in Bengal after Chaitanya's disappearance. A number of Bhaktisiddhanta Saraswati's disciples set up their own "houses," each of which functions independently. Similar patterns of inter-*math* discipline based on exclusion maintain the orthodoxy, and festivals and other practices assure their continued association. There is, however, little real cooperation among these *math*s or missions, whose relative success depends on the individual charismatic powers of their leaders. The recent attempt to create an association of Gaudiya Maths, the World Vaishnava Association, to foster cooperation and pooling of resources has not met with much success.

The method of preserving the disciplic lines in the Gaudiya Maths is clearly Pancharatrika in nature. The idea that one has to be an *uttama adhikari* or "un-conventional" spiritual master before one can take disciples has been aban-doned and the idea that one can take disciples in a "routine" manner accepted. The process of succession in these *maths* has, on the whole, been comparative-ly trouble free, though of course, heredity is not an option; in nearly every case, the parting *acharya* has named a single successor. ISKCON, the most success-ful of the Gaudiya Math's offspring, however, is a special case. ISKCON had its own set of succession problems. Within this worldwide organization, different situations in different countries have resulted in different real patterns being es-tablished; ISKCON's strength as a monolithic central institution is greatest in India and weakest in America, where the "religious free market" appears to favor the individualistic "intermediate" institutional model.

CONCLUSIONS

In my 1996 paper, I concluded that ISKCON's future depended somewhat on charismatic renewal within the movement. In the intervening years, the three directions of institutional development I pinpointed seem to have remained in place. The *ritvik* model subsumes any possibility of new charismatic leader-ship, putting "the seal on prophecy," so to speak; the other extreme, the open-ly charismatic model, is led by Narayana Maharaja, an outsider from the Gaudiya Math who rather directly makes claims of esoteric knowledge to which ISKCON's leaders are not privy. After the disastrous leadership of the eleven successors to Bhaktivedanta Swami, ISKCON itself has developed a middle way, in which a certain amount of charismatic leadership is given scope but is nevertheless subject to the approval or sanction of the governing body. On the whole, however, like any institution that seeks self-preservation, ISKCON is wary of the true charismatic leader, whose objectives are invariably destructive to existing power structures. As such, the attractions of Narayana Maharaja, and to a lesser extent, of other Vaishnava leaders outside the Gaudiya Math or even outside Gaudiya Vaishnavism itself, continue to cause a certain level of discomfort within the movement.

The reason for this is rather easy to pinpoint: Bhaktisiddhanta Saraswati placed so much emphasis on the need for "unconventional" leadership from a spiritual master, to the detriment of the "conventional" leadership of the caste Goswamis, continuously pointing to the ideal example of notoriously uncon-ventional Vaishnavas such as Gaura Kishor Das and Vamshi Das, that the pure-ly bureaucratic functionary leader ("guru by committee vote") pales in com-parison. In an age where the urge to personal religious experience dwarfs the idea of adherence to duty as a spiritual ideal, the attraction of the charismatic leader will no doubt continue to exercise a hold on seekers drawn to the Vaishnava path.

On the other hand, as the *ritviks* have pointed out, the concepts of *bhagavati diksha* and *bhagavata parampara* open the door to a kind of organization that does not specifically need charismatic leadership at every generational level. This permits institutions that are more rational in character. The contradiction here is that a certain amount of charismatic leadership is necessary for the promotion of even this idea if it is to take root in ISKCON itself. Whatever little successes the *ritvik* movement has had seem to be due to the banding together of disgruntled ex-ISKCON members rather than to any great shows of positive spiritual strength. It seems as though this splinter group is destined to remain marginal unless it can find that kind of leadership.

Within ISKCON itself, there do not seem at present to be any individuals who wish to exercise a uniquely dominant leadership over the movement as a whole by living out the traditional role of an institutional *acharya*. The bad experiences of the immediate postcharismatic phase have left a very deep mark in the consciousness of the current leaders. It is yet possible that the spirit of collegiality and even a certain degree of democracy may take root in the movement, though the problems involved in developing truly modern institutional structures are probably insurmountable in the immediate future.

NOTES

1. Harikrishan Goenka, ed., *Bhagavad Gita*, 16th ed. (Gorakhpur: Gita Press, 1946), 4.7.
2. Gita 10.42.
3. As stated succinctly by seventeenth-century Gaudiya Vaishnava *acharya* Vishvanath Chakravarti, in his hymns to the spiritual master (*Shri-Guru-devastakam* 7 [Bhakti Saranga Goswami, ed., *Stava-kalpa-druma* (Vrindavan: Imli Tala Mahaprabhu Mandir, 1959), 44].
4. Rupa Goswami describes the hierarchy of *avataras* in his *Laghu Bhagavatamrita* (B. V. Tirtha, ed. [Mayapur: Sri Chaitanya Math], 488) Gaurabda: *purusha, guna, lila, manvantara, yuga,* and *shakty-avesh.*
5. *Chaitanya Bhagavata* (4th ed., B. V. Tirtha, ed. [Mayapur: Shri Chaitanya Math, 1997]), Madhya 6.167–69: "If it is your intention to distribute devotion, then you must also give it to the women, the lower castes and the uneducated. Those who would withhold devotion or obstruct your devotees out of pride in their knowledge, wealth, social class or ability to practice austerities are most sinful. May they die and roast in hell, while the lowliest outcaste dances in joy at the sound of your holy name."
6. *Chaitanya Charitamrita* (2nd ed., B. D. Madhava, ed. [Kalikata: Shri Chaitanya Vani Press, 1992]), Antya 7.12–14.
7. There is much reason to believe that the connection to Madhva is a fabrication that became necessary in later times to legitimate the Gaudiya school outside of Bengal and has been preserved for its continued usefulness in this regard. S. K. De has voiced the principal arguments in his work *The Early History of the Vaishnava*

Faith and Movement (Calcutta: Firma KLM, 1986), 13–24. See also Friedhelm Hardy, "Madhavendra Puri" (*Journal of the Royal Asiatic Society* [1974]:23–41). Indeed, most scholars find these arguments against a Madhva connection to be persuasive, while only followers of Chaitanya Vaishnavism refuse to entertain the possibility. For the Gaudiya position, see B. V. Narayana Maharaja's *Five Fundamental Essays* (Mathura: Gaudiya Vedanta Samiti, n.d.), 55–76.

8. Sanatan Goswami's commentary to *Hari-bhakti-vilasa*, 2.1: "Since it is impossible for him to have directly instructed him [in the mantra], as the presiding deity of the consciousness, he is the supreme guru of all beings. Thus it is legitimate for [Gopal Bhatta] to call him his guru." Joseph O'Connell explains: "There is a standard explanation (or restatement) of the anomaly that Chaitanya, though founding an emergent tradition (or meta-*sampradaya*) of devotees, seems not to have bestowed *diksha* himself. It is to say that Chaitanya is the *samashti-guru* or collective spiritual master for the age, while his several associates are the *vyashti-gurus*, or particular spiritual masters" (forthcoming).

9. This incident is described in *Chaitanya Bhagavata*, Antya 5.222–229. According to the *Nityananda-vamsa-vishtara*, a later book, Chaitanya's instructions to Nityananda included the order to get married and to establish a hereditary line of gurus.

10. Ramakanta Chakrabarty, *Vaishnavism in Bengal, 1486–1900* (Calcutta: Sanskrit Pustak Bhandar, 1985), 235–38; Hitesranjan Sanyal, *Bangla kirtaner itihas* (Calcutta: K. P. Bagchi and Co., 1989), esp. ch. 10.

11. Both the doctrine of Chaitanya as the combined form of Radha and Krishna and that of the *pancha tattva* are credited to Svarupa Damodar, a close associate of Chaitanya in Puri. Though the *pancha tattva* idea seems to have come to Kheturi without passing through Vrindavan, the other certainly received potent force through the theological efforts of the Vrindavan school.

12. This doctrine was put to paper in the *Gaura-ganoddesha-dipika* by Kavi Karnapur, who was present at Kheturi, in 1572, around the same time as Kheturi.

13. The principle was that the possiblity of attaining the ultimate goal of spiritual life, a role in the eternal pastimes of Radha and Krishna, came by establishing a connection through disciplic succession with Chaitanya's original companions.

14. *Bhagavata-purana* 7.13.8 (Pandit Ramtej Pandeya, ed. [Chowkhamba Sanskrit Pratisthan, 1996]), quoted in *Bhakti Rasamrita Sindhu* (Haridas Das, ed. [Nabadwip: Haribol Kutir, 462 Gaurabda]), 1.2.113. This is taken as one of the ten principal prohibitions of devotional practice.

15. The reasons for this have not been fully explored, but may well be traced to local traditions, i.e., the strength of Tantrism in eastern India.

16. I borrow the terms "hard, soft and medium institutions" from Joseph O'Connell, who defines a hard institution as one "with centralized executive authority with coercive sanctions, and mechanisms for marshalling extensive mundane resources for community interests or for mobilizing adherents against external threats." Soft institutions are "symbolic means of articulating their cherished mode of loving devotion to Krishna, *prema bhakti*. Such 'soft' symbolic institutions are bound up with the production and utilization of religious literature (*sahitya, shastra*) and with a complex repertoire of recommended devotional practices (*sadhana*)." Intermediate organizational institutions in Gaudiya Vaishnavism are "diverse and diffuse networks of affiliation, formed through groups of religious mentors (*gurus*) and their disciples (*shishyas*). Typically, these groups are voluntary and hence noncoercive." From "Chaitanya Vaishnava Movement: Symbolic Means of Institu-

tionalization." in *Organizational and Institutional Aspects of Indian Religious Movements*, ed. J. T. O'Connell (Shimla: Indian Institute of Advanced Study; New Delhi: Manohar, 1999), 215–39.

17. Ibid.

18. See Hitesranjan Sanyal, *Social Mobility in Bengal* (Calcutta: Papyrus, 1981), 64.

19. There were others that laid claim to the charisma of one or the other of Chaitanya's associates, but of these only a few were non-Brahmins, and of the non-Brahmins, only the Thakurs of Shrikhanda had widespread influence.

20. In any case, as R. K. Chakrabarty argues, without a change in "existing economic organization," genuine social change was impossible (*Vaishnavism in Bengal* 345).

21. "The Impact of Devotion upon the Societal Integration of Bengal," in *Studies in Bengal Literature, History, and Society*, ed. Edward C. Dimock Jr. (New York: Learning Resources in International Studies, 1974); reprinted in *Studies on Bengal*, ed. Warren Gunderson (East Lansing: Asian Studies Center, Michigan State University, 1976), 33–42.

22. R. K. Chakrabarty, 324.

23. "Some Reflections on Initiation." March 19, 1999. www.bhajankutir.net/first-issue.html and subsequent issues, especially "Why Bhaktisiddhanta Saraswati Never Received Initiation from Gaur Kishor Das Babaji" at www.bhajankutir.net/first-issue.html/nitai-zine-vol-7/node5.html. For instance, the *tilaka* (sectarian marking) used by Saraswati and his disciples does not correspond to that of any existing disciplic line.

24. R. K. Chakrabarty, 398.

25. These articles were mostly succinct and prescriptive rather than descriptive, and dealt with most of the issues that spurred Saraswati to action. See Sukavak N. Dasa, *Hindu Encounter with Modernity: Kedarnath Datta Bhaktivinode, Vaishnava Theologian* (Los Angeles: Sanskrit Religious Institute, 1999), 211–16, 244–49. *Chaitanya-shikshamrita* (Kalikata: Sri Chaitanya Gaudiya Math, 497 Gaurabda), 102–11. *Sajjana-toshani* 2 (1885): 123, 142; 4 (1892): 121–24.

26. I have not seen this book, though no doubt it would shed some light on the development of Saraswati's thinking at this time.

27. Swami B. G. Narasingha, *The Authorized Sri Chaitanya Saraswata Parampara* (Bangalore: Gosai Publishers, 1998), 9. *Prabhupada Saraswati Thakur* (17). No firm date is given for this letter, so it may perhaps refer to the Balighai meeting, discussed below, where Bhaktisiddhanta Saraswati argues for a more fluid concept of the Varnashram system.

28. Though Bhaktisiddhanta Saraswati's vision was that Chaitanya Vaishnavism was a universal religion, and his social philosophy was meant to reflect this.

29. Rupa Vilasa Das, *A Ray of Vishnu* (Washington, Miss.: New Jaipur Press, 1988), 33

30. Nabadwip: Gaudiya Vedanta Samiti, 1995. It was first published in 1920, making it one of the Gaudiya Math's first books. An English translation has been prepared by Pundarik Vidyanidhi Das; I found this on the Internet. I can find no other details. Quotations here are from that translation, but page numbers refer to the Bengali edition.

31. *Sajjana-toshani*, Vol. 2. 1885, 123–24.

32. In Bengali society, there was in fact no system of four castes, but rather a two-tiered system consisting only of Brahmins and everyone else. A hierarchization of non-Brahmin castes existed, divided into six categories based on the degree to which Brahmins permitted intermingling with them. In the 1931 census, Brahmins repre-

sented about 7.5 percent of the Bengali population; 7.4 percent belonged to the other higher castes, i.e., Vaidyas, Kayasthas, Khatris, and Rajputs. See Census Commissioner, *Census of India, 1931* (Calcutta: Government of India central publication branch, 1932), 220–21.

33. Saraswati made much of the supposed currency of *tridandi sannyas* in the Ramanuja *sampradaya*, but there is not much evidence of any such practice. He also often identified Prabodhananda Saraswati, a Chaitanya contemporary, as being such a *tridandi sannyasi*, but there is absolutely no evidence anywhere to support this contention.

34. *anasaktasya vishayan yathartham upayunjataa | nirbandhah krishna-sambandhe yuktam vairagyam ucyate ||* Yukta-vairagya* is defined as the attitude of one who is detached from the objects of the senses, but uses them only inasmuch as they have utility in the service of Lord Krishna" (*Bhakti Rasamrita Sindhu* 1.2.255). It is unlikely that Rupa Goswami understood the concept in quite the same way that Saraswati did.

35. I have given the disciplic successions of Bhaktivinoda Thakur as given to his son Lalita Prasad Thakur and the *bhagavata parampara* delineated by Saraswati Thakur in my article, "The Parampara Tradition in Gaudiya Vaishnavism" (*Journal of Vaishnava Studies* 5 [1] [winter]: 151–82). Bhaktivinoda's *parampara* is also given by Shukavak Das. B. V. Narayana Maharaja's *Five Fundamental Essays* has given a rather interesting diagram attempting to combine the two kinds of disciplic succession. According to him, the *bhagavata parampara* includes the the *Pancharatrika*.

36. He justified this on the basis of *Bhakti-sandarbha* 210: "One should give up a mundane guru and take a spiritual guru." The traditional Vaishnavas hold that "mundane guru" refers to other authorities such as parents or village elders, not to a family guru, for this custom is approved in *Hari-bhakti-vilasa* (4.141), which quotes the *Brahma-vaivarta Purana,* "Even the vultures will not eat the dead corpse of the ungrateful one who abandons the guru in disciplic succession (*amnaya gatam*)."

37. See, for example, Swami B. V. Tripurari, *Sri Guru Parampara: Bhaktisiddhanta Saraswati Thakura, Heir to the Esoteric Life of Kedarnath Bhaktivinode* (Mill Valley, Calif.: Harmonist Publishers, 1998), 37–38.

38. Most Bengali Gaudiya Math authors seem to favor the term *bhagavati diksha*. See, for example, *Prabhupada Saraswati Thakur* (Eugene, Ore.: Mandala Publishing Group, 1997), 15 and Bhakti Promode Puri, *"Of Love and Separation"* (San Rafael, Calif.: Mandala Publishing Group, 2001), 48, 82, where it is translated as "esoteric initiation into Bhagavata Dharma." B. G. Narasingha says Bhaktisiddhanta Saraswati received *mantra diksha* in his book *The Authorized Chaitanya-Saraswata Parampara* (Bangalore: Gosai Publishers, 1998), 9. According to Rupa Vilasa Das, Gaura Kishor gave Bhaktisiddhanta Saraswati "initiation" and the name "Varshabhanavi Dayita Das." *A Ray of Vishnu.* (Washington, Miss.: New Jaipur Press, 1988), 18.

39. CC 3.3.240–1, 124. These translations are by A.C. Bhaktivedanta Swami, and Pundarika Vidyanidhi uses them throughout his translation of *Brahmana o Vaishnava*. Bhaktivedanta Swami translates *diksha* as "vow," which seems to fit the context. Neither Siddhanta Saraswati nor Bhaktivinoda Thakur has explained these verses in their commentaries to *Chaitanya Charitamrita*.

40. *Brahmana o Vaishnava,* 108. The context here is interesting, since Hari Das says that he has almost finished the *diksha*, which is a vow to complete a certain limited performance of chanting, i.e., chanting a certain number of Holy Names within in a predetermined period of time. A lengthy discourse on the history of initiation

is impossible here at this time. Suffice it to say that sacrifice is the original Vedic context where the word *diksha* was found. As Gonda, in his magistral article on *diksha,* correctly indicates, the Tantric (and Pancharatrika) rite of initiation is more closely modeled on the Brahminical *upanayana.* ("Diksha," in *Change and Continuity in Indian Religion* [The Hague: Mouton and Co., 1965], 444ff.). "According to the scriptural injunction, a Brahmin has three births: the first is from his mother, the second comes at the time of taking the sacred thread; the third comes with initiation into the sacrifice" (*Manava dharma-shastra. The code of Manu* [original Sanskrit text critically edited according to the standard Sanskrit commentaries, with critical notes, by J. Jolly (London: Trübner, 1887)], 2.169). It may be that Saraswati was in fact reverting to a more primordial concept of initiation as a genuine rebirth, or conversion, rather than a ritual formality of any kind.

41. *Bhagavata Purana* 12.3.52: *krite yad dhyayato vishnum tretayam yajato makhaiuh, dvapare paricaryayam kalau tad dhari-kirtanat,* where *paricarya* is taken to mean temple worship.

42. Ibid., 92.

43. Ibid., 103. These are: only a Brahmin devotee is eligible for liberation, the demigods are the foremost devotees, Lord Brahma attains *sayujya mukti* (merging in *Brahman*), and Lakshmi Devi is a *jiva.* The Baladeva text is from his commentary to *Tattva-sandarbha* 28.

44. Ibid.

45. Ibid., 119.

46. Bhakti Raksaka Sridhara Deva Goswami, *Sri Guru and His Grace* (San Jose, CA: Guardian of Devotion Press, 1983), 19.

47. Excerpted from the essay "Putana" printed in the January 1932 edition of *The Harmonist.* (available online at http://bvml.org/SBSST/putana.html).

48. This period was traumatic for most Gaudiya Math members, and most accounts of it are understandably vague. Thorough scholarly research of the postcharismatic phase of the Gaudiya Math would be most welcome.

49. All this appears to have been accompanied by personal problems. Ananta Vasudeva married one of his disciples. He liberated all his disciples to take initiation elsewhere and gave over the Gaudiya Mission to Bhaktikevala Audulomi Maharaja on the condition that he dress in white rather than the saffron of the Gaudiya Math *sannyasi*s. He then left for Vrindavan, where he lived out the rest of his life more or less as a recluse. Ex-disciples of Ananta Vasudeva formed a large contingent of the renounced residents of Radha Kund and *sri krishna chaitanya gaura gunadhama*, the *kirtana* promulgated by Puri Das, can still be heard there (Puri Das also came to accept that the congregational chanting of the *mahamantra* was not authorized). His abandonment of Bhaktisiddhanta Saraswati made him anathema in the rest of the *maths*, and left many of his admirers particularly disillusioned. Bhaktivedanta styled Bhaktivilas Tirtha as *guru bhogi,* "exploiter of the guru," and Puri as *guru tyagi,* "renouncer of the guru."

50. Calcutta: Karuna Das, 1964.

51. As noted earlier, *siddha pranali* involves the guru identifying the disciple's spiritual persona in Krishna's *lila* at the time of initiation.

[7]

BHAKTIVINODA AND SCRIPTURAL LITERALISM

SHUKAVAK N. DAS

I S IT POSSIBLE FOR A RELIGIOUS INSIDER to study his own tradition in a critical way and still maintain faith in that tradition? And if so, what is the precise nature of the critical approach that would permit such a study? Wilfred Cantwell Smith (1963) has pointed out that one of the objections most often directed to any scholarship undertaken by the religious insider is that the work is inherently unscholarly because it lacks necessary detachment and critical analysis.[1] On the other hand, the religious adherent often says that any scholarship performed by outsiders lacks an understanding of the essence of religious faith and therefore cannot adequately comprehend the tradition. On these grounds one could easily conclude that any scholarly study of religion is inherently inadequate, or that any apologetic study of religion is inherently unscholarly.

There are, no doubt, elements of truth in both arguments. The purpose of religion is to kindle faith, and to achieve this end there may be an emphasis on those facts and interpretations that nurture faith and a tendency to disregard the data that do not. Devotion is an appeal to the heart, whereas critical scholarship is an appeal to the mind. While both have their respective places, it is important to distinguish between them. How, then, does one strike a balance between critical scholarship and religious faith?

I eventually found a solution to this predicament in the writings of Kedarnath Datta Bhaktivinoda, the grandguru of A.C. Bhaktivedanta, whose first major work, the *Krishna-Samhita* (1879), I happened to find by chance. As I gradually translated the document I was amazed to learn that Bhaktivinoda was attempting to analyze Indian history and show the development of Vaishnavism according to what he called the *adhunika vada*, or the modern approach. Here was Bhaktivinoda taking a keen and discriminating look at Indian history and Vaishnava religious traditions according to the techniques of modern (nineteenth-century) critical scholarship. He offered a plausible date for the *Bhagavata* according to internal and extratextual evidence, pointed out corruption in the text, and brought attention to the human weaknesses of its author—all things that the religious insider seemingly should not do. At the same time, he obviously maintained firm faith in the Vaishnava tradition. In his *Krishna-Samhita* Bhaktivinoda was showing that it is indeed possible to take a critical look at one's own tradition, and at the same time maintain a deep and abiding faith within it. He is thus a possible role model for present-day members of the Chaitanya tradition grappling with the tension generated by the encounter of faith and reason.

THE *ADHUNIKA VADA*, OR THE "MODERN APPROACH"

Bhaktivinoda begins his *Krishna-Samhita* with an *Upakramanika,* or Bengali introduction, that was specifically written according to what he calls the *adhunika vada* or the "modern approach." The *Upakramanika* first establishes the dates of many important events of Indian history. The coming of the Aryans into Brahmavarta (India), their progressive migration from north to south, and the date of the *Mahabharata* war are all presented according to the methodology of what was then modern scholarship. It divided history into eight periods spanning 6,341 years, starting with the rule of the Prajapatyas and ending with British rule.

Bhaktivinoda cites the works of Archdeacon Pratt, Major Wilford, Professor John Playfair, and Mr. Samuel Davis—all British military officers or civil administrative officials who undertook historical research in India just prior to his own time. The *Upakramanika* further divides India's philosophical development into eight periods. The important feature of Bhaktivinoda's work is not this particular categorization of Vedic history or even the particular dating scheme that he suggests, but his evolutionary view. The idea that history leads to higher and higher levels of cultural and spiritual development is characteristic of nineteenth-century modernity. During the nineteenth century the influence of Darwin and Comte greatly supported this notion, which is reflected throughout Bhaktivinoda's work. In the *Samhita* portion of his *Krishna-Samhita* he interprets the ten incarnations (*avataras*) of Vishnu in a way that illustrates an evolutionary view of history:

Text

5. To whatever form of life the *jiva* [soul] goes, Sri Hari manifests through His inconceivable energy and plays with him in that way.

6. Sri Hari assumes the form of the Matysa *avatara* [incarnation] among fish, the form of Kurma among turtles, and the form of Varaha among *jivas* who possess a spine.

Commentary

When the *jiva* takes the form of a fish, Bhagavan becomes the Matysa *avatara*. A fish is spineless, but when the spineless state gradually becomes the hard shell state, the Kurma *avatara* appears. When the hard shell state gradually becomes a spine, the Boar (Varaha) incarnation appears.

Text

7. Midway (between man and animal) Nrisimha appears. Among dwarfs Vamana appears. Among uncivilized tribes Bhargava (Parasurama) appears. Among the civilized tribes the son of Dasharatha (Rama) appears.

8. When man attains full consciousness (*sarva-vijnana*), Bhagavan Krishna Himself appears.

9. According to the advancement in the heart of the *jiva*, the *avataras* of Hari appear. Their appearance in this world is never dependent on birth and action.

10. Analyzing the successive characteristics of the *jiva*, time in the *Shastras* [scriptures] has been divided by the *Rishis* [sages] into ten stages.[2]

Here the *Samhita* describes how each incarnation of God successively assumes a physical form to match the evolutionary development of the embodied soul (*jivatma*) from its most primitive invertebrate state to its highest vertebrate and intelligent state. Not only do these passages suggest the evolutionary theories of Darwin, they also reflect the view that the passage of time is synonymous with progress.

In a similar manner Bhaktivinoda analyzes history in terms of *rasa* or spiritual mood. He describes how there are five primary *rasas* (*shanta, dasya,* sakhya, vatsalya, and madhurya—peace, servitude, friendship, parental, and amorous) and how the various stages of Indian history exhibit each. He suggests that the dawn of Vedic civilization embodied *shanta rasa*, the peaceful mood. Later on, in successive ages, higher and higher stages of *rasika* development occurred. The *Ramayana* exhibits the *dasya rasa* (servitude) through Hanuman. Later on, Uddhava and Arjuna manifest the *sakhya rasa*, the friendly mood, and so on. He even describes how non-Vedic religions exhibit different *rasas*. Muhammad and Moses express *dasya rasa*, servitude, while Jesus embodies *vatsalya rasa*, the parental mood. Finally, with the advent of Chaitanya comes *madhurya rasa*, the quintessential amorous *rasika* mood. He compares the development of *rasa* in the world to the sun: each rises in the East and then follows its course to the West.

It is interesting that Bhaktivinoda never suggests a return to Vedic times, although he shows great respect and reverence for the past. He views Vedic culture as the foundation of Hindu culture but not something that India should return to. Life is dynamic and progressive, and just as the *shanta rasa* formed the foundations of Vedic civilization, so successive stages of spiritual and cultural development have occurred since that time. Today something higher, *madhurya rasa*, has arisen, so it would be regressive to return to *shanta rasa*. The ideas of Vedic culture are important in Bhaktivinoda's thinking. Indeed they are foundational, but they are not an absolute paradigm for modern emulation.

THREE KINDS OF SPIRITUAL SEEKERS

The *adhunika vada* was Bhaktivinoda's attempt to approach the study of Vedic history and geography from the perspective of the modern historian. He wanted to use the tools of modern comparative scholarship to show the antiquity of Vedic thought and thereby draw attention to the spiritual significance of Shri Krishna and Vaishnava culture. The *adhunika vada* was based on the premise that the existing religious traditions within Bengal had neglected the needs of the modern intellectual. Bhaktivinoda identified three types of spiritual seekers (*adhikaris*): *komala shraddhas*, *madhyamadhikaris*, and *uttamadhikaris*,[3] classified according to their ability to comprehend spiritual truth.

Komala shraddhas are people in the first stages of spiritual growth. They have simple faith. The expression *komala shraddhas* literally means people of "tender faith."[4] Their most common characteristic is their inability to see beyond their own subjective and parochial religious perspective. Next are the *madhyamadhikaris*, or people of middle faith. They are also known as *yuktyadhikaris*, or people capable of independent reasoning. Perhaps their most common characteristic is that they are plagued by profound religious doubt. Skepticism is the hallmark of the *madhyamadhikaris*. They are the intellectuals of society, who in Bhaktivinoda's time included many of the *bhadraloka*, the western-influenced urban elite of Calcutta. Above them are the *uttamad-hikaris,* or the enlightened *saragrahis,* naturally the rarest of all.[5] Bhaktivino-da's classification of spiritual seekers is analogous to Paul Tillich's three types of believers: primitive, doubting, and enlightened believers.

Komala shraddhas and *madhyamadhikaris* differ widely in their ability to understand spiritual truths and consequently in the way they must be approached for spiritual elevation. Bhaktivinoda writes: "Men have different rights according to their knowledge and tendencies. Only one with pure spiritual understanding can worship the pure spiritual form of God. To the extent that one is below this stage, one understands God accordingly. One at a low stage cannot realize the higher spiritual aspects of God."[6]

Unfortunately, pre-nineteenth century Hindu tradition had addressed the needs of *komala shraddhas* more than those of *madhyamadhikaris.*[7] Bhaktivinoda suggests that traditional forms of religious exegesis, the *tikas* and *tippanis* (commentaries), failed to address the modern concerns of the *bhadraloka,* and therefore his *Krishna-Samhita* was an attempt to fulfill that need. The problem, however, was even more complex. The *bhadraloka* lacked not only sophisticated religious texts or commentaries but also access to the intellectual side of their Hindu tradition, which was largely preserved in Sanskrit. Consequently, they were apt to reject the popular religious tradition as superstitious or irrelevant.

In fact, most Hindu texts were meant to be read with elaborate commentaries and living gurus to interpret them in more sophisticated ways, but in the absence of such textual and human aids, the *bhadraloka* were inclined to reject their traditions outright. The problem was further exacerbated by traditional commentaries that did not deal with modern critical issues. It was, therefore, the task of individuals like Bhaktivinoda to bridge the gap between tradition and modernity and create a relevant link between the past and the present.

In his *Krishna-Samhita* Bhaktivinoda tells us that texts like the *Mahabharata, Ramayana,* and Puranas present spiritual teachings to *komala shraddhas* through entertaining and superhuman stories, fantastic time calculations, and awesome descriptions of heavens and hells in order to inspire faith and regulate the activities of *komala shraddhas* for their ultimate progress.[8] This is what the *Bhagavata* calls *paroksha vada,* or the presentation of spiritual teachings through indirect means.[9] *Paroksha vada* often involves placing spiritual truths within historical or fictional narratives with the threat of punishment for failure or the promise of reward for compliant activities. In the *Tattva-sutra* (1893), Bhaktivinoda describes this:

Due to their instinctual nature, common people engage in worldly enjoyments. Their nature is generally inclined towards the gratification of their senses, but the scriptures try to reform them through various types of tricks, coercion or other strategies. Often the scriptures threaten the ignorant with the punishment of hell, or with the temptations of heaven. At other times they are purified by engagements suited to their nature.[10]

According to Bhaktivinoda, the popular approach of orthodox Hinduism, in which most of the *bhadraloka* had grown up, was the approach of Vedic culture presented for the benefit of *komala shraddhas*. It is a kind of religious literalism that involves only the most basic narrative level of *sastric* interpretation. In most cases, literal interpretations of this type do not appeal to the logical and rational minds of *madhyamadhikaris*; in fact, for them, these readings are intellectually and spiritually alienating. As a result, the Bengali *madhyamadhikaris* (the typical *bhadraloka*), when faced with rational alternatives, rejected their ancestral traditions and followed foreign philosophies or created their own rational systems of thought.[11] According to Bhaktivinoda, however, the *bhadraloka* need not restrict themselves to the perspective of *komala shraddhas*, but have the right and the obligation to examine their religious traditions from their own perspective. Spiritual truth is eternal, but how it is understood varies according to the capacity and the perspective of the individual.[12]

The *Krishna-Samhita* and the *Tattva-sutra*, to cite two examples, were not written for *komala shraddhas*; *shastra* can and should be presented in various ways to suit the intellectual and spiritual qualifications of a diverse audience, including all categories of *adhikaris*. But Bhaktivinoda warns that it is not always appropriate for *komala shraddhas* to hear what is written for *madhyamadhikaris*, as it may confuse and damage their tender faith,[13] as much as *madhyamadhikaris* feel alienated when subjected to the literal perspective of *komala shraddhas*.[14] Bhaktivinoda states that the whole point of his presentation is to show the antiquity of the Vedic tradition and the development of Vaishnava culture within it:

> Just when this pure Vaishnava dharma arose and how it developed in our country has to be determined, but before we discuss this we must discuss many other topics. Therefore, we will begin with the dates of the most important historical events of Indian history according to modern opinion. Then we will determine the dates of the many respected books. As we fix the date of these texts we will determine the history of Vaishnava dharma. Whatever seems clear according to modern opinion we will discuss. We examine time according to the ancient method, but for the benefit of people today we will rely upon the modern conventions.[15]

In other words, Bhaktivinoda is saying: My fellow *bhadraloka*, your minds are trained to accept the conclusions of rational analysis fashioned with the tools of modern scholarship, so we shall employ these tools to examine our religious traditions. Let us apply the techniques of modern textual criticism and historiography to the geographic and historical information of the *Puranas* and *Itihasas* to achieve a renewed understanding of our Hindu traditions. This was the *adhunika vada*.

Bhaktivinoda thus appealed to the western-educated *bhadraloka*, attempting to give them the confidence to follow their ancestral religious traditions by showing how those traditions could plausibly be redefined and reappropriated according to the culture of the modern world. By employing the approach of the *adhunika vada*, Bhaktivinoda extends himself beyond the parochial position of the traditional theologian and places himself in a position to peer back at his tradition through the eyes of the critical observer. This is the role of what he calls the true critic, one who:

> should be of the same disposition of mind as that of the author, whose merit he is required to judge. Thoughts have different ways. One who is trained up in the thoughts of the Unitarian Society or of the Vedant [*sic*] of the Benares School, will scarcely find piety in the faith of the Vaishnav. An ignorant Vaishnav, on the other hand . . . will find no piety in the Christian. This is because the Vaishnav does not think in the way in which the Christian thinks of his own religion. . . . In a similar manner the Christian needs to adopt the way of thought which the Vedantist pursued, before he can love the conclusions of the philosopher. The critic, therefore, should have a comprehensive, good, generous, candid, impartial, and sympathetic soul.[16]

The religious perspective that Bhaktivinoda describes here encompasses the perspective of the religious believer as well as the critical observer. The true critic eventually evolves into what Bhaktivinoda calls the *saragrahi*, or essence seeker.

Paul Tillich proffers a model of theology, which he calls the theological circle, that illustrates Bhaktivinoda's perspective. The area within the circle is the perspective of the religious insider and the area outside is the perspective of the religious outsider. Tillich suggests that it is the unique ability of the theologian to move on both sides of the theological circle. In the contemporary global context, the theologian must be able to step beyond the parochial perspective of the religious insider and critically examine that perspective from a position shared with the religious outsider.

Bhaktivinoda's use of the *adhunika vada* meant that he had to step beyond his own position—in this case the traditional perspective of the Chaitanya theologian—and move into the world of the religious outsider (to the Chaitanya Vaishnava tradition). The ability to step beyond one's own theological and philosophic perspective and appreciate the views of others without losing one's faith is the perspective of the *saragrahi*. He describes this as follows:

> Subjects of philosophy and theology are like the peaks of large towering and inaccessible mountains standing in the midst of our planet inviting attention and investigation. Thinkers and men of deep speculation take their observations through the instruments of reason and consciousness. But they take different points when they carry on their work. These points are positions chalked out by the circumstances of their social and philosophical life, different as they are in the different parts of the world . . . but the conclusion is all the same in as much as the object of observation was one and the same. They all hunted after the Great Spirit, the unconditioned Soul of the universe.[17]

Bhaktivinoda explains that the *saragrahi* is not attached to a particular theory or religious doctrine.[18] Even when an opposing opinion is offered, if it is presented according to sound reasoning, it can be worthy of respect and consideration. *Saragrahis* can perceive the essential truth in other religious perspectives because they are not limited to their own formulation of the truth. This irenic perspective relates well to the religious pluralism and cosmopolitanism of modernity.[19] The historical perspective of the *Krishna-Samhita* is in the spirit of the *saragrahi*.

TWO MODES OF RELIGIOUS UNDERSTANDING

Bhaktivinoda's *Krishna-Samhita* was a radical departure from the orthodox understanding of Vedic history, although by today's standards his Indian historiography is completely out of date. The fact that he employs the *adhunika vada* is a major innovation for the Chaitanya religious tradition. It is not difficult to understand how the British Orientalists, who were outsiders to Hindu tradition, could apply the tools of modern analysis to the Vedic traditions, but it is remarkable to find Bhaktivinoda, a Vaishnava insider, doing the same thing. We might expect that a historical study of the life of Krishna using modern methodology would diminish or even deny the divine aspects of his existence. So the question arises: How could Bhaktivinoda justify the use of the *adhunika vada* and at the same time maintain his faith in the spiritual integrity of the Vaishnava tradition? What was his theological basis for employing modern methods of critical analysis?

Let me give an example that shows that the problem was not just a concern for the nineteenth century but is still a real challenge for Chaitanya Vaishnavas today. I once presented a summary of Bhaktivinoda's analysis of Vedic history from his *Upakramanika* to an audience of Chaitanya Vaishnavas. I stated

Bhaktivinoda's view that the *Bhagavata Purana* might not be a work compiled by *the* Vedavyasa 5,000 years ago, as orthodox Vaishnava tradition teaches, but may be a work not older than 1,000 years, compiled by a southerner writing in the name of Vedavyasa. Bhaktivinoda had reached this conclusion by analyzing certain geographic and cultural aspects of the *Bhagavata*.[20] He was voicing an opinion arrived at through the use of the techniques of the *adhunika vada*.

A suggestion such as this coming from a secular scholar steeped in western criticism would not be unusual and could be easily deflected, but coming from Bhaktivinoda, a teacher from within the tradition, it cast a spell of disbelief over my audience. Many doubts arose: perhaps Bhaktivinoda did not actually believe these things but used them as a "preaching tactic"; perhaps he wrote his work when he was young and still learning but later came to reject these views; or perhaps my understanding of his perspective was incorrect.

I was approached by one respected participant who was greatly perplexed by the mere suggestion that Bhaktivinoda may have said that the *Bhagavata* was only 1,000 years old or that it was not written by *the* Vedavyasa. I realized that this individual was upset because I had challenged one of his most sacred beliefs, namely, the spiritual authority of the *Bhagavata*. What is more, by questioning his beliefs concerning certain historical details about that work, I had challenged his basic faith as a whole. The internal and subjective perspective of the traditionalist will not give credence to material facts that do not support and nurture religious faith.

I too wondered how Bhaktivinoda, a champion of Chaitanya Vaishnavism, could go to such lengths and question so many traditional beliefs yet maintain a strong and abiding faith in the authority of the *Bhagavata* and the Vedic tradition as a whole. Whereas so many of my respected colleagues were put on the spiritual defensive by even a small amount of such a discussion, the whole matter seemed insignificant to him.

Bhaktivinoda viewed religion in two components: one relating to this world and the other relating to transcendence. At the beginning of the *Upakramanika*, he writes:

> Scripture is of two types: that which relates to phenomenal matters (*artha-prada*) and that which relates to transcendent matters (*paramartha-prada*). Geography, history, astrology, philosophy, psychology, medicine, entomology, mathematics, linguistics, prosody, music, logic, yoga, law, dentistry, architecture, and the military arts, are all sciences which are *artha-prada*. . . . [On the other hand] that scripture which discusses the supreme goal of life is *paramartha-prada*, or transcendent.[21]

Knowledge relating to this world, even if it is derived from scripture, is subject to human analysis and logical scrutiny, whereas knowledge pertaining to transcendence is not subject to such logic and reasoning. Responding to criticism from religious colleagues, Bhaktivinoda states:

> With folded hands I humbly submit to my respected readers who hold traditional views, that where my analysis opposes their long held beliefs, they should understand that my conclusions have been made for persons possessing appropriate qualifications. What I have said about dharma applies to everyone, but with regard to matters which are secondary to dharma, my conclusions are meant to produce benefits in the form of intellectual clarification only for qualified specialists. All the subjects I have outlined in the Introduction concerning time and history are based on the logical analysis of *Shastra*. Whether one accepts them or not, does not affect the final spiritual conclusions. History and time are phenomenal subject matters (*artha-shastra*) and when they are analyzed according to sound reasoning much good can be done for India.[22]

Here Bhaktivinoda answers the charge that the *adhunika vada* is necessarily incompatible with sacred tradition, stating that matters secondary to dharma, and by this he means phenomenal knowledge, are subject to human analysis.

To illustrate how a sacred text may be scrutinized, Bhaktivinoda shows how a specific verse of the *Bhagavata* is incorrect. *Bhagavata* verse 12.1.19 states that the kings of the Kanva dynasty will rule for 345 years. Through logical analysis and in conjunction with other Puranic texts, Bhaktivinoda concludes that the correct figure is 45 years and not 345 years. Bhaktivinoda even says that Shridhara Swami, the original commentator of the *Bhagavata*, is mistaken in accepting the defective reading.[23] A more traditional way to reconcile a discrepancy of this type would have been to show how the number of years given in the *Bhagavata* is actually correct and not to state outright that the text is corrupt or that the original commentator was in error. For Bhaktivinoda those parts of *shastra* that are *artha prada*, i.e., in relation to this world, are subject to human scrutiny.

In another example he points out how the *Bhagavata* contains both phenomenal knowledge (*artha prada*) and transcendent knowledge (*paramartha prada*). During his descriptions of the heavens and hells in the *Bhagavata*, he writes:

> The *Bhagavat* certainly tells us of a state of reward and punishment in the future according to our deeds in the present situation. All poetic inventions [the various descriptions of heaven and hell], besides this spiritual fact, have been described as statements borrowed from other works in the way of preservation of old traditions in the book which superseded them and put an end to the necessity of their storage. If the whole stock of

Hindu theological works which preceded the *Bhagavat* were burnt like the Alexandrian library and the sacred *Bhagavat* preserved as it is, not a part of the philosophy of the Hindus, except that of the atheistic sects, would be lost. The *Bhagavat* therefore, may be styled both as a religious work and a compendium of all Hindu history and philosophy.[24]

By contrast, those parts of *shastra* that are strictly *paramartha prada*—in relation to transcendence—are not subject to rational analysis or human scrutiny. For Bhaktivinoda, "What is Divine is beyond human reasoning."[25] He is adamant in stating that the spiritual aspects of *shastra* are not open to rational analysis. Again he writes, "According to our *Shastra,* analysis of fundamental principles of theology and mystic insights are not subject to revision."[26] Such things cannot be approached through human reason, but only through direct perception by the soul, mystic insight.[27]

FAITH AND BELIEF

Bhaktivinoda's methodology of modern religious scholarship can be appreciated when we compare his work with that of Wilfred Cantwell Smith. Smith points out that one of the greatest stumbling blocks to the study of religion, for both the religious insider and the outsider, is the very concept of religion itself. He suggests that historically, "religion" is a vague and misleading term. To the insider it denotes religious faith, but to the outsider it denotes the hard data of a tradition. Smith proposes that we conceive of religion as two complementary categories, one, the historical cumulative tradition and the other, the personal faith of the individuals who take part in that tradition. Both tradition and faith exist in their own right, and together they form what we call religion.

This is similar to the distinction Bhaktivinoda makes. What Bhaktivinoda calls *artha prada*—the phenomenal side of a religious tradition—is nothing less than the cumulative religious tradition. What he calls *paramartha prada*—the transcendent side of religion, although not directly faith as Smith describes it—is an experiential reality that must be approached through faith. What Smith calls religious faith ultimately leads to what Bhaktivinoda terms *sahaja samadhi,* or a state of innate spiritual insight or intuition. For Bhaktivinoda, pure religious faith is the means by which an inner awareness of spiritual reality arises, and when that inner spiritual reality is expressed in physical terms, the cumulative religious traditions of the world arise.

Perhaps the most important feature of the cumulative tradition is that it lies within the realm of empirical history accessible to the rational mind and therefore can be the object of logic and comparative study. There is significant value in making the distinction between what lies within the realm of empirical observation and what lies beyond it because this allows the religious insider to differentiate between the two dimensions of the religious experience, to treat each area separately and thus keep the door open for higher perceptions.

Bhaktivinoda felt that the phenomenal could be the object of logical scrutiny, but that which transcended logic should be approached only by the innate seeing ability of the soul called *sahaja samadhi*.[28] Religious faith, unfettered by the rational process, is the key to unlocking that ability. *Sahaja samadhi* is a natural faculty of the soul that everyone possesses, though in most people it has been diminished due to occlusion by the rational mind. Religious mystics and saints are individuals who have reawakened this natural ability.

One important implication that arises from the differentiation of the phenomenal and the transcendent is the distinction between faith and belief.[29] Returning to our previous discussion about the date of the *Bhagavata*, the reaction of my audience, who became upset on hearing Bhaktivinoda's historical conclusions, was natural for those whose faith is rigidly tied to their belief system. They experienced faith in terms of their religious belief systems, considering faith and belief as virtually the same thing. They felt that faith was inseparable from certain historical conceptions. To tinker with one's belief system or revise one's view of history was to tinker with the foundations of religious faith itself. Bhaktivinoda, however, made a significant distinction between his faith and his belief.

When the religious person distinguishes between belief and faith, he is able to take a look at his religious tradition from a perspective that is not tied to vested intellectual and emotional interests. Religious faith becomes somewhat insulated from changes that may occur in the belief system as a result of critical research. This is why Bhaktivinoda could afford to make his presentation of Vedic history according to the *adhunika vada* or modern approach. His conclusion that the *Bhagavata* may be a work of only 1,000 years ago had no effect on his faith in the spiritual truths of that great work. Regardless of the *Bhagavata*'s historicity, Bhaktivinoda clearly points out that its value is in its expression of eternal spiritual principles:[30] in its capacity to elicit a response of faith, and not in who wrote it and when. The spiritual truths it embodies are its real significance.[31]

For Bhaktivinoda, faith is a living quality of the soul, and therefore faith in God is a natural condition of life.[32] Belief, on the other hand, is primarily a mental act that involves the holding of certain ideas in the mind. Belief is an expression of faith just as religious architecture and dance are expressions of faith. It is *artha prada* and, like all aspects of the cumulative religious tradition, it has the capacity to induce and nurture faith and is also the object of reason and logic by which it can be inspected, shaped, and molded. This explains why beliefs change so often and why those who fail to make the distinction between faith and belief often experience a crisis of faith when their beliefs are challenged.

In his *Upakramanika,* Bhaktivinoda could afford to show empirically how the Vedic historical and literary traditions may have developed. He knew that whatever he might believe about that development and however his beliefs might change as a result of his research would not necessarily affect his confidence in the spiritual essence of the Vedic/Vaishnava tradition. History and time are simply various aspects of the cumulative religious tradition.[33] Bhaktivinoda is able to conclude his critical assessment of Indian history by honestly saying that he has done his best and that future historians should attempt to do better:

> As far as possible, I have determined the chronology of the major events and important books according to the modern perspective. A *saragrahi,* however, is not attached to a particular view, so if, in the future, any of my conclusions are refuted by better reasoning, then those new conclusions are worthy of my respect and consideration. Indeed, there is much hope that future spiritual seekers and intellectuals will improve upon this matter.[34]

Since Bhaktivinoda makes the subtle but important distinction between the cumulative tradition and faith, he is able to keep the door open for continued empirical study of the cumulative tradition. The distinction he draws between the two, along with the separation of faith and belief, is basic to much of modern critical scholarship in religious theology. Theodore Parker makes a similar distinction in his sermon, "The Transient and Permanent in Christianity." Speaking of one who builds his faith solely upon human beliefs, Parker writes, "You will be afraid of every new opinion, lest it shake down your church; you will fear 'lest if a fox go up, he will break down your stone wall.' The smallest contradiction in the New Testament or Old Testament; the least disagreement between the Law and the Gospel; any mistake of the Apostles, will weaken your faith."[35]

If Chaitanya Vaishnavism is to become indigenous to the modern and the western world, then it must adapt to the conditions of modernity and the West. If Chaitanya Vaishnavism is to have a lasting position in and a positive impact on the West, then it must move beyond the literalism by which it entered the region and begin to develop new forms of intellectual expression and perspectives that are a part of the western intellectual and academic traditions. Bhaktivinoda's work provides the basis for such development.

NOTES

1. Wilfred Cantwell Smith, *The Meaning and End of Religion* (New York: Macmillan, 1963).
2. *Krishna-Samhita* (Mayapura: W. Bengal: Shree Chaitanya Math, 1960), *Samhita*, 3/5–10.
3. A more standard use of these three terms comes from the *Bhagavata Purana*, where they apply to three grades of *bhaktas* (*Bhagavata Purana*, trans. G. V. Tagare [Delhi: Motilal Banarsidass, 1976–78], 11.2.45–47). In the *Krishna-Samhita*, however, Bhaktivinoda uses these terms in a slightly different way, applying them to people in general and not exclusively to *bhaktas*.
4. *Krishna-Samhita, Upakramanika*, 3.
5. Ibid., 3.
6. *Jaiva-dharma* (Madras: Sree Gaudiya Math, 1975), 197–98.
7. *Krishna-Samhita, Upakramanika*, 4.
8. Kedarnath Datta, *The Bhagavat, Its Philosophy, Ethics and Theology* (Madras: Madras Gaudiya Math, 1959), 28; *Krishna-Samhita, Upakramanika*, 16, 199.
9. *Bhagavata Purana*, 11.3.44.
10. *Sajjana-toshani*, 1896:8.
11. *Krishna-Samhita, Upakramanika*, 4.
12. *Krishna-Samhita, Samhita*, 7.2.
13. *Krishna-Samhita, Upakramanika*, 56.
14. Ibid., 4.
15. Ibid., 11.
16. Datta, *The Bhagavat*, 8, 11.
17. Ibid., 9–10.
18. According to Bhaktivinoda, a religious sect (*sampradaya*) is characterized by three traits: physical (*alochaka*), cultic (*alochana*), and doctrinal (*alochya*). Physical traits are the external cultural differences that exist among the various religions, such as type and color of dress, sectarian marks (*tilaka*), the wearing of sacred articles, and so on. Cultic traits are differences of worship, which include the honoring of different rivers and places of geography, fasting times, dietary restrictions, etc. Doctrinal traits are differences based on interpretation of sacred texts, which conclude that God is immanent or transcendent, male or female, and so on. He points out that such differences are external and do not constitute the true essence of religious understanding. A *saragrahi* is able to see beyond these externals.
19. *Krishna-Samhita, Upakramanika*, 61.
20. *Krishna-Samhita, Upakramanika*, 57–59.
21. *Krishna-Samhita, Upakramanika*, 1.
22. *Krishna-Samhita, Vijnapana*, i–ii.
23. *Krishna-Samhita, Upakramanika*, 41.
24. Datta, *The Bhagavat*, 28–29.
25. *Sajjana-toshani*, 1895:7, *Tattva-sutra*, 186: *bhagavad-vishayati yuktir atita*.
26. *Krishna-Samhita, Upakramanika*, 197–98.
27. In *Datta-kaustubha* (Mayapura, W. Bengal: The Gaudiya Mission, 1942), verse 10, he states: "Direct perception is said to be obtained by either the material senses or the spirit soul directly. Similarly, inference may be performed in these two ways."

28. Bhaktivinoda himself never gives an English translation for this term, but he does describe it as a natural function of the soul to which everyone potentially has access. *Sahaja samadhi* is a state of cognition that is totally free of any kind of rational or conceptual processes (*vikalpa*). Elsewhere he describes it as *nirvikalpa-samadhi*. See *Krishna-Samhita, Samhita* 9/2e. I discuss *sahaja-samadhi* in *Hindu Encounter with Modernity* (Los Angeles: SRI, 1997), chapter 6.

29. W. C. Smith points out that many people, especially in the West, equate religious faith with belief because in Christianity the two have been made inseparable. Church theology, expressed in terms of doctrinal belief, is often set forth as a formal qualification for church membership. Smith writes: "Doctrine has been a central expression of faith, has seemed often a criterion of it; the community has divided over differences in belief, and has set forth belief as a formal qualification of membership" (13). The faithful have been distinguished by what doctrines they believe. Belief has even been translated into salvation—that all one has to do is believe certain creeds in order to obtain salvation. There is little doubt that in the West, with its long history of Christian influence, faith and belief have been made synonymous, or at least so tightly intertwined as to be indistinguishable.

30. *Krishna-Samhita, Upakramanika*, 56; appendix V, 16.

31. The distinction between religious faith and belief can also be shown to exist outside the religious field. In philosophy, for example, it is not what a philosopher believes but rather the individual's faith in philosophy that produces and sustains the beliefs, the particular philosophies. The same can be said about science. A person is a scientist because of his faith in science, in the spirit of science, and not because of his beliefs in the particular theorems, which unquestionably come and go.

32. Bhaktivinoda, *Tattva-viveka, Tattva-sutra, Amnaya-sutra*, trans. Narasimha Brahmachari (Madras: Sree Gaudiya Math, 1979), 18.

33. *Krishna-Samhita, Vijnapana*, i.

34. *Krishna-Samhita, Upakramanika*, 61.

35. Conrad Wright, *Three Prophets of Religious Liberalism: Channing Emerson Parker* (Boston: Unitarian Universalist Association, 1980), 147.

[8]

THE GURU, MAYAVADINS, AND WOMEN

Tracing the Origins of Selected Polemical Statements
in the Work of A.C. Bhaktivedanta Swami

EKKEHARD LORENZ

I N 1965, Bhaktivedanta Swami, a retired pharmaceuticals manufacturer from Calcutta, moved to New York, where he founded the International Society for Krishna Consciousness. In the following years he published his English translations of and commentaries on the *Bhagavad Gita* and the *Bhagavata Purana*. By paraphrasing the words of and repeatedly referring to the earlier Gaudiya Vaishnava writers in his books and lectures, he popularized these authors—perhaps for the first time—among a large English-speaking audience outside India. While these earlier commentators, in their writing, remained strictly within the boundaries of scriptural context, often limiting their notes to clarifications of syntax, grammar, and word meanings, with occasional quotes from other scriptures, Bhaktivedanta Swami added his own urgent and personal message. The contemporary world economy, politics, social development, education, and racial and gender issues are not uncommon topics in his commentaries. And while the works of his predecessor commentators had always remained reading matter for an elite minority, he wanted his books to be translated into all the languages of the world and distributed profusely.

Bhaktivedanta Swami's work is neither text-critical nor systematic. He basically drew from whatever sources happened to be easily available to him at the time. For his English translation of the *Bhagavad-Gita As It Is*,[1] he relied to a large extent on Dr. Radhakrishnan's English *Gita* translation.[2] His English translation of the *Bhagavata Purana* is based on a number of different sources. In his translation of the third book,[3] for example, there are a large number of stanzas that agree verbatim with C. L. Goswami and M. A. Sastri's earlier English translation of the text.[4] While Bhaktivedanta Swami continued to use their work when he translated the fourth book,[5] he no longer copied any of their translations verbatim. From the twenty-eighth chapter of book 4 to the thirteenth chapter of book 10,[6] his work is clearly based on the Gaudiya Math Bengali edition of the *Bhagavata Purana*.[7] Many of Bhaktivedanta Swami's translations in this part of his work are not rendered directly from the original Sanskrit, but from this Bengali translation.[8] His books, however, nowhere state the actual sources on which they are based.

Many explanations in Bhaktivedanta Swami's commentary on the *Bhagavata Purana* can be traced directly to the traditional Gaudiya Sanskrit commentaries that he used. It appears that in order to formulate his own commentary on a given stanza of the *Bhagavata Purana*, he would first glance at the notes of two or three of the earlier commentators, paraphrase fragments of their glosses, and then add his own elaborations.[9] He called his commentaries "Bhaktivedanta purports" and often suggested that they had not actually been written by himself, but that God, Krishna, had revealed them to him.[10] For the *Bhagavata Purana* alone, he produced 5,800 purports averaging 250 words in length.[11]

Not everything in the purports builds upon the earlier commentaries. There are many passages wherein Bhaktivedanta Swami clearly presents his own views—for example, when he dismisses the reports of the Moon landing in 1969,[12] debates scientific theories like Darwin's theory of evolution,[13] or condemns contemporary culture and morals when discussing the miniskirt fashion.[14] While it is easy to identify these statements as the author's own opinions, Bhaktivedanta Swami's purports also contain a range of statements that sound as if they were the conclusions of earlier commentators, but turn out to be his personal contributions when one compares them to all the commentaries that he possibly could have used.

To explore this aspect of Bhaktivedanta's commentaries, a list of about 150 most frequently recurring keywords in the Bhaktivedanta purports (such as *varna, brahmana*, "scholars," "women," "Mayavadis," etc.) was drawn up. Then, purport after purport was analyzed to see how many, and which, of those keywords corresponded to words in the traditional commentaries on the same stanzas. This procedure was repeated with all the purports to the *Bhagavad Gita* and 664 purports to the *Bhagavata Purana*,[15] with a view to eliminating those keywords that were common to both the purports and the traditional commentaries. As a result, a shorter list emerged of just those keywords that rarely or never had synonymous or equivalent expressions in any of the corresponding earlier commentaries. These fall into three distinct categories: statements about the position of the guru or spiritual master, statements about impersonalists or Mayavadins, and statements about women and sex.

THE POSITION OF THE GURU

Much of what Bhaktivedanta Swami writes about the guru repeats traditional Hindu views and is based on well-known Upanishadic statements that he either quotes or paraphrases: *yasya deve para-bhaktih* (*Shvetasvatara* 6.23), *tad-vijnanartham sa gurum evabhigacchet* (*Mundaka* 1.2.12), and *acharyavan purusho veda* (*Chandogya* 6.14.2). While the earlier commentaries also occasionally quote these aphorisms, Bhaktivedanta Swami employs them significantly more often, especially to underline the absolute position, superhuman qualities, and overall importance of the guru. The three above-mentioned passages, for example, appear 53 times in his purports, but only 12 of these occurrences have corresponding passages in earlier commentaries.

In the purports of Bhaktivedanta Swami's *Bhagavad Gita* alone, there are 138 statements about the spiritual master, but only in 24 of the cases did an earlier commentator refer to an equivalent word or concept.[16] In his purports to the second book of the *Bhagavata Purana*,[17] Bhaktivedanta Swami makes 141 statements about the position and importance of the guru, but only 7 of those statements can be linked to the commentaries on which his work is based.[18] The topic is clearly important to him. If the data from the *Gita* and the second book are representative, perhaps 89 percent of what he writes about the spiritual master's position and qualifications is not based on statements that earlier commentators made in the same context.

Given this unprecedented emphasis, it seems useful to consider how Bhaktivedanta Swami understood the role of the guru. He especially emphasizes how a person without a guru cannot know God:

Only Lord Krishna, or His bona fide representative the spiritual master, can release the conditioned soul.[19]

For one who does not take personal training under the guidance of a bona fide spiritual master, it is impossible to even begin to understand Krishna.[20]

Unless one is in touch with a realized spiritual master, he cannot actually realize the real nature of self.[21]

Time and again, Bhaktivedanta Swami also insists that the spiritual master be *bona fide*:

> A bona fide spiritual master does not mention anything not mentioned in the authorized scriptures.[22]

> The bona fide spiritual master is he who has received the mercy of his guru, who in turn is bona fide because he has received the mercy of his guru.[23]

> I am successful in my teaching work because I have not deviated one inch from my Spiritual Master's instruction.[24]

Moreover, he frequently states that, to be *bona fide*, the guru must be situated in the disciplic succession (*guru parampara*). In the introduction to his *Bhagavad Gita*, in his purports, and in letters to his disciples, he lists the names of the gurus in the disciplic succession, beginning with Krishna and ending with himself.

Elsewhere, Bhaktivedanta Swami repeatedly speaks about the guru's role as an educator; hence the name *gurukula* (house of the guru), which he gave to a network of boarding schools he created for ISKCON children:

> Everyone, and especially the Brahmin and *Kshatriya*, was trained in the transcendental art under the care of the spiritual master far away from home, in the status of *brahmacharya*.[25]

> Children at the age of five are sent to the *guru-kula*, or the place of the spiritual master, and the master trains the young boys in the strict discipline of becoming *brahmacaris*.[26]

> As soon as the children are a little grown up, they are sent to our Gurukula school in Dallas, Texas, where they are trained to become fully Krishna conscious devotees.[27]

Bhaktivedanta Swami also envisions the guru's role as family instructor:

> Any member of the family who is above twelve years of age should be initiated by a bona fide spiritual master, and all the members of the household should be engaged in the daily service of the Lord, beginning from morning (4 A.M.) till night (10 P.M.).[28]

Perhaps the most important mission of the guru—judging by the extent to which Bhaktivedanta Swami dwells on this topic—is to teach men about women and sex:[29]

During the first stage of life, up to twenty-five years of age, a man may be trained as a *brahmacari* under the guidance of a bona fide spiritual master just to understand that woman is the real binding force in material existence.[30]

His interpretation of *Bhagavata Purana* 7.12.1 illustrates that according to him, the guru exerts complete control over his married male disciples' sexual activities:

If the spiritual master's orders allow a *grihastha* to engage in sex life at a particular time, then the *grihastha* may do so; otherwise, if the spiritual master orders against it, the *grihastha* should abstain. The *grihastha* must obtain permission from the spiritual master to observe the ritualistic ceremony of *garbhadhana-samskara*. Then he may approach his wife to beget children, otherwise not. A Brahmin generally remains a *brahmacari* throughout his entire life, but although some Brahmins become *grihasthas* and indulge in sex life, they do so under the complete control of the spiritual master.[31]

None of the earlier commentators[32] has explained that *Bhagavata Purana* passage in this way. In fact, both Bhaktisiddhanta Saraswati and Ganga-sahaya took the word "guru" in this verse to refer to family elders, who advise the newly married boy about the proper time for begetting offspring.

Lecturing about the same topic before disciples in Bombay in 1976, Bhaktivedanta Swami claimed that Viraraghava Acharya, a fourteenth-century *Bhagavata* commentator, had expressed equally strong views regarding gurus, sex, and householders:

If a married man stick to one wife, and before sex, if he takes permission from his spiritual master, then he is *brahmacari*. Not whimsically. When the spiritual master orders him that "Now you can beget a child," then he is *brahmacari*. Srila Vira-Raghava Acharya, he has described in his comment that there are two kinds of *brahmacari*. One *brahmacari* is *naisthiki-brahmacari;* he doesn't marry. And another *brahmacari* . . . [a]lthough he marries, he is fully under control of the spiritual master, even for sex. He is also *brahmacari*.[33]

However, the Sanskrit commentary Bhaktivedanta Swami refers to does not state that a married man remains *fully under control of the spiritual master*. That commentary just names the two classes of celibate students, and explains that before one becomes a householder, anchorite, *sannyasin,* or even a lifelong celibate, one is known as *upakurvanaka,* a celibate who still has an option to marry.[34]

From these and other statements that Bhaktivedanta Swami makes about the guru, it appears that he envisions the master as an all-knowing, all-competent spiritual autocrat: a person without whose mercy the devotee is doomed, who is beyond criticism, and who exercises total control over the lives of his disciples. Bhaktivedanta Swami's statements about the position of the spiritual master take on special relevance since, in matters of epistemological conflict, his views are deemed ultimate, even over scripture, the traditional source of highest authority (see Conrad Joseph's essay in this volume).

MAYAVADINS

Another topic that received extensive coverage in Bhaktivedanta Swami's writings is what he calls "impersonalism" or "Mayavada philosophy." It is, however, not so much the philosophy he discusses but rather its proponents, the Mayavadins, or "impersonalists," as he calls them. He frequently describes them as foolish, less intelligent, or ignorant:

> The self-centered impersonalists, by their gross ignorance, accept the Lord as one of them.[35]

> The foolish impersonalists still maintain that the Lord is formless.[36]

> The less intelligent impersonalists cannot see the Supreme.[37]

In his purports to the *Bhagavata Purana,* Bhaktivedanta Swami makes more than 600 statements regarding Mayavadins and impersonalists. None of the 402 statements that are found in the purports to the second, third, and fourth books alone (which were examined for this essay), nor any of the 85 statements he makes about impersonalists and Mayavadins in his *Bhagavad Gita,* can be traced back to the earlier commentaries in the tradition.

While none of Bhaktivedanta Swami's statements about impersonalists in the above-mentioned sources can be traced to the sources he worked from, it can be shown that many of these statements were his passionate responses to expressions he found in the English source material on which his translations were based. For example, in his purport to *Bhagavad Gita* 8.3, he states:

> Impersonalist commentators on the *Bhagavad-gita* unreasonably assume that Brahman takes the form of *jiva* in the material world, and to substantiate this they refer to Chapter Fifteen, verse 7, of the *Gita.*[38]

It was Dr. Radhakrishnan who, in his edition (1948) of the *Gita,* commented: "*svabhava:* Brahman assumes the form of *jiva,* Chap XV, 7)"[39]

Another example of Bhaktivedanta Swami's dialogue with modern English commentaries is in his purport to *Bhagavad Gita* 9.11:

> Some of those who deride Krishna and who are infected with the Mayava-di philosophy quote the following verse from the *Shrimad-Bhagavatam* (3.29.21) to prove that Krishna is just an ordinary man.[40]

Again it is Radhakrishnan who wrote, commenting on the same passage from the *Gita:*

> In the *Bhagavata,* III, 29, 21, the Lord is presented as saying "I am present in all beings as their soul but ignoring My presence, the mortal makes a display of image worship."[41]

Thus Bhaktivedanta Swami's unnamed Mayavadin turns out to be Dr. Radhakrishnan.

It is not that Bhaktivedanta Swami was interested in Radhakrishnan's work or philosophy, but he apparently considered Radhakrishnan's English *Gita* a useful help in his own translation work. This is documented in the following passage from Hayagriva Das's book, *The Hare Krishna Explosion:*[42]

> Swamiji finally tires of my consulting him about *Bhagavad-gita* verses. "Just copy the verses from some other translation," he tells me, discarding the whole matter with a wave of his hand. "The verses aren't important. There are so many translations, more or less accurate, and the Sanskrit is always there. It's my purports that are important. Concentrate on the purports. There are so many nonsense purports like Radhakrishnan's and Gandhi's, and Nikhilananda's. What is lacking are these Vaishnava purports in the preaching line of Chaitanya Mahaprabhu. That is what is lacking in English. That is what is lacking in the world."
>
> "I can't just copy others," I say.
>
> "There is no harm."
>
> "But that's plagiarism."
>
> "How's that? They are Krishna's words. Krishna's words are clear, like the sun. Just these rascal commentators have diverted the meaning by saying, 'Not to Krishna.' So my purports are saying, 'To Krishna.' That is the only difference."

The translations of many stanzas in Bhaktivedanta Swami's first edition of his *Bhagavad Gita* seem to have been adapted from Radhakrishnan's English translation. When Bhaktivedanta Swami, in his translating work, came across passages in that book that didn't fit his own views, he produced vigorous attacks on "certain Mayavadins," who always remained unnamed.

A similar pattern can be found in the third and fourth books of the *Bhagavata Purana*. The English translations of many stanzas in Bhaktivedanta Swami's third book agree verbatim with the corresponding stanzas in the English Gita Press edition by C. L. Goswami and M. A. Sastri. In a letter to a disciple, dated 21 December 1967, Bhaktivedanta Swami wrote:

> Please send me the third Canto English translation of the *Shrimad-Bhagavatam* done by the Gita Press. You got these copies from the Gita Press for reference. I want the third canto, please send as soon as possible.[43]

When one compares the English translations of the stanzas in chapters 14 to 31 in Bhaktivedanta Swami's third book to those of the Gita Press English edition, one finds not only stanzas that have been copied verbatim but also a substantial number of stanzas that have been modified only slightly. Original translations are rare. By conservative estimation, up to 50 percent of the English translations in Bhaktivedanta Swami's rendition of the third book were actually copied from the Gita Press edition.[44] Considering the following excerpt from a letter that Bhaktivedanta Swami wrote to a disciple, one wonders why he chose to copy so much of the Gita Press translation, if he thought that it was so "full of Mayavada Philosophy":

> Gita Press is full of Mayavada philosophy which says Krishna has no form but He assumes a form for facility of devotional service. This is nonsense. I am just trying to wipe out this Mayavada philosophy and you may not therefore order for any more copy of the English Bhagavatam published by the Gita Press. The one which you have got may be kept only for reference on having an understanding of the Mayavada Philosophy which is very dangerous for ordinary persons.[45]

Incidentally, the purports to the third book contain more criticism of Mayavadins than any other part of Bhaktivedanta Swami's *Bhagavata Purana*. Apparently he reacted to Sastri and Goswami's interpretations of certain key terms. For example, in his purport to *Bhagavata Purana* 3.29.33, he writes:

> Sometimes Mayavadi philosophers, due to a poor fund of knowledge, define the word *sama-darshanat* to mean that a devotee should see himself as one with the Supreme Personality of Godhead. This is foolishness.[46]

Sastri and Goswami had indeed translated *sama-darshanat* (in *Bhagavata Purana* 3.29.33) as: "thus sees no difference between himself and Me."[47]

Anti-Mayavadin rhetoric in the purports to the fourth book of the *Bhagavata Purana* can also be accurately traced back to Sastri and Goswami's interpretation of certain keywords that caused Bhaktivedanta Swami to strongly disagree. For example, in his purport to 4.22.25, he notes:

> The word *brahmani* used in this verse is commented upon by the impersonalists or professional reciters of *Bhagavatam*, who are mainly advocates of the caste system by demoniac birthright. They say that *brahmani* means the impersonal Brahman.[48]

Here, too, Sastri and Goswami had rendered *brahmani* as "the attributeless Brahma."[49] The same authors (i.e., Radhakrishnan, Sastri and Goswami) of whose translations Bhaktivedanta Swami had availed himself became the targets of his numerous polemical remarks regarding their understanding of spirituality.

The large number of statements about Mayavadins that are found in the Bhaktivedanta purports to the *Gita* and the *Bhagavata Purana*, and the type and quality of these statements, have no precedent in the works of the earlier Gaudiya commentators.[50] There is, however, a certain tradition of dispute and debate with Mayavadins that can be seen in the *Chaitanya Charitamrita*, a chiefly Bengali hagiography of Chaitanya written by Krishnadas Kaviraja in 1615. Bhaktisiddhanta Saraswati, Bhaktivedanta Swami's guru, had written a Bengali commentary, the *Anubhashya*, on Krishnadas's work, in which he does elaborate on Mayavadins and impersonalists, Buddhists, Tattvavadins, *sahajiyas*, and other groups that were considered deviant or inimical to Gaudiya Vaishnavism, but these are topics that Krishnadas himself develops in his book. In his commentary on the *Bhagavata Purana*, however, the same Bhaktisiddhanta Saraswati rarely mentions Mayavadins. Following the earlier tradition, he keeps closely to the subject of the text under discussion.

Gaudiya Vaishnavas consider that the nucleus of the entire Bhagavata and its philosophy is found in four stanzas (*chatuh shloki*) in the second book of the *Bhagavata Purana*.[51] With reference to these four important verses, Bhaktivedanta Swami writes:

> The impersonal explanation of those four verses in the Second Canto is nullified herewith. Sridhara Svami also explains in this connection that the same concise form of the *Bhagavatam* concerned the pastimes of Lord Krishna and was never meant for impersonal indulgence.[52]

Here Bhaktivedanta claims that the famous fourteenth-century author Shridhara Swamin wrote in his *Bhavartha-dipika* commentary to *Bhagavata Purana* 3.4.13 that the *chatuh shloki* were "never meant for impersonal indulgence." In other words, he claims that Shridhara had formulated attacks against Mayavadins that were just as polemical as his own. In fact, Shridhara Swamin did *not* write this.[53] Never, in his entire commentary on the *Bhagavata Purana*, does Shridhara Swami mention "impersonal indulgence" or Mayavadins, not to speak of condemning the latter.

While it might be argued that this is an isolated example, it has far-reaching implications. One wonders why Bhaktivedanta Swami went so far as to tell his readers that Shridhara Swamin condemns impersonalist philosophy, when the fact is not only that Shridhara did not do this, but it is he, out of all the *Bhagavata* commentators, of whom it may be said that he had impersonalist leanings.[54] Could it be that Bhaktivedanta Swami was seeking to invest his statements with the authority of Shridhara Swamin, who is widely respected as the foremost *Bhagavata* commentator? This question is especially difficult to answer because Bhaktivedanta Swami never worked with competent Sanskrit editors, and it is hard to determine to what degree he was aware of such misrepresentations. What *is* known is that he repeatedly criticized or dismissed many of his disciples who gradually achieved a certain level of proficiency in Sanskrit.[55] Since anti-Mayavada polemics are highly conspicuous in ISKCON discourses (see also K. P. Sinha, *A Critique of A.C. Bhaktivedanta* [Calcutta, 1997]), a thorough investigation into what caused Bhaktivedanta Swami to formulate so many aggressive attacks on this group might help create a better understanding of his teachings and his movement.

WOMEN AND SEX

There is, within the Hare Krishna movement, a general awareness that Bhaktivedanta Swami made a large number of controversial statements about women. Some were written statements in his commentaries on the canonical Vaishnava scriptures, others were spoken statements in his lectures and conversations. While there is a general feeling that Bhaktivedanta Swami did not always mention pleasant things about women, an accurate assessment of how much of what he said was favorable and how much was unfavorable has never been presented.

A quantitative and qualitative analysis of all statements regarding women that Bhaktivedanta Swami made in his purports to the *Bhagavad Gita* and in his purports to five chosen books[56] of the *Bhagavata Purana* is presented below. Each of his 510 statements has been assigned to one of the following six categories:

1. Statements about women's sexuality and men's views of women as sex objects or sexually agitating objects that need to be avoided, e.g.: "women are always dressed in an overly attractive fashion to victimize the minds of men."[57]
2. Statements about women's qualities, e.g.: "It may be clearly said that the understanding of a woman is always inferior to the understanding of a man."[58]
3. Statements about women as belonging to a certain class or social group, e.g.: "Women, *Shudras* and even birds and other lower living entities can be elevated to the *achyuta-gotra*."[59]
4. Statements about restrictions concerning women, e.g.: "The woman must remain at home."[60]
5. General statements where "woman" simply means a person of the female gender, with no description or value judgment: "All over the world there are millions and billions of men and women."[61]
6. Other types of statements: "A barren woman cannot understand the grief of a mother."[62]

The analysis further ascertained whether any of the earlier commentators mentioned anything about women within the same scriptural context.

Eighty percent of all statements that Bhaktivedanta Swami makes about women in the six works investigated are negative statements, in the sense that they involve restrictions, list bad qualities, group women in socially inferior classes, or treat them as sex objects that have to be avoided. The figure of 80 percent is constituted as follows:

56% of all statements concern women as sex objects
8% are statements about women's class, status, or position
9% are restrictions that state that women should not be given any freedom
7% are statements about women having bad qualities

While "qualities" statements actually comprise 15 percent of the total, with half of them referring to "good" qualities, these are *only* mentioned in connection with specific women who are prominent figures in Hindu mythology: Kunti, Draupadi, Devahuti, Gandhari, and Sati. "Women in general," in other words, present-day living women, are *only* mentioned as having bad qualities.

For the *Bhagavad Gita* there are 7 out of 39 statements about women that can be related to the earlier commentaries; for the first book of the *Bhagavata Purana*, 12 out of 117 can be so related; for the second book, 4 out of 37; and for the eighth book, 16 out of 52. This means that 80 percent of Bhaktivedanta

Swami's statements about women, in the purports to these four titles, are his own contributions that do not represent statements that earlier commentators made in the same context. Reasonably similar results can be expected for the titles that were not included in this study.

While Bhaktivedanta Swami often made generalizing statements regarding Mayavadins,[63] he issued even more such broad generalizations about women:

> Generally all women desire material enjoyment.[64]

> Women in general should not be trusted.[65]

> Women are generally not very intelligent.[66]

> It appears that woman is a stumbling block for self-realization.[67]

Other statements that are not supported by the earlier commentators are Bhaktivedanta Swami's views on rape:

> Although rape is not legally allowed, it is a fact that a woman likes a man who is very expert at rape.[68]

> When a husbandless woman is attacked by an aggressive man, she takes his action to be mercy.[69]

> Generally when a woman is attacked by a man—whether her husband or some other man—she enjoys the attack, being too lusty.[70]

While sexuality is a topic that mainly comes up when Bhaktivedanta Swami focuses on women, he comments not only on their sexual morals but also on those of the Mayavadins:

> The answer anticipates the abominable acts of the Mayavadi impersonalists who place themselves in the position of Krishna and enjoy the company of young girls and women.[71]

In general, he depicts both groups as less intelligent, inferior, sexually incontinent, and downright dangerous.

In conclusion, then, since the historical and prolonged abuse of women in ISKCON has by now been acknowledged even by the most conservative elements in the movement (see Knott's and Muster's essays in this volume), a more systematic analysis of Bhaktivedanta Swami's statements about women and sex might be worthwhile, leading to a deeper and better understanding of the problem. ISKCON's polemical dismissal of other Hindu groups perceived to espouse "Mayavadin philosophy" (which includes almost every other Hindu group established in the West) is also an inherent part of ISKCON's self-definition and ethos that few would deny.[72] As Bhaktivedanta Swami was the founder of ISKCON, his derogations of Mayavadins and women and sex, coupled with his exaltations of the spiritual master, are not irrelevant to the attitudes demonstrated by his disciples. Since his statements in these areas have no parallel in the writings of his predecessor commentators, one is therefore led to search for links in his personal experiences. However, this research, and the question of how his views influenced his followers, falls under the academic rubrics of sociology or psychology of religion, rather than that of traditional Sanskrit commentarial exegesis.

Bhaktivedanta Swami's statements in the three areas treated here, namely the guru's position, Mayavadins, and women and sex, are bound to leave a certain impression on his readers. If the frequency of a particular type of statement exceeds a certain magnitude, then the context in which each particular statement appears loses relevance. What remains is the overall impression created by the sheer number of repetitions. In this particular case, that impression might very well be: *the spiritual master is good, beyond sexuality, and superior to all; Mayavadins are dangerous and bad; women and sex are dangerous and bad.* Within the Hare Krishna movement, Bhaktivedanta Swami's purports are considered as good as, and in case of conflict, superior to, scripture. History shows that the general mass of his followers indeed imbibed and lived by these ideas he conveyed.

NOTES

1. A.C. Bhaktivedanta Swami, *Bhagavad-Gita As It Is*, 2nd ed. (Los Angeles: Bhaktivedanta Book Trust, 1989).
2. S. Radhakrishnan, *The Bhagavadgita: With an Introductory Essay, Sanskrit Text, English Translation and Notes* (1948; reprint, Delhi: HarperCollins Publishers India, 1993).
3. A.C. Bhaktivedanta Swami, *Srimad-Bhagavatam: Third Canto,* 2 vols. (Los Angeles: Bhaktivedanta Book Trust, 1987).
4. C. L. Goswami and M. A. Sastri, ed. and trans., *Bhagavata Purana. SrimadBhagavata Purana,* 2 vols. Gorakhpur: Gita Press, 1971). (Gita Press had published this translation in multiple volumes already before 1967.)
5. See my discussion of his "polemic" against Sastri and Goswami below (section on Mayavadins), referenced by notes 48 and 49.
6. From book 4, chapter 28 of Bhaktivedanta Swami's translation of the *Bhagavata Purana* up to chapter 13 of book 10 (a total of 125 chapters), the breaking up of the *sloka-pada*s of the original Sanskrit text into numbered stanzas shows 100 percent agreement with the Gaudiya Math edition (see next note). The same errors (Sanskrit spelling errors, misplaced paragraphs, etc.) that occur in the Gaudiya Math edition are also found in Bhaktivedanta Swami's text.

7. *Srimad-Bhagavatam, Srimad-Gaudiya-bhashyopetam,* 2nd edition, 12 vols. (Maya-pur: Sri Chaitanya Math, 1962–69).

8. Explanatory notes that occur in the Gaudiya Math Bengali translation in paren-theses often appear without parentheses in Bhaktivedanta Swami's English trans-lations (as if they were part of the original Sanskrit text). Bhaktivedanta Swami's translation of *Bhagavata Purana* 5.25.1, for example, contains such a passage: "He is always in the transcendental position, but because He is worshiped by Lord Siva, the deity of *tamo-guna* or darkness, He is sometimes called *tamasi*" (A.C. Bhak-tivedanta Swami, *Srimad-Bhagavatam: Fifth Canto* [Los Angeles: Bhaktivedanta Book Trust, 1987], 872). The note in the Bengali edition reads: "*ei murti vastutah visuddha-sattva-mayi, tamogunavatara rudrera antare thakiya samhara-karyadi karena baliya ai murtike tamo-mayi bala haiyache*" (*Srimad-Bhagavatam, Pancama-skandha-matram* [Mayapur: Sri Chaitanya Math, 1969], 1802).

9. "No, no. I am taking help from all these Gosvamis and giving a summary." Inter-view with Professors O'Connell, Motilal, and Shivaram, June 18, 1976, Toronto, *The Bhaktivedanta VedaBase CD-ROM,* Sandy Ridge, NC: Bhaktivedanta Archives, 1995, record 499981.

10. "Sometimes I become surprised how I have written this. Although I am the writer, still sometimes I am surprised how these things have come. Such vivid description. Where is such literature throughout the whole world? It is all Krishna's mercy. Every line is perfect." *The Bhaktivedanta VedaBase CD-ROM,* Talk About Var-nashrama, S.B. 2.1.1–5, June 28, 1977, Vrindavana, record 561940.

    "I have tried to explain what is there in the *Bhagavatam,* expand it. That is not my explanation, that is Krishna's explanation. I cannot explain now. That moment I could explain. That means Krishna's . . . I can understand that. That the descrip-tion is very nicely given. Although it is my writing, but I know it is not my writing. It is Krishna's writing." *The Bhaktivedanta VedaBase CD-ROM,* Room Conversa-tion, September 4, 1976, Vrindavana, record 523163.

11. Bhaktivedanta Swami translated and commented up to chapter 13 of the tenth book of the *Bhagavata Purana.* The remaining 5,311 stanzas have been translated by his disciples, who also produced commentaries on 2,991 of these stanzas, trying to emulate, as far as possible, the style and spirit of their guru.

12. "Recently they have said that they have gone to the moon but did not find any liv-ing entities there. But *Srimad-Bhagavatam* and the other Vedic literatures do not agree with this foolish conception." Bhaktivedanta, *Srimad-Bhagavatam: Seventh Canto* (Los Angeles: Bhaktivedanta Book Trust, 1987), 804.

13. "Darwin's theory stating that no human being existed from the beginning but that humans evolved after many, many years is simply a nonsensical theory." Bhak-tivedanta, *Srimad-Bhagavatam: Fourth Canto,* 2:658.

14. "Kasyapa Muni advised his wife not to go out onto the street unless she was well decorated and well dressed. He did not encourage the miniskirts that have now be-come fashionable." Bhaktivedanta, *Srimad-Bhagavatam: Sixth Canto,* 832.

15. Purports from all ten books of the *Bhagavata Purana* have been analyzed. The number for each book of the *Bhagavata Purana* (from book 1 to book 10) is: 66, 121, 198, 130, 17, 9, 67, 29, 12, 15. These are all the purports where any given keyword turned up, with the exception of several cases where the purport contains a key-word but says nothing specific about it.

16. For his own commentaries on the *Gita,* Bhaktivedanta Swami had mainly relied on Baladeva *Vidya-bhusana,* a Vaishnava writer from Orissa, who lived during the

first half of the eighteenth century. His Sanskrit commentary on the *Bhagavad Gita*, the *Gita Vibhushana-Bhashya*, is the source of 22 guru statements in the *Bhagavad Gita*. Two statements can be traced to Vishvanatha Chakravartin, the seventeenth-century Vaishnava author of the *Sarartha-varshini-tika*. Both commentaries have been published in Baba Krishnadasa, ed., *Srimadbhagavadgita* (Mathura: Vik. Sam.), 2023.

17. The second book of the *Bhagavata Purana* is the shortest (391 numbered stanzas). Yet, in the 356 purports in which Bhaktivedanta Swami commented on this book, there occur more statements about the position and importance of the guru than in his purports on any other book. Like the *Gita*, this is one of the first books he wrote after coming to the West.

18. The following eighteen commentaries on the *Bhagavata Purana* were available to Bhaktivedanta Swami:

   Shridhara Svamin: *Bhavartha-dipika* (fourteenth cent.)
   Vamsidhara Pandita: *Bhavartha-dipika-prakasha* (1820–90)
   Radharamanadas Goswamin: *Dipika-dipani*
   Ganga-sahaya: *Anvitartha-prakashika* (1894–97)
   Viraraghavacharya: *Bhagavata-chandrika* (fourteenth cent.)
   Vijayadhvaja Tirtha: *Pada-ratnavali* (fifteenth cent.)
   Jiva Goswamin: *Krama-Sandarbha*, and *Brihad-krama-sandarbha* (only tenth book), (sixteenth cent.)
   Vishvanatha Chakravartin: *Sarartha-darshini* (seventeenth cent.)
   Shukadeva: *Siddhanta-pradipa*
   Giridhara-lala: *Bala-prabodhini* (1850–1900)
   Bhagavat-prasadacharya: *Bhakta-mano-ranjani*
   Sanatana Goswamin: *Vaishnava-toshani* (only tenth book), and *Brihad-vaishnava-toshani* (only tenth book), (sixteenth cent.)
   Vallabhacharya: *Subodhini* (sixteenth cent.)
   Madhvacharya: *Bhagavata-tatparya-nirnaya* (thirteenth cent.)
   Bhaktisiddhanta Saraswati: *Ananta-gopala Tathya* (1923–35); *Sindhu-vaibhava Vivriti* (1923–35)

19. Bhaktivedanta, *Bhagavad-Gita As It Is*, 7.14 purport, 383.

20. Ibid., 11.54 purport, 603.

21. Bhaktivedanta, *Srimad-Bhagavatam: Second Canto*, 2.3.1 purport, 136.

22. Bhaktivedanta, *Srimad-Bhagavatam: Fourth Canto*, 4.16.1 purport, 1:714.

23. Bhaktivedanta, *Srimad-Bhagavatam: Eighth Canto*, 8.16.24 purport, 556.

24. Letter to Brhaspati, Delhi, 17 November, 1971, *The Bhaktivedanta VedaBase CD-ROM*, record 594392.

25. Bhaktivedanta, *Srimad-Bhagavatam: Second Canto*, 2.2.30 purport, 116.

26. Bhaktivedanta, *Bhagavad-Gita As It Is*, 6.13–14 purport, 322.

27. A.C. Bhaktivedanta Swami, *The Nectar of Instruction* (Los Angeles: Bhaktivedanta Book Trust, 1975), 7.

28. Bhaktivedanta, *Srimad-Bhagavatam: Second Canto*, 2.3.22 purport, 170.

29. Women and sex are prominent topics in Bhaktivedanta Swami's purports, lectures, and conversations. No fewer than 50 passages in his purports mention that a guru must teach about these topics. Sex is mentioned in more than 300 purports; it appears more than 1,200 times in lectures and more than 1,000 times in conversations.

30. Bhaktivedanta, *Srimad-Bhagavatam: Second Canto*, 2.7.6 purport, 369.

31. Bhaktivedanta, *Srimad-Bhagavatam: Seventh Canto*, 7.12.1 purport, 690.
32. Here and in all other places where the expression "none of the earlier commentators" is used, it refers to the eighteen commentaries listed above.
33. Lecture: Srimad-Bhagavatam 7.12.1, Bombay, 12 April 1976, *The Bhaktivedanta VedaBase CD-ROM*, record 364741.
34. "*tatra garhasthyadivan naishthikam apy aupakurvana-purvakam eveti darshayitum tavad aupakurvana-brahmacharya-dharmma uchyante*" (Bhagavata-chandrika, 7.12.1), *Shrimad-bhagavata-mahapuranam: saptamam skandham*, ed. Krishnasankarah Sastri Sola: Sri Bhagavata-Vidyapithah, 1968, 441.
35. Bhaktivedanta, *Srimad-Bhagavatam: Second Canto*, 2.5.24 purport, 266.
36. Bhaktivedanta, *Bhagavad-Gita As It Is*, 7.24 purport, 402.
37. Ibid., 7.25 purport, 404.
38. Ibid., 8.3 purport, 417.
39. Radhakrishnan, *The Bhagavadgita*, 227.
40. Bhaktivedanta, *Bhagavad-Gita As It Is*, 9.11 purport, 469.
41. Radhakrishnan, *The Bhagavadgita*, 243.
42. Hayagriva Dasa, *The Hare Krishna Explosion : The Birth of Krishna Consciousness in America 1966–69* (New Vrindaban, W.Va.: 1985), 210–11.
43. Letter to Rayarama, San Francisco, 21 December 1967, *The Bhaktivedanta VedaBase CD-ROM*, record 580956.
44. The third book comprises 1,411 stanzas and these 18 chapters comprise 804 stanzas.
45. Letter to Rayarama, San Francisco, 7 March 1967, *The Bhaktivedanta VedaBase CD-ROM*, record 580012.
46. Bhaktivedanta, *Srimad-Bhagavatam: Third Canto*, 3.29.33 purport, 655.
47. Goswami and Sastri, ed. and trans., *Bhagavata Purana. SrimadBhagavata Purana*, 1:270.
48. Bhaktivedanta, *Srimad-Bhagavatam: Fourth Canto*, 4.22.25 purport, 177.
49. Goswami and Sastri, *Bhagavata Purana. SrimadBhagavata Purana*, 1:389.
50. Sometimes Madhva, the founder of the Dvaita school, is counted as a Gaudiya Vaishnava. While it is true that Madhva often attacked the Advaita doctrine in his commentaries on the *Gita* and the *Bhagavata Purana*, his attacks are far less frequent than and also rather different from Bhaktivedanta Swami's. In his entire *Bhagavata-tatparya-nirnaya* (Madhva's commentary on the *Bhagavata Purana*), for example, Madhva mentions the Advaita doctrine not more than thirty times explicitly; and on twenty occasions he mentions that those who hold Advaitin views will go to hell. None of these passages is elaborate.
51. Depending on the edition, these stanzas may be BhP 2.9.33–36 (*aham evasam . . . to . . . sarvatra sarvada*).
52. Bhaktivedanta, *Srimad-Bhagavatam: Third Canto*, 3.4.13 purport, 148.
53. Cf. *Srimad-bhagavata Shridhari Tika* (Varanasi 1988) (reprint of the earlier Nirnaya Sagara Press, Bombay edition); Commenting on the words *man-mahimavabhasam*, Shridhara explained, *lila'vabhasyate yena tat*, "that by which my pastimes are illuminated" (195).
54. Commenting on the words *tad-brahma-darshanam* in BhP 1.3.33, Shridhara wrote: *tada jivo brahmaiva bhavatity arthah; katham bhutam; darshanam jnanaika-svarupam*. Ibid., 47.
55. "I am practically seeing that as soon as they begin to learn a little Sanskrit immediately they feel that they have become more than their guru and then the policy is

kill guru and be killed himself." Letter to Dixit, Vrindaban, 18 September 1976, *The Bhaktivedanta VedaBase CD-ROM,* record 608866.

56. The highest frequency of women- and sex-related statements in Bhaktivedanta Swami's *Bhagavata Purana* occurs in his purports to the fourth book. However, in order to sample statements from a larger variety of contexts and to cover a broader interval of Bhaktivedanta Swami's creative period, books 1, 2, 3, 7, and 8 have been included in this analysis. The first book was written between 1959 and 1964 in India, before Bhaktivedanta Swami came to New York; the manuscripts for books 2 and 3 were produced sometime between 1967 and 1969; book 7 was completed in May 1976, and book 8 in September of the same year. These books thus span Bhaktivedanta's preaching career and are representative of his views on this matter over the last two decades of his life.

57. Bhaktivedanta, *Srimad-Bhagavatam: First Canto,* 1.17.24 purport, 971.

58. Bhaktivedanta, *Srimad-Bhagavatam: Sixth Canto,* 6.17.34–35 purport, 786.

59. Bhaktivedanta, *Srimad-Bhagavatam: Seventh Canto,* 7.7.54 purport, 407.

60. Bhaktivedanta, *Srimad-Bhagavatam: Third Canto,* 3.24.40 purport, 350.

61. Bhaktivedanta, *Srimad-Bhagavatam: Second Canto,* 2.3.1 purport, 135.

62. Bhaktivedanta, *Srimad-Bhagavatam: First Canto,* 1.7.49 purport, 392.

63. "Generally the impersonalists or monists are influenced by the modes of passion and ignorance." Bhaktivedanta, *Srimad-Bhagavatam: Second Canto,* 2.1.20 purport, 36.

64. Bhaktivedanta, *Srimad-Bhagavatam: Third Canto,* 3.23.54 purport, 299.

65. Bhaktivedanta, *Srimad-Bhagavatam: Eighth Canto,* 8.9.9 purport, 330.

66. Bhaktivedanta, *Bhagavad-Gita As It Is,* 1.40 purport, 67.

67. Bhaktivedanta, *Srimad-Bhagavatam: Second Canto,* 2.7.6 purport, 370.

68. Bhaktivedanta, *Srimad-Bhagavatam: Fourth Canto,* 4.25.41 purport, 478.

69. Ibid., 4.25.42 purport, 479.

70. Ibid., 4.26.26 purport, 542.

71. A.C. Bhaktivedanta Swami,*Krishna, The Supreme Personality of Godhead: A Summary Study of Srila Vyasadeva's Srimad-Bhagavatam, Tenth Canto,* rev. ed. (Los Angeles: Bhaktivedanta Book Trust, 1996), 1:315.

72. For recent efforts to redress such tendencies, see Shaunaka Rishi's position paper, mentioned in Mukunda Goswami and Anuttama's essay, as ISKCON's first official statement concerning its relationship with people of other faiths.

[9]

A.C. BHAKTIVEDANTA SWAMI'S PREACHING IN THE CONTEXT OF GAUDIYA VAISHNAVISM

PAUL H. SHERBOW

T HE WORLDWIDE PREACHING MISSION of A.C. Bhaktivedanta Swami was based on principles and practices received from his predecessors in the Gaudiya Vaishnava lineage, especially as enunciated by his spiritual master (*guru*) Bhaktisiddhanta Saraswati, and his guru's father, Kedarnath Dutt Bhaktivinoda. This essay presents a few such primary elements from that tradition, showing how they are and will remain vital for the continuation of the movement's spiritual dynamism.

GAUDIYA VAISHNAVA BACKGROUND AND LINEAGE

Abhay Charan De was born in Calcutta on September 1, 1896 to Gaura Mohan De. Related to the aristocratic Mullick family, the child was raised in an upper-class fashion. His father was a pious Vaishnava and his son was educated at home and initiated by the family priest (*kulaguru*). He attended Scottish Church College in Calcutta and, along with his classmates, refused his college diploma in 1920, inspired by the ideas of Mohandas Gandhi. Gandhi's movement continued to attract his attention, and he later accompanied Nehru from Allahabad to conferences in Calcutta. After college, young Abhay Charan began to write dramas at home, until Karttik Chandra Bose, a family friend, recommended him for a position with Bose Laboratories, where he worked until moving to Allahabad to start his own pharmaceutical business, Prayag Pharmacy, in 1923.

While residing in Calcutta in 1922, Abhay Charan first met his future spiritual master when a friend insisted that he accompany him to visit Bhaktisiddhanta Saraswati, founder of the Gaudiya Math, at his Calcutta headquarters. Engaged from childhood in devotional practice under his father's direction, Bhaktisiddhanta Saraswati thought of his own mission as the fulfillment of the work of his parent, Kedarnath Dutta Bhaktivinoda (1838–1914), a remarkably versatile Vaishnava author and magistrate in the Indian civil service, whose books had helped expose a more educated public to the teachings of Chaitanya Mahaprabhu, the sixteenth-century founder of Gaudiya Vaishnavism.[1] Educated in Calcutta during the Bengal renaissance of the early nineteenth century, Kedarnath Dutt began writing poetry and articles at an early age. He was friendly with Tagore family members and their Brahmo Samaj connections, and was well-read in the works of American Unitarians, Channing, Emerson, and Parker.

After entering the civil service in 1866, he held various posts in Orissa and Bengal as deputy registrar and deputy magistrate. Convinced of the importance of Chaitanya Mahaprabhu's movement, he entered fully into Gaudiya Vaishnava life, applying his writing talent to produce almost one hundred works in Bengali, Sanskrit, Oriya, Hindi, and English, which are of prime importance in understanding the scope of Bhaktivedanta Swami's mission.

Kedarnath Dutt Bhaktivinoda inspired his son, Vimala Prasad Dutt (1874–1937), in the systematic practice and dynamic propagation of Chaitanya's movement. After a brilliant student life and brief service as an editor and tutor, Vimala Prasad took up residence in Mayapura (near modern Nabadwip, West Bengal), identified by his father as the birthplace of Chaitanya Mahaprabhu. Completing a vow to chant a billion repetitions of Krishna's names in 1915, he accepted the renounced order of *tridanda-sannyasa* in 1918 under the name Bhaktisiddhanta Saraswati, and established Shri Chaitanya Math, a temple-monastery, in Mayapura. Founding the Gaudiya Math in Calcutta (1920), he expanded his activities through public preaching and publishing.[2] The Gaudiya Math gradually increased to 64 centers in India, Burma, and the United Kingdom by 1937. In line with his father's enthusiasm for distributing devotional literature, Bhaktisiddhanta Saraswati established printing presses at his regional centers, publishing monthly and weekly journals and a daily paper in Bengali, with editions in Hindi, Oriya, Assamese, and

English. By the time of his passing in 1937, Bhaktisiddhanta Saraswati had accepted several thousand disciples, and his dynamic teams of *sannyasi* and *brahmachari* preachers traveled across the country.

Although impressed by his meeting with Bhaktisiddhanta, it was not until a few years later in 1928 that Abhay Charan De again met preachers of the Gaudiya Math, when they visited his shop in Allahabad while canvassing for assistance to establish a local branch. Abhay Charan gradually became involved in the work of the mission, offering his services in both Allahabad and Bombay. He accepted initiation in 1933 in Allahabad, receiving the name Abhay Charanaravinda Das Adhikari. After his writings appeared in the institution's journals, his guru several times intimated that he should continue to expand his devotional writing.

In 1937, following the passing of Bhaktisiddhanta Saraswati, conflict among his senior disciples resulted in the departure of longtime manager Kunjavihari Vidyabhushana and others. A respected *brahmachari* disciple, Ananta Vasudeva, was nominated as spiritual successor (*acharya*) and continued in that position until he left the institution. A 1948 court decision divided the Gaudiya Math in two: Shri Chaitanya Math (headquartered at Shridham Mayapura, W. Bengal) and Gaudiya Mission (headquartered at Baghbazar, Calcutta), each with their branch *mathas*.[3] By this time, independent institutions had also been established by other prominent disciples of Bhaktisiddhanta Saraswati, such as Bhakti Rakshaka Shridhara (1895–1988), founder of Chaitanya Sarasvata Math (Nabadvip, 1941); and Bhakti Prajnan Keshava (1898–1968), founder of Gaudiya Vedanta Samiti (Calcutta, 1940), with both of whom Abhay Charanaravinda Das was intimately connected. He had first met Bhakti Rakshaka Shridhara in Allahabad in 1930. Later, both being stationed in Bombay, they worked closely together in the local preaching effort. In the early 1940s, they were next-door neighbors in Calcutta and spent long hours discussing devotional topics; their close relationship continued through their correspondence and occasional meetings when Bhaktivedanta Swami visited Bhakti Rakshaka Shridhara's Mayapura headquarters. Abhay Charan had hosted Bhakti Prajnan Keshava for several months as his houseguest in Allahabad, and he himself resided at the latter's centers in Nabadwip and Mathura at various times. All three godbrothers preached a strong and uncompromising doctrine inherited from their spiritual master.

In 1950, Abhay Charan left his home and family in Calcutta to live in Vrindavan, scene of Krishna's pastimes, as a *vanaprastha* (retiree), performing devotional practices and continuing to write. In 1959, prompted by a highly significant dream of Bhaktisiddhanta Saraswati calling him to accept the renounced order, he was given *sannyasa* by Bhakti Prajnan Keshava at his Keshavaji Gaudiya Math in nearby Mathura; his new name was Bhaktivedanta

Swami. Bhakti Prajnan Keshava gave all those who accepted *sannyasa* from him the title "Bhaktivedanta" (literally: "the purport of Vedanta is pure *bhakti*"), followed by one of 108 *tridanda-sannyasa* names. "Bhaktivedanta" is also among honorary titles customarily awarded to devotees, having been bestowed on Abhay Charanaravinda Das (by Gaudiya Sangha, 1947) to honor his learning. Wishing to also retain the initiatory name received from Bhaktisiddhanta Saraswati as a mark of humility and connection to his spiritual master, he usually included the initials "A.C." in front of his *sannyasa* name.

After his *sannyasa*, A.C. Bhaktivedanta Swami renewed his writing work and began planning to preach in America to fulfill his spiritual master's desire for the promulgation of Chaitanya's movement in the West. Arranging an opportunity to sail to the United States in 1965, although with hardly any operating funds, he managed to form a center in New York City by the summer of 1966, and established a new organization, the International Society for Krishna Consciousness (ISKCON). It expanded to San Francisco and Montreal (1967) and the number of centers in the United States grew swiftly, and soon disciples were dispatched to spread the movement in Germany and the United Kingdom. Public chanting (*sankirtana*) of the names of Krishna and the printing and distribution of literature were major activities in all centers. ISKCON Press was started in 1969 in Boston to publish Bhaktivedanta Swami's translations and *Back to Godhead* magazine; it moved to New York (1971) and later Los Angeles (1972), where it was transformed into the Bhaktivedanta Book Trust (BBT) to manage the international publishing and distribution of the society's literature. By 1977, original English editions had been in their turn rendered into Spanish, French, German, and, eventually, dozens of other languages.

Returning to India with a party of western disciples in 1970, Bhaktivedanta Swami concentrated much of his effort there for the next seven years, establishing major temples in Bombay, Vrindavan, and Hyderabad, and an international headquarters in Mayapura, West Bengal. Increasingly handicapped by illness, he passed away at his quarters in Vrindavan on November 14, 1977.

A.C. BHAKTIVEDANTA SWAMI'S MISSION IN THE CONTEXT OF GAUDIYA VAISHNAVISM

Chaitanya Mahaprabhu's teachings had been passed down through his associates in Bengal, Orissa, and, in particular, the six Goswamis of the Braj region of central north India, many of whom composed texts on various aspects of *bhakti* that were to form the canonical corpus of the movement. Their younger contemporaries, Narottama Das, Shyamananda, and Shrinivasacharya, were dynamic propagators of the movement in the sixteenth and seventeenth centuries, followed by commentators Vishvanatha Chakravarti and Baladeva

Vidyabhushana. In the late nineteenth and early twentieth centuries, Bhaktivinoda and his son Bhaktisiddhanta Saraswati emphasized the importance of this teaching lineage (*shikshaguru-parampara*) and re-published their translated works with commentaries. Bhaktivedanta Swami inherited this rich legacy of devotional literature along with a direct order from Bhaktisiddhanta Saraswati to write, publish, and distribute.

A.C. Bhaktivedanta Swami's subsequent translating and preaching work may be better understood by reference to the terms in which this philosophical legacy was expressed. The Gaudiya Vaishnava doctrines of God (*bhagavan*), the sentient beings (*jivas*), the material world (*jada-jagat*), and their mutual relationship (*sambandha-jnana*) will be briefly touched upon below with reference to the works of A.C. Bhaktivedanta Swami's immediate predecessors in disciplic succession.

God as Absolute Truth

In the initial verse of the *Bhagavata Purana*, the primary scripture of the Krishna sects, an outline of the Gaudiya Vaishnava concept of the Supreme Truth (*param satyam*) is presented in relation to the material world, the demigods, the living entities, the spiritual world, and consciousness. The verse's first words (*janmady asya yatah*), being identical with *Brahma-sutra* 1.1.2, led Vaishnavas to claim the *Bhagavata* as the original commentary on the Vedanta, as both texts were believed to have been composed by the same author.[4] In this initial verse, which should focus on the subject of the book it opens, it is notable that no personal name of a supreme deity is given. Considering the place that Krishna occupies in the *Bhagavata*, one would think that his name would be used here, or a name of Vishnu, or, at the very least, the term *ishvara*, God. The term used, however, is "supreme truth" (*param satyam*). Although these two words are understood by Vaishnava commentators to mean "supreme lord" (*parameshvara*), the use of this particular terminology in the first verse, as well as several other terms for Krishna early in the *Bhagavata*, is significant for understanding how the position of Krishna is seen in the Gaudiya Vaishnava tradition.

The Absolute has been described in the Upanishads as "one without a second,"[5] and the concept of the oneness of the Absolute is an integral part of Gaudiya philosophy.[6] The Absolute can be "one" because it is undivided (*akhanda*). Another verse in the *Bhagavata* (1.2.11) defines truth as *advaya-jnana*, "nondual knowledge," which is perceived in three phases: *brahman*, *paramatma*, and *Bhagavan*.[7] *Bhagavan*, the personal aspect of *advaya jnana*, realizable only through pure devotion (*shuddha-bhakti*), is accepted as the full (*purna*) perception of *advaya-jnana*; the other two aspects of truth are considered partial (*amshika*) or incomplete (*asamyak*).[8] Thus, of the three aspects of truth, Krishna (or Vishnu) is the ultimate knowable (*vedya*), and pure devotion (*shuddha bhakti*) the highest means of knowledge. This term, *advaya-jnana*, is vitally significant, as it distinguishes the absolute truth from all forms of relative truth, preventing the intellectual mind from subjecting Krishna to approaches based on inductive reasoning.

The term *advaya-jnana* is ubiquitous in the works of Bhaktisiddhanta Saraswati, where it is often used in conjunction with names of Krishna. In his English works it is usually translated as "Absolute Truth," and it appears in the same form in the works of Bhaktivedanta Swami. In fact, Bhaktivedanta introduces his translation of the *Bhagavata* with a reference to *advaya-jnana*: "The conception of God and the conception of the Absolute Truth are not on the same level. *Shrimad Bhagavata* hits on the target of the Absolute Truth . . . the Absolute Truth is one without a second and the *Shrimad Bhagavata* designates the Absolute Truth or the Summum Bonum as the *Param Satyam*." Since Gaudiya Vaishnavas accept the ultimate form of the Absolute to be the human (*narakirti*) form of Shri Krishna, the source of all sources including Vishnu, by identifying him with the terms "Absolute Truth," "one without a second," and "actual reality," Krishna and the category of *Vishnu-tattva* are distinguished, according to its followers, from narrower concepts of personal God that have developed throughout world cultural history. When it was suggested to Bhaktivedanta Swami during the founding of ISKCON in 1966 that the broader term "God Consciousness" would be preferable to "Krishna Consciousness," he rejected the recommendation, considering Krishna to include all less complete concepts of God and to be at once a more direct and intimate object of devotion (personal conversation with the author, 1970s).

Krishna is accepted by Gaudiya Vaishnavas as the highest form of the transcendental category (*Vishnu-tattva*).[9] Although possessed of unlimited powers, he appears as an ordinary child, adolescent, and adult, interacting with human society to accomplish his mission on earth. Deeds performed by Krishna and *avataras* of Vishnu distinguish them from all other entities. Beings at this transcendental level are thus not to be compared with the various demigods, such as Brahma, Rudra, or Indra, each of whom has a function to perform in the universal work of creation, maintenance, and destruction. Vishnu is the only independent being. As demigods are thus dependent ultimately on him, their worship is rejected as not useful in devotional practice, although Shiva is considered a special case,[10] and his worship is enjoined on Shiva-ratri. Otherwise, all demigods are to be offered respect and requested to bless one's progress in devotional service. Thus, Krishna and Vishnu are not to be considered as gods among other gods, but as the ultimate source of all existence, beyond compare, and with no competitors.

But, given the "oneness" (*ekatva*) or "undividedness" (*akhandatva*) of Krishna as the Absolute Truth, existing as one without a second, how is the multifarious universe created and how is it accommodated within the Absolute? This problem is solved in accordance with the *Shvetashvataropanishat* (6.8) by the existence of various categories of potency (*shakti*), which accomplish the work of creation and the existence of living entities without compromising the integrity of the Absolute. *Shakti* is not different from the Absolute as possessor of *shakti*; they are one, yet manifest in different forms. Basically, *shakti* manifests in three forms: spiritual (*chit-shakti*), material (*maya-shakti*), and multiple living entities (*jiva-shakti*).[11] It is through *maya-shakti* that the manifestation of the material universes is accomplished.

Thus, through the "transformation" (*parinama*) of various potencies (*vividha-shakti*), the Absolute retains its oneness. The Absolute possessor of power (*shaktiman*) is simultaneously different and nondifferent from his own power (*shakti*). This is the accepted philosophical position of the Gaudiya Vaishnava school—*achintya-bhedabheda*—in which the transformation of *shakti* is considered the only conclusion in accordance with the *Vedanta-sutra*, which states that *Brahman* is the creator, maintainer, and destroyer of the universe (*janmady asya yatah*), just as a touchstone is able to produce gold without being altered.[12] Although the Absolute exists simultaneously in his own form (*svarupa*), as well as power (*shakti*), all sentient beings (*jivas*), and matter (*pradhana*), he retains his nonduality. The entire universe, spiritual or nonspiritual, is an inconceivable (*achintya*) different and nondifferent manifestation of Sri Krishna.

Jíva

The living entity (*jiva*) is described in the *Chaitanya Charitamrita* as a particle of consciousness (*chit-kana*) expanded from the Absolute consciousness as a spark issues from a fire.[13] The Absolute and the living entities are thus spoken of as qualitatively one (*abheda*) yet having difference (*bheda*) in size and power, resulting in a relationship of predominant (the Absolute) and subordinate (the living entities). As the living entities possess not only limited power but also limited will, they are apt to err by allowing themselves to be overcome by God's material potency (*maya-shakti*). Because of this borderline existence between God's spiritual and material powers, the *jiva*'s power is known as "marginal" or "borderline potency" (*tatashtha-shakti*).[14] This spiritual nature of the living entities points to their relation with matter (of the material universe) and with spirit (other living beings and the Absolute). Although the Absolute manifests as the divided particles known as *jivas*, and thus appears as a multiplicity, he manifests no division; dualistic perception is never the same as nondual perception.[15]

When the *jivas* become averse to the service of God and attempt to enjoy the world, they automatically become subject to nonspiritual perception, which is under the power of *maya*, the material potency.[16] Bhaktivedanta Swami often used this eternal, spiritual nature of the living entities as a starting point in introducing the philosophy to his early students in the West. Drawing on the Upanishads and the first instructions of Krishna to Arjuna in the *Bhagavad Gita*,[17] where the former chastises the latter for not having practical understanding of the eternal spirit (*atma*) as opposed to the body and mind, a bridge could be made from there to devotional service (*bhakti*), the pure function of the spirit soul.

Bhakti

The living entities (*jiva*) are by nature pure consciousness (*chit*), but have the possibility of being covered by the darkness of ignorance when they turn away from the Absolute. In this condition, the mind of the *jiva* is compared to a mirror covered by dust.[18] As the dust is removed by surrender to spiritual practice, the mind-mirror begins to reflect the true nature of the *jiva*, and its spiritual function (*svadharma*) again becomes active.[19] This "eternal function of the soul" is completely different from what is conventionally understood by the term *svadharma*, which is *varnashrama*, the socioreligious function of an embodied soul determined by the type of body and mind covering it, and which changes from birth to birth. The eternal function of the soul (*nitya-dharma*) does not change and is the true *svadharma*.[20]

Gaudiya Vaishnava doctrine considers all forms of religion other than the inherent function of the soul (*atma-vritti*) to be forms of cheating. According to *Bhagavata* 1.1.2, the *dharma* it promulgates is "completely purged of all cheating" (*projjhita-kaitava*). Commentators interpret "cheating" as the four goals of man (*purushartha*): religion (*dharma*), economic development (*artha*), sense gratification (*kama*), and liberation (*moksha*). All these originate in desire for forms of personal sense gratification (*bhoga*), whereas true *dharma* is the function of the pure soul—service to the Absolute Truth. As personal enjoyment is antithetical to unselfish service, the former must be given up for service to be possible. The Gaudiya Vaishnava position is that Krishna is the only enjoyer (*bhokta*); all else is to be enjoyed (*bhogya*) by him. Any religion that has an element of desire for personal enjoyment at the expense of service is considered to be fraudulent. Bhaktisiddhanta Saraswati quotes a passage from the *Pushkara-samhita* stating that those desiring religion (*dharma-kami*) worship the Sun god, those desiring material gain (*artha-kami*) worship Ganapati, those desiring sense gratification (*kama-kami*) worship Shakti, and those desiring liberation (*mukti-kami*) worship Shiva.[21] Above these four levels is Vishnu as the Supreme Soul; pure Vaishnavism is the worship of Vishnu with no mundane reference. Thus, all religions are considered as lower or higher steps on a ladder culminating in the knowledge and service of Krishna, the undiluted function of the soul.

The eternal relationship between the pure souls and *Bhagavan* is considered to be as natural as that between iron and a magnet. As Bhaktivinoda puts it: "As iron is attracted by a magnet, so the natural action of the small (*anu*) consciousness toward the great consciousness (*maha chaitanya*) is the symptom of love (*priti*)."[22] In his notes on this verse, Bhaktivinoda explains that in their quality of consciousness (*chid-akaratva*), both God (*ishvara*) and the living entities (*jiva*) are one (*aikya*). Krishna attracts only the living consciousness,[23] and the mutual attraction of such conscious beings is eternal. Further, the attraction of the smaller consciousnesses by the large consciousness is also eternal. This is reflected in the material world by the attraction of atoms found by physicists.[24] As soon as obstructive association is abandoned, the attraction of the supreme will be activated. Bhaktivinoda writes that just as there is an eternal relationship (*nitya-sambandha*) between the sun and its rays, so the *jivas*, raylike particles, have a similar eternal relationship to the spiritual sun (*chinmaya-surya*).[25]

But wherever there is an absence of nondual knowledge of the truth, *maya*, or ignorance and unhappiness, ensues.[26] This is called the fallen position of mankind, wherein the souls migrate from body to body looking for their real home, suffering the pangs of material nature. As soon as the *jiva* turns away from its natural function of service, it falls into the clutches of "I" and "mine."[27] This error (*bhranti*) is the root of all problems and suffering in the material world. The service of one's material senses (*indriya-tarpana*) and the service of the Absolute with one's spiritual senses (*chid-indriya*) are completely different.[28]

Bhakti develops in the heart as the heart is cleared of all impediments; its growth is compared with that of a plant (*lata*), the seed (*bija*) having been given by the mercy of Krishna and guru.[29] Different seeds produce different plants.[30] To produce a pure *bhakti* plant (*bhakti lata*), the seed of genuine faith in the principles of *bhakti* must be received, requiring sincere receptivity on behalf of the disciple and substantial realization on the part of the guru.[31] Devotional principles nourish the plant, which develops from firm faith (*shraddha*) into steadiness (*nishtha*), taste (*ruchi*), attachment (*asakti*), feeling (*bhava*), and finally, pure love (*prema*).[32]

NECESSITY AND QUALIFICATIONS OF A SPIRITUAL MASTER (GURU)

At the time of initiation (*diksha*), when a disciple completely abandons all material considerations and surrenders to a spiritual master, the disciple's past sin (*papa*) is completely destroyed by the power of the mantra as conveyor of transcendental knowledge (*divya-jnana*), and by the disciple's understanding of his or her natural function as servant of the one Absolute.[33] As bell metal becomes gold through an alchemical process, initiation transforms the devotee into a spiritual instrument of service,[34] above all considerations of body, family, caste, creed, nationality, and past karma.[35] However, the essential ingredient is complete surrender (*sharanagati*). He or she must give up any material conception of spirituality and surrender body, speech, and mind to the service of godhead without qualification.

Bhaktisiddhanta Saraswati emphasized the vital distinction between the "descending" (*avaroha*) path of grace and the "ascending" (*aroha*) path of spiritual effort. The ascending path must take the help of logic (*tarka*) and speculation, but, in regard to matters that are inconceivable (*achintya*), these are ineffective.[36] Bhaktivedanta Swami regularly criticized efforts of "mental speculation" as not only useless for but also a great obstacle to Krishna-conscious progress, and instructed his scientifically trained disciples to establish the Bhaktivedanta Institute to oppose materialistic and purely mental approaches to knowledge. The only way to bypass the logical method is to accept the path of "descending" sound (*shrauta-pantha*) by the grace of a genuine spiritual master.[37] The master acts as a transparent (*svachchha*) medium for the transmission of Vedic truth.[38] The Gaudiya conception of the Veda or *shruti* "revealed scripture" is completely different from the academic one. Here the text is less important than the medium. In Bhaktisiddhanta Saraswati's view, "the enlivening flow of the nectar of the Absolute Truth in an undiluted form issuing from the mouth of a spiritual master in disciplic succession descending to the pure heart of a disciple affectionately engaged in service, that is '*shruti*.'"[39]

Bhaktivedanta Swami repeatedly stressed the importance of surrender to a genuine guru, and the recitation of Vishvanatha Chakravarti's *Gurv-ashtaka* (eight verses on the spiritual master) was an essential element of his daily morning program. Its final verse states that "by the grace of the guru one obtains the grace of God, and if one does not have the grace of the *guru*, no spiritual progress can be accomplished."[40] Obedience to the guru's order and principles was of paramount importance, and the terms "enjoyer of the guru" (*guru-bhogi*) and "renouncer of the guru" (*guru-tyagi*) were used to refer to those deviating from it. Bhaktivedanta Swami always credited the success achieved in his propagation work to his own fidelity to his spiritual master's orders.

THE UNIVERSALITY OF DEVOTIONAL SERVICE (*BHAKTI*)

As the only qualification for entering this process is genuine faith,[41] the Gaudiya Vaishnava path is universally available to Indians and non-Indians,

Hindus and non-Hindus, Christians, Muslims—anyone, irrespective of background. From the beginning of Chaitanya's movement in Bengal, Haridas Thakur and others of Muslim birth were participants. This openness received a boost from Bhaktivinoda's broad-minded vision in the late nineteenth century and was institutionalized by Bhaktisiddhanta Saraswati in the Gaudiya Math in the twentieth century. The widest example was demonstrated by A.C. Bhaktivedanta Swami's global mission from 1965 to 1977, wherein thousands of North and South Americans, Europeans, Africans, and Asians were introduced to the faith and became Gaudiya Vaishnavas by initiation and adoption of devotional practices.

Bhaktisiddhanta Saraswati gave Vaishnava initiation (*diksha*), including the *Gayatri mantra* and the sacred thread (*yajnopavita*), to his disciples according to the text of *Sat-kriya-sara-dipika*. These initiations were given without consideration of caste, in spite of strong objections by various communities in India. Bhaktivedanta Swami followed the same disregard for conventional caste distinctions determined by birth in accepting as disciples Americans and other westerners, categorized as "outcaste" in rigidly legalistic Hindu circles. In his preaching, Bhaktivedanta Swami usually defended the practice by verses of the *Bhagavad Gita* and *Bhagavata*,[42] which emphasize the importance of quality of character and work, rather than birth. The first Vaishnava *diksha* that he gave to a non-Indian took place in 1967 at Radha-Damodara Mandira, the temple of Jiva Goswami, in Vrindavan, where Bhaktivedanta Swami had resided prior to his 1965 departure for America, and the majority of his American disciples were given *diksha* in groups from April 1968. Bhaktivedanta Swami hoped that their full entrance into the Gaudiya Vaishnava lineage (*sampradaya*) and adoption of "divine orders and classes of life" (*daiva-varnashram-dharma*) would gradually spiritualize western society.

The ultimate stage in *varnashrama-dharma* was the renunciate (*sannyasa*) order. Bhaktisiddhanta Saraswati had awarded *tridanda-sannyasa*, the triple-staff renunciate order, in accordance with the prescriptions of a traditional text, the *Samskara-dipika*, to twenty of his senior disciples. The three sticks (*danda*) that the *sannyasi* constantly carries symbolize a threefold vow to serve the Supreme Lord with body, mind, and speech. These disciples preached the *Bhagavata* philosophy throughout India and, in their turn, have created hundreds of *tridandi-sannyasis*. Bhaktivedanta Swami gave the first *tridanda-sannyasa* to a westerner in 1967, and before passing away in 1977, had created many such American, English, German, and French *sannyasis*. In accordance with scripture enjoining men above the age of fifty to leave society for the forest, Bhaktivedanta Swami expected that disciples with genuine detachment would at some time take *sannyasa* to continuously travel and preach around the world, fully engaged in *bhakti*, devotional service to Krishna.

For the practitioner, *Bhagavata* 7.5.23 lists nine forms of *bhakti*: hearing (*shravana*), chanting (*kirtana*), remembering (*smarana*), serving the lotus feet (*pada-sevana*), ritual deity worship (*archana*), bowing (*vandana*), servitude (*dasya*), friendship (*sakhya*), and offering oneself (*atma-nivedana*). *Kirtana*, or chanting the Holy Name of God (*hari-nama*), was a special dispensation for the age of Kali promoted by Chaitanya as the only way to obtain love of God. His famous eight verses of instruction (*Shikshashtaka*) begin with praise of congregational chanting (*sankirtana*) of the names of Krishna. As the name of Krishna is considered identical with him (*abhinnatvan nama-naminoh*), God makes himself available through the chanting process. As the efficacy of chanting the holy names was so great, it was adopted as the "religion of the age" (*yuga-dharma*) for the entire world, and no other method was considered useful.[43] Chaitanya also gave guidelines for chanting: one was to be as humble as a blade of grass and as tolerant as a tree, demand no respect from others, and give respect to all.[44] The name could also not be successfully chanted without the benefit of transcendental association (*sat-sanga*), which helps the development of the inner soul function (*atmavritti-bhakti*); only when the spiritual heart and ear are vacant of mundane talk and pleasure will they become completely spiritual (*chid-anandamaya*).[45]

Chaitanya Mahaprabhu had dispatched preachers to spread the Holy Name, and he himself had converted many during his travels. Narottama, Shyamananda, and Shrinivasacharya had done much to spread the movement in the sixteenth century, and Bhaktivinoda had begun *nama-hatta* or chanting circles in villages around Bengal in the nineteenth century; much of his writing was on this topic. In the early twentieth century, Bhaktisiddhanta Saraswati organized large *sankirtana* ("congregational chanting") parties that paraded in procession through cities (*nagara-sankirtana*) or circumambulated holy sites chanting Krishna's name. When Bhaktivedanta Swami first arrived in New York, he arranged chanting at various yoga ashrams and public chanting in city parks. Congregational chanting was a major part of his thrice-weekly evening and daily morning classes held at each ISKCON center, and all disciples were required to complete a certain amount of individual chanting (*japa*) on consecrated prayer beads (*mala*).

OPPOSITION TO IMPERSONALISM

Following Bhaktisiddhanta Saraswati's example, Bhaktivedanta Swami crusaded against impersonalism, particularly the theory of illusionism (*Mayavada*) of the eighth-century Indian philosopher Shankara, which holds that all form, including that of Krishna himself, is ultimately illusory from the Absolute perspective. Vaishnava *acharyas* Ramanuja and Madhva had opposed Shankara's Absolute Nondualism (*Kevaladvaita*) with their philosophies of Qualified Nondualism (*Vishishtadvaita*) and Dualism (*Dvaita*)[46] respectively, and their successors have been engaged in a running battle with their Mayavadi counterparts ever since. According to Krishnadas Kaviraja's *Chaitanya Charitamrita*, Chaitanya himself had strongly condemned Shankara's explanations of the *Brahma-sutras*, prohibiting his followers from hearing or reading his works, and subsequent Gaudiya scholars such as Jiva Goswami, Vishvanatha Chakravarti, and Baladeva Vidyabhushana continued such criticism of Mayavada philosophy. Bhaktivinoda (1894) translated Kavipurnananda's *Tattva-muktavali* or *Mayavada-shata-dushani*, 119 verses revealing the defects in Mayavada.[47] In *Jaiva-dharma* (2, 15, 18) and other works, Bhaktivinoda critiques Mayavada rejection of the world's reality; and in his article "Who Is Called Mayavadi?" ("*Mayavadi kahake bali?*"), he brands them "spiritual offenders," as they reject Krishna's form, name, and pastimes as illusory (*mayika*).

In his *Anubhashya* on *Chaitanya Charitamrita*, Bhaktisiddhanta Saraswati discussed Shankara's interpretations of Vedanta,[48] repeatedly condemned impersonalism in his other writings, and encouraged bold preaching in this direction by his disciples (see Bhakti Prajnan Keshava's history of Mayavada [*Mayavadera jivani*] from the Vaishnava point of view).[49] A.C. Bhaktivedanta Swami continued this tradition with his strong objections to impersonalist concepts wherever encountered in his own missionary work. In his poetic homage to Bhaktisiddhanta Saraswati in 1935, the line "Impersonal calamity Thou hast moved," referring to his campaign against Mayavada, was highly appreciated by his spiritual master.[50] In the United States, he ridiculed promises of liberation through hatha yoga or meditational techniques such as Transcendental Meditation on the basis of verses from the *Bhagavad Gita*, *Bhagavata*, and *Chaitanya Charitamrita*, arguing that only congregational chanting (*sankirtana*) was effective in the present age (*kali yuga*). He repeatedly took issue in his articles ("*Muniganera Matibhrama*," *Gaudiya Patrika*, 1950s) and lectures with S. Radhakrishnan's comments on the *Bhagavad Gita* regarding Krishna's personality. He had exchanges with Professors Fritz Staal of the University of California-Berkeley and R. Zaehner of Oxford University over interpretations of particular *Gita* verses. In Vrindavan, he had once publicly challenged Swami Karpatriji, a famous *sannyasi* of the Shankara community and, following Vaishnava injunctions to avoid Mayavadi association, declined an invitation from Maharishi Mahesh Yogi in Rishikesh in 1976. Yet he on several occasions met with the famous blind Shankarite *sannyasi* Swami Gangeshvarananda, whom he claimed "was a devotee at heart."

A.C. BHAKTIVEDANTA SWAMI'S WRITINGS: TRANSLATIONS AND INDEPENDENT WORKS

Having a natural aptitude for writing from his youth, A.C. Bhaktivedanta Swami composed English articles and poetry in the 1930s for *The Harmonist*, Gaudiya Math's English journal, and Bengali and Hindi articles in the 1950s for *Gaudiya Patrika* and *Bhagavat Patrika*, publications of Gaudiya Vedanta Samiti, both of which he helped edit.[51] He was also briefly editor of Gaudiya Sangha's English journal (*Sajjana-toshani* [Delhi: Indraprastha Gaudiya Matha]). In 1944, he started his own fortnightly English magazine, *Back to Godhead*, consisting mostly of his own essays proposing solutions to local and world problems through pure devotional service (*bhakti* yoga). The magazine continued until 1960, and being later reestablished in New York (1966) with the assistance of western disciples, expanded internationally into German, French, Spanish, and other languages. The English *Back to Godhead* reached its highest circulation (500,000 per month) in the 1970s, but this has since decreased (the present circulation is 20,000 English-language copies bimonthly).

Bhaktivedanta Swami objected to currently available commentaries on the *Bhagavad Gita* as having been affected by impersonalism. He had earlier produced an English translation of the *Gita* in India (unfortunately lost), a Bengali verse edition (*Gitara Gana*),[52] and finally, *Bhagavad-gita As It Is*. Dictated on tape during his first years in the United States (1966–1967), and originally published with a reduced text (Macmillan, 1968), it was later published in a jumbo edition with Sanskrit text, transliteration, translation, and commentary (Macmillan, 1971). A more recent edition truer to the original dictation has since been published (Los Angeles: BBT, 1984). This is Bhaktivedanta Swami's most translated work, presently available in 96 languages.

Bhaktivedanta Swami followed the commentaries of Bhaktivinoda, Vishvanatha Chakravarti, and particularly Baladeva Vidyabhushana,[53] dedicating his translation to the latter, and often either directly translating or paraphrasing his *Vidyabhushana-bhashya* in the purports to *Bhagavad-gita As It Is*. In his fidelity to these commentaries, Bhaktivedanta Swami preached an uncompromising surrender to Krishna, the Personality of Godhead. *Bhagavad-gita As It Is* is not a straight translation of any one commentary. Bhaktivedanta Swami considered his understanding of scripture to be a fruit of all preceding *acharyas* in his line of disciplic succession (see the advertisement for his first English translation of the *Gita*,[54] where he lists his prominent spiritual predecessors), who are seen as descending in one unbroken stream (*sampradaya*). Thus Bhaktivedanta refers freely to relevant verses from the *Bhagavata*, *Chaitanya Charitamrita*, *Bhakti-rasamrita-sindhu*, or *Brahma-samhita*, and songs of Narottama Das.

Bhaktivedanta Swami's *Bhagavata* translation and commentary was begun in the late 1950s in India after a friend suggested that instead of writing devotional articles for journals, he should concentrate on books. He generally used an edition with eight classical Sanskrit commentaries on the *Bhagavata* published by Nityasvarupa Brahmachari (Vrindaban: Devakinandana Press, 1904); as well as that with commentaries by Vishvanatha Chakravarti, Madhva, and Bhaktisiddhanta Saraswati (Calcutta: Gaudiya Math, 1923–1935); among others. In his travels, Bhaktivedanta Swami always carried a handy one-volume Bengali-character edition of the *Bhagavata* with Shridhara's commentary. The black-covered book was a familiar sight, as Bhaktivedanta Swami often referred to it during his daily morning lectures.

Retiring each night at about 10 o'clock, Bhaktivedanta Swami would wake up as early as 1 A.M. to read the *Bhagavata* and dictate his translations and Bhaktivedanta purports into a tape recorder. He rarely missed a night of work. The first volume of his projected 60-volume work was published in India (*Shrimad Bhagwatam* [Vrindaban/Delhi: The League of Devotees, 1962]), and from 1969, volumes continued to appear year after year, followed by translations into German, French, Spanish, and other languages. By his passing in 1977, Bhaktivedanta Swami had completed 31 volumes (Los Angeles: BBT, 1972–77), up to the thirteenth chapter (*adhyaya*) of the tenth *skandha*, leaving the remainder unfinished (to be completed later by his disciples). Foresightedly, he had earlier translated the entire important tenth *skandha* in two volumes (*Krsna, The Supreme Personality of Godhead* [Boston: ISKCON Press, 1970]); and a section (Bhag. 10.20) translated with commentary in Vrindaban, 1961, was published as *Light of the Bhagavata* (Los Angeles: BBT, 1984). In addition, Bhaktivedanta Swami's lecture series on portions of the *Bhagavata*, such as the prayers of Kunti (*Bhag.* 1.8.18–43), have been published (*Teachings of Queen Kunti* [Los Angeles: BBT, 1978]).

Bhaktivedanta Swami's 17-volume translation and commentary on the seventeenth-century Bengali and Sanskrit *Chaitanya Charitamrita* of Krishnadas Kaviraja follows the commentaries of Bhaktivinoda (*Amrita-pravaha-bhashya*) and Bhaktisiddhanta Saraswati (*Anubhashya*). The *Chaitanya Charitamrita* was considered the entranceway for understanding the *Bhagavata* as well as the most complete and comprehensive presentation of Chaitanya Mahaprabhu's life and teachings, showing how the "religion of the age" (*kaliyu-ga-dharma*) appears in the form of Chaitanya Mahaprabhu's *sankirtana* movement. Another volume by Bhaktivedanta Swami, *Teachings of Lord Chaitanya* (New York, 1968), was based on five important conversations in *Chaitanya Charitamrita*.[55]

Rupa Goswami's *Bhakti-rasamrita-sindhu*, a key work for understanding the psychology of *bhakti*, was produced by Bhaktivedanta Swami in the form of a summary study, *The Nectar of Devotion: The Complete Science of Bhakti Yoga* (Los Angeles: BBT, 1970). An earlier translation, with Sanskrit text, word-for-word synonyms, and purports, appeared in *Back to Godhead* (vol. III, parts 17–22, 1960), but was not completed. These four books (*Bhagavad Gita, Bhagavata, Chaitanya Charitamrita,* and *Bhakti-rasamrita-sindhu*) were basic texts for ISKCON members.

Ishopanishat, with translation and commentary by Bhaktivedanta Swami, was partially serialized in *Back to Godhead* (vol. III, parts 23–25; vol. IV, part 1, 1960), and later reprinted in book form (Boston: ISKCON Press, 1969). Its first verse, highly regarded as a capsule of Vedic theology, presents a "god-centered" (*ishavasya*) view of the universe and was the basis for "The Peace Formula," a short tract written for distribution at anti–Vietnam War peace marches of the late sixties in New York and San Francisco.[56] Other texts translated by Bhaktivedanta Swami include *Shikshashtaka,* eight verses of instruction by Chaitanya Mahaprabhu; the eleven-verse *Upadeshamrita* of Rupa Goswami (as *The Nectar of Instruction* [Los Angeles: BBT, 1975]); and various *stotras.*

In conclusion, the sheer scope of Bhaktivedanta Swami's mission was ground-breaking even from within the universalistic context of Chaitanya Vaishnavism. Although not the first Gaudiya *sannyasi* to preach on western shores,[57] he was unquestionably the most successful, opening up the tradition to non-Hindus in unprecedented ways. His teachings, however, remained firmly grounded in the principles and doctrines of his predecessors in the Gaudiya Vaishnava tradition, especially those enunciated by his guru, Bhaktisiddhanta Saraswati, and his guru's father, Kedarnath Dutt Bhaktivinoda. Bhaktivedanta Swami charted the course all world religious teachers must negotiate: that between fidelity to a tradition and relevance to a time and place.

NOTES

1. Chaitanya Mahaprabhu (1486–1533) is considered by his followers as a direct appearance of the highest aspects of godhead. His movement developed mostly in Bengal, Orissa, and the Braj/Rajasthan regions of central northern India.
2. Bhakti Siddhanta Saraswati's most important works are commentaries on the *Chaitanya Charitamrita* (*Anubhashya*), *Chaitanya-bhagavata* (*Gaudiya-bhashya*), and *Srimad-Bhagavata* (*Gaudiya-bhashya*) in Sanskrit and Bengali.
3. A *matha* is a monastic institution for deity worship and the residence of renunciate monks or *brahmacharis,* as, for example, the historic *mathas* founded by Shankara and Madhva.
4. See Madhva in his *Bhagavata-tatparya* (on *Bhagavata* 1.1.1); Jiva Goswami, *Tattvasandarbha* (10); and Bhaktivinoda, "*Vastu-nirdesha,*" *Sajjana-toshani* (2/6).
5. *Chandogyopanishat* (6.2.1).
6. See the opening verses of Bhaktivinoda Thakur's Sanskrit treatises *Tattva-sutra* and *Amnaya-sutra.*

7. Bhaktivinoda describes *brahman* as the "impersonal, all-pervading, formless aspect of the Absolute," and *paramatma* as the "localized Absolute . . . in the heart of all beings." There are thus three different perceptions of Truth.

8. *Amrita-pravaha-bhashya* on *Chaitanya Charitamrita, Madhya,* 20.157 (Calcutta: Gaudiya Mission, 1958).

9. In *Bhagavata* 1.3.28—important for the Gaudiya Vaishnava doctrine that Krishna is the ultimate source of all *avataras*—Krishna receives special mention at the end of a long list of divine *avataras* as the personality of godhead himself (*krishnas tu bhagavan svayam*). Corroboration of Krishna's supreme position is also found in *Brahma-samhita*: "The supreme (*parama*) Lord (*ishvara*) is Krishna, having a form of *sach-chid-ananda*" (*Brahma-samhita* 5.1). This work had been found by Chaitanya during a pilgrimage to South India and brought back to Puri, where it was a favorite text. In 1967, the author and a godbrother found a copy of *Brahma-samhita*, with English translation by Bhakti Siddhanta Saraswati, in a New York bookstore and brought it to Bhaktivedanta Swami to inquire whether the book was authorized. Raising the volume to his forehead in respect, he surprised us by relating that he once had had the book "by heart" and recited it daily. Subsequently, verses were recorded and are presently played each morning at every ISKCON temple.

10. Bhaktivinoda writes (*Brahma-samhita-prakashini* 5.45): "Shambhu (Shiva) is not another 'controller' (*ishvara*) different than Krishna. Whoever conceives such difference (*bheda buddhi*) is an offender to the Supreme Lord. Shambhu's quality of being a controller (*ishvarata*) is dependent on the control of Govinda (Krishna). Therefore they are actually a nondifferent principle (*vastutah abheda-tattva*). Shiva is considered like yogurt compared to the original milk from which it has been altered by the addition of acid" (*Jaiva-dharma* [Nabadwip: Gaudiya Vedanta Samiti, 1988], 438).

11. *Chaitanya Charitamrita, Madhya* (20.111).

12. *Chaitanya Charitamrita, Madhya* (6.170–171).

13. *Chaitanya Charitamrita, Adi* (7. 116).

14. *Amrita-pravaha-bhashya* on *Chaitanya Charitamrita, Madhya* (20. 108–109).

15. *Anubhashya* on *Chaitanya Charitamrita, Adi* (5. 59–66).

16. *Anubhashya* on *Chaitanya Charitamrita, Adi* (5. 59–66).

17. *Kathopanishat* (2.2.12); *Bhagavad Gita* (2.11–30).

18. *Sanmodana-bhashya* on *Shikshashtaka* 1 (Mayapura: Chaitanya Matha, 3rd ed., 1971).

19. Op. cit.

20. *Jaiva-dharma* 3, 39.

21. *Pushkara-samhita* quoted by Bhakti Siddhanta Saraswati (*Shrichaitanya-darshane shri hsrila prabhupada bhakti siddhanta Saraswati thakura* [Shridhama Mayapura: Chaitanya Matha, 1974]).

22. *Datta-kaustubha* 67 (Calcutta: Gaudiya Mission, 1942).

23. *Shrichaitanya-darshane shri shrila prabhupada bhakti-siddhanta Saraswati thakura* (Shridham Mayapura: Chaitanya Matha, 1974), 1:171.

24. *Datta-kaustubha* 67.

25. *Prakashini* on *Brahma-samhita* 5.21 (Sridham Mayapura: Chaitanya Matha, 1958).

26. *Gaudiya-bhashya-vivriti* on *Bhagavata* (2.9.30).

27. *Gaudiya-bhashya-vivriti* on *Bhagavata* (3.9.6).

28. *Gaudiya-bhashya-vivriti* on *Bhagavata* (1.2.20).

29. *Chaitanya Charitamrita, Madhya* (19.151).
30. *Anubhashya* on *Chaitanya Charitamrita, Madhya* (19.151).
31. *Bhagavata* 11.3.21.
32. *Bhakti-rasamrita-sindhu* (1.4.15–16).
33. *Vishnu-yamala*, cited in *Hari-bhakti-vilasa* (2.9).
34. *Sattva-sagara*, cited in *Hari-bhakti-vilasa* (2.12).
35. *Chaitanya Charitamrita, Antya* (4.192–193).
36. *Mahabharata, Bhishma-parva* (5.12), cited by Jiva Goswami, *Tattva-sandarbha* (3).
37. *Gaudiya-bhashya-vivriti* on *Bhagavata* (1.2.21).
38. *Gaudiya-bhashya-vivriti* on *Bhagavata* (1.2.21).
39. *Gaudiya-darshana* (Calcutta: Gaudiya Matha, 1934), 98.
40. *Sarartha-varshini* on *Bhagavad Gita* (2.41).
41. *Chaitanya Charitamrita, Madhya* (22.62).
42. *Bhagavad Gita* 4.13 states that the fourfold caste system (*chaturvarnyam*) was created by Krishna according to categories of quality (*guna*) and work (*karma*). As birth (*janma*) is not mentioned here as a determining element, the verse is understood to support individual qualities in allocating social roles, rather than family of origin. *Bhagavata* 7.11.36 states that "in whomever the symptom of a certain caste is observed, he should be judged as belonging to that caste."
43. *Brihan-naradiya* (38.126); quoted in *Chaitanya Charitamrita, Adi* (7.76)
44. *Shikshashtaka* (4).
45. *Gaudiya-bhashya-vivriti* on *Bhagavata* (3.25.25)
46. See Madhva's *Mayavada-khandana*, etc.
47. See also Bhaktivinoda's preface to his Bengali summary of Baladeva's *Gita*.
48. See *Anubhashya* on *Chaitanya Charitamrita, Adi* (7.99–157).
49. Bhakti Prajnan Keshava, *Mayavadera jivani va vaishnava-vijaya* , 2nd ed. (Nabadwip: Gaudiya Vedanta Samiti, 1968).
50. The poem "Adore Adore ye all," was read in Bombay Gaudiya Math (January 1935) and later printed in *The Harmonist*.
51. These were subsequently reprinted from Calcutta by disciples (as *Vairagya-vidya* [Mayapura: BBT, 1977]) and later in English translation (*Renunciation through Wisdom* [Los Angeles: BBT, 1992]).
52. Calcutta: BBT, 1976. This has had the largest distribution of any of A.C. Bhaktivedanta Swami's writings.
53. Baladeva Vidyabhushana's exact dates are unknown (his commentary on Rupa Goswami's *Stavamala* is dated 1764). He is most renowned for his commentary (*Govinda-bhashya*) on the *Brahma-sutra*.
54. *Back to Godhead*, vol. I, part 1 (1944); *Sajjana-toshani*, 1950s.
55. *Teachings of Lord Chaitanya* consists of Chaitanya's conversations with Rupa Goswami, Sanatana Goswami, Prakashananda Saraswati, Sarvabhauma Bhattacharya, and Ramananda Raya.
56. *The Peace Formula* was also reprinted in *Only One Earth* (New York: United Nations Environment Programme, 1991).
57. Bhakti Siddhanta Saraswati had sent his *sannyasi* preachers B. H. Bon and B. P. Tirtha to Europe in 1933.

PART 3
Post-Bhaktivedanta
Controversies of Lineage

[10]

CLEANING HOUSE AND CLEANING HEARTS

Reform and Renewal in ISKCON

WILLIAM H. DEADWYLER (RAVINDRA SVARUPA DAS)

IN 1971 I BECAME A MEMBER of the International Society for Krishna Consciousness. I left one world to join another. Immersing myself in the life of a tightly knit temple commune, I radically restyled my exterior to mirror my utterly changed interior. I became a stranger in my own land. To cross the temple threshold was to pass from the material to the spiritual world, for temples were embassies of the kingdom of God. There the powers of material conditioning and desire had no sway. This is what I believed.

I have learned, by now, that transcendence is not so easily attained, that history does not so easily release us from its grasp. I have learned that the line between the godly and the ungodly is not congruent with the line separating ISKCON from non-ISKCON. I have learned that, like most in this world, I am committed—in my case deeply committed—to an institution that has done things that make me appalled and ashamed.

I joined ISKCON in my youth, when the society itself was young. Over the last quarter century we have matured together. Through struggle and difficulty, ISKCON has been forced to attain concrete awareness of its own limitations, and has, on the institutional level, enacted structures of self-criticism and self-correction. I want to set before you what I think is the central problem ISKCON has faced in that struggle. That problem arises out of both the internal dynamics of its spiritual endeavor and the historical situation in which it found itself.

ISKCON aims at creating "pure devotees"—people who serve God without personal motive and without interruption, who are free from all material desires. It is not thought that this is an ideal of which we must all, inevitably, fall short. On the contrary, ISKCON excels at instilling it as a practical aim. Though pure devotional service is an elevated state, it is attainable. Whenever ISKCON preaches this with confidence, it becomes highly effective in recruiting members and eliciting extraordinary levels of commitment. People join and remain because a sublime ideal seems achievable.

The potency with which ISKCON presents this ideal depends greatly upon the concrete, physical presence of a successful devotee who functions as an exemplary model, a paradigmatic individual. This personage—the guru, or *acharya* (one who teaches by his own behavior)—not only embodies the ideal for all to see but also delivers the divine grace by which others can become similarly advanced. Thus the institution itself requires devotees who appear, convincingly, to have realized the ideal.

Yet it is only to be expected that ISKCON would fall short of its high goals. Far more people are attracted to Krishna consciousness than are able to follow its principles. The real problem for ISKCON has not been its natural failings but rather an incapacity to deal constructively with them. Its more public shortcomings or scandals developed from a somewhat protracted refusal or inability to recognize its problems. In the minds of many devotees, they were simply not supposed to happen at all.

The difficulty for ISKCON was increased from the beginning, moreover, by the marginal social position of most of the early recruits. They were young and alienated—so much so that to join they became double dropouts—from mainstream society into the counterculture, from the counterculture into ISKCON. At the same time, certain countercultural attitudes were carried over into the unofficial culture of ISKCON.

"EASY AND SUBLIME"

When A.C. Bhaktivedanta Swami—known later by the honorific "Shrila Prabhupada"—began preaching in New York City in the second half of the 1960s, he characterized Krishna consciousness by a hendiadys that became something of a catchphrase: "simultaneously easy and sublime." This unlikely conjunction quite faithfully represented Shrila Prabhupada's received tradition from India.

Gaudiya Vaishnavism emerged in sixteenth-century Bengal as a reformed branch of a much older Vaishnava tradition. This reformation was the achievement of Shri Chaitanya Mahaprabhu (1486–1533). Somewhat like his European contemporary Martin Luther, Mahaprabhu stressed a direct, intimately personal relationship with God, unmediated by the traditional priestly offices and ritual formularies; and he was vigorous in extending this relationship to everyone, even the outcastes, the untouchables, and the fallen.

Vaishnavism had always propounded, as the highest salvation, a personal relationship with a transcendent God, whom it viewed as ontologically higher than the undifferentiated Brahman of the mysticism of negation (*Bhagavad Gita* 14.27). And Vaishnavism had always extended spiritual enfranchisement to traditionally disenfranchised people (*Bhagavad Gita* 9.32). Mahaprabhu developed both tendencies further. He taught, and practiced, a way of entering into relationship with God in his most private and confidential form.

According to Gaudiya Vaishnava theology, God has both a public and a private face. Manifesting his power and majesty (*aishvarya*), he is known as Narayana and is served in awe and reverence. However, when his beauty and sweetness (*madhurya*) overshadow his majesty, he is known as Krishna, the "all-attractive." Causing his confidential devotees to forget that he is God, Krishna enjoys rare intimacies with his devotee as friend or child or lover. Such intimacies, Chaitanya taught, are the highest achievement of the spirit, and they can be attained by pure devotion even in this life.

Chaitanya Mahaprabhu graciously offered such sublime relations with Krishna to all, even those considered degraded by culture or habit. Some of his prominent followers were recruited outside the pale of orthodox Hinduism. One was born a Muslim; two others had lost caste by serving the Turkish occupational government. This liberality was an affront to the hereditary caste Brahmins, who were shown scriptural text that stated, for example, that a pure devotee, no matter how low-born, is superior to the most well-qualified but nondevoted Brahmin (*Shrimad Bhagavatam* 7.9.10).

Mahaprabhu cited texts that claimed the practices of devotional service to possess such spiritual power as to elevate untouchables (*Shrimad Bhagavatam* 3.33.7) and aboriginal peoples (*Shrimad Bhagavatam* 2.4.18) to the highest position of Vedic culture. Furthermore, the practice of congregational chanting, the centerpiece of Chaitanya's reform movement, is natural and pleasing and requires no prior qualification whatsoever. Yet it possesses immense purifying potency.

Thus Chaitanya Mahaprabhu offered direct mystical entry into what amounts to the private life of God, and, by virtue of a process practicable by all, could liberally extend that offer equally to the low and the high, the ignorant and the wise, the damned and the saved. All this Shrila Prabhupada encapsulated in his conjunction "easy and sublime." "Easy," however, did not mean "cheap." The "easy" process was supposed to make one fully qualified for the sublime position. Advancement in chanting is evinced by the gradual disappearance of lust, greed, and anger from the heart; higher stages require the absence of all material desires (*virakti*). Chaitanya Mahaprabhu's liberality did not stop him from enforcing extremely strict standards among his followers.

This particular mixture of elements, transmitted quite faithfully by Shrila Prabhupada to America, did much to determine the inner tensions that produced the dynamic of ISKCON's development in the West.

PREACHING TO "WHITE ABORIGINES"

The demotic thrust of Vaishnava teaching provided theological justification for Shrila Prabhupada's coming to the West—for, by orthodox Hindu standards, westerners are *ipso facto* untouchables. Even so, Shrila Prabhupada had initially pictured his mission as directed toward the West's political and cultural elite. Several years before his journey, he had written in his English translation and commentary on *Shrimad Bhagavatam* (Vrindavan and Delhi: League of Devotees, 1962), that the work was "a cultural presentation for the re-spiritualization of the entire human society . . . meant for bringing about a revolution in the impious life of a misdirected civilization of the world." At that time he envisioned such a cultural revolution as coming from above:

> We are confident if the transcendental message of Shrimad Bhagavatam is received only by the leading men of the world, certainly there will be a change of heart and naturally the people in general will follow them. The mass [of] people in general are so to say tools in the hands of the modern politicians and leaders of the people. If there is a change of heart of the leaders only, certainly there will be a radical change in the atmosphere of the world siuation [*sic*].

As it turned out, the American establishment proved quite immune to the attractions of Krishna consciousness, but Shrila Prabhupada unexpectedly found a sympathetic reception among the hippies—"the spoiled children of society," as he once called them (*Shrimad Bhagavatam* 4.12.23, purport)—who had emerged as a group in the year of his arrival. He was often to note that the hippies were "our best customers" (letters to Gaurasundara das, 1969, and to Satsvarupa das, 1971), "immediate candidates of our Krishna Consciousness" (letter to Govinda dasi, 1969). The reason for such receptivity was that "the youth in the West have reached the stage of *vairagya*, or renunciation. They are practically disgusted by material pleasure from material sources" (*Shrimad Bhagavatam* 6.16.26, purport).

In a 1971 *Bhagavad Gita* lecture Shrila Prabhupada said that "these American boys" are "fed up with this materialistic way of life. They want something spiritual. But because there is no such information, there is no such leader, they are becoming hippies, frustrated and confused. And because here is something substantial, they are taking it. This is the secret of success of this Krishna Consciousness movement." In spite of having "reached renunciation," (*Shrimad Bhagavatam* 6.16.26, purport), American youth, for want of spiritual direction, disastrously took refuge in sex and drugs. The hippies appeared to Shrila Prabhupada as "morose" (*Shrimad Bhagavatam* 4.25.11, purport), "distressed," "wretched," "unclean," "without shelter or food" (*Shrimad Bhagavatam* 4.25.5, purport), "irresponsible and unregulated" (*Shrimad Bhagavatam* 5.6.10, purport), "lying idle, without any production" (*Bhagavad Gita* lecture, 1976), and so on. While the counterculture at one point made something of an icon of Shrila Prabhupada, he himself remained vigorously opposed to its standards and practices. For example, he wrote to Hayagriva das in 1969: "Anyway, we should be very much careful [not] to publish anything in our paper which will give impression to the public that we are inclined to the hippy [*sic*] movement.... I must tell you in this connection that if you have any sympathies with the hippy movement you should kindly give it up."

It is surprising that Gaudiya Vaishnavism could have been transplanted into the modern West at all. Yet it should not be surprising—especially to those acquainted with the history of religions—that its earliest followers should have largely been drawn from radically marginalized and alienated youth. Although Shrila Prabhupada may have hoped for a hearing from the establishment, he accepted the receptivity of the hippies as providential and relied on the potency of the holy name, vigorously preached, to achieve the requisite effect. And, indeed, the movement grew with extraordinary rapidity.

How did Prabhupada's deeply traditional and conservative message appeal to such radicalized youth? His powerful critique of modern material civilization, undertaken from a spiritual perspective, resonated strongly with his young hearers' own disillusionment. But the deep attraction was Shrila Prabhupada's ability to implant in us an extraordinary hope. He was able to establish the ideal of sainthood as a viable goal of life, a practical vocational aim. Young western men and women became convinced that they could attain direct experience of God in this life. Although Shrila Prabhupada made it very clear that such achievement demands uncompromising purity, his followers became convinced that, in spite of their own past actions and present conditioning, they could be elevated under his tutelage to that requisite standard.

Shrila Prabhupada's success brought him problems of its own. His follow-ers were young, immature, untrained, and inexperienced. Many suffered men-tal, moral, and spiritual disorders from their sojourn in the counterculture, if not in postwar America itself. In short, Shrila Prabhupada constructed his movement out of dubious raw material. To him, his effort was a matter of life or death; he was animated by a sense of extreme urgency. In a tempest one builds a shelter with whatever comes to hand; later, architects may criticize. Indeed, he knew well the defects of his handiwork. In the mid-seventies, a cer-tain ISKCON leader showed me a letter that Shrila Prabhupada had sent him. As I recall it, Prabhupada, writing about his difficulties managing ISKCON, had made the striking statement: "Krishna did not send me any first-class men. He sent me only second- and third-class men." Another leader told me Shrila Prabhupada had written him in nearly identical language. (I have been unable to find either letter in the present archive collection of Shrila Prabhu-pada's correspondence.)

The explosive growth of the early movement created a further problem. New people, immature and undertrained, had to assume positions of leader-ship and responsibility. For example, only eight months after joining the tem-ple in Philadelphia I was made president, with twelve or fifteen devotees under my care. But there was no one else to do the job, and I received on-the-job training with no immediate trainer. I can hardly remember my perform-ance without shuddering. I think that this was rather typical of ISKCON at the time.

Another difficulty arose from the intergenerational warfare of that era. A countercultural contempt for society and its institutions was absorbed into ISKCON in the early days (and in some cases remained for a long time). As a result, devotees were often unnecessarily hostile to and confrontational with established authorities (including their own parents); when those au-thorities responded in kind, it only confirmed our worst estimation. In some cases, the countercultural hostility became combined with notions extracted from our theology to produce a virulent antinomianism—something you will hardly find in, say, the *Bhagavad Gita*. This antinomianism later pro-duced the disaster in the West Virginia New Vrindavan community. Yet with all these early difficulties the movement still grew and developed, and even in trying times an extraordinary degree of spiritual facility was available to those who sought it.

One could argue that Shrila Prabhupada should have checked the expansion of his movement until his leaders could be properly trained by him. I am sure Prabhupada knew the risks, but from his perspective it would have been in-conceivable not to respond as energetically as possible to the God-given op-portunity to save souls. The positive results would be eternal; the negative, temporary. For my own part, I am deeply grateful for the risk he took in allowing the rapid expansion of ISKCON with all its attendant hazards and shortcomings. It saved me.

DEALING WITH SPIRITUAL FAILURE

It seemed to his early followers that Shrila Prabhupada offered them something unavailable in the religions they had been raised in: direct spiritual experience of God (*vijnana*, or "realized" knowledge), as opposed to mere doctrinal or "book" knowledge (*jnana*). *Bhakti yoga* is a spiritual discipline that aims to alter or "purify" consciousness so that the divine can become directly present to it, become a reality of immediate perception (*pratyaksha*) (see *Bhagavad Gita* 9.2). This systematic aim at experiential results gives *bhakti yoga* a common feature with modern science, and Shrila Prabhupada often translated *vijnana* as "science" and called *bhakti yoga* the "science of self-realization."

The practice of this science requires that one make oneself the subject of an experiment in the progressive purification of consciousness, which entails a fairly rigorous program of spiritual practices (*sadhana*), including rising each day before dawn to spend the first four or five hours in intense devotional exercises. During this time, two hours are set aside for chanting the Hare Krishna mantra on beads at least 1,728 times.

Furthermore, one has to strictly observe four prohibitions. The first prohibition, against eating meat, fish, or eggs, means, in its most rigorous understanding, that one ought only to eat food that has been sanctified by first being prepared for and offered to Krishna. The prohibition against taking intoxication means eschewing even the milder anodynes like tea and chocolate. The injunction not to gamble is meant to prohibit participating not only in wagering and games of chance but also in time-wasting diversions like sports, cinema, television, and so on. Finally, the injunction against illicit sex forbids sex not only outside of wedlock but even within marriage if it is not intended for procreation; for that purpose, sex can be engaged in one time in a month, within the period of the woman's fertility. The goal is to get through life with a minimum of involvement in sex, and not only in deed, but in speech and thought as well. Shrila Prabhupada called these rules "the regulative principles of freedom" (*Bhagavad Gita* 2.64). He made it starkly clear that self-realization and sense gratification are mutually exclusive, and he refused to compromise. His followers tended to attribute the dispirited condition of the routinized religions of their childhood precisely to institutional accommodations to sense gratification. Consequently, the very stringency of ISKCON's regulative principles became to many a hallmark of the society's validity and acted as an attractive, rather than repellent, factor.

In addition, the emphasis on stringent practice was closely linked to a charismatic outpouring of enthusiasm, manifest especially in *sankirtana*, group chanting of the names of God while dancing to drums and cymbals. This central practice illustrates the ability of devotional activities to produce an intense concentration of consciousness through the expressive engagement of the senses and feelings—a fundamental principle of *bhakti yoga*. The compelling energy generated by *sankirtana*, a contagious enthusiasm and a sense of exaltation, is enhanced by the affective channeling caused by the asceticism of the regulative principles. Conversely, the ability of devotional activities like *sankirtana* and *archana* (deity worship) to engage the feelings and senses can make adherence to the principles not an exercise in barren abnegation but rather a natural displacement of material activities by spiritual ones.

At any rate, not only did young people enthusiastically commit themselves with great self-confidence to the strict principles, but they rallied behind them as a sort of shibboleth, a distinctive validating feature of ISKCON that set it apart both from other, competing new religious movements from the East and from the mainstream denominations of the West.

From the beginning, ISKCON excelled in causing its members to internalize an extremely high ideal: that of a "pure devotee of Krishna," totally engaged in God's service without any personal motive and without interruption. Such a standard was visibly exemplified in Shrila Prabhupada himself, an *acharya*, or model, for all to emulate. Initiated devotees were expected to follow the principles rigorously, if not out of spontaneous love for God, at least out of dutiful obedience to the injunctions of scripture and guru.

It is only natural to expect that it would take a great and often protracted struggle for contemporary young secularized Americans to live up to their stringent new standards. Yet in the early culture of ISKCON such difficulties were not easily acknowledged. The shibbolethic role played by the regulative principles, and the fact that taking initiation vows was the only acceptable means of socialization within ISKCON, made strict following of the regulative principles a *sine qua non* of allegiance. At the same time, preaching aimed at producing swift conversions, a complete break with outside society, and a total immersion in temple culture. Naturally, temples filled with premature and tentative candidates under great internal and external pressure to profess a degree of commitment usually far in excess of the reality. Further, a lack of mature devotees who had passed successfully through the trials of spiritual development left most of the movement without experienced practical guides and counselors. All these factors combined to produce within ISKCON an inability to deal in a healthy and constructive manner with members' spiritual failings. Those problems could hardly even be acknowledged, let alone discussed.

The climate of ISKCON in those days strongly discouraged any frank and open confession of difficulty in following the principles. This was true not only on the institutional level but usually on the personal one as well. For example, when soon after joining the temple I confided my own normal problem to a slightly senior devotee, hoping for some forgiveness, practical advice, sympathy, and encouragement, my confessor showed alarm, astonishment, and anger; becoming aloof and stern, he simply delivered the judgment that I "could not be a devotee." Such experiences seem to have been all too typical. Concealment became the dominant mode of reaction. Devotees became isolated from one another, and real fellowship was baffled. The various unfortunate by-products of any religious group with a high demand for sanctity surfaced within ISKCON: bluffing, hypocrisy, intolerance, fanaticism, punctiliousness, fault-finding, and the substitution of minor for major virtues. (See Anton T. Boisen, *The Exploration of the Inner World* [New York: Harper and Brothers, 1936], 148.)

A steady stream of devotees joined the movement, and a steady stream left. In ISKCON jargon, they "blooped," fell back into illusion. Typically, a devotee would simply disappear, without any forewarning, often in the middle of the night. Sometimes this removal would be preceded by a period of withdrawal and depression, but often there would be no clue at all. An inquiry would later disclose a few devotees who had ascertained that the "blooped" one had had problems following the principles. He could not bring himself to admit it, and his sense of isolation and guilt drove him in silence from the community. Each such departure tended to create a community crisis. It rocked the faith of many members, whose own hold on Krishna consciousness was none too strong. Sometimes temple residents covertly envied the "blooped" devotee. At any rate, the community reacted to the departure as to a betrayal. Usually a communal postmortem would spontaneously take place, in which the faults and shortcomings of the departed devotee were dissected and condemned until the remaining members felt themselves secure and reassured.

To the bewilderment and, frequently, annoyance of the temple residents, many "blooped" devotees did not utterly vanish. They would maintain some contact with a temple member and join a network of other former members. They would show up at the Sunday feast and other public functions. They were always about, just on the periphery: "the shadow of ISKCON," as one temple devotee quipped. In society jargon these liminal people were called "fringies"—a term, by the way, now rarely heard. Because of the anger and resentment of temple residents, the treatment of "fringies" was often spiteful and rude. At best, the temple devotees were indifferent, because "you could not preach to fringies." Preaching was meant to persuade someone to join the temple community, but fringies were inoculated against such appeals.

They maintained some allegiance to Krishna consciousness, but had stabilized themselves on a platform the temple residents considered unsatisfactory, compromising on the regulative principles and engaging in an irregular program of devotional activities. Over the years the population of fringies steadily increased, yet ISKCON leaders and temple devotees did not acknowledge any duties or obligations toward them, nor give much value to their continuing allegiance. They represented failure, and the establishment wanted simply to disown them. Only in the late 1980s, at different rates in different locations, did the ISKCON leadership begin to acknowledge the "fringies" as "our people," as a genuine congregation to whom the temple should minister.

This belated recognition of a congregation illustrates the unwillingness of the movement to acknowledge the widespread failure to maintain long-term adherence to its own spiritual standards. ISKCON was finally forced to face the problem only when a crisis was produced by the fall down of a number of leaders who had become initiating gurus after Shrila Prabhupada's passing away in 1977. These gurus were all *sannyasis,* those who had taken supposedly irrevocable vows of celibacy and renunciation, and their fall from the standards became the crowning event in what had been a continuing failure among *sannyasis,* at a rate that approached 90 percent.

In 1969, three householder couples (*grihasthas*) had very successfully launched the Hare Krishna movement in London. Impressed by the way they could preach, Shrila Prabhupada encouraged marriage as a matter of policy. He explains his position in this 1971 Bombay *Bhagavad Gita* lecture (March 29):

Om Visnupada Paramahamsa Parivrajakacharya Asttotara Sata Shrimad Bhaktisiddhanta Saraswati Maharaja Prabhupada [Shrila Prabhupada's spiritual master]: He was creating more *brahmacaris* and *sannyasis* for preaching work, but I am creating more *grhasthas* [applause], because in Europe and America the boys and girls intermingle so quickly and intimately that it is very difficult to keep one *brahmacari.* So there is no need of artificial *brahmacaris.* . . .

So married life is called *grhastha-asrama.* It is as good as *sannyasa-asrama. Asrama* means where there is *bhagavad-bhajana* [glorification of God]. It doesn't matter whether one is *sannyasi* or one is *grhastha* or a *brahmacari.* The main principle is *bhagavad-bhajana.* But practically also, I may inform you that these married couples, they are helping me very much. . . . For practical example, I may say that one of my Godbrothers, a *sannyasi,* he was deputed [in the 1930s] to go to London for starting a temple, but three or four years he remained there, he could not execute the will [of his spiritual master]; therefore he was called back.

Now, I sent [three] married couples. All of them are present here. And they worked so nicely that within one year we started our London temple, and that is going on very nicely. [applause]

So it is not the question of a *brahmacari, sannyasi* or *grhastha*. . . . One who knows the science of Krsna and preaches all over the world, he is guru, spiritual master. It doesn't matter. So in Europe and America I am especially creating more *grhasthas*, families, so that they can take up this movement very seriously and preach, and I am glad to inform you that this process has become very successful.

Thus, when I joined ISKCON it was assumed that everyone would get married, and indeed, devotees were urged to do so. Marriages were arranged, usually without courtship, and each had to be approved by Shrila Prabhupada. But as early as 1971 Prabhupada was becoming concerned, as shown by this letter of July 5 to Hridayananda, one of his leaders:

> So far as R—— getting himself married, you must first discuss with him that this marriage business is not a farce, but it must be taken very seriously. There is no question of divorce, and if he will promise not to separate from his wife, then my sanction for the marriage is there; otherwise not. Recently too many couples have been drifting into Maya's waters, and it is very discouraging. So if he will agree on these points, then you can perform the marriage with my blessings.

Shrila Prabhupada's discouragement with the outcome of marriages continued to increase. Finally, in 1974, he simply refused to sanction any further marriages. (In my temple, there were no marriages between devotees for nearly a year, and then they were performed under my local sanction with a civil ceremony.)

Shrila Prabhupada's policy seemed to change. Throughout ISKCON, householder life underwent a radical devaluation. Scriptural condemnations of married life ("a dark well") received much play. Men were pressured to remain *brahmachari* (celibate), now held up as the normal state, with *sannyasa* a reward for achievement. The population of *sannyasis* increased dramatically. A genuine desire for transcendence, often commingled with an urge to acquire prestige, position, and power in ISKCON, propelled most of these young men into rash and improvident heroics. The persistence of desires they could neither acknowledge nor control began to erupt as intolerance and fanaticism. The social climate turned ugly: some *sannyasis* led campaigns against householders and even more against women, whose life in the movement at this time became extremely trying. Feelings grew so heated that in 1976 a clash in

North America between householder temple presidents and a powerful association of traveling renunciates exploded into a conflict so major that Shrila Prabhupada called it a "fratricidal war."

As one would expect, most of these young *sannyasis* could not sustain their commitment. There was a steady, even growing, exodus. Usually, an extreme sense of disgrace and shame, amplified by the merciless condemnation of the *sannyasi* community itself, propelled them into exile into the fringe or beyond.

Although the problems of *grihasthas* and *sannyasis* circulated widely through *sub rosa* channels of scandalized gossip, the movement could not bring itself openly to acknowledge the scope and significance of the difficulty. This was the state of affairs when Shrila Prabhupada passed away in November 1977, and ISKCON was transferred to the hands of his students, none of whom had had more than a dozen years' training. Eleven select members of the Governing Body Commission, a board of directors established by Prabhupada to continue leadership after him, were elevated to the position of initiating guru. (The two householders among them were quickly persuaded to take *sannyasa*.) The trend of *sannyasis'* falling down continued, however, and some of the new gurus were soon in trouble. Within ten years of assuming the role of living exemplars and *via media* to God for thousands of new devotees, six of them had quite spectacularly plummeted, and ISKCON's survival was in doubt.

"GURU REFORM"

The crisis of authority that then shook ISKCON to its foundations—and led finally in 1987 to a restructuring of the position of guru in the society—was not due exclusively to the spiritual immaturity of the leaders, although that was serious enough in itself. Those shortcomings were linked to a profound *structural* problem: the way in which the position of initiating guru had become institutionalized after Prabhupada. The problem arose because the conception of guru was based implicitly on a traditional model of an inspired, charismatic spiritual autocrat, an absolute and autonomously decisive authority, around whom an institution takes shape as the natural extension and embodiment of his charisma. Indeed, Shrila Prabhupada himself was such a guru. Yet from 1970, he had worked diligently to establish a quite different sort of leadership structure to continue after him. This was a model of management characteristic of distinctly modern institutions: a corporate board of directors, in ISKCON called "the Governing Body Commission" (GBC). The institutional and philosophical dilemma after Shrila Prabhupada's demise was this: how did gurus—who, according to Vaishnava theology, are direct representatives of God and worshiped "on an equal level with God"—fit within an organization functioning according to modern rational and legal modes under the direction of a committee? Although ISKCON's crisis of leadership and authority was precipitated by the fall-downs and deviations of gurus, it was ultimately addressed by a structural revisioning and reordering of the institutionalization of gurus in the society.

On May 28, 1977, during what turned out to be Shrila Prabhupada's terminal illness, a committee of seven GBC members was deputed to ask him how the function of initiating guru would be carried out in ISKCON after his departure. In response, Shrila Prabhupada said he would select some disciples to begin immediately performing all of the activities involved in giving initiation—approving the candidate, chanting on the beads, giving the name, and so on—acting as an officiating priest (*ritvik*) on his behalf. Those so initiated during Shrila Prabhupada's physical presence would be Shrila Prabhupada's disciples. After his demise, however, those same officiating gurus would, if qualified, become gurus in their own right. Those whom they initiated would be their own disciples, and Shrila Prabhupada would be their grand-spiritual master. On July 9, Shrila Prabhupada had a letter sent out announcing his selection of eleven of the twenty GBC members to begin acting at once as officiating gurus. Thus the GBC understood Shrila Prabhupada to have chosen the first initiating gurus to succeed him.

After Shrila Prabhupada's demise in November 1977, those eleven were immediately elevated above all others, even their GBC colleagues. Within the GBC, the gurus formed a special subcommittee, which held exclusive jurisdiction over all matters concerning gurus and initiation, including the power to appoint new gurus and to deal with any problems concerning gurus. The new gurus received the same ceremonial treatment that had been accorded Shrila Prabhupada. In every ISKCON temple room, there was reserved for Prabhupada an elevated ceremonial seat, called a *vyasasana*, that represented the spiritual authority of its occupier. After Prabhupada's demise, most temples installed a life-size statue of him on the *vyasasana*. Every morning, he was honored there with a ceremony called *guru puja*, during which the devotees sang a traditional hymn in praise of the guru while a priest performed the formal *arati* ritual of worship. New, somewhat lower *vyasasanas* were installed next to Shrila Prabhupada's, and there the new gurus also received daily *puja*, at the same time that Prabhupada was offered his. In point of fact, *two*—not one—*vyasasanas* were established for new gurus. The two smaller seats flanked Shrila Prabhupada's. The one on his right was consecrated to the exclusive use of the local zonal *acharya*. The one on the left, the "guest *vyasasana*," was occupied by any outside initiating guru who might be visiting.

Shrila Prabhupada had organized the GBC so that each member was responsible for activities in a particular geographical area, or "zone." With the advent of new gurus, those twenty or so zones became part of eleven greater zones, each having one of the initiating gurus as its head. That guru's zone would consist of the zone he managed as a GBC member, and then in most cases the zone or zones of other, nonguru GBC members. To all new recruits, the local zonal *acharya* was presented as *the* spiritual master. Although in principle a new devotee was free to choose his own guru out of the eleven, formidable social and institutional pressures directed his choice to one person only. Typically, a new devotee strongly attracted to taking initiation from a different guru would be relocated to that guru's zone.

The zonal *acharya* naturally exercised great *de facto* power, and the relation between the guru and the GBC (both individually and collectively) soon became a difficult and troubling issue. It seemed to many that Shrila Prabhupada had established two authority structures—that of the GBC and that of the gurus. Indeed, the gurus, with their sacred status, constantly emphasized by formal deference and ceremonial honors, and with their growing numbers of personally devoted followers, quickly eclipsed the GBC. Many gurus viewed the commission as a temporary, *ad hoc* expedient until the movement could be unified under the charismatic leadership of a single, "self-effulgent *acharya*," who would eventually emerge among the gurus, just as an emperor prevails among kings. Further, many gurus felt that the essential characteristic of a guru as an absolute authority was vitiated by the give-and-take of collegial relations within the GBC. Indeed, in response to the question about such a compromise of the guru's position, it was at one point officially stated that for the sake of the movement the gurus had *voluntarily* sacrificed the natural exercise of their absolute position for the relativity of working with the GBC.

The true position of the guru in ISKCON was most honestly and effectively proclaimed in symbolic terms, in the language, as it were, of furniture. I have noted the arrangement of twin *vyasasanas* established for the new gurus, which was instituted without any explanation of its significance. Indeed, I believe even those who established the system had not articulated its meaning to themselves but had acted mostly by instinct or intuition. Yet: why two seats? Why not only one upon which any new guru could sit? This question was not asked until the reform movement raised it in 1985. In fact the exclusive *vyasasana*, reserved for the sole use of the *acharya* of that zone, symbolized the seat of that guru as the head of the institution. That *vyasasana* indicated the absolute and autocratic guru of Hindu tradition. And that particular conception of the role of guru was in essential conflict with the GBC system established by Shrila Prabhupada.

The Sanskrit word *acharya* was commonly used in ISKCON as a designation for the initiating gurus, but the word has several meanings, and this ambiguity became the source of much difficulty. The fundamental sense is "one who teaches by example." It is generally synonymous with *guru*. However, *acharya* is a specific honorific for exceptional founders like Shankaracharya, Mad-hvacharya, and Ramanujacharya. Finally, *acharya* is specifically used to denote a guru who presides at the head of the institution. The *acharya* in this last sense denotes a traditional form of religious leadership in India, in which a charismatic individual attracts followers, and gradually, an institution forms about him. In this typically pre-modern style of leadership, the organization is a personal extension, a veritable embodiment, of that person. (Shrila Prabhupada referred to ISKCON as "his body.") The viability and credibility of the institution is largely a function of the perceived spiritual potency of the *acharya*. In India, the current *acharya* would appoint his successor from among his followers, and in this way the charisma would be transferred. Upon the demise of his predecessor, the successor *acharya* would ascend to the seat at the head of the institution. He would be ritually elevated over all his "godbrothers," and they would bring new members to him for initiation.

ISKCON, however, represents a departure from this archaic form of organization. Shrila Prabhupada emphasized that the society would not be managed after him by an *acharya*, but rather by the board of directors, the Governing Body Commission, that he formed in 1970. Shrila Prabhupada's intention, and his departure from the tradition of the institutional *acharya*, is shown in a striking way in his will. Traditionally, it was in the first article of his will that an *acharya* named his successor, passing his institution on to his heir as if it were his personal property. The first article of Shrila Prabhupada's will reads: "The Governing Body Commission (GBC) will be the ultimate managing authority for the entire International Society for Krishna Consciousness."

ISKCON thus represents a modernization of a religious tradition—the culmination of several generations of effort, not easily accomplished. Bhaktivinoda Thakur (1838–1914) was the first *acharya* in the tradition to receive a western-style education and to write in English. He envisioned a reformed and revitalized Gaudiya Vaishnava tradition functioning as a unified international preaching mission in the modern world. He instilled this vision in his son, Shrila Bhaktisiddhanta Saraswati Thakur (1874–1937), who was to become Shrila Prabhupada's guru. Bhaktisiddhanta Saraswati had constructed a preaching mission of more than sixty centers called the Gaudiya Math and even dispatched missionaries to Europe (without, however, much success). The Gaudiya Math was a vital, growing concern, yet soon after the demise of its founder, the organization fragmented. Shrila Prabhupada explains how this happened:

> Such disagreement among the disciples of one *acharya* is also found among the members of the Gaudiya Matha. In the beginning, during the presence of Om Visnupada Paramahamsa Parivrajakacharya Astottara-sata Sri Shrimad Bhaktisiddhanta Saraswati Thakura Prabhupada, all the

disciples worked in agreement; but just after his disappearance, they disagreed. One party strictly followed the instructions of Bhaktisiddhanta Saraswati Thakura, but another group created their own concoction about executing his desires. Bhaktisiddhanta Saraswati Thakura, at the time of his departure, requested all his disciples to form a governing body and conduct missionary activities cooperatively. He did not instruct a particular man to become the next *acharya*. But just after his passing away, his leading secretaries made plans, without authority, to occupy the post of *acharya*, and they split in two factions over who the next *acharya* would be. Consequently, both factions were *asara*, or useless, because they had no authority, having disobeyed the order of the spiritual master. Despite the spiritual master's order to form a governing body and execute the missionary activities of the Gaudiya Matha, the two unauthorized factions began litigation that is still going on after forty years with no decision. (*Chaitanya Charitamrita, Adi-lila*, 12.8, purport)

Other accounts, from Gaudiya Math sources, say that a Governing Body Commission was formed and operated for a while before the attempt to establish a single *acharya* shattered the organization. In any case, it is clear that the previous generation came to grief over the same issue that confronted ISKCON: of forming a unified preaching mission that did not depend on the direction of any one individual but rather of a collegial body, functioning cooperatively. Indeed, the *acharya* established over the Gaudiya Math suffered the same fate as later befell a number of the ISKCON *acharyas*: after being raised so high, he fell down from the principles of Krishna consciousness. From Shrila Prabhupada's perspective, all these spiritual problems must be considered the consequence of the disciples' disobedience of the order of the spiritual master.

The Gaudiya Math having failed, Shrila Prabhupada worked independently, establishing his own society and becoming its sole *acharya*. Had things gone better, he would have been one of many missionaries and preachers within a unified Gaudiya mission. In other words, Shrila Prabhupada's position as the autonomous guru at the head of ISKCON was, from his point of view, a second-best arrangement, the consequence of failure. Learning from that failure, Shrila Prabhupada set up a governing body, watched over it, and taught it how to function. For example, in 1975 he took the body through its first regular annual meeting, showing the GBC how to follow parliamentary procedure according to Robert's *Rules of Order*. Over time he tried to delegate as much management to the commission as possible, intervening only in crises. He made sure the whole movement understood that the GBC was being trained to continue at the head of the society after he was gone.

The GBC did carry on; no one tried to establish a single *acharya*. Yet the division of ISKCON into private initiating zones, the installation of the exclusive *vyasasana,* and the ritual elevation of the gurus far above their own godbrothers had implicitly established eleven *acharya*s of the traditional institutional type, each bearing the same relationship to his zone as Shrila Prabhupada had borne to the entire movement. The selection of the first eleven gurus became interpreted in accordance with the paradigm of the *acharya*'s appointment of a successor to the head of his institution. For example, in a book of homages to one of the new gurus, published in 1979, we read this: "Desiring to prepare his disciples for his departure, His Divine Grace Shrila Prabhupada very wisely selected eleven of his most intimate disciples to become both his material and spiritual successors."

At the same time, a growing number of Shrila Prabhupada's disciples felt there was something wrong with the position of new gurus in ISKCON. Many felt their godbrothers—or most of them, anyway—were simply unqualified for such a position. And when several *acharyas* began to engage in questionable or scandalous behavior, it was only with a struggle that the GBC established its right to exercise any authority over them. Even then, the commission's control remained more *de jure* than *de facto.*

After two gurus, Hamsadutta and Jayatirtha, were finally expelled from ISKCON, many Prabhupada disciples feared it only a matter of time before others fell or deviated. A California group circulated lengthy papers to argue that none of Shrila Prabhupada's disciples was fit to be an *acharya*. These dissidents refused to believe that Shrila Prabhupada could have hand-picked any of these (to them) obviously unqualified people, and they argued that the archival tape recording of the May 28, 1977 conversation had been doctored by the gurus. This group held that initiation must await the eventual emergence of the "self-effulgent *acharya*." This somewhat messianic notion failed to gain strength and the effort dissipated. Yet the idea that ISKCON needed a "self-effulgent *acharya*" continued as the shared presupposition of factions on the extreme "right" as well as the "left." On the extreme right were those partisans convinced that some one or another of the current zonal *gurus* was the expected "self-effulgent *acharya*," whose recognition awaited only the fullness of time. On the extreme left were those who held that none of ISKCON's leaders was remotely qualified to be an *acharya*, and until such time in the (remote) future a "self-effulgent *acharya*" should emerge, no one should presume to be a guru in his own right.

In the fall of 1984 a routine meeting of the temple presidents of North America turned into an open admission that nearly all present held deep misgivings about the position of the guru in ISKCON. Thus the "guru reform movement" was born. With the engagement of a significant number of second-tier leaders, an energetic and credible force took shape. While the presidents deeply believed something had gone drastically wrong, there was no clear idea of precisely what it was. At a follow-up meeting, I was assigned the task of preparing a research paper to uncover what had happened in the establishment of the gurus.

In my research, I found a 1978 letter written to a GBC member by Pradyumna das, who had a scholar's knowledge of Vaishnava traditions; the letter spelled out objections to the newly established guru system and provided the clue as to the precise problem. Elaborating on Pradyumna's insight, I prepared a paper arguing that, contrary to the desires of Shrila Prabhupada, the traditional post of the "institutional *acharya*" had been instituted in ISKCON and that this *acharya* system was essentially in conflict with the GBC system. This paper received the overwhelming endorsement of the North American temple presidents.

By this time, the "reform moment" had broadened far beyond the core group of temple presidents. For many, the really vital issue was not one of structure but of the perceived lack of spiritual qualifications among the present gurus. As a leader of the reform movement, however, I tried to focus our political effort on rectifying the structural problem. I was not blind to the spiritual shortcomings of some of the gurus. I even recognized that the structural problem was in part an institutionalization of a serious spiritual defect—that is, unacknowledged personal ambition. However, it was clear to me that the gurus hardly held the monopoly on spiritual deficiency. I was not at all sure that the reform group was that much purer—many of the attacks on the gurus were weighted by a generous load of envy, vengefulness, and *ressentiment*. In my view, what had gone wrong in ISKCON constituted a collective judgment on all of Shrila Prabhupada's disciples. After all, we agreed that Prabhupada's grace was equally available to all. Those who became gurus were among his "best men." If they were not good enough, every critic like me had to ask himself: "Why wasn't I any better?" I made the case that the first part of "guru reform" had to be personal reformation, a renewed dedication to the cultivation of spiritual life by all Shrila Prabhupada's disciples, the reformers most of all. It would not do to try to purify ISKCON as a substitute for purifying oneself.

Among those who focused on the lack of qualified people to be gurus, some thought the solution was to devise a way to continue the movement and yet eliminate the position of guru as far as possible. Initiations would continue, but the agent would be considered some sort of apprentice, or merely a formal ecclesiastical functionary. To my mind, these people were proposing an essential change in the tradition—the relation between guru and disciple—and not merely an adaptation to new circumstances. Most in this group also awaited the "self-effulgent *acharya*" to lead ISKCON, which, in the interregnum, would make do with semi- or demi-gurus. Captivated as they were by the image of the *acharya* as an absolute and infallible authority whose judgments were indubitably correct, and depending on such a person for their own spiritual security, they had no more enthusiasm for the give-and-take of a collegial body than for the absolutist gurus they opposed. It was my conviction that we had to retain the full-fledged position of guru, as delineated by scripture. Yet that position did not entail being the autonomous autocratic head of an institution; did not essentially disallow discussion, consultation, revision, and adjustment; and did not reject collegial decision making as a kind of *lese majesté*.

The zonal *acharya* position had held that it was intrinsic to the position of guru to be absolute, but the gurus would voluntarily sacrifice this for the sake of the movement. This implied that working with a GBC was an unnatural or artificial accommodation. In truth, the "voluntary sacrifice" looked quite *pro forma*. In response, I argued that it was essential for the *bona fide* guru to be *relative*. After all, Prabhupada stressed that the essential quality of a guru is that he strictly follows the order of his guru. He never becomes the master, but remains always the servant. Consequently, to be a guru in ISKCON it was essential to strictly follow the order of Shrila Prabhupada, who had decreed that all of us must serve cooperatively under the authority of the GBC. Hence, accepting the authority of the GBC board was not an option; it was necessary to guruship itself.

The first effort of the "guru reform movement" was to urge a strengthening commitment to spiritual purification on everyone's part. The second effort was to persuade the GBC to dismantle the zonal *acharya* system efficiently and decisively. We were able to put forward two proposals to the GBC, which, taken together, would accomplish the latter.

The first proposal was to make the process of authorizing new gurus radically more open. Initially, only the guru subcommittee had the power to appoint new gurus; in 1982, it was transferred to a three-fourths vote of the GBC. Under these restrictive procedures, by 1986, only some half dozen more gurus had been added. For a new guru to be provided with an exclusive initiating zone, one or more of the established gurus had to give up some territory. Such boundary changes required negotiations at the highest level. Most gurus seemed reluctant to shrink the area of their authority. From my perspective, the central intent of our proposal was to eliminate the implicit "property requirement" for becoming an initiating guru. This in turn would counter the steady disintegration of ISKCON produced by the zonal *acharya* model, which used common devotion to the reigning guru as the strongest unifying force. As a result, the separate zones became individually far more unified than ISKCON as a whole, which was becoming by the same process increasingly fragmented, turning into a kind of amphictyony of independently empowered leaders. The reform movement, in contrast, envisioned communities in which disciples of many different gurus could all work together for their common cause. The unifying personality was to be the founder-*acharya* of the institution, Shrila Prabhupada, the master of all subsequent gurus and disciples. This change could be achieved by removing the implicit property requirement for being a guru, by opening up the authorizing process and increasing the number of gurus.

Our second proposal was simply that there should be only one *vyasasana* other than Shrila Prabhupada's, to be occupied by any initiating guru. This proposal abolished the exclusive *vyasasana*, the symbol of the zonal *acharya*'s sovereignty. In religions, symbols and that which they symbolize are tightly unified; they could be said to interpenetrate. I realized therefore that if the symbol of the system were eliminated, it would go far to eliminate the system. This proposal also dealt with an impasse within the reform movement: there was little agreement on what to do about the rituals involving the gurus. This proposal simply to remove the exclusive *vyasasana* received a consensus and addressed the need to rectify the rituals, but it left the other issues of ritual until later.

Eventually, both these proposals were put into effect by the GBC. There are now more than fifty initiating gurus in ISKCON, all serving under the commission's direction and fully accountable to it. ISKCON regulations go out of their way to assure that new members are able to freely decide who their guru will be, and most temples have a diverse mix of disciples of different gurus working together. I believe we now have a movement organized the way Shrila Prabhupada wanted it. By itself that does not guarantee the purity of the members, but it is at least a necessary condition for it.

The reform movement was consolidated in 1987, when four more fallen or deviated gurus were removed and fifteen new members elected to the GBC, among them leaders of the reform movement. This has not put an end to controversy, of course. Implicit faith in authority has been shattered, and a number of devotees have gone to extremes to keep their faith in Shrila Prabhupada intact. They could not believe Shrila Prabhupada had intended his own disciples to be initiating gurus, and the "appointment tape" and "July 9 letter" continued to be reinterpreted. The left-wing challenge to gurus has undergone two further incarnations, resting on conspiracy theories and allegations of suppressed instructions of Shrila Prabhupada, who, it is now claimed, wanted the "officiating guru" or *ritvik* system to continue after his demise, so that Prabhupada himself (contrary to all Vaishnava teaching) would continue to initiate disciples posthumously. Thus Prabhupada is let "off the hook."

But he doesn't require this remedy. There is a failure to appreciate the problem Shrila Prabhupada faced in his last days. Certainly he knew his own disciples; he had no illusions about their spiritual qualification. Yet they were pressing for a selection of successor gurus, the ultimate position. Hamsadutta and Kirtanananda had already been rebuked by Shrila Prabhupada for overambitiously receiving *guru puja* "in the presence of the spiritual master." Had there been no indication from Shrila Prabhupada in this matter, there would likely have been chaos. Yet Prabhupada clearly did not want to give his sanction to unfit people. So he selected them without endorsing them. In response to the question of initiation after his departure, Shrila Prabhupada gave a list of "officiating gurus," designating them in an indirect or oblique manner. He expected them to become "regular gurus" in the future, but there was no "hand-picking of successors," no laying on of hands or anointing with oil, no transfer of power to some special and exclusive group. He also knew that some, like Kirtanananda, would initiate with or without his sanction, so he named them. If not, there would likely have been a schism in 1978 instead of 1987. To me, Shrila Prabhupada's solution was brilliant, the best that could have been done under the circumstances. The result would depend upon Krishna.

What ISKCON needed to achieve, at the cost of much conflict and suffering, was no easy thing. The problem was to take an ancient spiritual tradition, long isolated from the impact of modernity, and retrofit it for the modern world, while transplanting it at the same time from its native soil into multiple outside cultures and civilizations—all without vitiating or distorting its essential practices and doctrines. This task has been the endeavor of two generations, and it is far from complete. Reform and renewal must be perpetual engagements. A prerequisite is an ability to be frank and honest about one's own failures and shortcomings, both individually and socially. Only by such humility can ISKCON secure a viable and progressive future for itself.

[11]
THE GUARDIAN OF DEVOTION

Disappearance and Rejection of the Spiritual Master

in ISKCON After 1977

SWAMI BHAKTI BHAVANA VISHNU

THE AUTHOR IS A PRACTITIONER, not a scholar, of religion; as such, I have an obvious "insider" perspective on the topic under consideration. In our postmodern academic environment, it goes without saying that "accurate, objective accounts of . . . religious traditions simply do not exist in their own right. All accounts of religion are accounts by people who approach their study from a particular starting-point."[1] Thus, since objective accounts are impossible—whether authored by practitioners or scholars—disclosure of bias is perhaps the most appropriate and honest course of action.

Our readers are therefore invited to allow for my standpoint as a first-generation member of the disciplic succession of A.C. Bhaktivedanta Swami Prabhupada. Where I differ from other disciples of Bhaktivedanta Swami who have chosen to remain in ISKCON, and of particular relevance to this essay, is in my view that our disciplic line prominently includes Shridhara Goswami, the godbrother of Bhaktivedanta Swami. This claim is based on the long-term intimate relationship of Bhaktivedanta Swami and Shridhara Goswami,[2]

Bhaktivedanta Swami's direct instruction to his disciples to approach Shrid-hara Goswami with their philosophical inquiries after he had passed away,[3] and Shridhara Goswami's formal role as the *sannyasa* initiator of Bhak-tivedanta Swami's *sannyasa guru* (*sannyasa diksha param-guru*).[4]

The primary initiating spiritual master (*diksha-guru*) of both Bhaktivedan-ta Swami and Shridhara Goswami was Bhaktisiddhanta Saraswati Goswami, who founded the Gaudiya Math. During their spiritual master's lifetime, Shridhara Goswami was a highly respected senior disciple in the renounced order, while Bhaktivedanta Swami (then known as Abhay Charanaravinda Das) was a junior householder adherent who worked outside the mission. After Bhaktisiddhanta Saraswati's demise, Shridhara Goswami initiated Bhakti Prajnana Keshava Goswami, another godbrother, into the renounced order of *tridandi sannyasa*, and bestowed the title "Bhaktivedanta" upon Abhay Charanaravinda Das. Bhakti Prajnana Keshava Goswami, in turn, ini-tiated him into the renounced *sannyasa* order, and added the title "Swami" to the latter's name; thus Abhay Charanaravinda Das became known as Bhak-tivedanta Swami.

After the passing of Bhaktisiddhanta Saraswati Goswami, the close relation-ship of Shridhara Goswami with Bhaktivedanta Swami was akin to that of *shiksha-guru*, instructing spiritual master, and disciple. In the Gaudiya Vaish-nava tradition "the spiritual master who initiates according to the regulations of the *shastras* [scriptures] is called the *diksha-guru*, and the spiritual master who gives instructions for elevation is called the *shiksha-guru*."[5] The initiating and instructing spiritual masters are considered "nondifferent"—that is, one is not to make distinctions between them, even though they manifest in dif-ferent bodies.[6] Bhaktivedanta's own words best express his relationship with his senior godbrother:

> I took his [Shridhara Maharaja] advises [*sic*], instructions, very seriously because from the very beginning I know he is a pure Vaishnava, a pure devotee, and I wanted to associate with him and I tried to help him also. Our relationship is very intimate. After the breakdown of the Gaudiya Matha, I wanted to organize another organization, making Shridhara Maharaja the head.[7]

METHODOLOGY

We have chosen a methodological approach for this discussion that has im-plied assumptions, as all methodologies do. Being practitioners, we are as un-comfortable with approaches that go "no further than contorted taxonomies and thick descriptions" as with those with "an irrelevant preoccupation with the derogation of the truth content of religious beliefs."[8] Although we have scant formal training in anthropological, phenomenological, philosophical, sociological, historical, and theological approaches to the critical study of religion, we have tried to adopt a simplified regulative approach, derived from Lindbeck.[9] In Lindbeck's regulative approach,

> emphasis is placed on those respects in which religions resemble languages together with their correlative forms of life and are thus similar to cultures (insofar as these are understood semiotically as reality and value systems—that is, as idioms for the constructing of reality and the living of life). The function of . . . doctrines that becomes most prominent in this perspective is their use, not as expressive symbols or as truth claims, but as communally authoritative rules of discourse, attitude, and action.[10]

Our objective is to establish that certain "communally authoritative rules" regarding the nature and role of the spiritual master are applicable to our discussion, and that such rules constitute an important element in considering the history of ISKCON after 1977. They include (1) the indispensability of the spiritual master; (2) the fundamental identity of the initiating (*diksha*) and instructing (*shiksha*) spiritual masters; (3) the grave repercussions that ensue from rejecting the spiritual master or his instructions; and (4) the dire consequences that result from vilifying a Vaishnava. We will proceed to establish these four rules before considering the history of the institution.

Rule 1. A cursory study of the Gaudiya Vaishnava tradition suffices to establish the indispensability of the spiritual master. In this respect, the *Shvetashvatara Upanishad* (6.23) states: "Only unto those great souls who have implicit faith in both the Lord and the spiritual master, who is His manifestation and non-different from Him, are all the imports of Vedic knowledge automatically revealed."[11] (Although there are various, perhaps more literal, renditions of this verse into English, we have chosen to present a translation from within the Gaudiya Vaishnava tradition, for this particular exegesis constitutes a "communally authoritative rule" among Gaudiyas.) Furthermore, the *Bhagavad Gita*, perhaps the best known Indian scripture, recommends: "Learn the truth through surrender, submissive inquiry, and service. The self-realized soul, who has seen the truth, will enlighten you" (4.34).[12] Finally, the *Prema-bhakti-chandrika*, a specifically Gaudiya Vaishnava text by Narottama Das, unambiguously declares: "Fix your mind on the words emanating from the lotus mouth of the spiritual master. Place your hopes in nothing else. Affection for the guru's lotus feet is the ultimate goal, for by his mercy all of one's aspirations are realized."[13]

Rule 2. The fundamental identity of the initiating and instructing spiritual masters is amply established by Bhaktivedanta Swami in the introduction to chapter 1 of Krishnadas Kaviraja Goswami's *Chaitanya Charitamrita*: "the spiritual master . . . appears in two plenary parts called the initiating spiritual master and instructing spiritual master. They are identical because both of them are phenomenal manifestations of the Supreme Truth."[14] He expounds: "There is no difference between the shelter-giving Supreme Lord and the initiating and instructing spiritual masters. If one foolishly discriminates between them, he commits an offense in the discharge of devotional service."[15]

Rule 3. The grave repercussions that ensue from rejecting the spiritual master or his instructions after approaching and accepting his authority are made clear in *Shrimad Bhagavatam* (11.17.27): "A disciple should consider the teacher to be My very self and never disrespect him in any way."[16] Furthermore, Gaudiya Vaishnavas repeat the following verse by Vishvanatha Chakravarti every morning: "By the mercy of the spiritual master one receives the benediction of Krishna. Without the grace of the spiritual master, one cannot make any advancement."[17]

Rule 4. The dire consequences that result from vilifying a devotee (*vaishnava aparadha*) are stated in numerous passages in the Vaishnava literature. Vilifying a devotee is considered "the mad elephant offense,"[18] for it is said to destroy the creeper of devotion. This is of such importance that another of Bhaktivedanta's godbrothers, Bhakti Pramoda Puri Goswami, has dedicated an entire book to the subject.[19] *Vaishnava aparadha* is listed in the *Padma Purana* (BK 25.15) as the first and foremost of ten offenses to avoid in the chanting of the holy name, the central devotional practice for Gaudiya Vaishnavas.

> One can deliver himself from all offenses at the feet of the Lord by taking shelter of His holy name. But one cannot protect himself if one commits an offense at the feet of the holy name of the Lord. . . . The first offense is to vilify the great devotees who have preached about the glories of the Lord.[20]

There is no doctrinal dispute on these "communally authoritative rules" within the Gaudiya tradition. In this essay we will demonstrate, through historical and textual evidence, two essential points: that Bhaktivedanta Swami (the original initiating guru in ISKCON) instructed his disciples to approach Shridhara Goswami for clarification and application of Gaudiya Vaishnava philosophy; and that the failure to follow this mandate, and the eventual rejection and vilification of Shridhara Goswami by the ISKCON leadership, has resulted in the institutional chaos that continues to this day.

MISSION AND DISAPPEARANCE OF THE
INITIATING SPIRITUAL MASTER

Given the centrality of the spiritual master in Gaudiya Vaishnavism, it should come as no surprise that disturbances occur in the period after his disappearance (in this tradition, the spiritual master is said to appear and disappear, rather than be born and die, a usage that reflects the ontological position of the guru as the representative of God). These disturbances negatively affect the understanding and transmission of his spiritual teachings as well as his institutional arrangements. In this regard, Bhaktivedanta Swami wrote:

> When the acharya (guru) disappears, rogues and non-devotees take advantage and immediately begin to introduce unauthorized principles. . . . The acharya, the authorized representative of the Supreme Lord, establishes these principles, but when he disappears, things once again become disordered.[21]

The spiritual master comes to enlighten his disciples, but in his absence ignorance may once again prevail. This relapse may in part be attributed to human nature, but according to Gaudiya understanding, it also may be due to neglect or rejection of the instructions of the spiritual master.

Bhaktivedanta Swami traveled from India to the West in 1965, and in the short period before his disappearance in 1977, he translated and published more than 60 volumes of Vaishnava literature, circled the world 12 times, established more than 100 temples, and initiated thousands of disciples into a tradition[22] generally unknown in the West until that time. His disciples were mostly young men and women with little or no previous conception of the multifarious spiritual traditions of India, their sophisticated and intricate philosophies, or their arcane practices. If they had any knowledge of yoga and Indian religion, it was limited for the most part to a cursory acquaintance with the physical (external) procedures of hatha yoga, impersonal meditational practices, or the monistic philosophy of Shankaracharya. These had been popularized by a number of swamis and gurus, beginning with Vivekananda in 1893[23] and Yogananda in 1920.[24]

Later on, a veritable flood of gurus traveled west to promote their particular approaches to yogic practice. From Vishnudevananda[25] and the Divine Life Society to Maharishi Mahesh Yogi[26] and Transcendental Meditation—to mention two of the most popular—all advocated variant forms of *advaita vedanta* (impersonal monism). However, no one had attempted to convey the teachings of the exclusive theistic school of Gaudiya Vedanta. In fact, Indologists and religious scholars in the western world were scarcely aware of Gaudiya Vaishnava philosophy and practices before Bhaktivedanta Swami's presentation and exemplification of the tradition.

Gaudiya doctrine, technically known as *achintya bhedabheda tattva vada* (inconceivable and simultaneous difference and oneness), is a presentation of absolute reality that attempts to eschew the extremes of monism and dualism by interpreting material and spiritual realities as energies (*shaktis*) that are simultaneously one with but also different from the supreme personality of godhead. In traditional circles, a lifetime of disciplined study would be expected to understand and put into practice this doctrine, which incorporates and integrates aspects of Ramanuja's *vishishtadvaita vada* (qualified monism), Madhva's *tattva vada* (dualism), Nimbarka's *dvaita advaita vada* (monistic dualism), and Vishnuswami's *shuddhadvaita vada* (pure nondualism).[27]

It was improbable, if not altogether impossible, for the young western disciples of Bhaktivedanta Swami to imbibe and assimilate "the extremely subtle and rarified theology"[28] of Gaudiya Vedanta properly in a scant ten years, especially during a period of great organizational growth in which the rapid recruitment of new adepts required the constant repetition of the most basic instructions, rather than giving scope for delving into the finer points of doctrine. In this regard, Tamal Krishna Goswami, a prominent ISKCON leader and former secretary to Bhaktivedanta Swami, remarked, "Perhaps the most formidable, and certainly the first, obstacle to overcome was his Western audience's relative unfamiliarity with Chaitanya's teachings. He would have to unpack the densely encoded Sanskrit texts for his Western readers. . . . But Prabhupada quickly discovered that while his young American converts could easily modify their hippie habits to conform to the monastic discipline, it was far more difficult for them to leave behind their intellectual baggage."[29]

The literary canon of Gaudiya Vaishnavism includes the Vedas, Upanishads, Puranas, Itihasas, countless commentaries, and innumerable other devotional compositions. The six Goswami disciples of Chaitanya alone, who codified Gaudiya Vaishnava doctrine, produced more than 219 different works in Sanskrit.[30] Even Bhaktivedanta Swami's prolific pen could not make them all available—much less intelligible—to his western disciples in one decade. The *Bhagavad Gita* and the *Chaitanya Charitamrita*, translated into English by Bhaktivedanta Swami, are part of a much larger body of religious literature in Sanskrit and Bengali to which his disciples had virtually no access. His *magnum opus*, the multivolume translation and commentary on the *Shrimad Bhagavatam*, started in 1962, remained incomplete upon his disappearance in 1977. Also unfinished was his emergent effort to inculcate Krishna consciousness in the hearts and minds of western youth who were ill-equipped by reason of birth, culture, language, and upbringing to embrace the breadth and fathom the depths of the Gaudiya tradition.

In an essay entitled "Ending the Fratricidal War" (1985), Ravindra Svarupa Das, a member of ISKCON's Governing Body Commission (GBC), appointed guru, and onetime GBC Chairman, expressed the idea that ISKCON is a society of spiritual neophytes (*kanishtha adhikaris*):

> . . . the leaders, due to spiritual immaturity identify spiritual advancement with organizational advancement. . . . Although they know and intend better, the leaders of ISKCON repeatedly find themselves, to their dismay, involved in highly immature patterns of relationships with others. . . . This anomalous situation can only be attributed to an inheritance from the past.[31]

A decade later (February 1995), after countless upheavals, reforms, and contentious debates, Ravindra Svarupa Das reiterated that ISKCON remains a *kanishtha adhikari* society.[32] And still later, in 2000, he wrote:

> Spiritual immaturity often leads a *kanishtha-adhikari* to identify spiritual advancement with organizational advancement. He thinks that attaining prestige, power and the perquisites of office is evidence of spiritual advancement. Lacking the assets for real spiritual achievement, he substitutes organizational elevation, which he can attain through his cunning or political prowess. He therefore competes intensely with others for high office, and he comes to believe implicitly that one achieves a spiritually elevated state only by becoming victorious over others. In this way material competition becomes institutionalized in *kanishtha-adhikari* societies.[33]

THE INSTRUCTION TO SEEK INSTRUCTION

In an attempt to ensure that his teachings will remain intact after he is no longer physically present in this world, the guru may write books (extensively documenting his teachings), exemplify his teachings personally, give intimate instruction to his leading disciples, and sometimes organize an institution or movement to support the disciples in their daily practice and to distribute his teachings to future generations. From a disciple's perspective, although books, personal example, intimate instructions, and institutions are all very valuable, they are all the products of an enlightened individual, the *tattva darshi* of the *Gita*—one who has seen the truth. Without such an enlightened individual personally present, neophyte disciples may once again become submerged in ignorance. Bhaktivedanta Swami had the foresight to understand this important point, and therefore he instructed his disciples shortly before his disappearance: "In my absence, if you have any question regarding philosophy you may consult my Godbrother, Swami B.R. Shridhara Maharaja at Navadwipa."[34]

Shridhara Goswami joined the Gaudiya Math in 1926 after graduating from Baharampur College; four years later he was awarded the order of *tridandi sannyasa* by his guru, Bhaktisiddhanta Saraswati Goswami. Shridhara Goswami was recognized among his godbrothers as a profound thinker and was widely respected as a learned representative of the theistic conception of Gaudiya Vaishnavism. In this regard, his godbrother Bhakti Pramoda Puri Goswami observes:

From the very beginning of Pujyapada Shridhara Maharaja's life, his adherence to the devotional services of his own guru, Shrila Prabhupada [Bhaktisiddhanta Saraswati Goswami], was super-resplendent. . . . He would so superbly explain each and every word of Shri Gurudeva [Bhaktisiddhanta Saraswati] in such an intensely devotional, melodious way that we would be charmed.

. . . He was never known to give trouble to anyone in any way and never felt himself to be the loser when taking troubles from others. He was completely free from any tinge of malicious anger, which is opposed to pure devotional service. He would always heartily try, with great patience, to resolve any problems arising from the conflicts or disputes between his godbrothers. A natural, simple, and most cordial behavior was always seen on the part of this spotless personality setting an exemplary standard for the *brahmacharis* [celibate students] and *sannyasis* [renounced monastics] of our mission.

In light of his divine knowledge, qualities, devotional services, [and] realization in the field of pure devotional *siddhantas* . . . he is always most worshipable to this insignificant *jiva* soul as one of my *shiksha-gurus*.[35]

Bhaktisiddhanta Saraswati Goswami greatly appreciated Shridhara Maharaja's writings and stated publicly, regarding his presentation of Gaudiya philosophy: "I am satisfied that after me what I came to say, that will stay, that will remain."[36] Moreover, Shridhara Goswami's commentary on the Gayatri mantra, "Sri Gayatri Nigudartha,"[37] was prized by the members of the Gaudiya family as an unprecedented and significant contribution to Gaudiya Vaishnavism.[38]

Bhaktivedanta Swami and Shridhara Goswami lived together in the same quarters for many years during and after the well-known disintegration in the 1940s of the Gaudiya Math, the formal institution of their spiritual master, Bhaktisiddhanta Saraswati Goswami. During this period of intimate exchange, Bhaktivedanta Swami "wanted to organize another organization, making

Shridhara Maharaja the head."[39] Bhaktivedanta Swami held Shridhara Goswami in the highest regard, as the record of their long and intimate relationship through almost five decades demonstrates:

So, we are very fortunate to hear His Divine Grace, Om Vishnupada Paramahamsa Parivrajakacharya Bhakti Rakshaka Shridhara Maharaja. By age and by experience, in both ways, he is senior to me. I was fortunate to have his association since a very long time, perhaps in 1930.[40]

So, by guru and Vaishnava, whatever position I have got it is by guru's mercy and the blessings of the Vaishnava. Otherwise, how I may have? So, I wish that Shridhara Maharaja may bestow his blessings as he was doing always, and may Guru Maharaja help me so I can do some service. By his grace it has become successful. I have no credit. I do not know how things are happening, because I am not at all qualified: *chadiya vaishnava seva, nishtara payeche keba* [without serving an ideal Vaishnava, who can be delivered from the clutches of *maya*]?[41]

What Shripada Shridhara Maharaja has directed, I take it on my head. He is my always well-wisher. After the departure of Prabhupada [Bhaktisiddhanta Saraswati Thakur] it is appropriate that I should accept his direction. . . . [42]

So, if you are actually sincere to take instructions from a *shiksha-guru*, I can refer you to the one who is most highly competent of all my Godbrothers. This is B.R. Shridhara Maharaja, whom I consider to be even my *shiksha-guru*, so what to speak of the benefit that you can have by his association. So, if you are serious about the advancement of your spiritual life, I will advise you to go to Shridhara Maharaja. It will be very good for your spiritual benefit, and I will feel that you are safe. When I was in India with the others, we lived with Shridhara Maharaja. You can also make arrangements for your other Godbrothers to go there in the future.[43]

In the first quotation of this series, Bhaktivedanta Swami refers to Shridhara Goswami in the formal address and with the full appellation reserved for the most revered spiritual masters in the Gaudiya tradition (His Divine Grace, Om Vishnupada Paramahamsa Parivrajakacharya). In the second one, he expressly asks "that Shridhara Maharaja may bestow his blessings as he was doing always." And in the third and fourth, he explicitly defines their relationship as one in which Shridhara Goswami assumes the role of his *shiksha-guru*, instructing spiritual master. Furthermore, as early as 1969[44] and up until his disappearance in 1977,[45] Bhaktivedanta Swami encouraged his closest disciples to accept the instruction of Shridhara Goswami, as they themselves initially acknowledged:

> He [Bhaktivedanta Swami] has given explicit desires, but he told us that, on other technical points and other matters of philosophy, if there was question we should approach you [Shridhara Goswami].[46]

> . . . Shridhara Swami, who Shrila Prabhupada said we should consult about philosophy and practical points.[47]

ISKCON leaders were manifestly impressed with Shridhara Goswami, as is evident from the following recorded exchanges between them:

> Our Guru Maharaja [Bhaktivedanta Swami] was kind upon us, so you are kind upon us. I find no difference at all in how you [Shridhara Goswami] are blessing us. When I used to come every year to Mayapur, my whole purpose in coming was fulfilled when I would be in his [Bhaktivedanta Swami's] association. So similarly, now I am feeling that as I have come here, that my purpose is being fulfilled, whenever I am in your association.[48]

> I take it that Prabhupada is speaking to us through you [Shridhara Goswami].[49]

> Shridhara Maharaja's instructions are nondifferent than Prabhupada's.[50]

Following the instruction of Bhaktivedanta Swami, ISKCON's Governing Body Commission (GBC) approached Shridhara Goswami in March 1978 (five months after the disappearance of Bhaktivedanta Swami) for clarification on particular points regarding the position of the new initiating gurus.[51] For over two continuous years the leaders and members of ISKCON regularly took guidance and instruction from Shridhara Goswami in philosophical matters. On several occasions, when fighting and confusion broke out among the new gurus, Shridhara Goswami guided the institution through troubled times:

> I think it's very encouraging for everyone to hear how our spiritual uncle Shrila Shridhara Maharaja . . . [is helping us] . . . I thought the issues they discussed were very significant for my disciples, especially because of the answers given by Shrila Shridhara Maharaja, and the way the GBC members responded to him, bringing about a resolution under Shrila Shridhara Maharaja's guidance. Just before his disappearance, His Divine Grace Shrila Prabhupada, our beloved spiritual master and the Founder-Acharya

of ISKCON, said that we should go to his Godbrother Shridhara Maharaja for guidance on philosophy, after the disappearance of Shrila Prabhupada. So, this talk of October certainly showed the GBC doing this, and Shrila Shridhara Maharaja fulfilling this role, as Prabhupada requested he do for the disciples of Shrila Prabhupada.[52]

Some ISKCON leaders belatedly suggest that Shridhara Goswami should be held responsible for the internal problems that developed in ISKCON after the disappearance of the institution's founder. In particular, blame has been assigned to him for the zonal *acharya* (guru) system established in ISKCON in 1978, in which new devotees were directed to accept initiation from whatever guru had administrative responsibility over the particular geographic zone where they happened to encounter the movement (see Deadwyler's essay in this volume).

In the controversy over the zonal *acharya* system, Shridhara Goswami gave explicit direction from the very beginning that such a system of initiations in ISKCON would not be a good idea.[53] He suggested to the leadership that newcomers in Krishna consciousness should be given time to hear from different people and then choose to whom they would submit according to their faith (*shraddha*), not according to the dictates of geography. To this effect, Shridhara Goswami stated in March 1978:

> According to his *shraddha* [faith] a newcomer should be given some time. Who will come to be initiated, he should be given some time for a fair period of time to hear from different persons and then the *shraddha*, the faith, will be awakened. Will be considered (by faith) to whom he will submit. Do you follow?[54]

Ignoring this advice, ISKCON leaders implemented the zonal *acharya* system, which has left the society reeling and in a state of disorder for the past twenty-four years.

LETTER OF PRADYUMNA TO SATSVARUPA GOSWAMI

Shortly after the eleven initiating gurus assumed their positions in 1978, Pradyumna Das, a senior disciple of Bhaktivedanta Swami, perceived anomalies in their conduct. Concerned that the new gurus were transgressing proper Vaishnava etiquette by assuming an elevated status and in their behavior toward their nonguru godbrothers,[55] he consulted with Shridhara Goswami about the standard understanding of guru protocol in the Gaudiya *sampradaya*. Encouraged by Shridhara Goswami's comprehensive explanations,

Pradyumna, paraphrasing what he had heard,[56] wrote a letter to Satsvarupa Goswami,[57] a GBC member and one of the eleven new gurus, wherein he comprehensively expressed his fears for ISKCON's future, gave a detailed explanation of Gaudiya Vaishnava *sadachara* (etiquette) in regard to the guru, and proposed steps for rectification.

The GBC's immediate response to this letter was to expel Pradyumna from ISKCON. Some gurus defended their opulent worship by stating that they were following the standard set by the Founder-*Acharya*, Bhaktivedanta Swami.[58] However, Ravindra Svarupa writes, "The force of this position is somewhat weakened when it is seen how its proponents tend to be selective in its application."[59] Years later, after much protest by godbrothers,[60] it was openly acknowledged by the GBC that the statements in Pradyumna's letter were entirely accurate.[61] However, it wasn't until 1999 that the GBC issued an official apology to Pradyumna Das for neglecting his lucid advice.[62]

Despite having received Pradyumna's foreboding letter in 1978 and personally hearing such instructions innumerable times from Shridhara Goswami, Satsvarupa Goswami in his "Revised Guru Worship" paper of 1985 pleaded ignorance, that "we did not know what to do [in regard to excessive guru worship] because there was no precedent or scriptural rule that told us specifically what to do." Rather than admit their faults and their neglect of Shridhara Goswami's pertinent advice for the well-being of ISKCON, leaders such as Jayapataka Swami[63] and Tamal Krishna Goswami[64] attempted to blame Shridhara Goswami for their own past deviations.

A careful study of Shridhara Goswami's instructions and the policies implemented by the GBC over the years shows that the GBC was very selective in its application of those instructions. Shridhara Goswami was consulted on certain issues, but his advice for reform was repeatedly ignored and misconstrued.[65] It was only after repeated requests by godbrothers that the ISKCON gurus were forced to implement the very reforms he had advised from the beginning.[66]

REJECTION OF THE INSTRUCTING SPIRITUAL MASTER

In August 1980, the relationship between ISKCON leaders and Shridhara Goswami was on the verge of a serious breakdown. Bhakti Caru Swami (a member of ISKCON's Governing Body Commission) related the following to Shridhara Goswami: "Prabhupada gave an instruction that if we have any difficulty then we should come to you, but they (GBC) are deliberately neglecting that instruction of Shrila Prabhupada."[67] Again in 1982, Bhakti Charu Swami repeated: "Maharaja, time will prove that they [ISKCON leaders] are wrong, and you are right."[68]

The leaders of ISKCON were in the beginning very satisfied and encouraged by the guidance they received from Shridhara Goswami,[69] although they did not follow it closely. None of the society's leaders or members felt that Shridhara Goswami posed any danger to Bhaktivedanta Swami's movement. On the contrary, they felt very fortunate to have the guidance and blessing of the most senior Gaudiya Vaishnava in Bengal, and ISKCON's elite GBC gurus regularly attended his talks. Shridhara Goswami was known by his followers as the venerated Guardian of Devotion, and ISKCON considered itself privileged to have his guidance. He was seen as a conciliator, not an aggressor, and his affectionate help was always welcome whenever the disciples of Bhaktivedanta Swami faced any difficulties.[70]

But all was not well. The society experienced repeated problems, mostly concerning the new gurus. ISKCON advocated the position that the new gurus were pure devotees of Krishna (infallible souls) and that they could never fall down to material ignorance. There were heated debates over the gurus' infallibility, and ultimately anyone who did not accept it was ejected from the movement and branded as envious.

Although many disciples of Bhaktivedanta Swami were forced to leave the movement between 1979 and 1980, the concerns surrounding the new gurus did not diminish. Eventually it became known to the general membership of ISKCON that several of the new gurus (purportedly abstemious and celibate monks) were indulging in sex and intoxication. Shridhara Goswami tried his best to make peace among the fighting groups of ISKCON members by repeatedly suggesting that they "Call for a meeting."[71] The leaders (particularly the new gurus) did not care for his advice, and in 1982 they officially severed ties with him and declared him the enemy of Bhaktivedanta Swami, ostensibly because his "presentation of Krishna consciousness often differs from that of Shrila Prabhupada."[72]

In many cases intimidation, threats of violence, and even actual physical assault were employed by ISKCON leaders to deter members from communicating or associating with Shridhara Goswami. Jayadvaita Swami, an ISKCON guru and long-time leader, recalled the dynamic over this issue: "The GBC [ISKCON's Governing Body Commission] displayed naiveté, incompetence, crudeness, offensiveness, and gross self-interest in dealings with B.R. Shridhara Maharaja."[73] Increasing self-interest produced such insensitivity that the ISKCON leaders even abused Shridhara Goswami directly and personally. Shridhara Goswami was reduced to saying:

I am an old man. I am tired, exhausted. I am very, very sorry (crying). Really I say with folded palms that you are ill-treating me. I am very sorry. Swami Maharaja [Bhaktivedanta Swami] was so affectionate, I also treated with such affection to him. And rudely you are behaving towards me. I am very much mortified for that, but what can I do? I am a small man.[74]

The tears of Shridhara Goswami broke the hearts of many sincere followers and disciples of Bhaktivedanta Swami who perceived him as ISKCON's affectionate well-wisher.[75] A more candid explanation for ostracizing Shridhara Goswami, the Guardian of Devotion, is perhaps the fact that many members of the society began to follow him instead of accepting the dictates of the new gurus. ISKCON Law #12.5.9 1 codified the institution's reaction to this perceived threat:

A. In obedience to the instruction of His Divine Grace A.C. Bhaktivedanta Swami Prabhupada, the GBC directs that the members of ISKCON should respect all senior Gaudiya Vaishnavas outside ISKCON, but should not intimately associate with them, personally or through printed or recorded media, for guidance, teaching, instruction, or initiation as their presentation of Krishna consciousness often differs from that of Shrila Prabhupada in emphasis, balance and other aspects of both teaching and practice.

B. This resolution is intended to apply categorically to all ISKCON members. ISKCON leaders' first responsibility is to give considerate direction, guidance, and counseling to any ISKCON devotees personally affected by this resolution so as to bring them back to the path set by Shrila Prabhupada.

In any case, those who continue to act in violation of this resolution are subject to sanctions by temple presidents and GBC zonal secretaries, who may exercise their discretion to prohibit any such devotees from living on ISKCON properties or participating in ISKCON functions.

Those who persist in violating this resolution are cautioned they may be reported to the GBC Executive Committee for immediate action or action at the following year's annual GBC meeting. The Executive Committee is hereby given authority to suspend any violator from ISKCON.[76]

Although the GBC rejected Shridhara Goswami's advice in 1982 and launched a rancorous propaganda campaign[77] in order to discourage its members from further associating with and taking instruction from him,[78] not all ISKCON members complied. Perceiving that Bhaktivedanta Swami's instruction to take advice from Shridhara Goswami had been discarded, and that ISKCON leaders had rejected and personally insulted the Guardian of Devotion, the loyal followers of Shridhara Goswami both inside and outside ISKCON were outraged.[79] This reversal in policy toward him led to the first major schism after the disappearance of the institution's founder. Those members who felt enlightened by Shridhara Goswami and who understood his instructions as being in complete harmony with the teachings of Bhaktivedanta Swami were eventually forced out of ISKCON.

Jayadvaita Swami acknowledged that:

> The GBC and its members have allowed, have failed to halt, have defended, have encouraged, and have deliberately brought about mistreatment and persecution of innocent persons.[80]

The hard-line approach served no real purpose, except to alienate more members. According to several sources, ISKCON had more than 5,000 full-time members at the time of the schism,[81] the immediate result of which was that in 1981–82 more than 500 devotees left ISKCON worldwide. The devotees who have left since then are now counted in the thousands. Currently many ISKCON temples worldwide are severely understaffed, a number of them are permanently closed, and as of early 2002, at least 12 more have declared bankruptcy.

Of the more than 5,000 disciples initiated directly by Bhaktivedanta Swami, it is estimated that only between 5 and 20 percent are active in ISKCON today. The exact figure is not known precisely, yet estimates range from 500[82] (5 percent of initiated disciples) to 1,000 worldwide[83] (20 percent of total). And in an article entitled "Where Have All the Krishnas Gone?" the *Boston Phoenix* reported that there are scarcely 800 ISKCON members left in the United States today, disciples and grand-disciples of Bhaktivedanta Swami included.[84] One can therefore conclude that the previous rapid growth of ISKCON was reversed after the expulsion of the followers of Shridhara Goswami.

THE GUARDIAN OF DEVOTION

ISKCON is no longer the only organized representative of the Gaudiya tree in the West. In addition to the many other devotees who have left ISKCON and are pursuing and propagating Gaudiya Vaishnavism independently, the followers of Shridhara Goswami established a printing press in 1982 and began the systematic publication and distribution of his teachings in the western world on a large scale. The highest concentrations of devotees to initially leave ISKCON and follow Shridhara Goswami resided in Central and South America, where a dozen temples with all their residents gave up all formal connection with ISKCON and formed their own Krishna consciousness societies.

Since then, followers of Shridhara Goswami have established and manage temples and other centers in Murwillumbah (Australia); Vienna (Austria);

Buenos Aires, Mendoza, and Tucumán (Argentina); La Paz (Bolivia); Sao Paulo, Rio de Janeiro, Resende, Porto Alegre, Florianapolis, and Parana (Brazil); Sofía (Bulgaria); Antofagasta, Arica, Calama, Catemu, Concepción, Copiapó, Cuarnilahue, Iquique, La Serena, Linares, Santiago, Temuco, Tocopilla, and Valparaíso (Chile); Arbelaez, Armenia, Barranquilla, and Belalcazar (Caldas); Bogotá, Bucaramanga, Cali, Cartagena, Cúcuta, Florida, and Granada, Ibagué, Manizales, Medellín, Neiva, Pasto, Pereira, Popayán, Santa Marta, Tuluá, Ubaté, and Villavicencio (Colombia); San José (Costa Rica); Baños, Puyo, Guayaquil, Quito, and Rio Bamba (Ecuador); El Salvador; Saru Lautoka (Fiji); Berlin and Freiburg (Germany); Guatemala; Tegucigalpa (Honduras); Budapest, Nandafalva, Szeged, Eger, Gyor, Debrecen, and Pécs (Hungary); Navadvipa, Calcutta, Chiriamore, Hapaniya, Bamunpara, Jagannatha Puri, Orissa, Mathura, Vrindavan, Mayapura, Sri Rangapatna, Mysore, and Bangalore (India); County Kildare (Ireland); Usmate-Velate (Italy); Perak, Kuala Lumpur, and Sitiawan (Malaysia); Yucatan, Guadalajara, Nuevo León, Colonia del Valle, Tijuana, Veracruz, Orizaba, México, D.F., and Michoacán (Mexico); Buiten and Amsterdam (Netherlands); Auckland (New Zealand); Arequipa, Callao, Cuzco, Huancayo, Chiclayo, Ilo, and Lima (Peru); Manila (Philippines); Coimbra (Portugal); Moscow and St. Petersburg (Russia); Singapore; KwaZulu Natal, Johannesburg, and Pietermaritzburg (South Africa); Thun (Switzerland); Ankara (Turkey); London (U.K.); Soquel, Philo, and San Jose, CA, Boston, MA, Oaklyn, NJ, Maui and Honokaa, HI, West Pawlet, VT, and Miami, FL (U.S.A.); and Caracas and Isla de Margarita (Venezuela). There are also numerous devotees in Belgium, Croatia, Mauritius, Puerto Rico, Serbia, and various cities in the United States.[85]

ISKCON is not only losing members but also confronting enormous challenges that threaten its survival. As the GBC concluded at its 1996 special meeting in Abentheur, the house is on fire:

> The movement faces serious social problems. Devotees are dissatisfied, confused about their responsibilities and hampered in achieving their full potentials. Everyone is suffering, leaders as well as rank-and-file. Women, children and cows are unprotected and abused. Many who for years dedicated themselves to preaching and devotional service are now outsiders. Others are "hanging on" with diminishing hope of finding a secure, decent life in ISKCON. Others who should be free to be models of renunciation and spiritual leadership are perceived to be entangled with money and power.[86]

Such problems have not escaped the attention of the media. The *Hindustan Times*, India's largest English-language newspaper, noted:

Times haven't been exactly smooth for the Hare Krishna cult these past few years, the ISKCON boat being rocked off and on by controversies ranging from child abuse, rape, suicide and bitter factional fights in India and other parts of the world.[87]

Warring ISKCON factions have now dragged one another into the American and Indian court systems, where they seek to settle their differences. It is ironic that after rejecting the guidance of Shridhara Goswami, ISKCON has submitted to a mundane judicial system for clarification of philosophical disputes. It is important to note that although ISKCON leaders cast aside Shridhara Goswami's repeated advice regarding the zonal *acharya* system (1978 GBC session[88] and numerous later sessions[89]), proper treatment of nonguru godbrothers (1978 and later sessions[90]), and excessive guru worship (18 August 1980),[91] all of his instructions proved to be correct[92] and were officially implemented by the GBC without giving Shridhara Goswami credit.

I have acknowledged my own contextuality as a follower of Shridhara Goswami in conformity with the ideals of postmodern academic disclosure of bias. From this perspective, it is our assessment that the difficulties that developed in ISKCON after Bhaktivedanta Swami's disappearance were caused by disobedience of the instruction of the spiritual master and vilification of his highly respected and intimate godbrother, Shridhara Goswami. They are predictable outcomes of the rejection of the spiritual master, according to the "communally authoritative rules" that Gaudiya Vaishnavas accept universally. Bhaktivedanta Swami's dictum to accept the guidance of Shridhara Goswami as instructing spiritual master was ISKCON's singular prospect for continued spiritual growth and healthy development after the disappearance of the Founder-*Acharya*.[93] Until the leadership once again accepts the order of Bhaktivedanta Swami to abide by the instruction of Shridhara Goswami (available through his writings and the guidance of his senior disciples) and contritely apologizes for offending the pure devotee, ISKCON cannot claim to represent the Gaudiya tradition faithfully.

During late 2001 and early 2002, Swami B.G. Narasingha met extensively with ISKCON GBC representatives Bir Krishna Das Goswami, Guru Prasad Swami, and Keshava Bharati Das to discuss some issues pertaining to the society's relationship with Shridhara Goswami. Foremost was the erroneous but persistent attempt by prominent ISKCON leaders to blame Shridhara Goswami for the adoption of the disastrous zonal *acharya* system after the disappearance of Bhaktivedanta Swami.

At the 2002 Annual Meeting, held in Mayapura, India, during the month of March, the ISKCON Governing Body Commission (GBC) approved the following resolution, by a vote of 26 in the affirmative and one abstention.

403. Shripad Shridhar Maharaja and the Zonal Acharya System

Whereas, a committee composed of Bir Krishna Das Goswami, Guru Prasad Swami and Kesava Bharati Das met and discussed with Bhakti Gaurava Narasimha Swami the issue of Shripad B.R. Shridhar Maharaja's relationship to the establishment of the zonal-acharya system in ISKCON;

Whereas, the GBC Body recognizes that there may be a mistaken perception in some circles that the GBC holds Shripad B.R. Shridhar Maharaja responsible for ISKCON's acceptance of the zonal-acharya system;

[STATEMENT] Resolved, That the impression that may exist in some circles that the GBC Body regards Shripad B.R. Shridhar Maharaja as responsible for ISKCON's accepting the zonal-acharya system is erroneous. The GBC Body realizes that regardless of how the zonal-acharya system evolved, it alone is responsible for its acceptance and implementation. Any imputation that Shripad B.R. Shridhar Maharaja is responsible is wrong. In this regard the GBC Body would like to restate, as per resolution 76 of the 1987 Annual General Meeting, that "ISKCON devotees should strictly avoid hearing or speaking personal criticism of Shripad B.R. Shridhar Maharaja."

The adoption of this resolution is both a current manifestation and a harbinger of profound changes in the society founded by A.C. Bhaktivedanta Swami Prabhupada. We hope that the thesis presented in this essay—that the multifarious problems faced by ISKCON since the disappearance of Bhaktivedanta Swami are due, in no small measure, to offenses against Shridhara Maharaja and refusal to accept his perfect instruction—will be further validated by the society's gradual and welcome return to the fold of orthodox Gaudiya Vaishnavism.

NOTES

1. P. Connolly, ed., *Approaches to the Study of Religion* (London and New York: Cassell, 1999), 1.
2. Bhaktivedanta Swami and B.R. Shridhara Goswami, Room Conversation, 17 March 1973 (BBT Archives 730317RC.MAY), first two paragraphs missing from BBT translation. Available online as an MP3 audio file: http://www.gosai.com/tattva/.
3. Bhaktivedanta Swami, room conversation with disciples (Tamal Krishna Goswami, Hansadutta-Das, Swami B.V. Tripurari and others), witnesses' testimony (recording not available), Vrindavan, India, October 1977. Corroborating statements of leading disciples presented later: Jayapataka Swami (note 46), Giriraja Goswami (note 47), Satsvarupa Goswami (note 52), and Bhakti Charu Swami (note 67).

4. Bhaktivedanta Swami was ordained into the *sannyasa* order by Bhaktiprajnana Keshava Goswami, a *sannyasa* disciple of Shridhara Goswami.

5. Bhaktivedanta Swami, Cc. Madhya 8.128, purport, Bhaktivedanta VedaBase 4.11.

6. "The initiating and instructing spiritual masters are equal and identical manifestations of Krishna, although they have different dealings. Their function is to guide the conditioned souls back home, back to Godhead." Bhaktivedanta Swami, SMD (new98) 2.5, Other Important Instructions Concerning the Spiritual Master, Bhaktivedanta VedaBase 4.11 (Sandy Ridge, NC: Bhaktivedanta Archives).

7. Bhaktivedanta Swami and B.R. Shridhara Goswami, Room Conversation, 17 March 1973 (BBT Archives 730317RC.MAY).

8. E. T. Lawson and Robert N. McCauley, *Rethinking Religion: Connecting Cognition and Culture* (Cambridge: Cambridge University Press, 1990), 1.

9. G. A. Lindbeck, *The Nature of Doctrine: Religion and Theology in a Postliberal Age* (Philadelphia: Westminster Press, 1984), 32–45.

10. Ibid., 17–18.

11. Quoted in Swami B.P. Puri Maharaja, *The Art of Sadhana* (San Francisco: Mandala Publishing Group, 1999), 111.

12. Ibid., 98.

13. Ibid., 110.

14. Bhaktivedanta Swami, *Chaitanya Charitamrita*, Adi 1: the Spiritual Masters, Bhaktivedanta VedaBase 4.11.

15. Ibid., Adi 1.47.

16. B.P. Puri Maharaja, *The Art of Sadhana*, 106.

17. Vishvanatha Chakravarti, "Eight Prayers to the Guru," in Bhaktivedanta Swami, Bhaktivedanta VedaBase 4.11.

18. Bhaktivedanta Swami, Cc. Madhya 19.156, purport, Bhaktivedanta VedaBase 4.11.

19. B.P. Puri Maharaja, *The Heart of Krishna* (San Francisco: Mandala Publishing Group, 1995).

20. Bhaktivedanta Swami, SB 2.1.11, purport, Bhaktivedanta VedaBase 4.11.

21. Bhaktivedanta Swami, *Shrimad-Bhagavatam*, 4.28.48, purport, Bhaktivedanta Book Trust, 1975.

22. Vaishnavism, the worship of Vishnu, is represented in India by four main schools, or *sampradayas*. Gaudiya Vaishnavas are members of the Brahma-Madhva *sampradaya*, which was reformed by Shri Krishna Chaitanya Mahaprabhu 500 years ago.

23. Swami Vivekananda represented Hinduism at the first World Parliament of Religions in Chicago in 1893. Subsequently he was invited to speak all over America and Europe.

24. In 1920 Yogananda was a delegate to an international congress of religious leaders in Boston. He established the Self-Realization Fellowship in 1925.

25. Swami Vishnudevananda founded and directed the International Shivananda Yoga Vedanta Centers in the USA and Canada.

26. Maharishi founded Transcendental Meditation and the Spiritual Regeneration Movement in 1957.

27. For a succinct, if somewhat heterodox summary of Gaudiya Vaishnavism, see S. K. De, *Early History of the Vaishnava Faith and Movement in Bengal*, 2nd ed. (Calcutta: K. L. Mukhopadhyata, 1961).

28. E. C. Dimock Jr., *The Place of the Hidden Moon: Erotic Mysticism in the Vaishnava-sahajiya Cult of Bengal* (Chicago: University of Chicago Press, 1989), xviii.

29. Tamal Krishna Goswami, *The Perils of Succession: Heresies of Authority and Continuity In the Hare Krishna Movement*, www.iskcon.com/ICJ/5_1/5_1perils.htm.

30. Dimock Jr., *The Place of the Hidden Moon*, 77.

31. Ravindra Svarupa, "Ending the Fratricidal War," unpublished manuscript, 1985; available at http://www.harekrishna.asn.au/speakers/ravindra_svarupa_prabhu/spiritual_reform.doc.

32. Ravindra Svarupa Das, Public Statement to ISKCON members, Mayapur, India, 1995.

33. Ravindra Svarupa Das, "Pillars of Success: The Principles and Practices of Reform in ISKCON," *ISKCON Communications Journal* 7 (2) (Dec. 1999); http://www.iskcon.com/icj/7.2/72rsd.html.

34. Bhaktivedanta Swami, room conversation with disciples (Tamal Krishna Goswami, Hansadutta Das, Swami B.V. Tripurari and others), witnesses' testimony (recording not available), Vrindavan, India, October 1977.

35. B.P. Puri Goswami, *Exalted Glorification of Parama-Pujyapada Shrila Shridhara Dev* (Mayapur: Gopinatha Gaudiya Math, 1993).

36. Remarks to his *sannyasa* disciple, Shrauti Goswami, and to Shriyukta Aprakrita, in Swami B.A. Sagar, *Shrila Guru Maharaja, His Divine Pastimes and Precepts in Brief* (Nabadwip: Sri Chaitanya Saraswata Matha, 1994), 48.

37. Shridhara Goswami, *Subjective Evolution of Consciousness* (San Jose, CA: Guardian of Devotion Press, 1989), chapter 12, "The Gayatri Mantra." Available online: http://www.gosai.com/tattva/.

38. B.P. Puri Goswami, *Exalted Glorification of Parama-Pujyapada Shrila Shridhara Dev* (Mayapur, Bengal: Gopinatha Gaudiya Matha, 1993).

39. Bhaktivedanta Swami and B.R. Shridhara Goswami, Room Conversation, 17 March 1973 (BBT Archives 730317RC.MAY), available online: http://www.gosai.com/tattva/.

40. Ibid.

41. Ibid.

42. Bhaktivedanta Swami, Letter to Govinda Maharaja, 29 January 1969.

43. Bhaktivedanta Swami, Letter to Hrishikesa Das, 31 January 1969.

44. Ibid.

45. Bhaktivedanta Swami and B.R. Shridhara Goswami, Room Conversation, March 1977 (SSM Archives 770300RC.SM).

46. Jayapataka Swami, Room Conversation of GBC body with B.R. Shridhara Goswami, Navadvipa, India, March 1978 (SSM Archives 780300SM.GBC). Available online: http://www.gosai.com/tattva/.

47. Giriraja Swami, Letter to GBC, 16 September 1978.

48. Tamal Krishna Goswami, Bhaktivedanta Swami's secretary, GBC member, and new guru, Room Conversation with B.R. Shridhara Goswami, Navadvipa, India, 26 February 1981 (SSM Archives 810226SM.ST).

49. Rameshvara Swami, GBC member and new guru, Room Conversation with B.R. Shridhara Goswami, Navadvipa, India, 5 March 1981. (SSM Archives 810305SM.ST).

50. Achyutananda Das, "Autobiography of A Jewish Yogi," unpublished manuscript.

51. GBC body, Room Conversation with B.R. Shridhara Goswami, Navadvipa, India, March 1978 (SSM Archives 780300SM.GBC). Available online: http://www.gosai.com/tattva.

52. Tape recording, 21 October 1980, Swami Satsvarupa; in author's possession.

53. GBC body, Room Conversation with B.R. Shridhara Goswami, Navadvipa, India, March 1978 (SSM Archives 780300SM.GBC).

54. Ibid.

55. "Somehow or other, large numbers of Shrila Prabhupada's disciples feel strongly disturbed, discouraged, bitter, offended, confused, angry, or unhappy because of their relationship with their godbrothers who have 'accepted the mantle' as initiating gurus." Jayadvaita Swami, 1982 letter to GBC.

56. Pradyumna Das, series of 1978 Room Conversations with Shridhara Goswami (SSM Archives).

57. Pradyumna Das, Letter to Satsvarupa Goswami, 7 August 1978. Available online: http://www.gosai.com/tattva/.

58. "Specifically regarding the guru-puja, we took the precedent of Prabhupada himself, who accepted a daily guru-puja and considered it an important function." Guru Worship Reform, Satsvarupa Goswami, 21 September 1985. Letter to disciples; in author's possession.

59. Serving Shrila Prabhupada's Will, Ravindra Svarupa, 14 September 1985. Unpublished manuscript distributed among ISKCON members; copy in author's possession.

60. Somaka Maharaja, "In Search of Harmony," 1994. Article distributed by Somaka Maharaja; copy in author's possession.

61. Pradyumna's lucid statement of the misunderstanding [*acharya* implementation in ISKCON] would be difficult to improve on. Reading this letter seven years after it was written, one is astonished by the perspicuous way Pradyumna spells out the issue and by the accuracy with which he foresees the evil consequences of this misunderstanding. Ravindra Svarupa, Under My Order . . . , Reflections on the Guru in ISKCON, unpublished manuscript, 17 August 1985, 4.

62. "The GBC Body extends its heartfelt apologies to Shriman Pradyumna Das Adhikari for any offences caused in its dealings with him in 1978–9. During this period Pradyumna Prabhu wrote to the GBC via Satsvarupa Das Goswami warning them of serious repercussions with the Zonal Acharya system in his letter dated 7th August 1978. Unfortunately Pradyumna Prabhu's good advice was not taken seriously. In retrospect the GBC Body and ISKCON could have benefited greatly by heeding his well-meant and pertinent observations. Although it is now many years hence, we nevertheless wish to state publicly that we sincerely regret the actions and words of the GBC Body that contributed to his leaving his active service in ISKCON. We unreservedly and humbly beg the forgiveness of Pradyumna Prabhu for any offences caused to him by our dealings." 403 Action Order, B. APOLOGY TO PRADYUMNA PRABHU FROM GBC BODY, 1999 GBC Resolutions, http://www.vnn.org/world/WD9903/WD31–3455.html.

63. 1998 Vyasa Puja Offering to Swami Bhaktivedanta, Jayapataka Swami, http://www.vnn.org/editorials/ET9809/ET08–2172.html.

64. See Tamal Krishna Goswami's own "The Perils of Succession: Heresies of Authority and Continuity In the Hare Krishna Movement", n.d., http://www.iskcon.com/ICJ/5_1/5_1perils.htm.

65. Ibid. Tamal Krishna Goswami quotes Shridhara Goswami's advice (SSM Archives 780300SM.GBC) that the guru must be autonomous, but fails to mention that Shridhara Goswami states in the same session that such advice is not possible prac-

tically to apply in such a large society as ISKCON, thus erroneously drawing his conclusion that Shridhara Goswami's advice is wrong. Tamal Krishna Goswami also fails to mention that countless question-and-answer sessions in 1978, 1980, 1981, and 1982 were attended by himself, as well as by a significant number of other prominent ISKCON leaders (transcriptions available), where all such guru reform instructions (zonal *acharya*, guru opulence, and guru expansion) were carefully re-iterated in painstaking detail by Shridhara Goswami. Time and the GBC's own admission has shown such advice to be correct.

66. "Is the GBC going to recognize that in the letter that Pradyumna Prabhu wrote to Satsvarupa Maharaja in '78 he pointed out all the defects that in '87 due to so many fall downs they had to admit?" Somaka Maharaja, "In Search of Harmony," 1994.

67. Bhakti Charu Swami, Room Conversation with B.R. Shridhara Goswami, 19 August 1980 (SSM Archives 810819SM.ST).

68. Bhakti Charu Swami, Room Conversation with B.R. Shridhara Goswami, 5 February 1982 (SSM Archives 810205SM.ST).

69. Shridhara Goswami counseled ISKCON's GBC to expand the number of new gurus (1978 GBC session); reduce excessive guru worship (18 August 1980); establish a nonzonal *acharya* system based on the faith of initiates (1978 session); maintain and promote proper treatment of nonguru godbrothers (1978 GBC session); and adopt a proper vision of first-initiated disciples of Bhaktivedanta Swami who took *mantra diksha* (second initiation) from a godbrother guru (1978 GBC session).

70. Tape recording, 21 October 1980, Swami Satsvarupa (see note 48); Tape recording, February 1982, Bhakti Charu Swami: "And I have been seeing that for the last four years Maharaja, you have been giving them a chance. You are always taking their side. You are always trying to support them."

71. B.R. Shridhara Goswami, Room Conversation, Navadvipa, India, 18 August 1980 (SSM Archives 800818SM.ST).

72. 1982 GBC Resolution, codified as ISKCON Law #12.5.9 1, *ISKCON Law Book* (updated 1996).

73. Jayadvaita Swami, "Several Grievances Against the Members of the GBC," 1987, http://www.islandnet.com/krsna/vada/iskcon/grievanc.htm.

74. B.R. Shridhara Goswami, Room Conversation, Navadvipa, India, 5 March 1982 (SSM Archives 820305SM.C).

75. "Please accept my humble obeisances and apologies for my remarks in a letter written some time ago. . . . In this state of confusion and concern for the welfare of the society so loved by my spiritual master, I allowed myself to be coerced into writing a letter that was meant to minimize your exalted position and question your credibility in the matter of management." Apology letter to Shridhara Goswami, Achyutananda Das, 22 November 1982.

76. *ISKCON Law Book* (updated 1996).

77. *Purity Is the Force*, Official GBC Publication, 1982. Original points and refutation available online, http://www.gosai.com/tattva/, as are numerous smaller ISKCON publications and position papers.

78. "All kind [*sic*] of offenses against H. H. B. R. Shridhara Maharaja were broadcasted, but the apologies to Shridhara Maharaja were not at all publicized." Somaka Swami, *In Search of Harmony*, 1994.

79. Swami B. B. Vishnu, *Our Affectionate Guardians* (Delhi: Gosai Publishers, 1996); available online: http://www.gosai.com/tattva/.

80. Jayadvaita Swami, "Several Grievances Against the Members of the GBC," 1987, http://www.islandnet.com/krsna/vada/iskcon/grievanc.htm.

81. J. Gordon Melton and Robert L. Moore, *The Cult Experience: Responding to the New Religious Pluralism* (New York: The Pilgrim Press, 1984 [3rd printing; 1st printing 1982]).

82. ISKCON Reform Movement paper, attributed to Adikarta Das, "Respecting the Order of the Guru": "Adi's Ad-Hominems Don't Add Up," http://farsight.members.beeb.net/adikarta2.htm.

83. Ibid.

84. Dorie Clark, "Where Have All the Krishnas Gone?" *Boston Phoenix*, 2 February 2001.

85. Personal communication and Internet research on the missions of B.S. Govinda Maharaja, B.A. Paramadvaiti Maharaja, and B.G. Narasingha Maharaja.

86. "Social Development Report," ISKCON Commission for Social Development, February 1998. Quoted in E. B. Rochford Jr., "Prabhupada Centennial Survey: A Summary of the Final Report." Available online: http://www.iskcon.com/ICJ/7_1/71rochford.htm.

87. *Hindustan Times*, Calcutta, 24 September 2000.

88. "These eleven, they will extend themselves. From this point, it will be—the area of the acharyaship will be extended. Then gradually twenty-four or more, but it will spread from this point, extend-bigger, bigger, bigger. That you may do, to keep the spiritual characteristic of the extension of the acharya board."

89. **Bhakti Charu Swami:** But these *acharyas*, they are not teaching their disciples to show respect to their godbrothers. Sometimes the opposite.

     Srila Shridhara Maharaja: Then my suggestions to keep the unity are that a person of one zone may accept a guru of another zone. Free choice by *shraddha*. He who has preference for one *acharya* but is compelled to accept one whom he considers to be lower, that is an anomaly. That zonal arrangement is against free choice. Also, new appointments of *acharyas* from amongst the brothers who are considered fit, that sort of position should also be there (Room Conversation, 1 February 1982; original recording and transcript in author's possession).

90. Ibid.

91. "According to my consideration, as I hear it, the grandeur of the acharya, the puja of the present acharyas, it is undesirable and too much and that will create some difficulty. It should be modified. The way in which the acharya puja has been established, that should be modified to suit the circumstances and some adjustment with the godbrothers should be made. A protocol, a spiritual protocol should be evolved which may not be very harmful to the body, to the association, the ISKCON organization."

92. "A near unanimous decision has been reached by the senior devotees, that the present system of zonal *acharyas* should be changed" (Satsvarupa Goswami, guru reform letter, 21 September 1985). "It has become more apparent that daily guru-puja [for the present ISKCON gurus] is questionable" (Satsvarupa Maharaja, "Terms and Policies for Revised Guru Worship," 1985). "Somehow or other, large numbers of Shrila Prabhupada's disciples feel strongly disturbed, discouraged, bitter, offended, confused, angry, or unhappy because of their relationship with their

godbrothers who have 'accepted the mantle' as initiating gurus" (Jayadvaita Swami, 1982 letter to GBC). Copies of documents in author's possession.

93. The instruction of Swami B.R. Shridhara Goswami to his spiritual nephews was very extensive and delved into all the essential aspects of Krishna consciousness. Details of those instructions and exchanges with ISKCON leaders through good and bad times have been thoroughly documented in the book *Our Affectionate Guardians*. Entire book available online: http://www.gosai.com/tattva/.

[12]

THE NO CHANGE IN ISKCON PARADIGM

KRISHNAKANT DESAI, SUNIL AWATRAMAMI
(ADRIDHARAN DAS), AND MADHU PANDIT DAS

THE DEVELOPMENT OF SCHISMS within a religion after the demise of its founder is surely nothing new. Perhaps what distinguishes the current dispute raging within the Hare Krishna movement from earlier altercations is the sheer scale of documentation, litigation, and public acrimony surrounding it. From this point of view it makes a fascinating and well-documented study of a contemporary worldwide religious movement in crisis over a matter of fundamental importance to its practitioners, the issue of disciple ownership in the absence of the Founder-*Acharya* (guru).

The dispute centers on what system His Divine Grace A.C. Bhaktivedanta Swami Prabhupada (henceforth Shrila Prabhupada) intended for the process of spiritual initiation (*diksha*) within the movement he founded. The current Governing Body Commission (GBC) of the International Society for Krishna Consciousness (ISKCON) maintains that Shrila Prabhupada ordered his own disciples to succeed him as *diksha* gurus after his "departure" (a period we will refer to as post-*samadhi*); whereas the reformists (or "revivalists" as they prefer to be called) under the leadership of the ISKCON Revival Movement (henceforth IRM), contend that the system that was in place before his "departure" (pre-*samadhi*) should simply have continued without change. The latter group points to the last signed directive from Shrila Prabhupada, dated July 9, 1977, issued to all the leaders of the movement, which formalized and extended the system of initiation already in place via the use of ceremonial priests or *ritviks* who were to give initiation on Shrila Prabhupada's behalf. The directive is as follows:

ISKCON INTERNATIONAL SOCIETY FOR KRISHNA CONSCIOUSNESS
Founder-Acharya: His Divine Grace A.C. Bhaktivedanta Swami Prabhupada

July 9, 1977

To All G.B.C., and Temple Presidents

Dear Maharajas and Prabhus,

Please accept my humble obeisances at your feet. Recently when all of the GBC members were with His Divine Grace in Vrindavan, Shrila Prabhupada indicated that soon He would appoint some of His senior disciples to act as "ritvik"-representative of the acharya, for the purpose of performing initiations, both first initiation and second initiation. His Divine Grace has so far given a list of eleven disciples who will act in that capacity. . . . [1] In the past Temple Presidents have written to Shrila Prabhupada recommending a particular devotee's initiation. Now that Shrila Prabhupada has named these representatives, Temple Presidents may henceforward send recommendation for first and second initiation to whichever of these eleven representatives are nearest their temple. After considering the recommendation, these representatives may accept the devotee as an initiated disciple of Shrila Prabhupada by giving a spiritual name, or in the case of second initiation, by chanting on the Gayatri thread, just as Shrila Prabhupada has done. The newly initiated devotees are disciples of His Divine Grace A.C. Bhaktivedanta Swami Prabhupada, the above eleven senior devotees acting as His representative. After the Temple President receives a letter from these representatives giving the spiritual name or the thread, he can perform the fire yajna in the temple as was being done before. The name of a newly initiated disciple should be sent by the representative who has accepted him or her to Shrila Prabhupada, to be included in His Divine Grace's "Initiated Disciples" book. Hoping this finds you all well.

Your servant,
Tamala Krsna Gosvami
Secretary to Shrila Prabhupada

Approved: A.C. Bhaktivedanta Swami

Immediately post-*samadhi*, the GBC suspended this *ritvik* system and introduced the "zonal *acharya*" system, whereby the 11 *ritviks* appointed on July 9, 1977 became powerful gurus who divided the world into separate geographical zones and initiated thousands of disciples on their own behalf. This system was modified in the mid-eighties with the "multiple *acharya* successor system" (henceforth M.A.S.S.), wherein it was taught that *all* of Shrila Prabhupada's disciples could become *diksha* gurus as long as they acquired a majority "no objection vote" from the GBC body.

The following essay is argued from the point of view of the revivalists who maintain that this *ritvik* system should have continued unchanged, and this being the case, both the zonal *acharya* and M.A.S.S. guru systems are deviations from the order of the Founder-*Acharya*. In the view of the revivalists, Shrila Prabhupada should have remained the sole initiating *diksha* guru within ISKCON post-*samadhi*, just as he was pre-*samadhi*. His disciples, we argue, were meant to act as *shiksha* gurus, that is, in an "instructing" capacity only. (The *diksha* guru is authorized to initiate his own disciples and receive worship from them on a par with worship offered to God, whereas the *shiksha* guru simply instructs and acts as a humble assistant to the *diksha* guru).

The first part of this essay is an abridged version of one submitted to the GBC at their annual meeting in 1999,[2] which precipitated two attempts to expel the revivalists along with a countering High Court action taken against the GBC in Calcutta by the revivalists. Added as a postscript is an account of an event that occurred after the initial writing of this essay, concerning an armed attack on the IRM regional headquarters in Calcutta by hundreds of armed devotees from the ISKCON world headquarters in Mayapur, West Bengal.

SHRILA PRABHUPADA'S BLUEPRINT FOR ISKCON

During the period of his physical presence, or pre-*samadhi*, Shrila Prabhupada gave the blueprint for how ISKCON was to operate. He personally established all the necessary standards, systems, processes, and teachings that were to govern ISKCON for the rest of its existence. ISKCON was set up legally to run solely under the authority of Shrila Prabhupada and was intended to last a very long time (Shrila Prabhupada mentioned ten thousand years); for its duration it would be bound to the initial parameters set by its founder. Thus, there was to be complete continuity between the way ISKCON ran while he was physically present and the way it ran after he was gone. Any proposed change therefore would need to be expressly supported by an authorizing instruction from Shrila Prabhupada if it were to be legitimately carried out within the institution.

This principle is well understood and accepted as axiomatic by members of ISKCON. Standards such as the morning program, chanting sixteen rounds of *japa* (mantra meditation) on beads, and the four regulative principles[3] were all set in place by Shrila Prabhupada specifically for ISKCON. Everyone accepts that these things were meant to endure throughout the lifetime of the society. No devotee would ever dare propose changes to these standards given by Shrila Prabhupada. Since he worked out every aspect of how ISKCON should run, managing the society was to be reasonably straightforward, involving simply the preservation, continuation, and expansion of what was already given and established. This concept of not changing anything we shall call the "No Change in ISKCON Paradigm" (henceforward, NCIP).

NCIP

In theory at least, ISKCON is governed by the NCIP, with the GBC and members expected to maintain and apply only those standards and practices directly given by Shrila Prabhupada. The very idea of change and speculation is entirely antithetical to the constitution of ISKCON, and from the very beginning this principle was enshrined within society law:

> The GBC has been established by His Divine Grace A.C. Bhaktivedanta Swami Prabhupada to represent Him in carrying out the responsibility of managing the International Society for Krsna Consciousness of which He is the Founder-*Acharya* and supreme authority. The GBC accepts as its life & soul His divine instructions and recognises that it is completely dependent on His mercy in all respects. The GBC has no other function or purpose other than to execute the instructions so kindly given by His Divine Grace and preserve and spread His Teachings to the world in their pure form.[4]

This resolution was passed specifically to define exactly how ISKCON would be managed, and was directly approved by Shrila Prabhupada. It specifies very clearly the responsibilities and boundaries for the GBC, which would be responsible for running the society. "The GBC has no other function or purpose than to execute the instructions so kindly given by His Divine Grace," and it must keep intact and apply only that which Shrila Prabhupada has taught: "and preserve and spread His Teachings to the world in their pure form."

These being the two key aspects of GBC governance, it is clear that the commission members were intended as the natural guardian angels of the NCIP. The authority of the GBC (and hence the NCIP) to reign supreme throughout every aspect of ISKCON, for as long as it exists, is further specified in Shrila Prabhupada's "Last Will and Testament":

1. The Governing Body Commission (GBC) will be the ultimate managing authority of the entire International Society for Krishna Consciousness.[5]

To ensure there was no doubt about how ISKCON was to be run for its duration, the very first item of the will opens with a statement reinforcing the NCIP. Item 1 makes it clear that the scope of the GBC is complete and ultimate for the lifetime of the institution. This means that the NCIP is also complete and ultimate, since acting within the NCIP is the very definition of the GBC as given above. The term "ultimate managing authority" is often misunderstood to grant the GBC far more power than ever intended, by interpreting it to mean members are empowered to do as they please. Such an interpretation seems to get carried away by the word "ultimate," and confuses the fact that the GBC is the topmost managing authority for ISKCON, as stated in the will, with how it was supposed to manage, which is not stated in the will. The way it was meant to manage is set out in the articles of definition, as already given, which were personally approved by Shrila Prabhupada and which make it clear that all management must be undertaken solely within the parameters of the NCIP. Thus Shrila Prabhupada set a balance. The "ultimate" authority of the GBC is checked by the fact that it must use this authority for one purpose, to preserve and execute the instructions and teachings given by Shrila Prabhupada. This "ultimate" authority can only be used to keep Shrila Prabhupada's instructions and teachings absolute, and absolutely the same. Since there is no power to change, but only the power to "maintain," potential GBC abuses are checked, for as soon as the power is used inappropriately the commission is acting outside the boundaries set by Shrila Prabhupada.

That the opening statement of the will supports the NCIP is further reinforced by the very next clause:

2. Each temple will be an ISKCON property and will be managed by three executive directors. The system of management will continue as it is now and there is no need of any change.[6]

So however ISKCON was managed *pre-samadhi* was meant to continue for the duration of the institution. Here we see Shrila Prabhupada directly spelling out the NCIP.

Strong evidence supporting the paradigm is also found in Shrila Prabhupada's books. It is accepted without dispute by all in ISKCON that these are the "law books" for the society, to guide it for its entire lifetime. Shortly before his passing Shrila Prabhupada instructed:

If death takes place, let it take here. So there is nothing to be said new. Whatever I have to speak, I have spoken in my books. Now you try to understand it and continue your endeavour. Whether I am present or not present, it doesn't matter.[7]

This indicates that the books are applicable for the post-*samadhi* period just as for the pre-*samadhi* period, not written specifically for either time frame. It also means that the teachings and standards personally established by Shrila Prabhupada and mentioned in his books are applicable during both periods. It follows therefore that the books were written to support an ISKCON that was meant to continue unchanged.

As indicated, the NCIP is not in any sense alien to modern-day ISKCON. In most areas of the society's theology, practice, and management, this paradigm is vigorously enforced, with devotees proclaiming proudly that they will never deviate from what Shrila Prabhupada taught. When there has been any perceived deviation, strenuous attempts have been made to return to Shrila Prabhupada's standards as practised and taught pre-*samadhi*. The very idea of "change" or "speculation" within ISKCON is severely frowned upon. Thus the NCIP is already, in theory at least, the guiding principle for management.

Thus we have established the NCIP as an ongoing principle applicable to every area and aspect of ISKCON. Therefore, unless otherwise demonstrated, the vitally important process of initiation must also automatically be covered by this paradigm, since the proofs above did not make any reference to a special clause on the subject of initiation. This in itself is enough to establish that the system of initiation that was in place pre-*samadhi* should continue throughout the lifetime of ISKCON without change.

To further strengthen this assertion we will now show how the issue of initiation has been *explicitly* included to apply within the NCIP, and argue that with this being the case, there should be no reason to exempt initiation from the NCIP that is otherwise so staunchly defended by the GBC.

JULY 9, 1977 DIRECTIVE

To preclude any possibility of the GBC legitimately attempting to claim initiation's exemption from the NCIP, Shrila Prabhupada issued an institutional directive on July 9, 1977, quoted earlier, clearly outlining the application of the NCIP to the area of initiation. This directive was issued and sent out to all the leaders and managers of ISKCON as the policy to be implemented from that point on. The directive simply formalized, with some amendments, the practice that had been common in ISKCON for many years, namely, that the system of initiation was to consist of ceremonial priests or *ritviks* giving initiation on Shrila Prabhupada's behalf. The amendment meant that the practice could continue in ISKCON without the need for any physical involvement from Shrila Prabhupada, and it became enshrined as the official policy for the whole movement to follow under the management of the GBC.

This directive was highly significant since traditionally in Hindu religious institutions the *acharya,* or spiritual head, issues a document shortly before his departure detailing how the guru succession of the institution is to be handed over, often to a certain named individual. However, with this directive Shrila Prabhupada made it clear to the whole movement that the arrangements already in place, with him as the sole initiating guru for the whole movement, would continue. All new recruits to the movement would be "initiated disciples" of Shrila Prabhupada, with the named representatives acting only as that, representatives. This point is made three times in a directive that is very short (two paragraphs) and to the point. This was the final communication on this matter, issued only 120 days before Shrila Prabhupada's passing away and after the "Last Will and Testament" had already been registered.

In Shrila Prabhupada's will we find the following instruction regarding the appointment of future executive directors for certain ISKCON properties in India:

> The executive directors who have herein been designated are appointed for life. In the event of the death or failure to act for any reason of any of the said directors, a successor director or directors may be appointed by the remaining directors, provided the new director is *my initiated disciple* following strictly all the rules and regulations of the International Society for Krishna Consciousness as detailed in my books, and provided that there are never less than three (3) or more than five (5) executive directors acting at one time.[8]

Here we see a post-*samadhi* arrangement for the institution, consistent with the 9 July directive, using the same language, that could only be implemented if the directive was implemented. This is because in the absence of the July 9 directive there would be no arrangement for the production of future initiated disciples of Shrila Prabhupada, and thus the pool of potential executive directors would soon be exhausted once the disciples Prabhupada had personally initiated had all died out. For a movement that was meant to continue for ten thousand years this would have been quite a significant oversight. Thus the will also enshrines the NCIP specifically in relation to initiation.

To seal the case, Shrila Prabhupada's books, which are accepted by the whole movement as setting the standard for how ISKCON should operate under the NCIP, specifically set out how initiations should be done:

> Thus in the beginning the students of our Krsna consciousness movement agree to live with devotees, and gradually, having given up four pro-

hibited activities—illicit sex, gambling, meat-eating and intoxication—they become advanced in the activities of spiritual life. When one is found to be regularly following these principles, he is given the first initiation (*hari nama*), and he regularly chants at least sixteen rounds a day. Then, after six months or a year, he is initiated for the second time and given the sacred thread with the regular sacrifice and ritual.[9]

Due to the necessity of these activities, we do not immediately initiate disciples in the International Society for Krishna Consciousness. For six months, a candidate for initiation must first attend *arati* and classes in the *shastras*, practice the regulative principles and associate with other devotees. When one is actually advanced in the *purascarya-vidhi*, he is recommended by the local temple president for initiation. It is not that anyone can be suddenly initiated without meeting the requirements. When one is further advanced by chanting the Hare Krsna mantra sixteen rounds daily, following the regulative principles and attending classes, he receives the sacred thread (brahminical recognition) after the second six months.[10]

So we can clearly see that the books make specific reference to the initiation system to be applied in ISKCON. This can only refer to being initiated by Shrila Prabhupada, since this is exactly what happened pre-*samadhi* in precisely the manner described above: the local authorities approved a person when he or she was qualified per the requirements outlined by Shrila Prabhupada, and that person was then considered initiated by Shrila Prabhupada in a ceremony conducted by one of his representatives on his behalf. And by the NCIP, the above is exactly what should happen post-*samadhi*. There is no mention of the adjustments that would be required to operate a multiguru system as currently exists. Such a system could not follow the above-stated model since it would require many different procedures to accommodate the many new *diksha* gurus, along with the terms and means of choice and verification of acceptance. (At present there are some eighty gurus operating officially within ISKCON, so some hitherto unmentioned selection process would be needed on the part of the disciple to choose his preferred guru and for that guru to agree.)

And if ISKCON were to adopt exactly the same procedures as described by Shrila Prabhupada above, it would have to abandon the current M.A.S.S. Furthermore, if ISKCON were to adopt the procedures above, the process for *diksha* would be identical to that which was operating pre-*samadhi*, so why then would the identity of the *diksha* guru change? If everything else is running identically to the way it was pre-*samadhi*, why should this one aspect be arbitrarily changed? Thus the books explicitly mention the system of initiation, and this must be applied in line with the NCIP.

So pervasive is this paradigm that even the current GBC has incorporated it into its authorized position paper—"On My Order Understood."[11] This paper has also been added as an appendix to the *ISKCON Law Book*. There the GBC states:

> If an advanced devotee's spiritual qualities are "self-effulgent," devotees may naturally accept him as an "*acharya*" or advanced or realized spiritual master and his association and guidance will be sought, but the GBC cannot "rubber stamp" him nor change ISKCON's system of management consequently. ISKCON will continue to be managed as Shrila Prabhupada provided without "change" by the GBC. That is Shrila Prabhupada's instruction.[12]

Note, here, that the GBC not only agreed with the NCIP thesis put forward in this essay but also did so specifically in the context of the issue we are discussing—the emergence of a highly realized spiritual master. Even in such an extreme situation, the GBC insists that ISKCON adhere rigidly to the NCIP, just as we have argued thus far.

We have demonstrated that the NCIP forms an integral part of Shrila Prabhupada's mission; that the system of initiation to be applied throughout the lifetime of ISKCON must also fall under the NCIP; and that this system of initiation was set out explicitly in separate instructions in the last days before Shrila Prabhupada's departure. We have also shown that even the current GBC has agreed with the NCIP, having incorporated it into the *ISKCON Law Book*.

Obviously, in order to alter the initiation system and make such a dramatic change to the way the institution ran (effectively usurping its spiritual head), the quality of evidence required would need to be impressively unambiguous and overwhelmingly clear. In summary, it would need to take the above into account, with the evidence needed consisting of direct instructions from Shrila Prabhupada of unparalleled magnitude and definitiveness; and, since we are speaking of making a change in the NCIP that was being implemented and managed by the GBC, the instructions would have to be directed to the GBC, so it would be able to implement them. We would need such clear unequivocal instructions to be present in pre-*samadhi* GBC resolutions, the last will and testament, the books, and directives to the whole movement. Instructions only received privately by individuals or on a one-off basis by a fraction of the institution do not satisfy the requirement to make an institutional change. Changes must be directed to the managers of the institution in order to be applicable at all levels.

THE EVIDENCE PUT FORWARD

The officially accepted explanation that purports to validate this monumental exception to the NCIP is found in a paper by Ravindra Svarupa Das (to be referred to as the author), the chairman of ISKCON's Governing Body Commission at the time of writing. Entitled "Cleaning House and Cleaning Hearts: Reform and Renewal in ISKCON" (henceforward *CHCH*) and published in this volume, it was originally presented to the Vaishnava Academy conference held in Wiesbaden, Germany in January 1994, and outlines the dynamics and rationale behind the "guru reforms" he engineered within ISKCON in the mid-1980s, which underpin the movement's current policy. He supports his case with the five following assertions:

1. That guru reform was based on implementing Shrila Prabhupada's expressed instructions on the guru;
2. That Shrila Prabhupada wanted a GBC system, as opposed to a single *acharya* system;
3. That Shrila Prabhupada's own guru had also wanted a GBC system, as opposed to a single *acharya* system;
4. That the *ritvik* alternative had to be rejected because it was not "traditional"; and
5. That guru reform solved the "crisis" that the zonal *acharya* system had created.

These assertions are examined carefully in the response paper entitled "The False Dawn of Guru Reform," which can be found on the IRM Web site.[13] For our purposes here we shall just look briefly at assertions 1 and 2, since 3, 4, and 5 are largely irrelevant to the case of what Shrila Prabhupada himself established within ISKCON. In other words, he was perfectly at liberty to establish an institution with management systems different from those employed by his own spiritual master (3), that parted with tradition (4), and that was meant to continue regardless of whatever perceived crisis might or might not arise (5). The response paper proves that even these irrelevant assertions are also false.

With regard to assertion 1, which is of course directly relevant, the author makes great play of the fact that the guru reforms he instituted meant: "we now have a movement organized the way Shrila Prabhupada wanted it." Yet he also admits that a central feature of this organization, namely the existence of a multitude of successor gurus to Shrila Prabhupada, was not the answer Prabhupada gave to the GBC when pressed by them as to how initiations would continue in his absence (on May 28, 1977):

In response, Shrila Prabhupada said he would select some disciples to begin immediately performing all of the activities involved in giving initiation—approving the candidate, chanting on the beads, giving the name, and so on—acting as an officiating priest (*ritvik*) on Shrila Prabhupada's behalf. (page 161 above)

Here the author states that Shrila Prabhupada's answer to how initiations would be carried out after his *departure* would be through his selection of *ritviks*. As we have shown, *ritviks* (also called officiating *acharyas*) are priests who act as representatives for the *existing* guru, and thus operate as an *alternative* to successor gurus. The author claims that Shrila Prabhupada gave the following instructions in a recorded room conversation: "After his demise, however, those same officiating gurus to be selected by Shrila Prabhupada would, if qualified, become gurus in their own right."

Let us look at the only section of this conversation the author could be alluding to:

TAMAL KRISHNA GOSWAMI: No. He is asking that these *ritvik acharyas*, they are officiating, giving *diksha*, (there) . . . the people who they give *diksha* to, whose disciples are they?

SHRILA PRABHUPADA: They are his disciples.

TAMAL KRISHNA GOSWAMI: They are his disciples.

SHRILA PRABHUPADA: Who is initiating . . . his grand-disciple . . .

SATSVARUPA DAS GOSWAMI: Then we have a question concerning . . .

SHRILA PRABHUPADA: When I order you become guru, he becomes regular guru. That's all. He becomes disciple of my disciple.[14]

It is hard to see from the above how the author arrived at his conclusions, since there is no mention of either Shrila Prabhupada's demise or the need of the selected *ritviks* to become qualified in direct conjunction with their becoming initiating gurus. Rather, Shrila Prabhupada states categorically that there must first be a specific order ("when I order") before such activity can commence. If the author had such an order as evidence, we assume he would have presented that. We are left only with the author's own admission: that Shrila Prabhupada's response to the question of how initiations would go on after his departure was that he would recommend some *ritviks* to perform them. The fact that no such explicit order for *diksha* gurus exists is admitted when the author states that the authority for the *ritviks* to become gurus came from the GBC's "understanding" that this was to be the case:

In July, Shrila Prabhupada selected eleven members of the GBC (then twenty in number) to begin acting at once as officiating gurus. Thus the GBC understood Shrila Prabhupada to have chosen the first initiating gurus to succeed him. (page 161 above)

This is the same GBC that also "understood" that it was meant to operate a zonal *acharya* system for nearly a decade, which the author also asserts was a serious deviation. He goes on to state that his guru reforms were in reality based on little more than his "conviction" that ISKCON must continue to have new *diksha* gurus: "It was my conviction that we could retain in ISKCON the full-fledged position of guru, as delineated by the Scriptures."

It would seem then that today's ISKCON is replete with *diksha* gurus as a result of the author's personal "conviction" and the GBC's "understanding," rather than through any explicit order to this effect from the movement's founder. Again in relation to the May 28 conversation, the GBC asserts that the July 9 policy directive introduces itself as being the output of this conversation. Therefore, by definition, one need not be overly concerned with the conversation since we already have the official written record in hand (the July 9 letter). Thus the GBC's attempts to interpret this conversation as somehow contradicting or overturning the directive are self-defeating, since it insists that this is the conversation referred to at the outset of the directive, and hence by its own argument the two must match.

Assertion 2, that Shrila Prabhupada wanted a GBC system rather than a single *acharya* system, is clearly false since even while he was physically present as the "single institutional *acharya*" for ISKCON, Shrila Prabhupada worked to establish a fully operational GBC that managed the movement from as early as 1970. This fact is admitted by the author: "Yet starting in 1970, Shrila Prabhupada had worked diligently to establish a quite different sort of leadership structure in ISKCON, a structure, he repeatedly emphasized, that would continue after him."

The author thus agrees that the GBC system, as established in ISKCON in 1970, was to continue after Shrila Prabhupada's departure; he further agrees that the GBC was set up simply to manage on behalf of the single institutional *acharya*, Shrila Prabhupada, and not as a mechanism in place of rule by a single institutional *acharya*: "As time went on he tried to turn as much management over to the GBC as possible, intervening only when there were crises." This is clearly spelled out in the document that was used to incorporate the GBC in 1970:

As we have increased our volume of activities, now I think a Governing Body Commission (hereinafter referred to as the GBC) should be established. I am getting old, 75 years old, therefore at any time I may be out

of the scene, therefore I think it is necessary to give instruction to my disciples how they shall manage the whole institution. . . . My duty was to
first appoint twelve (12) persons to my free choice amongst my disciples
and I do it now and their names are as follows. . . . These personalities are
now considered as my direct representatives. While I am living they will
act as my zonal secretaries and after my demise they will be known as Ex-
ecutors. . . . The purpose of the Governing Body Commission is to act as
the instrument for the execution of the Will of His Divine Grace [Shrila
Prabhupada].[15]

It is made clear here that the GBC's function after the departure of the
acharya is no different from its function during his presence—to act as the instrument for executing the will of the single institutional *acharya*. All that
changes, as necessitated by the law of probate, is the language, as the living representatives previously designated as "zonal secretaries" are now called "Ex-
ecutors." This renders invalid the argument that the eventual departure of the
acharya by its very nature necessitated a change in the system of corporate governance for ISKCON.

The author has argued strongly that the single institutional *acharya* had
deemed that the governance of ISKCON would actually continue after his departure, not with a successor *acharya*, but solely via the GBC:

Shrila Prabhupada's intention, and his departure from the tradition of
the institutional *acharya*, is shown in a striking way in his will. Traditionally, it was in the first article of his will that an *acharya* named his successor, passing on his institution to his heir as if it were his personal property. The first article of Shrila Prabhupada's will reads: "The Governing
Body Commission (GBC) will be the ultimate managing authority for the
entire International Society for Krishna Consciousness." (page 163 above)

The author is correct that the GBC acts as the instrument that replaces the
"traditional" system of successor *acharya* (thus contradicting his own argument that the *ritvik* system must be rejected on the basis of its not following
"tradition"). It does not, however, replace the system of rule via a single institutional *acharya*, for its very purpose is to maintain the rule of Shrila Prabhupada in the absence of the "traditional" successor. This is made crystal clear by
the definition and purpose of the GBC. Now it is obvious that the selection of
ritvik priests by Shrila Prabhupada to continue initiations in ISKCON is an
arrangement not just consistent with a system of corporate governance based
around the GBC but actually *absolutely essential*; for the single institutional
acharya would need *ritviks* to ensure that he could continue to function in his

capacity in the same manner when absent as when he was present. An evaluation of "Cleaning House and Cleaning Hearts" reveals that that Ravindra Svarupa's highly influential position presented therein is based on flawed reasoning and no discernable direct evidence from Shrila Prabhupada.

REASONS PRESENTED FOR THE SUSPENSION OF THE NCIP

There are two other categories of indirect evidence used in defense of the GBC's suspension of the NCIP in relation to initiation, namely evidence from the repeated orders to "become guru" and evidence from the nature and history of the *parampara* (the historical succession of gurus). Let us examine each in turn.

Regarding the first category of evidence, it is claimed that Shrila Prabhupada has many times instructed his disciples to "become guru." In fact, this evidence itself falls into two categories: references to "becoming guru" in connection with the *amara ajnaya* verse, dicussed below; and references to "becoming guru" in connection with the "law of disciplic succession." Evaluating the above evidence according to the criteria outlined earlier, we note that none of it is given in any institutional form. Rather, it is given either in unpublished private letters to individuals or in lectures to a small fraction of the movement. In sum, the GBC was established to manage solely on the basis of the instructions received from Shrila Prabhupada. Its members can only implement the July 9 directive in accordance with whatever other direct instructions they may have received in this regard. We have seen that there are no instructions in the books or other institutional directives that affect the implementation of this directive. The GBC was given no managerial mandate to avoid implementing institutional directives by searching twenty years later for other instructions Shrila Prabhupada may have spoken privately on a one-off basis.

Further, we find that the explanatory purports to the *amara ajanya* verse state that: "it is best not to accept any disciples."[16] Yet this evidence is put forward to justify accepting disciples, lots of them! In conclusion, there is no instruction issued to the institution authorizing an individual to take up the role of *diksha* guru in ISKCON once Shrila Prabhupada departs. This would be the very minimum required to overturn the July 9 directive and radically change the NCIP that Shrila Prabhupada set up for ISKCON.

Regarding the second category of indirect evidence used in defense of the GBC's suspension of the NCIP, namely, evidence from the nature and history of the *parampara*, it is argued that the concept of change in the issue of initiation is inherent due to the need to maintain the historical succession of gurus. The *parampara* seems practically defined by change alone, with each link in the disciplic succession being succeeded by another in due course of time. This is not disputed. This is why we specifically called the paradigm, "No Change in ISKCON," not "No Change Eternally." The issue is—does Shrila Prabhupada need to be succeeded within the lifetime of his institution in order to continue the *parampara*? Or more specifically, should he be succeeded upon his physical departure, since the argument put forward is that historically *diksha* has always been performed only when a *diksha* guru was physically present at the moment the initiation ceremony took place? Shrila Prabhupada did not give any such instructions in the entire canon of his teachings (indeed, the GBC members have themselves conceded that Shrila Prabhupada's lack of physicality does not prevent him from transmitting *diksha*, by admitting to everyone in ISKCON, via the latest GBC resolutions, that Shrila Prabhupada is transmitting *divya jnana*—transcendental knowledge—which is the "principal active ingredient of *diksha*"[17]). On the contrary, in a specific question-and-answer exchange to do with the *parampara*, Shrila Prabhupada stated that the manner of the *parampara's* continuation after his departure would be unchanged:

GANESHA: Shrila Prabhupada, if the knowledge was handed down by the saintly kings, *evam parampara-praptam* [*Bhagavad Gita* 4.2], how is it that the knowledge was lost?

SHRILA PRABHUPADA: When it was not handed down. Simply understood by speculation. Or if it is not handed down as it is. They might have made some changes. Or they did not hand it down. Suppose I handed it down to you, but if you do not do that, then it is lost. Now the Krsna consciousness movement is going on in my presence. Now after my departure, if you do not do this, then it is lost. If you go on as you are doing now, then it will go on. But if you stop.[18]

Here Shrila Prabhupada tells us exactly *how* the *parampara* must be continued after he departs—"go on as you are doing now." This is exactly what the NCIP states. There is nothing from the concept of the *parampara* that necessitates a change in the initiation system authorized by Shrila Prabhupada. Thus the evidence forwarded by the GBC falls far short of the criteria necessary to make their exemption to NCIP in the highly charged and supremely significant area of spiritual initiation.

CONCLUSION

In this essay, we have argued that the NCIP is applicable to ISKCON, and in particular to initiation; that no instructions from Shrila Prabhupada authorizing a deviation from the NCIP are present, especially in the matter of initiation; and that as a result, there is no discernible justification for having changed the system of initiation, and in that way removed Shrila Prabhupada from his position as ISKCON's sole initiating *acharya*. Shrila Prabhupada unequivocally defined the respective roles he and the GBC were to have within ISKCON:

> The GBC should all be the instructor gurus. I am the initiator guru, and you should be the instructor guru by teaching what I am teaching and doing what I am doing. This is not a title, but you must actually come to this platform. This I want.[19]

These roles were formalized in the signed institutional directive of July 9, 1977, which established the *ritvik* system. We have seen no document or approved resolution from Shrila Prabhupada authorizing any change to this system, let alone terminating it and inventing a new one. We fear that unless the GBC reinstitutes the *ritvik* system, the movement will continue to flounder, or at worst, disintegrate completely. Indeed, the current GBC chairman, Ravindra Svarupa Das, who has represented the opposing argument in this same publication, stated in a private letter to fellow GBC members that ISKCON is "polarized and disintegrating."

POSTSCRIPT

The IRM's philosophical challenge to ISKCON's current multiguru system came to a head on the weekend of April 27–29, 2001, when the IRM's regional headquarters in Calcutta was stormed by representatives of ISKCON and IRM supporters were physically assaulted with weapons. This incident caused shock waves throughout India, with several national newspapers and television news bulletins reporting the event. The following accounts appeared in leading Indian newspapers:

> The city Police on Saturday arrested 72 devotees and monks of the International Society For Krishna Consciousness (ISKCON) who went on a rampage and clashed inside its Kolkata Temple office. Assistant Commissioner of Police (South Division) Prasanta Chatopadhyay, and four constables were injured while trying to separate the warring sadhus. . . . On Saturday, devotees and monks were arrested from the temple office on the charge of unlawful assembly, police said. About 150 devotees and monks of ISKCON's Mayapur temple arrived here last (Friday) night, and tried to "evict the outsiders" in the ISKCON's Albert Road temple office. This led to heated scuffles and exchanges, police said. (*Times of India*, April 28, 2001)

Seventy two ISKCON Mayapur devotees were arrested by the Shake-speare Sarani Police on charges of rowdyism on Saturday morning. They have been kept in Police custody. Sources say that more than 250 ISKCON Mayapur devotees barged into the ISKCON Revival Movement office on Albert Road on Friday evening and tried to assault IRM President Adridharana Das who, they claimed, is no more the president. Adridharana Das had filed a case against 70 ISKCON Mayapur Gurus who claimed they were the chief leaders of the ISKCON Movement. Das said ISKCON only had one leader—Shrila Prabhupada. This has been the major bone of contention between the two factions. They assaulted the 15 IRM devotees who lived inside the temple and held them hostage for the entire night. They again assaulted the IRM devotees on Saturday night. (*The Asian Age*, April 28, 2001)

Trouble at the temple has been brewing for some time. [Adridharan] Das had filed a case against over 70 gurus over a year ago, alleging that their authority was contrary to the legally binding directives of Shrila Prabhupada, rightfully the sole initiating guru for ISKCON. The case is now being heard at Calcutta High Court. . . . 'The Governing Body Commission', alleges Das, who is also chairman of the ISKCON Revival Movement, 'comprises gurus who have unauthorisedly set themselves up as new initiating gurus, siphoning off donations and followers. . . . We have finally summoned the courage to question this illegal system, by which gurus are elected as spiritual leaders. I have filed a case against these gurus. It is under their instructions that these disciples have come today to attack the temple', said Das, amidst an atmosphere of tension. Das, president of over 20 years, appointed by Prabhupada himself, claimed he has received weekly death threats since filing the case. (*Calcutta*, April 27, 2001)

ADRIDHARANA'S FIRST-HAND ACCOUNT OF THE EVENTS

On the afternoon of Friday, April 27, 2001, 100 members from the guru-controlled ISKCON temple in Mayapur stormed into the Calcutta temple. The mob immediately demanded to forcefully take possession of the temple and began to occupy parts of the building. Those who tried to stand in their way were physically attacked. When I came down from my office to confront them, a huge crowd of them rushed to attack me. The police were called, and most of the assailants were removed, with some of them jailed.

However, around 25 of them had sneaked into the temple room and began chanting hymns to evade arrest, claiming that they had simply come to take part in the temple services. A few police officers were put on guard outside the temple to prevent a further invasion. By the time the temple closed that evening, these 25 members from Mayapur were still inside, refusing to leave. By midnight a crowd of 300 to 400 had congregated outside the temple, with many having been bused in from Mayapur especially for the event. They began demonstrating and pressuring the local police to allow them in to take over the temple, and have myself and the other residents removed.

The local police soon became overwhelmed by the crowd, and about 25 Mayapur members managed to climb the walls at the back of the temple and gain entry. Once inside, they joined up with the 25 Mayapur members who were already inside. As we were to later discover, all 50 of them were heavily armed with knives, machetes, chains, nails, and hammers. They had also brought eight changes of locks with them. Clearly this was a carefully planned operation to forcibly occupy the temple through violence.

Coordinating all this from outside was the Chief Executive of Mayapur, who was at the head of the 300-strong crowd, and who was shouting instructions both verbally and via his cell phone. He had also organized about 50 hired professional "heavies" armed with metal bars, who were dressed in security uniforms and were standing outside waiting to charge in. Heavily armed to the teeth, and outnumbering the temple residents by 3 to 1, these 50 members of the Mayapur gang quickly ran amok and took over the whole temple. All the temple devotees were threatened with severe violence if they tried to intervene. The local police, who were trying their best to keep the huge crowd at bay, were powerless to do anything, as those inside forcibly took possession. At this point the Chief Executive of Mayapur phoned the GBC member for India and informed him that the temple was now "taken" and the IRM supporters were ousted. Very quickly the news spread over Mayapur and the higher echelons of ISKCON that "Calcutta had fallen into GBC hands."

The 50 Mayapur members waited for reinforcements from the huge crowd outside, to assist in "officially" taking the temple over and ousting myself and all the other residents. However, these reinforcements never came, for at around 1 A.M., extra police from outside the area arrived and dispersed most of the crowd. As morning approached, we were effectively held hostage by these armed attackers, as they waited for extra help to come. Yet with most of the outside crowd cleared, our captors began to realize that their occupation was not going according to plan, and began to act in an increasingly desperate fashion. They threatened the residents, ripped out phone lines, and performed random acts of vandalism, damaging temple furniture.

The other temple residents and I waited for the arrival of extra police from outside the area to come to our rescue. At 10:30 A.M., two huge police trucks with more than 100 policemen pulled up with three large empty police vans in tow. In seconds, they swarmed over the whole temple, shouting, "Get the Mayapur *goondas* [criminals]." Forming snatch squads, they immediately seized and arrested the 50 Mayapur members who were inside. The assailants dropped their weapons and tried to flee, but were rounded up and bundled into the police vans. The entire police operation was over in 10 minutes. The police also arrested more than 20 members from the crowd outside the temple, which had begun to form again in the morning and which had been cheering on the assailants inside. To prevent an immediate recurrence of such violence, 30 policemen were posted on 24-hour guard at the ISKCON Calcutta temple.

The net result of this incident was that around 70 members of the Mayapur gang were arrested and spent time in jail, and are now bailed out to appear before the court again to face formal charges.

The media were not slow in broadcasting this news. Every TV station in West Bengal, as well as others with national reach, broadcast this story repeatedly on their headline news bulletins. The tens of millions of viewers were shown a graphic display of the weapons the assailants had brought, including knives, chains, and machetes. I was also personally interviewed by a combination of local, national, and international TV stations on Saturday following the attack and arrests, including *Khas Khaber*, *Taja Khaber* (the most popular Bengali news programs in West Bengal); HNBC; CYGNUS; and ETV.

NOTES

1. The disciples listed at this point in the letter are: His Holiness Kirtanananda Swami, His Holiness Satsvarupa Das Goswami, His Holiness Jayapataka Swami, His Holiness Tamala Krishna Goswami, His Holiness Hridayananda Goswami, His Holiness Bhavananda Goswami, His Holiness Hamsadutta Swami, His Holiness Rameshvara Swami, His Holiness Harikesha Swami, His Grace Bhagavan Das Adhikari, His Grace Jayatirtha Das Adhikari. (The latter two were still householders at the time, hence the difference in their title.)

2. The entire paper can be found on the ISKCON Revival Movement's Web site at: www.farsight.members.beeb.net or www.come.to/irm.

3. Upon taking initiation into the Hare Krishna movement, candidates have to vow to strictly abstain from intoxication, meat-eating, gambling, and sexual relations outside the act of procreation.

4. Definition of GBC, Resolution 1, GBC minutes 1975, emphasis added. Available from www.archives.org and www.chakra.org.

5. Opening Statement, Shrila Prabhupada's Last Will and Testament. Available from irm@ntlworld.com.

6. Shrila Prabhupada's Last Will and Testament.

7. Arrival Address, Vrindavan, 17 May 1977, *Conversations With Shrila Prabhupada*, vol. 33 (Los Angeles: Bhaktivedanta Book Trust, 1991), 193.

8. Statement 3, Last Will and Testament, emphasis added.

9. *Shri Chaitanya-Charitamrita*, Adi-lila, 17.265, purport, single-volume edition (Los Angeles: Bhaktivedanta Book Trust, 1992), 336.

10. Ibid., Madhya-lila, 15.108, purport, 800.

11. *Gurus and Initiation in ISKCON*, GBC, 1995. Available from www.archives.org and www.chakra.org.

12. *ISKCON Law Book* (Mayapur: ISKCON GBC Press, 1997) (emphasis added).

13. See note 2.

14. *Conversations With Shrila Prabhupada,* vol. 33, 269–70.

15. The Direction of Management, 28 July 1970. Available at http://www.prabhupada.com.

16. *Shri Chaitanya-Charitamrita*, Madhya-lila, 7.130, purport, 538.

17. See paper, "GBC Endorse *Ritvik* By Mistake," on IRM Web site: www.farsight.members.beeb.net or www.come.to/irm.

18. Room Conversation, 9 May 1975, Perth, Australia, *Conversations With Shrila Prabhupada,* vol. 12 (Los Angeles: Bhaktivedanta Book Trust, 1989), 303.

19. Letter to Madhudvisha, 4 August 1975, *Letters From Shrila Prabhupada*, vol. 5 (Los Angeles: The Vaishnava Institute in association with the Bhaktivedanta Book Trust, 1987), 2884.

[13]

THE "ROUTINIZATION OF CHARISMA" AND THE CHARISMATIC

The Confrontation Between ISKCON and Narayana Maharaja

IRVIN H. COLLINS

THE SUCCESSION OF SPIRITUAL AUTHORITY is a matter of deep and abiding concern for every religious institution that seeks to perpetuate its influence over the generations. It is of especially critical importance in the intermediate and often turbulent years following the demise of a charismatic religious founder—before the teachings and practices of that teacher can become established as an indisputable, fixed tradition. The history of all the world's great religions—Buddhism, Christianity, Islam, and Hinduism alike—highlights how divisive the matter of who becomes the next successor can be.[1]

The dynamics involved in the transition of authority from charismatic founder to successor, along with the continuity of the religious tradition itself, are inherently complex and contingent upon historical context and relevant circumstances. In the early Christian church, for example, St. Paul, who was considered an *outsider* if not heretical by Jesus' original disciples, was assimilated into Christianity as one of its greatest saints and preachers.[2] On the other hand, Martin Luther, a sincere and well-meaning reformer from *within* the Catholic tradition, was thoroughly ostracized and banished from it. Nonetheless, Luther's writings (along with those of other reformers such as Calvin) became so influential that they resulted in the Protestant Reformation, the greatest schism in Christian history. Then again, we have the case of St. Francis of Assisi: not only was his deviance tolerated but, shortly after his death, he was even granted sainthood, and his followers were accommodated into the greater diversity of the Catholic Church as one of its prominent orders, the Franciscans. These few examples suggest that the future course of an entire religious tradition can be imperiled—or preserved—by the advent of maverick preachers and reformers and by how they are dealt with by the presiding religious hierarchy.

This paper will trace the history and ongoing dynamic of an escalating confrontation between ISKCON and the followers of Narayana Maharaja, a senior *sannyasi* from a branch of the Chaitanya Gaudiya tradition outside of ISKCON. Using Weberian insights, it will first touch upon the increasing institutionalization of ISKCON in its postcharismatic phase, and then, using Narayana Maharaja as a case study, discuss the vulnerability of an organization confronted with the appeal of a charismatic preacher outside the parameters of its authority.

ISKCON'S POSTCHARISMATIC PHASE:
A WEBERIAN PERSPECTIVE

Charisma, in its purely religious sense, is defined as "a special gift or grace." Indeed, in the Chaitanya tradition the *guru* or spiritual preceptor is referred to as "His Divine Grace." A mystical understanding of charisma is, of course, inherently subjective, but nonetheless overlaps Weber's own definition of the term as "a certain quality of individual personality by virtue of which one is set apart from ordinary men and treated as endowed with supernatural, superhuman, or at least specifically exceptional power or qualities."[3] Selengut notes that charismatics or prophets gain particular influence during times of social and cultural crisis and preach that a more meaningful and satisfying life can be realized by following their particular teachings.[4] Regarding ISKCON, he observes:

> To his followers, Prabhupada was such a [charismatic] person, the bearer of an ultimate and salvationist truth available to them if they were loyal and obedient to his directives. . . . The successful development of ISKCON in America must be seen, then, as largely the result of Prabhupada's leadership.[5]

But charisma is inherently unstable and tends to become institutionalized or routinized.[6] The very effort to attain success, to perpetuate the movement's mission and spread it beyond the immediate band of disciples—even during the charismatic leader's own lifetime—"introduces the need for mechanisms of coordination, supervision and delegation."[7] As a religion becomes more bureaucratic and "rational strategy replaces utopian aspiration,"[8] the imparting of its spiritual knowledge and practices also becomes more routine. Although the charisma of the leader is a major factor in a religious movement's initial success, this is inevitably followed by institutionalization and a shift to "rational-legal forms of authority and administration."[9] Wallis informs us how this process, over time, results in "the development within the movement of a leadership cadre or body of officials with vested interests in the maintenance of the organization or movement structure, who seek to adapt the organization to ensure its survival, and the maintenance of their interests."[10] Organized religions have thus historically treaded the same path followed by all bureaucratic institutions.

Bhaktivedanta Swami's own guru, Bhaktisiddhanta Saraswati Goswami, who pioneered the establishment of a worldwide organization for Chaitanya Vaishnavism, the Gaudiya Math, was fully aware of the teleology of religious institutions:

> The idea of an organized church in an intelligible form, indeed, marks the close of the living spiritual movement. The great ecclesiastical establishments are the dikes and the dams to retain the current that cannot be held by any such contrivances. They, indeed, indicate a desire on the part of the masses to exploit a spiritual movement for their own purpose. They also unmistakably indicate the end of the absolute and unconventional guidance of the bona-fide spiritual teacher.[11]

Bhaktivedanta Swami was similarly concerned about the increasing institutionalization of his own burgeoning society. When one leading disciple misunderstood his position as a GBC (Governing Body Commission) member to be more like that of a modern CEO and attempted to centralize finances and administration, the swami sternly reprimanded him:

> Do not centralize anything. Each temple must remain independent and self-sufficient. That was my plan from the very beginning, why you are thinking otherwise? Once before you wanted to do something centralizing with your GBC meeting, and if I did not interfere the whole thing would have been killed. Do not think in this way of big corporation, big credits, centralization—these are all nonsense proposals. . . . Management, everything, should be done locally by local men. . . . Krishna Consciousness Movement is for training men to be independently thoughtful

and competent in all types of departments of knowledge and action, not for making bureaucracy. Once there is bureaucracy the whole thing will be spoiled.[12]

While Bhaktivedanta Swami has been recognized for his ability to harness the power of organization, capital, and followers to spread his spiritual mission around the world in the span of a few short years, he never succumbed to their beguiling influence, as did other "charmistic *gurus*"[13] [*sic*]. Rather, Bhaktivedanta Swami was prepared to suspend the GBC, disband ISKCON, and even forsake his disciples should they betray his ultimate objectives, which were avowedly spiritual.[14] By all accounts, the swami was never attached to the comfort, power, prestige, or position that accompanied his success. Thus, while keenly aware of the drawbacks of institutions, he was able to employ these organizational means without compromising his principles or being adversely affected.

As evinced by both Bhaktivedanta Swami and his own guru, we should note two potentially crippling consequences that can arise from the institutionalization of religion. First, it deprives a religious tradition of its original vitality, compromising its spiritual ideals with mundane considerations and gradually overburdening it with an inflexible hierarchy.[15] Second, the bureaucratic forms that evolve effectively suppress the power of charismatic saints and reformers to revive the tradition with new energy or infuse it with fresh insights. While on the one hand, an institution can provide structure that conserves a religious tradition and safeguards its truths from the wanton attacks of heretics and deviants; on the other hand, the same structure of authority can prevent an institution from correcting itself when it has gone astray and delay improvements when significant changes are called for. The perennial sociological conundrum again confronts us: humankind cannot live without religion yet cannot quite live with it either.

As in the case of ISKCON, new religious movements that manage to survive the loss of charisma after the demise of the founder inevitably face deep and continuing sources of internal conflict in their postcharismatic phase, conflict that often results in factionalism and splintering. Bhaktivedanta Swami's death in the fall of 1977 was a major turning point for ISKCON's development all over the world, since this left the society with no single heir apparent ("self-effulgent *acharya*"[16]) to lead it; thus, subsequently an elite of Bhaktivedanta's most prominent disciples consolidated themselves as his collective successors. Within ten years, however, the majority of these eleven "zonal *acharyas*" were either removed by the GBC or had fallen from spiritual grace. The far-reaching consequences of these successive apostasies cannot be overestimated. Of the original eleven guru successors from 1977, seven were suspended or abdicated their roles in ISKCON, one recently died, and another remains in virtual seclusion, leaving only two functionally active. In the fallout, roughly two thirds of all ISKCON members became, at one time or another, spiritual "orphans."

As its pool of secondary charismatics has diminished, ISKCON has progressively accommodated itself to a policy of institutionally certified gurus, a process Weber calls the "routinization of charisma." In other words, institutional and rule-bound criteria supersede the charismatic. Such a transformation in organizational dynamics can then alter the nature of religious experience itself. A candid remark from one of the leaders in this process of "guru reform"—who now acts as both GBC member and guru himself—illustrates just how serious these consequences can be: "I joined ISKCON to become a mystic, but instead I have become a bureaucrat."[17] If "mystic" refers to that which is sacred, then "bureaucrat" would seem to imply that which has become profane.

As Rochford, a lifelong ISKCON observer, notes, it seems clear that pressures to control the gurus and the guru institution through bureaucratization of the guru role will only increase as individual ISKCON gurus continue to "fall down" and become involved in scandal and controversy.[18] The cycle of apostasy and resultant controversies, followed by efforts to reform the institution (efforts which place further restrictions on the gurus), promises to further divest the guru institution of any charismatic religious authority it might have had. As a result of the more stringent bureaucratic controls on ISKCON's current gurus and the further subversion of their charismatic authority for the sake of institutional stability, two distinct developments have emerged.

First, as long as the spiritual acumen of current gurus remains open to question and they primarily act as bureaucratically controlled "functionaries" of ISKCON, Bhaktivedanta Swami's own charismatic authority and stature as the Founder-*Acharya* rises in comparison. This has had the effect of posthumously magnifying Bhaktivedanta Swami's prominence to Christ-like proportions. ISKCON convention now heralds him as a last-of-the-prophets for the next ten thousand years.[19] Notwithstanding the swami's physical absence, ISKCON members attempt to adjust for the loss of charisma by stressing Bhaktivedanta's enduring presence in the form of his books and instructions—typically to the neglect of other recognized authorities within the Chaitanya tradition. Radical advocates of this view go a step further and argue that all subsequent generations of the swami's followers should also be considered his *direct* disciples. This latter interpretation characterizes the *ritvik* doctrine, presented in the previous chapter, which disavows any charismatic authority other than Bhaktivedanta Swami himself.

The second repercussion of this routinization of the guru is that ISKCON has become vulnerable to charismatic *sadhus* (holy men or saints) from other branches of the Chaitanya lineage outside the jurisdiction of ISKCON. Narayana Maharaja, as a recognized patriarch of that tradition, is a salient example of one such individual.

The Narayana Maharaja crisis provides an interesting case study: ISKCON, initially an iconoclastic movement that set itself apart from the mundanity and spiritual vacuity of conventional mainstream society,[20] has itself, at least in the eyes of its critics, become a bureaucratic institution that has lost its own charismatic effervescence, and thus become prey to charismatic individuals hovering on its own horizons. As Weber notes, the decisive element distinguishing the prophet or charismatic from the priest is that the latter lays claim to authority by virtue of his service in a sacred tradition, while the charismatic's claim is based on personal revelations and magnetism.[21] So, given the routinization of ISKCON's spiritual leadership—which increasingly resembles the functions of Weber's priest, particularly among its now-outlawed *ritvik* element—Narayana Maharaja's appeal as a senior and charismatic member of the lineage, with claims to more profound realizations of the tradition's esoteric truths than ISKCON leaders', has enticed large numbers of disenfranchised and disillusioned devotees to his orbit of influence outside the jurisdiction of ISKCON. Equally as predictable, this has elicited a furious backlash from the society's orthodoxy.

NARAYANA MAHARAJA'S RELATIONSHIP WITH ISKCON

We cannot understand ISKCON's controversy over Narayana Maharaja without first examining the history of their relationship. Like any family, they share a common past.

Before coming to America, over the span of half a century, Bhaktivedanta Swami had made lasting friendships with many members of his guru's organization, the Gaudiya Math (i.e., his "godbrothers"). Most notable among these were B.R. Shridhara Maharaja and Narayana Maharaja's own guru, B.P. Keshava Maharaja, from whom he would later take *sannyasa*. Even after leaving India, the "Swami" (as he was affectionately known) maintained connections with his godbrothers, hoping they would join with him in his worldwide preaching mission:

So practically there is no difference of opinion in our missionary activities, especially because we are all deriving inspiration from His Divine Grace Bhaktisiddhanta Saraswati Goswami Maharaja [Bhaktivedanta's guru]. I think all our God-brothers are doing the same missionary activities without a doubt, but still the regrettable fact is we are doing all separately, not in conjunction.

I think if my Godbrothers would have attempted similarly, preaching centers would have been established all over the world by this time. Therefore, I wish that my Gaudiya Mission should send their preachers and establish different centers in different parts of the world. That will fulfill the mission of [our Guru Maharaja].

If the Gaudiya Mission decides to send their representatives in all other parts of the world, I can help them in this matter. Similarly, I would also expect cooperation from all our Godbrothers in the matters where I require their help. This mutual cooperation can be established immediately.[22]

Unfortunately, the swami's vision never materialized, although this remained his heartfelt desire.[23] He was obliged to establish the International Society for Krishna Consciousness by his own efforts, for his godbrothers never offered assistance when he requested it.[24] There was one exception, however: Narayana Maharaja—who was not exactly a godbrother, being a disciple of Bhaktivedanta Swami's godbrother, Keshava Maharaja, but a spiritual nephew.

From their introduction in 1947, Narayana Maharaja reverentially accepted Bhaktivedanta Swami as his *shiksha guru*, instructing spiritual master, on a par with his own teacher, Keshava Maharaja. In the years before Bhaktivedanta came to America, Narayana Maharaja worked closely with him as co-editor of two magazines: the Bengali *Gaudiya Patrika* and the Hindi *Bhagavata Patrika*.[25] Over the course of two decades, they became friends, traveled, preached, discussed philosophy, ate meals and shared many intimate times together. Narayana Maharaja would cook for Bhaktivedanta Swami and cared for his needs as the situation called for it. When Narayana Maharaja noticed how the renounced swami was becoming sick by sleeping on the cold stone floor in an unheated room during winter, he asked the swami why he didn't purchase a bed. Bhaktivedanta Swami replied, "I need every *paisa* [penny] for printing my books." Seeing his friend so unconcerned for his personal comfort, Narayana Maharaja went out and collected the funds to buy him a bed. Another time, the Maharaja had to entreat the swami to undergo surgery for elephantiasis, since Bhaktivedanta distrusted western allopathic medicine. Again, Narayana Maharaja paid for the operation with money he had personally collected.[26]

In one of his most significant acts of friendship, Narayana Maharaja urged Bhaktivedanta Swami to accept the renounced order (*sannyasa*) and influenced his own guru, Keshava Maharaja, to encourage him likewise. As the swami himself later recalled: "Upon the repeated insistence of Shri Narayana Maharaja, Shrila Keshava Maharaja bestowed boundless mercy upon this unwilling and blind person by forcibly giving me *sannyasa*."[27] In 1959, Bhaktivedanta Swami accepted the sacred order from Narayana Maharaja's guru at a service organized and officiated by Narayana Maharaja. As history has shown, this set the course for what would become a most extraordinary preaching career.

Bhaktivedanta Swami's affection for his spiritual nephew was also beyond doubt. As the swami would later write to Narayana Maharaja from America: "I think that in all the Gaudiya Matha, you are the best *sevaka* [assistant]." In another letter, Bhaktivedanta Swami wrote: "Our relationship is certainly based upon spontaneous love. From the first time I saw you I have been your constant well-wisher."[28] If we consider that these letters were written almost twenty years after their first encounter, this would seem to indicate an unalienable connection. From their very first meeting, there was mutual acknowledgment of a deep and abiding friendship, a relationship that the swami continued to reaffirm over the years.

While Bhaktivedanta Swami had close ties with many members of the Gaudiya Math, Narayana Maharaja proved to be a friend he could count on. In those first critical years, when Bhaktivedanta Swami was trying to establish a foothold for the Krishna Consciousness movement in the West, Narayana Maharaja supplied whatever he requested from India—books for translation, musical instruments (*karatalas* and *mridangas*), deities for temples, and even his favorite sweet (*pera*). Whenever the swami asked for something to be sent from India, Narayana Maharaja went out of his way to purchase, pack, and ship it. (This was no small task in premodern, rural India.) When the swami turned his attention to establishing a center in India after his successes in the West, it was Narayana Maharaja whom he requested to purchase land for him in the Vrindavan area.

Narayana Maharaja reportedly received several hundred letters from Bhaktivedanta Swami (mostly in Bengali and Hindi), which would have been many more than the swami wrote to any other person.[29] Narayana Maharaja was the only one to greet Bhaktivedanta when he first returned to India after preaching in the West. More significantly, the Swami asked Narayana Maharaja to assist him in his preaching activities abroad:

> When he was in New York, he requested me that, "You should come with me. I am alone and I will like to do something here, so you should come." I told him that, "my *guru* is here and I am serving him. When he will return to Bengal, I may come." "Oh, very good. You should serve your *Gurudeva,* but when you have the chance, you should certainly come and join me." I said "Yes, I will come."[30]

Perhaps the most compelling testimony to their intimate relationship—and what would be Narayana Maharaja's final tribute to a lifelong friend—was when the Swami requested him to preside over his burial rites after his demise.[31]

Narayana Maharaja was also the last person to communicate with Bhaktivedanta Swami before the latter passed away on November 14, 1977.[32] Over the span of thirty years, Narayana Maharaja thus proved to be a trustworthy and faithful friend.

In subsequent years, Narayana Maharaja would continue to volunteer his services to ISKCON in significant ways. During the protracted *De vs. ISKCON* court case in the 1980s, he inconvenienced himself several times, despite a heart condition, to travel across India (Mathura to Bombay) to testify on ISKCON's behalf. In 1990, Ravindra Svarupa (now one of Narayana Maharaja's most outspoken critics) journeyed along with other ISKCON leaders to Narayana Maharaja's *math* to question him about the philosophical and historical validity of the *ritvik* doctrine. Along with publishing Maharaja's remarks, Ravindra Svarupa would subsequently write in the *ISKCON Journal*:

> Narayana Maharaja is a well-wisher of ISKCON and its devotees, and his judgment and discrimination are held in high regard. As one steeped in the Gaudiya Vaishnava tradition, he would have a perspective well worth hearing. . . . Moreover, we thought it would be particularly interesting to consult with him in this case since the main promulgators of the posthumous-*ritvik* doctrine . . . used to inquire from Narayana Maharaja extensively on the subject of *guru*.[33]

Narayana Maharaja was respected as "the best friend of ISKCON"—that is, until ISKCON's leadership abruptly repudiated that relationship in 1995.

A SEISMIC SHIFT: ISKCON'S PERCEPTIONS OF NARAYANA MAHARAJA

In 1995, the annual GBC meeting produced the following resolutions:

> The members of ISKCON should respect all senior Gaudiya Vaishnavas outside ISKCON, but should not intimately associate with them, personally or through printed or recorded media, for guidance, teaching, instruction, or initiation as their presentation of Krishna consciousness often differs from that of Shrila Prabhupada in emphasis, balance and other aspects of both teaching and practice. . . . Those who continue to act in violation of this resolution are subject to sanctions by temple presidents and GBC zonal secretaries, who may exercise their discretion to prohibit any such devotees from living on ISKCON properties or participating in ISKCON functions . . . [and] to suspend any violator from ISKCON.[34]

Although he was not named, everyone knew that this edict was directed specifically at Narayana Maharaja and amounted to an outright ban on associating with him in any way, shape, or form—not in person, not by audio- or videotape, not by literature. What drastic change in circumstances could have provoked such a sudden, deep, and irreparable rift between ISKCON and such a close friend and well-wisher?

Prior to this edict, in the years following the Swami's demise, ISKCON members from around the world could visit Narayana Maharaja's *math* in India without invoking any official reprimand from the institution. They were free to inquire about philosophical specifics of Gaudiya theology and listen to the Maharaja's narrations of Krishna *katha*, elaborations on the stories of the *Bhagavata Purana*. As an elder, austere, and learned Vaishnava, Narayana Maharaja had an obvious appeal, and his discourses started to attract an increasing number of senior ISKCON members. But when such high-profile leaders and GBC members began to "submit to an authority outside of ISKCON" and form an elite, cultlike following, a vigorous protest from the conservative wing of the institution was finally provoked. The threat this maverick group within ISKCON posed, with the possibility of it growing into a full-blown schism, culminated in the 1995 GBC resolution outlawing Narayana Maharaja.

Philosophically, ISKCON leaders felt particularly disturbed by Narayana Maharaja's apparent focus on *rasalila katha*, meditation on the conjugal pastimes of Krishna with the *gopi* cowherd women, a topic that had become a virtual taboo in ISKCON since the Swami had deemphasized it to his neophyte disciples in the 1960s and 1970s. The major points of contention noted in the GBC resolution were that "Some ISKCON members had become overly involved in confidential topics of *rasika bhakti* [imitative devotion] under the influence of Gaudiya Vaishnavas outside of ISKCON," and "the recent proliferation in ISKCON of literature focusing on '*rasika-bhakti*' . . . and other subject matter suitable only for highly advanced souls represent[s] a departure from Shrila Prabhupada's orders."

Initially, the senior members who had been attracted by Narayana Maharaja defended themselves against the allegations of disloyalty and deviance. They attested experiencing an overall deepening of their Krishna consciousness as a result of Narayana Maharaja's influence. But perhaps more insidious from ISKCON's perspective was their conviction that, "Prabhupada, they believed, was now guiding them in the person of Narayana Maharaja."[35] This unpretentious admission of faith in Narayana Maharaja set off alarm bells. Any hint that someone could be equal to or greater than the Swami was considered heretical and utterly intolerable to the ISKCON orthodoxy, since it was interpreted as overshadowing Bhaktivedanta Swami's preeminent role as "the Founder-*Acharya* of ISKCON."[36] In the wake of the systemic successor guru apostasies and the concomitant loss of faith, there was great suspicion of any charismatic authority beyond that of Bhaktivedanta Swami, especially from outside ISKCON.

In 1994, tensions came to a head at the celebration commemorating Bhaktivedanta Swami's taking *sannyasa*, traditionally held at Narayana Maharaja's *math*, where the actual event had taken place thirty-five years previously. During the proceedings, Narayana Maharaja stated that "there were many higher teachings that Prabhupada could have given had his disciples been more advanced." This implied that the Swami's missionary work was elementary and that ISKCON devotees were now ready for a more advanced stage of Krishna consciousness that he (Narayana Maharaja) could provide.[37] When some of the aforementioned senior leaders took the opportunity to glorify Narayana Maharaja rather than the Swami, the rumblings of discontent from those who took these remarks as belittling to "Shrila Prabhupada" (as the Swami is known in ISKCON) erupted into an outcry, and the issue became the primary focus at the next annual GBC meeting in 1995. A swift and summary declaration of heresy was issued. The offending leaders, now repentant, were chastised, subjected to a set of reformatory penances, and then allowed to continue with their managerial functions under the condition that they sever all ties with the elderly *sannyasi*. A major schism was thus averted, at least among these particular senior members.

Rank-and-file devotees were not able to jettison their relationship with the charismatic *sannyasi* quite so easily, however. Almost two hundred devotees had taken "spiritual shelter" with Narayana Maharaja after being orphaned by their previous ISKCON gurus, who had fallen from their vows. Another hundred disciples of Gaura Govinda Maharaja, a charismatic and thus highly controversial ISKCON guru who had recently passed away, were also drawn to Narayana Maharaja due to the similarity in their moods, and had thus accepted him as a *shiksha guru*, "instructing spiritual master." Suddenly, all these devotees found themselves in violation of the GBC ban. Because they were unwilling to give up their source of heartfelt spiritual inspiration to an institutional dictum, they were forced out of ISKCON in the brouhaha that followed. Scores of devotees, such as the head *pujari* (priest) in Murwillambar, Australia and the temple president in Birmingham, England, who had both served faithfully in ISKCON for fifteen to twenty years, were ejected from the society immediately.

Up to this point, the ISKCON devotees going to Narayana Maharaja's *math* in India were limited to those who either lived in India or who could make the extensive and costly journey there. The new threat of excommunication provided further disincentive. The next year, however, as if in defiance of the GBC's ban, an international cadre of former ISKCON members arranged for

Narayana Maharaja to begin traveling in the West: if devotees could not come to Narayana Maharaja, then Narayana Maharaja would go to them. After the first world tour in 1996 proved a resounding success, these extensive preaching tours became a yearly gala affair in many places across the globe. Because of their familiarity with ISKCON, the organizers chose locations convenient to ISKCON centers, thus bringing Narayana Maharaja to the society's doorstep—indeed, to wherever it happened to have its strongest following. Over the next few years, hundreds upon hundreds of disaffected ISKCON members assembled at these gatherings to hear from Narayana Maharaja, attracted by his charismatic qualities. Many devotees even renounced their ISKCON "priestlike" gurus—although they were institutionally certified as being in "good standing"—and took reinitiation from Narayana Maharaja. Though the numbers are now beginning to level out, a significant portion of ISKCON's worldwide congregation has left the parent organization and affiliated with Narayana Maharaja's following. Narayana thus poses a serious and ongoing threat to ISKCON.

Since Narayana Maharaja's preaching tours in the West were primarily targeting long-standing ISKCON followers and congregation members, ISKCON saw this as blatant poaching. From their perspective, it appeared that Narayana Maharaja was striking back at ISKCON with a vengeance. The society was not slow in retaliating. Numerous letters and position papers were hastily written by senior GBC members delineating the alleged deviations of Narayana Maharaja and his followers. These regularly appeared on ISKCON Web sites[38] and were widely publicized to members to alert them of the imminent "danger" of associating with Narayana Maharaja. A letter signed by 350 ISKCON members in the U.K., for example, made the following strongly worded protest to the Maharaja's upcoming visit:

> Throughout the year, and especially at the times of your visits, this *yatra* [branch of ISKCON] is under siege to convert to your line of thought. Our respectful entreaty is that you and your followers stop trying to recruit ISKCON members to your line of thought. We would like to live in an atmosphere of mutual respect with other Vaishnavas, free from intimidation and harassment, respected for our own realization of what it means to be a *Prabhupadanuga* [follower of Prabhupada].[39]

In contrast to other GBC resolutions, which typically went all but unnoticed, the GBC mobilized all of the organizational means at its disposal to alert members of this new threat. Newsletters, temple circulars, and the routine preaching during classes were utilized to ensure that ISKCON members were kept informed. Several prominent temple communities in Australia, England,

and Los Angeles even went beyond GBC resolutions by enjoining *a priori* bans of anyone who affiliated themselves with Narayana Maharaja. According to ISKCON law, "excommunication" was a penalty to be applied judiciously according to an individual's specific misbehavior. Now Narayana Maharaja's followers and sympathizers were being banned categorically without due process or any recourse to appeal.

A thunderstorm of accusations and counterarguments naturally ensued between the two groups as Narayana Maharaja's followers, who all had once been ISKCON members, attempted to defend their faith and philosophical positions. Their response papers were published on non-ISKCON Web sites[40] and in any other venues that they could find, including covert leaflets. Initially, many heated discussions flared up in and around ISKCON communities. In time, however, as dissidents to the GBC policy became increasingly subject to excommunication, protest from within ISKCON was all but extinguished. As the two groups are now completely polarized and divorced from each other, interaction has practically ceased. With no forum to promote fair-minded discussion, few moderates left to maintain any common ground, and no ISKCON leaders willing to sponsor reconciliation, there does not seem much hope for any resolution between the two groups anytime in the near future.

A perusal of the various letters and position papers from ISKCON on the Narayana Maharaja issue highlights the following salient points, indicating either intractable differences or deep-rooted misunderstandings:

1. Shrila Prabhupada was perfect and complete, and supplied everything necessary for complete spiritual realization in his books. His disciples and followers thus need not look elsewhere for spiritual guidance.
2. Prabhupada had stressed that *rasalila katha*, Krishna's amorous liaisons with the *gopis*, was a subject for liberated souls and not for spiritual neophytes. Narayana Maharaja's focus on such topics indicates that his views on this and other matters depart from those of Bhaktivedanta Swami.
3. Narayana Maharaja is minimizing Bhaktivedanta Swami by claiming to be presenting more elevated esoteric teachings.
4. Narayana Maharaja's claim that Bhaktivedanta Swami had asked him to safeguard his mission and disciples, especially his purported claim to be Bhaktivedanta Swami's designated successor, is false and disingenuous, and his representation of the intimacy he enjoyed with Bhaktivedanta Swami overblown.
5. Narayana Maharaja's followers' claim that ISKCON gurus are neophyte or spiritually bankrupt, and that without submitting to Narayana Maharaja's authority devotees can no longer advance spiritually, is also false and presumptuous.

6. Narayana Maharaja is breaking Vaishnava protocol by reinitiating ISKCON devotees whose gurus are in good standing, and by allowing his followers to actively and consciously target ISKCON members and engage in aggressive and duplicitous modes of proselytizing.
7. Narayana Maharaja associates inappropriately with some of his female disciples, and thus exhibits symptoms of *sahajiya*[41]—the display in mundane body and relationships of actions that belong only to the spiritual body and its relationships (specifically, intimate relationships with young women in perverted imitation of Krishna's pastimes with the *gopi* cowherd girls).

Any one of these charges was vilification enough, but all together they were completely damning. ISKCON's allegations, in turn, were considered misinformed, false, disingenuous, and exaggerated by Narayana Maharaja's followers. For instance, the term *rasika bhakti*, which ISKCON often used to point the finger at Narayana Maharaja, was termed a misnomer.[42] Unfortunately, from the very beginning, the GBC never made any honest attempt to verify its misgivings about him and discuss their differences. Once the commission had issued its ban on Narayana Maharaja, the fatal blow to the relationship was struck. It was tantamount to an unprovoked declaration of war, because up to that point, he was not doing anything different than he had ever done. In retrospect, ISKCON's internal politics and insecurity about its own leadership fomented the entire debacle, thus generating a mutual sense of animosity that was previously unknown. As each side has projected its own anger and mistrust into the words and actions of the other, the cycle of accusations and recriminations has spiraled out of control.

In one of the last meetings between a senior ISKCON leader and Narayana Maharaja, Hridayananda Maharaja acknowledged that the GBC never offered Narayana Maharaja the opportunity to defend himself before banning him and his followers in 1995.[43] Despite this admission of fault, no ISKCON apology was forthcoming. Rather, the GBC continued to insist there were genuine concerns behind its complaints, particularly about reinitiation of and the proselytizing to ISKCON members. The conversation thus ended in a stalemate, and no follow-up was scheduled. While several individual ISKCON leaders have approached Narayana Maharaja to apologize, none of them was willing to step forward and help reverse the society's retributive policies against him.

COMPASSION, BETRAYAL, AND ANGER: NARAYANA MAHARAJA'S PERSPECTIVE ON ISKCON

Narayana Maharaja was deeply offended and hurt by the unceremonious abandonment by ISKCON leaders who had been frequenting his *math* (ashram) up until 1995. From his perspective, it was *they* who had come to *him* for guidance and inspiration, and he had always made time for them, spending many hours in discussions and cultivating what he had thought was an honest and friendly relationship. In his view, his interaction with ISKCON devotees, whether in India or the West, was a continuation of his duties to Bhaktivedanta Swami, and to the greater Chaitanya mission:

> I want to take the dust from Shrila Bhaktivedanta Swami Maharaja's lotus feet by going to the places he preached. . . . I have come here to give his message to the entire world. He has planted seeds, and they have somewhat grown, but they are lacking water. Swamiji has given me that water which is *hari-katha* [stories about Krishna]. . . . I have come to help the sincere devotees who are unhappy due to long term lack of good association.[44]

> Eighty or ninety percent of the devotees have left ISKCON. I want that ISKCON becomes more and more powerful. Everyone should be strengthened, and everyone should preach all over the world, just as Swami has preached.[45]

> Swamiji preached in the West and my *Gurudeva* preached in India, yet they spoke the same message. Their love for Krishna is the same. Their teachings are the same. Their service for Mahaprabhu [Chaitanya] is the same. One was in the International Society for Krsna Consciousness and the other in the Gaudiya Vedanta Samiti. But both are in the family of Chaitanya Mahaprabhu (*Gaura parivara*), so there is no need to quarrel.[46]

There are striking similarities between the sentiments expressed by Narayana Maharaja and those of the Swami (as previously quoted). From both their perspectives, there is only *one* Chaitanya lineage and no "separate branch," as ISKCON now conceives itself. It also seems ironic that Narayana Maharaja criticizes ISKCON with the same voice of authority that the Swami criticized his parent institution, the Gaudiya Math. He says: "They don't know what it means to be *Rupanuga* [followers of Rupa Goswami, the primary disciple of Chaitanya] so they have concocted this expression *Prabhupadanuga* [follower of Prabhupada] as if they belong to some new line, thinking that ISKCON is outside of the Gaudiya line."[47]

In addition to its intralineage isolationism, Narayana Maharaja feels that ISKCON has degenerated into factionalism and squabbling, and thus lost touch with Vaishnava decorum and the basic goals of spiritual practice (*bhakti*):

> Although they had taken initiation from a great personality, they are now quarreling with each other for control of their center and all the devotees.

One of them had become *guru*, and he had been controlling all [in Calcutta]. The second party, the *ritviks*, had no faith in him, and they themselves wanted to control all ISKCON. Both sides were saying, "We are the real ISKCON." Who is the real ISKCON?[48]

A Vaishnava will be *akinchana*, without any sense of proprietorship, and *dinahina*, very humble and not quarreling with anyone. Why are the godbrothers quarreling? Are they quarreling for *bhakti*? They are only quarreling because they are greedy for mundane achievement.[49]

Narayana Maharaja further criticizes ISKCON for its obsession with quantitative results—book distribution, temple construction, etc.—rather than the qualitative cultivation of devotion (*bhakti*):

Some are telling that you should always be distributing book and making money for your whole life, and this will take you to Goloka Vrindavan [the kingdom of God] in the service of *gopi-prema* [love of God in the mood of the *gopis*]. This is quite absurd. . . . They should know that this book distribution alone will not be sufficient to achieve the final goal. . . . Why are they falling down? They are blaspheming persons for their own gain, and when collecting donations in the name of *guru*, they are giving 25% and 75% profit is coming into their own pockets. . . . Swamiji has written everything. Everything [all the details of advancing through the various stages of *bhakti*]. . . . But [they] have no chance to go through these books, because [they] are always only distributing and distributing. But this will not take us to that higher goal.[50]

In Narayana Maharaja's critique, proficiency in the external activities of devotion is not automatically equivalent to internal spiritual advancement. Without the infusion of inspiration that comes as a direct result of spiritually advanced and exemplary association, the "regular" or "routine" discharge of devotional service (*vidhi marga*) tends to become mechanical and make practitioners complacent. In resonance with Weber, the association of genuinely charismatic saints (*sadhu sanga*) is therefore extolled in Gaudiya theology as indispensable because it is the primary catalyst for advancement in devotion. While religious institutions can play a vital role in facilitating spiritual experience, they are not intrinsic to it. Vaishnavism, like most forms of Hindu spirituality, is essentially a mystic path, a process of *self*-realization.

Narayana Maharaja was particularly indignant about the charges of *sahajiya*, inappropriate conduct with his female disciples in imitation of Krishna's pastimes with the *gopis*, leveled against him, especially with the backdrop of the seemingly endless spectacle of ISKCON's scandals and *sannyasi* fall-downs. Who were *they* to throw stones at him?

> They think I am involved with women. Can anyone say this? Do I drink and smoke, or do any bad habits? Do I wear my *sannyasa* dress when I come to my room in the *mandira* [temple], and I change my cloth when I go to other countries? And about money? I want pure hearts only, I don't want money. So who is *sahajiya* [a cheap imitator]? Myself or those who are telling like this? You can decide. Those who are telling like this and who are not following these instructions are *sahajiya*. . . . Krishna has given you the intelligence to meditate on all these things. Don't accept blindly. Don't believe their rumors and propaganda. Today in *kali-yuga* [the present world age], propaganda and rumors are the most prominent weapons, but a Vaishnava is not affected by all these things.[51]

As for the emphasis on esoteric teachings, *raganuga bhakti* (spontaneous rather than rule-bound devotion), Narayana Maharaja has repeatedly contended that if Bhaktivedanta Swami were physically present today he would surely give such higher, esoteric teachings.[52] There is an interesting exchange from the early days of ISKCON between Bhaktivedanta Swami and one of his disciples who had studied in the Gaudiya Math that would seem to give some credence to this. The disciple was complaining to the Swami that whenever he mentioned anything about such higher topics to fellow disciples, they would become angry and dismiss it as "a bunch of Gaudiya Math nonsense," and say, "[the Swami] never taught us that!" Bhaktivedanta Swami assured him, "Everything is coming, they will also know it."[53] This same disciple then recalled a lengthy discussion with Bhaktivedanta Swami on esoteric aspects of Gaudiya philosophy to which the Swami expressed no aversion. Indeed, upon this disciple's prompting, Bhaktivedanta responded by translating and then publishing Rupa Goswami's *Upadesamrta* (The Nectar of Instruction), which exhorts readers to come to this higher level of *raganuga bhakti* by declaring it the "essence of all advice."[54] As a charismatic teacher, Narayana Maharaja has taken it as his specific mission to enlighten devotees with these esoteric teachings.

One of Bhaktivedanta Swami's primary concerns was that Krishna's affairs with the *gopis*, which Gaudiya theology holds to represent the highest intensity of divine love, not be misunderstood as mundane sexual dealings. But the swami's words of caution never constituted an outright ban, nor did they necessitate developing a phobia about the topic:

> The policy should be that people [should] not understand the *gopis* [to be] like ordinary girls. . . . You should be careful to present the *gopis*. It does not mean that "We shall not utter even the name of *gopis*. We have

taken vow to boycott the *gopis*." No. They are our worshipable devotees. How can we avoid them?[55]

CONCLUDING REFLECTIONS

ISKCON's conflict with Narayana Maharaja is not the idiosyncratic clash of personalities, but the inevitable consequence of a deep-rooted organizational strategy. Its exclusion of next-of-kin charismatics has not been limited to Narayana Maharaja. Rather, the 1995 GBC ban reiterates a long-standing ISKCON policy to censure any senior member of the Gaudiya tradition outside its own jurisdiction. And as Gelberg notes, this policy of isolationism has deprived the institution of potentially invigorating renewal and rejuvenation:

> Individual immersion in ISKCON's parent tradition is also limited by ISKCON's self-imposed quarantine against other contemporary forms of Chaitanya Vaishnavism in India. Competition among Vaishnavite *gurus* in India for disciples has played a role, as has Prabhupada's abhorrence of perceived heresies on the part of other teachers and sects. Thus Prabhupada deliberately isolated his inexperienced Western disciples from Indian Vaishnavas in general to keep them from potential contamination. A certain kind of orthodoxy may have been preserved, but potentially nourishing contact with exemplary persons within the living tradition in India was enjoined. Such insularity has caused psychological and cultural inbreeding within ISKCON that has weakened its spiritual fabric and engendered an unhealthy elitism with regard to other forms of Chaitanya Vaishnavism. ISKCON's virtual isolation from the contemporary wellsprings of its Indian roots has deprived devotees of an important potential source of inspiration and invigoration.[56]

From a Weberian perspective, such self-imposed quarantine is all but inevitable as charisma becomes stagnant and routinized, and an originally dynamic institution is threatened, in its turn, with external forms of charisma claiming greater and more exhilarating truths—which, in this case, are the esoteric teachings Narayana Maharaja feels it is his calling to impart.

It is true that Chaitanya authorities including Bhaktivedanta Swami have cautioned against public disclosure of the apparently sensual pastimes of Krishna's *rasalila*, and it is true that some of the lectures of Narayana Maharaja deal with subjects that may be considered esoteric from the perspective of a novice.[57] It is also true that Narayana Maharaja, on specific occasions, has spoken on confidential texts like *Shri Vilapa-kushumanjali* at the request of certain senior ISKCON leaders during friendlier times. However, these classes were conducted selectively and in private, not in public. Moreover, most of the devotees who comprise the inner audience of Narayana Maharaja have been practitioners for twenty years or more and, like himself, have lived exemplary lives as ascetics and celibates. Furthermore, even from an ordinary standpoint, a distinguished scholar has the prerogative to teach advanced subjects at his own discretion.

Narayana Maharaja's presence and preaching provoke a number of deeper considerations. If Bhaktivedanta Swami were still physically present, would he be explaining the same teachings to those who had been following him for thirty years as he would to those who had just recently adopted the process of Krishna consciousness? If Bhaktivedanta Swami forbade a recently converted disciple in 1969 to read an esoteric scripture due to the newcomer's fledgling commitment to *bhakti* and the high moral standard of celibacy that such study entailed, would he still have denied such a disciple access to that scripture thirty years later (in 1999)—or for the rest of his life, for that matter—despite the disciple's having developed maturity and stability in spiritual practice over the years?

Taking a phobic position against *raganuga bhakti*, the undisputed culmination of Chaitanya devotional praxis, entails asserting that everyone is banned forever from reading the writings of the Goswami disciples of Chaitanya on the grounds that Bhaktivedanta Swami may have restricted his new disciples from doing so decades ago. There can be little doubt that Bhaktivedanta Swami desired all of his followers to study the esoteric teachings of the Goswamis in due course:

> Unless one follows the six Gosvamis . . . one cannot be a bona fide spontaneous lover of Krsna [*raganuga bhakti*]. In this connection, Shrila Narottama dasa Thakura says, *rupa-raghunatha-pade haibe akuti kabe hama bujhaba se yugala piriti* [When will I become very eager to study the books of the Goswamis]?[58]

> To follow Chaitanya Mahaprabhu means to follow the six Gosvamis, because these six Gosvamis were directly instructed by Chaitanya Mahaprabhu to spread this movement. . . . And they have given us this invaluable literature. There are so many other literatures, of which the *Bhakti-rasamrta-sindhu,* we have translated into English: *Nectar of Devotion.* So try to follow this book. *Rupa-raghunatha-pade haibe akuti.*[59]

The implications of ISKCON's puritanical stance on *raganuga bhakti* produce further dichotomies. If after thirty years, none of Bhaktivedanta Swami's disciples is qualified to read certain Gaudiya literatures, then is the process of *bhakti* that he propagated ineffective, or, at best, productive of only rudimentary results? If ISKCON tries to impose unconditional legislation as to the esoteric level of literature that its practitioners are qualified to study, then is it not denying the possibility of degrees of eligibility among individuals in its community, as well as the possibility of attaining the stated goal of the lineage?

> Real *bhakti* . . . that is *raganuga-bhakti*. This *raganuga-bhakti*, we have to come after surpassing the *vaidhi-bhakti* [regulative process]. In the material world, if we do not try to make further and further progress in devotional service, if we are simply sticking to the *shastric* [scriptural] regulation process and do not try to go beyond that. . . . The *shastric* process is *kanishtha-adhikara*, lowest stage of devotional service. . . . This is nice beginning, but one has to go above this. . . . If I become satisfied only with these regulative principles for worshiping . . . but if I have no other idea, then *sa bhaktah prakrtah smrtah*. *Prakrta* means on the material platform. . . . So any devotee can fall down if he remains *prakrta-bhakta*. So he has to raise himself above this in the *madhyama-adhikara* [intermediate stage]. . . . Therefore, if we do not associate with the advanced devotees, *uttama-adhikari*, if we simply want to remain in the lowest stage of devotional service, then we are not making progress. Then we shall simply enjoy the material field, without entering into the spiritual platform.[60]

From the perspective of the sociology of religion, ISKCON has entered into a phase of denominationalism—the development wherein religiosity is judged in terms of being a card-carrying member of an institution rather than of a person's sincere interest in spiritual activities, and the obligation to conform to group norms tends to overshadow the individual's need to advance spiritually. This creates serious repercussions for any ISKCON member who finds a source of inspiration outside. The term "outside ISKCON"—whether in terms of reading non-ISKCON approved literature or taking association with Vaishnava authorities outside the institution—has now become so emotionally fraught and politicized that it is equated with disloyalty to Bhaktivedanta Swami.

At the risk of stating the obvious, denominations do not live on "spirit" alone; institutions require concrete resources for their subsistence. Irrespective of theological differences or spiritual hierarchies, the influence of an itinerant charismatic such as Narayana Maharaja on an institution's manpower and support base is unlikely to be welcome. As its congregation and potential financial contributions are siphoned away, the institution may take the convenient recourse of demonizing the perceived culprit. Add to this that, since this schism erupted, Narayana Maharaja, in true charismatic style, openly defies GBC authority, preaches against its policies, and proclaims it is his mission to reform its catechism, and confrontation becomes inevitable.

ISKCON's attempts to remain rigidly exclusive must inevitably prove counterproductive. The farther the society continues down the path of routinization, the more its membership will be tempted to look elsewhere for inspirational role models; its bland institutional authority will stand in uninspiring contrast to itinerant charismatics, who will appear more attractive by comparison. In the decade prior to Narayana Maharaja's emergence as a charismatic teacher, the Swami's godbrother B.R. Shridhara Maharaja also attracted significant numbers of disaffiliated and disillusioned ISKCON members. There have been other contenders as well—Shrila Shridhara Maharaja's successor, B.S. Govinda Maharaja; B.P. Puri Maharaja (now deceased); B.V. Puri Maharaja, etc. It seems safe to assume that the confrontational dialectic between the charismatic and the institution is perpetual, and ISKCON will continue to face such external challenges.

The emergence of charisma *within* the group can be no less problematic. The tension that was brewing between ISKCON and Gaura Govinda Maharaja prior to his demise is a case in point. Gaura Govinda Maharaja was an elderly Indian disciple of Bhaktivedanta Swami and Vaishnava by birth, thus more senior, learned, exemplary, and inspirational than the younger westerners who comprised the majority of ISKCON's gurus. While a full discussion is beyond the scope of this essay, suffice it to say that Gaura Govinda Maharaja was also perceived as a threat. The GBC was concerned about the devotees who were flocking to his ISKCON temple in India from other ISKCON temples. The GBC was on the verge of taking disciplinary action against the Maharaja for his outspoken opinions—defying the commission's decisions on such theological matters as *guru tattva* (the truth about guru) and the origin of the soul—when he passed away.

Charisma, by its very nature, can only be subversive to the established conventions of institutionalized religion. Religious institutions, in their turn, have little recourse, short of conceding their own claims of legitimacy, but to counter the iconoclastic claims of the charismatic. However, given their formidable potential influence, it would seem prudent for a religious hierarchy to deal with charismatic teachers and outspoken reformers wisely. For it is next to impossible to turn back the clock and change the past once a major religious schism has erupted.

NOTES

1. Larry Shinn, *The Dark Lord* (Philadelphia: Westminster Press, 1987), 47.
2. While scholars obviously differ in their views about church history, the line between heterodoxy and heresy is certainly a fine one. Sometimes that sharp line is drawn only because of the times and prevailing political atmosphere. Cf. *A History of Heresy* by David Christie-Murray (1976; reprint, London: Oxford University Press, 1989).
3. Max Weber, *The Theory of Social and Economic Organization* (New York: Oxford University Press, 1947), 358 59.

4. Charles Selengut, "Charisma and Religious Innovation: Prabhupada and the Founding of ISKCON." *ISKCON Communications Journal* 4(2) (1999): 4.
5. Ibid.
6. Weber, *The Theory of Social and Economic Organization,* 364.
7. Roy Wallis, "Charisma, Commitment and Control in a New Religious Movement." In: *Millenialism and Charisma,* ed. Roy Wallis (Belfast: The Queen's University, 1982), 116.
8. Roy Wallis, *Salvation and Protest: Studies of Social and Religious Movements* (New York: St. Martin's Press, 1979), 137.
9. Ibid., 130.
10. Ibid., 137.
11. Bhaktisiddhanta Saraswati, "Putana." Originally published in *The Harmonist* (*Sree Sajjanatoshani*) (Calcutta: Gaudiya Mission) Jan. 1932. Available online: http://www.bvml.org/SBSST/putana.htm.
12. A.C. Bhaktivedanta Swami, Letter to Karandhara, 22 December 1972. In: *Srila Prabhupada's Letters 1965–1977* (Culver City, CA: The Vaisnava Institute, 1987), 2183.
13. Charisma can also be deceptive and imply something suspect or fake. Hence Bhaktivedanta Swami's quip about "charmistic" gurus (see *Conversations,* 31 October 1976 [Vrindavan, India: Vedabase, 1998], 76031rc.vrn).
14. A.C. Bhaktivedanta Swami, Letter to Hamsaduta, Sydney, 11 April 1972. *Srila Prabhupada's Letters,* 1958–59.
15. In other words, the institution becomes an end in itself. Aside from spiritual principles, even basic social ethics are compromised to cover tracks, protect the church's hierarchy, and maintain the status quo. The current child molestation scandals plaguing ISKCON and the Catholic Church come to mind.
16. A.C. Bhaktivedanta Swami, Letter to Rupanuga Tirupati, 28 April 1974 (Vedabase, 1998). Also: "If Guru Maharaja could have seen someone who was qualified at that time to be *acharya* he would have mentioned. Because on the night before he passed away he talked of so many things, but never mentioned an *acharya*. His idea was *acharya* was not to be nominated amongst the governing body. He said openly you make a GBC and conduct the mission. So his idea was amongst the members of GBC who would come out successful and self effulgent *acharya* would be automatically selected [*sic*]." *Srila Prabhupada's Letters,* 2476. In the Gaudiya tradition, an *acharya* usually refers to a guru who is the sole head of an institution or sectarean lineage (a guru is anyone who accepts disciples). Thus there may be a number of gurus, but only one *acharya*.
17. Personal correspondence, December 1996.
18. E. Burke Rochford, "Prabhupada Centennial Survey: A Final Report." *ISKCON Communications Journal* 7 (1) (1999).
19. To uphold this view, ISKCON devotees routinely invoke a somewhat obscure quote from Bhaktivedanta Swami that gained wide currency, "My books will the law books for human society for the next ten thousand years," spoken on a single occasion to Tamal Krishna Goswami in a private conversation. (Personal communication, Tamal Krishna Gosvami to Ekkehard Lorenz, 2 November 2000).
20. See Stillson Judah's ground-breaking study, *Hare Krishna and the Counterculture* (New York: Wiley, 1974).
21. Max Weber, *Sociology of Religion,* trans. Ephraim Fischoff (Boston: Beacon Press, 1964), 46.

22. A.C. Bhaktivedanta Swami, Letter to Bhagavata Maharaja, 21 August 1969. *Srila Prabhupada's Letters,* 1001.

23. Before passing away, Bhaktivedanta Swami again repeated his great hope for a unified preaching mission in his final conversation with Narayana Maharaja, 8 October 1977, "My Shiksha-Guru and Priya Bandhu," 36.

24. The context may have also provided little scope for assistance. After the demise of Bhaktisiddhanta Saraswati, the preaching mission was a fractured institution, with rivaling leaders each busy conducting their own separate *maths* (temple-ashrams). These godbrothers were generally poor and had few resources or manpower at their disposal. The one institution that was in a position to lend the swami substantial resources, the Gaudiya Mission in Calcutta, declined his requests on sectarian grounds: they would not sponsor him or offer any assistance because he was not a member of their *math.*

25. B.V. Narayana Maharaja, "A Brief History." In *Their Lasting Relation* (Delhi: Harmony Press, 1997), 4.

26. Conversation with Narayana Maharaja. Badger, California, May 1998; personal recording. Also see ibid.

27. A.C. Bhaktivedanta Swami. "Letter of Condolence" to Shripad Trivikrama Maharaja, 22 October 1968. In B.V. Narayana Maharaja, *Their Lasting Relation,* 39.

28. A.C. Bhaktivedanta Swami, Letter to Narayana Maharaja, 28 September 1966. In *Letters from America to Srila Narayana Maharaja* (Mathura: Gaudiya Vedanta Press, 1997), 15.

29. Ibid., 60. ISKCON contests this number as highly exaggerated. To date, only about thirty of these letters are still extant; the rest were supposed to have been destroyed in a fire.

30. B.V. Narayana Maharaja, "A Brief History," 4. Although he is highly educated in Hindi, Bengali, and Sanskrit, Narayana Maharaja's grasp of English is somewhat basic.

31. Conversation, 8 October 1977, in Satsvarupa Dasa Goswami, *Srila Prabhupada Lilamrta,* vol. 6 (Los Angeles: Bhaktivedanta Book Trust, 1984), 399–401. The honor of presiding over the funeral rites of an *acharya* is traditionally entrusted to his successor, or in the case of a father, to his eldest son.

32. Recollection by Bhagavata Dasa, in Narayana Maharaja, *My Shiksha-Guru and Priya Bandhu. Remembrances by Srila Bhaktivedanta Narayana Maharaja* (Mathura: Gaudiya Vedanta Press, 1999), 46.

33. Ravindra Svarupa, "Conversation with H.H. Narayana Maharaja," *ISKCON Journal* 1 (1) (1990): 21.

34. GBC Resolution #73, Mayapur, 1995.

35. Tamal Krishna Goswami, "Heresies of Authority and Continuity in the Krishna Movement." *Journal of Vaisnava Studies* 8 (1) (1999): 132.

36. It is significant to note that the swami stipulated that the title "Founder-*Acharya*" should appear along with his name on all ISKCON letterhead, publications, and official notices.

37. Tamal Krishna, Goswami, "Heresies of Authority and Continuity in the Krishna Movement," 134.

38. See http://narasimha.net/ISKCON-protection/ for a selection of these.

39. Submitted by Shivarama Swami, GBC for UK, to CHAKRA Web site, June 14, 2001.

40. www.vnn.org, www.gaudiya.net, www.purebhakti.com, etc.

41. Per Gaudiya Vaisnava canon, *sahajiya* (imitative devotion) is a highly charged heresy.

42. According to B.V. Aranya Maharaja, a former ISKCON member and now one of Narayana Maharaja's leading disciples, *rasika bhakti* is a fabricated charge. ISKCON leaders had accused Narayana Maharaja of the *sahajiya* heresy, but, unable to substantiate this charge with much more than hearsay, they coined a new term, *rasika bhakti*, with no historical validity, and then accused him of that.

43. Conversation, Narayana Maharaja and Hridayananda Maharaja, Three Rivers, California, 5 June 2000; personal notes.

44. B.V. Narayana Maharaja, "My Mission in the West." Lecture in San Francisco, 30 June 1996. In *Their Lasting Relation*, 16.

45. Ibid.

46. B.V. Narayana Maharaja, "Nectar Sprinkles in Australia" (pamphlet) (Mathura: Gaudiya Vedanta Press, 1998).

47. B.V. Narayana Maharaja, comments at the "disappearance" (paraphrased from Hindi). Dauji Mandira, Vrindavan, India, October 2000; personal notes.

48. B.V. Narayana Maharaja, Morning Lecture Transcript, "Two Drops of Nectar." Eugene, Oregon, 30 April 2001.

49. Ibid.

50. B.V. Narayana Maharaja, *The Essence of All Advice* (Mathura: Gaudiya Vedanta Press, 1998), 26. The gurus who left ISKCON often absconded with substantial bank accounts and ISKCON resources. A recent settlement with one ex-guru was reportedly worth over one million dollars.

51. Ibid., 20. At over eighty years old, Narayana Maharaja has passed an exemplary life as a renunciant for fifty years, constantly surrounded by fellow monastics, and with no record of anyone in his guru's mission ever deviating from their vows. To suggest that Maharaja maintains any illicit connections with women would seem a dubious argument at best.

52. B.V. Narayana Maharaja, "Remembrances at 26 2nd Ave." In *Their Lasting Relationship*, 26.

53. "Conversation with Hrishikeshananda," Mayapur, 1973. Available online: www.vnn.org: Editorial 10/21/1998—2391.

54. A.C. Bhaktivedanta Swami, *The Nectar of Instruction* (Los Angeles: Bhaktivedanta Book Trust, Text 8, 1976). Devotion in practice (*sadhana bhakti*) is classified under two divisions: regulated service (*vaidhi bhakti*) and spontaneous attraction (*raganuga bhakti*). The neophyte/esoteric controversy revolves around the question of at what point an aspirant is qualified to benefit from a higher order of teachings.

55. A.C. Bhaktivedanta Swami, Conversation, Boston, 24 December 1969 (Bhaktivedanta Vedabase, 1998, 691224.dc.bos).

56. Steven J. Gelberg, "The Call of the Lotus-Eyed Lord: The Fate of Krishna Consciousness in the West," in *When Prophets Die: The Post Charismatic Fate of New Religious Movements*, ed. T. Miller (Albany: SUNY Press, 1991), 159.

57. These lectures can be downloaded from the Internet: http://www.gaudiya.net.

58. A.C. Bhaktivedanta Swami, *Chaitanya Charitamrita, Madhya-lila* 22.153 purport (Los Angeles: Bhaktivedanta Book Trust, 1974).

59. A.C. Bhaktivedanta Swami, *The Nectar of Devotion* lectures, Bombay, 5 January 1973 (Vedabase, 1998).

60. A.C. Bhaktivedanta Swami, *Srimad-Bhagavatam* lectures 1.2.33, Vrindavan, 12 November 1972 (Vedabase, 1998).

PART 4
Heresies

[14]

DOCTRINAL CONTROVERSY AND
THE GROUP DYNAMIC

CONRAD JOSEPH (KUNDALI DAS)

I N 1994–95, a long-simmering doctrinal controversy came to a boil in
ISKCON. It turned around the question, Where did the souls in this
world originally come from? Did they fall down from Vaikuntha, the
kingdom of God? Did they come here from some other place? Were they always here? Concerned devotees were not satisfied with the stock response of
the society's leaders, which was that souls fall here from Vaikuntha, for it
seemed inconsistent with other parts of the Gaudiya philosophy. They kept
pressing the question. Eventually the issue reached an inflamed emotional
pitch. In the end, although the leaders of ISKCON never delivered a sound
philosophical explanation for their verdict, based on scripture, those who disagreed with the official position were dubbed heretical.

Part 1 of this paper presents a case study of that doctrinal controversy. Here
I show five things: (1) a significant number of ISKCON members consider it a
virtue to take the founder's words as absolute, that is, uncritically or blindly; (2)
the methodology ISKCON commonly uses for determining doctrinal deviation, because it is not based on rigorous epistemological procedure, is arbitrary;

(3) several of ISKCON's top scholars—and the GBC as a whole—have a fundamentally wrong understanding of the scriptural tradition they represent; (4) ISKCON's concept of heresy results in confusion, because it is not based on proven deviation from divine revelation or scriptural canon but on perceived deviation from the teachings of ISKCON's founder, Swami Prabhupada; (5) the inescapable outcome of these four failings is that ISKCON commits heresy against its own tradition.

In part 2, using this case study as a backdrop, I pursue a broader discussion of the dynamics within ISKCON, drawing primarily on Erich Fromm's and Abraham Maslow's theories of social psychology. I conclude by stating briefly the key step in addressing the problem of destructive group dynamics.

PART I

Though ISKCON has a bulky law book, it has no official definition of heresy. Accordingly, we must deduce its position from the official reaction to events deemed heretical, and from unofficial published statements of some of ISKCON's long-standing leaders. One such leader, the late Tamal Krishna Goswami, besides being a Governing Body Commission (GBC) member and guru, is a respected ISKCON academic. At the annual meeting of the American Academy of Religion (New Orleans, 1996), he presented a paper entitled, "The Perils of Succession: Heresies of Authority and Continuity in the Hare Krishna Movement." So far the most thorough treatment of the topic in print, it subsequently appeared in the *ISKCON Communications Journal* (5 [1] [June 1997]). Citing Joseph Tyson (1984:410), Tamal Krishna Goswami defines heresy as follows:

> The word heresy is derived from a Greek word meaning "choice." It had been used to designate the particular teachings of philosophical schools, and it denoted the opinion that each one had chosen. Christian writers began to use the term and soon gave it a pejorative significance. To them it indicated that a person had chosen a human opinion and rejected divine revelation. In this sense heresy has an evil significance, and the heretic is considered evil.

All orthodox systems of Indian spirituality accept the divine origin of the Vedic scripture, so the Gaudiya tradition implicitly agrees with Tyson that heresy means choosing a human opinion over divinely revealed scriptural canon. When we look at Tamal Krishna Goswami's application of the term "heresy," however, he is inconsistent with his own stated definition. Issues that should merely be called controversy are labeled heresy. For instance, he so labels a 1976 power struggle between the ascetics of ISKCON and the house-holders. This was a power play that involved no canonical dispute as such, though it greatly displeased Prabhupada, for it threatened schism among his followers. Another misplaced item on Tamal's list is the controversy that erupted when some ISKCON members wanted to emphasize the esoteric aspect of *bhakti*, which focuses on the erotic pastimes of Krishna. That episode also incurred the extreme displeasure of Prabhupada, who considered his disciples' interest in spiritual eroticism premature, but it hardly qualifies as a rejection of divine revelation. There were two occurrences of such emphasis on premature eroticism in ISKCON's history. Confirming his misapplication of heresy, Tamal Krishna Goswami listed them both as instances of heresy.

Tamal Krishna Goswami, in summarizing the GBC's resolution, states: "Regarding philosophical controversies, Prabhupada's instructions and personal example are to be the first and primary source for ISKCON's devotees. Vedic literatures, the writings of the past *acharya*s, and even the current teachings of any bona fide non-ISKCON *acharya* must be viewed through Prabhupada's teachings." This suggests that for the GBC, Prabhupada's utterances are the yardstick for truth claims, not an epistemological analysis of the divine revelation of scripture. We will see more evidence to this effect.

According to the GBC's outlook on doctrinal controversy, to question, sift, and sort the statements of Prabhupada, even in light of canonical statements and the views of previous commentators in the Gaudiya line, is to risk being heretical. Instead, one should do the reverse, understand all matters by filtering them though Prabhupada's explanations. Indeed, to this effect, Tamal Krishna Goswami cites Hridayananda Das Goswami, long-time GBC member (now retired), and respected ISKCON academic with a Harvard Ph.D.: "The members of ISKCON, who live perpetually at the feet of Shrila Prabhupada, may speculate how Shrila Prabhupada's statements are true, but they may not challenge his statements, or claim that they are false. This is precisely what it means to accept Shrila Prabhupada as the founder-*acharya*."

Hridayananda Das Goswami, one of the main players in the controversy under discussion, has clearly articulated his orientation: the line between heresy and orthodoxy is not based on the divine revelation of scripture but on Prabhupada's utterances. To question these, or to examine any contradictory statements with a critical eye, is unacceptable scholarship, in Hridayananda's view, and unacceptable conduct for a follower of Prabhupada. And this orientation, he says, "is precisely what it means to accept Prabhupada." So, if Prabhupada said brass is gold, for example, a good disciple can try to justify how his statement is true, but does not dare have a goldsmith test a sample. Accept his opinion as your own; if it is questioned, generate arguments to bolster his words and you are the true believer. Tamal Krishna Goswami agrees with this stance. Thus, to follow Prabhupada, in the eyes of two of ISKCON's leading lights, means to do so uncritically, blindly.

For several years prior to 1994, the question of the fallen soul's origin was high on the agenda of the GBC's Philosophical Committee. Eventually, the chair of that committee, Suhotra Swami, gave up his post, declaring that the committee was unable to resolve the question. Meanwhile, in an unrelated development, Satyanarayana Das and Kundali Das[1] were both involved in translating and commenting on the *Sandarbhas*,[2] a six-part treatise by Shri Jiva Goswami, a prominent disciple of Chaitanya in the sixteenth century and one of the principal formulators of the Gaudiya philosophy. All Gaudiyas accept Jiva Goswami's exegesis as the most systematic and conclusive work on Chaitanya's philosophy.

Word got out that Kundali and Satyanarayana's view on the origin of embodied souls in this world, reflecting Jiva Goswami's teachings, was that no one falls from the spiritual realm, but rather the souls were always here in the *samsaric* material world. Not knowing any of the evidence or reasoning from these two authors, another reputed ISKCON academic, Drutakarma Das, circulated a vitriolic e-mail to the GBC members on August 24, 1994 making serious charges against them. His message revealed a fervor that did not invite discussion: "To kill Shrila Prabhupada's teachings (by whimsically explaining them away) is to kill Shrila Prabhupada. So let him [Satyanarayana] go and publish his nonsense interpretations elsewhere. At least we will know that we have preserved Shrila Prabhupada's teachings intact and insured against that thing Shrila Prabhupada most feared, that we would change or relativize what he taught us." From his words it is clear that Drutakarma, like Tamal Krishna Goswami and Hridayananda Das Goswami, believes that to question Prabhupada's words is to "relativize" his teachings, a vile deed. Conversely, the height of virtue and righteousness must be to take Prabhupada literally and without question.

Did Prabhupada teach this to his disciples? Was this his mission in coming to the West? Did he try to establish a cult of personality? He wrote more than 60 books, and his recorded lectures and conversations are in the hundreds. More than 4,000 of his letters are archived, and there are several films of him as well. So there is no shortage of data we can examine to see what most typifies his orientation, his personality, and his character. Such an examination shows that he taught that scripture, not quoting and counterquoting his own words, is the litmus test for truth claims: "The process of speaking in spiritual circles is to say something upheld by the scriptures. One should at once quote from scriptural authority to back up what he is saying" (*Bhagavad Gita* 17.15, purport). Prabhupada's view accords with Tyson's definition of heresy. Then how and why did some of his most learned followers end up with the very opposite idea of what he was all about?

Drutakarma's vitriol raised the controversy to an emotional pitch that precluded any equitable procedure or due process. He backed the leaders into a corner over the translation efforts of Kundali and Satyanarayana. He also authored an unpublished manuscript, "Once We Were with Krishna," which was circulated via the Internet. In it he laid out his understanding of what came to be called "the *jiva* issue." Kundali and Satyanarayana were prevailed upon to respond to both his e-mail and his book. Initially, they refused, sensing that a philosophical discussion was hopeless. Eventually, however, a further missive from Drutakarma Das appeared in an Internet discussion group for ISKCON members. In an attempt to exalt Prabhupada's greatness and show love for him, Drutakarma made claims implying that Prabhupada had started his own line of discliplic succession, the "Prabhupada Parampara," or "Prabhupada Sampradaya," which is something Prabhupada never claimed for himself. Rather, he insisted that he did not add or subtract anything from his predecessors.

At this point, Kundali and Satyanarayana resolved to respond to Drutakarma and to clear up the *jiva* issue for posterity. In the spirit of open debate, they decided to write a book refuting Drutakarma's idea that the souls in this world originally fell from the spiritual world. They would do this via an epistemological analysis and show that Prabhupada's final conclusion on the question agreed with his predecessors in the Gaudiya lineage. The book was called *In Vaikuntha, Not Even the Leaves Fall*.[3]

In researching Prabhupada's statements about the origin of the soul, Kundali and Satyanarayana found that at different times he in fact had given three different kinds of responses to the question:

1. Typically, his answer was that all living entities were once with Krishna, but misused their free will and opted out of that perfect situation. As a result they fell from the spiritual kingdom to the material world. Now, in the human form of life, they have the chance, by perfecting their *bhakti*, to return to Krishna's kingdom.

2. At other times, notably when Prabhupada was not responding directly to the *jiva* question from disciples but addressing it in the context of a lecture or in his writings, he was emphatic that no one falls from Vaikuntha (*Bhag.* 3.16.26, purport): "The conclusion is that no one falls from the spiritual world, or Vaikuntha planet, for it is the eternal abode."

3. Sometimes Prabhupada discouraged dwelling on the question: "What does it matter how you got here? If you are drowning, the important thing is to get out of the ocean. Solve this problem. Later you may understand how it happened." In a variant of this category of response, Prabhupada sometimes compared it to arguing whether the fruit fell

from the tree because the bird flew off the branch or the fruit fell first, causing the bird to take off; in other words, the question was a fruitless speculative enterprise.

In short, on some occasions Prabhupada said that the souls did fall from the Kingdom of God; on others, that they did not; and sometimes he discouraged dwelling on the issue at all.

One naturally assumes that all three versions cannot be the conclusive truth under the Gaudiya view; but how to ascertain the correct one? Despite the assertions of Tamal Krishna Goswami, Hridayananda Goswami, and Drutakarma, quoting Prabhupada back and forth will never solve the problem, because those who are fortified with counterquotes in support of the version they favor will simply not accept the opposing view. A better approach would be to turn to epistemology. This would be impartial and conclusive. As Will Durant (1961) pointed out, epistemology is more a part of science than philosophy proper, because its purpose is to validate truth claims.[4] So in efforts to settle possible heretical deviation, epistemology is indispensable.

To Kundali and Satyanarayana, therefore, their task seemed simple. They had only to apply the standard epistemological proofs to each of Prabhupada's three replies to the *jiva* question and see which one had the support of scriptural canon. It was not a matter of lacking faith in Prabhupada, relativizing him, or one-upmanship over the institution's leaders. It was a matter of reconciling Prabhupada with revelation and rendering a service in resolving a controversy they did not even start. As it happened, the very text they were working on, the six-part exegetical work of Jiva Goswami, mentioned earlier, details the Gaudiya epistemology in *Tattva Sandabha*, the first of the six-part treatise. Jiva Goswami explains that the Gaudiya epistemology is essentially a triad composed of scriptural testimony (*shabda*), inferential reasoning (*anumana*), and direct perception or experience (*pratyaksha*).

Scriptural testimony, which for Gaudiyas is the same as divine revelation, is considered infallible because it is not of human origin and is therefore free of the four human defects—making mistakes, being deceived, cheating, and having imperfect senses. Reason (*anumana*) and sense perception (*pratyaksha*) are not considered as reliable because, having human origin, they are subject to the four defects. It is important to note, however, that despite these defects, Jiva Goswami does not reject reason and direct experience as sources of knowledge. While they are not as reliable as revelation, they are valid means of knowledge. His point is that though not totally reliable, they are not totally invalid, either—they just cannot stand as independent means but must work in concert with revelation.

Indeed, to properly understand revelation, so there is no inconsistency between different statements in the scriptures, reason (*anumana*) is essential.

Consequently, Baladeva, another major formulator of Gaudiya thought in the nineteenth century, was careful to mention in his treatise on *Vedanta Sutra* that while revelation is the source of understanding, we must not leave out reason. Commenting on *Sutra* 1.1.3, Baladeva writes: "*Uha*, or right reasoning, is that by which we find out the true sense of a scriptural passage by removing all conflicts between what precedes and what follows it. But one should abandon all mere dry speculation."[5]

Dry speculation means attempting to understand the subject matter without referring to the revelation of scripture, whereas right reasoning is the attempt to reconcile the various utterances of scripture, resulting in a clear understanding. Prabhupada taught this epistemological method to his disciples:

The devotee in the first or uppermost class is described as follows. He is very expert in the study of relevant scriptures, and he is also expert in putting forward arguments in terms of those scriptures. He can very nicely present conclusions with perfect discretion and can consider the ways of devotional service in a decisive way. . . . The first-class devotee never deviates from the principles of higher authority, and *he attains firm faith in the scriptures by understanding with all reason and arguments. When we speak of arguments and reason, it means arguments and reason on the basis of revealed scriptures.* (29–30; italics mine)[6]

As for sense perception (*pratyaksha*), the third epistemological proof, that too has its role. In the *Bhagavad Gita* (9.2) Krishna declares that because *bhakti* gives "direct perception of the self by realization, it is the perfection of religion." Revelation, then, when properly understood and applied via reason, culminates in direct experience, the final measure of any truth claim. Thus, the three methods of knowledge work together, with revelation essentially guiding the other two.

As the quote above shows, Prabhupada was aware of and taught proper epistemological procedure. Further, implicit in his encouragement to subject Chaitanya's teachings to the cold light of reason (*vichara*) is the invitation to do the same with his own words as well:

Nyaya-kovidah means *nyaya-nipuna*. *Bhagavad-duta*s, those who are *gosvami*s, they place everything with *nyaya*, or logic. Their instructions are not blind, dogmatic. *Naya-kovidah*. Everything, what is said by Krsna or His representative, they are not dogmas. Those who are not representative of Krsna, they will say simply dogmas . . . in *Bhagavata* religion, *Bhagavata-dharma*, there is no dogma. Chaitanya Mahaprabhu's *Bhagavata-dharma*, the *Chaitanya-Charitamrita*'s author, Krsnadasa Kaviraja Gosvami, says, therefore, that *caitanyera dayara katha karaha vicara. Vicara* means you just try to understand the gift of Lord Chaitanya by logic, *vicara*. Don't follow blindly. Following blindly something, that is not good. That will not stay. But one should take everything with logic . . . the servants of God, they put everything in logic. *Caitanyera dayara katha karaha vicara*. . . . Study the Chaitanya's philosophy with logic and argument. . . . Don't go by sentiment.[7]

Also, in commenting on *Gita* (4.34), the central verse supporting the rule of surrender to the guru, Prabhupada writes: "In this verse, both blind following and absurd inquiries are condemned." In the same purport, he stresses that a disciple must seek "a clear understanding" via submissive service and questioning the guru. From this and the passage above, we see that the dogmatic orientation implicit in the statements of Hridayananda Das Goswami, Tamal Krishna Goswami, Drutakarma, and others is not Prabhupada's outlook. His rational and epistemologically sound approach rules out the method of anyone who advocates that the primary category of proof is Prabhupada's statements, not scriptural canon, and that a follower's task is simply to reconcile scripture with Prabhupada rather than reconcile Prabhupada with scripture. Such a mindset suggests literalism, dogmatism, fanaticism, and the inevitable confusion these traits bring, because like any other thinker in history (or any scriptural text), Prabhupada said many things that require intelligent consideration and reconciliation in order to derive a clear understanding. This means all his utterances cannot have equal weight in every context. Literalism flies in the face of Prabhupada's own stated aim, which was to inspire a class of thoughtful, reasonable people who would assimilate the Gaudiya philosophy so well they would eschew all dogmatism in establishing its tenets.

How can a sincere disciple validate all Prabhupada's statements when he gives three different answers on the same question? Even the most zealous blind follower is hard put by this requirement to go three ways at once. Indeed, Tamal Krishna Goswami, Drutakarma, and Hridayananda Das Goswami could not go three ways themselves; they favor one of the three answers, though in every case their verdict was reached without applying the Gaudiya epistemology. The GBC body could not go three ways either, or it would not have had a philosophical committee working on the issue for several years, nor would it have an official ruling favoring only one of the three options—a ruling, we shall see, in which it does not acknowledge the aforementioned "conclusion" of Prabhupada that no one falls from the spiritual world, or reconcile this with its verdict.

Also relevant is why among ISKCON members there is a general failure to understand and apply Gaudiya epistemology properly, despite Prabhupada explaining Jiva Goswami's version. Part of the confusion is because, typically, when ISKCON members discuss reason and sense perception, they equate "fallible" with "invalid," and from this basic miscalculation, distort their whole approach to epistemology, and, ultimately, to Gaudiya Vaishnavism itself. They strive to eliminate, or at least undermine, two out of the three proofs and leave only revelation standing.

This tendency is seen in another essay that appeared in the *ISKCON Communications Journal* entitled, "Doubt and Certainty in Krishna Consciousness."[8] The author, Suhotra Swami, also a GBC leader, guru, and former chair of the GBC's Philosophical Committee, initially argues correctly for the interrelationship between revelation and reason, but quickly sets this aside and proceeds to undermine reason, instilling in the unsuspecting reader a disdain for reason rather than a heightened awareness of its utility and importance when combined with or guided by revelation, which is the actual Gaudiya standpoint.

There is an interesting subtext to this practice. Since *shabda*, or revelation, loosely interpreted, also means "hearing from authority," eliminating reason and sense perception takes on a special significance in the ISKCON context, especially since followers are not supposed to question the authority of divine revelation, for to do so brings their faith into question. Before long "authority" in the scriptural context is used interchangeably with "authority" in the organizational sense—human authorities. This occurs in Tamal Krishna Goswami's application of the term in his paper on heresies of authority, and the same is implied in Suhotra Swami's essay on doubt and certainty. According to him, ultimate authority for an ISKCON member is not divine revelation, as upheld by Jiva Goswami and other recognized Gaudiya masters. Suhotra Swami's last sentence in his opening paragraph unwittingly redefines authority, putting the guru and other devotees on a par with revelation: "Therefore, when a devotee of Krishna is asked about the certainty of his beliefs he usually answers by quoting authority: *guru* (the spiritual master), *shastra* (the Vedic scriptures) and *sadhu* (other devotees respected for their realization of the teachings of *guru* and *shastra*)." Thus, Suhotra Swami does not explain Gaudiya epistemology at all, but substitutes a new triad in its place. Instead of the triad Jiva Goswami taught—revelation, reason, and direct experience—he posits revelation, guru, and respected saintly persons. He elevates guru and respected devotees (which includes GBC members, among others) to an equal footing with canon.

There is an explanation for this confusion. Suhotra Swami's triad is part of the Gaudiya system, but it is not part of epistemology proper, a distinction he fails to make. In the tradition, his trinity functions as a frame of reference in the sense that one may confer with a more experienced lawyer for insight about the law but should recognize that his expert opinion is not itself the law; it should be in accord with the law, but one does not blindly assume that it is. Similarly, even after applying the proper proofs for truth claims—scriptural canon, reason, and experience—one may still want to confer with a guru or a saintly person, to seek confirmation that one has applied the method correctly and arrived at the right conclusion. That is the proper utility for the triad Suhotra Swami advocates as the actual epistemological method. For him, revelation, guru, and "respected saintly persons" are all equal and interchangeable authorities. Accordingly, if challenged, a devotee invokes authority to justify his beliefs rather than explaining them with logical arguments, which is an abstruse way of saying a devotee blindly follows authority.

These leading devotees are not atypical examples within ISKCON. Their writings are read across the society, yet no readers challenge the philosophical blunders they propound. This in turn suggests that for a large segment of Prabhupada's followers, their guru became what Erich Fromm called "the voice of swallowed authority," an authority so idolized—and so feared—that none dares examine his words with a critical eye, even when he is teaching precisely such an analytical approach to life itself: "Don't follow blindly. Following blindly something, that is not good. That will not stay. But one should take everything with logic . . . the servants of God, they put everything in logic. *Caitanyera dayara katha karaha vicara.* . . . Study Chaitanya's philosophy with logic and argument. . . . Don't go by sentiment."

Sentiment is the very thing in evidence here, substantiated by a twisting of the Gaudiya teachings. I suggest that the mindset reflected in the words and attitudes of Tamal Krishna Goswami, Hridayananda Goswami, and Drutakarma Das, and indirectly in the words of Suhotra is endemic in ISKCON. The same confusion is reflected in the GBC resolution regarding the book that Kundali and Satyanarayana wrote to air their side of the controversy.

To assess the book, the GBC formed a nine-member subcommittee. The chair was Ravindra Svarupa Das, another highly respected ISKCON academic as well as a reputed ISKCON reformer. Out of the nine, however, only two members, Ravindra Svarupa and Jayadvaita Swami, read the book they were to pass judgment on. These two told the others what to think, and the committee voted to ban the book. In ISKCON two members of a jury can hear a case and decide the verdict. In this case, the jury was composed of top leaders in the society and none of them protested the ethos involved. That committee in turn informed the GBC body what to think, and the body ruled on the issue in 1995, telling the whole society in turn what to think. GBC resolution number 79 for that year reads as follows:

1. *Vaikuntha* is that place from which no one ever falls down. The living entity belongs to Lord Krsna's marginal potency (*tatashtha shakti*). On this we all agree. The origin of the conditioned life of the souls now in this material world is undoubtedly beyond the range of our direct perception.

We can therefore best answer questions about that origin by repeating the answers Shrila Prabhupada gave when such questions were asked of him:

"The original home of the living entity and the Supreme Personality of Godhead is the spiritual world. In the spiritual world both the Lord and the living entities live together very peacefully. Since the living entity remains engaged in the service of the Lord, they both share a blissful life in the spiritual world. However, when the living entity, misusing his tiny independence, wants to enjoy himself, he falls down into the material world" (Srimad-Bhagavatam 4.28.54, purport).

No ISKCON devotee shall present or publish any contrary view as conclusive in any class or seminar or any media (print, video, electronic, etc.).

2. In resolving philosophical controversies, the teachings, instructions, and personal example of His Divine Grace A.C. Bhaktivedanta Swami Prabhupada shall be the first and primary resource for ISKCON devotees. We should understand Vedic literature, the writings of previous *acharya*s, and the teachings of current bona fide *acharya*s outside ISKCON through the teachings of Shrila Prabhupada. Where we perceive apparent differences, we may attribute them to our own lack of understanding or (more rarely) to "differences among *acharya*s." When *acharya*s apparently differ, we shall defer to what is taught by His Divine Grace, our Founder-*Acharya*.

3. The GBC rejects the speculation that Shrila Prabhupada, while teaching about the original position of the *jiva*, did not mean what he said. The GBC finds this speculation unwarranted, poorly supported, unintentionally offensive to Shrila Prabhupada, and, as a precedent, dangerous.

The GBC therefore directs that, effective immediately, the book *In Vaikuntha, Not Even the Leaves Fall* shall be prohibited from sale and distribution at all ISKCON centers and by all ISKCON entities. The GBC members and temple presidents shall be responsible for carrying out this resolution. The GBC appreciates Satyanarayana Dasa's willingness to withdraw the book.

One readily sees the singular consistency between the GBC's attitude and the examples already cited from Tamal Krishna Goswami, Hridayananda Goswami, Drutakarma Das, and Suhotra Swami—emphasis on Prabhupada's words without any pretense of canonical support. Rather than actual philosophy, Prabhupada's name is invoked, making it difficult to disagree with those invoking it for fear of being perceived as argumentative with the founder, which is believed to be a mode of conduct unthinkable to his authentic follower. To question too keenly can instantly ruin the credibility of a questioner, regardless of the true motive or the actual content of the inquiry. Credibility is not all that may get ruined. Those with power may feel justified in teaching a lesson to punish the offensive questioner in any way they see fit. The clear point is that the entire GBC body labors under a conception that to question Prabhupada, or to appear to disagree with him, is heretical. It appears that ISKCON's top leaders learned to parrot Prabhupada's words, and are unable to apply his teachings in terms of the Gaudiya norms.

Moreover, not content to merely suppress the opposition, the next year the GBC published an official rebuttal to the banned book. No doubt the ethos of airing to the public only one side of a debate says something about the inner workings of ISKCON. The book, called *Our Original Position*,[9] had three authors, Gopiparanadhana Das, a Sanskrit scholar and translator, widely regarded in ISKCON as an authority on Gaudiya philosophy, and the aforementioned Suhotra Swami and Hridayananda Goswami. In the preface, Hridayananda Das Goswami reveals the book's slant when he declares that it is not his aim to resolve the issue, but "simply to restore within ISKCON the proper spiritual culture within which we may study the issue. The proper spiritual culture is to submissively accept the statements of our Founder-*Acharya* as fact, and then try, through devotion and service, to realize the purport of his statements."

According to Hridayananda Das Goswami, it is not proper spiritual culture to cleave to Gaudiya epistemology in studying the issue, but to accept as fact whatever Prabhupada said, even if he gave three different replies to the same question. Yet none of the three authors could accept all three replies as equally valid, for their book echoed the verdict of the GBC resolution. So it is not even a matter of accepting unequivocally all three versions of what Prabhupada said, but rather of accepting the one approved by ISKCON authorities: ignore divine revelation, ignore reason, ignore Prabhupada's "conclusion," or be guilty of heresy.

Kundali and Satyanarayana opted to stick to canon and the philosophical approach to Gaudiya Vaishnavism. Their research turned up no scriptural statements supporting the view that souls fell here from the spiritual world. On the other hand, there are numerous statements saying that residents of the spiritual world cannot fall down to the material world. (Ironically, even the GBC resolution states this before proceeding to contradict itself.) The souls in this world, as stated in *Gita* 13.20, are here "beginninglessly" (*anadi*). They never fell here from elsewhere. Hence, the word "fallen" in the expression "fallen soul" refers, not to some past event, but to the soul's existential condition in this world, which is a fallen situation.

The banned book, based on research in more than 80 works covering all schools of Vaishnavism and consistent with the Gaudiya epistemology, agrees with the second of Prabhupada's answers cited earlier—"The conclusion is that no one falls from the spiritual world, or Vaikuntha planet, for it is the eternal abode." Kundali and Satyanarayana felt, therefore, that when they agreed with the authority of the scripture and with the expressed conclusion of Prabhupada, and when both these versions made logical sense, then the charge of heresy leveled against them was a terrible blunder, a rationalization for some other motive, a testimony to the deep-seated irrational dynamics and political rivalry within ISKCON, or perhaps all three. Whatever the truth of the matter, by disagreeing with "the conclusion" and by not practicing proper epistemological procedure, the accusers fit the charge of heresy more than the accused.

PART 2

ISKCON's handling of the above controversy seems to hint at a more widespread condition in the organization, and the following excerpt from an e-mail sent by Bhakti Tirtha Swami to his fellow GBC members confirms this impression:

> If we just go back and reflect on our last Mayapur meeting. Our major problems that we all had to deal with were all leadership oriented. For example, abuse of philosophy; abuse of financial resources; abuse of children; abuse of women; abuse of cows; spiritual weaknesses; lying; and yes, corruption. Some of you remember, at one point in the meeting, I brought up that just writing in one hour's time, I listed approximately 15 terms we were using in our discussions that were all battle tactic terminology . . . such terms as, wiping out the opposition, attacking them first, destroying them once and for all, our second plan of attack, eliminating the competition, getting something on the person, etc. . . . we were spending most of our energies in a combative mentality.[10]

This leader paints a bleak picture of the inner workings of ISKCON. He reveals a mindset that, perforce, can only negatively influence attempts at problem solving from the leadership on down. Language such as "combative mentality" reveals that, in general, the leaders see issues in terms of power, not truth; this shows how the handling of something like the *jiva* issue could be politicized and subsequently bungled.

Exploring the deeper implications of the GBC's "battle tactic" mentality is vital, because leadership sets up the atmosphere that prevails in a group, so insight into the leadership's mindset is a good gauge of the overall mindset. Another reason to diagnose the group's condition is that even when leaders resolve to address the problems in their organization, they often make the mistake of treating the symptoms rather than the root cause. Therefore, the problems tend to recur, each time in perhaps a slightly different guise. Indeed, diagnosing group behavior calls for a great deal of integrity and realism, and a determination to go beneath the surface causes and beyond cosmetic solutions. Leaders should not be satisfied with mere relief if they want a cure.

Such an attitude is usually hard to come by among committed members of a group, especially when that group claims lofty spiritual ideals. Both the leaders and followers tend to have blind spots about the number and severity of their problems. They usually lack the critical eye required for self-analysis. Their denial leads to cover-ups, typically justified as being in the best interest of the group. For example, members of ISKCON may rationalize their hush-ups as being "for the preaching," though such measures almost always backfire with greater consequences than frank honesty from the outset.

Another denial strategy groups use to protect themselves from the truth while trying to appear realistic, aware, and proactive is to openly admit the group's shortcomings, then hurriedly redirect attention to a "more positive picture"—the grand achievements of the group—thereby avoiding deeper issues that need addressing. A common variation on this tactic is to exalt all who bring good news and condemn all who bring bad news. Good news about the group is seen as tacit proof of the messenger's dedication to the cause, no matter how exaggerated (or untrue) the information may be. Bad news, no matter how accurate, means the messenger harbors ill will for not giving a rosy picture. Such messengers are rarely seen as loyal opposition, expressing love and concern for the group. Recognizing this limitation in the corporate world, companies sometimes call in outside consultants for problem solving.

There is no shortage of data and theories for diagnosing problems of group dysfunction today. Since the industrial revolution and then the phenomenon of Nazism, we have been challenged to understand what transpires in whole societies and organizations that enables a range of offenses against human dignity, even within well-intentioned groups. This phenomenon came to be called "groupthink," when the views held by members of a group in the name of doing good, even in the name of religion, are so insular and at odds with civilized norms and basic moral values, or even the ideals of the group itself, that its members are able to do unethical or evil things that they would never do as individuals.

A number of social scientists have tried to penetrate to the roots of this problem. In his preface to *Religions, Values, and Peak Experiences*,[11] Maslow attempts to describe how and why spiritual institutions end up working against their lofty ideals:

> Most people lose or forget the subjectively religious experience, and re-define Religion as a set of habits, behaviors, dogmas, forms, which at the one extreme becomes entirely legalistic and bureaucratic, conventional, empty, and in the truest meaning of the word, anti-religious. The mystic

experience, the illumination, the great awakening, along with the charismatic seer who started the whole thing, are forgotten, lost, or transformed into their opposites. Organized Religion, the churches, finally may become the major enemies of the religious experience and the religious experiencer.

Maslow saw that when the organization favors "big R religion" (organized religion's emphasis on the legalistic and bureaucratic), it may turn followers into depersonalized, unreasoning, mechanical performers, into ciphers. The results are the opposite of what the group claims to strive for. Members become very much like the corporate world's "organization man." This trend never culminates in authentic religious experience; rather, it enslaves and cripples the spirit of the would-be devout. Prabhupada warned his followers about this, echoing his sixteenth-century predecessor, Rupa Goswami, who cautioned that while too lax a practice of *bhakti* is inadequate, a too mechanical approach destroys it. In 1972 Prabhupada wrote to a leader who favored increasing centralization and bureaucracy:

> The Krishna Consciousness Movement is for training men to be independently thoughtful and competent in all types of departments of knowledge and action, not for making bureaucracy. Once there is bureaucracy the whole thing will be spoiled. There must be always individual striving and work and responsibility, competitive spirit, not that one shall dominate and distribute benefits to the others and they do nothing but beg from you and you provide. No.

Thus, despite ISKCON's numerous visible achievements, despite capturing market share in the areas of conversions, acquiring properties, and so on, Bhakti Tirtha's message indicates that the institution is moving in the direction indicated by Maslow, the opposite direction from that intended by the founder.

There are implications for both the leaders and the followers who succumb to the authoritarian atmosphere of "might makes right" and gaining power. Erich Fromm (1994)[12] outlines the devastating effect of authoritarian systems and how they dehumanize both the perpetrators and the victims. As a social psychologist, he considers the inner workings of the group paramount in shaping the person, more so than the ideals the group espouses. When it comes to religion, Fromm argues that the doctrines and beliefs of various sects are not as important as the dynamics within the group itself, of which there are essentially two kinds: authoritarian and humanitarian.

In the authoritarian system, the institution looms large over the lives of its members, including even the leaders, undermining individuals' capacity to think for themselves and subverting the voice of conscience, which is replaced by the voice of "swallowed authority." Power is to be respected more than truth and no distinction is made between rational and irrational authority figures. Regardless of any other variables, those who have titles, positions, and power assume that they must win in all conflicts of opinion with subordinates. This gives rise to the battle tactic thinking Bhakti Tirtha mentions, "wiping out the opposition, attacking them first, destroying them once and for all, our second plan of attack, eliminating the competition, getting something on the person, etc." Consequently, institutional agendas; coercing others to the will of the leaders; closing ranks against all opposition, real or imagined; and punishing socially and economically those who rock the boat all take precedence over reason and the cornerstone values of truth, love, and justice. In this depersonalized atmosphere, people become objects.

In contrast to the impersonal authoritarian setup, Fromm believes that the humanitarian atmosphere fosters individuality, people's inherent creative and productive potential. It encourages the flowering of the individual's powers of reason, sense of conscience, and respect for human dignity, and a heightened concern for truth, love, and justice. He considers these vital elements in any claim to religious life, regardless of theology, creed, ritual, and any other sectarian concerns.

In the humanitarian system, when there is conflict, reason is the main technique for resolving it, and there is concern for due process. It is unthinkable to manipulate the life of another human being or bend a person to one's will, especially in God's name. Indeed, Prabhupada didn't bully or coerce his disciples; he reasoned with them. He indicated the important role of reason when he advised in letters to his disciples that disagreements between them should be settled through discussion.

In the authoritarian system, however, there is a "combative mentality." In case of a conflict of interest, those with power cannot risk rational, equitable proceedings. They may try to appear to do so, but they really believe they have to win at any cost, fearing that any other outcome means a loss of face for themselves and a loss of power. So, as seen in the handling of the doctrinal controversy of the "*jiva* issue" detailed in part 1, truth and justice suffer. Ironically, in this situation both the leaders and the followers are victims, because when we dehumanize others, we dehumanize ourselves as well. We lose touch with our humanity and become victims of the same affliction found in bureaucratic mazes the world over. In "The Sickness Unto Death," Kierkegaard gives an insightful description of this condition he calls "loss of self":

> The biggest danger, that of losing oneself, can pass off in the world as quietly as if it were nothing; every other loss, an arm, a leg, five dollars, a wife, etc., is bound to be noticed.[13]

Such people are unaware that they are self-alienated. They go on thinking, feeling, willing, and acting as if normal, but something vital at the core is missing—a conscience. Not surprisingly, therefore, "being lost to oneself" is on Krishna's list of demonic symptoms in the *Bhagavad Gita* (16.9). Clearly, when a religious institution fosters this condition, we have what Maslow feared, the transformation of religious experience into its antithesis. In ISKCON, for example, people assume the right to say who is a true Prabhupada devotee, when it turns out they themselves have neither the spirit nor the intent Prabhupada wanted in his followers.

Another destructive consequence of authoritarianism is that sycophancy is elevated to a virtue. Indeed, it becomes a vital survival skill. The upshot is that the organization ends up with two kinds of corrupt people, those corrupted by power and those corrupted by weakness. The weak are corrupt because their will has atrophied, become too crippled to address the abuses of power. They learn to go along to get along, in effect endorsing and enabling the dysfunctional situation, invariably out of fear of punishment economically and socially, usually through isolation from the group.

ISKCON members have ample reason to fear exclusion from the group because they vow to follow four regulative principles—no meat-eating, no gambling, no intoxication, and no illicit sex (meaning no sex unless for procreation). These last two principles prove difficult for most members, even within the group. Outside the group, they prove virtually impossible. This is one reason isolation from the group is a major concern for ISKCON members. This fear can go unnoticed, yet it can cripple the will, easily causing individuals to endure things they would not ordinarily, such as being victims or perpetrators of the transgressions in Bhakti Tirtha's e-mail.

We know that people corrupted by power cannot be authentically religious, but what about those corrupted by weakness? Can people with crippled wills achieve true religious experience? Theologically, of course, a believer will not claim to know how God's grace will be apportioned. Psychologically, however, Fromm (1978), quoting Freud, notes: "Feelings of powerlessness are not authentic religious feelings." Following Freud, Fromm criticizes the kind of dynamic in which a crippling of the will is imposed by religious authorities, "thereby causing the impoverishment of the intellect." The *Bhagavad Gita* begins with Arjuna in a state of powerlessness, of fear and trembling, but by the end, specifically through Krishna's influence, he became firm and free from doubt, ready to cope with life's challenges, which is authentic religious experience.

Another vital factor in a group is the coercive power of peer pressure. Fromm argues that as individuals, our innermost nature is not usually irrational, but we can become irrational when influenced by the group mind or the demands of irrational authorities. He holds that group psychology is very similar to individual psychology. Thus, the group mind, which he terms the "social unconscious," is the social equivalent of the individual unconscious, which operates in the background of conscious awareness yet exerts a powerful influence over personal motivation and behavior.

In the group context, owing to what Fromm calls "man's sheep nature," the social environment is a compelling force to conform, to fit in and be "normal." To survive, to avoid peers punishing us socially and economically, we learn to twist our perceptions and to act as expected, rather than from our own conscience. We don't just act but also learn to think and to feel as approved by the group. Over time we become "social characters" rather than our authentic selves. This becomes habit, and it is rationalized in the conscious mind as a virtue; in this way, it goes unnoticed. A new convert to ISKCON naturally wants to be accepted, and that means conforming, and so begins the process of becoming inauthentic to oneself, of tuning out the voice of conscience, and a diminished capacity for critical thinking.

Fromm considers the pressure the group mind exerts on the individual the most powerful technique of coercion, an unconscious force that gains control over the individual. Sadly, this condition can be amplified in systems of authoritarian religion, because believers are doubly motivated to avoid rocking the boat, fearing both social backlash and a loss of spiritual fellowship. For an ISKCON member there is an added fear: incurring the displeasure of a key authority figure—the guru. Displeasing the guru could mean the end to one's bid for spiritual salvation, being cast into untold lifetimes of rebirth and suffering in the material world. The resultant fear is analogous to something familiar to many, the fear of eternal damnation that afflicts fundamentalist Christians. It is quite likely that this is at the heart of devotees', even ISKCON's best intellectuals', inability to think analytically about Prabhupada's utterances, as shown in the handling of the *jiva* issue. They get stuck on "Prabhupada said" rather than learning to philosophize properly according to his teachings. Having substituted his thoughts for their own, when they quote and counterquote him out of fear of putting his words under scrutiny, they actually think they are discussing philosophy and thinking analytically.

In the *Gita* (16.1), at the top of Krishna's list of "divine qualities" is fearlessness (*abhayam*), followed by "purification of one's existence" (*sattva samshuddi*), indicating a progression where freedom from fear is a foundation and not an outcome of spiritual progress. This makes sense, because just to have proper understanding of scripture, for example, a person needs to be without fear so as to freely weigh the variables in the instructions of divine revelation. However, an authoritarian atmosphere, or the subtle coercion of the group mind, or swallowing uncritically the guru's words (or divine revelation) works against this freedom. Fear causes panic, a condition that impairs the faculties and prevents clear thought about the nuances involved in grasping spiritual wisdom. Fear impairs us even in practical matters, not only abstract issues. Then, out of fear, people may bully and coerce those who are not fearful, to "save" them and get them back in line.

Another related point Fromm makes is that typically in authoritarian religion sin is no longer disobedience to God but disobedience to powerful church authorities. Reality is defined by the group mind or by the leaders, not by each individual's critical assessment of the data in his or her life. The more one conforms, the more one's volition and reason become crippled; yet those who conform are rewarded by the group, hailed as sincere, loyal to the cause, spiritually advanced, and so on. They are rewarded with promotions in the hierarchy, all of which reinforces the illusion of spiritual progress. They become attached to the respect and the perks, adding yet another impediment to their capacity to function rationally. Those who don't conform are presumed sinful in some sense.

In the big R setup, spiritual progress is no longer a matter of self-transformation but of getting on the corporate fast track. In this system, then, it is questionable whether those who emerge as leaders are in fact spiritually awakened. More likely they are just the best conformers, the ones who turn out least threatening to the system, though their leadership position is seen as a sure sign of their spirituality. In truth, they are more self-alienated than self-realized, having shown a proven capacity for suppressing the voice of conscience, perhaps too long ago to remember; like the naked emperor in the children's fairy tale, they are unaware of their condition.

One particularly insidious outcome of this scenario is that people will be masochistically servile to those above them in the hierarchy and sadistically domineering to those below, which, again, is dehumanizing to both perpetrators and victims. This accords with Maslow's view that the opposite of religious experience becomes the reality after the founder passes. Indeed, Prabhupada warned his followers that after his passing chaos would ensue. He held that personal ambition is the cause of the chaos. Maslow believes a misplaced emphasis on the big R issues is the cause. Fromm would agree with both these reasons, but points to a still deeper cause that seems to make chaos unavoidable even if no personal ambition is a factor. In his view, no matter how sincere the successors to the founder of a religion may be, they will still inadvertently take the organization to a "new promised land."

Fromm believed that the instinctive response of all successors to the founder of a religion is a move to consolidate power. This may not initially have any untoward motive; the new leaders simply do not live in the same experience or spiritual state as the departed founder and so are not as securely anchored in their spirituality. Yet they want to do their level best to have a smooth transition, to show that collectively they can fill the shoes of the founder and thereby bind the faith of the flock to the new leadership. From this understandable motive, they naturally move to consolidate power, for how else can they convince the masses that things will go on as usual? Paradoxically, embedded in this seemingly reasonable effort is the seed of the chaos Prabhupada and Maslow cautioned about.

The instinctive move to consolidate power then prompts leadership to give a misplaced emphasis in the group dynamic. Instead of striving to establish the aforementioned humanitarian atmosphere as their first priority, they may emphasize the externals, the bureaucracy, the "power over" mode of dealing with one another, Maslow's whole list of big R concerns. This in effect diminishes the quality of life in the organization. In *Psychoanalysis and Religion*,[14] Fromm sums up the impact of the move to consolidate power:

> It is the tragedy of all great religions that they violate and pervert the very principles of freedom as soon as they become mass organizations governed by a religious bureaucracy. The religious organization and the men who represent it take over to some extent the place of family, tribe, and state.

Here, Fromm alludes to the coercive power of peer pressure to override our volition and shape us into automated social stereotypes. About such people, Mark Twain said: "They think they think."[15] In reality, they think the thoughts they ought to think, those approved by the family, tribe, or state. The religious bureaucracy and community replace these influences, perhaps more effectively, because, unlike in the family, tribe, and state, in the religious community people believe their eternal salvation is at stake. For all these reasons, Prabhupada wrote, "Once there is bureaucracy the whole thing will be spoiled."

Fromm further notes:

> They [the new leaders] keep man in bondage instead of leaving him free. It is no longer God who is worshiped but the group that claims to speak in his name. This has happened in all religions. Their founders guided man through the desert, away from the bondage of Egypt, while later others have led him back toward a new Egypt though calling it the Promised Land.[16]

This new direction does not call for a new official doctrine replacing the founder's teachings, although that may also happen. However, in ISKCON, taking a Frommian perspective, *bhakti* may no longer mean something enacted between the individual and God; it may come to mean something enacted between the individual and ISKCON. Thus the mission is deviated from its original spirit, for the people who speak in the name of cooperation and love for the founder, really believing that they are doing him the optimum service, actually divert his followers to a new promised land in his name.

A progression emerges, linking the ideas of Fromm, Maslow, and Prabhupada into a causal chain: an innocent move to consolidate power, then the struggle to hold on to power, and finally the succumbing to the seduction stemming from that very power. In his analysis of group evil, M. Scott Peck (1985)[17] traces how personal ambition can suddenly enter the minds and hearts of people who may not have entertained any such private agendas previously. He makes the point that an administration, like a living organism, has a blind, unreasoning instinct to survive. Those with power want to keep it, usually with the best intentions, but in wresting to hold on to power, they become attached to a position and may begin to compromise their respect for human dignity, demanding rather than commanding respect. The result is a decline in the inner workings of Bhakti Tirtha's group, for both leaders and followers.

This analysis suggests that the chaos Prabhupada warned about, and confirmed by Bhakti Tirtha's e-mail, could be entirely owing to ignorance of group dynamics. The new leaders simply didn't know that their top priority as successors should be maintaining a live-and-let-live humanitarian ethic. People may enlist in groups with the best of intentions but unwittingly get sidetracked along the way. This assessment may disappoint some ISKCON critics who are perhaps keen to see sinister motives as the sole cause of the society's present predicament, and the leaders as contemptible individuals. They may think that such an analysis gives an excuse to the guilty and ill-intentioned; however, it does not mean other factors such as personal ambition were not operative as well, perhaps even before Prabhupada's passing. Thus, we might consider whether Fromm, Maslow, and Peck offer some insight into a root cause of the problems destabilizing ISKCON.

These observations suggest that even if every leader were selfless and sincere from the very beginning, free of any ulterior motive, nevertheless an inadvertent slide into the authoritarian mode or big R religion might still have taken place, owing to an instinctive move to consolidate power. Hence the chance that ISKCON could have charted a different course than the one it has followed since 1977, the year of Prabhupada's passing, seems unlikely.

Given Prabhupada's warning about chaos after his passing, given ISKCON's sorry state of affairs as summed up in Bhakti Tirtha's letter, and given the views of Maslow about the pitfalls of big R religion, along with Fromm's analysis about how and why new leaders of religious groups invariably deviate from the mission, the question naturally arises: What is the solution to the type of group dysfunction just described?

If the root cause is alienation from self, loss of conscience, and an escape from responsibility by giving over one's volition to the group, then the remedy is to reclaim what has been lost. In the words of Scott Peck:

> The plain fact of the matter is that any group will remain inevitably potentially conscienceless and evil until such time as each and every individual holds himself or herself directly responsible for the behavior of the whole group, the organism of which he or she is a part.[18]

Such group members give more consideration to the dictates of conscience than to external authority. They will not easily do things that will compromise their self-respect, their integrity. People are like the bricks that make up the institution; if the integrity of each brick is sound, the edifice they make is likely to be sound. So the cure for loss of conscience is to take the step that will oblige one to hear the voice of conscience and resolve to become a person of integrity.

In other words, all members of a group should be taught about the pitfalls of group dynamics and the leaders should knowingly strive to eliminate the tendency in the group setting for people to fall into the roles of leaders or sheep. They must strive to make a society of all leaders, according to individual capacity, and to inspire every member to become conscientious, civic-minded, and responsible for the entire group. In short, ISKCON's leaders should train members to be "independently thoughtful," as the founder wanted for the Krishna Consciousness movement.

BIBLIOGRAPHY

Bhaktivedanta, A.C. *The Beginning.* Los Angeles: Bhaktivedanta Book Trust, 1996.
——. *The Bhagavad-gita As It Is.* Los Angeles: Bhaktivedanta Book Trust, 1993.
——. *Collected Lectures on Srimad Bhagavatam.* Los Angeles: Bhaktivedanta Book Trust, 1993.
——. *The Nectar of Instruction.* Los Angeles: Bhaktivedanta Book Trust, 1991.
——. *Shrila Prabhupada Siksamrta.* Los Angeles: Bhaktivedanta Book Trust, 1992.
——. *Srimad Bhagavatam.* Mumbai: Bhaktivedanta Book Trust, 1987.
Tyson, Joseph B. *The New Testament and Early Christianity.* New York: Macmillan, 1984.

NOTES

1. Kundali Dasa is a well-known social critic of ISKCON. See Kundali Dasa, *Our Mission,* 4 vols. (New Delhi: ABHAYA Books, 1995–1999).
2. Satyanarayana Dasa and Kundali Dasa, *Tattva Sandarbha of Srila Jiva Goswami* (Vrindavan: JIVAS, 1995).
3. Satyanarayana Dasa and Kundali Dasa, *In Vaikuntha, Not Even The Leaves Fall* (Vrindavan: JIVAS, 1994).

4. Will Durant, *The Story of Philosophy* (New York: Washington Square Press, 1961).

5. S. C. Vasu, *The Vedanta-Sutras of Badarayana with Commentary of Baladeva* (New Delhi: Munshiram Manoharlal Publishers, 1979).

6. A.C. Bhaktivedanta Swami, *The Nectar of Devotion* (Los Angeles: Bhaktivedanta Book Trust, 1982), 29–30.

7. Lecture, Calcutta, 6 January 1971, in A.C. Bhaktivedanta Swami, *Collected Lectures on Srimad Bhagavatam* (Los Angeles: BBT, 1993).

8. *ISKCON Communications Journal* 3 (2) (Dec. 1995).

9. Hridayananda Dasa Goswami, Suhotra Swami, and Gopiparanadhana das Adhikari, *Our Original Position* (Stockholm: ISKCON GBC Press, 1996).

10. E-mail sent to a GBC Internet discussion group, 16 May 2000.

11. A. H. Maslow, *Religions, Values, and Peak Experiences* (New York: Penguin, 1994).

12. Erich Fromm, *Escape from Freedom* (1969; reprint, New York: Holt, 1994).

13. S. Kierkegaard, *The Sickness Unto Death* (London: Penguin, 1989).

14. New Haven: Yale University Press, 1978.

15. Mark Twain, *Letters from the Earth* (New York: Harper and Row, 1991).

16. Ibid.

17. *People of the Lie* (New York: Simon & Schuster, 1985). See also *The Road Less Traveled and Beyond* (New York: Simon & Schuster, 1997).

18. Ibid.

[15]

HERESY AND THE *JIVA* DEBATE

HOWARD RESNICK (HRIDAYANANDA DAS GOSWAMI)

I N 1995, the leaders of the International Society for Krishna Consciousness (ISKCON) asked me to address a raging controversy among its
members over the theological issue of the origin of the soul. The chief
source of this controversy was a book published the year before under the
name *In Vaikuntha, Not Even the Leaves Fall.*[1] The authors, Satyanarayana Das
and Kundali Das (hereafter simply "the authors"), argued essentially that
ISKCON's view that souls in this world dwelled originally with God in the
spiritual world and then fell to this world was illogical and heretical to
ISKCON's own Gaudiya Vaishnava tradition. Since Shrila Prabhupada himself
often espoused this "illogical" and "heretical" position, and since both authors
were active disciples of Shrila Prabhupada, they argued that in teaching this,
Shrila Prabhupada was consciously speaking falsely, claiming to be true what
he knew to be untrue, and that he did this "for the sake of preaching."

The claim that Shrila Prabhupada's disciples, within his own spiritual society
that he had founded and developed, could at will declare portions of his teachings to be false, illogical, and deviant, and the further claim that Shrila Prabhu-

pada had consciously lied to achieve a practical effect in the world, caused considerable commotion within ISKCON. After approximately one year of heated debate, from 1994 to 1995, the Governing Body Commission of ISKCON (GBC) decided to publish a book refuting the authors' claims. At the GBC's request, I agreed to write the introduction and the first eight chapters of the book, which the GBC Press published in 1996 as *Our Original Position*.[2] That volume provided far-reaching and sound evidence demonstrating that Shrila Prabhupada did not deviate from his tradition in teaching that souls fall from the spiritual world; that this teaching does not contradict what we know to be true about the soul and God; and that this teaching is not inherently illogical.

Although the authors have never published in any medium a refutation of *Our Original Position*, Kundali curiously continues to argue that his position, and not that of ISKCON, rests on logic and tradition. He further criticizes ISKCON's general handling of heresy and orthodoxy.

At the request of this volume's editor, I will not rehearse in this essay the weighty evidence and sound reasons given in *Our Original Position*, but rather shall consider the specific issue of heresy and orthodoxy in ISKCON. To accomplish this, I will first briefly discuss these concepts within religions in general, and then consider how ISKCON has dealt with them, using as an example the specific theological dispute that took place over the origin of the souls presently living in the material world. I will conclude by discussing where ISKCON seems to be headed in regard to heresy and orthodoxy.

I shall utilize the relevant definitions of the terms "heresy" and "orthodoxy" from my *American Heritage Dictionary*, as follows:

> heresy: "an opinion or a doctrine at variance with established religious beliefs"
> orthodoxy: "adhering to the accepted or traditional and established faith, especially in religion"

It seems self-evident that a religious group that claims to know the nature of, and the means to achieve, highest truth, and that further claims to be practicing and preserving such privileged metaphysical insights, will endeavor to safeguard its orthodoxy and orthopraxis in the face of internal and external challenges. The group's members will typically see such efforts as exceedingly important for the intact survival of a divine mission upon whose success the world may depend.

Moreover, in our increasingly globalized world, hardly any religious group operates in a totally monolithic cultural context, and one serious about maintaining its identity must seek in some manner to regulate its reciprocal contacts with the world, and thus must have some sense of heresy and orthodoxy.

ISKCON claims to be teaching absolute truth and the best means to realize it. Thus that ISKCON acts to preserve orthodoxy and exclude heresy, as understood within ISKCON, seems to be an almost banal datum in and of itself. Less banal are the particular means by which it arrives at its conception of orthodoxy and heresy, and then seeks to preserve the former and exclude the latter. We shall study ISKCON's conception using the origin-of-the-soul debate as a focus.

In the volume, *In Vaikuntha, Not Even the Leaves Fall*, and in his article published in this volume, Kundali Das essentially claims the following:

1. ISKCON defines heresy and orthodoxy exclusively as (respectively) deviation from or adherence to the teachings of its founder, Shrila Prabhupada.
2. At times Shrila Prabhupada's statements deviate from tradition.
3. Thus through its unthinking, literalist mode of interpreting and following Shrila Prabhupada's teachings, ISKCON becomes heretical to its own Gaudiya Vaishnava tradition.
4. A good example of this is ISKCON's heretical stand on the theological issue of the origin of the soul.

I will now consider these points in turn.

In response to Kundali's co-authored book, several members of ISKCON published *Our Original Position*. I was perhaps the main author of that volume and my essay appears first in it. Comparing the use of evidence in the two books, we discover that the authors quote Shrila Prabhupada as an authority more than twice as often as I do. In the first eight chapters of *Our Original Position*, I directly quote Shrila Prabhupada twenty-three times. In contrast, the authors quote Shrila Prabhupada fifty-two times.

In my introduction to *Our Original Position*, I stated that the members of ISKCON accept Shrila Prabhupada's philosophical statements as authoritative and that in difficult or controversial matters, we try to see in what sense Shrila Prabhupada's statements are true. Indeed, Shrila Prabhupada himself often stressed that the statements of a guru must be corroborated by *shastra* (scripture) and *sadhu* (other saintly teachers). In *Our Original Position*, we clearly show that Shrila Prabhupada's teachings on the origin of the soul do not in fact contradict other authorities; and in the six years since that book was published, Kundali has failed to refute the scholarly arguments raised in that volume.

It must be borne in mind that Shrila Prabhupada never claimed to be leading the only authentic Vaishnava or Gaudiya Vaishnava movement. He made it clear to his disciples that other Vaishnavas in other institutions were also receiving the grace of Krishna and that without ISKCON they would be successful in their spiritual lives. Those who choose to participate in ISKCON do so

because they have satisfied themselves as to the authenticity of Shrila Prabhupada's teachings. If Kundali or any other person is not so satisfied, that person
has every right and freedom to pursue their spiritual life in another institutional context. ISKCON affirms and respects that right and recognizes the genuine spiritual achievements of people in other institutions.

Similarly, those disagreeing with Shrila Prabhupada's statements on a specific issue should respect his right to found and lead an institution based on his
teachings. Kundali repeatedly claims that we may reject some of Shrila Prabhupada's explicit teachings by alleging that Shrila Prabhupada knowingly lied
to us as a "preaching strategy." Kundali has failed to provide a single objective
bit of evidence to substantiate this allegation. If a member of ISKCON may
simply declare, without the slightest bit of objective evidence, that this or that
teaching of Shrila Prabhupada is false, and that Shrila Prabhupada knowingly
lied to us, then what is to prevent any ISKCON member from insisting that we
reject Shrila Prabhupada's other teachings on the same grounds?

Kundali claims that the entire weight of tradition supports his view, but *Our
Original Position* provides massive evidence to show that this is patently false.
Yet without refuting any of that evidence, Kundali continues to make the same
claim.

At the very least, a neutral observer would instantly recognize that *Our Original Position* deeply problematizes the authors' position by demonstrating with
all sorts of evidence that the Gaudiya Vaishnava tradition has historically taken
a complex view on the issue of the origin of the soul, and that Shrila Prabhupada's paradoxical teachings on this topic reflect that complexity. Thus we are
justified in accepting, and not rejecting, Shrila Prabhupada's complex teachings on this subject.

Shrila Prabhupada taught that souls originally dwelled with Krishna in the
spiritual world, and he also taught that souls do not fall from the spiritual
world. If one considers these two teachings to be a contradiction, as Kundali
does, then he or she may seek to resolve the problem by declaring, as Kundali
does, that some of Shrila Prabhupada's statements are false, being ad hoc in-
ventions intended to accomplish a pragmatic missionary goal, at the moment
only. Or he or she may choose, as I did, to find truth in both statements, treating them not as a contradiction but rather as a paradox.

My *American Heritage Dictionary* defines "paradox," in the first instance, as
"a seemingly contradictory statement that may nonetheless be true." Wisdom
traditions often use paradoxes for at least one obvious reason: a paradox, precisely because it is contradictory on the surface, forces us to go beneath the
surface, to plumb the depths of the teachings.

I fail to see how reaching this conclusion, that there are paradoxes in Shrila
Prabhupada's teachings, is less intellectually demanding than simply tossing

out those statements that seem disconcerting or annoying. As stated earlier, *Our Original Position* provides broad evidence from within the Gaudiya Vaishnava tradition to show that Shrila Prabhupada's paradoxical claims on the soul's origin are firmly rooted in that tradition. If this is the case, then the authors err when they claim that Shrila Prabhupada's teachings on the origin of the soul isolate him from his historical tradition.

Also, as mentioned above, *Our Original Position* has problematized the authors' puzzling view that every relevant authority says one and the same thing about the soul's origin. Apart from this topic, though, are there other instances in which Shrila Prabhupada plainly is at odds with his tradition?

In reply, I would again say that ISKCON is a society of those who believe and claim that Shrila Prabhupada effectively taught to the world absolute spiritual knowledge within the historical Gaudiya Vaishnava tradition. Our claim is simply that *within ISKCON and not within the world in general*, one who claims that Shrila Prabhupada taught a false doctrine takes on a burden of proof. Kundali believes he has met that burden of proof. But *Our Original Position* has succeeded, in my view, in deeply problematizing, if not plainly refuting, that claim.

Finally, let us consider whether ISKCON dealt fairly with the controversy over the origin of the soul. It must be the case that due to the human imperfection of all those who lead in this world, ISKCON too surely dealt imperfectly with this issue. Yet if there is any justice whatsoever among human beings, then surely also there are imperfect adjudications that meet minimum standards of fairness. I have no doubt that ISKCON's response to the origin-of-the-soul controversy meets these standards. The true irony of the case is this: before the authors' insistence that there was only one correct view on this matter, a campaign that culminated in their publication of *In Vaikuntha*, the devotees of ISKCON held diverse positions on this theological issue. There was no serious demand for orthodoxy and much free discussion took place. ISKCON had not officially published a single book, or even article, insisting on a single way of seeing this matter. Shrila Prabhupada made paradoxical statements on the topic, and this paradox held a perennial dialogue in place.

It was in fact the authors (and before them, the former Ravanari Das in another book) who insisted formally that this paradox must be rejected, that one view must be forever discarded and a single position on the matter be adopted by all reasonable people. In other words, it was the authors who raised the flag of orthodoxy. In response, ISKCON studied the matter and published a scholarly refutation. The authors did not present a serious response to *Our Original Position*, and in a final touch of irony, ISKCON has again returned to a somewhat diverse position on this issue. In other words, within ISKCON different devotees hold different views on what is surely a paradoxical issue. Because, unlike the authors, neither side in this issue stridently demands that everyone adopt their view—in other words, because neither side demands that theirs be taken as an orthodox view—ISKCON leadership does not respond. The situation on the ground in ISKCON, before and after Kundali, is one of diverse views on the origin-of-the-soul issue. The brief period of serious orthodoxy in ISKCON on this matter was a response to the authors' own demand for orthodoxy in support of their position.

In conclusion, Shrila Prabhupada founded a spiritual society and named it ISKCON. With unfailing candor and transparency, he explained that ISKCON's purpose was to offer to the world the spiritual teachings of Gaudiya Vaishnavism, as he had learned them from his guru. Shrila Prabhupada always made clear that there were other authentic institutions teaching Gaudiya Vaishnavism in a somewhat different way, but that those who chose to work in ISKCON should honor the wishes of its founder.

On the specific issue of the origin of the soul, ample and significant evidence shows that those who choose to follow Shrila Prabhupada do not thereby isolate themselves from the Gaudiya Vaishnava tradition from which ISKCON derives its religious authority. To the best of my knowledge, ISKCON, in general, does not inordinately concern itself with orthodoxy and heresy, and on this specific issue, again hosts a complex dialogue that honors the teachings both of Shrila Prabhupada and of the entire Gaudiya Vaishnava tradition, and that reflects the somewhat paradoxical nature of this inescapably recondite area of theology.

NOTES

1. Delhi: JIVAS (Jiva Institute of Vaisnava Studies), 1994.
2. ISKCON GBC Press, 1996.

PART 5
Social Issues

[16]

AIRPORTS, CONFLICT, AND CHANGE IN THE HARE KRISHNA MOVEMENT

E. BURKE ROCHFORD JR.

To promote social change in accordance with its ideological prescriptions, every social movement must act on the environment in which it operates. If a movement wants to disseminate its message and mobilize the resources required to reach its goals (i.e., people, power, and money), leaders and members alike must develop outward-reaching strategies. In reaching out, however, a movement becomes subject to public scrutiny and evaluation. Public interest and response—whether favorable, neutral, or hostile—in turn affect its growth and survival, as a number of investigators of social movements have noted. The public's response can influence the resource mobilization opportunities available to a movement, its choice of recruitment strategies, the kind of opposition it encounters, the nature of its goals and values, and its overall prospects for survival and prosperity (McCarthy and Zald 1974; Snow 1979; Rochford 1987; Zald and Ash 1966).

In this chapter, I examine ISKCON's emerging resource mobilization strategies during the 1970s in light of the American public's changing attitudes toward the Hare Krishna movement. I then analyze how ISKCON's strategies and public image have in turn influenced its overall patterns of development in America by describing and analyzing an activity known within ISKCON as *sankirtana*. Originally the term denoted a practice by which Krishna devotees went out into public places to chant, distribute literature, recruit new members, and solicit donations, but by the mid-1970s in ISKCON, it had begun to take on a more monetary character. The first of this chapter's three sections presents a natural history of ISKCON's use of public places during the 1970s. The second details the changes in ISKCON's public place strategies that began in 1973. The third section describes and analyzes the ways in which the public backlash toward ISKCON influenced both its choice of strategies and its overall history as a social movement during the 1970s.

A HISTORY OF ISKCON'S USE OF PUBLIC PLACES

Public places have been crucially important in the development of ISKCON in the United States. They have been important for the movement's recruitment efforts and for raising financial support for its communities. My 1980 devotee survey revealed that 42 percent of ISKCON's members in the United States were recruited through public place contacts with movement members (Rochford 1985:152).[1] The distribution of literature and other forms of public solicitation—seeking donations and selling various consumer goods in public places—financially supported ISKCON's expansionary efforts up until the mid-1980s.[2]

Beginning in 1968, Srila Prabhupada instituted the practice *Hare Nama*[3] as a means of preaching Krishna Consciousness, recruiting members, and raising money in public settings. Until 1972, ISKCON's communities were almost completely supported by groups of devotees venturing out into the streets and other public places to distribute literature and seek donations. As one longtime ISKCON member explained:

When I joined the movement in '71, the whole temple went out each day. There were twelve to fifteen people at that time. We chanted in the street from eleven in the morning until six in the evening. Half the group chanted and half stood on the corners, with *dhotis* and *telac* on, extending a BTG [*Back to Godhead* magazine] out saying [to people passing by] 'Take one.' And each devotee would come home with $8, $10. Average income to the temple each day was between $50 and $75. But our rent was only $400 a month, so it was enough (Philadelphia 1982).

The strategy of combining the movement's missionary goals with collecting money became standard ISKCON policy throughout the 1970s. In 1971, ISKCON established the Bhaktivedanta Book Trust in Los Angeles to publish Prabhupada's translations and commentaries on the *Bhagavad Gita, Shrimad Bhagavatam*, and other Vedic scriptures. Prabhupada instructed his disciples to distribute his books in volume.[4] Between 1972 and 1974, ISKCON members did so primarily in shopping malls and parking lots across Canada and the United States. While these locations proved effective for ISKCON's distribution of literature, a major change took place in 1974 that had a revolutionary impact on the future of that distribution.

Under constitutional protections provided by the First Amendment (*Murdock v. Pennsylvania*, 1942)[5] ISKCON shifted its *sankirtana* efforts from the streets and parking lots into airports, national parks, and state fairs. When these public locations were opened to *sankirtana* between 1974 and 1976, ISKCON's literature distribution increased dramatically. As table 16.1 indicates, *sankirtana* devotees in 1976 distributed more than 18,000 hardback books per week throughout Canada and the United States. At the Los Angeles International Airport alone, devotees were handing out as many as 5,000 to 6,000 each week in 1976. Literature distribution doubled each year between 1974 and 1976, then declined modestly until 1979, when it began to fall off significantly.

TABLE 16.1 Average Amount of ISKCON Literature Distributed Weekly in the United States and Canada by Year*

Year	# of Weeks	Large Books	Small Books	(Total)	Communities Reporting	(Average)
1974	(36)	1,748	6,830	19,570	(28,148)	(12)
1975	(45)	3,434	5,759	40,750	(49,943)	(18)
1976	(32)	18,406	8,555	118,724	(145,685)	(24)
1977	(42)	23,393	5,203	93,693	(122,294)	(25)
1978	(51)	28,976	4,014	91,813	(124,803)	(26)
1979	(52)	20,442	6,634	75,640	(102,715)	(21)
1980	(19)	11,985	1,724	19,921	(33,630)	(18)
1981	(26)	10,456	5,692	35,594	(51,743)	(18)
1982	(41)	11,852	22,273	24,534	(58,659)	(20)

*These data are compiled from ISKCON's weekly *Sankirtana Newsletter*, which began in 1974. I have computed weekly figures because the *Sankirtana Newsletter* was not published consistently during the 1974–1982 period.

Economically, the growth in book distribution resulted in a financial boom for the movement. ISKCON members received an average of $4 to $5 as a donation for each of the large books they distributed to members of the public. With a cost to the movement of approximately $2.50 per book, ISKCON made considerable profit from the large volume given out. If we take the conservative figure of $4 received for each book, ISKCON grossed over $13 million between 1974 and 1978 on hardback books alone.[6]

As a result of this financial prosperity, ISKCON purchased half a dozen new and larger temples in 1975 and 1976. The decision was based on the assumption that the movement's ranks would continue to grow and that book distribution would continue to expand as it had in these years. By 1975, however, ISKCON's recruitment numbers had already begun to decline (Rochford 1985:276–78) and in 1977, book distribution began to level off as well.

It was in the midst of the apparent affluence of the movement in 1975 and 1976 that the seeds of ISKCON's coming decline were being planted. The mass distribution of books brought large sums of money into the organization, but this was not because the public had become more receptive to Krishna Consciousness. On the contrary, the rapid growth reflected ISKCON members' use of a variety of interactional strategies meant to increase the volume of literature distributed and to maximize the financial return from each book. These changes ultimately altered the very structure and purpose of *sankirtana* and brought the movement into conflict with the public. From the public's perspective, *sankirtana* was seen as motivated more by financial concerns than by religious principles.

FROM PREACHING TO SELLING: MICROSTRUCTURAL CHANGES IN SANKIRTANA

As early as 1973, a number of changes were already under way in ISKCON's *sankirtana* practices. Initially, these changes appeared to reflect no more than ISKCON's continuing search for more effective missionary practices.[7] By the end of the 1970s, however, *sankirtana* strategies were becoming ever more financial in character. A devotee who joined in 1971 provided a description of the changes that took place:

> Even in the early seventies Prabhupada was saying, "Just a magazine [*Back to Godhead*]. If they can give a quarter, fine." So you would preach to them [people met in the street] and then ask, "Could you just give a quarter donation?" And if they didn't give it to you [we] just let them go. It was no big deal then. . . . We didn't want to pressure anyone, we just wanted to give them a taste of Krishna. (Los Angeles, 1978)

But, as this devotee further explained, *sankirtana* had undergone a fundamental change by the middle of the decade-:

> While there was some trouble with devotees being aggressive [in their *sankirtana* efforts], up until '74 and '75 it was limited and excusable really. If there were any problems it was just the immaturity of the devotees and it came off that way. But then you saw the aggressive sort of thing. Finances became important. Everything became conscious, organized. You could see there was a change. Not just goofy mistakes like before. They were organized. (Los Angeles 1978)

While this insider's account is suggestive, it ultimately says little about the interactional dynamics underlying the changes in *sankirtana*. In the following discussion, I will look at four such interactional changes that reflect ISKCON's different uses of public settings.

CHANGES IN THE TARGETS OF THE DEVOTEES' CONTACT ATTEMPTS

With the decline of the counterculture in the early 1970s, public places became less productive locations for recruitment purposes. The youth of the counterculture were no longer available in large numbers in communities such as the Haight-Ashbury district in San Francisco and the Bowery on the Lower East Side of New York. ISKCON therefore shifted its public efforts mostly into airports to take advantage of the better prospects for distributing the movement's literature. With this shift, members began seeking out a range of social groups in these public places that would not have gained much attention previously.

Systematic observation of the devotees' book distribution efforts at the Los Angeles International Airport in 1980 revealed that they generally sought out people who would have little or no prospect of becoming ISKCON members, or who would not even be sympathetic to the movement's message. This conclusion is based upon observations of 103 attempted contacts between devotees and people in the airport. These contacts fell into several categories.

First, devotee distributors often attempted to make contact with older people. Forty-five percent of the people they contacted were over the age of 35 (based on my own age estimates). A substantial number of these people were 50 years of age or older. Because ISKCON can accurately be considered an age-graded association, which favors participation and interest by the young, it seems unlikely that people over the age of 30 could be considered serious candidates for preaching and recruitment. For the devotees surveyed in 1980, the average age upon joining the movement was 21. Only 8 percent of the devotees sampled had been over the age of 30 at the time they joined. Moreover, the average age of members at the time of the survey was 27.

Second, one third of the people contacted by the devotees were of Asian extraction, including many Japanese. While in some measure this high frequency of attempts at contacts with Asians is an artifact of the ISKCON distributors' proximity to a Japanese airline, the devotees did choose to take up their positions in this area out of a range of other possibilities in the airport terminal. Only one Asian person was among the devotees surveyed in 1980 (excluding members originally from India). One reason these people might be preferred targets is suggested by the finding that they were both more likely to stop and talk with the devotees upon contact and more likely to purchase a book than other social groups contacted.

Third, the vast majority—three fourths—of the people contacted by ISKCON members were men. Since airports tend to have a higher proportion of men than women, one might suppose that men were the favored targets because of their sheer numbers. It seems, however, that other reasons were involved. Observation revealed that even women who passed close to devotees were generally overlooked in favor of male subjects (Rochford 1985:142–43). Men make better prospects for contact and interaction because of the dynamics of male-female encounters in public settings (Goffman 1977; Gardner 1980, 1995). Because of this they were favored targets for ISKCON solicitations (see Rochford 1985:139–47).

CHANGES IN THE DEVOTEES' PRESENTATIONS OF SELF

As any door-to-door salesman can attest, making a sale to a stranger who has not expressed an interest in a particular product is a difficult task. When the salesman is a member of a religious group that is defined by the public as peculiar, strange, or perhaps even threatening, this job becomes even more problematic. While for traditional religious organizations and for a number of the Christianity-based new religions (e.g., the Unification Church and the Children of God/Family), such selling can be accomplished rather easily, for ISKCON members, winning over potential donors presents a unique problem because they have taken on the identity equipment (Goffman 1963) of a traditional eastern culture. To help overcome the stigma attached to their appearance, devotees have devised a number of strategies to disguise their identities during *sankirtana*. In 1973, ISKCON members began wearing conventional clothes to conceal their identity as Hare Krishna devotees (shirts, pants, and wigs for the men and dresses for the women).

Something new has been added to the Hare Krishna movement: the toupee. Numerous male members are wearing hairpieces on their shaved pates these days while they are distributing literature. And both sexes are shedding the orange saffron robes in favor of more traditional dress in public. "We sort of freak out people with our normal appearance," said Krishna member John Robertson, 27. "Our culture is so aesthetic that people get upset when they see anything religious." (*Los Angeles Times*, 19 March 1976)

Beginning in 1975, *sankirtana* devotees began to alter their appearances in more extreme ways in an effort to upgrade their respectability in the eyes of the public. I encountered this when walking down Westwood Boulevard in Los Angeles one afternoon in December, when a Santa stopped me on the street and offered me a candy cane.

SANTA: Ho, ho, ho. Have you been a good boy this year?

I responded that I had indeed. The Santa asked, "Would you give a donation to help needy people throughout the world?"

EBR: What kind of help?

SANTA: (raising his money bucket to reveal some small pictures on the side) Book publishing, education, and food distribution.

At this point I recognize the pictures and the organization name ISKCON written on the side.

EBR: Oh, that's a nice thing to be doing.

As I reached into my pocket for some change, the Santa held the bucket up high to expose numerous dollar bills. After I had put the money into the bucket, the Santa handed me a *Back to Godhead* magazine and said, "I am part of a movement that is seeking to alter people's consciousness, through yoga and meditation." (Los Angeles 1975)

By taking on roles that the public can interpret as respectable and harmless, the devotees gain special license to approach people in public settings. In Goffman's (1963) terms, the devotees project a public image that allows them to be seen as opening persons, thereby facilitating their *sankirtana* efforts.

CHANGES IN THE STRUCTURE AND CONTENT OF *SANKIRTANA*

Beginning in 1975, ISKCON devotees began employing *sankirtana* tactics that were meant to maximize the financial returns from literature distributed. The following interaction between the author and a male ISKCON member at the

Los Angeles International Airport in 1981 shows the ways in which preaching had become secondary to the goal of raising money:

DEVOTEE: Sir! Sir! Where are you flying today?

EBR: Oh, I'm just here to pick someone up who's flying in.

DEVOTEE: Look what we have for you. We have already given away hundreds today. Everyone is getting one and here is yours. (*He hands me a copy of the Bhagavad Gita.*)

EBR: Thanks, I appreciate that. This will give me something to read while I wait. (*I start to move away, but he opens another text exposing pictures of artwork.*)

DEVOTEE: Uh, we do ask for a donation to cover the cost of publishing. Give a donation.

EBR: Sure, how much do you want?

DEVOTEE: As much as you can. If you give ten dollars that would really help.

EBR: (reaching for my wallet) I can't give ten. How about a couple of dollars? (I open my wallet and pull out two one-dollar bills, but in so doing I expose a ten-dollar bill.)

DEVOTEE: (*looking over my shoulder*) Would you mind exchanging that ten-dollar bill for some ones? I have a lot of ones.

EBR: Sure (giving him the ten).

DEVOTEE: (He reaches into his pocket and pulls out a handful of bills, none of which are one-dollar bills. He has nothing but fives and tens and grabs one of the fives.) Could you give five?

EBR: No, I'm a student. I don't have much money. How about four?

(The devotee reaches into the other pocket, pulls out a number of one-dollar bills, and then gives me six one-dollar bills.)

In this interaction, the devotee made use of a practice known as the "change-up." Having gotten agreement from me to pay for the book, he then tried to obtain a large bill. With the bill in hand, he was able to bargain further for a higher price.

More systematic evidence of this profit-seeking motive is provided by a study conducted by the Portland Airport authorities in 1976. Of the 154 people interviewed[8] who had been contacted by ISKCON members in the airport terminal, 52 percent stated that they had not been aware that the person they had encountered was a member of any religious organization. Also, a number of these airport patrons who had been aware that the person they had contacted represented a religious group had no idea that the group was ISKCON; many of them reported that they thought the money was to be used for a Christian charity. More telling is the finding that 89 percent of these respondents reported that the ISKCON member who had contacted them had made no effort whatsoever to discuss religious principles of any sort (Port Authority of Portland 1976).

CHANGES IN THE OBJECTS DISTRIBUTED IN PUBLIC PLACES

A major change took place beginning in 1977. When book distribution began to level off during that year, many ISKCON communities began to experience economic difficulties. As literature distribution continued to decline over the next five years, ISKCON as a whole faced increasingly serious financial problems. To help bring money into the movement's communities, members began to sell a variety of consumer goods in public settings. In contrast to book distribution, during which individual devotees could take it on themselves to preach, the practice of "picking," as it is referred to by the devotees, affords little or no opportunity to carry out any missionary activities.

Picking is a form of public solicitation that involves seeking straight donations on behalf of a worthy cause (e.g., to feed needy people) or selling nonreligious products to strangers in such locations as rock concerts, shopping centers, roadside rest areas, and, in California, at the Department of Motor Vehicles. Items sold include candles, record albums, candy, cookies, prints of artwork, American-flag lapel pins, and buttons (supporting various sports teams and recording artists). When involved in picking, devotees wear conventional clothing to disguise their identity as Hare Krishna converts.

Between 1977 and 1979, the devotees sometimes distributed literature when picking. After that, this practice became less common and was actively discouraged by the leaders in many ISKCON communities because it often interfered with making a sale. A male devotee, who picked at rock concerts on the East Coast in 1980 in order to help finance the many building projects going on at ISKCON's West Virginia farm community, explained why the devotees in his area stopped giving out Krishna books when selling records:

> We had to stop giving out books at rock concerts. People would realize that we were devotees and they would just tear them up anyway. I mean,

these are sex-and drug-crazed people. There is no point in giving them Krishna like that. They won't read the book anyway. (Cleveland 1980)

The inability to preach Krishna Consciousness often created considerable distress for *sankirtana* devotees. A woman from the Los Angeles ISKCON community contrasted her feelings about book distribution and picking in a 1980 interview:

EBR: When you distribute books, does it feel like a different kind of thing than doing records?

DEVOTEE: I do books and records. When you're doing the books it's different because you are giving them Krishna. But you see, a lot of times when you're doing records you can't give them a book. A lot of times they won't take them. Right now I am fried out on doing these records. . . . I want to go and preach to people. I actually want to tell them about Krishna. I'm a devotee. I want to spread Krishna Consciousness, not sell records. (Los Angeles 1980)

The decision of ISKCON's leaders to favor picking at the expense of book distribution effectively blocked putting forward the movement's missionary goals in public places. This form of solicitation works quite differently from book distribution because it involves no presumption that the buyer has any interest in ISKCON or in the philosophy of the movement.[9]

STRATEGY, PUBLIC DEFINITION, AND DECLINE

As a number of investigators of social movements have noted, the developmental pattern of any movement is neither fixed nor solely determined by its goals and ideology (Snow 1979; Rochford 1987; Zald and Ash 1966). Instead, its history is strongly influenced by the dynamic interplay between its values, goals, and strategies and the way these are defined and reacted to by the public.

In the early 1970s, the recruitment tactics and information-spreading efforts of the new religions became a public issue in the United States. A countermovement of anticultists emerged, bent on discrediting such groups and shaping public opinion against them. The anticult movement sought to influence the public's view of the new religions through the media, conventional church organizations, chambers of commerce, civic groups, and an extensive lobbying campaign directed at state and federal legislators (Shupe and Bromley 1979, 1980). Bromley and Shupe describe the ideology and how it was used to legitimize the tactics of those opposing the cults:

Conversion to new religions was explained in terms of brain washing, drugging or spot hypnosis; this explanation effectively reduced "converts" to "victims." The remainder of the anti-cult ideology provided the rationale for such manipulative and abusive practices. Leaders of new religions were portrayed as authoritarians and charlatans who exploited their young followers for power and profit. Thus, these groups were not religious at all but merely self-aggrandisement schemes masquerading as religions to avoid taxation and criminal prosecution. Since conversion was neither voluntary nor to a legitimate religion, even forcible removal hardly represented a serious infringement of constitutional rights or personal freedom. (1982:4)

While the claims of the anticultists have proved largely unfounded (Bromley and Shupe 1981), the anticult movement was largely successful in mobilizing what had been an innocent bystander public into a struggle against the cults, which by the mid-1970s had become a publicly defined social problem. As a result, ISKCON and the other new religions came to be viewed as threatening.[10]

Because of this strong public opposition, ISKCON's mobilization strategies were greatly narrowed; the movement had few options and chose to pursue covert and illegitimate tactics to help assure its survival. The choices were particularly limited in ISKCON's case because its exclusive communal structure and sectarian beliefs precluded financial strategies that otherwise might have been available (e.g., outside employment). To have chosen this alternative would have involved changes in the movement's exclusive structural arrangements, which would have in turn risked the commitment of its membership. Most critically, working outside the devotee community might well have resulted in members forming social ties with nondevotee co-workers, which might have acted as countervailing ties, threatening members' commitment to ISKCON and Krishna Consciousness. ISKCON therefore began to further stress the financial side of *sankirtana* at the expense of missionary activities. As book distribution began to level off and then decline after 1977, ISKCON's public place strategies shifted once again. Picking became the dominant financial tactic.

These changes in ISKCON's *sankirtana* practices during the middle and late 1970s further shaped and rigidified the public's image of ISKCON as a deviant and threatening cult. By employing tactics that were viewed as coercive, financially motivated, and lacking in religious content, ISKCON helped to mobilize public opinion against its beliefs and way of life. The public became keenly aware of devotees in airports and other public places and actively sought to avoid contact with them.[11] But more formal and systematic efforts were also instituted to control ISKCON's use of these settings. In the mid-1970s, airports, state fairs, and other public facilities throughout the United States began to legally challenge ISKCON's *sankirtana* practices. The authorities argued that ISKCON was using tactics that were more financial than religious and that therefore it should be denied First Amendment privileges. Despite a wealth of legal precedents in its favor, ISKCON faced a stiff challenge in protecting its free access to public spaces. As the member largely responsible for opening public settings to *sankirtana* explained in a 1983 interview, the movement's tactics became the grounds for legal attempts to limit its access :

> While it was initially easy to open these various public places to *sankirtana*, suddenly everything began to change. When we [ISKCON] came back to fight time, place, and manner regulations, we had a hard time. They [airports, etc.] would say: "Look what you are doing. You are using the change-up on people and other practices of this sort simply to get money from them. We don't think First Amendment rights are at issue." So they would get the judge thinking that we were involved in fraud. As a result, we could no longer assert *pure* First Amendment rights. (Philadelphia 1983)

Initially, the courts reacted only by imposing limitations on ISKCON's use of public settings. These included restrictions on where ISKCON members could distribute literature in a particular public facility and how many devotees could distribute it at any one time, and/or time limitations on *sankirtana*. In addition, in the late 1970s, state fairs in several states won legal rulings confining ISKCON members to booths, thereby limiting the devotees' access to fair patrons (*ISKCON v. Barber, Young, and Garlick,* 1980; *ISKCON v. Evans,* 1977; *ISKCON v. State Fair of Texas,* 1978).

Several state courts, beginning in 1977 and 1978, began hearing lawsuits aimed at denying ISKCON's right to engage at all in public place solicitation. Airports in Los Angeles, Seattle, Chicago, and other locations initiated litigation meant to bar ISKCON members from airport facilities. Public zoos and a number of state and county fairs from California to New York brought legal actions aimed at ending *sankirtana*. Finally, in 1978, O'Hare International Airport in Chicago was closed to *sankirtana*. As one ISKCON leader explained in 1982, the public reaction that had been generated by the movement's practices was largely responsible:

> While book distribution went up and up between 1974 and 1977, the public reaction was also building. And then bam, there was a chain reaction: O'Hare [airport in Chicago] went down and there was litigation to get us

out of other airports and public places. . . . The airport managers used to discuss with each other at their conventions: "How do we get the Hare Krishnas out?" (Philadelphia 1982)

In 1981, the U.S. Supreme Court ruled (*Heffron v. ISKCON*, 1981) that ISKCON members did not have the legal right to distribute literature and solicit donations at state fairs throughout the country. Because of this decision and a number of other legal rulings that either restricted or prohibited *sankirtana*, ISKCON discontinued or limited literature distribution in a number of public places, particularly airports.

Even as ISKCON faced being discredited by the anticult movement, the public, and the courts, it also began to face criticism from within. A growing number of members began openly to question the movement's *sankirtana* practices, to the extent that ISKCON's legitimacy as an instrument for putting forward the cause of Krishna Consciousness was challenged. As one long-time member explained in a 1982 interview:

One thing that you have to realize is that from the beginning to the end, the change-up and so forth were very controversial within the movement. Some devotees were sensitive to how the public would react and realized from experience that karmis [members of the public] weren't stupid. They were going to figure it out in due course of time and it was all going to come back on us. . . . Some leaders grossly underestimated the consciousness of the people who were coming into contact with the devotees. They seemed to think that people didn't realize that they were being manipulated. . . . But some of us knew that sooner or later it was going to come down. It was a mistake to become unethical with the people. (Philadelphia 1982)

The controversies surrounding the movement's money-gathering strategies led to an erosion of member commitment and to mounting internal conflicts, factionalism, and a growing number of defections (Rochford 1985:191–220). The loss of ISKCON credibility in the eyes of a part of its membership became a major cause of ISKCON's decline during the late 1970s. While external challenges could be interpreted as no more than a deepening of the general persecution of ISKCON and the cults, internal challenges to the authority of the organization brought ISKCON to the edge of organizational crisis. As Zald and Ash (1966) argue, the decline and failure of a movement organization is often the result of strategies that place the organization's legitimacy in doubt from *within*. By altering the purpose of *sankirtana*, ISKCON's leaders unwittingly set off a process that led to their being discredited, which ultimately undermined the organization's legitimacy and helped to hasten the decline of Hare Krishna in America.

POSTSCRIPT

In recent years the most common question I receive from people when they find out that I have been studying the Krishna Consciousness movement is: "Whatever happened to the Hare Krishnas?" This is usually followed with: "Do they still exist? I never see them anymore." The fact is the Hare Krishnas in North America are only rarely seen in public places these days, and are found distributing books in only a limited number of major airports in the United States. From a movement that was once financed more or less exclusively by the distribution of Prabhupada's books and other objects in public places, ISKCON's North American communities today receive little support from *sankirtana*. The decline of this source of revenue has resulted in the demise of ISKCON's traditional communal structure and the subsequent transformation of ISKCON from a sectarian movement to one that is increasingly congregational in form (Rochford 1995a, 1997, 1998).

Sankirtana throughout the 1970s represented the foundation of ISKCON's sectarian world (Rochford 1998). Yet as we have seen, book distribution declined beginning in 1977 and then plummeted in the following years. While picking made up for the revenue shortfall in the short run, this practice remained controversial and was officially discontinued as an organizational strategy in the late 1980s. Without an economic alternative capable of supporting the movement's membership within a communal context, ISKCON faced a major turning point in its North American development. Members, especially those with families, were forced to seek work in the conventional labor market (Rochford 1997). For most this also involved setting up households outside of ISKCON's communities. Devotee families became self-supporting and increasingly independent. Freed from the authority and control of the leadership, yet wanting to raise their families in a devotee environment, many householders formed enclave communities nearby an ISKCON temple. There they interact with other devotees, worship at the local temple and, in some cases, send their children to the temple day school. By 1990 the nuclear family had effectively displaced communalism as the basis of ISKCON's social organization.

The overall effect of these changes was the disintegration of ISKCON's traditional communal structure and, with it, the movement's sectarian way of life (Rochford 1995a, 1997). In struggling to meet the needs of nuclear family life, many devotees became far less involved in the collective life of ISKCON (Rochford 1995a). In working jobs outside the communal fold many also became increasingly involved in the conventional society, withdrawing their involvement in and commitment to the movement's religious beliefs and practices and to ISKCON as a religious organization (Rochford 2000).

The demise of *sankirtana* left ISKCON without a means to support an *oppositional* religious culture based on a communal structure. ISKCON underwent dramatic change, becoming a congregationally based movement in North America and increasingly throughout much of the world (Rochford 1995b, Rochford 2000).

REFERENCES

Bromley, David and Anson Shupe. "Financing the New Religions. A Resource Mobilization Approach." *Journal for the Scientific Study of Religion* 19 (3) (1980): 227–39.

——. *Strange Gods: The Great American Cult Scare.* Boston: Beacon Press, 1981.

"11 Linked to Krishna Cult Indicted in Narcotics Case." *Los Angeles Times,* 6 November 1979.

Gardner, Carol Brooks. "Passing By: Street Remarks, Address Rights, and Urban Women." *Sociological Inquiry* 50 (3–4) (1980): 328–56.

——. *Passing By: Gender and Public Harassment.* Berkeley: University of California Press, 1995.

Goffman, Erving. *Behavior in Public Places.* New York: The Free Press, 1963.

——. "The Arrangement Between the Sexes." *Theory and Society* 4 (3) (1977): 301–31.

"The Hare Krishna Cover-up." *Los Angeles Times,* 19 March 1976.

"Hare Krishna Arsenal Discovered at Ranch." *Los Angeles Times,* 16 March 1990.

"Krishna Arms Caches Draw Police Scrutiny in California." *New York Times,* 9 June 1980.

"Krishna Cult Members Hustle Millions in Cash From Public." *Fresno Bee,* 27 June 1980.

McCarthy, John and Mayer Zald. "Tactical Considerations in Social Movement Organizations." Paper presented at the meetings of the American Sociological Association, August 1974.

Messinger, Sheldon. "Organizational Transformation: A Case Study of a Declining Social Movement." *American Sociological Review* 20 (1955): 3–10.

National Broadcasting Corporation (NBC). *Prime Time with Tom Snyder.* 1 July 1979. New York. Television broadcast.

Port Authority of Portland, Oregon. *Portland International Airport Study on the Activities of Hare Krishna Members.* Portland, Oregon, 1976.

Rochford, E. Burke, Jr. *Hare Krishna in America.* New Brunswick, NJ: Rutgers University Press, 1985.

——. "Shifting Public Definitions of Hare Krishna." In Ralph Turner and Lewis Killian, eds., Collective Behavior, 3rd ed., 258–60. (Englewood Cliffs, NJ: Prentice-Hall, 1987).

——. "Family Structure, Commitment, and Involvement in the Hare Krishna Movement." *Sociology of Religion* 56 (2) (1995): 153–75.

——. "Crescita, Espansione e Mutamento nel Movimento Degli Hare Krishna." *Religioni e Sette nel mondo* 1 (1) (1995): 56–80.

——. "Family Formation, Culture, and Change in the Hare Krishna Movement." *ISKCON Communications Journal* 5 (2) (1997): 61–82.

——. "Child Abuse in the Hare Krishna Movement: 1971–1986." *ISKCON Communications Journal* 6 (1998): 43–69.

——. "Hare Krishna in North America and Europe." *Social Compass* 47 (2) (2000): 169–86.

Shupe, Anson and David Bromley. "The Moonies and the Anti-cultists: Movement and Counter-Movement in Conflict." *Sociological Analysis* 40 (4) (1979): 325–34.

——. *The New Vigilantes: Anti-Cultists, Deprogrammers, and the New Religions.* Beverly Hills: Sage, 1980.

Snow, David. "A Dramaturgical Analysis of Movement Accommodation: Building Idiosyncrasy Credit as a Movement Mobilization Strategy." *Symbolic Interaction* 2 (2) (1979): 23–44.

Zald, Mayer and Roberta Ash. "Social Movement Organizations: Growth, Decay and Change." *Social Forces* 44 (1966): 327–41.

Court Cases Cited

Heffron v. ISKCON, 49 U.S.L.W. 3802, 1981.

Murdock v. Pennsylvania, 319 U.S. 105, 63 S. Ct. 870, 87 L. Ed. 1292, 1942.

ISKCON v. Barber, Young and Garlick, 506 N.Y. 147, 1980.

ISKCON v. Conlisk, 374 ILL. 1010, 1973.

ISKCON v. Evans, 440 U.S. 414, 1977.

ISKCON v. Rochford, 425 ILL. 734, 1977.

ISKCON v. State Fair of Texas, 461 TX. 719, 1978.

NOTES

This is a revised and expanded version of "Airports and Public Places," previously published in E. Burke Rochford Jr., *Hare Krishna in America* (New Brunswick, NJ: Rutgers University Press, 1985).

1. I conducted a nonrandom survey of six ISKCON communities in the United States in 1980. Data were collected from 214 adults in Los Angeles, Denver, Port Royal (a farm community in Pennsylvania), New York, and Boston. My sample represents approximately 10 percent of the total ISKCON population in the United States in 1980.

2. Even though distribution of Prabhupada's books and public solicitation provided the primary source of revenue for ISKCON's communities, other monies came from the sale of Spiritual Sky incense. In 1969 in New York City, ISKCON began producing and distributing this incense as a way of raising money to support the movement. The sale of incense was not, however, a major source of revenue for all of ISKCON's communities. Some chose to distribute incense, while others decided to rest their financial security solely upon the distribution of literature.

3. *Sankirtana* involves three types of activities in public places: Book distribution is the practice whereby devotees venture into airports and other public places to distribute for money Prabhupada's translations of the Vedic scriptures; *Hare Nama* usually involves a group of devotees going out in public to chant and preach and may or may not involve literature distribution; "picking," which will be discussed

later in the chapter, involves selling products to the public for money. It generally does not involve literature distribution.

4. The decision to combine missionary activity with money making was made by ISKCON's founder, Shrila Prabhupada. He instructed his disciples that book distribution would provide for ISKCON's financial needs and allow the movement to pursue its missionary goals at the same time. Prabhupada actively discouraged the development of other forms of business enterprise that might have helped support ISKCON. In fact, the ex-business manager of ISKCON's incense business, Spiritual Sky Scented Products, argued in a 1977 interview that the company's financial potential was never fully realized because Prabhupada had failed to support it.

5. In *Murdock v. Pennsylvania* (1942) the Supreme Court held that the Jehovah's Witnesses could not be held to a city ordinance requiring the purchase of a permit in order to conduct door-to-door solicitations and sales of religious literature. The fact that religious literature was sold rather than donated did not transform religious activity into a commercial enterprise, according to the court. While ISKCON was ultimately protected under the First Amendment, the movement nevertheless was forced initially to enter into litigation to secure its rights with regard to practicing *sankirtana* (*ISKCON v Conlisk*, 1973; *ISKCON v. Rochford*, 1977; *ISKCON v. Evans*, 1977).

6. Another indication of how much ISKCON made from its *sankirtana* practices is suggested by the financial report of the Berkeley ISKCON community, which cited *sankirtana* income of $1.1 million in 1977 and of $877,325 in 1978, according to its application for property tax exemptions in Alameda County (*Fresno Bee*, 27 June 1980).

7. Beginning as early as 1971, ISKCON members began to experiment with various strategies to increase their literature distribution and, thereby, the amount of money that could be raised through donations. The first major innovation was the introduction of "sales mantras." Instead of standing on the street and offering people passing by a copy of the movement's magazine, *Back to Godhead*, the devotees came up with the idea that people would be more likely to stop and talk if a printed card with the Hare Krishna mantra was offered first. Only after the person took the card and stopped would the devotee offer the magazine. This simple strategy resulted in ISKCON members distributing substantially more literature and therefore raising more money as well. As one devotee explained, "Instead of a devotee being able to bring home $10, he could now bring home $25 or $30, by that simple change. So then you could distribute so many more magazines and also fix up your temple and do so many things to preach Krishna Consciousness" (Philadelphia, 1982).

8. The people interviewed by airport staff were selected randomly. At the time of the study, ISKCON members were distributing books as well as other nonreligious items to people in the airport terminal.

9. Messinger (1955) notes a similar development within the Townsend movement as this group faced decline in the late 1930s and early 1940s in the United States. As it lost mass support, it faced growing financial difficulties. To bring money into the organization, members were urged to purchase a variety of consumable goods bearing the Townsend name (e.g., Townsend candy bars, toilet soap, and health foods). Purchase of these items did not signify any degree of commitment to the Townsend movement or its goals and ideology. As Messinger argues, this period in the movement's development involved a "striking shift from programmatic matters to concern(s) with promoting . . . product(s)" (1955:8).

10. ISKCON's public image as a threatening movement was also strongly influenced by two major controversies that received national media attention. In 1979, people claiming to be either current or former ISKCON members were charged by authorities in California with possession and smuggling of drugs (*Los Angeles Times* 1979). ISKCON officials denied any movement involvement, claiming that these people were not members in good standing. In 1980, a major controversy emerged that had far-reaching consequences for ISKCON's public image. Law enforcement officials in a community north of San Francisco uncovered what was described as "a cache of weapons and ammunition" in an ISKCON farm community (*Los Angeles Times* 1980; *New York Times* 1980). The leader of the community, one of the eleven guru successors to Prabhupada after the latter's death in 1977, was arrested and charged in the case. While charges were later dropped, the incident had a significant impact on ISKCON's public image, following as it did closely on the heels of the tragedy at Jonestown in 1978. Irrespective of the facts in either of these cases, the media coverage further influenced the public's view of ISKCON. The weapons incident, in particular, was used repeatedly by the anticult movement in its efforts to discredit ISKCON and the other new religions (see Rochford 1987).

11. The public's awareness of ISKCON members' work in public settings was influenced by several factors: (1) insofar as ISKCON claims to have distributed 100 million pieces of literature by 1982, many members of the public had first-hand experience with the devotees' *sankirtana* tactics and actively sought to avoid further contacts; (2) the media's coverage of ISKCON often described Krishna members' deceitful *sankirtana* tactics (*Fresno Bee* 1980; *Los Angeles Times* 1976; NBC 1979); (3) there have been a variety of formal and informal efforts by authorities in charge of public facilities subject to ISKCON's *sankirtana* practices to inform their patrons of the devotees' presence and purposes. In a number of locations (e.g., the Los Angeles International Airport, Sea World in San Diego), signs warning the public of the Krishna activities were displayed around the facilities' entrances. At the Denver zoo in 1980, I observed an employee standing outside the exit at closing time, warning zoo patrons as they left that ISKCON members were awaiting them and requesting that they not contribute any money; and (4) anticultists have sought to disrupt ISKCON's *sankirtana* efforts in public settings by approaching people talking with a Krishna member and informing them of the identify of their contact (Bromley and Shupe 1980).

$\begin{bmatrix} 17 \end{bmatrix}$

HEALING THE HEART OF ISKCON

The Place of Women

KIM KNOTT

U NDERSTANDING AND ANALYZING the place of women in this western Vaishnava movement is no easy matter. It requires a careful consideration of a variety of sources, including primary scriptural sources, the writings and sayings of Prabhupada, sociological research by interested outsiders, and the many contributions on the subject, both scholarly and personal, by ISKCON devotees.[1] Why is all this necessary? First, it is evident from the recent state of the debate within the movement—much of which may be viewed on Web sites associated with ISKCON[2]—that the place of women in Krishna Consciousness is informed by both its scriptural and its historical legacy. Second, it is clear that any account of the identity and roles of women and men must conform to the intentions and teachings of the movement's founder, Shrila Prabhupada.[3] Third, as ISKCON is a preaching movement the *raison d'être* of which is to spread the name of Krishna, its principles must be lived out according to "time, place, and circumstance." It follows that an understanding of the situation of women and men in this movement is related to comparable issues outside it, as the outside world not only provides new members and sympathetic outsiders but also the social and legal context for the movement and its members, and thus its ultimate mundane authority. Most important, the positions of women and men are a function of real social relations within ISKCON, between leaders and grassroots members, different generations of disciples, reformers and revivalists, celibate and married devotees, husbands and wives, parents and children.

No outsider, however knowledgeable, could ever hope to do justice to all these sources, the views of the various constituencies, and the complex relations among them. No devotee could do so either. The purpose of this chapter cannot be to offer a fully comprehensive and neutral account of women in ISKCON; rather, its aims are to provide a context for understanding attitudes to the place of women in the movement, to identify some of the principal participants in the debate, and to survey, in brief, events from the mid-1970s onward.[4] No author could be neutral in pursuit of these aims, as we are all interested when it comes to matters of gender. I am a feminist outsider who has written about ISKCON and the debate about women within it since the mid-1980s.[5] Being a western feminist does not endear me to any of the parties within ISKCON who debate this issue, though it makes me more personally sympathetic to those women and men who argue for women's full participation.

The title of the chapter is borrowed from the conclusion to a presentation by Vishakha Dasi given with others of the ISKCON Women's Ministry to the Governing Body Commission (GBC) at its annual meeting in Mayapur in 2000.[6] It is significant because it recognizes "women in ISKCON" to be a process, not merely a debate or an issue of the day. As such, it will not be settled by a series of resolutions or even a catalogue of changes, but is rather the gradual working out of the legacy, teachings, practices, and relations I mentioned earlier. Vishakha's identification of this process with the "heart" of ISKCON not only indicates its centrality for her and other women but also signals the view articulated by many, that the women problem is everyone's problem. It damages the family unit, now the most common living arrangement among ISKCON devotees;[7] it threatens the future of the broader community of devotees; and it cripples the spiritual progress of all individuals, female and male.

> Prabhupada used to say that we are not impersonalists, we do not see Krishna alone . . . we are eternally a family and to understand that is to understand Krishna Consciousness. When, due to injudicious policies or our own immaturity and ignorance, basically half the family in ISKCON is cut off from what could be much more meaningful participation, then actually all of us are cut off. . . . If we are denied the normal spiritual relationships with mothers, with sisters, with daughters, nieces . . . we are actually being denied our own self-realization. . . . The realization of that

eternal spiritual personality actually comes by relationships, because to be a person means to have relationships with other persons.[8]

The centrality for the health of the movement of the problems faced by women was indeed acknowledged by the GBC in Mayapur in 2000. In their resolutions (Section 500), they stated,

> that many of the social issues that confront us are exacerbated because the voice of our women, who are the mothers and daughters of our Krishna Conscious family, have been hushed and stifled due to misinterpretation of our Vaishnava philosophy, and thus the human and interpersonal needs of our devotees have been minimised.[9]

The embeddedness of the women problem in ISKCON's social and spiritual life, and its consequences for the future, will be a subject to which I shall return after discussing the movement's teachings on equality, gender, and *dharma*.

EQUALITY AND THE SOUL: THE STARTING POINT

Women themselves have to transcend the bodily conception of life and become liberated from the mundane social sexual rat race. And of course men have to raise *their* consciousness. Spiritual life begins with the realization that one is not the material body but an eternal spiritual soul, and the designations "male" and "female" refer only to the material body. So ultimately they have nothing to do with the soul or self.[10]

Devotees may differ on other matters regarding the women issue, but no one dissents from this view. Many articles written on the subject of women in Krishna Consciousness by devotees have made this their focus of attention.[11] Most external commentators have also acknowledged it, J. Stillson Judah, for example: "Regardless of their social positions, the souls of female devotees are to be considered of equal value with their male counterparts."[12] Like many religions, then, this movement teaches spiritual equality. All the souls (*jiva*) are distinct from one another, and are both of the same quality and nature yet separate from the supreme soul, Krishna.[13]

The self-realization sought in Krishna Consciousness is not primarily the liberation of the soul from the round of rebirth (*samsara*), although this is a by-product of the process, but the attainment and perfection of a relationship of loving service to God. *Bhakti yoga* or devotional service is both the path and the goal, and it is open to anyone. Success upon it depends not only on keeping the regulative principles (abstention from meat and other unacceptable foodstuffs, alcohol and drugs, illicit sex, and gambling) but especially on a "service attitude," a position of surrender to Krishna, the spiritual master or guru, and all the other devotees. Egoism, pride, envy, and greed, whether they are directed to material or spiritual attainments, are signs of deviation from the realization that one is by nature a servant. In Krishna Consciousness it is essential to recognize the dutiful nature (*dharma*) of the soul as well as the body. While the latter is dependent on one's social position, stage of life, and gender, the former is eternal (*sanatana*). It is the constitutional nature of the soul to be a servant of God. The perfection of this natural role was embodied by Chaitanya Mahaprabhu and eternally exemplified by Radha, the beloved consort of Krishna. It is only through her that devotees, both male and female, ultimately can approach him.

This explains why devotees writing on the subject of women in ISKCON return again and again to this philosophical starting point. This is where their concept of equality has its roots. What is more, the success of the self-realization of the soul is measured against the "service attitude" of Radha.[14] Therefore, in theory, it is not that women on the path of Krishna Consciousness must aspire to or imitate male spiritual practice, but that all devotees, whether female or male in body, must adopt what might be called a "feminine" approach to spirituality.[15] This "feminine" approach is essentially an attitude—spiritual, mental, and physical—of surrender and service to others, and ultimately to Krishna, who manifests a "masculine" approach. Femininity and masculinity, as manifested transcendentally in Radha and Krishna, are eternal values, not merely cultural constructions.

This is important for several reasons. First, the spiritual role model for all devotees is apparently "female" (though her transcendental form is nonmaterial). Second, the "feminine" approach of surrender and service is recommended for all. We see it manifested by Arjuna in the *Bhagavad Gita* as well as by Radha. Thirdly, women, by virtue of their social and cultural conditioning in Indian and western societies, are in many ways better practiced in this attitude or approach than men. Many men—and some women—have found it difficult, for example, to surrender to a spiritual master, and there have been battles in the history of ISKCON over the issue of serving God through his representative, the guru. Most women, it is said, seem to have less problem accepting this aspect of the philosophy or the practical consequences of obedient and submissive behavior.[16] There are, naturally, a number of women newcomers who, while attracted to Krishna, find the notion of submission initially objectionable on the grounds that it reminds them of the very oppression from which, as intelligent women, they are trying to escape. It will be pointed out to them, however, that there is a world of difference between material submission and spiritual submission, the one leading to oppression, the other to liberation.

The basic philosophy of Krishna Consciousness concerning the soul is one of spiritual equality. At this level, the women problem is largely irrelevant. Devotees are the first to admit, however, that they are *aspiring* to live on what they call "the spiritual platform"; they have not achieved it yet. Equality may exist on this ideal level, but, at the level of conventional experience, it is threatened by all the circumstances of material and social embodiment.

EQUALITY AND THE BODY

Although in the philosophy of Krishna Consciousness the soul is eternal and the body merely impermanent, the latter cannot and should not be ignored. The body is there to enable the soul to experience service to God. The opportunity of human embodiment is to be treasured for providing this occasion for liberation. Human beings may respond to God's call in a way that other living beings may not, and they may experience, albeit in a qualified way, the pastimes of Krishna. But human embodiment also provides many opportunities for entrapment. Living out a spiritual path in which the body is used with care as a vehicle for liberation is extremely difficult. The way is full of material temptations. It might be easier if all bodies were the same, like all souls, but they are not. They are different, each one having a unique *dharma* or dutiful nature. This *dharma* differs according to social situation (*varna*) and stage of life (*ashram*). And, traditionally, both of these differ according to gender.[17] Formally, according to classical Hindu scripture, women were excluded from the requirements of *varnashram dharma* and had their own *dharma*. Various women in the Vaishnava texts exemplified different aspects of this, e.g., Kunti, Draupadi, Devahuti, and Sita. Although all these women were strong and devout, their roles were generally supportive. They expected to serve their husbands (though difficulties arose in this even for these women) and to find spiritual fulfillment and material protection in doing so.[18] These roles (*stri dharma*) derived from an understanding of women's nature. It was associated with *prakriti*, matter, and *maya*, illusion. Their bodies were formed for procreation, and this process bound them to material nature to a greater degree than men. What is more, the beauty of their form made them potentially dangerous both to men on the spiritual path (hence they were perceived to be a problem to be avoided) and to the honor of families (as a result of which they were to be protected at all times by male relatives). As we shall see, this traditional view of women's nature and roles has been influential in the women issue in ISKCON.

Although devotees come across these ideas in scripture regularly, the teachings of the movement focus more on the problems of dealing with our material bodies while striving to make spiritual advancement. As all *jivas* or souls are embodied materially until spiritual realization is attained, this is a problem for both women and men. But different bodies are differently problematic, and there does seem to be a common view among devotees that the woman's body is the more entrapping for a soul in search of liberation for the reasons given above.[19]

What was Prabhupada's view of these matters? It seems clear from his commentaries, lectures, and conversations that he endorsed the view of the potential liability of a woman's body both for the soul that resides within it and for others. However, he was most adamant on the point that *bhakti yoga*, the path of Krishna Consciousness, provided the possibility of transcending the body, whether female or male. The recollections of his earliest devotees strongly support this. Yamuna Devi Dasi recalls his repeated references to the adage, "Never trust a woman or a politician," followed quickly by the rejoinder to her that "you are not a woman, you are a Vaishnava."[20] On record also is Prabhupada's response to the question raised by two of his earliest devotees about whether their womanhood held back their spiritual advancement. "Yes," Prabhupada answered. "If you think of yourselves as women, how will you make any advancement? You must see yourself as spirit-soul, eternal servant of Krishna."[21]

This was his first point, then, that being a *Vaishnavi*, a true servant of Krishna, changed the terms of the debate about women. Additionally, through his behavior and teachings he demonstrated that, *as Vaishnavis*, women devotees—irrespective of their material form compared to men—were equally acceptable as servants of Krishna, equally empowered with intelligence, equally open to spiritual advancement and to contributing to the advancement of others. In engaging *Vaishnavis*, he created "an analytical exception" in relation to the nature and role of women.[22] Of the many occasions when Prabhupada enunciated this,[23] I shall cite just two. Women were among his first disciples, and he expected them to take up the opportunities that arose in devotional service according to their talents and ability, just as he did his male disciples: "I have always accepted the service of women without any discrimination."[24] To record his acceptance of women disciples, as if in answer to his traditionally minded critics, Prabhupada wrote in his purport to a verse from *Chaitanya Charitamrita*: "both the boys and the girls are being trained to become preachers, those girls are not ordinary girls, but are as good as their brothers who are preaching Krishna Consciousness."[25]

WOMEN AND DHARMA: THREE LEVELS OF MEANING

As I hope I have made clear, spiritual equality is fundamental to the movement's principal teaching that "I am not this body." Furthermore, material inequalities—whether of gender or *varna*—are overridden in the common pursuit of *bhakti yoga*. There is equality on the path of spiritual advancement. However, as Radha Devi Dasi has suggested in an article on international law and women's rights in ISKCON, this principle has yet to be fully accepted in the movement: "There is a feeling in ISKCON that souls in women's bodies are not equal, but suffer instead from serious mental and emotional deficits."[26] How does this view arise?

A major difficulty stems directly from the teachings of the movement on *dharma* as they relate to women, and concerns the use of three different levels of meaning. These are not always clearly distinguished and, as a result, have led to a certain amount of confusion both inside and outside ISKCON. For example, devotees speak of participating both in *varnashram dharma*, social nature and its attendant responsibilities, and in *bhagavata dharma*, divine nature.[27] In fact, Krishna Consciousness, as a radical *vaishnava bhakti* movement, offers the latter as a challenge to old, brahminical orthodoxies. Devotees remind us frequently of the promise in the *Bhagavad Gita* of spiritual realization to women and *shudras* as well as those from twice-born groups. Surely, it is the teaching on humanity's divine nature and duty in service to Krishna, on *bhagavata dharma*, that is of greatest importance in Krishna Consciousness. Or is it? There is certainly a recognition of *ashram*, the different stages of life, in the movement. And, although Prabhupada initiated male and female devotees as Brahmins, there is a common parlance of *varna dharma* at work, devotees seeing themselves as engaged according to their nature in *shudra* or *kshatriya* activities and so on. And how do women fit into all of this? Should they obey the normative Hindu prescriptions laid down in *Manusmriti* on a woman's duty (*stri dharma*), which place them outside the conventions of *varnashram dharma*, or does their position in ISKCON's *bhagavata dharma* render them immune from these? These difficulties are compounded by devotees' references to "Vedic" culture and ideals. Are they trying to live out a philosophy and practice derived centuries previously in a different social and cultural context? Should women devotees try to live in a "Vedic" manner, and what would that mean in practice?[28]

What is ISKCON's understanding of *dharma*, particularly as it applies to women? To answer this, it is helpful to distinguish among three distinct understandings of dharma, which might best be designated "Vedic," "Hindu," and "Krishna Conscious."[29] Although devotees frequently refer to their aspiration to live according to "Vedic" prescriptions, at the theological level a distinction is made between the Vedic way of life per se and the ideal, "Krishna Conscious" way of life or *bhagavata dharma*. The account that follows, particularly with regard to the concept of "Vedic" culture and ideals, conforms with a devotional scholarly view but not necessarily with any view held by scholars outside the movement.[30]

The "Vedic" way of life was specific to a particular period of time and a particular people, who lived out their relation to God in a particular social form.[31] In "Vedic" *varnashram dharma*, men served God through their spiritual masters, and women served God through the men who protected them: their fathers, husbands, or sons. Because they understand this social system to have been developed in a different time and place, and by a people who knew perfectly how best to serve God, the devotees do not see it as unequal or oppressive. The men did not abuse their positions by using them as mechanisms for the pursuit of power over women, and women served God by supporting the male members of their family. In this arrangement, the husband was the wife's spiritual master, *patidev*.[32] This view of social life has a mythic and historical reality for devotees.

The "Hindu" system of *varnashram dharma* also has a historical reality, but it relates to a different period, that of the dark age of *kali yuga*. The "Hindu" social system, according to devotees, is a function of this age, during which Indians have continued to live by the social rules of Vedic *varnashram dharma*, but these have become distorted in practice. In *kali yuga* the path of spiritual life has been obscured, and people resort to the lesser goals of material and sensual gratification. What was once a spiritually legitimized system of social organization has become a caste system, and thus a means of oppression. Women are still expected to serve, but, instead of offering spiritual guidance and protection, men exploit and oppress them. Similarly, although *varnashram dharma* is not indigenous to the West, Europe and America in *kali yuga* have experienced a similar period of social and moral degradation in which the distortion of old social structures and principles has led to the exploitation of women. This, as devotees see it, has led to the rise of feminism: women have been oppressed by the very people who they were told were supposed to protect them and their interests, and their natural response has been to attempt to take control of their own lives, to protect themselves. When such women come into ISKCON, unsurprisingly, they wish to resist any hint of male protection. They want to take charge of their own bodily needs and spiritual advancement.

And difficulties may certainly arise as a result of this. The Hare Krishna movement is not a "feminist" movement. As we saw earlier, it understands the essential natures of masculinity and femininity to be different, and believes, *ideally*, that men and women should have separate and different natures and roles while being spiritually equal. That women and men cannot be expected to behave in conformity with their ideal "Vedic" types is conceded unwillingly in the cold reality of *kali yuga*. And this brings us to the "Krishna Conscious" view of *dharma*, or *bhagavata dharma*.

The "Krishna Conscious" view is an attempt to apply the Vedic "service attitude" to *kali yuga*. The aim is not to imitate the Vedic system of *varnashram dharma*, but to use it for guidance in a troubled period.[33] This cannot be achieved by introducing the system wholesale and expecting it to work. This, as the devotees see it, is the failing of the "Hindu" system. For this reason, in the "Krishna Conscious" system, men and women are seen not only as spiritually alike but also as materially alike in the sense that they are ultimately responsible for their own spiritual welfare, with guidance from a guru. Both men and women take gurus, and when they marry, although the women are responsible for bearing and raising children and the men for supporting them in this, both are expected to serve Krishna and the spiritual master in the best way they can, be this cooking, gardening, teaching, sewing, managing, writing, or whatever. Women are not seen as intrinsically less intelligent or less able. *Kali yuga* has changed the ground rules. One disciple asked Prabhupada, "Should I live like in Vedic times, and simply serve my husband and child?" He replied, "No, you have a talent as a writer, you should write articles for newspapers and propagate Krishna consciousness."[34] The test, then, is not whether a woman's role or activity is Vedic, but whether it helps to spread Krishna Consciousness.[35]

Following the Vedic ideal in this dark and dangerous age of *kali yuga*, then, does not mean that women should submit to the whims of their husbands but that both parties should do whatever is best for serving Krishna. In the Vedic period this would naturally have meant service through the husband; in *kali yuga* it means service through the spiritual master by whatever means is most conducive. If a woman feels that her spiritual life is best practiced through serving her husband she may focus on this; if she feels that she can serve best through cooperative independence, she may cultivate her career in conjunction with sharing the care of her family with her husband. Furthermore, as Prabhupada wrote in a letter to a disciple,

> The actual system is that the husband is the spiritual master to his wife, but if the wife can bring her husband into practicing this process [of Krishna Consciousness], then it is all right that the husband accepts the wife as the spiritual master. Chaitanya Mahaprabhu has said that anyone who knows the science of Krishna should be accepted as spiritual master, regardless of any material so-called qualifications, such as rich or poor, man or woman, or *brahmana* or *shudra*.[36]

The changing demands of the contemporary situation are illustrated in the thought-provoking comments of two male devotees:

> We had to become friends in Krishna Consciousness, because I couldn't become that *varnashram* husband—the one that is so respectable that the wife would automatically do everything, as soon as I come home she would wash my feet and whisper pleasantries in my ears. That's not real life for ISKCON devotees today.

I'd like to challenge the supremacy of the male body for realization. . . . It seems to me that that concept actually belongs to *varnashram dharma*. *Bhagavata dharma* doesn't actually place a stress on male or female. When you go to any place of worship, there's always more women than men there—church, temple, mosque, even. . . . Vrindavan, even in Radhakund, there's at least as many women as men there. So I really wonder if it's true, on the *bhagavata dharma* platform, that women can't make progress as easily as men.[37]

In the first we see the welcome recognition by a male devotee that it is not only women but men who have been affected by the changes brought about in *kali yuga*. A relationship of equality and partnership came about as a result of the impossibility of either party living up to the "Vedic" ideal. In the second, in a powerful challenge to the common assumption that the female body is unsuited to the path of spiritual realization, the speaker affirms the radical nature of the "Krishna Conscious" system or *bhagavata dharma* for overturning the problems of material embodiment. Together these examples confirm that *kali yuga* demands new approaches from both female and male devotees, and that the most appropriate strategies conform not to "Vedic" ideals (impossible to achieve in *kali yuga*) or "Hindu" practice (the failure of Vedic *varnashram dharma*) but to *bhagavata dharma*, the Krishna Conscious spiritual path.

Needless to say, these complex levels of interpretation have led to many misunderstandings among both external commentators on ISKCON and society members themselves. Devotees continue to strive for clarification about Prabhupada's own view of the relationship of *varnashram dharma* and *bhagavata dharma*. My opinion is that the ambiguities of this relationship are not likely to be resolved once and for all in a movement that accepts as fundamentally authoritative both scripture and guru. Ancient texts speak of philosophical ideals and social principles that were worked out for distant places and times; living teachers have to interpret these in the light of contemporary circumstances while not losing the impetus for real spiritual revolution. The need to balance a commitment to ideals and the wisdom of a spiritual tradition situated in a real time and place inevitably elicits mixed messages, those spoken out of an appreciation of ideals and those framed in the experience of the hard realities. It is commendable in the face of this tension that the founder of the Hare Krishna movement made a philosophy and practice that had once been largely closed to women available to them, allowing them effective equality with men and the opportunity to serve in the same ways *despite* his own cultural background and the ideal prescriptions of his tradition. He acted in accordance with the spirit of *bhagavata dharma*, in the manner of Chaitanya, and in the specific context of *kali yuga* as it manifested itself in the West, thus taking into consideration time, place, and circumstance. But was Prabhupada's good practice sustained?

LIBERATION: A MALE PROJECT?

While this book is concerned principally with events that took place after the death of Prabhupada in 1977, it is 1974 that is commonly cited as the critical year for the decline in women's participation in ISKCON.[38] Until then, women devotees had led very full and diverse lives in devotional service, strongly supported by their spiritual master.[39] The records and testimonies of the earliest ISKCON *Vaishnavis* attest to this,[40] with notable examples being Yamuna's experience of leading *kirtana* and singing in public, Vishakha's roles as principal cook and photographer, Yadurani's and Malati's memories of giving classes and public lectures, the experiences of Janaki and Govinda Dasi as personal servants to Shrila Prabhupada, Varanasi's as temple commander, Jyotirmayi's as chief of the Book Trust. Many of these women and other female disciples of Prabhupada had ritual roles, not least of all Shilavati, who was head *pujari* at the Los Angeles temple. Yamuna and Govinda Dasi were recommended by Prabhupada as founder members of the GBC. Many women were sent, in partnership with their husbands, to open temples in territories uncharted by ISKCON. For those who were not married, Prabhupada established the *brahmacharini ashram*, a celibate community for women, unique at that time in the *Gaudiya Vaishnava* tradition.

These opportunities were not offered grudgingly.[41] Rather, Prabhupada expressed himself as grateful for the young people—male and female—whom Krishna brought before him for engagement in devotional service, and he challenged those in India who criticized his acceptance of women disciples. Furthermore, he developed tender relationships with those who gave up everything to follow him and help his cause: his letters to Janaki, his earliest female disciple, movingly attest to his appreciation of her talents and service, his desire to see her advance in Krishna consciousness, and his love for his "naughty daughter" and "young mother."[42]

In the United States by 1974, women's participation in ISKCON was waning with the growth of the *sannyasa ashram* for men and a consequent change in attitudes to women's nature and status.[43] The recognition of a stage of spiritual service for men beyond that of *grihastha* led to a devaluation of householders and women in the minds of many devotees. *Sannyasa* was seen by some as a superior stage; it also raised the status of celibacy as the preferred state for spiritual advancement.[44] It displaced women: wives became objects to be cast off in pursuit of a greater goal; all women became despised for their potential to deflect renunciates from spiritual advancement.[45] This led to the segregation of women from men, and to their ritual demotion: they were moved to the back of the temple during worship, were removed entirely during the chanting of *japa*, were stopped from direct involvement in deity worship and from paying obeisances in front of the *vyasasana*, and were made to follow after men in everything. The consequences of these restrictions and of the change in attitude to women were dramatic, leading to a cycle of degradation that was to affect women, men, and children and relationships between them, between the different *ashrams*, and between those inside and outside the movement.[46]

> In our society, unscrupulous men, often in managerial positions, have abused and neglected women. Under these conditions, women lose their sense of worth as beloved daughters of Shrila Prabhupada and lose their voice within the assembly of devotees. With no standing in the devotional community, women, especially those abandoned by their husbands, become degraded and cannot protect their children. Children become like orphans, "unwanted progeny," as Arjuna says in *Bhagavad-gita*, not recognised as the "Vaikuntha children" they are by birthright. Instead of the "future saviours of the world," as one *gurukula* promotional piece states, second-generation devotees become angry, frustrated and want to sue ISKCON because of their pain. . . . Our sexist and inhumane behaviour reflects badly on Shrila Prabhupada and taints his movement in the eyes of the world.[47]

Many of the alterations that led to this cycle of degradation occurred during Prabhupada's time—though after he had relinquished effective day-to-day management of ISKCON temples. There is evidence that, when discriminatory practices were brought to his attention, he did his best to reassert the philosophy of Krishna Consciousness on Vaishnava equality of opportunity and his own practice of nondiscrimination.[48] However, it is also suggested that he tolerated some occurrences in order "to allay the fears of . . . the newly celibate male population"[49] and to help them with the difficulties engendered by their choice of a renunciate lifestyle. The frustation he felt at times, however, was reflected in his oft-repeated comment that, if male devotees had a problem with the presence of women, then they—not the women—should be the ones to deal with it: let the men "go to the forest," was his exasperated retort.[50]

After Prabhupada passed away in 1977, the management of ISKCON passed into the hands of the GBC, and spiritual authority passed to a group of male initiating gurus, all *sannyasis*, who were not sympathetic to calls for the reinstatement of opportunities for women. According to two women who experienced ISKCON in this period, "Times were difficult. . . . Conditions for women living in the temples became abysmal, and the terms 'protection' and 'exploitation' seemed practically interchangeable."[51] It was not until the late 1980s, however, that criticisms about the treatment of women and their exclusion from active participation in the movement began to make their way into print.

THE REASSERTION OF WOMEN WITHIN ISKCON: VAISHNAVIS AND THEIR CRITICS

The small number of articles written about women in ISKCON before the mid-1980s appeared in publications intended for a wide audience, especially *Back to Godhead*.[52] Not wishing to expose internal problems to public view, they asserted not only the spiritual equality at the heart of the movement's philosophy but also the equality of opportunity for women within it. It was not until later in the decade that a greater openness about the reality of women's situation came about. But this was not without cost. In a lecture delivered at the first conference of the ISKCON Women's Ministry in 1997, Pranada Dasi looked back on her endeavors some ten years previously to share her concerns with the GBC (in a letter that was then published in the *Vaishnava Journal*):

That letter sealed my fate, as I stood alone for my Godsisters, as a black sheep of my family. I was told I was a demon destroying Prabhupada's movement, and I received the most controversial label: Pranada is a women's libber. Labels are just labels, but they have the ability to discount human beings and create social rejection. . . . And what was my great sin to receive such rejection? I suggested women should give *Bhagavatam* classes and were authorized to do so by Shrila Prabhupada.[53]

Female and male devotees gradually began to acknowledge publicly the degree of damage that had been done through the failure to tackle women's second-class status. The newsletter *Priti-Laksanam*, an uncensored channel of communication in which women's issues could be aired, was established. A conference was organized by ISKCON Communications in Europe in 1992 on the issue of women, at which women and men spoke. In 1994 the Governing Body Commissioner for Germany, Harikesha Swami, declared that discrimination against women must stop in his area, and instituted a new regime of equality for women in temple life.[54] Then, in 1996, an American woman devotee (Sudharma Dasi) attained guest status on the GBC where, with the help of sympathetic members, she was able to form the ISKCON Women's Ministry. The new ministry held its first international conference in Los Angeles in December 1997. Sudharma Dasi was joined on the GBC by Malati Dasi in 1998.[55] Their presence, together with the active work of the women's ministry, led to the issue of women in ISKCON being given a serious hearing at the annual

GBC meeting in Mayapur in 2000. The presentations by senior women devotees called for an apology for the mistakes of the past, recognition of the importance of women for the health of the movement, and the reinstatement of women's participatory rights. These were accepted, and resolutions were passed with the purpose of prioritizing the provision of "equal facilities, full encouragement, and genuine care and protection for the women members of ISKCON."[56]

Presenting these positive steps in this way may give the impression that they were attained systematically without a struggle. In fact, there was much opposition to change. The most organized campaign took the form of an electronic conference (GHQ) started in 1998 with the intention of gathering support to contest the demands of reformers and those involved in the women's ministry. Using military images, contributors saw their purpose as the organization of "a counteroffensive against the feminists who are a plague in our movement."[57] An early contribution to the e-mail conference was more specific, listing the following objectives: no women in leadership positions, no women allowed to give classes or lead *kirtana*, the termination of the women's ministry (and the removal of its concerns to the *grihastha* ministry), the banning of "feminist philosophy," and the censorship of ISKCON media for "feminist" contributions.[58] The conference continued to generate short contributions and longer articles (e.g. "Women's Rights . . . and Wrongs," "ISKCON Law: What About Husbands?," "Critical Analysis of 'Women in ISKCON'") in response to reforms and initiatives by women.[59]

Opponents of progress for women focused their attention on challenging the claims made by senior *Vaishnavis*.[60] Against the examples of Prabhupada's inclusion of women they set counterexamples, citing his statements about the inferiority of women's intelligence, their untrustworthiness and weakness. Drawing on the call for participation rights and substantive rights for women in the movement,[61] they cited Prabhupada's negative responses to secular, liberal calls for equal rights for women. They rejected statements made by women devotees who distanced themselves from secular feminism.[62] Attempting to offer a positive suggestion in addition to counterclaims, they called for the formal reestablishment of the "Vedic" notion of womanhood, thus repudiating the commonly cited principle at the heart of calls for reform for women, of "time, place, and circumstance."

CONCLUSION

It is this last point that has proved critical in engaging support for change within ISKCON, whether it be in relation to women, family life, the treatment of children, relations with outsiders, or dialogue with other religions. Time, place, and circumstance have been seen as intrinsic to the movement's evangelical focus on spreading the name of Krishna responsively. Chaitanya is cited as the exemplar in demonstrating this, and Prabhupada his studious follower in enacting it in another, quite different age. He stated its importance repeatedly, most notably in his commentary on the spiritual activities of Chaitanya, in which he stressed the need to find "the ways and means by which Krishna consciousness may be spread" and "the possibility of renunciation in terms of country, time and candidate."[63] What is more,

> Prabhupada himself was constantly changing—not in his essential beliefs and devotional relation to Krsna, but in the decisions he made to meet new circumstances and take advantage of new opportunities.[64]

Having come to the West and observed its social life and spiritual needs, Prabhupada took upon himself the responsibility—unusual by *Gaudiya Vaishnava* standards—to engage women as well as men in communicating the name of Krishna to every town and village, according to their abilities, propensities, and stage of spiritual advancement. He saw them as instruments given to him by Krishna to facilitate this mission. But this was not his only criterion for involving women in the widest possible range of devotional activities. While criticizing the secular women's rights movement, he stressed three aspects of equality in the development of his own movement. First, in engaging disciples in spiritual life, he did not discriminate on the basis of status, gender, race, or age. Second, he exercised equanimity in seeking to identify the individual characteristics and propensities of each of his disciples. Third, he saw the path of Krishna Consciousness as transformational for all those on it, lifting them above material designations.

In 2001, ISKCON was in the process of attempting to renew itself according to these principles, having been criticized by sympathetic outsiders as well as reforming insiders for its treatment of women, its failure to acknowledge their contribution and to reopen its roles and structures to their full participation.[65] What was at stake was the memory of Prabhupada, the future of the movement he founded, and its place in the wider society. The damage to the health of ISKCON through the treatment of its women members was acknowledged by the GBC in its resolutions in 2000, and a new regime introduced. The authority and durability of these changes will now be tested to ensure that participation within ISKCON, fulfillment on the path of Krishna Consciousness, and spiritual liberation are cleared of obstacles and truly opened up for women. As one senior devotee said, given that the theology of *Gaudiya Vaishnavism* presents a woman's body as the more difficult body for spiritual advancement, "Why make it more difficult?"[66]

NOTES

1. Articles that deal specifically with women in ISKCON, mostly authored by women devotees themselves, are listed in later notes. Relevant writing by scholarly outsiders on this subject includes my own articles (see note 5), and work by Janet Jacobs, "The Economy of Love in Religious Commitment: The Deconversion of Women from Non-traditional Religious Movements," *Journal for the Scientific Study of Religion* 23 (2) (1984): 155–71; Susan Jean Palmer, *Moon Sisters, Krishna Mothers, Rajneesh Lovers: Women's Roles in New Religions* (Syracuse, NY: Syracuse University Press, 1994); and Elizabeth Puttick, *Women in New Religions: In Search of Community, Sexuality and Spiritual Power* (Basingstoke: Macmillan, 1997). On the wider *vaishnava bhakti* movement and gender issues, see *Journal of Vaisnava Studies* 3 (4) (special issue on "Vaisnava Women"), 1995; Steven J. Rosen, ed., *Vaisnavi: Women and the Worship of Krishna* (Delhi: Motilal Banarsidass, 1996); and Katherine Young, "Srivaisnava Feminism: Intention or Effect?" (*Sciences Religieuses/Studies in Religion* 12 (2) (1983), 183–90.

2. See the women's page of www.chakra.org, and the site launched by opponents of the Women's Ministry, www.ghq.org.

3. There is recognition within ISKCON, however, that the words of Shrila Prabhupada are open to a variety of interpretations arising from selectivity, context, and motivation.

4. The main sources for this account were ISKCON's own discussions and writings in *Back to Godhead*, *Priti-lakshanam*, and *ISKCON Communications Journal*; the tapes, papers, and reports relating to seminars and conferences (particularly the first ISKCON European Communications Seminar, Germany, 1992; the first ISKCON Women's Ministry Conference, Los Angeles, 1997; and the European Women's Ministry Conference, Radhadesh, 1998); and, latterly, the contributions to Web sites associated with ISKCON (my thanks to Maria Ekstrand for providing details of these). Relatively little use has been made of scholarly studies by outsiders, as they have often reflected internal views rather than adding anything new, exceptions being Janet Jacob and Susan J. Palmer (see note 1), who have offered psychological and sociological interpretations, respectively. A source of potential interest is the Prabhupada Centennial Survey, undertaken by E. Burke Rochford Jr. in the late 1990s, of devotees worldwide (nearly 2,000 in total). Detailed findings on gender have yet to be published, but a brief discussion may be found in E. Burke Rochford Jr., "Prabhupada Centennial Survey: A Summary of the Final Report," *ISKCON Communications Journal* 7 (1) (1999): 11–26.

5. My earlier articles on women in ISKCON were: "Men and Women, or Devotees? Krishna Consciousness and the Role of Women," in U. King, ed., *Women in the World's Religions, Past and Present* (New York, Paragon House, 1987), 111–28 (reprinted in a new edition in 1994); and "The Debate About Women in ISKCON," *Journal of Vaisnava Studies* 3 (4) (1995): 33–50 (also published in *ISKCON Communications Journal* 3 [2] [1997], and in S. J. Rosen, ed., *Vaisnavi: Women and the Worship of Krishna*). Some passages from these earlier articles form the basis of the sections on "Equality and the Soul," "Equality and the Body," and "Women and Dharma."

6. Vishakha Dasi, "Prabhupada's Ladies and Soul Concern," from "Women in ISKCON: Presentations to the GBC, March 2000," *ISKCON Communications Journal* 8 (1) (2000) (electronic version: www.iskcon.com/ICJ).

7. E. Burke Rochford Jr., "Family Formation, Culture, and Change in the Hare Krishna Movement," *ISKCON Communications Journal* 5 (2) (1997): 69.

8. Hridayananda Maharaja, "The Importance of Women in ISKCON," paper presented to the first ISKCON Women's Ministry conference, Los Angeles, December 1997.

9. GBC Resolutions pertaining to the position of women in ISKCON: Section 500, Holy places and spiritual communities, see www.chakra.org/articles/2000/05/02/gbc.women.in.iskcon/index.htm. See also "Conclusion" in "Women in ISKCON: Presentations to the GBC, March 2000."

10. Sitarani Dasi, "What's the Role of Women in Krishna Consciousness? A Krishna Conscious Woman Explains," interview in *Back to Godhead* 12 (1982): 11–12.

11. This was particularly so in the 1980s; see Sitarani Dasi, "What's the Role of Women," also Satarupa Dasi, "I Am Not This Body," interview in *Who Are They?* (Los Angeles: Bhaktivedanta Book Trust, 1982), 17; Vishakha Dasi, "Women in Krsna Consciousness: Questions and Answers," *Back to Godhead* 16 (3–4) (1981): 6. In the 1990s, the focus shifted from spiritual equality to the importance of equality of opportunity within Krishna consciousness; see "Equality and the Body" below.

12. J. Stillson Judah, *Hare Krishna and the Counterculture* (New York: Wiley, 1974), 86. See also Angela Burr, *I Am Not My Body: A Study of the International Hare Krishna Sect* (New Delhi: Vikas Publishing House, 1984).

13. This philosophical stance of identity-in-difference is known as *achintya bhedabheda*. See O. B. L. Kapoor, *The Philosophy and Religion of Sri Chaitanya* (Delhi: Munshiram Manoharlal, 1977); Steven J. Gelberg, ed., *Hare Krishna, Hare Krishna: Five Distinguished Scholars on the Krishna Movement in the West* (New York, Grove Press, 1983); and Shrivatsa Goswami, "Achintya Bhedabheda," in Steven J. Rosen, ed., *Vaisnavism: Contemporary Scholars Discuss the Gaudiya Tradition* (New York: Folk Books, 1992), 249–60.

14. For a full discussion of Radha's love for Krishna and its significance for spiritual advancement in Gaudiya Vaishnavism, see Steven J. Rosen, "*Raganuga bhakti*: Bringing Out the Inner Woman in *Gaudiya Vaisnava sadhana*," in S. J. Rosen, ed., *Vaisnavi: Women and the Worship of Krishna* (Delhi: Motilal Banarsidass, 1996), 113–32.

15. The articles I wrote in 1987 and 1995 on women in ISKCON opened with an account of the early morning activities of the male *brahmacharis* in the Boston temple. Its purpose was to illustrate the feminine service attitude of Krishna devotees, irrespective of their material gender. Satyaraja Das reflected on this issue: "Gaudiya Vaisnavism . . . exalts the feminine side of reality as supreme. . . . This emphasis of feminine spirituality . . . is something that we've yet to explore [in ISKCON]." *Priti-laksanam* 4 (1992): 11.

16. Urmila Dasi, "Prabhupada's Views on Women," www.chakra.org, 2 September 2001.

17. The Krishna consciousness view of *varnashram dharma* is described by A.C. Bhaktivedanta Swami Prabhupada in his purports to chapters 3 and 4, *Bhagavad-gita As It Is* (Los Angeles: Bhaktivedanta Book Trust, 1983) and to canto 7, *Srimad Bhagavatam* (Los Angeles: Bhaktivedanta Book Trust, 1987). Several contemporary views may be found in the *ISKCON Communications Journal*: Krishna Dharma Das, "Towards Varnashrama Dharma: A Constitution for ISKCON" (4 [1994]: 69–79); Ravindra Svarupa Das, "ISKCON and *Varnashram-dharma*: A Mission Unfulfilled" (7 [1] [1999]: 35–44).

18. The tensions experienced by such heroic women have been discussed by Vishakha Dasi, "Humility, Chastity, Surrender, Protection. What Do They Mean?," paper presented to the ISKCON Women's Ministry conference, 1997; Satya Dasi, "Female Ascetics: A Look through Puranic Glasses," paper presented to the ISKCON Women's Ministry conference, 1997; Hridayananda Maharaja, "The Importance of Women in ISKCON."

19. For discussions of the nature of male and female bodies for spiritual advancement, see Ravindra Svarupa Das, "The Position of Women in ISKCON," ISKCON European Communications Seminar, 1992; Urmila Dasi, "Prabhupada's Views on Women."

20. Yamuna Dasi, "Shrila Prabhupada's Transcendental Sweetness and Beauty," from "Women in ISKCON: Presentations to the GBC, March 2000," *ISKCON Communications Journal* 8 (1) (2000).

21. Satsvarupa Das Goswami, *Shrila Prabhupada-lilamrta*, Vol. 3: *Only He Could Lead Them, San Francisco/India, 1967* (Los Angeles: Bhaktivedanta Book Trust, 1981), 150.

22. Radha Dasi, "Participation, Protection and Patriarchy: An International Model for Women's roles in ISKCON," *ISKCON Communications Journal* 6 (1) (1998): 36.

23. See Jyotirmayi Dasi, "Women in ISKCON in Prabhupada's Time," a paper presented at the ISKCON Women's Ministry conference, 1997 (accessible on the women's page of www.chakra.org); Yamuna Dasi, "Shrila Prabhupada's Transcendental Sweetness and Beauty"; Vishakha Dasi, "Prabhupada's Ladies and Soul Concern."

24. From a letter to Guru Das in 1972, quoted in Jyotirmayi Dasi, "Women in ISKCON in Prabhupada's Time."

25. Purport to *Chaitanya Charitamrita* Adi 7.31–32, quoted in Vishakha Dasi, "Humility, Chastity, Surrender, Protection."

26. Radha Dasi, "Participation, Protection and Patriarchy," 32.

27. The tension between *varnashram dharma* and *bhagavat dharma* was explored by devotees at a European communications seminar in 1992. The lecturer, Ravindra Svarupa Das, pointed out that both are mentioned in the writings of Shrila Prabhupada and that it is difficult always to see how the two should fit together in practice ("The Position of Women in ISKCON Today").

28. Radha Dasi refers to the problems underlying devotees' use of the term "Vedic" as both a means of defining behavioral norms for women and of judging their actual behavior ("Participation, Protection and Patriarchy," 41).

29. These particular designations were explained to me in an interview with Garuda Das, who also discussed this issue in "Dharma: Nature, Duty, and Divine Service," *Back to Godhead* 15 (12) (1980): 7–13. The distinctions between these different perspectives were also alluded to by Satsvarupa das Goswami, *Living with Scripture*, vol. 1 (Philadelphia: Gita Nagari Press, 1984), 61; Sitarani Dasi, "What's the Role of Women?," 26; Ravindra Svarupa dasa, "The Position of Women in ISKCON Today."

30. I discussed the relationship between these perspectives in "Problems in the Interpretation of 'Vedic' Literature: The Perennial Battle Between the Scholar and the Devotee," *ISKCON Communications Journal* 2 (1994).

31. The Vedic period is held by devotees to form the latter part of the age previous to this one, *dvapara yuga* (about 5,000 years ago).

32. This ideal "Vedic" view of *varnashram dharma* and *stri dharma* conforms with that presented in the classical Hindu lawbook, *Manusmriti*. However, devotees would

see the practical attempt to live out the prescriptions of Manu in India in the last 2,000 years as "Hindu" rather than "Vedic" and as representing the distortion of the ideal system of *varnashram dharma* in the dark age of *kali yuga*.

33. See Ravindra Svarupa Das, "Position of Women in ISKCON," and Visakha Dasi, "Prabhupada's Ladies and Soul Concern."

34. Testimony of Bhibavati Dasi, quoted in Jyotirmayi Dasi, "Women in ISKCON in Prabhupada's Time," 11.

35. Radha Dasi, "Participation, Protection and Patriarchy," 36. This view, however, contrasts with the one articulated by some men in the movement who call for the reestablishment of Vedic culture here and now, and criticize women activists for their rejection of Vedic teachings and norms regarding male/female roles, e.g., Jivan Mukta Das, "ISKCON Law: What About Husbands?," www.ghq.org, 29 February 1999.

36. From a letter to Shilavati Dasi, 14 June 1969, quoted in Vishakha Dasi, "Prabhupada's Ladies and Soul Concern."

37. These reflections formed part of the discussion about the situation of women in the Hare Krishna movement at the European communications seminar, 1992 ("The Position of Women in ISKCON Today," part 2).

38. Vishakha Dasi and Sudharma Dasi, "Introduction" to "Women in ISKCON: Presentations to the GBC, March 2000," *ISKCON Communications Journal* 8 (1) (2000). Jyotirmayi Dasi suggests the same date for a noticeable decline in women's involvement in France ("Women in Prabhupada's Time," 4)

39. This is not contested in ISKCON. In his summary report of the Prabhupada Centennial Survey, conducted in 1998, E. Burke Rochford Jr. records that the vast majority of the 1996 devotees questioned agreed "that Prabhupada viewed his male and female disciples as spiritual equals. And there is evidence that Prabhupada implemented policies and procedures that were meant to be inclusive of women." "Prabhupada Centennial Survey: A Summary of the Final Report," 22.

40. Jyotirmayi Dasi, "Women in Prabhupada's Time"; contributors to "Women in ISKCON: Presentations to the GBC, March 2000" (especially Yamuna Dasi and Vishakha Dasi); Satsvarupa dasa Goswami, *Shrila Prabhupada-lilamrta*, vols. 2 and 3 (Los Angeles: Bhaktivedanta Book Trust, 1980, 1981).

41. Saudamani Dasi, presentation in "Women in ISKCON: Presentations to the GBC, March 2000," *ISKCON Communications Journal* 8 (1) (2000); Jyotirmayi Dasi, "Women in Prabhupada's Time," 3.

42. Vishakha Dasi and Sudharma Dasi, "Introduction."

43. The movement's first *sannyasi* was Kirtanananda Swami, who was initiated into the *sannyasa ashram* in August 1967 (Satsvarupa dasa Goswami, *Prabhupada* [Los Angeles: Bhaktivedanta Book Trust, 1983], 133–34). Numbers of *sannyasis* began to increase in the early 1970s. The mantle of *sannyasa* was one women were unable to take on. Whereas Prabhupada had initiated them, giving them *brahmacharini* status, and thus allowed them to become Brahmins (though they did not wear the sacred thread) and *pujaris*, they were not formally allowed to renounce the world and wander as *sannyasinis*. The explanation for this is that renunciation would separate a woman devotee from the sources of her protection, e.g., a husband or temple authorities, and this might expose her to danger and exploitation.

44. These views were not endorsed by Prabhupada: "Household life is not repugnant: it is favourable"; "Better to prove yourself first by being ideal householder and

forget all this nonsense [of taking *sannyasa*]" (from letters to Dayananda and Mahatma quoted in Jyotirmayi Dasi, "Women in Prabhupada's Time," 19).

45. Critiques by women devotees of the impact of *sannyasa* on men within ISKCON may be found in *Back to Godhead* (Jan./Feb. 1991): 11–13, and Jyotirmayi Dasi, "Women in Prabhupada's Time."

46. This cycle has been powerfully depicted by Jyotirmayi Dasi, "Women in Prabhupada's Time," 5–7. See also Bimala Dasi on the repercussions of male *sannyasa* for women and children, "The Anomaly of the Single Mother in ISKCON," paper presented at the ISKCON Women's Ministry conference, 1997. The link has been made between the treatment of women in ISKCON and occurrences of domestic abuse and child abuse: see Bimala Dasi; and Sudharma Dasi, presentation in "Women in ISKCON, Presentations to the GBC, March 2000." E. Burke Rochford Jr. makes the link between the demotion of the *grihastha ashram* and family life, and the abuse of children in "Child Abuse in the Hare Krishna Movement: 1971–86," *ISKCON Communications Journal* 6 (1) (1998): 43–70.

47. Rukmini Dasi, presentation in "Women in ISKCON: Presentations to the GBC, March 2000," *ISKCON Communications Journal* 8 (1) (2000).

48. Letter to Ekayani Dasi, 1972, quoted by Pranada Dasi in "With Redoubled Strength," *Vaishnava Journal* 1988: 34–39. See also Prabhupada's response in Mayapur in 1976 to the fears about *brahmachari* entanglement in family affairs (Hari Sauri Das, *A Transcendental Diary*, Vol 1. [San Diego: HS Books, 1992], chapter 9).

49. Vrinda Dasi, "Change Ourselves, Then the World," *Priti-Laksanam* 4 (1992): 9.

50. Pranada Dasi, "With Redoubled Strength," 38; Jyotirmayi Dasi, "Women in Prabhupada's Time," 10, 15.

51. Vishakha Dasi and Sudharma Dasi, "Introduction." The power of this comment is lost to a reader not fully conversant with the language of gender in ISKCON. As I suggested earlier, the notion of "protection" is central to an understanding of women in Krishna consciousness (deriving from the "Vedic" conception that women should be protected by male relatives at all times). For discussions of "protection" by women devotees, see Radha Dasi, "Participation, Protection and Patriarchy" and Vishakha Dasi, "Humility, Chastity, Surrender, Protection."

52. Sitarani Dasi, "What's the Role of Women"; Vishakha Dasi, "Women in Krishna Consciousness: Questions and Answers"; Satarupa Dasi, "I Am Not This Body."

53. Pranada Dasi, "Yesterday, Today and Tomorrow," paper presented at the first ISKCON Women's Ministry conference, 1997.

54. In Germany in the mid-1990s, the situation for women devotees was different from that in the United States: about one third of ISKCON National Council seats were held by women, as were a similar proportion of temple presidencies (Daya Dasi, "ISKCON Germany: Perspectives on the Past and Lessons for the Future," *ISKCON Communications Journal* 3 [1994]: 37–42). For details of the statement by Harikesa Swami, see Jyotirmayi Dasi, "Women in Prabhupada's Time," 20–21.

55. I am grateful to Vishakha Dasi and Sudharma Dasi for this brief history of events ("Introduction" in "Women in ISKCON: Presentations to the GBC, March 2000).

56. These resolutions can be found in "Women in ISKCON: Presentations to the GBC, March 2000," and in Madhusudani Radha Dasi, "GBC Resolutions Pertaining to the Position of Women in ISKCON," www.chakra.org, May 2000 (reposted 29 November 2002).

57. Ardhabuddhi Das, "Conspiracy to Terminate the ISKCON Women's Ministry," *VNN Vaishnava News*, www.vnn.org, 18 November 1998.

58. E-mail from Shyamasundara Das to GHQ, 2 October 1998, in Ardhabuddhi Das, "Conspiracy to Terminate the ISKCON Women's Ministry."

59. These may be found in Dharma-kshetra, www.ghq.org.

60. See Jivan Mukta Das, "ISKCON Law: What About Husbands?" for an example of this approach.

61. This call was made persuasively by Radha Dasi, a Harvard-educated lawyer, in "Participation, Protection and Patriarchy."

62. An example of the rejection by *Vaishnavis* of the feminist tag may be found in Sitala Dasi, presentation in "Women in ISKCON: Presentations to the GBC, March, 2000," *ISKCON Communcations Journal* 8 (1) 2000. See also Satyaraja Das, "Feminism and the Quest for God," *The Vedic Observer*, n.d.

63. *Chaitanya Charitamrita, Adi-lila*, chapter 7, purport of verse 32; *Chaitanya Charitamrita, Madhya-lila*, chapter 23, purport to verse 105. Both quoted in Jyotirmayi Dasi, "Women in Prabhupada's Time," 2–3. E. Burke Rochford Jr. has seen this focus on time, place, and circumstance as Prabhupada's principal sociological contribution ("Analyzing ISKCON for Twenty-five Years: A Personal Reflection," *ISKCON Communications Journal* 8 (1) (2000).

64. Sitala Dasi, presentation in "Women in ISKCON: Presentation to the GBC, March 2000."

65. Outsiders critical of ISKCON's policy and practice regarding women have included Julius Lipner ("ISKCON at the Crossroads?," *ISKCON Communications Journal* 2 [1994]: 24), Gavin Flood ("Hinduism, Vaishnavism, and ISKCON: Authentic Traditions or Scholarly Constructions," *ISKCON Communications Journal* 3 [2] [1995]: 13), Kim Knott ("The Debate About Women in the Hare Krishna Movement," 103–5), and E. Burke Rochford Jr. ("Prabhupada Centennial Survey," 22–23).

66. Ravindra Svarupa Das, "Position of Women in ISKCON."

[18]

LIFE AS A WOMAN ON WATSEKA AVENUE

Personal Story I

NORI J. MUSTER

FROM AGES TWENTY-TWO TO THIRTY-TWO I was a devotee at the western world headquarters of the International Society for Krishna Consciousness, located at 3764 Watseka Avenue in West Los Angeles. Although a native Californian, I dressed in saris, followed the four regulative principles enjoined on ISKCON members (no meat-eating, intoxication, gambling, or sex outside of marriage), attended early morning services to chant *japa* (repetition of the Hare Krishna mantra) and *kirtana* (congregational chanting), and dedicated my heart to the beautiful Lord Krishna. Although there were some bright spots and good friendships, we women lived under a cloud of chauvinism and outright hatred of our gender. I look back on my ten years in the movement with regret.

I sum up my experience as a woman in the following way: it was about trying to remain as innocent as a child in a family with a lot of secrets. The elders never spoke about the drug money flowing through our "zone," nor did they honestly discuss the gurus' various problems. They also hid the child abuse and made it taboo to criticize any leader for anything. I spent a lot of energy forcing myself to look straight ahead, ignoring gossip, rumors, and my own gut feelings. I was like a horse with blinders on; a blind follower.

When I joined in 1978, ISKCON's leadership consisted of multiple patriarchs who divided the globe into eleven zones. Each zone had an all-male retinue of gurus, commissioners, ministers, temple presidents, directors, trustees, and department heads. In addition, the organization sponsored a priesthood of celibate men called *sannyasis*, who traveled around the world enforcing the doctrines of the society's Governing Body Commission (GBC).

The daily schedule on Watseka Avenue started at 4 A.M. with religious services in the temple building, including sermons from the scripture *Shrimad Bhagavatam*. The book contains chauvinistic purports, such as: women's breasts are "agents of *maya* [illusion] meant to victimize the opposite sex."[1] Rather than attempting to minimize or modernize these sorts of statements, most *Bhagavatam* speakers embellished them with even more degrading statements about women. They said it was our bad karma that we were born as women and that our only hope of salvation was through serving a male guru. They preached that our brains were half as big as those of men, and that our bodies were ten times more lusty than male bodies. They said it was a sin for a woman to look at a man's face; therefore, some of us acquired the uninformed, humiliating, and sorry behavior of turning to the wall if we were alone and a man passed by. They barred us from teaching the *Shrimad Bhagavatam* class and leading the morning *kirtanas*. With practice, most of us could have learned to handle these responsibilities, but our participation would have been a threat to the "celibate men." Their cruel words, reinforced with official policy, had a demoralizing effect. The words, "I'm sorry I'm wearing a sari," ran through my head for years after leaving ISKCON.

ISKCON had a concept of utopia called "Vedic civilization," which was supposedly based on the ancient Hindu civilizations in India described in the *Shrimad Bhagavatam* and other scriptures. The ideals were lofty, but I never experienced the society actually living up to any kind of utopian standard. One aspect of this Vedic civilization that was completely lost on ISKCON was the culture of respect for women: we were never treated as "genteel Vedic mothers." We simply had low self-esteem. The men thought it was Vedic to spit on the ground to demonstrate their resentment toward women. They got their cue from a stanza in the scriptures that said: "Since I have been engaged in the transcendental loving service of Krishna, realizing ever-new pleasure in Him, whenever I think of sex pleasure, I spit at the thought, and my lips curl with distaste."[2]

ASHRAM LIFE

In ISKCON, women were supposed to work obediently without questioning the leadership. If a woman acted out of character, the other women corrected her. All temples had self-appointed female monitors who went around correcting other women and telling them what to do. For example, once when I was a young devotee, I raised my hand and asked a question at the end of a *Bhagavatam* class. Afterward, a woman told me that my behavior was rather brazen, considering the number of traveling *sannyasis* in the audience. The practice of women correcting and criticizing women was widespread; most of us participated in it at least part of the time. Sometimes women ended up in tears after receiving more corrections than they could handle in one morning.

When I moved to Watseka Avenue I lived in the new *bhaktin* (female devotee) *ashram* (dorm) with four other new women and a housemother called a *bhaktin* leader. I have terrible memories of the experience, which I described in my book, *Betrayal of the Spirit*.[3] The temple authorities moved us into another apartment, then gave us an ever-changing series of *bhaktin* leaders, and finally closed down the *ashram*. The few new *bhaktins* who were left were eventually moved into the newly opened women's *sankirtana ashram* (*sankirtana* had become the common name for airport solicitation, even though the word historically refers to public devotional chanting). The new *ashram* consisted of two one-bedroom apartments on the top floor of a building, across the street from the former *bhaktin ashram*. A door was installed to join the two apartments, and these provided lodging for approximately sixteen women.

The new *ashram* had female leaders, which was quite an improvement over the former arrangement where a man lived with and slept with (molested) all the *sankirtana* women. Once, while I was still in college, I visited Watseka Avenue and met some of the *sankirtana* women who lived in the former *ashram*. They took me back to their living quarters and introduced me to their male leader. At the time I had absolutely no idea what was going on. In retrospect, I now remember the experience as scary, because of the disgusting way he looked me over. It was as if he thought I might someday become one of his victims.

Due to numerous complaints, the GBC passed resolutions in 1977 and 1978[4] to end the practice of male leaders for women's *sankirtana* parties. The Los Angeles *ashram* closed down in 1978, but the arrangement continued in Berkeley under the guru Hamsadutta Swami, with the addition of drugs and rock 'n' roll, and in New Vrindavan, West Virginia, under the guru Kirtanananda Swami, with the additional features of prostitution and physical abuse. In 1998, I interviewed a former *sankirtana* woman from New Vrindavan who told me that her male *sankirtana* leader would drop the women off at bars, where they would wait by the exit and offer to do anything a man wanted in exchange for money. I used to hear "rumors" about it, but 1998 was the first time someone told me about it first hand.

The new *sankirtana ashram* closed down within a year, but the system worked eventually with good women leaders like Gouri (now deceased), Vrindavan-vilasini, and Yadurani. With passing years the specter of the scandals faded. However, back in 1978, most of my roommates had just come out of the abusive situation. I even knew a woman who had a child from her time in a *sankirtana ashram*.

After a few weeks of living in the *ashram*, I caught the flu and had a fever for at least three months. The female *sankirtana* leaders told me to rest and chant "Hare Krishna" instead of sending me to a doctor. When I finally got to a doctor, he gave me a shot of antibiotics and scolded me for waiting so long. Doctors cost money, and the temple policy was that until a devotee could get on MediCal (a public assistance program that was available to nuns and monks in California before 1980), they had to be satisfied with natural healing.

SHRILA PRABHUPADA AND THE
TREATMENT OF WOMEN

Women who lived in India during the early days of ISKCON told me that ISKCON's founder, Shrila A.C. Bhaktivedanta Swami Prabhupada, always made sure that his women disciples were treated well and that they felt included. He personally took care of details like making sure that they had adequate living quarters, good food, and even rides to events. When the devotees went places as a group, Shrila Prabhupada invited the women to ride with him in his car to make sure they got there. He set it up so that women could stand at the front in the temples to behold the altars (*darshan*); he encouraged women to give *Bhagavatam* class and lead *kirtana*; and he nominated two women, Yamuna and Govinda, to the Governing Body Commission (GBC). Unfortunately, an elitist and rowdy band of male disciples, headed by the late Tamal Krishna Goswami, turned all this around so that women were counted out of GBC positions. *Sannyasis* received all the advantages, while women generally got the worst accommodations, waited at the end of the food line, and prayed at the back of the temple. When these changes took place in the mid-1970s, people who resisted were either silenced or forced out. By the time I joined, the controversy was settled: women's place as second-class citizens was cemented and thoroughly institutionalized.

Although the organization was blatantly slanted in favor of men, many followers of both genders were in denial. The first time I met devotees and attended a lecture at their Sunday feast, I questioned the speaker, Radha Vallabha, general manager of the Bhaktivedanta Book Trust (BBT), about the place of women. He told me that ISKCON considered women to be spirit souls and therefore completely equal with men. Looking back now, I realize he was in denial, and so was I most of the time.

In the p.r. department, where I worked for Mukunda Goswami, I was sheltered from the worst ISKCON had to offer. Our department was a close-knit family where we respected each other. Actually, there were several women who wrote for the p.r. department, so I had good company. Also, we had constant interaction with the outside world. I believed women and men were equal in ISKCON because the people I knew treated me well and valued my work. I started as a p.r. secretary and later became associate editor of the monthly newsletter *ISKCON World Review*. During my last two years, I did nearly the entire paper single-handedly. However, I also knew that due to my gender, I was a thorn in the side of at least one guru, who protested: "The worst thing about this paper is that it's written by a woman!"[5]

In Los Angeles, the BBT had women working in the publishing house, legal offices, photo department, ISKCON Cinema, and other art departments. Usually these women became successful through a combination of skill in their field and the right personality to navigate a chauvinistic bureaucracy. In my ten years on Watseka Avenue, I knew many of these women because the p.r. department and the BBT were financially linked. For several years after leaving the *sankirtana ashram* I roomed with other BBT women. One year I lived with the female artists who painted illustrations for the BBT books. Those were good times that reminded me of my college dorm experience. In another *ashram* I lived with Koumadaki, secretary for the L.A. guru, Rameshvara, and with Sita, a typesetter at the Spanish BBT. These two dedicated and generous Prabhupada disciples were my strongest role models. They navigated ISKCON's chauvinism with a mixture of tolerance, humor, and rebellion.

My experiences in the BBT women's *ashram*s were good, but in the 1980s the BBT became more decentralized and its presence on Watseka Avenue dwindled. Whole divisions left, and all my artist and publishing friends moved away. After that, I shared an apartment with the other p.r. secretary, and then for about a year I had an apartment to myself. Another privilege I enjoyed was constant contact with my father, who volunteered his time as a p.r. consultant for ISKCON. Having him nearby helped me keep my sanity, and eventually his support made it possible for me to decide to leave the organization. Meanwhile, the other *sankirtana* women on Watseka Avenue had to renounce their "material" families, accept ISKCON as their "real" family, and live in overcrowded conditions.

The *sankirtana* women woke up at 3 A.M. to chant, then worked long days at the airport soliciting donations. The ones I knew were genuinely dedicated to Krishna, but to please the gurus, they remained naïve about ISKCON politics. Many of them were my friends. We danced and chanted in temple services, but on some levels I felt alienated from them. I dealt with top-secret matters that Mukunda and Rameshvara told me I wasn't allowed to talk about with anyone outside the p.r. department.

TRAGIC CASES, CRIMINALS, AND VICTIMIZED WOMEN

During my years on Watseka I met many wonderful women and I've kept a few friends from those times, who have also moved on with their lives. But along with the relatively healthy women, I also met some clinically depressed and psychotic women. For several years in the 1980s there was a woman living in the *sankirtana ashram* who had a psychiatric disorder. She constantly exhibited eccentric behaviors, such as lying down on the floor during *kirtanas*. Nevertheless the temple leaders tried sending her to the airport to solicit donations. I once saw her grab money out of a traveler's wallet, stash it in her bag, and repeat Sanskrit phrases until the person walked away. She eventually left the temple to live with her relatives.

ISKCON also harbored criminal women, and I met a few of them. One of the female *sankirtana* leaders ran away from Watseka Avenue with the temple's airport shuttle driver to get married and deal drugs. Before leaving, they kidnapped his children from a previous marriage while he held the mother at gunpoint. The children were only reunited with their mother years later when she was dying of cancer. Another woman I knew was convicted of enabling her husband to molest children at the Watseka Avenue nursery school. Both husband and wife served time in jail. She was quiet; my sense was that she also had a psychiatric disorder. I interviewed another woman from the East Coast who told me that when she was a new *bhaktin* they trained her to shoplift for the deity department. She and an older woman would go on shopping sprees where they stole beaded *saris*, jewelry, and other expensive items to decorate the altars and dress the deities.

Even though the vast majority of ISKCON women were not criminals, if they joined as adults, they willingly participated in a sick culture and took on dysfunctional attitudes and behaviors. However, it was a different story for the girls born into the movement or brought in as children. These innocent souls were often abandoned to the schools at the age of five. In certain schools during the 1970s and 1980s, children grew up communally, deprived of the bare necessities, including love, and they often received an inadequate education. Girls and boys suffered physical and sexual abuse as well as humiliating punishments. The schools taught girls to be ashamed of their bodies and young female minds. A dear friend named Subhadra who grew up under these conditions told me that she has a frightening image of her shame as a black hole in the center of a beautiful multifaceted diamond.

Abuse of a woman's children was the worst thing that could happen to someone in ISKCON. In addition to the children suffering long-term trauma, many of the mothers have never recovered. I had one friend who confided that she felt she had alienated her new husband because of her constant grief over one son from a previous marriage who was hurt in ISKCON schools.

Gurus and temple leaders also arranged marriages for girls who were barely eleven or twelve years old. The men, who were typically much older, emotionally, physically, and sexually abused their child brides while the parents and everyone else in the organization looked the other way. One guru, Hridayananda Goswami, wrote, "These early marriages show our concern for not letting women become polluted," and he promoted and defended the practice in GBC meetings.[6]

There were also instances of women who joined as adults who were forced into arranged marriages with abusive men. In my research I interviewed a family who lost their daughter to ISKCON in 1980. The people at the temple said she had moved to India with her "husband." The family accepted that and believed it until 1994, when they learned that their loved one had been brutally murdered and buried under the name of a Jane Doe fourteen years earlier.

I had some degrading experiences as a woman on Watseka Avenue, but for some women, life in ISKCON was tragic. There is mounting evidence of an alleged conspiracy among the leaders to allow wife beating. One of the most outspoken proponents of spousal abuse was the guru Kirtanananda, who explained on national TV that it's okay to slap a woman who disobeys. He compared it to training a dog. The culture of wife beating was widespread in ISKCON, although I never knew about it when I was a member.

CONCLUSIONS

In ISKCON temples, the deity of Lord Krishna is always standing side by side with his consort, Shrimati Radharani. The Jagannatha deity (Krishna) appears with his sister Subhadra and brother Balarama. Lord Rama appears with the Goddess Sita, and the scriptures say that Lord Chaitanya was an incarnation of Radha and Krishna in one body. Since the deities themselves honor women, it is ironic that the women of ISKCON came to accept their inferior status as normal, as though it were mandated in the scriptures.

ISKCON could have up to 50 percent women *kirtana* leaders, *Shrimad Bhagavatam* reciters, and gurus. The GBC could resolve that women may go anywhere inside the temple room and participate freely in the cultural life of ISKCON. While it is possible that ISKCON may someday change, lingering attitudes ensure that that will be difficult: ISKCON is the way it is because a majority of the men want it that way.

In the 1990s there were hopeful developments, such as the formation of the women's ministry. Along with some of the adult children of ISKCON, it held open forums to air these issues. A tense moment came in September 1999, when men assaulted a group of women inside the ISKCON temple in Vrindavan, India, during a morning *kirtana*. Allegedly they did it because the women were trying to get to the front. The controversy over this incident brought women's issues to a head, and nine women addressed the all-male leadership at the March 2000 GBC meeting. However, little changed. It's still rare to see women lead the pre-dawn *kirtanas* or teach the morning *Bhagavatam* class. There are several women temple presidents now, but only one woman on the GBC and not even one woman guru. Attitudes have also remained fixed. Some devotees in ISKCON still try to argue that the child abuse was the victims' karma. Elsewhere, the practice of arranging marriages continues. A young college student told me that an ISKCON temple president tried to convince her to marry one of his "disciples" as recently as December 2001.

In the thirty-seven-year history of ISKCON, women have married, divorced, had children and grandchildren, lost loved ones, aged, and suffered their humiliations in silence. In my opinion, ISKCON's policies toward women have been unacceptable. Even more destructive would be to manufacture a whitewashed version of the history and try to pass it off as fact. These are real dramas that have affected families over several generations. It is a difficult history to recall, but the lessons are valuable. I believe it is important to study and record what happened, so that future generations of Shrila Prabhupada's followers may be spared the grief that the first three generations of women have had to endure.

NOTES

1. *Shrimad Bhagavatam* 4.25.24, purport.
2. The stanza "*yadavadhi mama chetasah*" appears in *Bhakti-rasamrita-sindhu* 2.5.72, by Rupa Goswami (sixteenth century), to illustrate the transcendental sentiment of *jugupsa rati*, love in disgust or ghastliness. Shrila Prabhupada mentions the verse at least six times in his purports in *Shrimad Bhagavatam* and more than fifty times in his lectures, conversations, and letters. However, in some of these instances (SB 4.24.25, 9.18.39, 9.19.16, and other places) he attributes the quote to the tenth-century devotee Yamunacharya. The verse has also been attributed to the poet Bilvamangala Thakur in connection with his renunciation of material life after receiving spiritual instructions from Chintamani. Further, the quote is in *Gaudiya-kanthahara*, a Gaudiya Math verse book published in 1926 and used in the Gaudiya Math in India around the time Shrila Prabhupada met his guru, Bhaktisiddhanta Saraswati Thakur, founder-*acharya* of the Gaudiya Math. The literal translation is: "Since the time my mind was trained to enjoy the lotus feet of Krishna, which are the abode of ever newer *rasas*, whenever previous sex with a

woman is being remembered—Alas! there is distortion of the mouth and profuse spitting [or: "my mouth distorts and I drool profusely]." Special thanks to Dr. Ekkehard Lorenz and Dr. Maria Ekstrand, as well as members of the Dharma Mela discussion boards at HareKrsna.com, for supplying this information.

3. For a description of life in the new *bhaktin ashram*, see chapter 3 of *Betrayal of the Spirit* (Urbana: University of Illinois Press, 1997).

4. The 1977 GBC resolution said: "Regarding [women's] *sankirtana* parties—Resolved: The philosophy that the man *sankirtana* leader is the eternal husband and protector of the woman in a women's party is rejected. The philosophy of the man *sankirtana* leader as the representative of the spiritual master—and not the husband—should be preached instead" ("GBC Meetings: March 1–4, 1977, Mayapur Chandrodaya Mandir," 1977 GBC Resolutions [ISKCON document, author's collection] item 22, 6). The following year, a GBC resolution called for a committee to "correct difficulties regarding women's [*sankirtana ashrams*] in Berkeley and Los Angeles within three months' time" ("GBC Meetings," item 4, 1). The same resolution also called for a committee to correct *sankirtana* irregularities in New Vrindavan.

5. See description in *Betrayal of the Spirit* 168. The guru Hridayananda was a consistent foe of *ISKCON World Review*'s expanded editorial policy, 1986–88, and its editors.

6. Hridayananda Goswami wrote this in a letter to the P.R. department (quoted in *Betrayal of the Spirit* 74).

[19]

CHILD ABUSE AND THE HARE KRISHNAS

History and Response

DAVID WOLF

THIS CHAPTER WILL DESCRIBE the history of child abuse and neglect in the International Society for Krishna Consciousness (ISKCON), as well as the organization's response and the effects of child abuse on the organization.

A.C. Bhaktivedanta Swami Prabhupada, the founder of the modern-day Hare Krishna movement, desired to establish schools for the purpose of educating children to develop and manifest brahminical qualities, such as self-control, peacefulness, purity, honesty, wisdom, and tolerance, and ultimately to become responsible Vaishnavas to lead a respiritualization of human society. Prabhupada envisioned these boarding schools, or *gurukulas*, to be based on the ancient Vedic model of education, while also facilitating the needs of a dynamic preaching movement in the current age. Prabhupada wrote (*Letters* 21 November 1971): "The old system of *gurukula* should be revived as the perfect example of a system designed to produce great men, sober and responsible leaders, who know what is the real welfare of the citizens."

ISKCON opened its first formal school in Dallas, Texas in 1971. By 1974 there were about 100 children in the school, most of whom were under nine years old. By the early 1980s ISKCON had more than a dozen *gurukulas* in North America, as well as several schools on other continents. By the end of the 1980s, most ISKCON schools had become day schools, abandoning the *gurukula*, boarding-school model. Today, the vast majority of the children of the Hare Krishna movement attend state-supported schools (Rochford 1998). A major reason for this is the physical, sexual, and psychological abuse suffered by many of the children who attended ISKCON schools.

PREVALENCE AND TESTIMONIES

In 1998 the ISKCON Youth Ministry conducted a nonrandom survey of former *gurukula* students ("*gurukulis*") to determine levels of abuse in *gurukula*. One hundred fifteen responded to the survey, including 40 males and 75 females, ranging in age from 15 to 34. The average year that the respondents left Hare Krishna schools was 1989. Twenty-five percent described that they suffered sexual abuse in school for more than one year, and 29 percent reported that they suffered sexual abuse for a period of between one month and one year.

Regarding physical abuse, 31 percent of respondents stated that in *gurukula* they were repeatedly hit by a teacher or someone two or more years older than they were, to the point that marks were left on their body, and 37 percent reported that they knew of friends being repeatedly hit, resulting in marks on their body.

The survey contained 40 questions addressing various types of emotional mistreatment. Some results include 47 percent reporting that they were humiliated in front of other children, 16 percent stating that conversations with their parents were monitored, 26 percent that they were chastised for no apparent reason, 29 percent that they were punished for questioning the reason for a school rule or procedure, and 16 percent that they were ordered to rewrite a letter to relatives that reported negatively on the *gurukula*. Twenty-five percent of the respondents stated that they felt unloved and uncared for while they were in school.

On the survey were 18 questions concerning child neglect. Responses included 27 percent stating that they sometimes received insufficient food in *gurukula*, 16 percent that there was sometimes a lack of sanitary water to drink, 26 percent that they sometimes lacked necessary clothing, 27 percent that they sometimes lacked appropriate medical attention, and 24 percent that they experienced not being believed when they told school staff that they were sick, causing the illness to worsen.

Though the survey has many shortcomings, including sampling method and size, it is the only reasonably formal quantitative study that has been conducted on the topic of prevalence of child abuse in ISKCON. Another important consideration in assessing the results is that the vast majority of respondents were from western backgrounds, though some of them attended schools in India. Based on the work and findings of the Association for the Protection of Vaishnava Children (APVC), it would be expected that Indian-born *gurukula* graduates would report higher rates of some types of maltreatment, including sexual and physical abuse. Another limit to the generalizability of the survey results is that those who completed the questionnaire are probably more favorable to and involved with the ISKCON organization and Krishna Consciousness than the average youth who was raised in ISKCON, many of whom have no connection with ISKCON temples, the ISKCON Youth Ministry, or any other entity affiliated with the Hare Krishna movement. The sample for the survey was one of convenience, including people to whom the ISKCON Youth Ministry had relatively easy access.

As of January 2002, the APVC has received allegations of child maltreatment against more than 300 people. About 60 percent are reports from before 1992. That year is used as a marker because 1991 is the final year from which there are clusters of allegations connected with an ISKCON school. Specifically, in 1991 an investigation revealed extensive child abuse and neglect in the school in Mayapur, India. About 70 percent of the 300 alleged perpetrators were directly ISKCON-related, meaning that the accused was representing ISKCON at the time of the alleged incident or that the alleged abuse occurred on ISKCON property. About 30 percent of the reports involve allegations of abuse in the congregation; post-1991, the proportion of congregational reports is higher. These incidents are relevant to the APVC because they may involve a congregation member who is an active participant in temple functions, and who may have access to children during those functions. These figures therefore reflect the number of alleged perpetrators connected with ISKCON. For each there are often several victims, and for each victim there are often many incidents of child abuse. More than 80 percent of the cases involve accusations of sexual abuse, and many cases include accusations of more than one type of child abuse.

Though extensive research has been done on the frequency of child abuse in society, lack of clarity in definitions, as well as variance in research designs and formats, makes it difficult to estimate its prevalence. Studies have reported substantial variance in the rates of child sexual abuse, ranging from 4 to 62 percent, though an estimate generally accepted is that in the United States one in three females and one in five males will experience some form of sexual abuse before the age of 18 (Whetsell-Mitchell 1995). Population survey findings estimate that approximately 1.5 percent of children are subjected to very severe violent behavior each year in the United States, and more than 10 percent of children are victims of less severe parental physical maltreatment (Kolko 1996). Psychological maltreatment is recognized as the primary type of abuse in about 11 percent of the approximately 3 million cases of child abuse and neglect reported annually in the United States (Hart, Brassard, and Karlson 1996). Approximately 2.5 percent of children in the United States are reported each year as suffering from neglect, and approximately 40 percent of these cases are substantiated. Of course, it is probable that the actual incidence is much higher than reporting statistics indicate, as neglect often leaves no visible scars and is frequently undetected. Also, many victims of neglect and abuse are too young to speak about the treatment they experience (Farrell-Erickson and Egeland 1996).

From these statistics, indeterminate as they may be, the following can reasonably be suggested with regard to child abuse in the Hare Krishna movement relative to the incidence in the general population of the United States. While the incidence of child sexual abuse in ISKCON has been about the same as, or perhaps slightly higher than, in the general population, the prevalence of physical child abuse, psychological child abuse, and child neglect has probably been greater.

For many ISKCON children, who were raised in an atmosphere of oppression and fear, exacerbated by prolonged separation from their parents, a common experience of childhood in the boarding school (*ashram*) was one of terror and entrapment. Caution is advised in interpreting statistics when trying to understand the experience of these children. Statistics tend to strip the context from a situation, reducing a multidimensional experience to a few numbers (Tyson 1995) and thus depriving the reader of a comprehensive understanding. In regard to the topic at hand, numbers alone cannot convey the experience of, for example, an eight-year old boy separated from his parents by thousands of miles, being sexually molested every night by people in positions of authority, far bigger and stronger than him, with no one to share these horrifying experiences with, lest he be severely beaten for speaking. Therefore, this chapter contains some first-hand statements from child abuse victims, to give faces to the numbers and to provide insight into the varieties of abusive situations experienced by ISKCON children.

A former student in a boarding school in India describes a typical beating by one of the teachers:

> It would go something like this: a slap to the face, another slap to the other side of the face. When the person being assaulted would cover their face, he would hit them on the back/top of the head. Then as the person

crouched down, he would hit them on the back. As they doubled over from the previous blow, he would hit them in the chest or stomach. They would lurch one way or the other and so on and so on. It was like a dance.

Another student from the same school wrote:

[Name of teacher] had taken [name of student], then 8 years old, outside to the hallway for not chanting *japa*. Thirty seconds later or so, the solid concrete and brick wall noticeably shook with the sound of a deep, dull thud. Towards the end of the *japa* period, [name of teacher] came in smiling and really proud of himself. He showed off his fist that had 2 bleeding knuckles. "I went to punch him," he laughingly told his other teacher comrades, "but he ducked out of the way." . . . He really was the worst nightmare of *gurukula*, mainly for one reason. [Name of teacher] made it quite clear he was more than capable and willing to truly kill or handicap any one of us. He went out of his way to convince me of that and I am very sure he did so with other children. . . . What makes it so unforgivable was that the others, headed by the principle [*sic*] . . . did very little to discourage that attitude in [name of teacher]. . . . With the worst of his beatings, he decided to leave me locked up in a room for 2 weeks. He was very concerned someone might see the 6 and 12 inch wide blackish purple and bright red bruises all over my back, arms, legs and face . . . It was a month before most all the bruises were healed.

In another *ashram* school in India, an investigation revealed confirmed reports of dozens of instances of child sexual abuse, most perpetrated by older students or young adults in the school, against younger boys. The report on one 19-year old stated: "abused several younger boys, threatened many boys." A report on a 14-year-old described, "Repeatedly abused at a young age and was involved with many other boys." Another report stated, "Fondled about 8 boys and attempted worse." A report on a 17-year-old stated: "teacher of mantrachanting. Was abused when younger. . . . Repeated incidents of homosexual attack of many boys of different ages. Threatened many boys. Encouraged other older boys to engage in similar activities. . . . Known as a bully throughout the *gurukula* . . . eventually confessed to nearly everything." A description of a 10-year-old reported: "Abused smaller boys, including a five year old." The investigation revealed four generations of boys who were abused and became abusers, with violations including many incidents of forcible penetration.

A young woman reported that in the early 1980s, when she was about six years old and in an *ashram* school in New York, she was sent to the office of a school administrator. "Normally he would just smack us, by tricking us in a way, thinking the smack would come from that side, and quickly he would slap with the other hand instead. But this time, he first tricked me, and then took the blue fly-whopper from the windowsill and continuously whacked me all over the head, not just the face." Describing another incident, she stated, "[Name of teacher] came in, with a big stone in his fist. I was all alone with him there. Then he hit me in the stomach with that stone. I fell to the ground with pain and cried. As I got up he hit me again in the same way. I had a strong pain in my stomach. Then he ordered me to go to my class room." Narrating an incident when she was in her early teens, she wrote, "While driving, [name of teacher] would pinch and tickle [name of sister] continuously, and quite hard, too. I didn't like this and told him to stop. . . . He continued to tease her, so I moved into the middle of the back seat and punched his arm to get him to stop. . . . Then he grabbed my right breast with his right hand and squeezed it. I was shocked and upset. It was quite painful. When I told him that he cannot do such things he simply said that I had asked for it. . . . During the entire rest of the journey, including our stay with him in the hotel room in Brooklyn that night, I was quite panicked and stuck together with my sister like anything."

An official decision of the APVC, on the case of a perpetrator of child sexual abuse who violated several children while on the staff of an ISKCON nursery school in the United States, quotes from the decision of a State of California jury.

> We further find . . . the said defendant . . . engaged in substantial sexual conduct, to wit, penetration of the rectum of the victim by foreign object, said victim being a child under the age of eleven years. . . . We further find the allegation that at the time of the commission of the above offense, said defendant . . . occupied a position of special trust, to wit, teacher, caretaker, and committed an act of substantial sexual conduct . . . penetration of the rectum of the victim by the penis . . . oral copulation . . . penetration of the vagina of the victim by a foreign object . . . masturbation of defendant by victim or of said victim by said defendant.

A former student in an *ashram* described the behavior of a teacher as follows. "[Name of teacher] would pull me under water every day until I couldn't breathe. I lived in constant fear of water. . . . He slapped us all the time, making a game of it."

A devotee youth describes a former temple president in Northern Europe:

> One day me and the TP went there in the middle of the day, he said he wanted to be in peace, but I didn't understand what he wanted me there for . . . he suggested that we wrestle like in India boys used to do. I told him that I don't want to wrestle him. He said 'don't be so shy' so he lift-

ed me up and started to tickle me and grab me in funny places, hugging me really tightly.

A principal's assistant in a *gurukula ashram* in South America admitted to several times sexually abusing a preadolescent boy.

A youth in North America wrote of an incident in 1983:

One day while talking to my mother on the phone about how I disliked the *gurukula*, [name of teacher] listened on the other line. He became angry that I was complaining to my mother and when the call was over he beat me. He used a paddle made from 2 inches x 6 inches lumber, leaving bruises from the middle of my back to the back of my knees. I also had facial bruising from being slapped.

A young woman in Australia wrote that she was "sexually abused for a period of fourteen months" in the 1980s by the temple president. She continued, "Today, the main thing I am battling with is the faith I have lost in ISKCON."

A long-time *gurukula* teacher and headmaster in North America, who became a leading figure in ISKCON's attempts to combat child abuse, was exposed in 1998 as a child molester.

This chapter is about child abuse in ISKCON, and therefore that is what is being described. A comprehensive perspective on the experiences of the children of the Hare Krishna movement is not being presented. In the course of interviews with former students the APVC has received, even from youth who have been severely abused, and even in relation to some of the worst abusers, many positive statements of sweet and pleasant experiences growing up in *gurukula*. One *gurukuli*, who was badly mistreated for many years as a child in ISKCON, related, "India—it was just so phenomenally cool, especially back then. Vrindavan is so dramatic, from the peacocks, and the monkeys . . . the festivals, so much color, the dress, the temples, all so gorgeous. . . . I had so many spiritual experiences that I'm grateful for. And there was a great deal of camaraderie. And a lot of really cool devotees. Even some of the abusers were there for you, when you had problems with other teachers. . . . Actually, the real story, beyond the abuse, is why so many of the gurukulis remain in Krishna consciousness. It's the hand of Krishna, the attractiveness of Krishna." One young woman who suffered tremendously in *gurukulas* throughout her childhood and adolescence related that, surprising even to herself, through all of her experiences she would remember verses from the *Bhagavad Gita*, learned as early as age five, that would carry and inspire her through the roughest times. She expressed appreciation for the austerity, the *sadhana*, and other Vedic principles that she imbibed, though naturally she remained hurt and outraged at the abuse, the neglect, and the damage done to the spirit and confidence of herself and her friends. Many *gurukula* veterans told of great affection they had for some teachers, whose caring and loving attention, in spite of difficult circumstances, stood in stark contrast to an otherwise harsh childhood experience.

CAUSES

Several elements in an organization or program tend to decrease the susceptibility of children to abuse. To reduce the risk, all personnel involved in an organization or activity should be screened and receive some form of child protection training. Also, the parameters of activities and relationships should prevent isolated contact between an adult and a child. Another important factor is that increased parental participation translates into decreased vulnerability for children. Additionally, the physical facilities should make it difficult for perpetrators to effect abuse. For example, there should be abundant lighting and windows, and access by outsiders should be carefully monitored and regulated. Perhaps most important, an organization serving and interacting with children should ensure that the children receive child protection education. Despite all preventive measures, there is a significant possibility that a child will be approached by a person with abusive intentions. A child who has received child protection education has a better chance of avoiding abuse (Patterson 1995).

Analyzing ISKCON's school and temple situations from the 1970s through the early 1990s, we find that in many instances the environment was very conducive to child abuse. In ISKCON, children were separated from their parents, often on different continents, and sometimes for more than a year without any contact. The APVC has received many reports from parents that their instincts screamed at them not to leave their children at the school, but they did so, thinking that they had no choice if they wanted to be regarded as good devotees. *Ashram* teachers, who had intimate contact with children day and night, were admitted to the school staff without completing the most rudimentary application form, and often without receiving even basic training in child protection, discipline techniques, or academic instruction. Moreover, teachers and administrators were strained and overburdened in many ways, including a severe lack of resources and being forced to accept students they did not want in numbers that the school could not handle. This was a formula for even the most conscientious and cool-headed staff members to mistreat students on occasion, and to allow those with decidedly bad intent to prey on ISKCON's children.

Rochford (1998) asserts that until the early 1980s, children born within ISKCON were characteristically depicted as spiritually pure by dint of taking birth in a devotee family. By the mid-1980s, however, as many of the children entered young adulthood and did not manifest the conventional symptoms of devotion to Krishna, ISKCON leadership tended to adopt a deprecatory attitude toward them, often labeling them as "karmis," or materialists. Both of these attitudes served as convenient excuses for ISKCON leadership to avoid investing even minimal resources in educating and caring for these children. In the first instance, it was assumed that the children would become pure devotees of Krishna, simply as a result of their fortunate circumstances of birth, and thus it was considered that not much investment in them was required. In the later framework, ISKCON leaders considered that, no matter what arrangements they made, the children would not turn out good, so it was no use to devote resources to them. That is, rather than look at the mistakes they made in attempting to institute the system of traditional *gurukula*, they assumed that they managed things properly, and that, perhaps due to the degraded nature of the children and householder parents, the results were regrettable.

A central principle of Vedic philosophy and lifestyle is *yukta vairagya*, or dovetailing everything, even apparently material products and affects, in the service of spirit. By such utilization material energy transforms into spiritual energy. Applying this principle to family life, Prabhupada wrote, "As for detachment from children, wife and home, it is not meant that one should have no feeling for these. They are natural objects of affection" (*Bhagavad Gita* 13:8–12, purport). Clearly Prabhupada meant the *gurukula* experience of the children of ISKCON to be austere and disciplined, relative to the comforts and intemperateness of western life, but also replete with caring and affection and filled with the exhilaration and adventure that comes from learning and growing in a loving communal atmosphere. His novitiate followers frequently went to excess, overemphasizing the renunciation aspect of the Vedic lifestyle at the expense of properly understanding the importance of natural human affections, and Prabhupada often needed to rectify his wayward disciples in this regard. In response to a superficially and prematurely renounced parent, Prabhupada wrote on March 23, 1973, "Why should the parents not feel attachment for their children, that is natural" (*Letters*).

Daner (1992) conducted a case study of the Hare Krishna movement in the early 1970s. Illustrating devotee parents' unusual detachment from and apparent neglect of their children, she reported on an interview with a visitor to a Hare Krishna temple who stated: "After lunch I went back to the basement for a while to help out, but first I played a little with the small children who seemed to be craving for attention. When I withdrew, the children tried to get attention from other passers-by, who just shoved them aside. I guess I also expected the mothers to cast me a smile upon seeing me play with their children. But there was none of that and it disturbed me somewhat." The mentality reflected is very remote from Prabhupada's mood when he writes to a mother with a similarly undeveloped understanding of renunciation: "I am simply surprised that you want to give up your child to some other persons, even they are also devotees. For you, child-worship is more important than deity-worship. . . . These children are given to us by Krishna, they are Vaisnavas and we must be very careful to protect them" (*Letters*, 30 July 1972).

Rochford (1998) conducted a survey in 1992–1993 in which 63 percent of *gurukula* graduates agreed, and 26 percent strongly agreed, with the statement, "The *ashram gurukula* primarily served the interests of parents and ISKCON, rather than the spiritual and academic needs of children." ISKCON's attempts at *gurukulas*, especially during the 1970s and 1980s, often served primarily economic purposes, allowing parents to contribute full time to the preaching mission or, increasingly over the years, temple financial support, with child education and even proper child care substantially disregarded. Rochford writes, "From an institution meant to train and educate, the *gurukula* instead became the functional equivalent of an orphanage" (58).

Due to the factors described in this section, including untrained staff overburdened with excessive responsibilities and lack of resources and parental involvement, the *gurukula* experience for many children was one of isolation and bitterness. However, some schools in ISKCON during the same period largely avoided instances of child abuse. Reasons for this include staff members who, despite the harsh circumstances, were able to caringly mentor and educate their students, thus establishing a trusting and protective relationship. Also, in some schools parents were more involved, thus decreasing the chances of abuse.

RESPONSE

Through the 1980s ISKCON leadership did not mount a concerted effort to combat child abuse. One GBC member stated that in the late 1980s, when he tried to address the issue with the GBC body, a response he received was that it was a *grihastha* issue and did not actively concern them. When there were reports of rampant child sexual abuse in one of the *ashram* schools in India, the ISKCON education minister wrote letters to the authorities, urging them to deal with the situation responsibly, but to no avail, and the abuse continued for several more years. In other instances *gurukula* principals removed child sexual abusers from their schools when transgressions were disclosed, only to find the same abuser working with children in a different ISKCON school a few months later. The APVC has received dozens of reports from former ISKCON children, describing how they disclosed the abuse or tried to tell about it, but instead of meeting with concerned, responsible action, were beaten and threatened by school and temple authorities, or at best ignored. Often they were scolded and told that it was offensive to speak in such a way about their teacher and a Vaishnava Brahmin. Obviously such responses discouraged and intimidated them and others from revealing the abuse, and this caused re-victimization of the children by the organization itself.

Though by today's standards ISKCON's responses to child abuse in the organization were far from adequate, this must be considered in terms of general awareness of the issue in the outside world. It wasn't until the late 1970s and more so in the early 1980s that professional journals published extensively about child abuse, especially sexual abuse, and its effects. The harsh reality of its pervasiveness was just becoming known (Whetsell-Mitchell 1995), and this awareness was slow to reach the insulated ranks of ISKCON. Jenkins (1996) described clergy sexual abuse as "a model example of a social problem that undergoes mushroom growth, receiving virtually no attention from media or policy makers before about 1984–1985, yet becoming a major focus of public concern within a few years" (3). Many ISKCON leaders have expressed remorse at their lack of wisdom in dealing with child mistreatment in the past. One wrote, "I just wish I had deeper realizations about the education of children and wasn't such an impractical purist and fundamentalist." Another stated, "Of course, since that time we have been educated about child abuse and what to do when it comes up."

In 1990 the ISKCON Governing Body Commission (GBC) passed resolution 119, which attempted to establish a system of investigating, reporting, and preventing incidents of child abuse. Although the GBC supplied no practical means to enforce its elements, the resolution did provide some common-sense guidelines for dealing with cases of suspected child abuse, and it conveyed the message that ISKCON acknowledges that child abuse in its communities is a serious issue.

Meanwhile, former students were beginning to make their voices heard, in the form of newsletters and reunions, and the stories of the abuses they suffered were increasingly publicized. At a meeting in Florida in May 1996 of ISKCON leaders in North America, a group of former *gurukula* pupils spoke to the assembled devotees, sharing their stories of suffering. Das (1998) wrote, "The leadership of ISKCON, particularly the GBC, simply had to address the issue of past abuses or face a crippling credibility crisis. . . . An entire generation of children had been subjected to horrendous treatment. . . . The children, now adults, had complained before and no one had listened. But, their voice had now been heard collectively. . . . In addition, the children, now young adults . . . organized themselves" (74).

As a direct result of the 1996 meeting, the organization Children of Krishna formed. It is managed by a board of directors consisting of ISKCON youth and senior ISKCON devotees, and issues grants to assist Vaishnava youth with educational and vocational development, as well as with mental health therapy and organizing devotee youth projects. For more than five years Children of Krishna, although not an ISKCON organization, has been funded by donations from the society's leaders and others concerned about the young generation of devotees.

As the former *gurukula* students aged they became increasingly willing to speak about their experiences, and thus, through Web sites, newsletters, and individual communication, the extent and severity of abuse in ISKCON's past became increasingly known. In 1997 the GBC established the ISKCON Child Protection Task Force, whose assignment was to develop a comprehensive plan for ISKCON to address past, present, and future cases of child abuse, as well as a system for child protection education. The task force was composed of ISKCON youth, leaders, and devotees with professional credentials in social work and law.

At the annual GBC meetings early in 1998, the commission ratified a lengthy report issued by the task force. The report called for the establishment of an ISKCON Central Office of Child Protection, which became known as the Association for the Protection of Vaishnava Children (APVC) and opened in April 1998. The main functions of the APVC, as outlined in the task force report, are to investigate and adjudicate cases of alleged child abuse in ISKCON, both past and present; to establish a grant program specifically for people who suffered mistreatment when they were children under the care of ISKCON; and to assist ISKCON schools and temples in developing child protection programs.

The APVC has given grants to more than 80 young adults, at an average of slightly under $2,000 per grant. Mainly these funds have been used for therapy and college education.

The APVC works with ISKCON educational authorities and regional and local management bodies to organize child protection screening and education programs throughout ISKCON. Information packages have been sent to schools and temples throughout the world that explain basic principles for screening volunteers and employees. Another function of the APVC is to assist temples and schools to organize child protection teams. These teams provide information on child protection issues and hear concerns, in accord with principles of confidentiality, from community members, including children, about child abuse. Further, the teams serve as a liaison between the devotee community and governmental law enforcement and social service authorities. Early in 1998, in an ISKCON community in North America, a child abuse case surfaced. After notifying state law enforcement and social service departments, the local ISKCON child protection team assisted state workers with the investigation. Law officers and child protective investigators commended the devotees for helping with elements of the investigation that otherwise could not have been thoroughly explored.

Despite the successes of the prevention and education efforts of the APVC and concerned temples and schools around the world, monitoring and evaluating local child protection efforts remains difficult. Though many reasonably effective child protection teams have been established throughout the ISKCON world, most temples still do not have a team, and many still lack basic awareness of the principles of child protection. The APVC has worked with those temples and schools that have shown interest to institute child protection programs, though the association has not been able to follow up on the many temples that have not responded to its mailings. One former *gurukula* student in North America recently wrote to the APVC, "I am saddened when I tell you that unfortunately your services have not reached way out here. . . . The [name of temple] temple is really struggling as a community. I have never felt safe having my child be free on and around the temple property alone. I have stopped going there altogether in the past two years because it has gotten so strange."

In its role as a guidance, resource, and information center on child protection issues for devotees around the world, the APVC has compiled a list of ISKCON members and friends with experience in mental health and social service fields as a reference for temples and schools. The association handles thousands of letters (e-mail and regular mail), hundreds of phone calls, and dozens of in-person interviews each year. Such interactions include many diverse situations. A devotee concerned about a situation in his Vaishnava community requests advice: a fourteen-year-old girl is planning to marry a man in his thirties. A representative from a temple child protection team wants guidance on how to deal with a congregational devotee in his fifties whose history seems shady and who likes to associate and play with young children; single parents often leave their children with him. *Gurukula* veterans, or their parents, call to speak about what they went through and are experiencing in connection with abuses in the *gurukula.* Devotees call or write to discuss an official decision from the APVC, requesting interpretation of its elements and inquiring about its enforcement. A devotee mother asks for advice, reporting that her three-year-old daughter told her earlier in the day that her father (the former husband of the mother) touches her private parts when she stays at his house on weekends; the mother remains anonymous, as she doesn't want to report the allegations in or out of ISKCON, due to fear of the father. Devotees write or call to ask about APVC investigative and adjudicatory procedures.

The original task force report estimated that the APVC would need to investigate and adjudicate about a dozen or two dozen cases of alleged child abuse in ISKCON's past. As described above, the APVC has received accusations against more than 300 people, and only a small number of the alleged incidents occurred since the association was established in 1998.

When the APVC receives allegations of child abuse, the process of investigation begins. Results are given to an adjudicative panel that includes child protection judges who are veteran members of ISKCON and who have received training in the basic principles of recognizing child abuse. This training consists of an intensive four-day seminar that includes material on types of abuse, typologies of abusers, investigative procedures, confidentiality, and dealing with personal biases. In July 1998, a child protection judges training was held in North America, with ten devotees participating in the seminar conducted by two professional social workers, which included lecture and discussion sessions by an expert in forensic psychology, a pediatrician who specializes in child abuse issues, and a nationally renowned psychologist in the field of counseling for victims of child abuse. In June 1999, a similar seminar was held in Italy, and another was conducted in Florida in 2001.

After receiving an investigative case packet, the panel of three judges determines whether any of the allegations is valid. If it is decided that at least one of the allegations is true, then the panel meets with the director of the APVC to ascertain a rectification plan and sentence for the perpetrator. The foremost consideration is the safety of the children. The plan also considers factors such as personal and institutional moral obligations, care and restitution for the victims, the message ISKCON wants to convey about child protection, punishment of the perpetrator, degree of remorse of the abuser, reform of the abuser, and several other mitigating and aggravating factors. Restrictions are in proportion to the offense, and can extend to complete excommunication from the society.

It should be noted that the investigative and adjudicative procedures of the APVC are not a replacement for the functions of state authorities. The APVC merely determines the relationship of an alleged perpetrator with ISKCON. It directs and assists all temples, schools, and projects in learning and following their local laws regarding child abuse and mandated reporting of it.

To date, the APVC has adjudicated about 75 cases, and has been involved in investigating and giving advice on more than 100 others. ISKCON members, including abuse victims, temple managers, parents, and even perpetrators, have expressed appreciation for the standard procedures for case processing it utilizes. For example, recently, after reviewing a case file on allegations of severe child sexual abuse, the APVC director spoke on the phone with the alleged perpetrator, who had been distanced from ISKCON for several years. At first he was very skeptical about cooperating. After the director explained the function and procedures of the association, however, he was enthusiastic about participating in the process, because he wanted his relationship with ISKCON, which had been unclear from his own perspective and that of the temple managers, to be resolved. He confessed to some of the accusations on the phone, and later sent a complete report to the APVC after the office sent him a formal letter. The association has heard from many people in diverse life situations, including therapists specializing in abuse issues, child psychologists, *gurukula* veterans, parents of victims, legal professionals, senior ISKCON devotees, and ministers from other religious traditions, who have stated that they are very impressed with its processes for addressing cases of child abuse and with the fact that ISKCON has established an office for the sole purpose of child protection. A forensic psychologist who has been consulted by the APVC stated, "I very much applaud the work of the Association for the Protection of Vaishnava Children. I am impressed by your commitment and sacrifice. So many groups do lip service to protection of children, but your organization really epitomizes the ideal of taking action in this area." Whetsell-Mitchell (1995) provides research evidence demonstrating that the trauma for a child abuse victim is lessened if he or she sees that there are consequences for the offender, and if those consequences are publicized. In this and other ways, the APVC has provided some relief for victims of child abuse in ISKCON.

After a case is resolved by an official decision, it is not over as far as APVC involvement. Many of the decisions require close follow-up on items such as a psychological evaluation for the perpetrator, restitution payments, enforcement of restrictions on perpetrators, and inquiries about the decision from devotees.

Shortly before the task force report was issued, a committee of devotees, separate from the task force, critiqued it. The committee's main concerns with the system proposed by the task force were that it contained "Loop holes that can be used by abusers who have 'friends in high places,'" and that the body of appeal for APVC official decisions is the GBC Executive Committee (Dasa 1998). These concerns have proven to be warranted. Though the GBC has allowed the APVC to process and adjudicate the great majority of cases, the few instances where the commission has intervened have been cases involving people close to the ISKCON power structure. In one case, involving a *sannyasi* and initiating guru who fondled a preteen girl, the GBC instructed the APVC not to adjudicate. As the case is high-profile, the APVC has received many inquiries from devotees regarding its status and the *sannyasi*'s position in ISKCON. Turning to the GBC Executive Committee for answers, the APVC has received elusive and inconsistent responses and false guarantees of action over a period of several years.

In another instance, also involving a *sannyasi* and initiating guru, the GBC Executive Committee overturned an element of the APVC official decision, thus lightening one of the restrictions on the perpetrator. Also in this case, the *sannyasi* didn't comply with some aspects of the official decision, such as restrictions on where he could speak publicly as an ISKCON representative, and these violations were permitted by the GBC, with no censoring of those who declined to enforce the decision.

Currently there are a few other cases involving devotees with leadership roles. The standard APVC processing of some of these is being contested by many ISKCON leaders, as (to summarize their views) they believe that whatever may have happened in the past, these devotees should be free to use their experience and talents to serve ISKCON, without being substantially inhibited by restrictions from the APVC. A common scriptural argument on which such views, in these and other cases, are frequently based is the *Bhagavad Gita* verse 9:30, where Krishna declares, "Even if one commits the most abominable action, if he is engaged in devotional service he is to be considered saintly because he is properly situated in his determination." A common counterargument is that, even if this verse genuinely applies to the people under investigation, that does not obviate the necessity for the society to demonstrate that there are consequences for misconduct. In 2001 the GBC amended the appeal procedure for official decisions of the APVC so that the GBC Executive Committee and ISKCON Justice Minister have less of a role in the appeal process.

EFFECTS AND ANALYSIS

Rochford (1998) asserts that ISKCON's child abuse crisis may account, more than any other factor, for the loss of trust in ISKCON leadership. That leadership's lack of credibility is clear in the responses to the survey conducted by the youth ministry, though faith in the tenets of Krishna Consciousness and Prabhupada remains strong among former *gurukulis*. About 85 percent responded that they believe Krishna is God and that Shrila Prabhupada is a pure devotee of God, 73 percent stated that they consider themselves a devotee of Krishna, and more than 72 percent replied that they believe that Prabhupada's books have the solutions to the problems of the world. This contrasts with 28 percent responding that they believe that ISKCON has the solutions to the problems of the world, and only 23 percent responding that they are serving under the direct guidance of an ISKCON spiritual master or ISKCON authority. However, 82 percent stated that they believe that ISKCON has hope for improvement. One Vaishnava youth who conducted an informal survey of his cohort in a devotee community in North America found that 92 percent favored disconnecting the community from the GBC, with the other 8 percent not caring enough about the matter to offer an opinion.

The APVC commonly receives testimonies from youth who were raised in Prabhupada's movement, describing dedication and love for Krishna and Prabhupada and anger at ISKCON and its leadership. One former student wrote, "It's only because of Prabhupada that I have any connection to the movement, otherwise I'd be happy to see the whole thing go to hell." A young woman who was severely sexually abused in ISKCON as a child stated, "Though I have never ever lost my faith in the Mahamantra [the primary mantra chanted by followers of Krishna], I have, over the years, lost my faith in ISKCON." Several senior *gurukula* veterans have related endearing personal contacts they had with Prabhupada when they were children, describing instances where Prabhupada showed his personal concern for the children and took decisive action to improve *gurukula* facilities. One young woman who was sexually abused as a child by a temple leader wrote, "My lawyer was pushing for me to prosecute the society. . . . But because I understood it was the society of the Supreme Lord and Shrila Prabhupada, I didn't want to do that. I hoped that something could be resolved within the society. A number of different magazines . . . have offered me money for my story, but . . . not wanting to drag Prabhupada through the mud, I have refused so far to give the story to them. . . . At the moment I am not very involved with the temple. . . . I would like to be in a lot of ways, but it hurts me going there, so I worship Krishna in my home. . . . At the time of my abuse my parents were acting as fully surrendered devotees to the society. The society didn't protect me at the time, and continues to not consider what happened to me. . . . By going to the temple I feel like I am giving in to those who have hurt me . . . I can accept that [name of abuser] is basically crazy, but the GBC and TPs [temple *pujaris*] are still in positions of responsibility and should know better than to act in the way they did."

Not surprisingly, some people did abandon their Krishna Consciousness as a result of the child abuse they suffered. A devotee mother of three children, all of whom experienced violent child abuse within ISKCON, declared, "They now want nothing to do with Krishna Consciousness, what to speak of ISKCON."

Many parents and *gurukula* veterans believe ISKCON's efforts to help its youth to be disingenuous, emerging only under great pressure and for the purpose of protecting the organization more than from a sincere desire to help the victims and make amends for the past. As evidence, some point to leaders who were authorities at the time when child mistreatment was rampant and who continue to feign ignorance and innocence in relation to past abuses. During the summer of 2000 a group of Vaishnava youth who gathered in New Vrindavan specifically to discuss the issue of leadership and management of ISKCON strongly favored the idea that all GBC members, and especially those who were members before 1991, should resign their posts, in order to convey acknowledgment of and remorse for the neglect of the children in the movement.

Sipe (1990) explains that child abuse perpetrated by clergy has effects on victims that are particularly devastating. Apart from the well-documented, long-lasting physical and psychological effects, such abuse also tends to profoundly damage the spirituality of the victims, as well as their families and other community members. It is evident that the entire community of Prabhupada's followers has been severely affected by the extensive child abuse in the movement, and by the organization's failure, perhaps until recently, to adequately acknowledge and address the issue. Sipe, commenting on child abuse in Christian churches, cites questions that are relevant for ISKCON's situation: "How will the child be able to perceive the Church and clergy in the future as unselfish, loving representatives of the Gospel and Body of Christ? What happens to the child's perception of the sacraments as administered by the clergy? As an adult, will the victim come to view the hierarchy of the Church as hypocritical and weak for not having prevented the abuse or putting a stop to it once it was discovered?" (365).

Jenkins (1996) explains that an understanding of a society's concerns and fears can be gleaned by evaluating the context in which it analyzes its social problems. With regard to child abuse in ISKCON, a majority of Prabhupada's followers have evaluated the problem in terms of issues such as the schooling system, hierarchical authority, institutional control, the role of family in the society, and the position of renunciants. Carlson and Carlson (1994), describing an instance of child sexual abuse callously mishandled by parish authorities, write, "families with children started trickling away from the church. All families with children eventually left the church" (11). Similarly, masses of devotees, though perhaps retaining their faith in Prabhupada and the practices of Krishna Consciousness, have left ISKCON, or have at least rejected the authority of the GBC. Many *grihasthas* feel that the renunciant hierarchy of ISKCON has been glaringly disconnected from the concerns and interests of most devotees, and that the child abuse calamity was a manifestation of this. This has led to distrust of both institutionalized ISKCON schools and the authority structure of the organization.

As a result, parents are arranging other means for educating their children, and devotee communities are becoming less dependent, managerially and spiritually, on the international GBC body. It should be noted that the trend toward devotee parents not enrolling their children in ISKCON schools began in the early 1980s, before the prevalence and severity of child maltreatment in the schools was widely known. This was largely due to an economic downturn for the temples, schools, and parents. Awareness of the abuses that took place, and the attitude and reactions of many ISKCON leaders to these abuses, have made parents very reluctant to entrust their children to ISKCON. As a result of the child abuse crisis and many other issues of integrity, devotees are increasingly convinced that the GBC lacks moral authority to guide Prabhupada's movement, and many no longer identify the essence of the movement itself with the GBC and the institutional hierarchy.

There has been a lawsuit against the GBC and ISKCON, filed by people who were maltreated when they were children under the care of the society. Many ISKCON youth have expressed to the APVC that, though they have a deep attachment to Krishna and Prabhupada in their hearts, their disgust with the indifference, insensitivity, and lack of basic decency of ISKCON leadership has led them to consider suing ISKCON.

According to Jenkins (1996), a sect shields itself from external criticisms by providing a common enemy against which members can unite, whereas in a church, organizational beliefs are less likely to contradict prevailing social views, and thus isolated offenses will not generally be perceived as reflective of debilitating structural flaws. In ISKCON's past, when excessive physical punishments or perverse sexual crimes against children were covered up or justified with rationalizations, devotees were more likely to accept the assertions of authorities, in order to preserve the sect and protect it from the outside. Some common rationalizations included disparaging the protests of child abuse as being simply a western concoction, a hysteria imbibed from modern materialists who know nothing of Vedic educational principles or effective child discipline, an exaggeration concocted by whiners, and equating an adult having sex with children with a sexual relationship between two consenting adults, both instances being regarded as a "fall-down." The remedy for an adult who sexually violated children would often be to get married or to relocate. Currently, the vast majority of devotees are concerned that their religion be integrated into society as a church, rather than a cultish sect, and thus such responses as were formerly accepted are rejected in favor of views more representative of the larger society, including an emphasis on rehabilitation and mental health therapy, and involving governmental social service and law enforcement agencies when child abuse is suspected. Jenkins, describing the effect of child abuse scandals on the American Catholic Church, wrote, "In the 1980s the American Catholic church was still sufficiently different to excite criticism, but its members no longer responded by 'circling the wagons,' as they had so predictably in the past . . . Whereas once the religious institutions would have been thought worthy of enforcing internal standards of behavior and morality, the current trend is to seek external controls from the civil and criminal law, and to impose the value systems of nonreligious groups. . . . The clergy-abuse scandals demonstrated a near-collapse of public confidence in the integrity of church institutions" (159–62). Similarly, ISKCON is clearly sufficiently different from mainstream society to attract public outrage for scandals such as child abuse, but the great majority of devotees are no longer inspired to rally around the organization in defense of ineffective institutional policy and practice.

By publicizing its history of child abuse in its own *ISKCON Communications Journal* (June 1998), ISKCON has displayed integrity by admitting past failures to protect children. Also, the efforts of the APVC, which is funded by the GBC, have met with substantial approval and respect from devotees and people in the greater community. However, these efforts have not significantly alleviated the cynicism about the GBC itself, as many of Prabhupada's followers consider its efforts as too little too late, and merely a pretense of concern.

Such skepticism is fueled by a perception that the GBC remains entangled in a web of corruption, practically forcing its members to continually sacrifice the integrity of the organization for the sake of protecting some interest of the GBC body, its members, or those who serve its members. Katz (1977) explains that organizations commonly shield members whose misconduct may bring embarrassment by obscuring outsiders' perceptions of internal enforcement of norms and by protecting wrongdoers from outside criticism. Such tactics may in the short term protect the image of the organization, but often at the expense of creating a self-defeating labyrinth forcing leaders to continually weaken the internal authority of the organization by not enforcing codes of ethical conduct. In ISKCON, continuing to the present, leaders have shielded subordinates from consequences for committing child abuse, which allows superiors to secure authority at the expense of the respect of most members of Prabhupada's movement, who, over time, detect the machinations. The technique of nonenforcement has also been used in ISKCON, especially in high-profile cases. Katz writes, "Decisions not to enforce become corrupt when, instead of strengthening the authority of persons in officially superordinate positions . . . they strengthen the independent authority and illegitimate purposes of the persons granted lenience. . . . The formal hierarchical relation may reverse by imperceptible degrees, with the result that the superordinate becomes an agent of the subordinate's morality" (9). This has happened in the GBC, with the body's strength and influence diminishing as a result of continually allowing child abusers to maintain positions and influence in the organization.

An issue confronting the GBC and APVC is whether and to what extent the association should process and adjudicate cases of people who served as GBC members in locations where there was extensive child abuse. Even in dealing with cases of neglect of supervision by *gurukula* headmasters in schools where abuse was extensive, the APVC has met with strong opposition from GBCs who have worked closely over the years with the principals (or former principals). Buckley (1997), deliberating on a similar issue in regard to the Catholic

Church, reflects on the appropriate fate of bishops who were supervisors in places where child sexual abuse occurred. "One wonders, in respect of that bishop in Dallas, and the two bishops in Ireland and Canada, whether a public mortification isn't appropriate. Resignation, or at least withdrawal from the diocese, or at least a leave of absence of several years in a monastery, is a sign of pain felt, and sacrifice merited" (87). In ISKCON, though the GBC is taking commendable measures to deal with past child abuse and to prevent repetition of mistakes in the future, there is incredulity from devotees because many leaders who were in authority when horrendous child abuse happened retain their positions. Further, the perception is that, as individuals, many of these leaders have not adequately accepted responsibility for the mistreatment of children. This is felt as an ongoing organizational character failing that continues to plague the community.

CONCLUSION AND CURRENT STATUS

In the past ISKCON markedly failed to protect its children. A psychologist who had contact with some of the victims and testimonies related to one of the *gurukula ashrams* remarked on the similarity of the atmosphere in the schools and descriptions of concentration camps.

This chapter has referred to superficial renunciation and the position of renunciants in the ISKCON society, as these are perceived as significant contributing factors to the history of child abuse and the organization's inability to effectively address the issue. It is important to note that such false renunciation is not defined in terms of *ashram*. Most *sannyasis* and *brahmacaris* in the organization have been genuinely supportive and appreciative of the efforts of the APVC, and have shown sincere concern for the child abuse victims; conversely, there have been *grihasthas* in leadership positions who have been unresponsive and negligent in child protection duties. As the movement matures, we can hope and expect that the membership of all *ashrams* will similarly mature, and all will cooperate to protect vulnerable populations, as is done in a civilized society.

Vaishnava philosophy asserts that a true spiritualist transcends material responsibilities but does not neglect them, for in honest spiritual endeavor they are subsumed and fulfilled. Superficial renunciation implies an assumption of greater spiritual advancement than actually obtained, at the expense of neglecting basic and essential duties in the material realm. In assuming too much about their spiritual position, members of ISKCON irresponsibly neglected fundamental duties, such as protection of dependents, that form the foundation for a humane society. Thus, the devotee community needs to focus on and integrate such core elements of civilized development, which of course is intrinsic to Vedic culture and fundamental to Prabhupada's mission. Otherwise, intelligent, respectable people will not be attracted, and those who do take shelter in the organization will continue to be exploited.

Based on talks with professionals in many fields, as well as research on other religious groups, ISKCON's establishment of an international office dedicated to child protection appears to be unique among denominations. As former students hear from their friends about the efforts of the APVC, they are increasingly willing to tell their stories to the association, to expose the abusers, and to thereby help prevent others from being similarly mistreated. Thus, ISKCON is in some measure gradually restoring its trustworthiness. Pope John Paul II, in his apology in 2001 for damage from child sexual abuse by clergy, promised "open and just procedures" to respond to abuse complaints. He further expressed commitment to "compassionate and effective care for the victims, their families, the whole community, and the offenders themselves." Thus, other denominations, such as the Catholic Church, are seeking to establish programs and systems similar to what ISKCON has been developing through the APVC.

However, as described above, intervention by the GBC in some cases is perceived, by *gurukulis* and many other devotees, as politically motivated and symptomatic of a leadership lacking integrity, seeking to protect self-serving interests at the expense of truly leading and serving Prabhupada's mission and followers. Additionally, lack of personal admissions of irresponsibility and neglect, and even of the true extent of the child abuse, on the part of GBC members and other leaders who were in responsible positions when the abuse was prevalent, continues to erode trust in and respect for ISKCON leadership. Besides furthering its current efforts to protect children and deal with past cases, ISKCON would benefit from mandating child protection training for all who accept leadership positions. This would help ensure that organizational decisions consider child protection needs and concerns. Toward this goal, the GBC organized one full day of child protection training at its annual meetings in 2001.

Child abuse in ISKCON has substantially decreased, though one obvious reason is that relatively few parents place their children under the care of the society. The majority of current cases received by the APVC involve allegations of abuse occurring in the congregation, not in temples and schools. In analyzing the present and future of child abuse in ISKCON, we must at least acknowledge definitional issues of what constitutes "ISKCON" and a member of ISKCON. Increasingly, devotees are not identifying themselves with the organization, or at least not with the authority structure of the international organization. Institutional certification of a school is not nearly as meaningful as in the past. Now, devotee parents are more conscientious about personally acquainting themselves with school policies and staff before entrusting their children there.

Among most schools that are clearly part of ISKCON, compliance with accepted child protection standards, such as screening of staff and students, prohibition of corporal punishment, ensuring that an adult and a child are not alone, and mandating child protection education for all members of the school, are far greater than they were a decade ago. If ISKCON wants to develop more schools and convince parents to send their children to them, then adherence to such standards must continue to increase so that schools and temples are safe and attractive for all who attend. Otherwise, institutional control and authority will continue to diminish, as Prabhupada's followers, who are committed to ensuring that the future will be a better and happier place for their children, create temples for worship and schools for education outside of ISKCON.

REFERENCES

Buckley, William F., Jr. "Buggery in Church." *National Review*, 15 September 1997, 86–87.

Carlson, D. and M. Carlson. "Child Molestation: One Family's Experience." In J. T. Chirban, ed., *Clergy Sexual Misconduct: Orthodox Christian Perspectives*, 1–39. Brookline, MA: Hellenic College Press, 1994.

Daner, F. J. *The American Children of Krsna: A Study of the Hare Krsna Movement*. Stanford: Stanford University Press, 1992..

Das, B. S. "ISKCON's Response to Child Abuse: 1990–1998." *ISKCON Communications Journal* 6 (1) (1998): 71–79.

Farrell-Erickson, M. and B. Egeland. "Child Neglect." In J. Briere, L. Berliner, J. A. Bulkley, C. Jenny, and T. Reid, eds., *The APSAC Handbook on Child Maltreatment*, 4–20. Newbury Park, CA: Sage Publications, 1996.

Hart, S. N., M. R. Brassard, and H. C. Karlson. "Psychological Maltreatment." In Briere, J., Berliner, L., Bulkley, J. A., Jenny, C., & Reid, T (Eds) *The APSAC Handbook on Child Maltreatment*.. pgs. 72–89, Sage Publications.

Jenkins, P. *Pedophiles and Priests: Anatomy of a Contemporary Crisis*. Oxford: Oxford University Press, 1996.

Katz, J. "Cover-up and Collective Integrity: On the Natural Antagonisms of Authority Internal and External to Organizations." *Social Problems* 25 (1) (1977): 3–17.

Kolko, D. J. "Child Physical Abuse." In J. Briere, L. Berliner, J. A. Bulkley, C. Jenny, and T. Reid, eds., *The APSAC Handbook on Child Maltreatment*, 21–50. Newbury Park, CA: Sage Publications, 1996.

Patterson, J. *Child Abuse Prevention Primer for Your Organization*. Washington, D.C.: Nonprofit Risk Management Center, 1995.

Swami, Bhaktivedanta. *Bhagavad-gita As It Is*. Los Angeles: Bhaktivedanta Book Trust, 1972.

Swami, Bhaktivedanta. *Letters from Srila Prabhupada*. Los Angeles: Bhaktivedanta Book Trust, 1986.

Rochford, E. B., Jr. and J. Heinlein. "Child abuse in the Hare Krsna Movement: 1971–1986." *ISKCON Communications Journal* 6 (1) (1998): 43–69.

Sipe, A. W. R. *A Secret World: Sexuality and the Search for Celibacy.* New York: Brunner/Mazel, 1990.

Tyson, K. *New Foundations for Scientific Social and Behavioral Research: The Heuristic Paradigm.* Needham Heights, MA: Allyn and Bacon, 1995.

Whetsell-Mitchell, J. *Rape of the Innocent: Understanding and Preventing Child Sexual Abuse.* Washington, D.C.: Taylor & Francis, 1995.

[20]

FIFTEEN YEARS LATER:
A CRITIQUE OF *GURUKULA*

Personal Story II

GABRIEL DEADWYLER (YUDHISHTHIRA DAS)

MY LAST YEAR IN *gurukula* and my last intimate involvement with ISKCON was in 1986, when I was fifteen years old. Devotee children born then would themselves be fifteen years old now, and they have experienced a very different upbringing than my peers and I. Most have not attended boarding-school *gurukulas*. The entire movement has also changed, and I think (and hope) that the few *gurukulas* that still exist, and, more important, the attitudes of ISKCON leaders, parents, and educators, have changed as well. Still, with the benefit of hindsight, I wish to discuss several things that were obviously not clear to the leadership, educators, parents, and members of ISKCON fifteen years ago.

The first of these I will call the antinomian heresy, which, while referring to a development in Christian history and therefore not perfectly applicable in this case, is a good term for the idea that spiritual perfection places one above the law. In my youth, many devotees operated as if they and ISKCON were above not just the law in a strictly legal sense, but also the basic moral laws of civilized behavior, especially among those who claim to be religious. Many devotees seemed to have taken the passages in scripture that seem to suggest that anyone engaged in Krishna's service is without faults and beyond reproach[1] as a license to engage in, or look the other way at, all kinds of criminal and immoral behavior justified in the name of Krishna. Anyone who's been around ISKCON over its lifetime will know what I'm talking about (one need only consider the ISKCON slang term *scam-kirtana,* which illustrates this).[2]

The most horrible results of this attitude were *gurukula* teachers and administrators not treating sexual and physical abuse of children as crimes that must be reported to civil authorities so the perpetrators could be prosecuted. Instead, when incidents of sexual abuse came to light they were ignored or hidden. *Gurukula* administrators often seemed more concerned with protecting the reputation of the schools and of ISKCON than with the protection and welfare of the children. They usually treated sexual abuse as a "fall-down" that could be rectified by better spiritual practice (*sadhana*). In almost every case, perpetrators were simply counseled to practice better *sadhana* to reduce their sexual desires, and in some cases, they were not even removed from their position as teachers but simply quietly transferred to another school. For myself and many others, incidents that occurred in the first *gurukula* in Dallas, when we were barely five years old, had long-term consequences for all our lives. Thus, from the very beginning, the lives of *gurukulis* (the children of the *gurukula*) were "spoiled"—to use Shrila Prabhupada's term[3]—by personal exposure and the exposure of their classmates to criminal sexual activity and frequent physical abuse. I remember no lawful response by *gurukula* or ISKCON leaders to any of this.

As noted above, there have been many instances of what I've called antinomian thinking in ISKCON's culture, and child abuse is only the most egregious. As recently as May 2000, I was at a conference in New Vrindavan at which sociologist Burke Rochford urged ISKCON leaders to make institutional changes to prevent abuses of authority.[4] One of the devotees in attendance insisted that ultimately people do bad things due to spiritual defects and that therefore, better spiritual practice is the only real cure. Thus the philosophical opinion that ISKCON's institutional and practical problems have only a spiritual solution is not entirely gone.

However, one has only to extend this logic to analogous situations in life to appreciate its absurdity. Should a devotee about to get on an airplane be more concerned that the pilot and crew have the proper training or that they are devotees in good standing? Does a devotee in need of an operation insist that the surgeon and hospital staff chant the Hare Krishna mantra and strictly follow ISKCON's regulative principles before allowing the procedure? Yet, at one point in *gurukula*'s history, it was felt that training and qualifications for teachers—such as a degree in education—were to be avoided because they would only contaminate the devotee teachers with "karmi"[5] ideas. And while faith is an important ingredient in theistic belief systems, it often seemed that *gurukula* teachers had faith and only faith, rather than real plans based on practical principles. They were convinced that *gurukula* was the best possible educational experience for the children under their care simply because they had good intentions and faith in Shrila Prabhupada and Krishna. I hope that ISKCON leaders, and especially parents and educators, have since realized that while spiritual practices like faith in guru and Krishna are important foundations of ISKCON, they cannot replace practical intelligence and expertise. Whatever spiritual perfections result from being a devotee of Krishna, no one is above the law or too good for civilized behavior.

I would think that by now, everyone connected with ISKCON has heard of the abuses we suffered in *gurukula*. Some *gurukulas* and some teachers were much better than others, so not everyone lived a horror story, but the stories are not exaggerations. The tremendous difficulties many former *gurukulis* have gone through, both in the schools and then later in life as they tried to come to terms with their experiences, are almost too much to bear. I don't want to dwell on these here, except to say the obvious: that they must never happen again. There is absolutely nothing in the philosophy of Krishna Consciousness that condones sexual abuse. I hope that now that ISKCON knows that such abuse happens even in religious societies, and that if it diligently keeps the standards that the Child Protection Office has put in place, the abuse will not happen again.

In terms of physical abuse, there may be some complications in definition. ISKCON educational philosophy emphasizes strict discipline and obedience to authority. Furthermore, it involves separation of children and parents, isolating the children from mainstream society, and attendance at *mangala-arati* (the 4:00 A.M. worship of the deity) and the rest of the four- to five-hour morning program in the temple (mantra meditation, scriptural study, etc.). It also values other practices of devotional life conducted in the name of austerity (*tapasya*), such as having few possessions and sleeping on simple bedding. Some of my peers have argued that all these principles are inherently abusive. I would not go that far, but I do agree that these principles can and often did become abusive in the hands of fanatical teachers. Thus, while physical abuse of children can happen in any circumstances, aspects of ISKCON educational philosophy may easily be followed to the point of fanaticism and become abusive. Teachers and parents must use their practical intelligence to avoid this. Children may wake up early and attend *mangala-arati*, but they must get enough sleep; some *gurukulas* were good about this, but many were not. A simple lifestyle is not abusive, but lack of basic facilities and affectionate loving care, as occurred in many *gurukula*, certainly is. Discipline is not abusive, but beatings, threats of beating, and an atmosphere of intimidation certainly are. The principle, as Shrila Prabhupada himself said several times, is not to force.[6] Tragically, this aspect of his instructions was largely ignored by teachers and parents alike.

I've heard that some devotees think the *gurukula* system was great and everything would have worked out fine for us, but somehow "demons" got involved and abused some of the children, and that's why we *gurukula* alumni are not all full-time devotees and why some of us have even become antagonistic toward ISKCON. Blaming so-called "demons" or even placing all the blame on *gurukula* administrators and teachers (who certainly deserve a large share of it) is clearly a way to ignore larger institutional failings and avoid self-examination (see Rochford 1998 for an excellent sociological analysis of this issue).[7] Like those leftists who claim that the history of the Soviet Union doesn't accurately reflect communism because the Soviet Union was never really communist, I have some sympathy with those who see the history of *gurukula* as so marred by sexual and physical abuse that it tells us little about an ideal "Krishna Conscious" education. Nevertheless, I think the leaders, parents, and educators of ISKCON should understand that graduates of even a perfect *gurukula*, who have never suffered from any form of abuse, will still have to contend with a host of problems as they grow older.

The crux of the problem is that Krishna Consciousness and modern culture are as culturally far apart as you can get, and in many ways they are in direct opposition. Most devotees recognize this. In fact, in becoming devotees they specifically seek an escape from modern culture, which they view as an increasingly abhorrent product of the present degraded age. Thus they enthusiastically transform not only their beliefs but also every aspect of their lives, from what they read, what they do, and whom they associate with to their clothing, hairstyle, diet, and even their very names. But what about their children, born into the movement?

I remember over the years many devotees joyfully telling me how happy I must feel and how lucky I must consider myself to be a *gurukula* boy. I always found that a strange comment. First of all, I didn't always think it was that cool to be a *gurukuli*, subject to authoritarian rules like standing in line to go to the temple, made to wear an ugly yellow *dhoti* (traditional male attire), forbidden to ride bikes around the farm, and not allowed even to talk to girls. But mostly I found it strange because this was the only life I knew. I had nothing to compare it with, and in no way had I chosen it. Those who joined the movement imagined *gurukula* as an amazing gift, because while they had made a choice to change their lives, renounce the material world, and become devotees of Krishna, they found so many ingrained impurities and material attachments within themselves from their pre-devotee life. To have grown up without those impurities was the stuff of their dreams, and when I look back to how really innocent we all were, I guess I can understand that enthusiasm.

My point is that adult devotees join the Hare Krishna movement by choice. They have often seen it all and done it all before they become devotees and finally find their home at the feet of Shrila Prabhupada and Krishna. No matter what pressures they may have experienced to "shave up" or "move in" and not to "bloop,"[8] as adults, they are ultimately involved with ISKCON of their own free will. In fact, the whole basis of *bhakti yoga*, or devotional service in loving relationship with Krishna, is one of choice. Children born into ISKCON, however, do not really make that choice and cannot until they are independent, that is, until they reach adolescence.

Before then, *gurukulis* are more or less parrots. We danced, we sang, we chanted mantras, recited *Bhagavad Gita* verses, and even preached the philosophy, but it was all we knew. Many even took formal initiation from a guru, but the vows were meaningless, as time has shown. Our complete absorption in the devotee lifestyle was not an expression of deep spiritual realization but simply the natural capacity of children to be inculcated in their culture, be it the American one or the ISKCON one. When we began to be independent, growing from obedient *gurukula* kids into free-thinking adults, the two completely dissimilar cultures clashed. No one had prepared us for this, and in fact the abuses we suffered made it much worse. Consequently, almost all of us have had the most difficult time. As long as there is this difference between American culture and ISKCON culture, each *gurukuli* (or, at least, American *gurukuli*) will face this clash and the choices it brings. I hope in the future, children of ISKCON will have more help and be better prepared than we were.

When I graduated from the *gurukula* in Vrindavan I had a *Bhaktishastri* degree, which means I knew the *Bhagavad Gita* and other scriptures rather well. I also had some skill at reading and writing, mostly developed through the study of scriptures, and a smattering of Sanskrit. But I had received only the most basic rudiments of the social sciences and mathematics, and I had absolutely no science education. I was qualified to be an outstanding temple devotee but had no training with which to do anything else, like enter college and pursue a career. It seems I was never expected to even want to do that. Actually, from quotations I have read from Shrila Prabhupada, this type of academic focus seems more or less what he wanted. Interested overwhelmingly in a religious education, he specifically instructed that the goal of *gurukula* was to create preachers and devotees of high character and sense control, and that advanced academics and higher education like university were neither desired nor required.[9] So perhaps the fact that at fifteen I found myself with basically only a religious education is not a failure to realize *gurukula* ideals, but to be expected from the very concept of *gurukula* as envisioned by Shrila Prabhupada.

What does seem a clear failure is that no one seemed to know what to do with us when we were done with *gurukula*, especially if we didn't want to be full-time devotees. In my case, when there was nothing more for me to learn in the *gurukula* system, I served for a while as the typist for one of Shrila Prabhupada's senior disciples. That didn't last long, and now that I understand just how difficult fifteen-year-olds can be, I'm surprised it lasted as long as it did. At the Gita Nagari farm in Pennsylvania, they tried to have the teenagers work as devotees (i.e., as unpaid volunteers), and after much strife, that too failed. No one knew what to do with all of us, and more than that, once we started experimenting with the outside world, there was often outright hostility toward us. It seemed no one had even considered that teenagers might not want to live the life of devotee monks, that everyone assumed that since we had experienced the "higher taste" of love of Krishna we would never want "sense gratification." It was a shock that we wanted to eat ice cream, to watch television and movies; that we were fascinated with American culture—not to speak of the near heart attacks when we engaged in those activities that potentially involved breaking the ISKCON "regulative principles," like associating with girls.

My father (Ravindra Svarupa) describes in one of his articles how early devotees had no idea how to relate to "fringies" (those on the fringe of ISKCON society).[10] Well, adolescent *gurukulis* were (and I think always will be) fringies with a vengeance. Even to this day—for example, at our reunions—we cause problems because of our "fringe" behavior. One day we'll be running around and swimming in shorts and bikinis, boys and girls freely mixing, listening to rock and roll or hip-hop, and the next day we'll be at the Sunday temple program in *dhotis* and *saris* singing and dancing in the *kirtana*, congregational chanting sessions (and probably with better pronunciation and musical skills than many of the convert devotees). No one had any idea that something like this would happen, no one had any idea how to respond when it did, and it seems some still don't know how to respond. Everyone was scrambling—parents, whose children had not grown up with them and so didn't even know their children very well; temple authorities, who didn't know how to deal with troublemakers you couldn't just kick out of the temple; and we kids were especially scrambling, for we had to face not only the normal troubles of any adolescent but also this additional, unbelievable clash between the ISKCON culture we grew up in and the larger world that we were now more or less free to enter.

I believe that an upbringing that does not prepare *gurukula* kids to face this dichotomy, and more than that, does not provide at some point the basic academic and social building blocks to be a success in the secular world, should they choose to enter it, is a disservice to ISKCON's children. Considering that Shrila Prabhupada envisioned *gurukula* as ending at fifteen, and that the

American system of education continues secondary education until eighteen, there can be flexibility in simultaneously maintaining the strict spiritual principles of *gurukula* without impairing the secular future of the students. This may be a moot point since most devotee children are now educated in secular schools and straddle both worlds from the beginning, but my peers and I had to figure all this out more or less on our own.

It was very frustrating for me that I had spent months in minute study of Vaishnava texts like *Nectar of Devotion* and years memorizing Sanskrit grammar through traditional methods, yet when I wanted to take the SATs for college admission, I didn't know what sine or cosine were. I feel even more for the girls, many of whom were not even given the scriptural education the boys received, for at least that education improved my reading and writing. Instead they were taught that their role was as an obedient wife, that academics and advanced philosophy were not necessary for them, and that they would be best off learning to cook, sew, and clean. The simple fact, which may now seem obvious but was not imagined in the past, is that, given the renunciation required, relatively few *gurukulis* are going to end up being full-time temple devotees. Therefore, at some point they will need to receive the education and social tools to allow them to live and work in the secular world if they choose to do so.

As far as this choice is concerned, I think it is important to note that this will most naturally be an issue between the adolescent and his or her parents. One of the problems in the past was that parent-child relationships were neglected in ISKCON, which made them all the more difficult when we kids reached adolescence. *Gurukula* authorities strictly insisted that all ISKCON children be separated from their parents in *gurukula*, even when some children and parents clearly should not have been apart. In some cases they actively kept children and their parents from communicating, because they thought the parents were too much "*maya.*"[11] Even if we accept that a boarding school (*ashram*) education under the daily care of a teacher is the best arrangement for a spiritual education, it seems obvious that a child's relationship to his or her parents cannot be neglected or given second-class status. But for many ISKCON children—and for various reasons, some the parents' fault—this is exactly what happened.

In my own case, even though I spent more time between five and fifteen years of age in the *ashram* than I did with my parents, and as much as those experiences and teachers have shaped me, my connection to my parents is more visceral and enduring and means much more to me, both then and now, than my connection with *gurukula*. If my parents had been less involved with my life while I was in *gurukula*, if they had reacted to my choices as I grew older with hostility or resentment, if they had not been forgiving, open-minded, and supportive as I made my choices and ultimately became my own person, I would have had an incredibly more difficult time. When an adolescent leaves *gurukula*, and especially if he or she chooses to leave the community of ISKCON, that person's only real connection in life, and to Krishna Consciousness as well, will be with the parents. Thus whatever may be the spiritual value of transcending bodily attachments, a child's relationship with his or her parents cannot be neglected or diminished, even if, or perhaps *especially* if, the child goes to a boarding school.

Another issue of choice that every adolescent *gurukuli* will face is sexuality and relationships between the sexes. I remember my last year in *gurukula*, when I was fifteen (and I trust we all remember what it was like to be that age), one of my teachers discovered I had a crush on a certain girl. He gave me a little lecture, telling me: "Don't get involved with girls. They'll only bring you trouble." Whether he was right or wrong, that particular instruction was out my other ear in record time. I wanted nothing more than exactly that kind of trouble. Now I don't intend to argue that ISKCON has to change its principles and condone sex outside of marriage. Shrila Prabhupada clearly wanted strict *brahmacharya*, and celibacy is of course recognized in many religious traditions as an important spiritual practice. However, it was a problem that my teacher's only option seemed to be to tell me: "No, you can't." I suppose he or my parents could have "arranged" my marriage, as is the Hindu and often ISKCON practice, but considering that, if I'm not mistaken, 100 percent of the marriages of young *gurukulis* have already ended, I don't think that marriage at that time would necessarily have been a better option. I must admit I have no easy solution to this problem, and ISKCON is not the only religious community to face it. However, because American culture practically celebrates dating and premarital relations, how to deal with sexuality is a major part of the vastly complex set of choices that devotee adolescents will face.

As far as relationships between the sexes, while I was in *gurukula*, we boys were allowed no contact with girls whatsoever. This made our adolescence and our first forays into the wider world that much more awkward and difficult. American boys and girls relate with each other throughout their lives, and in the mainstream world of work and school, men and women relate with each other all the time, and not always with sex in mind. The fact that boys and girls coming out of *gurukula* had absolutely no experience in relating with members of the opposite sex was an added burden. America is not a village society in India in which only a limited number of boys and girls will ever be potential mates for each other, all the families know each other, the roles of the sexes are exclusively defined, and common societal obligations outweigh personal desires. America is a much more complicated social scene, and if ISKCON children enter that world, how are they going to be prepared for it? As it was, we often became sneaky and hypocritical, because most of us did find ways to at least talk to girls. We all went through many tribulations and embarrassments, boys and girls alike, when we were finally exposed to the wider world. Again, I don't have an easy answer, but this is a difficulty that all ISKCON teenagers will face and that ISKCON parents and educators in the past did not understand, predict, or plan for in any way.

I have been criticizing my *gurukula* upbringing, but now I would like to share what I think was valuable about it. Of course, from a "Krishna Conscious" perspective there is no question of the priceless value of even the most minor association with Krishna, His holy name, and His devotees, and the fortunate opportunity to begin this rare human life as a devotee. However, I would like to address the *gurukula* experience from the perspective of someone who has made the choice to enter the secular world, to become sometimes more American than devotee, and to reject some of the spiritual values I was taught, at least for a time. In other words, what do I now feel I gained from *gurukula*, which is essentially a religious education, even though I have left the religious movement?

The most obvious thing is that *gurukula* made us tough. Especially those of us who went to school in India felt that, since we'd survived that experience, we could survive anything—sleep anywhere, make do with whatever—and not let it get to us. An example of this is when I joined the Civil Air Patrol, which is a U.S. Air Force auxiliary search-and-rescue organization that teenagers can join. One summer I attended their eased-down basic training and wilderness survival camp held for ten days in the Pocono Mountains of Pennsylvania. Many of the other teenagers couldn't take being yelled at or missed their parents, but none of that even fazed me. Even the real military training I later received never really fazed me: I knew how to obey orders, and I knew how to make do with few comforts. I had been yelled at by people who I had seen hit kids with impunity, and I knew the drill instructor couldn't do that (not to speak of the older kids in the Civil Air Patrol, who were simply imitating drill instructors). A lot of us *gurukulis* felt and feel this pride, and it is largely a result of the hardships we faced. Actually, many of our "austerities" were just the result of a standard of living that is fairly normal for countries like India. In many ways, we had received an education in how much of the world lives. I personally consider that experience something valuable as I now live in the relative luxury of the United States. This is not to deny that it was sometimes terrifying (for example, when I was seriously ill in a hospital in Mathura) and that I was often homesick, and one certainly can't overlook the overwhelming context of abuses. But I survived it, and I believe I'm stronger for it.

Another thing I treasure from my upbringing is music, especially drumming. Without realizing it at the time, I had an excellent foundation for becoming a musician. Every day I played *mridanga* drum and sang in the *kirtanas*. Skills like that become second nature the more they are practiced in the cruchial years of development before the age of twelve, and while artistic development is a life-long quest, I have been blessed with a head start in certain skills. It is one of my greatest pleasures to play music with people, and I can thank my upbringing for opening that door for me. Many of my peers, too, find pleasure and fulfillment in similar artistic endeavors, like dancing, writing, fashion, and cooking, the skills and inspiration for which they first learned in *gurukula*.

I mentioned above the vast difference, almost complete opposition, between ISKCON culture and American culture. As an adolescent living in America after leaving *gurukula* I found this difference very embarrassing. I had no knowledge or any idea about how to relate to American culture. I had none of the "culture-specific" skills, and I basically went on a crash course. I watched hours of television, rented hundreds of movies, listened to top-40 radio, made my first nondevotee friends in the Civil Air Patrol, got a job, and eventually attended the local community college. I felt very lonely and really just wanted to be a normal American teenager, to fit in somehow, like any adolescent wants to.[12] At the time I was resentful that my parents had joined the movement and raised me so differently, and I remember thinking that if I wasn't able to get into college and become a naval officer so that I could fly jet planes, if my upbringing had ruined my chances at this dream, I would hold a lifelong grudge against my parents and ISKCON.

Fifteen years later I don't hold that grudge at all, and what is more, in many ways I have come to treasure the differences that I once despised. Even if I don't always apply them or have complete faith in them, the beliefs and ideas that were my first philosophy give me ways to analyze the world and to try to understand life that most Americans cannot conceive. The understanding of the soul and how it transmigrates, the interactions of the modes of nature,[13] the philosophy of simultaneous oneness with and difference from God, the intricacies of developing a loving relationship with God, and the wealth of stories that are certainly among the world's greatest literature are all gifts of my upbringing. Now that I'm not so frightened to be different and am as comfortable living in American culture as I used to be in ISKCON culture, these differences are almost what define me. This tension between the two and this almost dance I do on the edges of both is in many ways who I am. I don't really want to become all American, but nor do I want to be a full-time devotee.

This straddling of cultures is not unique to *gurukulis*. I recently read Pollock and Reken's book *The Third Culture Kid Experience: Growing Up Among Worlds*,[14] in which they discuss the challenges and benefits of growing up in more than one culture. It was a great comfort, not so much because it gave me a lot of new information—it was like reading an excellent presentation of many of my own disorganized and scattered thoughts—but because I realized that many people around the world straddle cultures the way we do and it seems we all have similar issues. In a way I already sensed this. My best friends in life have almost always been other "third culture kids," from my former classmates in *gurukula,* with whom I feel the strongest bonds, even when I don't see them for years, to a college roommate who attended high school in Ecuador, to a girl-friend who grew up in East Berlin until she was fifteen years old. Without going into the details, I think that even if *gurukulis* later reject the religious and spiritual aspects of their upbringing, we can still find value in it if we manage to meet the challenges and embrace the benefits of being "third culture kids."

Very often devotees present their arguments based on quotations from Shrila Prabhupada and argue from within the philosophy of Krishna Consciousness. Here I have just given my opinions on *gurukula* based on my own experiences. However, the essential aspect of *gurukula* is the instructions of the guru (the very term *gurukula* means "[living in] the residence of the guru"). In that respect, the instructions of Shrila Prabhupada will remain a guiding principle of ISKCON *gurukula* education, and I think it is as fundamental an American right as any other that ISKCON can pursue this religious vision, as long as it doesn't break the law. However, as I argued in the beginning, this spiritual pursuit must be done with practical intelligence, wisdom, kindness, and love, principles that Shrila Prabhupada himself expressed but that many of his followers have failed to apply.

A former schoolmate of mine has written eloquently of his loving personal exchanges with Shrila Prabhupada—what he called Prabhupada's magic—contrasted with his sufferings in *gurukula.* Somehow or another, in the history of *gurukula* and ISKCON at large, such loving personal relationships were sorely lacking. Too often, instead of cultivating loving relationships, with all the give and take, compassion, and understanding they involve, those in authority have had destructive or even abusive personal relationships with those in their care, or they have been impersonal in their dealings by expecting every child or every devotee to fit in the same box. I hope that with practical intelligence, and by developing their loving personal relationships, the devotees of ISKCON, especially the leaders and parents, can avoid the terrible blunders of the past and realize the glorious potential one hopes Krishna Consciousness can help realize.

NOTES

This paper is a condensed version of a presentation at the 2001 Vaishnava Family and Youth Conference. The full text appears in *ISKCON Communications Journal* Vol. 9, No. 1, September 2001.

1. For example, *Bhagavad Gita* 9:30–31.
2. *Sankirtana* is the term used in the Gaudiya tradition to refer to the public chanting of the Hare Krishna mantra. By extension, the term came to be used in ISKCON to also refer to the distribution of books and soliciting of donations that accompanied

this public chanting, but was soon used just for the collection of money irrespective of context. ISKCON's internal critics coined the term *scam-kirtana* to refer to the duplicitous side of such fund raising.

3. "When the boys and girls are ten years old, they should be separated. At that time, special care should be taken, because once they become victims of sexual misbehavior, their lives are spoiled" (Letter to Satsvarupa dasa Goswami, 4 October 1973, quoted in Bhurijana Dasa, *The Art of Teaching: Raising Our Children in Krsna Consciousness* [Vrindavana: VIHE, 1995], 366).

4. "ISKCON's leaders must be careful about how they interpret organizational problems. . . . They must not fall prey to the individualizing of what are fundamentally social problems" ("Analyzing ISKCON for Twenty-Five Years: A Personal Reflection," *ISKCON Communications Journal* 8 [1] [June 2000]).

5. The term "karmi'" is used in ISKCON to refer to nondevotees who work for themselves rather than dedicating everything to Krishna.

6. For example, "Keep them always happy in Krsna consciousness, and do not force or punish, or they will get the wrong idea" (Letter to Satsvarupa Das, 16 February 1972, quoted in Bhurijana Das, *The Art of Teaching*, 373).

7. "Child Abuse in the Hare Krishna Movement: 1971–1986." *ISKCON Communications Journal* 6 (1) (June 1998).

8. In ISKCON jargon, "shaving up" refers to new male recruits shaving their heads before "moving in" to the temples, where they are encouraged not to "bloop," or return to the secular world.

9. For example: "They should have knowledge of Sanskrit, English, a little mathematics, history, geography, that's all" (Letter to Aniruddha Das, 16 February 1972, quoted in Bhurijana Das, *The Art of Teaching*, 376); or: "Their academic education should consist of learning a little mathematics and being able to read and write well. No universities. Higher education they get from our books" (Letter to Chaya Devi Dasi, 16 February 1972, also quoted in *Art of Teaching*, 365).

10. See Ravindra Svarupa Das, "Cleaning House and Cleaning Hearts: Reform and Renewal in ISKCON," *ISKCON Communications Journal* 3 (1) (Jan.-June 1994) (pt. 1) and *ISKCON Communications Journal* 4 (2) (July-Dec. 1994). A revised version of this paper is included in this volume.

11. *Maya*, in traditional Hindu thought, refers to the power of illusion that causes the pure soul to misidentify with its temporary covering of the body, and, by extension, the relationships associated with the body such as family, and children, etc. Too much attachment to such relationships is perceived as detrimental to spiritual progress.

12. See E. Burke Rochford Jr., "Education and Collective Identity: Public Schooling of Hare Krishna Youths," in *Children in New Religions*, ed. Susan J. Palmer and Charlotte E. Hardman (New Brunswick: Rutgers University Press, 1999) for more details of the difficulties devotee children faced when entering the wider world.

13. All aspects of human life and psychology, in traditional Hindu thought, are influenced by three *gunas*, "modes of nature" (see *Bhagavad Gita*, chapters 14, 17, and 18).

14. David C. Pollock and Ruth E. Van Reken, *The Third Culture Kid Experience: Growing Up Among Worlds* (Yarmouth, ME: Intercultural Press, 2001).

[21]

RACE, MONARCHY, AND GENDER

Bhaktivedanta Swami's Social Experiment

EKKEHARD LORENZ

AN INTERNET SEARCH FOR THE STRING *"varnashram dharma"* produces more than 450 matches. Today, 50 years after Bhaktivedanta Swami mentioned *varnashram* for the first time in a public speech, members of the Hare Krishna movement continue to cherish his vision of a perfect society. The majority of matches refer to the sites of organizations that profess allegiance to the teachings of Bhaktivedanta Swami. One such organization, the Bhaktivedanta Archives, introduces their latest book, *Speaking About Varnashram*, and states:

> Criticizing a modern society based on industrialism, materialism, and a callous disregard for the workers who support it, Shrila Prabhupada calls for a spiritualized social structure. Citing *Bhagavad-gita*, he advocates *varnashram dharma*, a social institution in which people gain spiritual satisfaction and spiritual advancement by doing their daily work as an offering to God.[1]

Another Web site dedicated to the propagation of Bhaktivedanta Swami's teachings mentions how *varnashram dharma* can bring about peace and happiness:

> There is a natural system of social organization which can bring about a peaceful society where everyone is happy. This system is described in the timeless Vedic literature of India and it is called Varnashram dharma.[2]

Apart from mainstream ISKCON, organizations such as the General Headquarters, the Florida Vedic College, and the Bhaktivedanta College all offer extensive *varnashram* study materials compiled from the teachings of Bhaktivedanta Swami. The Florida Vedic College offers a degree "Master of Arts in Vedic Philosophy," which includes graduate-level studies of *varnashram dharma*,[3] while the Bhaktivedanta College offers credits for its courses in *varnashram dharma* and "Applied Varnashram Studies."[4]

While there is no consensus within present-day ISKCON regarding what exactly *varnashram dharma* is, many trust that introducing *varnashram* principles would improve the health of the movement. The General Headquarters,[5] for example, argues that Bhaktivedanta Swami's mission can only be accomplished by means of vigorous propagation of his *varnashram* teachings. They especially call for strict implementation of Bhaktivedanta Swami's teachings regarding women, family, and sexuality in a future Vedic society.[6] Many faculty members of the above-mentioned Bhaktivedanta College are also leading members of the General Headquarters. Others, less radical, believe that most of the problems plaguing today's ISKCON can be traced to its members' failure to apply *varnashram dharma* principles in their own lives. While they do not promote the (re)introduction of *varnashram dharma* for the entire world, they call to attention Bhaktivedanta Swami's instructions to organize ISKCON itself as a *varnashram dharma* society, so that it might serve as an attractive model. In a recent paper discussing difficulties in the implementation of *varnashram dharma* in ISKCON, William H. Deadwyler, a leading member of ISKCON's Governing Body Commission (GBC), states that the foremost problem he and his colleagues are facing is that ISKCON "has no brain."[7] Like the General Headquarters and the Bhaktivedanta College, he too perceives the solution as an increased and systematic study of the books and teachings of Bhaktivedanta Swami.[8]

Before exploring in detail what Bhaktivedanta Swami had to say about *varnashram dharma*, it might be in order to quote a general definition. A. K. Majumdar defines *varnashram dharma* as: "rules of conduct enjoined on a man because he belongs to a particular caste and also to a particular stage of life, such as, 'a Brahmin *brahmacharin* should carry a staff of *palasha* tree.'"[9] What exactly did Bhaktivedanta Swami teach about *varnashram dharma*, that up to this day many of his followers believe that its principles can turn the world—or at least ISKCON communities—into a better place?

THE LOWEST OF MANKIND

The earliest available reference to *varnashram dharma* occurs in a speech, "Solution of Present Crisis by Bhagwat Geeta," delivered by Bhaktivedanta Swami in Madras in 1950, fifteen years before he founded his ISKCON movement in the West.[10] Listing the causes of what he refers to as a crisis, he mentions among other things, "No training of human civilization. Varnashram Dharma."[11] Bhaktivedanta Swami's idea of such training was first concretely outlined in a series of articles, "The Lowest of Mankind," "Purity of Conduct," and "Standard Morality." Published in Delhi between 1956 and 1958, they appeared in *Back to Godhead*, his bimonthly magazine that he called "an instrument for training the mind and educating humanity to rise up to Divinity in the plane of the spirit soul."[12]

In "The Lowest of Mankind" he declares that 99.9 percent of all humans are morally despicable (Sanskrit: *naradhama*), because they do not follow the regulations of *varnashram dharma*:

> It is the duty of the guardians of children to revive the divine consciousness dormant in them. The ten processes of reformatory ceremonies as enjoined in the *Manu-Smriti*, which is the guide to religious principles, are meant for reviving God consciousness in the system of Varna Ashram. Nothing is strictly followed now in any part of the world and therefore 99.9 percent populations are Naradhama.[13]

Referring to the *garbhadhan samskara*, which he considers to be the most essential of the aforementioned ten ceremonies, he argues in "Purity of Conduct" that Hinduism lost its special significance since *varnashram dharma* is no longer followed:

> The *Garbhadhan Samskara* is also a checking method for restricting bastard children. We do not wish to go into the details of the *Garbhadhan Samskara* or any other such reformatory processes but if need be we can definitely prove that since we have stopped observing these reformatory processes—the whole Hindu society has lost its special significance in the matter of social and religious dealings.[14]

And in "Standard Morality" he states that the *varnashram* system "is schemed for fulfilling the mission of human life by suitable division of departmental activities"[15]—a reference to *varnas*.

ISKCON SHALL SAVE THE WORLD

After 1965, when the International Society for Krishna Consciousness was founded, the need to reintroduce *varnashram dharma* worldwide became a central and recurring theme in Bhaktivedanta Swami's books and talks:

> The Krishna consciousness movement, however, is being propagated all over the world to reestablish the *varnashram-dharma* system and thus save human society from gliding down to hellish life.[16]

> In order to rectify this world situation, all people should be trained in Krishna consciousness and act in accordance with the *varnashram* system.[17]

> The Krishna consciousness movement is therefore very much eager to reintroduce the *varnashram* system into human society so that those who are bewildered or less intelligent will be able to take guidance from qualified Brahmins.[18]

Bhaktivedanta Swami apparently believed that all problems would be solved, the world situation would be rectified, and humanity would be saved from hellish life if only people could be made to accept guidance from his ISKCON Brahmins. Declaring that "without *varnashram-dharma*, materialistic activities constitute animal life,"[19] he repeatedly identifies *varna sankara*, mixed-caste people—or "unwanted population," as he would also call them—as a key factor contributing to contemporary world problems:

> *Varna-sankara.* There is no *varnashram*; therefore all the children, they are *varna-sankara*. And as soon as there is *varna-sankara* population, the world becomes hell. Therefore we are trying to check—"No illicit sex"—to stop this *varna-sankara*.[20]

> There are so many talks about to keep the *varnashram* intact for peaceful condition of the society, and the modern problem, the overpopulation.... So there is no question of overpopulation. The question is *varna-sankara*. *Varna-sankara*, that is the problem.[21]

But though he often declared that his movement was meant to reestablish *varnashram dharma*, Bhaktivedanta Swami occasionally admitted that it was no longer possible to do so: "Nobody can revive now the lost system of *varnashram dharma* to its original position for so many reasons."[22] "Nor is it now possible to reestablish the institutional function in the present context of social, political and economic revolution."[23]

THE PROGRESSIVE MARCH OF THE CIVILIZATION
OF THE ARYANS

The Sanskrit word *aryah* is not uncommon in the stanzas of the *Bhagavata Purana*. It is mainly used in the sense of "noble" or "respectable," but never as a racial designation. Bhaktivedanta Swami, however, speaks extensively about "the Aryans"—at least twenty-five of his purports and over a hundred lectures and conversations contain lengthy elaborations on the topic. He places all those whom he calls "non-Aryan" in a category similar to his "unwanted population," thus dividing humans into two groups: a large group of *varna sankara* and non-Aryans on one side, and a small group of Aryans, i.e., those who follow *varnashram,* on the other: "Those who traditionally follow these principles are called Aryans, or progressive human beings."[24] "The Vedic way of life," he writes, "is the progressive march of the civilization of the Aryans."[25] "In the history of the human race, the Aryan family is considered to be the most elevated community in the world."[26]

Most of Bhaktivedanta Swami's statements define "Aryan" in social, religious, and cultural terms. However, in more than one fifth of his statements he clearly describes or defines them in racial terms:

The Aryan family is distributed all over the world and is known as Indo-Aryan.[27]

The Aryans are white. But here, this side, due to climatic influence, they are a little tan. Indians are tan but they are not black. But Aryans are all white. And the non-Aryans, they are called black. Yes.[28]

Dravidian culture. Dravida. They are non-Aryans. Just like these Africans, they are not Aryans . . . Shudras, black. So if a Brahmin becomes black, then he's not accepted as Brahmin.[29]

On other occasions Bhaktivedanta Swami presents a mixture of both racial and sociocultural views regarding Aryans, such as when he appealed to his young western audiences:

So we all belong to the Aryan family. Historical reference is there, Indo-European family. So Aryan stock was on the central Asia. Some of them migrated to India. Some of them migrated to Europe. And from Europe you have come. So we belong to the Aryan family, but we have lost our knowledge. So we have become non-Aryan practically.[30]

You French people, you are also Aryan family, but the culture is lost now. So this Krishna consciousness movement is actually reviving the original Aryan culture. Bharata. We are all inhabitants of Bharatavarsha, but as we lost our culture, it became divided.[31]

So on the whole, the conclusion is that the Aryans spread in Europe also, and the Americans, they also spread from Europe. So the intelligent class of human being, they belong to the Aryans, Aryan family. Just like Hitler claimed that he belonged to the Aryan family. Of course, they belonged to the Aryan families.[32]

SCIENTIFIC ARYANS

Bhaktivedanta Swami used the expressions "Vedic civilization," "Aryan civilization," and "*varnashram-dharma*" as practically synonymous,[33] and said that the purpose of his movement was "to make the people Aryan."[34] On numerous occasions he stated that this message was aimed at the intelligentsia:

This movement is meant for intelligent class of men, those who have reason and logic to understand things in a civilized way, and who are open-hearted to receive things as they are.[35]

It is not that everyone will be able to understand this philosophy. Still if some intelligent section of the human society understands it, there will be tremendous change in the atmosphere.[36]

It is not a sentimental movement. It is meant for the learned scholars and highly situated person.[37]

Intelligent class of men will take this *sankirtana* movement for his spiritual elevation of life. It is a fact, it is scientific, it is authorized.[38]

That *varnashram dharma* was something ancient and scientific turns out to be also the opinion of Kedarnath Datta Bhaktivinoda (father of Bhaktivedanta Swami's guru), who, almost one hundred years earlier, had introduced the term *vaijnanika varnashram*. In *Hindu Encounter with Modernity*, Shukavak N. Dasa writes: "The system of *varnas* and *ashrams* that Bhaktivinoda refers to is not the traditional caste system of his time. In his opinion the existing caste system was only a remnant of the ancient and scientific *vaijnanika-varnashram* system."[39] Bhaktivinoda's son Bimal Prasad, who later founded a Vaishnava organization in India and became known as Bhaktisiddhanta Saraswati, or Siddhanta Saraswati, explained his movement, the Gaudiya Math, in the following manner:

This institution has undertaken the task of re-establishing the system of *daiva-varnashram* for reinstating such persons in the proper functioning of true Brahmins as have forgotten the principle of the *dharma* of jivas as servitors to Vishnavas [*sic*] and have been consequently running after the function of Kshatriyas, Vaishyas, etc.[40]

Countless statements in the books, lectures, and conversations of Bhaktivedanta Swami—himself a disciple of Bhaktisiddhanta Saraswati—suggest that he shared the views of his direct predecessors. He too believed that in bygone ages a divine and scientific social system had existed in India, and like Bhaktisiddhanta Saraswati, he too founded a movement whose express mission it was to reestablish what he often referred to as the "perfectional form of human civilization," *varnashram dharma*.

VARNASHRAM IN THE BHAKTIVEDANTA PURPORTS

Unlike the earlier *Bhagavata* commentators, who hardly ever, and if at all, then only briefly, mention *varnashram* in their glosses, Bhaktivedanta Swami gives this topic great attention. Of the 113 purports in which he discusses it in his *Shrimad Bhagavatam*, only 13 coincide with occasions where earlier commentators interpret certain words as referring to *varnashram*.[41] Most of Bhaktivedanta Swami's purports that discuss *varnashram* appear in a context where the topic had not been mentioned either in the text of the *Bhagavata Purana* itself or in any of the commentaries that he is known to have used.[42]

There are also cases in which Bhaktivedanta Swami backs his *varnashram* elaborations with references to earlier commentators that factually find no support in their original glosses. Here is just one example: "According to Viraraghava Acharya, such protection means organizing the citizens into the specific divisions of the four *varnas* and four *ashrams*. It is very difficult to rule citizens in a kingdom without organizing this *varnashram-dharma*."[43] Viraraghava, however, does not mention *varnashram dharma* in his commentary to this particular verse or in his commentaries to the directly preceding or following verses.[44]

In Bhaktivedanta Swami's written commentaries, the Bhaktivedanta purports, to the *Bhagavad Gita*, the *Bhagavata Purana*, and the *Chaitanya Charitamrita,* there are all together three hundred explicit statements about *varnashram dharma*. These can be divided into five groups, namely statements about the status, purpose, restrictions, structure, and history of *varnashram dharma*.

The largest group, comprising 35 percent of all statements, concerns the status of *varnashram dharma*. Typical expressions in this category state that *varnashram dharma* is:

the perfectional form of human civilization.[45]
the beginning of human civilization.[46]
the natural system for civilized life.[47]
the beginning of actual human life.[48]
the beginning of the distinction between human life and animal life.[49]
the most scientific culture.[50]
a religion.[51]

Bhaktivedanta Swami's statements about the purpose of *varnashram dharma* form the second-largest group with 32 percent. Statements typical for this category express that its purpose is:

to protect women from being misled into adultery.[52]
to train the follower to adopt the vow of celibacy.[53]
to train everyone so that the money is spent only for good causes.[54]
to turn a crude man into a pure devotee of the Lord.[55]
to prevent human society from being hellish.[56]
to make sure that the good population would prevail.[57]
to uplift all to the highest platform of spiritual realization.[58]
to satisfy the Supreme Lord.[59]

The third category, with 16 percent of all statements, deals with rules and restrictions imposed by *varnashram dharma*:

One has to retire from family life in middle age.[60]
Small boys after five years of age are sent to become *brahmachari* at the
    guru's *ashram*.[61]
The *varnashram-dharma* scheme forbids or restricts association with
    women.[62]
A human being is expected to follow the rules and regulations of *varna*
    and *ashram*.[63]

The fourth category (14 percent) deals with the structure of, and people in, *varnashram dharma*:

The scientific system of *varnashram-dharma* divides the human life into
    four divisions of occupation and four orders of life.[64]
The irresponsible life of sense enjoyment was unknown to the children of
    the followers of the *varnashram* system.[65]

The fifth category, with only 3 percent of all statements, treats *varnashram dharma* from a historical perspective:

Indian civilization on the basis of the four *varnas* and *ashrams* deteriorated because of her dependency on foreigners, or those who did not follow the civilization of *varnashram*. Thus the *varnashram* system has now been degraded into the caste system.[66]

"WE ARE TRYING TO TRAIN SOME BRAHMINS TO GUIDE HUMAN SOCIETY"

In all of his books as well as throughout his lectures and conversations, Bhaktivedanta Swami shared his vision of establishing *varnashram dharma* worldwide. He was convinced that it was a practical sociopolitical structure that modern governments could implement, and that his movement would facilitate this by creating qualified Brahmins through some sort of suitable training or education:

> At present this Krishna consciousness movement is training Brahmins. If the administrators take our advice and conduct the state in a Krishna conscious way, there will be an ideal society throughout the world.[67]

> We are therefore creating Brahmins. We are not creating Shudras. Shudras are already there.[68]

> They have no brain how to make the society peaceful and prosperous. They are Shudras. They have no intelligence. There is necessity of creating Brahmins and Vaishnava. This movement is meant for that purpose.[69]

> We train them in austerities and penances and recognize them as Brahmins by awarding them sacred threads.[70]

> There is a great need of Brahmins. Therefore, in the Krishna consciousness movement, we are trying to train some Brahmins to guide human society. Because at present there is a scarcity of Brahmins, the brain of human society is lost.[71]

While Bhaktivedanta Swami repeatedly spoke or wrote about training that would produce Brahmins, he delivered only very few concrete instructions about what exactly such training should consist of. When asked by a disciple how a Brahmin should be trained, he replied:

> He must be truthful, he must control the senses, control the mind. . . . He must be tolerant. He should not be agitated in trifle matters. . . . He must be always clean. Three times he must take bath at least. All the clothing, all, everything is clean. This is brahminical training. And then he must

know all what is what, knowledge, and practical application, and firm faith in Krishna. This is Brahmin.[72]

On another occasion he wrote to a disciple in India about his vision of a *varnashram* college. He thought that in such a college he could produce certified Brahmins who would then receive degrees from a local university. But in this letter too, there are no details about the training itself, only a list of desired end results:

> As desired by you, I can immediately take up the task of opening a center there and to open a varna-asram college there affiliated by the university. In this college we shall train up pure Brahmins, (qualified Brahmins), Kshatriyas and Vaishyas. That is the injunction of *Bhagavad-gita*. . . . This system should be introduced. They must sit for proper examination after being trained. So, if we start a varna-asram college in terms of *Bhagavad-gita* instructions and approved by *Shrimad-bhagavatam*, why the university will not give degree to a qualified person as approved Brahmin.[73]

"KSHATRIYAS, THEY HAVE TO LEARN HOW TO KILL"

The above letter shows that Bhaktivedanta Swami not only wanted a Brahmin training but also had plans for *kshatriya* and *vaishya* training. Training Brahmins appears to have occupied the highest rank on his priority scale, but training *kshatriyas* was definitely important to him. However, the type of *kshatriyas* that he most often talked about were kings and rulers rather than common soldiers or administrators:

> A Kshatriya should not be a coward, and he should not be nonviolent; to rule over the country he has to act violently.[74]

When asked by a disciple how the *kshatriya* training in the planned *varnashram* college was to be organized, he replied:

> Just like material subject matter, Kshatriya, or the Brahmins, Kshatriya, as they are described in the *Bhagavad Gita*, what are the symptoms of Brahmin, what is the symptoms of Kshatriya. The Kshatriyas should be taught how to fight also. There will be military training. There will be training how to kill.[75]

Kshatriya students in the ISKCON *varnashram* college were to practice killing:

Just like Kshatriyas, they have to learn how to kill. So practically, they should go to the forest and kill some animal. And if he likes, he can eat also.[76]

There is no single instance where Bhaktivedanta Swami speaks about *kshatriya* training without mentioning killing. While he might not have considered it to be the most important aspect of that education, he does stress this aspect:

You can kill one boar. Some disturbing elements, you can kill. You can kill some tiger. Like that. Learn to kill. No nonviolence. Learn to kill. Here also, as soon as you'll find, the Kshatriya, a thief, a rogue, unwanted element in the society, kill him. That's all. Finish. Kill him. *Bas.* Finished.[77]

It is not that because the Kshatriyas were killing by bows and arrows formerly, you have to continue that. That is another foolishness. If you have got . . . If you can kill easily by guns, take that gun.[78]

All the royal princes were trained up how to kill.[79]

The killing is there, but the Brahmin is not going to kill personally. . . . Only the Kshatriyas. The Kshatriyas should be so trained up.[80]

A Kshatriya, he is expert in the military science, how to kill. So the killing art is there. You cannot make it null and void by advocating nonviolence. No. That is required. Violence is also a part of the society.[81]

"MONARCHY I HAVE SAID, BECAUSE THE POPULATION ARE ASSES"

Bhaktivedanta Swami often spoke about the ideal monarch: "So the kings were very severe to punish unwanted social elements,"[82] and from his many outspoken statements against democracy it appears that he envisioned a return to monarchy:

Nowadays it is constitutional, democratic government. The king has no power. But this is not good for the people. The democracy is a farce. At least, I do not like it.[83]

The so-called democracy under party politics is nonsense. Monarchy . . . I have said. That day I was in remarking that "This democracy is the government of the asses," because the population are asses and they vote another ass to be head of the government.[84]

On some occasions Bhaktivedanta Swami would denounce democracy as "de-moncracy" or "demon-crazy." Referring to Indira and Rajiv Gandhi, he asks: "She and her son are the destiny of India? A woman and a debauch? They can do whatever they like. It's a farce condition. That so-called democracy is non-sense demoncracy."[85] Two months later he asserts that democracy had not yet arrived in India:

> This democracy is a demon-crazy. It has no value. It is simply waste of time and effort and no feeling, demon-crazy. I do not know who intro-duced this. In India still there is no demon-crazy. Indian king always. Everyone is taking part in politics. What is this nonsense? It is meant for the Kshatriyas. They can fight and defend.[86]

In a lecture in London in 1973, Bhaktivedanta Swami told his audience that his movement could help turn the British monarchy into some sort of Krishna conscious rule:

> So again the monarchs, where there is monarchy, little, at least show of monarchy, just like here in England there is, actually if the monarch be-comes Krishna conscious, actually becomes representative of Krishna, then the whole face of the kingdom will change. That is required. Our Kr-ishna consciousness movement is for that purpose. We don't very much like this so-called democracy.[87]

In numerous purports in his *Shrimad Bhagavatam* he describes the advantages a *varnashram*-based monarchy would have over democratic governments:

> Monarchy is better than democracy because if the monarchy is very strong the regulative principles within the kingdom are upheld very nicely.[88]

> In such dealings, a responsible monarchy is better than a so-called dem-ocratic government in which no one is responsible to mitigate the griev-ances of the citizens, who are unable to personally meet the supreme ex-ecutive head. In a responsible monarchy the citizens had no grievances against the government, and even if they did, they could approach the king directly for immediate satisfaction.[89]

> When monarchy ruled throughout the world, the monarch was actually directed by a board of Brahmins and saintly persons.[90]

> The modern democratic system cannot be exalted in this way because the leaders elected strive only for power and have no sense of responsibility.

In a monarchy, a king with a prestigious position follows the great deeds of his forefathers.[91]

Gradually the democratic government is becoming unfit for the needs of the people, and therefore some parties are trying to elect a dictator. A dictatorship is the same as a monarchy, but without a trained leader. Actually people will be happy when a trained leader, whether a monarch or a dictator, takes control of the government and rules the people according to the standard regulations of the authorized scriptures.[92]

Statements like the last one, in which Bhaktivedanta Swami declares that he favors even dictatorship above democracy, are by no means rare:

So monarchy or dictatorship is welcome. Now the Communists, they want dictatorship. That is welcome, provided that particular dictator is trained like Maharaja Yudhishthira.[93]

I like this position, dictatorship. Personally I like this.[94]

Bhaktivedanta Swami's appreciation for dictatorship is further underlined by his generally approving remarks about Hitler. While he often mentions Hitler to give an example of materialistic scheming, he nevertheless calls him a hero and a gentleman:

Why should our temples support or denounce Hitler. If somebody says something in this connection it must simply be some sentiment. We have nothing to do with politics.[95]

So these English people, they were very expert in making propaganda. They killed Hitler by propaganda. I don't think Hitler was so bad man.[96]

Hitler knew it [the atom bomb] . . . everything, but he did not like to do it. . . . He was gentleman. But these people are not gentlemen. He knew it perfectly well. He said that "I can smash the whole world, but I do not use that weapon." The Germans already discovered. But out of humanity they did not use it.[97]

Sometimes he becomes a great hero—just like Hiranyakashipu and Kamsa or, in the modern age, Napoleon or Hitler. The activities of such men are certainly very great, but as soon as their bodies are finished, everything else is finished.[98]

Therefore Hitler killed these Jews. They were financing against Germany. Otherwise he had no enmity with the Jews. . . . And they were supplying.

They want interest money—"Never mind against our country." Therefore Hitler decided, "Kill all the Jews."[99]

VAISHYAS

Bhaktivedanta Swami did not have much to say about *vaishyas,* or the mercantile class, as he would often call them. "Vaishyas should be trained how to
give protection to the cows, how to till the field and grow food," was his standard comment regarding their place in a *varnashram* society.[100] When asked
how *vaishyas* should be trained in his *varnashram* college and whether they
should learn how to do business, he replied:

> We are not going to open mills and factories and . . . No. We are not going
> to do that. That is Shudra business. The real business is that you produce
> enough food grains, as much as possible, and you eat and distribute.
> That's all. This is business. He does not require any so high technical ed-
> ucation. Anyone can till the ground and grow food.[101]

Two years later, in a conversation with Indian politicians, he restates his opinion that *vaishyas* do not require education:

> So therefore I say that there must be educational institution for training
> Brahmin, Kshatriya especially. And Vaishyas, they do not require any ac-
> ademical area. . . . They can learn simply by associating with another
> Vaishya.[102]

When talking about *vaishyas,* Bhaktivedanta Swami often brought up the
following rule, apparently designed by himself: "Kshatriyas and Vaishyas are
therefore especially advised to give in charity at least fifty percent of their accumulated wealth."[103] This 50-percent charity tax might have been an early attempt to inspire followers not living in the temple to financially support his
movement:[104]

> The householder should earn money by business or by profession and
> spend at least fifty percent of his income to spread Krishna consciousness;
> twenty-five percent he can spend for his family, and twenty-five percent
> he should save to meet emergencies.[105]

> *Grihasthas,* those who are in householder life outside, are expected to con-
> tribute fifty percent of their income for our society, keep twenty-five per-
> cent for family, and keep twenty-five percent for personal emergencies.[106]

The system did not become the norm in ISKCON during Bhaktivedanta Swami's time, probably because most members preferred to remain in the temples, even after getting married, rather than practice "householder life outside." And after his death, when many moved out of the American temples, the 50-percent rule was practically never followed.

SHUDRAS

Regarding the question whether *shudras* should be counted among the Aryans, Bhaktivedanta Swami made conflicting statements: "Shudras means non-Aryan. And Aryans, they are divided into three higher castes."[107] "Aryans are divided into four castes."[108] His remarks regarding training for *shudras* are also contradictory. When asked what kind of training they should receive in his *varnashram* college, he replied:

> "Do this." That's all. Yes. That is also training, to become obedient. Because people are not obedient. . . . So obedience also require training. If you have no intelligence, if you cannot do anything independently, just be obedient to the other, higher three classes. That is Shudra. . . . Little arts and crafts can be trained up to the Shudras.[109]

On a different occasion, however, he asserts that *shudras* do not require any training at all:

> Shudras does not require any training. Shudra means no training. Ordinary worker class. Otherwise other three, especially two, namely the Brahmins and Kshatriyas, they require very magnificent training.[110]

On the whole, Bhaktivedanta Swami's attitude toward *shudras* appears to be rather negative. While he depicts the other three *varnas* in positive or at least neutral terms, his description of *shudras* sounds harsh, spiteful, and condescending. Most of his remarks begin with the words "Shudra(s) means," typically followed by:

> ordinary people; the laborer class; once-born; the lowest class of men; non-Aryan; worker; the black man; he must find out a master; one who has no education; almost animal; without any culture; fourth-class men; ordinary worker; dog; no intelligence, little better than animals; they do not know what is the aim of life, just like animal; just like a dog; he becomes disturbed; one who is dependent on others; they are ignorant rascals; unclean; equal to the animal; no training; fools, rascals.[111]

It is hard not to perceive racist undertones in many of Bhaktivedanta Swami's statements about *shudras*. According to his understanding, people of black or dark skin color, as well as native Americans, are *shudras*, third-class, degraded, and less intelligent:

> Shudras have no brain. In America also, the whole America once belonged to the Red Indians. Why they could not improve? The land was there. Why these foreigners, the Europeans, came and improved? So Shudras cannot do this. They cannot make any correction.[112]

> A first-class Rolls Royce car, and who is sitting there? A third-class negro. This is going on. You'll find these things in Europe and America. This is going on. A first-class car and a third-class negro. That's all.[113]

> But his bodily feature, he was a black man. The black man means Shudra. The Brahmin, Kshatriya, Vaishya, they were not black. But the Shudras were black.[114]

In the last statement Bhaktivedanta Swami is commenting on the passage "*nrpa-linga-dharam shudram*," from *Bhagavata Purana* 1.16.4. The verse mentions the evil spirit Kali, describing him as "a *shudra* having royal insignia." Neither the verse nor any of the earlier commentators mention that this personality should have been black. It looks like Bhaktivedanta Swami considered having black skin color and being evil to be closely related features. He certainly considered black people to be ugly: "Such action of the cupid is going on even on the negroes and beastly societies who are all ugly looking in the estimation of the civilized nations."[115]

In February 1977, less than a year before his death, Bhaktivedanta Swami expressed regret about the fact that America had abolished slavery. In a room conversation, which later received the title "Varnashram System Must Be Introduced," he referred to African Americans as follows:

> Shudra is to be controlled only. They are never given to be freedom [*sic!*]. Just like in America. The blacks were slaves. They were under control. And since you have given them equal rights they are disturbing, most disturbing, always creating a fearful situation, uncultured and drunkards. What training they have got? They have got equal right? That is best, to keep them under control as slaves but give them sufficient food, sufficient cloth, not more than that. Then they will be satisfied.[116]

It was probably not at all unusual for Bhaktivedanta Swami to reason in these ways, for, as he had once told his disciples: "So the Kiratas, they were always slaves of the Aryans. The Aryan people used to keep slaves, but they were treating slaves very nicely."[117] And that the Kiratas were Africans he had explained many times: "Kirata means the black, the Africans."[118]

One wonders how Bhaktivedanta Swami, who repeatedly identified "the intelligent class of men" as the main target of his preaching, could present to them his program of turning back the clock by several centuries of human social thought and still expect it to be favorably received. Although he had often stressed that his message was meant for "the intelligent class of men," he had just as often declared that the entire world population were *shudras*: "At the present moment, they are Shudras or less than Shudras. They are not human beings. The whole population of the world."[119]

Bhaktivedanta also thought that he and his movement could take over some government and rule some part of the world: "However, in Kali-yuga, democratic government can be captured by Krishna conscious people. If this can be done, the general populace can be made very happy."[120] On other occasions he urged his followers not to take his message lightly. He promised doom and gloom to those who failed to accept and follow his instructions: "Don't think that Krishna consciousness is a joke, is a jugglery. It is the only remedy if you want to save yourself. Otherwise, you are doomed. Don't take it, I mean to say, as a joke. It is a fact."[121] He thought that his *varnashram* college could save the world, and that even the *shudras* would come to like it:

> Unless they take to Krishna consciousness, they'll not be saved. The *varnashram* college has to be established immediately. Everywhere, wherever we have got our center, a *varnashram* college should be established to train four divisions: one class, Brahmin; one class, Kshatriya; one class, Vaishya; and one class, Shudra. But everyone will be elevated to the spiritual platform by the spiritual activities which we have prescribed. There is no inconvenience, even for the Shudras.[122]

ASHRAM

In the classical *varnashram* system there are four *ashrams*, stages of life: *brahmacharin, grihastha, vanaprastha,* and *sannyasa* (celibate student, married householder, celibate recluse, and celibate mendicant). In Bhaktivedanta Swami's vision of establishing *varnashram dharma* worldwide, there was also a plan for what might be called "*ashram* training." However, throughout his books and lectures he focuses only on training for the first *ashram*: celibate student. While he does speak about *grihasthas,* he does not mention anywhere that they would require some sort of training, and the *vanaprastha* topic is virtually absent. The *sannyasa ashram* could in a way be seen as an extension of the celibate student status, but if one considers how freely Bhaktivedanta Swami turned his young male disciples without much preparation into fully ordained *sannyasins*, it seems that even *sannyasa* training was not much of a priority for him.

In contrast, there is an abundance of references to training young boys to become exemplary—lifelong, if possible—celibates. One thing that most of Bhaktivedanta Swami's statements regarding *brahmachari* training have in common is the emphasis on the need to start it as early as possible. He typically mentions five years of age as being the "Vedic standard," and consequently urges his disciples to send their children to his ISKCON *gurukula* schools at this age at the latest:

> Children at the age of five are sent to the *guru-kula,* or the place of the spiritual master, and the master trains the young boys in the strict discipline of becoming *brahmacharis.*[123]

> In the system of *varnashram-dharma,* which is the beginning of actual human life, small boys after five years of age are sent to become *brahmachari* at the guru's *ashram.*[124]

> The Krishna consciousness movement encourages marriage not for the satisfaction of the genitals but for the begetting of Krishna conscious children. As soon as the children are a little grown up, they are sent to our Gurukula school in Dallas, Texas, where they are trained to become fully Krishna conscious devotees. Many such Krishna conscious children are required, and one who is capable of bringing forth Krishna conscious offspring is allowed to utilize his genitals.[125]

Encouraging one of his disciples to send her son to the school in Dallas, he wrote:

> Recently I have visited our Gurukula school in Dallas, and I was quite satisfied how the boys and girls are being trained up to be ideal Vaishnavas. This training from an early age is important, and I also was fortunate to have received such training when I was a child.[126]

The above statement by Bhaktivedanta Swami, however, should not be misunderstood to mean that he too was sent away from home to a distant *gurukula* at the age of five. He attended a regular, secular day school in Calcutta. Still, he was convinced that it was beneficial for the children of his disciples to be separated early from their parents:

That is a good proposal, that parents should not accompany their children. Actually that is the *gurukula* system. The children should take complete protection of the Spiritual Master, and serve him and learn from him nicely. Just see how nicely your *brahmacharis* are working. They will go out in early morning and beg all day on the order of the guru. At night they will come home with a little rice and sleep without cover on the floor. And they think this work is very pleasant. If they are not spoiled by an artificial standard of sense gratification at an early age, children will turn out very nicely as sober citizens, because they have learned the real meaning of life. If they are trained to accept that austerity is very enjoyable then they will not be spoiled. So you organize everything in such a way that we can deliver these souls back to Krishna—this is our real work.[127]

Bhaktivedanta Swami never missed an opportunity to canvass for the Dallas *gurukula*. He taught that "real affection" for one's child means to send the child away from the parents to his Bhaktivedanta *gurukula*, if possible already at the age of four:

Rather, all of our children should go to Dallas when they are four and begin their training program there. In Dallas, they have full facility approved by me, I have personally seen that they are doing very nicely there. . . . But our affection is not simply sentimental, we offer our children the highest opportunity to become trained up in Krishna consciousness very early so as to assure their success in this life to go back to Godhead for sure. That is real affection, to make sure my child gets back to Godhead.[128]

Now we have gone to Dallas where I am visiting in the Gurukula school. It is very first class school and church and I think it is better than Los Angeles Temple. We have got very many children here and I am teaching the way how to give them instruction in Krishna consciousness. It is the first class place to send your son when he is old enough to come here.[129]

In this letter Bhaktivedanta Swami writes that he is personally teaching "the way how to instruct the children." He was apparently concerned to win the trust of the parents, and to assure them that things were conducted in responsible ways and under his supervision. Typical instructions regarding child education that he often gave to parents, teachers, and leaders are:

Therefore our young men must be trained at the earliest age to not be attached to so many things like the home, family, friendship, society, and nation. To train the innocent boy to be a sense gratifier at the early age when the child is actually happy in any circumstance is the greatest violence.[130]

You should give all freedom to your child for five years, and then, next ten years, you should be very strict, very strict, so that the child may be very much afraid.[131]

Unfortunately, this training is lacking all over the world. It is necessary for the leaders of the Krishna consciousness movement to start educational institutions in different parts of the world to train children, starting at the age of five years.[132]

Every mother, like Suniti, must take care of her son and train him to become a *brahmachari* from the age of five years and to undergo austerities and penances for spiritual realization.[133]

As education begins at the age of five years, similarly, Krishna consciousness, or *Bhagavata-dharma,* should be taught to the children as soon as the child is five years old.[134]

But in spite of all these detailed instructions, it appears that something went wrong in the Dallas *gurukula* and sometime in 1976 it was threatened with closure. Bhaktivedanta Swami's effort to save the project by appealing to the parents not to withdraw their children from the school shows how important *ashram* training was to him. In a circular dated 4 March 1976, he wrote to the parents:

My Dear parent,

Please accept my blessings. There has been a serious mistake. I do not wish that Gurukula should be closed down in Dallas. So you kindly arrange to send your child back to Gurukula.[135]

Bhaktivedanta Swami was in fact quite adamant when it came to the question of child education. When one of his disciples, herself a *gurukula* teacher, reminded him that he had once said that "some parents can keep their children with them and teach themselves,"[136] he rebuked her:

You follow that, *brahmachari gurukula,* that I've already explained. That should be done. Don't bring any new thing, imported ideas. That will not be helpful. It will be encumbrance. "My experiment with truth"—Gandhi's movement. Truth is truth. "Experiment" means you do not know what is truth. It is a way of life, everything is stated there, try to train them. Simple thing.[137]

When he says: "You follow that, *brahmachari gurukula*," Bhaktivedanta Swami refers to a passage from *Bhagavata Purana* 7.12.1 (*"brahmachari gurukule"*), wherein it is stated that a celibate student should live at the guru's *ashram*. He insisted that his instructions, based on his understanding of certain scriptural passages, had to be followed with absolute obedience. He thus disliked the idea that children should stay with or be taught by their parents. In fact, he regarded separation from the parents to be a vital aspect of the child's spiritual education. That boys should be separated from their parents at the age of five was a rule based on Bhaktivedanta Swami's interpretation of *Bhagavata Purana* 7.6.1: *"kaumara acharet prajno,"* "the wise should begin worship in childhood," a passage he quoted over a hundred times in his books and lectures. The personality who speaks this passage is the child saint Prahlada, who, along with the child saint Dhruva, became the emblem of childhood *bhakti* success in Bhaktivedanta Swami's preaching.

Bhaktivedanta Swami was so convinced of the superiority of his *gurukula* schooling system that he instructed one of his leading disciples to organize the schools in such a way that even non-ISKCON members would want to send their children there:

> They should be given only what they will eat, so that nothing is left over, and while bathing they can wash their own cloth. Your country, America, will become so much degraded that they will appreciate if we are revolutionary clean. Our revolutionary medicine will be experimented on these children, and it will be seen in America to be the cure. So make your program in this way, and encourage nondevotees or outsiders to enroll their children with us for some minimum fee, and you will do the greatest service to your country and its citizens by introducing this.[138]

> Now I am concerned that the Gurukula experiment should come out nicely. These children are the future hope of our Society, so it is a very important matter how we are training them in Krishna consciousness from the very childhood.[139]

In the above-quoted passages Bhaktivedanta Swami refers to his instructions regarding child education as "revolutionary medicine." He speaks about "the Gurukula experiment," and orders his disciples to test his "medicine" on their children. Many years later ISKCON leaders were forced to acknowledge that the outcome of his "experiment" was radically different than expected.

Most of Bhaktivedanta Swami's statements about child education leave no doubt that he was mainly thinking about how to train boys. As far as girls were concerned, he appears rather reserved:

> Girls should be completely separated from the very beginning. They are very dangerous . . . No girls. . . . They should be taught how to sweep, how to stitch . . . clean, cook, to be faithful to the husband. They should be taught how to become obedient to the husband. Little education, they can. . . . They should be stopped, this practice of prostitution. This is a very bad system in Europe and America. The boys and girls, they are educated—coeducation. From the very beginning of their life they become prostitutes. And they encourage.[140]

When asked whether his *varnashram* college would be open for women also, he replied:

> For men. Women should automatically learn how to cook, how to cleanse home. . . . Varnashram college especially meant for the Brahmin, Kshatriya and Vaishya. Those who are not fit for education, they are Shudras. That's all. Or those who are reluctant to take education—Shudra means. That's all. They should assist the higher class.[141]

WOMEN'S ROLE IN THE ISKCON *VARNASHRAM* MODEL

While Bhaktivedanta Swami was known to have been kind and accommodating in dealings with his women disciples, most of what he wrote about women in his books, lectures, and conversations appears rather negative. (For a detailed analysis of Bhaktivedanta Swami's statements about women, see E. Lorenz, "The Guru, Mayavadins, and Women: Tracing the Origins of Selected Polemical Statements in the Work of A.C. Bhaktivedanta Swami," in this volume.) Just like with *shudras*, he does not have much good to say about women:

> Women are generally not very intelligent.[142]

> Women in general should not be trusted.[143]

> Generally when a woman is attacked by a man—whether her husband or some other man—she enjoys the attack, being too lusty.[144]

> It may be clearly said that the understanding of a woman is always inferior to the understanding of a man.[145]

One gets the impression he saw women primarily as wombs, used by the Aryans for the purpose of perpetuating a race of saintly heroes. "The whole purpose of this system is to create good population,"[146] writes Bhaktivedanta Swami about *varnashram dharma.* "According to Vedic rites, the breeding of child is very nicely enunciated. That is called *garbhadhan-samskara.*"[147] When Bhaktivedanta Swami speaks about women in the context of *varnashram,* he inevitably brings up the topics of bad population, adulteration, prostitution, *varna sankara,* women's lesser intelligence, and the lifelong control of women by men:

> Women cannot properly utilize freedom, and it is better for them to remain dependent. A woman cannot be happy if she is independent. That is a fact. In Western countries we have seen many women very unhappy simply for the sake of independence. That independence is not recommended by the Vedic civilization or by the *varnashram-dharma.*[148]

> And Shudras, they are not taken into account. In the similarly, woman class, they are taken as Shudra, Shudra. . . . Woman class, are taken less intelligent, they should be given protection, but they cannot be elevated.[149]

> If women become prostitute, then the population is *varna-sankara.* And *varna-sankara* means unwanted children. They become practically nuisance in the society. . . . If *varna-sankara* population is increased, then the whole society becomes a hell. That's a fact.[150]

What Bhaktivedanta Swami might have had in mind when he used the word "prostitute" can perhaps be guessed from his statements about the former Indian prime minister, Indira Gandhi:

> PRABHUPADA: And Indira was doing that. Indira and company. . . . She is a prostitute; her son is a gunda. . . .

> TAMALA KRISHNA: She seems to have been one of the worst leaders so far.

> PRABHUPADA: She is not leader, she is a prostitute. Woman given freedom means prostitute. Free woman means prostitute. What is this prostitute? She has no fixed-up husband. And free woman means this, daily, new friend.[151]

His greatest concern seems to be how to avoid *varna sankara.* Again and again this topic comes up when women are mentioned in the *varnashram* context:

> When women become polluted, no fixed-up husband—that is pollution for woman, no chaste, no chastity—then this *varna-sankara* will come out.

And when the world is overpopulated by *varna-sankara,* it will become a burden. Therefore it so became, atheist, *varna-sankara,* demons.[152]

If the woman becomes widow, then there will be *varna-sankara* population. *Varna-sankara* population means a population who cannot say who is his father. That is *varna-sankara.* Or which caste does he belong, what is his father, what is his family. No, nothing, no information. That is called *varna-sankara.*[153]

The last statement speaks for itself: a widowed woman is "by default" a prostitute. The less intelligent women are so prone to degradation that unless they are kept under the tight control of men, they are sure to become pregnant, and the result will be the dreaded *varna sankara.* Bhaktivedanta Swami therefore advises his disciples: "And being the weaker sex, women require to have a husband who is strong in Krishna consciousness so that they may take advantage and make progress by sticking tightly to his feet."[154]

IMPLEMENTATION OF *VARNASHRAM* IN ISKCON

Bhaktivedanta Swami's declaration that his writings were "meant for bringing about a revolution in the impious life of a misdirected civilization" appears in the preface to each published volume of his commentaries to the *Bhagavata Purana.*[155] What sort of impression did his teachings about *varnashram dharma* leave in the minds of his disciples? Did they try to implement his *varnashram* instructions?

One ISKCON project in which some—perhaps the most far-reaching—of Bhaktivedanta Swami's *varnashram* instructions came to be implemented was the Bhaktivedanta *gurukula* in Dallas. Jeff Hickey, former Jagadish Das, who had been appointed by Bhaktivedanta Swami as his "education minister" and was in charge of the entire ISKCON *gurukula* education, recently appeared on a TV show and commented on his involvement:

JEFF HICKEY: I really believed that I was doing the best for my children. I thought that this was a divine system that would give them the best training for the future that they were going to meet.

JOHN QUINONES: You were looking out for your child's best interest?

JEFF HICKEY: I thought so.

JOHN QUINONES (VO): Jeff was 19 when he became a Hare Krishna devotee in 1968. He followed the teachings of this man, the guru who brought the movement to America. Swami Prabhupada, who died in 1977, is still the most revered man in the religion. The swami put Jeff in charge of the Dallas school, then appointed him to be his minister of education, even though Jeff admits he had absolutely no experience in the field. It was Jeff who kept the children away from their parents. Now, he regrets following the swami's orders.

JEFF HICKEY: It is my opinion that he didn't know what he was doing, and that he—he made a huge mistake by separating the children from their parents and—and really, like, crushing their emotional lives.[156]

Another, rather brief project was the attempt to run a *varnashram* college in New Vrindavan, West Virginia. Many of Bhaktivedanta Swami's statements quoted in the present paper are taken from a morning walk conversation recorded in Vrindavan, India, in March 1974. It was after this morning walk that the idea of a *varnashram* college began to circulate, and sometime in April the first *varnashram* college was started. Hiranyagarbha Das, who had been appointed "headmaster" of the *varnashram* college, remembers his involvement in the project:

The experiment was short-lived. We lasted only 8 months or so. In December, I took the boys on a book distribution trip to Buffalo and Toronto, and then returned to Dallas, where I unilaterally put an end to the experiment. I can't remember any real repercussions from that.[157]

When asked whether ISKCON members in those days showed any awareness of how violent some of Bhaktivedanta Swami's instructions regarding Kshatriya training actually were, Das replies:

Not really. Even so, in New Vrindavan, while I was there, Kirtanananda brought in some ex-military devotees who spent a bit of time setting up a Kshatriya group in the community. The mood was pretty militaristic at the time. I read somewhere that K. deliberately exploited (and maybe even fabricated) an incident in which some rough types attacked the temple in order to build up this kind of fortress mentality. It infected the Varnashram College to some degree also. We had some military type discipline—marching to the Hare Krishna mantra, etc. Eventually, we see where all this led to in New Vrindavan.[158]

Regarding how a person's *varna* was to be determined in *varnashram* college, Bhaktivedanta Swami had once said that this "will be tested by the teachers, what for he is fit. He will be test [sic] by the guru."[159] When asked whether any such testing was actually practiced in the *varnashram* college, Das explained:

> As I said above, this was not really touched upon, because Prabhupada confused the issue by assuming that everyone who came to the temple was automatically a Vaishnava and beyond being even a Brahmin, and therefore able to do any kind of work "to teach and set example." So, stupidly, everyone in the movement was simply dumped onto the sankirtana [canvassing] party to collect [money], without consideration for his or her individual character or propensities.[160]

In 1981, four years after Bhaktivedanta Swami's death, two of his leading disciples, Robert Campagnola and Jay A. Matsya,[161] coauthored *Varnashram Manifesto for Social Sanity,*[162] a volume dedicated to Bhaktivedanta Swami, "the real father of the modern varnashram system."[163] The book was controversial. Some felt that it was overly fanatical and could lead to public relations problems for ISKCON—which it actually later did: the anticult movement and the Orthodox Church in Russia used passages from the book to prove that ISKCON was driving a dangerous political agenda and could be potentially harmful to society. A detailed study of the 215-page text, however, reveals that Matsya and Campagnola faithfully repeat Bhaktivedanta Swami's teachings on *varnashram dharma*:[164]

> In the present period of the earth's history, the books of His Divine Grace A. C. Bhaktivedanta Swami Prabhupada are the absolute foundation upon which all individual and collective spiritual progress depends. Since the departure of His Divine Grace from this mortal world, his disciples have inherited the task of expanding the original Vedic knowledge for the benefit of materially attached humanity. No one can become fully spiritually enlightened without the help of transcendental literature written by Shrila Prabhupada and his authorized disciples. Nor can anyone completely change human society for the permanent good without these books' clear and powerful guidance.[165]

While William H. Deadwyler finds the *Varnashram Manifesto* to be "spectacularly unpersuasive,"[166] it cannot be denied that Matsya and Campagnola's views on child education completely agree with Bhaktivedanta Swami's teachings:

> From the early years of life, children should hear correct knowledge of the material and spiritual realities. They should learn to understand the difference between matter and spirit, and the predominance of spirituality

over material ignorance. By chanting songs and *mantras* that glorify the Supreme Lord, they should put this knowledge into action and thus purify their consciousness. The self-centeredness and selfishness of childhood are a form of material contamination. Young children desire to be the controllers and enjoyers of their little world. Expert at manipulating their parents by crying and smiling, young children have complete opportunity to maintain the illusions that they are their material bodies and the whole world is subject to their beck and call. Such illusions must be dealt with as soon as the child's cognitive powers develop. Behind the carefreeness and glee of childhood lurk dormant, strong material desires. Although young children are sometimes believed to be "innocent and pure," there is no question of actual innocence or purity; there is only the question of time. Because young children's bodies and sensual powers have not fully developed and matured, they do not yet have the ability to manifest their inherent material desires. But as soon as the biological light turns green, they begin to contemplate and execute their formerly dormant desires for sense gratification. Hence, in a *varnashram* society, when children reach the age of five, the Brahmins will begin to train them in the correct understanding of the purpose of human life. When from an early age children develop the crucial qualities needed to conquer over material desires that will later arise to disturb them, then society is spared from many social problems.[167]

CONCLUDING REMARKS

Bhaktivedanta Swami left no doubt in his writings that he wanted his movement to save the world by establishing *varnashram dharma*:

> So we shall have a unique position all over the world provided we stick to the principles, namely unflinching faith in Spiritual Master and Krishna, chanting not less than 16 rounds regularly and following the regulative principles. Then our men will conquer all over the world.[168]

Given the hurts that ISKCON members have inflicted on one another in their endeavor to please their guru, it can hardly be seen as unfortunate that they ultimately failed to fulfill his dream of taking over the world. While Bhaktivedanta Swami did not leave concrete instructions on how to go from modern democracy to a *varnashram*-based monarchy, he hoped to convince the intellectual elite of the world with the help of a perfect educational model: his Bhaktivedanta *gurukula*. There he wanted to create perfect Vaishnava Brahmins, children of exemplary character, who, by dint of their spiritual purity, would be able "to ignite the sacrificial fire without matches, solely by chanting mantras."[169] Other papers in this volume have discussed the results of this *gurukula* educational experiment.

ISKCON is presently trying to come to grips with its past. There have been official statements acknowledging that abuse of children in the Bhaktivedanta *gurukula* was a fact, and that it is regretted. There have also been official GBC resolutions regarding the treatment of women. Here too, regret for past abuses has been expressed. Efforts are under way to create an ISKCON that is not friendly and accommodating toward *sannyasins* and celibate males only, but also to families, women, and children. However, in the society's attempts to examine its past and to understand what went wrong and why, very little progress has been made in identifying the underlying causes. The consensus seems to be that the movement was too liberal in its enrollment procedures, and that for this reason "bad elements" managed to enter, even into the leading echelons. Another popular explanation is that the members failed to correctly understand and execute Bhaktivedanta Swami's perfect instructions.

It is a theological dogma in the movement that Bhaktivedanta Swami is a pure representative of God, incapable of error, all-knowing, and absolutely good. Since Bhaktivedanta Swami taught that criticism of a pure devotee was *the* most serious and devastating impediment to spiritual progress,[170] a question that ISKCON leaders presently do not dare to consider is to what degree his teachings contributed to past abuses. It is no secret that many ISKCON leaders knew about the abuse, for example, of women and children, but often did not perceive this as in any way contrary to Bhaktivedanta Swami's teachings. It used to be standard to first of all examine whether a current practice was justifiable in the light of Bhaktivedanta Swami's teachings; it was—and still is—always secondary to ask whether any such practice agrees with commonly accepted ethical or social norms.

NOTES

1. http://www.prabhupada.com/publishing.html.
2. http://krishna.org/ctfote/varnash.html.
3. http://www.floridavediccollege.edu/masters.htm.
4. SS: Vedic Social Science; SS201: Varnashram Dharma—Vaisnava Social Responsibility. 3 Credits. Prescribed social duties in light of Vaisnavism; SS202: Applied Varnashram Dharma Studies—6 Credits. Prerequisite SS201. A study of Varnashrama by studying the lives of famous Vedic personalities and how they integrated Varnashrama Dharma into the fabric of their lives. http://bhaktivedanta-college.org/index.htm.
5. The General Headquarters home page: http://www.ghq.org/index.html.
6. "'It is ISKCON's responsibility to revive Vedic culture. Feminism—the ideology of female occupational equal rights—is diametrically opposed to the principles of

prescribed duties. Therefore a feminist Vaisnava is an oxymoron." "Vaisnavism and Social Responsibility," http://ghq.org/download/.

7. Ravindra Svarupa Dasa (William H. Deadwyler), "ISKCON and Varnashrama-Dharma: A Mission Unfulfilled," *ISKCON Communications Journal* 7 (1) (June 1999): 41.

8. "You will recall that Prabhupada originally thought that ISKCON would perform the brahminical function for the rest of society—'I have come to give you a brain.' Prabhupada based this effort on books. By books he could transmit the Vedic heritage, and through books he could instruct and train large numbers of followers, who, by studying his writings systematically and practising their teachings, could advance to the mode of goodness and beyond." Ibid.

9. A. K. Majumdar, *Concise History of Ancient India : Vol. 3, Hinduism: Society, Religion & Philosophy* (Delhi: Munshiram Manoharlal, 1983), 1.

10. Lecture at Sri Goudiya Math, Royapettah, Madras, 10 September 1950, *The Bhaktivedanta VedaBase CD-ROM: Pre-1965 Writings* (Sandy Ridge, NC: Bhaktivedanta Archives, 1995), record 13681–13749.

11. Ibid., record 13722.

12. A.C. Bhaktivedanta Swami, Back to Godhead *1944–1960 The Pioneer Years: A Collection of* Back to Godhead *Magazines Published between 1944 and 1960* (Los Angeles: Bhaktivedanta Book Trust, 1994), 75, BTG vol. 3 part 1, 1 March 1956.

13. Ibid., 88, BTG vol. 3 part 3, 5 April 1956.

14. Ibid., 114, BTG vol. 3 part 7, 5 June 1956.

15. Ibid., 155, BTG vol. 3 part 14, 20 November 1958.

16. A.C. Bhaktivedanta Swami, *Srimad Bhagavatam: Fifth Canto* (Los Angeles: Bhaktivedanta Book Trust, 1987), 5.19.19 purport, p. 713.

17. A.C. Bhaktivedanta Swami, *Srimad Bhagavatam: Fourth Canto* (Los Angeles: Bhaktivedanta Book Trust, 1987), 4.14.20 purport, p. 671.

18. A.C. Bhaktivedanta Swami, *Srimad Bhagavatam: Tenth Canto* (Los Angeles: Bhaktivedanta Book Trust, 1987), 10.8.6 purport, p. 336.

19. A.C. Bhaktivedanta Swami, *Srimad Bhagavatam: Seventh Canto* (Los Angeles: Bhaktivedanta Book Trust, 1987), 7.15.36 purport, p. 859.

20. Room Conversation with Sanskrit professor, other guests, and disciples, 12 February 1975, Mexico, *The Bhaktivedanta VedaBase CD-ROM* (Sandy Ridge, NC: Bhaktivedanta Archives, 1995), record 444187.

21. Ibid., Lecture at World Health Organization, Geneva, 6 June 1974, record 379897.

22. Essays: Perfection at Home—A Novel Contribution to the Fallen Humanity, *The Bhaktivedanta VedaBase CD-ROM: Pre-1965 Writings*, record 14311.

23. A.C. Bhaktivedanta Swami, *Srimad Bhagavatam: Second Canto* (Los Angeles: Bhaktivedanta Book Trust, 1987), 2.4.18 purport, p.216.

24. A.C. Bhaktivedanta Swami, *Srimad Bhagavatam: Third Canto* (Los Angeles: Bhaktivedanta Book Trust, 1987), 3.12.35 purport, 1:524.

25. A.C. Bhaktivedanta Swami, *Srimad Bhagavatam: First Canto* (Los Angeles: Bhaktivedanta Book Trust, 1987), 1.18.45 purport, p. 1049.

26. A.C. Bhaktivedanta Swami, *Srimad Bhagavatam: Fourth Canto*, 4.20.26 purport, 2:39.

27. Ibid.

28. Lecture: Srimad-Bhagavatam 6.1.6, Bombay, 6 November 1970, *The Bhaktivedanta VedaBase CD-ROM*, 1995, record 356922.

29. Ibid., Room Conversation, 2 August 1976, Paris, record 514967.

30. Ibid., Lecture: *Bhagavad-gita* 10.4–5, New York, 4 January 1967, record 335380.

31. Ibid., Lecture: *Srimad-Bhagavatam* 2.1.5, Paris, 13 June 1974, record 349711.

32. Ibid., Lecture: *Bhagavad-gita* 9.3, Melbourne, 21 April 1976, record 334397.

33. Ibid., Lecture at World Health Organization, Geneva, 6 June 1974, record 379907: "So really Indian civilization or Aryan civilization, Vedic civlization, means *varnashrama-dharma.*"

34. Ibid., Press Conference, Mauritius, 2 October 1975, record 469812.

35. Ibid., Letter to: Kirtanananda, Montreal, 30 June 1968, record 582228.

36. Ibid., Letter to: Bali-mardana, Nairobi, 9 October 1971, record 594201.

37. Ibid., Lecture: *Sri Chaitanya-Charitamrita, Madhya-lila* 20.100–108, Bombay, 9 November 1975, record 368302.

38. Ibid., Lecture: *Bhagavad-gita* 2.18, Hyderabad, 23 November 1972, record 323377.

39. Shukavak N. Dasa, *Hindu Encounter with Modernity: Kedarnath Datta Bhaktivinoda Vaishnava Theologian* (Los Angeles: Sri, 1999), 212.

40. Bhaktisiddhanta Saraswati, *Shri Chaitanya's Teachings*, part 1 (Madras: Sree Gaudiya Math, 1975), 312.

41. Viraraghava Acharya, for example, commenting on the word *lokanam,* explains that it refers to the followers of *varnashrama dharma*: "*lokanam varnashramavatam.*" Shridhara Svami, commenting on the word *setavah,* explains that it refers to the boundaries of *varnashram dharma*: "*setavo varnashrama-dharma-maryadah.*" *Srimad Bhagavata Sridhari Tika* (1988; reprint, Bombay: Nirnaya Sagar Press, 1950), 7.8.48, p. 689: "*setavo varnashram-dharma-maryadah.*"

42. In only 29 out of 113 purports that mention *varnashram,* Bhaktivedanta Swami comments on *Bhagavata Purana* passages that contain obvious keywords like *varna, ashram,* or *dharma.*

43. A.C. Bhaktivedanta Swami, *Srimad Bhagavatam: Fourth Canto,* 4.29.81 purport, 2:791.

44. Krsnasankara Sastri, ed., *Srimad-bhagavata-mahapuranam caturthah skandhah* (Sola: Sri Bhagavata-Vidyapithah, 1966), 4.29.81 srimad viraraghavavyakhya, p. 762. What Viraraghava actually wrote is, "*tatah prachinabarhih praja-shristau tadrakshane cha sva-putran anujnapya svayam tapas chartum kapilashramam agat.*" "Having instructed his sons about increasing and protecting the subjects, Prachinabarhi went to Kapilashram to perform austerities."

45. A.C. Bhaktivedanta Swami, *Srimad Bhagavatam: Seventh Canto,* 7.3.24 purport, p. 152.

46. A.C. Bhaktivedanta Swami, *Bhagavad-Gita As It Is* (Los Angeles: Bhaktivedanta Book Trust, 1989), 2.31 purport, p. 117.

47. A.C. Bhaktivedanta Swami, *Srimad Bhagavatam: First Canto,* 1.2.13 purport, p. 108.

48. Ibid., 1.5.24 purport, p. 272.

49. Ibid., 1.16.31 purport, p. 935.

50. Ibid., 1.8.5 purport, p. 403.

51. Ibid., 1.13.24 purport, p. 739.

52. A.C. Bhaktivedanta Swami, *Bhagavad-Gita As It Is,* 1.40 purport, p. 67.

53. A.C. Bhaktivedanta Swami, *Srimad Bhagavatam: Second Canto,* 2.6.20 purport, p. 313.

54. A.C. Bhaktivedanta Swami, *Srimad Bhagavatam: Fourth Canto,* 4.16.10 purport, 1:725.

55. A.C. Bhaktivedanta Swami, *Srimad Bhagavatam: First Canto,* 1.2.2 purport, p. 89.

56. A.C. Bhaktivedanta Swami, *Srimad Bhagavatam: Tenth Canto,* 10.8.6 purport, p. 436.

57. A.C. Bhaktivedanta Swami, *Bhagavad-Gita As It Is,* 1.40 purport, p. 66.

58. A.C. Bhaktivedanta Swami, *Srimad Bhagavatam: Third Canto,* 3.22.4 purport, 2:206.

59. A.C. Bhaktivedanta Swami, *Srimad Bhagavatam: Fourth Canto*, 4.20.28 purport, 2:44.
60. A.C. Bhaktivedanta Swami, *Srimad Bhagavatam: Fifth Canto*, 5.13.8 purport, p. 438.
61. A.C. Bhaktivedanta Swami, *Srimad Bhagavatam: First Canto*, 1.5.24 purport, p. 272.
62. Ibid., 1.11.36 purport, p. 641.
63. A.C. Bhaktivedanta Swami, *Srimad Bhagavatam: Sixth Canto* (Los Angeles: Bhaktivedanta Book Trust, 1987), 6.3.13 purport, p. 154.
64. A.C. Bhaktivedanta Swami, *Srimad Bhagavatam: First Canto*, 1.15.39 purport, p. 880.
65. Ibid., 1.5.24 purport, p. 272.
66. A.C. Bhaktivedanta Swami, *Srimad Bhagavatam: Third Canto*, 3.21.52 purport, vol. 2, p. 198.
67. *The Journey of Self-Discovery* 7.1, *The Bhaktivedanta VedaBase CD-ROM*, record 316824.
68. Ibid., Lecture: *Srimad-Bhagavatam* 2.3.1, Los Angeles, 19 May 1972, record 349873.
69. Ibid., Initiation Lecture Excerpt, London, 7 September 1971, record 374193.
70. A.C. Bhaktivedanta Swami, *Srimad Bhagavatam: Sixth Canto*, 6.5.39 purport, p. 310.
71. A.C. Bhaktivedanta Swami, *Srimad-Bhagavatam: Ninth Canto* (Los Angeles: Bhaktivedanta Book Trust, 1987), 9.2.23–24 purport, p. 48.
72. Morning Walk, "Varnashrama College," Vrindavan, 14 March 1974, *The Bhaktivedanta VedaBase CD-ROM*, record 426878.
73. Ibid., Letter to: Prabhakar, Honolulu, 31 May 1975, record 604402.
74. A.C. Bhaktivedanta Swami, *Srimad Bhagavatam: Fourth Canto*, 4.12.10 purport, 1:555.
75. Morning Walk, "Varnashrama College," Vrindavan, 14 March 1974, *The Bhaktivedanta VedaBase CD-ROM*, record 426806.
76. Ibid., record 426856.
77. Ibid., record 426912.
78. Ibid., record 426916.
79. Ibid., Lecture: *Bhagavad-gita* 1.28–29, London, 22 July 1973, record 321203.
80. Ibid., Lecture: *Bhagavad-gita* 2.36–37, London, 4 September 1973, record 324206.
81. Ibid., Lecture: *Srimad-Bhagavatam* 1.7.28–29, Vrindavan, 25 September 1976, record 344572.
82. Ibid., Lecture: *Srimad-Bhagavatam* 2.3.17, Los Angeles, 12 July 1969, record 350225.
83. Ibid., Lecture: *Bhagavad-gita* 1.28–29, London, 22 July 1973, record 321203.
84. Ibid., Room Conversation, Indore, 13 December 1970, record 396710.
85. Ibid., Morning Conversation, Bombay, 11 April 1977, record 552458.
86. Ibid., Morning Conversation, Vrindavan, 23 June 1977, record 561228.
87. Ibid., Lecture: *Bhagavad-gita* 1.31, London, 24 July 1973, record 321250.
88. A.C. Bhaktivedanta Swami, *Srimad Bhagavatam: Fourth Canto*, 4.13.19–20 purport, p. 626.
89. Ibid., 4.21.6 purport, 2:63.
90. Ibid., 4.22.45 purport, 2:212.
91. A.C. Bhaktivedanta Swami, *Srimad Bhagavatam: Sixth Canto*, 6.4.11 purport, p. 200.
92. A.C. Bhaktivedanta Swami, *Srimad Bhagavatam: Ninth Canto*, 9.13.12 purport, p. 425.
93. Lecture: *Bhagavad-gita* 1.4, London, 10 July 1973, *The Bhaktivedanta VedaBase CD-ROM*, Sandy Ridge 1995, record 320926.
94. Ibid., Room Conversation, Bombay, 21 August 1975, record 467143.
95. Ibid., Letter to: Dr. Wolf, Honolulu, 20 May 1976, record 607891.
96. Ibid., Room Conversation, Toronto, 17 June 1976, record 499762.

97. Ibid., Morning Walk, Bombay, 20 November 1975, records 476348–476350.
98. A.C. Bhaktivedanta Swami, *Srimad Bhagavatam: Fourth Canto*, 4.25.10 purport, p. 435.
99. Conversation During Massage, Bhubaneswar, 23 January 1977, *The Bhaktivedanta VedaBase CD-ROM*, records 540250–540252.
100. Ibid., Morning Walk, "Varnashrama College," Vrindavan, 14 March 1974, record 426808.
101. Ibid., record 426814.
102. Ibid., Conversation with Seven Ministers of Andhra Pradesh, Hyderabad, 22 August 1976, record 521531.
103. A.C. Bhaktivedanta Swami, *Srimad Bhagavatam: Fourth Canto*, 4.12.10 purport, 1:555.
104. Bhaktivedanta Swami never referred to his followers and supporters as a "congregation": "We are not a church. It is true that our congregation is not increasing, simply the inmates are becoming more numerous. We should be classified as a residential temple. . . . We simply have a bigger family therefore our temple is bigger." Letter to: Karandhara, Auckland, 21 February 1973, *The Bhaktivedanta VedaBase CD-ROM*, record 598178.
105. A.C. Bhaktivedanta Swami, *Srimad Bhagavatam: Third Canto*, 3.21.31 purport, 2:178.
106. A.C. Bhaktivedanta Swami, *The Science of Self-Realization* (Los Angeles: Bhaktivedanta Book Trust, 1978), ch. 6, 205.
107. Lecture Excerpt, Montreal, 27 July 1968, *The Bhaktivedanta VedaBase CD-ROM*, record 375748.
108. Ibid., Lecture, Seattle, 7 October 1968, record 376098.
109. Ibid., Morning Walk, "Varnashrama College," Vrindavan, 14 March 1974, records 426818–426828.
110. Ibid., Lecture: *Srimad-Bhagavatam* 3.1.10, Dallas, 21 May 1973, record 351445.
111. All statements compiled from public lectures given by Bhaktivedanta Swami between 1966 and 1976; *The Bhaktivedanta VedaBase CD-ROM*, records 325375, 321872, 324287, 373118, 375748, 376098, 348074, 321762, 346644, 364869, 373118, 341145, 321762, 349874, 342416, 352085, 327836, 343560, 343561, 345037, 440043, 359218, 451445, 359947.
112. Ibid., Discussions with Shyamasundara Das: John Dewey, record 383864.
113. Ibid., Room Conversation, Mauritius, 5 October 1975, record 470657.
114. Ibid., Lecture: *Srimad-Bhagavatam* 1.16.4, Los Angeles, 1 January 1974, record 348074.
115. Ibid., *Srimad-Bhagavatam: Second Part* (From Seventh Chapter 2nd half to Twelfth Chapter of the First Canto, Delhi 1964), *Pre-1965 Writings of Srila Prabhupada*, 1.11.36 purport, record 5739. Bhaktivedanta Swami's editorial team later edited the reference to "negroes" out of this passage. In the 1987 Bhaktivedanta Book Trust edition it reads: "Cupid's provocations are going on, even among beastly societies who are all ugly-looking in the estimation of the civilized nations" (p. 642).
116. Ibid., Room Conversation, "Varnashrama System Must Be Introduced," Mayapura, 14 February 1977, *The Bhaktivedanta VedaBase CD-ROM*, record 543832.
117. Ibid., Morning Walk at Villa Borghese, Rome, 26 May 1974, record 435756.
118. Ibid., Lecture: *Srimad-Bhagavatam* 1.16.8, Los Angeles, 5 January 1974, record 348176.
119. Ibid., Morning Walk, "Varnashrama College," Vrindavan, 14 March 1974, record 426904.
120. A.C. Bhaktivedanta Swami, *Srimad Bhagavatam: Fourth Canto*, 4.16.4 purport, 1:718.

121. *Srimad-Bhagavatam* 1.7.25, Vrindavan, 22 September 1976, *The Bhaktivedanta Ved-aBase CD-ROM*, record 344514.

122. Ibid., Morning Walk, Vrindavan, 12 March 1974, record 426651.

123. A.C. Bhaktivedanta Swami, *Bhagavad-Gita As It Is,* 6.13–14 purport, p. 322.

124. A.C. Bhaktivedanta Swami, *Srimad Bhagavatam: First Canto,* 1.5.24 purport, p. 272.

125. A.C. Bhaktivedanta Swami, *The Nectar of Instruction* (Los Angeles: Bhaktivedanta Book Trust, 1975), purport, p. 7.

126. Letter to: Tulsi, Mayapur, 12 October 1974, *The Bhaktivedanta VedaBase CD-ROM*, record 602204.

126. Ibid., Letter to: Satsvarupa, Delhi, 25 November 1971, record 594508.

128. Ibid., Letter to: Satyabhama, Hyderabad, 23 March 1973, records 598314–598315.

129. Ibid., Letter to: Krishna Das, Dallas, 9 September 1972, record 597098.

130. Ibid., Letter to: Jayatirtha, 76–01–20, record 606815.

131. Ibid., Lecture: *Srimad-Bhagavatam* 7.6.1, San Francisco, 6 March 1967, record 361415.

132. A.C. Bhaktivedanta Swami, *Srimad Bhagavatam: Fourth Canto,* 4.12.23 purport, 1:573.

133. Ibid., 4.12.34 purport, p. 587.

134. Lecture: London, 12 July 1972, *The Bhaktivedanta VedaBase CD-ROM*, record 379028.

135. Ibid., Letter to: Parent, Mayapur, 4 March 1976, records 607395–607396.

136. Ibid., Room Conversation, Paris, 31 July 1976, record 514761.

137. Ibid., record 514762.

138. Ibid., Letter to: Satsvarupa, Mayapur, 28 February 1972, record 595543.

139. Ibid., Letter to: Satsvarupa, New York, 11 April 1973, record 598384.

140. Ibid., Morning Conversation, Bombay, 29 April 1977, records 556479–556491.

141. Ibid., Morning Walk, "Varnashrama College," Vrindavan, 14 March 1974, record 426865.

142. A.C. Bhaktivedanta Swami, *Bhagavad-Gita As It Is,* 1.40 purport, p. 67.

143. A.C. Bhaktivedanta Swami, *Srimad Bhagavatam: Eighth Canto* (Los Angeles: Bhaktivedanta Book Trust, 1987), 8.9.9 purport, p. 330.

144. Ibid., *Fourth Canto,* 4.26.26 purport, p. 542.

145. Ibid., *Sixth Canto,* 6.17.34–35 purport, p. 786.

146. Ibid., *Seventh Canto,* 7.11.13 purport, p. 657.

147. Lecture: *Bhagavad-gita* 3.21–25, New York, 30 May 1966, *The Bhaktivedanta Ved-aBase CD-ROM*, record 325569.

148. A.C. Bhaktivedanta Swami, *Teachings of Lord Kapila* (Los Angeles: Bhaktivedanta Book Trust, 1988), 43.

149. Lecture: *Bhagavad-gita* 9.29–32, New York, 20 December 1966, *The Bhaktivedanta VedaBase CD-ROM*, record 335067.

150. Ibid., Lecture: *Bhagavad-gita* 2.13, Hyderabad, 19 November 1972, record 322847.

151. Ibid., Room Conversation, April 5, 1977, Bombay, record 551678–551680.

152. Ibid., Lecture: *Srimad-Bhagavatam* 1.8.34, Bombay, 14 October 1974, record 345749.

153. Ibid., Lecture: *Srimad-Bhagavatam* 1.16.12, Los Angeles, 9 January 1974, record 348242.

154. Ibid., Letter to: Madhukara, Bombay, 4 January 1973, record 597847.

155. A.C. Bhaktivedanta Swami, *Srimad Bhagavatam: First Canto,* Preface, p. xxiii.

156. Childhood of Shame, *ABCNEWS,* Monday, 27 November 2000, http://abcnews.go.com/onair/abcnews/transcripts/2020downtown_001127_harekrishna_trans.html.

157. Personal communication, 7 March 2001.

158. Ibid. Das probably refers to events described in: John Hubner and Lindsey Gruson, *Monkey on a Stick: Murder, Madness and the Hare Krishnas* (New York: Harcourt Brace Jovanovich, 1988).

159. Morning Walk, Hyderabad, 20 April 1974, *The Bhaktivedanta VedaBase CD-ROM*, record 433800.

160. Personal communication, 7 March 2001.

161. Former Harikesha Swami and Devamrita Swami; Harikesha Swami left ISKCON in 1998, Devamrita Swami remains in a leading position in the movement.

162. Harikesa Swami Visnupada, *Varnashrama Manifesto for Social Sanity* (Los Angeles: Bhaktivedanta Book Trust, 1981).

163. Ibid., title page.

164. Even the title of their book echoes words he wrote in India in 1956: "The atheist is requested herewith for his own benefit and for the benefit of all concerned—not to indulge in any more attempt of insanity. The whole world is already infected with an epidemic of insanity. The whole world is now full with men of unclean habits. And to save the world from further deterioration for human habitation, the atheist should give up the mode of irresponsible life under the influence of blind materialism and take to the path of 'Buddhiyoga' as mentioned in the Bhagwat Geeta." Back to Godhead *1944–1960 The Pioneer Years: A Collection of* Back to Godhead *Magazines Published between 1944 and 1960* (Los Angeles: Bhaktivedanta Book Trust, 1994), 95, BTG vol. 3 part 4, 20 April 1956.

165. Harikesa Swami Visnupada, *Varnashrama Manifesto*, 132.

166. William H. Deadwyler, "ISKCON and Varnashrama-Dharma," 40.

167. Ibid., 123–24.

168. Letter to Tamal Krishna, Gurudasa, London, 23 August 1971, *The Bhaktivedanta VedaBase CD-ROM*, record 593851.

169. I cannot find the source of this popular quote, which is commonly attributed to Bhaktivedanta Swami, but it is well known in ISKCON circles.

170. "Even though one is very much advanced in devotional service, if he commits offenses at the feet of a Vaishnava, his advancement is all spoiled. . . . The most grievous type of *vaishnava-aparadha* is called *gurv-aparadha,* which refers to offenses at the lotus feet of the spiritual master." A.C. Bhaktivedanta Swami, *Srimad Bhagavatam: Fourth Canto,* 4.21.37 purport, pp. 111–12.

"It is said, therefore, by Vaishnava authorities that even the most intelligent person cannot understand the plans and activities of a pure devotee. . . . He is above all materialistic criticism, just as Krishna is above all criticism." A.C. Bhaktivedanta Swami, *Bhagavad-Gita As It Is,* 9.28 purport, pp. 491–92.

"A devotee should be fixed in the conclusion that the spiritual master cannot be subject to criticism and should never be considered equal to a common man." A.C. Bhaktivedanta Swami, *Sri-Chaitanya-Charitamrita: Antya-Lila* (Los Angeles: Bhaktivedanta Book Trust, 1996), 3.11 purport, p. 217.

PART 6
Reevaluations

[22]

ON LEAVING ISKCON

Personal Story III

STEVEN J. GELBERG

SINCE MOST DEVOTEES eventually leave ISKCON (A.C. Bhaktivedanta Swami Prabhupada correctly predicted that the great majority of his disciples would ultimately abandon the movement), the leaving experience itself (and its aftermath) is certainly one of the core experiences in the life of most devotees, and therefore worthy of reflection and discussion.

It's hard to imagine an experience more wrenching, more potentially disorienting, than leaving a spiritual community or tradition to which one has devoted years of one's life. To lose faith in a comprehensive system of ideas that have shaped the consciousness and guided all actions, to leave a community that has constituted the social world and defined social identity, to renounce a way of life that is an entire mode of being, is an experience of momentous implications.

Especially when the community/tradition defines itself as the repository and bastion of all goodness, meaning, truth, decency, and meaningful human attainment, it may require a major psychological effort to reorient both to one's own self and to the wider world. Internally, those leaving must work to rediscover and reclaim their own unique, personal sources of meaning and to live authentically from those inner depths. Externally, they must learn how to deal with the vast territory beyond the gates of the spiritual enclave—a place that has for so long been viewed as a dark and evil abode unfit for human habitation. Very often devotees no longer content living in ISKCON prolong their stay simply out of fear of the demonized world.

This reorientation to self and reentry into the world is no small task, and it's more easily finessed with the support of others who've traveled a similar path. Though I've had little to do with ISKCON for nearly 16 years now, I still feel a certain kinship with devotees, both past and present. How could I not? I devoted fully 17 years (ages 18 to 35—my youth) to a life of Krishna Consciousness in the association of similarly committed devotees. Virtually all my friends and acquaintances were devotees. I absorbed Prabhupada's teachings into the depths of my being and preached them with an enthusiasm born of serene confidence in their absolute truth and efficacy. I dedicated myself both to encouraging a deeper immersion in Vaishnava spirituality on the part of my fellow devotees (through editing such books as *The Spiritual Master and the Disciple* and *Namamrta: The Nectar of the Holy Name*) and to cultivating respect and appreciation for ISKCON among intellectuals and scholars (as with my volume of interviews, *Hare Krishna, Hare Krishna: Five Distinguished Scholars on the Krishna Movement in the West* [Grove Press, 1983]).

Though my way of thinking and mode of being have changed considerably since leaving the movement, I cannot forget all my brothers and sisters who have shared the Krishna Consciousness experience. We all entered ISKCON driven by a need to know and experience truth, enlightenment, peace, bliss. I, like most devotees, felt an inexplicable attraction to the supernaturally beautiful, blue-skinned boy Krishna; to the strangely beautiful music of the Hare Krishna *mahamantra*; to the promise of transcendence. Therefore, I cannot help but feel a special kinship with them.

Most devotees experience doubts, now and then, about the truth of Krishna Consciousness, or about its relation to their personal spiritual and psychological growth. In my last few years in the movement I certainly did. And I know that, in spite of claims to the contrary, there are powerful disincentives to openly express such doubts.

Doubts, however, may be the voice of one's own inner self, the self that doesn't always exactly reflect the exterior "system" of Krishna Consciousness, that protests being shaped and molded into something it is not. Notwithstanding outer loyalty to ISKCON and its parent tradition, if the inner self is not being addressed, respected, honored, allowed to grow, provided means of expression, that authentic self is, sooner or later, going to raise a protest. When that voice first begins to speak, it can be quieted with regimental thinking, louder chanting, externalized activity, or simple denial. But sometime down the road it is bound to return, a little louder, a little more insistent; and at some point there will be no choice but to acknowledge it.

I would like, now, to address that inner voice and answer it with my own. I have, by the way, no malicious intent in doing so. I'm no anticultist or any other species of crusading ideologue. I've nothing to gain personally from this exercise except the pleasure of speaking words that I think need to be spoken to old friends and friends yet unknown.

Allow me to relate some of the reasons I left ISKCON after so many years of committed service. I've organized my reflections into several sections, which follow.

WHERE ARE THE PURE DEVOTEES?

As I think back, it seems that the factor that initially set in motion my gradual disillusionment with ISKCON was my growing awareness that, judging by its own criteria for success, ISKCON had, quite simply, failed as a spiritual movement. It became increasingly and inescapably obvious that the society was not fulfilling its own stated primary goal: to create "pure devotees"—to skillfully and successfully guide serious practitioners to those sublime states of spiritual consciousness elaborately described in the scriptures and endlessly reiterated in the movement's teaching forums.

There are, of course, devotees who seem peaceful, content, full of sincere purpose and conviction, high-spirited, and enthusiastic. And it is true that most devotees have experienced, at one time or another, uplifting feelings from chanting, seeing the deity, etc. But what of the more developed and sustained spiritual states described by such terms as *bhava* and *prema*? What of the love of Krishna that flows from the depths of one's being, overwhelms the mind and heart, and utterly transforms one into a holy person whose very presence inspires sanctity in others? Is ISKCON actually producing such manifestly Krishna-conscious people? Need I ask?

To account for this embarrassing lack of pure devotees in ISKCON, members are forced to enact a version of "The Emperor's New Clothes": do their best to convince themselves and others that certain high-profile devotees are, indeed, pure devotees, and proclaim that those who don't acknowledge their status are either not yet advanced enough for such discernment or are "envious fools." Or, alternatively, they must redefine the term "pure devotee" in such a broad, generous manner as to include the greatest number of devotees possible (e.g., all those aspiring to be pure devotees, all those following their initiation vows, etc.).

Some few, highly self-motivated, highly disciplined devotees do apply themselves to the principles of *bhakti* yoga and taste the fruits of their efforts.

But for the overwhelming majority of members, spiritual life in ISKCON is largely defined by a perpetual struggle against the base material instincts. They go on, year after year, hoping against hope that, "One day, yes, one day, a day far off in the future, one magic and wonderful day, I shall become a pure devotee."

After many years in the movement I came to the conclusion that whatever other success the society may enjoy—the proliferation of shaved heads and *saris*, numbers of temples opened, books distributed, celebrity endorsements procured—in the absence of the creation of highly evolved Krishna-conscious people, it's all an empty show.

ETHICAL FAILURE AND INTELLECTUAL DISHONESTY

Over the course of my years in ISKCON I became alarmed at the extent to which people who joined the movement in part as a reaction against the pervasive dishonesty in interpersonal dealings in mundane society, permitted themselves to become clever, sneaky, and two-faced in the name of promulgating truth. However hard it may be to admit, "the end justifies the means" has long been a defining and controlling ethic in the movement. Based on the presumption that tricking, deceiving, and cajoling illusioned souls to financially subsidize and otherwise support ISKCON represents a "higher" morality, devotees are taught to say and do almost anything if it can be justified in the name of "preaching." From the new devotee in the street extracting money from outsiders through blatant dissimulation to the most intellectually and socially sophisticated devotee skillfully packaging ISKCON in such a way as to most effectively win friends and undermine enemies, the ethic of pulling the wool over the benighted eyes of nondevotees in order to save their souls is the same.

Though this may appear justified from the point of view of a certain self-serving, contrived "spiritual" ethic, in practice it encourages a fundamental disrespect and superior attitude toward those for whom it claims feelings of compassion, and a manipulative, controlling attitude toward those it claims to liberate. Though some of the grosser manifestations of that cheating ethic have been tempered in recent years, the basic mindset, as far as I can see, hasn't changed, because it is rooted in ISKCON's presumption of moral superiority.

Another kind of dishonesty fundamental to the movement is intellectual: a learned orientation by which devotees' chief philosophical project ceases to be the sincere and disciplined effort to open themselves to truth and becomes to study, memorize, internalize, preach, and defend an already defined, predigested, prepackaged "truth." Instead of undertaking a genuinely open-minded, open-hearted quest for knowledge, they simply wave the banner of received "truth," however much it may or may not address the reality or facts at hand.

This tenacious defense of received "truth" in the face of potentially disconfirming realities represents, I suggest, an act not of courage but of cowardice, an ultimately futile attempt to defend a fragile existential security masquerading as enlightened certainty. I am continually amazed, and in retrospect somewhat embarrassed, by my own and other ISKCON intellectuals' easy willingness to sacrifice intellectual honesty in order to fortify our own and others' imperfect faith—to wave our tattered little banner of truth in the face of the wealth of contradictory ideas and multitextured realities surrounding us.

HARD HEARTS

I can recall, throughout my years in ISKCON, often being disappointed with the behavior of leaders, who seemed to care little for the personhood of the devotees under their command. There's a certain hardness of heart that comes from subordinating people to principles, defining the institution itself as preeminent and its members as merely its "humble servants."

This rhetoric of submission has, of course, a certain ring of loftiness: the idea of devotees striving together, pooling their energies and skills, sacrificing personal independence and comforts in order to serve the Glorious Mission. The trouble is, this creates a social and interpersonal environment in which the particular needs of individuals are devalued, downplayed, and postponed indefinitely—leaving the individual devotee sooner or later feeling used and abused. Through my years in ISKCON I became increasingly, painfully, and sadly aware of the ways in which, in the name of "engaging devotees in Krishna's service," leaders and administrators at all levels treat those "under" them in a patronizing, condescending, heavy-handed and authoritarian manner— viewing and dealing with their subordinates not as unique individuals possessing rich and complex inner lives, but as units of human energy to be matched to the necessary tasks at hand. I recall leaders criticizing, even ridiculing the very notion that special attention should be paid to the individual psyches and needs of devotees—who dismissed such concerns as mere sentimentality, unnecessary coddling, a lack of tough-mindedness, and destructive of the mandated qualities of humility and surrender.

This hard-nosed, hard-hearted attitude, this insensitive disregard for the individual, this almost cynical exalting of the principles of humility and surrender to ensure that the floors get swept and the bills paid, leaves many devotees, especially those low on the institutional totem pole, feeling betrayed. When the frustration, anxiety, and disappointment reach a high enough level, many simply leave, having become (understandably) bitter and vindictive.

SEXY CELIBACY

Most devotees will acknowledge that ISKCON's prohibition against "illicit sex" (any sex other than to conceive children in marriage) is the hardest ascetic principle to observe, the cause of the greatest difficulty among devotees, and (with the possible exception of disillusionment with ISKCON per se) the most common cause of "fall-down" from Krishna Consciousness.

Without debating the merits of celibacy in spiritual life, it's fair to say that the typical devotee, over time, is going to violate the celibacy rule. Desire for sex appears in everyone's life sooner or later, to one degree or another, in one form or another. From the guru lecturing from his throne down to the new recruit cleaning the bathroom, devotees think about sex, fantasize about it, or indulge in it (with other willing devotees, old lovers, outside contacts, whomever) if they think they can get away with it. This rather obvious fact isn't openly acknowledged in ISKCON because it's a source of significant embarrassment to devotees, who view indulgence in sex as disgusting, disgraceful, and a sign of personal failure—and, further, because they're forever boasting to nondevotees that their enjoyment of a "higher taste" is evidenced most conclusively by their disinterest in mundane sense gratification.

To be frank, there is something very sad, tragic even, in the spectacle of sincere spiritual aspirants endlessly struggling against and denying sexual feelings, continually berating themselves for their lack of heroic detachment from the body, seeking dark corners in which to masturbate, or, finding themselves "attached to" another devotee, planning and scheming "illicit" encounters. All this cheating and hypocrisy, guilt and shame, denial and cover-up, make a pathetic sham of ISKCON's ascetical conceit.

After many years in ISKCON, the whole celibacy fetish began to appear to me a bit suspect. Why the abysmal failure of most devotees to be uncompromisingly celibate? Why the pervasive inability to perform an act of renunciation that ISKCON defines as a precondition not only of serious spiritual practice but of civilized human life? Why this fundamental problem in the society?

Some devotees feel it's due to some innate deficit in the consciousness of westerners (we're too lusty); others blame it on devotees' chronically flawed performance of *bhakti* yoga (offensive chanting, etc.); a few contend that Prabhupada passed on Gaudiya Vaishnava practice imperfectly (by omitting certain necessary mystical elements in the initiatory process); some say it's a natural consequence of co-ed *ashrams* (and periodically suggest that the temples be rid of women). Whatever the cause, the fact remains that most devotees fall far short of serene celibacy, finding themselves deeply rooted in a physical body that by its very nature desires to touch and be touched, to feel the warmth of another human being.

So strong is that natural human desire that in order to avoid it, to repress the desire for it, one must paint the most exaggeratedly negative picture of it possible, envisioning sex as a purely wild, disgusting animal act. But consider: is lovemaking really just bestial humping and grunting? Does it have no connection at all to feelings of love, caring, appreciation, affection? Certainly, like any other human activity, sex can be beautiful or ugly. It can be an act of gross, selfish, piggish abandon, or it can be an expression of affection, a gentle act of mutual pleasuring, even a catalyst for feelings of emotional and spiritual oneness. It is only through a deliberate denial of past personal experience, or of intuition, that one can obliterate such memories or preempt such capacity for imagining.

My purpose here is not to advertise the glories of sex, but to note the problems associated with outlawing it—and also to make the radical suggestion that perhaps it is possible to be a spiritual person, a person of goodness, compassion, wisdom, sensitivity, awareness, under whatever spiritual banner, without denying and repressing one's implicit sensuality.

DISRESPECT FOR WOMEN

If ISKCON had truly been the glorious spiritual movement it advertises itself to be, with its only defect being offensive attitudes and discriminatory policies toward women, my then wife Sitarani and I still would have felt fully justified in abandoning the organization to which we'd devoted our lives. It became increasingly difficult for us to tolerate (and to defend among the scholars and students it was our duty to "cultivate") the raw, unreflective, juvenile, boys-club mentality of the movement—the official, insulting view of women as childlike, irrational, irresponsible, emotional, and wild unless controlled by a man.

It's not at all surprising that ISKCON would be a woman-fearing, woman-hating, woman-exploiting institution. A male-centered religion that defines sex as the enemy of spirituality naturally is going to define the object of men's sexual desire as the enemy personified: woman becomes chief antagonist in the holy drama of man transcending. Women, thus stigmatized, are to be tolerated at best—allowed to exist on the fringe in an officially reduced status, their wanton energies mercifully channeled into the service of men—and, at worst, to be officially and systematically denigrated, shunned, and, not infrequently, abused emotionally and sexually.

A movement that can allow a brand-new male recruit to feel superior—simply because he's got a penis—to a seasoned woman devotee who's been refining her consciousness for decades; a movement that can encourage a husband to feel at ease bossing his wife as if he were a Maharaja and she a coolie, as if she were placed on earth simply to serve and satisfy him—as if Krishna must be pleased by such a display of proper hierarchical dealings between the sexes—is going to invite the ridicule of outsiders, as well as incite pangs of conscience in its own thoughtful members. It's a wonder that any self-respecting woman tolerates such attitudes and treatment, and it's to her credit (I suppose) that she endures such abuse so as to remain connected to a spiritual tradition that she feels, or hopes, is wiser and grander than that.

For a time, Sitarani and I felt content with being "liberal" on the issue—with lending our weight, for example, to efforts to allow the occasional woman to give a lecture, lead a *kirtana*, or have a vote on the temple board. But we grew tired of struggling to put the best possible spin on the issue when questioned by discerning college students and others, of having to employ our intelligence and savvy in the supposedly noble quest of covering up for an organization unabashedly sexist.

When we finally left the movement, we felt greatly relieved to be free from a social and political environment that so denigrated women and positive feminine principles. ISKCON is, after all, such a determinedly male institution: all that obsession over power, control, order, hierarchy, protocol, and competition, not to mention all the chest-pounding martial rhetoric: "conquering the senses, destroying illusion, defeating enemies, smashing demons."

What of the beautiful "feminine" qualities of Shri Chaitanya and his followers? What of gentleness, humility, empathy, love, compassion, spiritual protection and nurturance, delicacy of emotion and of interpersonal dealings? While devotees pay occasional lip service to these acknowledged Vaishnava qualities, in practice it's the cherished male qualities of tough-mindedness, aggressiveness, and the power to dominate and manipulate others that the ISKCON establishment promotes and rewards.

SPIRITUAL DEPERSONALIZATION

A final factor in my cumulative decision to leave ISKCON was philosophical: a growing awareness that however much wisdom and beauty may be found in a particular religious tradition, no one tradition, no one system, can speak fully for any individual. Whatever the possible transcendent origins of a spiritual path, it is passed down through human beings: wise, insightful, saintly perhaps, but distinct, individual people nonetheless, with their own distinctive life histories, experiences, temperaments, and ways of thinking, feeling, and communicating. Though there was much in Krishna Consciousness that I found deeply meaningful and appealing, I began to realize (subtly, slowly, over a long period of time) that, short of simply obliterating my own thoughts and feelings, I could not blindly, automatically accept every word of the scriptures (e.g., women are inferior to men, thunder and lightning come from Lord Indra, the Sun is closer to the Earth than the Moon, etc.)

More important than such difficulties, however, was my growing sense that there was something unnatural, something artificial and forced, about the very idea of having to completely supplant my own thoughts, reflections, insights, and intuitions about myself, the world, and my own experience with a prepackaged, preapproved system of ideas and doctrines that, whatever its origins, has evolved through countless hands and been refracted through many minds and sensibilities through the centuries. I began to feel (though it took a long time to admit it to myself) that this is an unrealistic and unfair demand to be made upon anyone, however "imperfect" we may be, because it dishonors the integrity and particularity of who we, in our essential individuality, are.

I came to feel that there is something ultimately impersonal about the notion that we are utterly different from what we presently feel ourselves to be, that our manifest personality is simply the product of an unnatural, illusioned state, and that to "transcend" this felt, immediate sense of self we must submit to the authority of certain authorized people for radical reeducation—cutting ourselves off, more or less, from any ideas, influences, and individuals that might possibly remind us of the selves we mistakenly felt we were.

Now, whatever the beauties of the spiritual path, there is something slightly ominous about a spiritual system that so utterly and uncompromisingly devalues me as I directly know and experience myself, that would make me doubt and question my every perception, my very sense of reality, a system that would have me submit, body and mind, to certain "authorities" about whom I've seen no conclusive evidence of perfection—whose spiritual status is tenuous at best (in light of the periodic scandals involving those advertised in ISKCON as "pure" and "perfect").

Must spiritual life really depend upon such an extreme act of self-abnegation, such a wholesale rejection of personal experience? Are truth and wisdom to be so radically abstracted from my own consciousness, the depth of my own being? Is turning a blind eye and deaf ear to my inner vision and voice really in my best interest? Is this self-denial really "humility"—a rational recognition of personal limitations—or ultimately little more than a form of self-shaming and self-negation?

I began to sense that true spirituality cannot be reduced to a corporate, conformist, authoritarian structure. On the contrary, it honors and trusts the individual spirit enough to allow it to seek its own path, make its own mistakes, find its own way, by listening to its own intuitions and acknowledging the various sources of wisdom that present themselves throughout life's journey. I realized, ultimately, that for all ISKCON's talk of freedom, liberation, escaping conditioned modes of being, the prevailing mentality in ISKCON is, in fact, characterized by a distinct fear of freedom: an anxiety about personal quest, a fear of trusting the moment, of opening to the unexpected, of allowing the mind and heart to remain receptive, curious, vulnerable, adventurous.

IS THERE LIFE AFTER ISKCON?

That such a question might even occur to a devotee is itself a telling comment on the ISKCON mindset. In seventeen years of Krishna Consciousness I sat through literally thousands of *Bhagavad Gita* and *Srimad-Bhagavatam* classes (a great many of them my own!) in which I was regaled with nightmarish images of the world looming outside the walls of ISKCON, warned repeatedly of the miseries to come should I foolishly wander outside our fortifications. In a place where higher spiritual experience is in short supply, it is necessary, indeed, to create powerful disincentives to leaving—even if they must be based on exaggeration and fear-mongering.

But the world, as it turns out, is not the unrelieved chamber of horrors described in *Bhagavatam* classes. It's a mixed bag, just like ISKCON. Yes, there are all manner of terrible things: war, poverty, disease, sexual abuse, racism, and many more. One cannot help but affirm that the world is a place pervaded by suffering and cruelty. But in the midst of all that darkness and craziness there is good as well. To begin with, there are many good-hearted people who come to the aid of those who are disadvantaged, persecuted, misunderstood, mistreated, who try to relieve others of suffering in myriad ways.

Out here in the wider world there are also many who seek truth, meaning, and beauty through artistic self-expression. At their best, all of the arts—painting, music, dance, literature, and so on—support a quest for truth, beauty, and sublimity. One has only to open oneself to the works of master creators—wander a fine arts museum, hear a great symphony, witness a ballet, lose oneself in a great novel or poem—to experience the depths and heights of the human spirit. There are infinite riches to be seen, heard, experienced, and absorbed.

Over the past several years I've immersed myself in fine art photography—both as a working artist and as a student of the history and aesthetics of the medium—and derive profound satisfactions therefrom. Through creative photography I've discovered in myself new capacities for seeing, intuiting, feeling, creating, communicating. I'm currently working on a book that explores the spiritual dimensions of the medium.

Besides artistic expression, which is my own path, there are other venues for living a meaningful life: intellectual pursuits, works of compassion (both within and outside of formal institutional and career contexts), teaching, and a thousand other forms of honest, meaningful activity. And there are, of course, a world of spiritual paths and practices to explore. Leaving ISKCON, one is pleasantly surprised to discover that many people are devoted to a spiritual path—seeking, through various means, to become more aware, more sensitive, and more compassionate, and working to integrate spiritual truths into their daily lives. And, of course, many former ISKCONites continue on the Vaishnava path, but in ways they feel retain an integrity and humanism largely missing in ISKCON itself.

Once you step outside the gates of ISKCON, you discover that it's the quality of your own consciousness and heart that determines what sort of person you're going to be and what sort of life you're going to live. You do not suddenly and automatically fall into wanton debauchery, become a demon, or go mad. Nor are you forced to assume an attitude of uncritical acceptance. It's quite possible to remain acutely aware of the limitations and imperfections of human society and maintain a creatively ambivalent relationship with it, while constructing a safe, sane, and meaningful space for yourself within it.

Out here in the wider world there are people who are good and decent, who share one's values, and whose friendship can be nourishing and deepening. People who've left ISKCON also often find profound satisfaction in developing the kinds of deep, intimate, loving relationships that they missed as celibate *brahmacharis* and *brahmacharinis*, or as married people caught in unsatisfying, hierarchical, sexless (or sexually abusive) relationships.

Well, that's more or less what I wish to say. This essay is a revised, slightly shortened version of one I wrote several years ago, which has been available online for the last few, and apparently widely read and discussed. If the e-mails I continue to receive from readers, both inside and outside ISKCON, are any indication, I've spoken to, and for, many. For that I'm grateful.

[23]

ON STAYING IN ISKCON

Personal Story IV

MICHAEL GRANT (MUKUNDA GOSWAMI)
AND ANUTTAMA DAS ADHIKARI

The truth suffers more from the heat of its defenders than
the arguments of its opponents. —William Penn

SINCE ITS INCEPTION IN 1966, the International Society for Krishna
Consciousness (ISKCON) has grown into a worldwide institution. As is
clear from the other papers in this volume, many problems, both internal and external, have accompanied this growth, impeding the movement's
progress and causing many members to leave the institution, some of them
joining other organizations in the greater lineage of Gaudiya Vaishnavism. In
this essay we outline the reasons why we chose to stay within the ISKCON institution, and present our perspective: that through reform and other forms of
direct confrontation with difficulties, there is hope that a healthy ISKCON will
ultimately emerge and that the movement will achieve its mission.

We shall define "staying in ISKCON" as "subscribing to the teachings and
practices of A.C. Bhaktivedanta Swami while supporting and identifying oneself as part of the organization he founded, namely, ISKCON." Following the
desires of its founder, A.C. Bhaktivedanta Swami, ISKCON, the International
Society for Krishna Consciousness, attempts to bring about a change in world
consciousness by educating people on how to become Krishna (God) con-

scious. Shrila Prabhupada, as his followers call him, prophesied that this change would occur, and that it would inevitably involve political and social change. In his estimation, ISKCON would effect this process well after its founder's physical demise.

The seven purposes of ISKCON (originally written in 1953) are as follows:[1]

1. To systematically propagate spiritual knowledge to society at large and to educate all peoples in the techniques of spiritual life in order to check the imbalance of values in life and to achieve real unity and peace in the world;
2. To propagate a consciousness of Krishna, as he is revealed in the *Bhagavad Gita* and *Shrimad Bhagavata* scriptures;
3. To bring the members of the society together and nearer to Krishna, the prime entity, thus to develop the idea within the members, and humanity at large, that each soul is part and parcel of the quality of God (Krishna);
4. To teach and encourage the *sankirtana* movement, congregational chanting of the holy name of Krishna as revealed in the teachings of Lord Shri Chaitanya Mahaprabhu;
5. To erect for the members and for society at large a holy place of transcendental pastimes, dedicated to the personality of Krishna;
6. To bring the members closer together for the purpose of teaching a simpler and more natural way of life;
7. With a view toward achieving the aforementioned purposes, to publish and distribute periodicals, magazines, books, and other writings.

Our vision is that ISKCON's seven purposes are achievable, even though some, especially numbers one and three, appear to be "missions impossible." Besides these purposes, a statement made by Shrila Prabhupada's spiritual master indicates just how difficult ISKCON's mission is. He said that the Krishna Consciousness movement would be successful when the high court judges are wearing *tilaka* (the clay forehead mark of a Krishna devotee).[2] Such lofty and seemingly unrealistic goals challenge us both psychologically and intellectually.

The kinds of reasons that we identify for remaining a part of ISKCON are principally three: psychological, intellectual, and spiritual. First, the psychological component includes the "feeling" that ISKCON is the right place for us to be. It encompasses, among other things, personal friendships, a sense of community, love for the founder and his mission, love for his organization, and a fondness for ISKCON's culture—fine art, sculpture, architecture, food, dance, music, drama, deity attire, books, and hospitality.

Second, we find ISKCON intellectually engaging. The teaching of the Vaishnava literature, most notably the *Bhagavad Gita* and the *Bhagavata Purana*, as well as the lectures by ISKCON's founder, stimulate our philosophical quest for truth. We have found a depth of theoretical knowledge and practical wisdom that constantly challenges our minds. We find this knowledge to be ever fresh and intellectually invigorating.

Third, an equal, perhaps even more prominent component is our spiritual belief. We are continually involved in learning and teaching processes related to the theological realms of human existence. As practitioners of *bhakti*, devotional yoga, we see spiritual knowledge as something not accessed solely through absorption of theological facts or memorization of philosophical precepts but also acquired through acts of practical devotion. ISKCON provides satisfaction for our spiritual inclinations and, through its outreach programs, gives us a practical framework for performing devotional service, thus helping us realize the transcendent and develop love for the supreme being.

We are certain that Krishna is the supreme being and the intimate friend of all living beings. We are also convinced that the best way to please and develop our love for Krishna is to serve Shrila Prabhupada, Krishna's devotee and emissary. We are sure that the best way to prove our love for Shrila Prabhupada is to serve and assist his institution, and, indeed, Prabhupada specifically stated: "Your love for me will be shown by how much you cooperate to keep this institution together after I am gone."[3] In our view, staying in ISKCON is the most effective way to repay the debt we owe him and the most effective means to share the beauty and mystery of Krishna with the world. Prabhupada identified himself as an integral part of the society, often declaring that ISKCON was his own body. We support this and assert that his vision is not fully achievable outside of ISKCON.

Shrila Prabhupada did say that his own disciples could "spoil everything."[4] But ISKCON has faced many external difficulties over the years, starting from the early days of the organization. To list but a smattering of these: a real estate agent cheated disciples who wanted to purchase a better property for the New York temple (1967); the British government prohibited ISKCON's biggest annual festival in that country (1974). German police raided ISKCON's Schloss Rettershof temple, Gestapo-style; drove resident devotees in paddy wagons into nearby Frankfurt; interrogated, photographed, and fingerprinted all of them; and detained 73 devotees for eight hours and booked two on charges that were later dropped (1974). Arsonists destroyed a Prabhupada deity in Fiji (1989); a hurricane blew away the Puerto Rico temple (1989); paid hoodlums demolished the first Hare Krishna temple in Mumbai (1973); the government of Argentina banned ISKCON (1976); major earthquakes toppled deities in San Francisco and Los Angeles (1989 and 1994); devotees died in Soviet prisons and psychiatric "clinics" (1983 to 1986); a Liberian firing squad killed seven innocent ISKCON members (1984); Armenian, Yugoslavian, and Georgian bigots beat resident devotees and ransacked temples, and several cases came to light in which police unnecessarily brutalized devotees (Rostov 1995, Krasnodar 1996). In what became external adversity's high-water mark, a U.S. jury ordered the movement in 1977 to pay plaintiffs US$36 million in the highly publicized "Robin George case" (a suit that was ostensibly about a teenage girl who turned against ISKCON after having been helped by devotees to hide from her parents, but was in fact fueled by the "anticult" movement in California).[5]

To most of these external roadblocks, ISKCON's response was somewhat predictable, and in many cases responsible. Its leaders sought to correct the difficulties and to ensure that such problems would not recur. For example: in response to the "Robin George case" ruling, ISKCON stopped accepting minors into the movement without parental consent, and in response to charges of unethical or illegal fund-raising strategies, ISKCON refrained from raising funds in ways that would cause national governments to suspect the entire movement of wrongdoing. The society also put in place improved security measures on temple premises and obtained full government permission for all details of festivals, especially those organized on national landmarks. Members regularly met with police and government officials. Devotees built new structures out of better materials and rebuilt with greater durability damaged and destroyed property.

More internal, personal problems were also always with the movement, becoming more prominent in the 1990s. Conspicuous with their shaved heads and robes or *saris*, most members, even leaders, have had to grapple with "being different," and all have had to fight the temptations of, to use ISKCON-speak, the "material world," especially intoxication and sex (ISKCON requires all initiated devotees to foreswear intoxication, meat-eating, gambling, and extramarital and nonprocreational sex). Over the years, many members have succumbed to sensual demands, and some have left the movement as a result.

To list a sample from the spectrum of such internal problems that plagued ISKCON in its earlier years: a devotee shot dead another devotee who was having an affair with the former's wife (1970); a group of ISKCON members claimed to have attained the highest level of spiritual realization and started their own club to promote this "higher level of consciousness," leading Prabhupada to personally intervene (1970); some devotees were discovered to be actively promoting that Shrila Prabhupada was Krishna himself (1970); the Governing Board Commission (GBC) suspended New Vrindavan, one of the movement's largest U.S. devotee communities, for deviation and criminal activities (1987); and errant devotees were arrested for smuggling heroin and hashish (1975 and 1977 respectively). In addition to these individual incidents, there have been more widespread internal problems. For example, a majority of early ISKCON arranged marriages have ended in separation and divorce, and, in the 1990s, many apostasies and parallel Gaudiya Vaishnava groups arose and proliferated via the Internet, and significant numbers of devotees left ISKCON to join them.

Perhaps the most catastrophic calamity to befall the movement occurred almost immediately after Shrila Prabhupada's passing on November 14, 1977. A misconstrued system of governance ensued, and ISKCON lived through what came to be known as the "zonal *acharya* system." Eleven ISKCON gurus began to eclipse ISKCON's General Board of Commissioners, the GBC, which is the movement's ultimate managing authority, and became gurus and islands unto themselves, managing the society on a regional basis with little concern for the world as a whole. This structure occluded Prabhupada's vision of a global ISKCON.

ISKCON's second generation is also a matter of grave concern. In some areas of the world many new members may be joining, but what about the children of current devotees? Will they remain a part of the society, and if so, to what extent? In 2000, a number of children of devotees filed a lawsuit against the movement, claiming sexual, physical, and psychological abuse and neglect in ISKCON's boarding schools. The civil lawsuit in the U.S., launched by some of them against the organization or parts of it, is a grim indicator that some of ISKCON's second generation may be opting out.[6]

During his time with us, Prabhupada often stepped in and did what he could to ease critical situations that bewildered managers and senior disciples. He was trying to teach that enlightened leaders should be, among other things, problem solvers. He taught by practice and precept that institutions, like cars or other technological constructs, are not perfect. They have to be repeatedly observed from all angles, maintained, repaired, changed, and upgraded. Some of ISKCON's early responses to these internal problems can only be described as failures. Managers' inability to govern and lead in an enlightened fashion, combined with harsh or insensitive treatment of adult members in many communities, have caused internal weaknesses resulting in the thinning of frontline ranks. Also, the movement sometimes upheld substandard leaders, turning a blind eye to serious personal defects. Many marriages were "arranged" or gone into hastily without due deliberation, and too many understandably ended in divorce.

On the other hand, ISKCON has often acted responsibly and instituted changes aimed at preventing such internal calamities from recurring, and it is such changes that ultimately give us hope. Notwithstanding a delay of several years and much damage, ISKCON's management, unaided by Prabhupada's personal presence or intervention, eventually dismantled the zonal *acharya* guru system and declared it anathema. After the criminal activities of the previously mentioned New Vrindavan community were discovered, members of ISKCON's top leadership, including the GBC, helped the police and the courts land convictions. Leaders have also put in place a women's ministry, through which the first woman to sit on the GBC began her tenure in 1998. Child protection teams and youth programs have been established, and several hundred thousand dollars have been given in grants for education and therapy to former students of ISKCON's schools. Legal and financial accounting systems, academic and interfaith activities, task forces assigned to help leadership restructure itself, a temple support team dedicated to raising standards of accountability, and alternative dispute resolution and ombuds systems are all post-Prabhupada developments in ISKCON. In addition, a series of examinations meant to assure that spiritual titles and deferment are offered only to those truly and officially deserving is in place. These steps are the beginnings of serious reform. Moreover, an uncompromising demand that ISKCON members practice what they preach and fully embody the qualities the scriptures state they must embody is being put forward by an increasing number of devotees, internal reformers, and communications specialists.

Another troubling phenomenon that some members are attempting to redress concerns a type of spiritual hubris in which devotees feel superior to others. Historically, this has caused numerous problems in relationships both within ISKCON and between its members and the greater society. This type of arrogance raises the question of tolerance toward other religions. Shaunaka Rishi, ISKCON's director of communications for Europe and editor of the *ISKCON Communications Journal*, has squarely confronted and addressed the interfaith issue. He drafted ISKCON's first official statement concerning its relationship with people of other faiths. The final declaration, which was adopted by the GBC executive committee, includes this excerpt:

> In ISKCON we consider love of a Supreme personal God to be the highest form of religious expression, and we recognize and respect this expression in other theistic traditions. We respect the spiritual worth of paths of genuine self-realization and search for the Absolute Truth in which the concept of a personal Deity is not explicit. Other communities and organizations advocating humanitarian, ethical and moral standards are also valued as being beneficial to society.[7]

This position paper, which continues for several pages, was published in the *ISKCON Communications Journal* and sent to more than 700 academics worldwide. Numerous academic and interfaith forums have recently helped demonstrate that not all ISKCON leaders think the movement is "God's gift to the world." While some decry all such effort as too little too late, those operating these programs see them as well-chosen remedial responses to the growing pains of an organization founded only thirty-six years ago.

Nonetheless, ISKCON's difficulties devastated swaths of its membership, who left the movement. Some thought that facing the kinds of obstacles outlined above simply wasn't worth the personal sacrifice they had made and would have to make in the future, or that facing sometimes blatant hostility from the greater society was too overwhelming and perhaps unnecessary. Others felt that ISKCON's internal problems would never be overcome. And, as noted above, some left ISKCON because they felt its demands for no meat-eating, no intoxication (including use of coffee, tea, and cigarettes), no "illicit" sex, and no gambling were excessive and impractical. They felt ISKCON was failing by making unrealistic and unnatural demands on its initiates.

We do not intend, here, to pass judgment regarding whether the reasons that people have left ISKCON are emotional or rational, or whether they are valid or invalid. But we do feel strongly that ISKCON leaders need to conduct critical analyses and learn how to respond when substantial numbers of members exit. This has not always been done. Instead, those who have left have often been blamed for not being serious enough about their spiritual lives. Clearly, such an approach is not constructive for a movement that wishes to grow into an organization with worldwide impact.

We have elected to remain a part of ISKCON because we are convinced that problems are natural and inevitable. We remember well that Prabhupada told us we shouldn't be surprised at how many leave the movement but at how many stay. We think that the dedication and sincerity of those who remain will eventually bring to the movement the kind of leadership that Shrila Prabhupada expected. We have seen reform and correction taking place, and we see it continuing and accelerating. Michael Langone, of the "anticult" American Family Foundation, praised ISKCON's recent efforts at reform and acknowledged the efficacy of change that is initiated from and takes place within an organization.[8] In our perspective, ISKCON has learned from its mistakes and its reforms are slowly setting in. We are convinced that its mission will prevail and that ultimately the movement will help to bring about social change globally. Admittedly we want to be on a winning team, but our team must advocate, we feel, "ultimate truth," beauty, and goodness; and it must also hold out hope for improving the quality of life for billions of people. We believe that it does.

ISKCON's goals call for a sea change in the world and carry an unspoken social agenda. We are convinced that through rededication to purity, honest assessment, and adaptability, ISKCON can succeed, despite all past and present obstacles. While pained by the welter of difficulties facing the movement, we have seen recent signs that it is starting to unravel these problems and will eventually solve them. However, we continually scrutinize ISKCON, because we are convinced that effective reform has to come from within, and it must include accountability, integrity, basic morality, ISKCON core values, and good character. At all levels within the organization, disciples of Shrila Prabhupada must improve their own commitment to the standards of integrity he demanded of his followers.

It is easy to blame others for our problems. ISKCON's detractors, internal and external, will likely continue for the life of the organization. Their effect, however, will be measured not so much by their skills but by how ISKCON and its members respond to them. Today ISKCON has learned how to deal more effectively with external aggression such as government harassment, bigoted populaces, "deprogrammer" kidnappings (now passé), cheating business tactics, cultural condescension, and general intolerance. We now need to become more effective in dealing with the internal problems. Prabhupada indicated that one must become "conscious" before becoming "Krishna conscious," and he exhorted his followers to at least become "ladies and gentlemen." Improvement begins when there are full recognition and admission of mistakes and wrongdoing as well as heartfelt apologies to those wronged. Conflicts of interest and corruption must be eliminated before reform can take place. Many devotees have left Shrila Prabhupada's society, dissatisfied by what they perceive as a lack of support or love from those supervising them.

We may measure growth by how many people receive initiation, the numbers of books devotees distribute, how many temples ISKCON opens each year, how many times the name of Krishna is vibrated in public, the quantity of *prasadam* (spiritual food) ISKCON members distribute, how many festivals they put on, or the number of new members joining each year. Some point to such statistics as indisputable signs of growth. But such progress can be short-term or even imaginary. Quantity is a poor substitute for quality. If foundational support is crumbling, and if many are leaving and many more are voicing heartfelt distress because they are not getting the love and sense of community they expected from ISKCON, there must be cause for alarm as well as internal systemwide reform.

Given all of ISKCON's difficulties, would it not be best to abandon such an organization? If an institution's problems are systemic and seem unsolvable, as some would argue, would it not be prudent to jettison it altogether and seek out affiliation with more seemingly member-friendly associations? As a matter of fact, it is a Vedantic principle that identification with one's body or nation is a lower form of consciousness,[9] so does the same hold true for people who identify and stay with organizations in the first place?

Although loyalists can be victims, fidelity has a positive dimension too. It turns out to be a principal reason for staying in ISKCON. In her best-selling book, *The Healing of America*, Marianne Williamson argues that the United States cannot be "the home of the brave" until it has made reparations with Native Americans, African Americans, and the people of Vietnam. Williamson shows that patriotism includes components of conscience, loyalty, and love.[10] This is relevant to ISKCON's present efforts to reach out to the children, women, and all others who have been mistreated by the institution.

Are devotees starry-eyed? Blinded by love? Love, including pure spiritual love, is a mysterious phenomenon. Most people who stay in ISKCON say they do so because they "love Prabhupada," ISKCON's founder, or because they still believe his society is the best place to learn how to love Krishna. This love may exist in the realm of irrationality, feelings, and subjectivity, but it is valuable nonetheless. Some who remain say they feel they would be betraying Prabhupada if they were to withdraw from the organization he founded, no matter how much of a muddle it might be in.

One might also add, without attempting to shift responsibility, that the difficulties that haunt ISKCON are not unique. Experience and discussions with leaders of many other religious organizations have shown that the types of problems ISKCON encounters also occur in most organizations. In fact, some faith groups in the United States have had to confront more grave and more frequent difficulties than those of ISKCON. While commonality cannot be cause for complacency or insouciance, we often have to force ourselves to remember that ISKCON's problems are not so different from those that happen every day in our own worlds and at home, within our families, communities, countries, and countless other organizations, religious and otherwise. Successful organizations have learned how to openly meet and overcome their obstacles.

This, we suggest, is the key issue. As members of ISKCON, how do we correct the faults we find in Shrila Prabhupada's society? Some choose to improve their individual lives by leaving ISKCON, just as they joined to improve themselves. Others, such as ourselves, stay, believing that reform, both of ISKCON and of individual hearts, is best accomplished within the association of Prabhupada's intimate ISKCON family.

In an important letter, Prabhupada wrote that problems would always exist because, "It is the nature of the living condition to always have some fault." He said that internal clashes occur "because devotees are persons," and that differences would therefore be inevitable.[11] Prabhupada has stated that mistakes should become pillars of our success.[12] This means that a management learning curve needs to be established, individually and collectively, if ISKCON is to solve its problems. We view recent institutional actions, such as those noted above, as positive developments and have confidence that they will grow and

eventually be instrumental in curing the troubles that have beleaguered the society. We think ISKCON will get on the right track and succeed in achieving
Shrila Prabhupada's goals. But we cannot be heedlessly optimistic about any
future. Leaders can still, as Prabhupada said, "spoil everything." Time and
again, he urged his followers to employ vigilance and caution,[13] and "organization and intelligence."[14] Clearly, change must begin with our own individual hearts. We, as devotees, must ask this question: "Can we be committed to
help ISKCON focus on the integrity and spiritual maturity that Prabhupada
intended for his organization?"

Our faith and love for Prabhupada's organization, and the association of
devotees who constitute it, keep us in it today. By staying with ISKCON we feel
close to him. Willingness and enthusiasm to make the worst better and the
best better are key factors in staying with any organization. Attitude and vision
are what tend to prevail, and reason, irrespective of how abundant, how expert, or how persuasive it may be, will not necessarily change attitudes. Points
of view will always differ, sometimes slightly and sometimes diametrically, because there are faults and glories in every person, endeavor, and organization.
People choose their association and pin their futures on what works best for
them. Institutions can support individual initiative; they can also dampen and
extinguish it. The authors have elected to stay and help make ISKCON what
its founder wanted it to be, no matter how difficult or how long the effort. We
love ISKCON, with all its defects. We also love its ideals, its prayers, its hopes,
and its aspirations.

In summary, then, staying in ISKCON is ultimately an act of faith. No matter how hard we may try to reason it all out, we are here because we want to
be here. We tolerate the opposition of the world and the agonizing internal
problems mainly because we believe that Shrila Prabhupada's teachings represent the consummate philosophy of life; there is no better place for us to be;
ISKCON will overcome the evils afflicting it; and Krishna Consciousness is the
best mechanism for attaining love of God and achieving positive spiritual
change in the world—even if it takes centuries for an ISKCON groundswell to
alter the global landscape. The spiritual purity of ISKCON's members and the
conviction that the founder would want us to remain and help renovate,
reengineer, and, when necessary, reinvent the society's structure and leadership have all contributed to our decision to remain. The numerous difficulties
the International Society for Krishna Consciousness has encountered over
three decades encompass widespread organizational and personal failures.
But, while they still have much to learn, ISKCON's members have learned a lot
from their mistakes. Emotional, intellectual, and spiritual fulfillment, as well
as the ongoing implementation of serious reform, keep us in the movement.

NOTES

1. See http://www.iskcon.com/about/mission.html.
2. Bhaktivinoda Thakur, *Shri Chaitanya Shikshashtikam,* 4th ed., trans. Sar Bijoy Krishna Rarhi (Chenai, India: Gaudiya Math, 1998), 115, 138.
3. Satsvarupa dasa Goswami, *Srila Prabhupada Lilamrta* (Los Angeles: The Bhaktivedanta Book Trust, 1980), chap. 52.
4. In at least one lecture and two letters, Prabhupada used the phrase "spoil everything," to indicate how devotees could ruin what he had started. Bhaktivedanta Swami, lecture on *Bhagavad-gita,* 1.43., London, 30 July 1973, *Bhaktivedanta Vedabase* (published by Bhaktivedanta Archives, Los Angeles: The Bhaktivedanta Book Trust International, 1998); Bhaktivedanta Swami to Bali Mardan, Calcutta, 5 March 1972, *Bhaktivedanta Vedabase*; Bhaktivedanta Swami letter to Madhumangala, Hyderabad, 18 November 1972, *Bhaktivedanta Vedabase.*
5. The case was settled out of court fifteen years later for a fraction of the initial judgment.
6. This is not to ignore that civil litigation in the United States is often driven by money- and fame-hungry attorneys.
7. Shaunaka Rishi Das, "ISKCON in Relation to People of Faith in God," *ISKCON Communications Journal* 7 (1999): 1.
8. Michael D. Langone wrote, "the reform group within ISKCON appears to recognize that some of the organization's behaviors and practices need to be subjected to ethical accountability. . . . Even if the reform movement is not fully confronting the organization's problems, its capacity to bring about constructive change is much greater than that of its critics. . . . Reform that grows from within an organization has a much greater chance of success than reform that outsiders try to impose." "Cults, Psychological Manipulation and Society: International Perspectives—An Overview," *ISKCON Communications Journal* 7 (1999): 53.
9. "One who identifies his self as the inert body composed of mucus, bile and air, who assumes his wife and family are permanently his own, who thinks an earthen image or the land of his birth is worshipable, or who sees a place of pilgrimage as merely the water there, but who never identifies himself with, feels kinship with, worships or even visits those who are wise in spiritual truth—such a person is no better than a cow or an ass." Hridayananda Das Goswami, ed., *Srimad Bhagavatam* (Los Angeles: Bhaktivedanta Book Trust, 1989), canto 10, chap. 84, verse 13, p. 455.
10. Marianne Williamson, *The Healing of America* (New York, Simon & Schuster, 1997), 317-18.
11. Bhaktivedanta Swami, letter to Aitreya Rishi, Mumbai, 4 February 1972; *Bhaktivedanta Vedabase*, Bhaktivedanta Archives (Los Angeles: Bhaktivedanta Book Trust International, 1998).
12. "One should not be discouraged in the discharge of devotional service. Failures may not be detrimental; they may be the pillars of success." Bhaktivedanta Swami, *Light of the Bhagavata* (Hong Kong: Bhaktivedanta Book Trust, 1984), verse 43: commentary.
13. Prabhupada used the word "cautious" at least 155 times in books, conversations, lectures, and personal letters (*Bhaktivedanta Vedabase*, published by Bhaktivedanta Archives, Los Angeles: The Bhaktivedanta Book Trust International, 1998).

14. "'Do you think this movement can go on without me?' Prabhupada asked. Giriraja was astounded that Prabhupada had called him in the middle of the night to ask him this. 'I think,' said Giriraja, 'that as long as we are sincere and go on chanting Hare Krishna and follow the principles, the movement will be successful.' Shrila Prabhupada was silent. When he spoke, each word seemed to come with great effort. He uttered the word organization. Then he said, 'Organization and intelligence. Is there anything else?'" Satsvarupa dasa Goswami, *Shrila Prabhupada Lilamrta*, chap. 54.

[24]

RE-VISIONING ISKCON

Constructive Theologizing for Reform and Renewal

THOMAS HERZIG (TAMAL KRISHNA GOSWAMI)
AND KENNETH VALPEY (KRISHNA KSHETRA DAS)

SINCE THE DEMISE OF ITS CHARISMATIC FOUNDER in 1977, the International Society for Krishna Consciousness (ISKCON) has faced a growing institutional disaffection among its initiated membership. In outreach, if results are judged quantitatively, a slackening of missionary fervor has failed to attract new recruits to replenish the diminishing ranks of its full-time members. An official survey conducted in 1998 has found ISKCON's underlying problems to be largely sociological.[1] Rarely is the theology deemed suspect. It is regarded as sacrosanct, as if to tamper with it is to court disaster.

ISKCON's founder, A.C. Bhaktivedanta Swami Prabhupada (1896–1977), a disciplic successor to the sixteenth-century ecstatic Shri Chaitanya (1486–1533),[2] emphasized clear literary sources and subcontinental enculturation to validate social change in the contemporary global order—a future he hoped to forge by legitimating a reenvisioned past. But any amalgam of past and present is never entirely homogenous. For a self-consciously traditional movement, fixed on the one hand by the mammoth literary canon of its founder, confronted on the other by the ever-changing conditions of time, place, and circumstance, consequent tensions are a natural outcome.

ISKCON's initial efforts within the counterculture and its reverse missionary endeavors in India and the Hindu diaspora are well documented, as is the postcharismatic turmoil that has beset its ranks. To date, however, this large body of social scientific research has at best exposed the strain of ISKCON's premodern appeal against modern realities and postmodern assumptions, stopping short of in-depth theological analysis and problem solving. This paper begins to fill the lacuna by identifying likely locations—flexible postulates and porous boundaries—hospitable to theological construction.

The authors, both active leaders within ISKCON and at the same time academics, feel a dual obligation, on the one hand to ISKCON, on the other to academe. Ideally, one finds in one's different affiliations a mutuality of interests and methods; practically, this is not always the case. As a work in progress meant to encourage dialogue within and between these two fields of discourse, the position advanced in this essay is at best exploratory, not advocacy. If ISKCON feels our probing too insistent, or if the academy feels we have held back and not dug deeply enough, we request each to recognize the constraints under which we operate and to appreciate that ours is indeed a delicate tightrope act.

The term "theology," despite and perhaps because of its obvious Christian currency, has circulated widely enough now to defy sectarian limits and finds acceptance even amid nontheisms: thus "Buddhist Theology."[3] It should therefore come as no surprise that ISKCON's founder Prabhupada, ever willing to adopt "skillful means," also takes possession of the term to describe his theology.[4]

We, too, will theologize, but we will do so employing a long-respected Chaitanya Vaishnava hermeneutic that organizes theological inquiry into *pramana* (the means to acquire valid knowledge) and a threefold *prameya* (the object of valid knowledge): *sambandha* (relationship), *abhidheya* (process), and *prayojana* (motive or goal).[5] Prabhupada's explanatory translation to a defining Chaitanyaite text unpacks the terms' essential meanings:

> The Vedic literatures give information about the living entity's eternal relationship with Krishna, which is called *sambandha*. The living entity's understanding of this relationship and his acting accordingly is called *abhidheya*. Returning home, back to Godhead, is the ultimate goal of life and is called *prayojana* (*Chaitanya-Charitamrita* 2.20.124).[6]

The great advantage of this schema is the confidence it has enjoyed from Shri Chaitanya's earliest theologians to his most recent exponents. The congeniality of a familiar system is obvious, particularly when for most traditions explicit doctrinal originality is regarded not as a virtue but as a deviation. Let us start by discussing *pramana*.

In contradistinction to the current aversion to an absolute, ahistorical vo-
cabulary of any sort, Gaudiya Vaishnavism insists upon the capacity of *valid*
knowledge (*prama*) to reveal and circumscribe the true nature of an object as
it actually is. For the followers of Chaitanya, *shabda* (from *shabd*, to sound) is
revelation, not just verbal testimony, and is the only ultimate source of valid
knowledge in which epistemological certainty resides. In addition to the Vedas
and Upanishads, *shabda*'s divine status is extended to all of the tradition's chosen texts. Jiva Gosvamin (1513–1598), the tradition's preeminent theologian,
lists ten *pramanas*, which he then collapses into three—*pratyaksha* (sense perception), *anumana* (inference), and *shabda*—before concluding that only the
last, *shabda*, is independently reliable in revealing the absolute. Prabhupada
follows Jiva.[7]

The Chaitanya Vaishnava tendency to diminish other *pramanas* like *pratyaksha* and *anumana* enables Prabhupada to make remarkably little allowance for
modernity. His exegetical method, while clear and theological, above all, is literal. Applying it to texts like the *Bhagavata Purana* (also known as the *Shrimad
Bhagavatam*), replete with detailed cosmographies and genealogical histories, he
considers the intent of the original authors and the meaning for the believing
community today to be the same, with the conviction that the plain meaning
discernible in the text *now* is what it was *then*. For example, Prabhupada reads as
accurate the Puranic accounts of creation, without reducing them, either historically or culturally. Whatever there is in his exegesis of theological reflection, ritual performance, or moral obligation is not sufficiently sophisticated to impress
those who decry his explications as naïve realism (an unsupportable one-to-one
correspondence between depiction and reality)—though whether such a judgment of any well-reasoned perception is fair may be seriously questioned.[8]

In ISKCON, literalism often is equated with intellectual chastity. Thus: "The
members of ISKCON, who live perpetually at the feet of Shrila Prabhupada,
may speculate *how* Shrila Prabhupada's statements are true, but they may not
challenge his statements, or claim that they are false. This is precisely what it
means to accept Shrila Prabhupada as the founder-*acharya*" (Hridayananda
1996:viii). The author of this statement is paraphrasing an instruction he himself received from Prabhupada. Indeed, this view is the guiding ethos for VAST
(Vaishnava Academic Studies), a moderated ISKCON Internet forum.

If ISKCON wishes to avoid the label of naïve realism, a number of strategies
suggest themselves. One is to also acknowledge the strength of *pramanas* other
than *shabda* in order to make conditional allowances for historically contingent, "relative" knowledge. Prabhupada himself shows that this may be done.
While certainly favoring revelation over reason and perception, for audiences
unfamiliar with the text tradition he makes ample use of logic and everyday examples. Further, following the lead of nineteenth-century theologian Bhak-

tivinoda Thakur (1838–1914),[9] ISKCON can reexamine its traditional texts and reappropriate them in ways consistent with modernity, discerning the symbolic through critical scholarship. As with Bhaktivinoda's experiments, this would provide a new dimension to *sambandha*, the area to which we next move.

Sambandha's connotative sense embraces numerous ontological categories. As well as the godhead's nature, the living being, and the world, *sambandha* signifies the action of the godhead and its infinite energies as they relate with each other, a subject treated in a manner unique to this school under the axiomatic principle of *achintya-bhedabheda* (inconceivable simultaneous difference and identity).

To Bhaktivinoda, matters of phenomenal knowledge (i.e., Puranic history and cosmology) are particularly amenable to rational analysis, even if transcendence (i.e., Krishna, *bhakti*, etc.) is not. In his innovative *Krishna-samhita*, thousands of *yuga*-cycles of Prajapatis and Manus are compressed to conform to an Indian history of some 6,000 years complete with migrating Aryans, and Mogul and British rule. The same time frame is linked to a progressive intellectual history encompassing all major texts, assigning the *Bhagavata*, for example, to an anonymous ninth-century Dravidian origin. Krishna and his abode's supremacy are rationally established, his incarnations tied to human evolution, his *lila* framed within a discussion of the limitations of human language, and his destruction of demons related metaphorically to the removal of corresponding obstacles to devotion.

Whether a clearly nineteenth-century Bengali *bhadralok* hermeneutic responding to historically and culturally specific assumptions is any longer appropriate is not the issue; that a person who is widely credited with inaugurating modern Chaitanya Vaishnavism makes every effort to accommodate modern intellectualism is. More important than the particular hermeneutic is its motive and method. Similar progressive theologizing may be necessary if ISKCON is to embody Shri Chaitanya's mood of magnanimity (*audarya*). Unlike many of Bhaktivinoda's contemporaries who willingly sacrificed much about Krishna that offended them,[10] revisionism along the lines Bhaktivinoda practiced need not be revolutionary. Moderate theologizing that harnesses "tradition as a modality of change" (Waldman 1986) can express fidelity and continuity with the past while forging connections to the present and future.

The status and role of women within ISKCON is an area to which this approach may be applied to great advantage. Normally a topic for the praxis-rich province of *abhidheya*, its problems may be traced to ontological confusions; hence, its placement under *sambandha*.

Some of Prabhupada's statements seem blatantly sexist, yet he opened his movement to women. Though offered fatherly affection by Prabhupada, women in the eyes of his male disciples were like Maya (the illusory energy)—

both encoded female. Like Maya, they were seen as threatening to men's spiritual progress. Initially accorded equality by Prabhupada, women in ISKCON were gradually disenfranchised, tolerated more than welcomed. This had disastrous consequences: their stigmatization affected ISKCON's social fabric to such an extent that at present, despite much conscious effort to right the situation, the society has yet to recover.[11]

Kim Knott (1995) has problematized ISKCON's difficulties reconciling traditional models with modern realities, juxtaposing the theoretical gender equality of a soul-based theology in which the feminine divine Radha is the exemplar *par excellence* with *stri dharma* (the duty of a woman) understood as three distinct levels of meaning within Prabhupada's teachings—*bhagavat dharma* (divine duty), "Vedic" *varnashram dharma* (ancient notion of duty based on orders and stages of life), and "Hindu" *varnashram dharma* (its modern interpretation).

The multivalent weighting of the founder's statements has, and will continue to have, a decisive bearing on ISKCON's history. If ISKCON is to be rid of residual sexism, a theology is needed that interprets his comments in the spirit of *bhagavat dharma*, taking into account the hard realities of present life, even if in doing so the principles of *varnashram dharma* are set aside. The unfair sexual bias implied by the Maya narrative needs reworking to reflect the Chaitanya Vaishnava perspective of the feminine gender generic to all souls, including those who are male-embodied. This would certainly be in keeping with the spirit of *bhakti* in pan-Indian religious history, as Fred Smith points out: "In Sanskrit grammar, *bhakti* is feminine, just as *yoga*, *dharma*, and *yajna* (sacrifice) are masculine. Not just grammatically, however, but substantially, did the rise of *bhakti* . . . redress the imbalance of the masculine and feminine forces in (official) Indian religion" (Smith 1998:30).

Can our agenda be pushed further? A radical discontinuity with Chaitanya Vaishnava theology within the realm of *sambandha* might mean, for example, blurring the divide that separates personalists from impersonalists. Traditionally, Vaishnavism has defined itself over and against Advaita Vedanta. The Chaitanyaites have framed their entire discussion of *sambandha* around explicating the nested tripartite model of ultimate reality as *brahman*, *paramatma*, and *bhagavan*. While maintaining that *bhagavan* alone is the full expression of this highest truth, under the school's axiomatic principle of *achintya-bhedabheda* (inconceivable difference and identity simultaneously), they can claim, much as Advaita Vedantists do, that reality is nondual and one without equal (*advaya-jnana-tattva*).[12]

Still, only faint praise is given *brahmavadins*, while *mayavadins* are censured with the harshest rhetoric.[13] Indeed, Prabhupada defines his mission in terms of their defeat.[14] To be fair, the reverse is equally true: those adhering to the *advaita* viewpoint often depreciate the Vaishnavas. Impersonalists and Vaishnavas rarely perceive each other as fellow travelers, despite having much in common. For ISKCON, at times this has meant alienating many in its diasporic Indian congregation who feel confused, if not deeply offended, by what they perceive to be sectarian conflict in ISKCON's condemnation of revered people, past and present, because of impersonal beliefs.

Can this rhetoric of exclusivity be toned down to move toward an internal pluralism? In the *Gita* (4:11), Krishna exemplifies a spirit of responsiveness: "As they surrender unto Me, I reward them accordingly."[15] It should be possible to adjust the balance that presently favors difference over identity without sublating the unique realization of the *jnanin* (*brahman*), the *yogin* (*paramatma*), or the *bhakta* (*bhagavan*).[16]

Looking outside the Chaitanya Vaishnava tradition, apparently competing, extratraditional views of the godhead may be assessed in proportion to their ability to marshal numerous relational models of the godhead, the living entities, and the world. Images of transcendence from beyond the tradition that resonate with Gaudiya theology could amplify the understanding of Krishna's multiple roles in Vrindavan as friend, son, and lover, and through his expansions and incarnations, in numerous other relationships, not the least as overseer *paramatma* of the bound *jiva*.[17] Both outside and inside, the flexibility of ontological categories needs to be tested further if a theology of accommodation is to replace one of exclusion.

Within the tripartite schema of *sambandha-abhidheya-prayojana*, asymmetrical disjunctions between inherited tradition and actual contingency are most noticeable within the division of *abhidheya*—process or execution—to which we now turn. Here, *bhakti*, devotional practice, is the process leading to the ultimate goal of Krishna *prema* (love of Krishna). Over centuries, *bhakti*'s discursive formulations have massaged whatever traditional rigidities resisted the flux of contingency.

Bhakti receives detailed explication throughout the Chaitanya Vaishnava canon. Despite its inclusivist character, both its definition and its eulogy emphasize transcendent efficacy and superiority: *bhakti* as a mode of living is thoroughly different from and independent of *karma*, *jnana*, and *yoga*, those orientations or practices otherwise typically celebrated in pan-"Hindu" texts.[18] Rupa Gosvamin (1489–1564) and other systematizers following Shri Chaitanya offer what they believe to be a comprehensive program of practice leading to spiritual perfection. Rupa's elaboration on *bhakti* begins with a sixty-four-item list comprising "rule-governed practice" (*vaidhi-sadhana-bhakti*) followed by "attraction-governed practice" (*raganuga-sadhana-bhakti*). These are followed in turn by matters pertaining to our third methodological category, the goal (*prayojana*)—*bhava* and *prema bhakti*.[19]

Flowing underneath Rupa Gosvamin's several categories and subcategories of Krishna *bhakti* are two orientations, one "vertical," the other "horizontal" or "lateral." "Vertical *bhakti*" (O'Connell, unpublished) refers to all aspects of practice and attitude emphasizing hierarchy, the paradigmatic distinction being that of the godhead Krishna and the *bhakta* (i.e., the Vaishnava practitioner as subordinated servant of Krishna). "Lateral *bhakti*" refers to not only the dimension of mutuality that characterizes devotional feelings between one *bhakta* and another but also that between the godhead and the *bhakta*, wherein sweetness and proximity supersede majesty and distance. To date, ISKCON's missionary priorities, arguably, have made greater purchase on the vertical, hierarchical vector. An important constructive strategy would be the recovery of a neglected principle of balance and interdependence between these two modalities.

A point of departure is an often-quoted verse fragment from the revered seventeenth-century Vaishnava poet Narottama Das: *Sadhu-shastra-guru bakya, hridaye koriya aikya*, "making the statements of saintly persons, scripture, and preceptors unified within my heart [. . . may I attain *prema*]."[20] Saintly persons, scripture, and preceptors comprise the body of authority we are referring to here as tradition. Emphasizing the vertical principle of authority, ISKCON members often inadvertently distance themselves from Narottama Das's verse, failing to recognize that the living practitioner, as a recipient of tradition, is the implied "final arbiter" among these three representatives of traditional authority. Indeed, the practitioner is not simply a passive recipient of tradition; rather, through active engagement, she or he participates in and inevitably reinvents tradition. When examining these three sources of authority in terms of lateral reciprocity, the role of the practitioner is of crucial importance on the vertical/lateral grid.

Such an exercise might best begin with the last of the aforementioned three authorities, the guru.[21] Chaitanya Vaishnava literature abounds in narratives and explications about guru-disciple relations that emphasize the guru's authoritative position. Scriptural lessons instruct a disciple to regard him- or herself as a veritable fool in the presence of the guru, who is to be seen and worshipped as a direct manifestation of the supreme lord, Krishna.[22] Obviously, such a theology is open to potential abuse, as ISKCON experienced after Prabhupada's demise. The excesses of the hierarchical model of guruship victimized many of the successor gurus and their followers. Yet a careful study of Chaitanyaite literature also reveals a counternarrative of intimacy and collegial reciprocity that nuances the hierarchical emphasis. Arjuna, for example, reminds readers of the *Bhagavad Gita* of his intimate relationship to Krishna even as he begs pardon for any indiscretions before Krishna's *Virat-rupa* (universal form).[23] In Krishnadas's *Chaitanya Charitamrita*, Shri Chaitanya receives instruction from Ramananda Raya, who otherwise serves as Chaitanya's follower if not disciple.[24]

If, as Chaitanya Vaishnavism claims, the relationship between guru and disciple in some ways replicates that of the *bhakta* and Krishna, one would expect to see in it a parallel dynamic of reciprocity based on deemphasizing vertical polarity. As suggested earlier, a notable Chaitanyaite strategy is to undercut divine majesty to make way for unrestrained intimacy between the lord and his associates. Similarly, the guru, to further a disciple's understanding of and participation in Krishna's intimate pastimes, may subdue his own authority in favor of cooperative reciprocity, thus encouraging the disciple to think and act as a *partner* in the mutual pursuit of spiritual perfection.

An important consequence of this element of partnership in the traditional master-servant model would be a deeper sense of spiritual community. Hierarchy emphasizes exclusionary relationships: identification with one's guru to the exclusion of collegial relations (with *all* spiritual aspirants, Vaishnava or otherwise), results in sectarianism. Within the guru-disciple relationship, tempering hierarchy with communality would develop a much-needed mutuality among fellow practitioners in ever-widening circles of participation.

Participation is central to the Chaitanya Vaishnava account of *bhakti*. Karen Prentiss, in her recent book *The Embodiment of Bhakti*, argues that *bhakti* is most fully understood to be "a theology of participation in God and the ability to reach God" (27). Participation suggests reciprocity, the idea of exchange or sharing contained in *bhakti*'s verbal root—*bhaj*. What is further implied is a "cybernetic" principle of *appropriateness of response*—a sensitivity to immediate circumstance—in other words, the pragmatic dimension of *bhakti*. Openness and flexibility in interpretation permits the revelatory basis of the tradition to remain susceptible to contemporary experience, to coalesce as a crystallized conviction within each practitioner's heart.

Looking at Narottama Das's second source of traditional authority—the *sadhu*—through a *Bhagavata Purana* definition, we find virtues that deny any specific cultural identity. One who exhibits tolerance, mercy, friendliness to all, and peacefulness and is without enemies is a *sadhu* (*Bhag.* 3.25.21). This suggests that people beyond those accepted customarily as *sadhus* in India deserve to be considered as such. This nonsectarian reckoning obliges Chaitanya Vaishnavas to acknowledge and welcome a wide range of people as genuine spiritual participants from whom wisdom may be gleaned.[25] But what of their spiritual practices? Must these fall within Rupa Goswamin's sixty-four categories to be accepted as *bhakti*? Perhaps not. Chaitanyaite practices centered on chanting names of God, hearing and recitation of devotional texts, and worship of divine images need to be reexamined in the context of a broader spectrum of practitioners.

To the objections that our proposed reassessment of guru and *sadhu* will wither before the stipulations of Narottama Das's third source of authority, namely, *shastra*, our basic claim is that interpreting scripture is a perpetual process of reappraisal by the reader or hearer. Practitioners must admit this openly for tradition to serve a vital, liberating function in their lives. That for the disciple the guru is the central interpreter and that *sadhus* are secondary interpreters cannot obscure the fact that the "end user," the practitioner, is the final interpreter.[26] As "Protestant" as this may sound, it simply recognizes that although scripture maintains boundary structures to delimit those qualified to interpret, the very nature of print culture and mass distribution democratizes the system.

The hermeneutical circle or interpretative horizon of scripture for modern readers has exploded out into the entire range of presently available texts drawn from an ever-increasing spectrum of religious and secular traditions. Canonical works no longer enjoy the seeming autonomy they once had, nor are they impervious to scrutiny from outside readers. The top-down, "vertical" process of receiving spiritual truth from infallible scripture is now, more than ever before, faced with the pervasive presence of a multiplicity of voices that challenge the privileged position of any one of them.

Shri Chaitanya is remembered best perhaps as one constantly given to ecstatic states, absorbed in Krishna *prema*. This, after all, is the *prayojana*, the motive or goal to which Chaitanya Vaishnavas aspire, and the final division of our study. Much of the Chaitanyaite prescriptive as well as narrative literature conduces to bring about *prema*, the ripened fruit of *bhakti*. Liberation is conceived not as the nondual union of Advaita Vedanta but in terms of active *seva* (cherished service) in relation to the godhead, ideally, an intimate reciprocity between the *sevya* and the *sevaka*—Krishna and his devotee.

While love for Krishna (*prema*) remains the tradition's normative goal, its achievement is open to question. Since the passing away of ISKCON's founder, its members often appear uncertain, in practice if not in theory, about the basis of attaining Krishna *prema* and about how to recognize such love once it manifests. The texts abound in theory, and narrative exemplars are plentiful enough. The confusion arises largely from the importance the founder, Prabhupada, gave to his mission and from his stress upon "rule-governed practice" (*vaidhi-sadhana-bhakti*) rather than "attraction-governed practice" (*raganuga-sadhana-bhakti*). This emphasis, though in apparent contradistinction to previous preceptors, closely parallels that given by his own guru, Bhaktisiddhanta Saraswati (1874–1937).[27]

In framing the problem, polarities suggest themselves. Is Krishna Consciousness a state of internal ecstasy or manifest missionary enthusiasm? If the latter, did Prabhupada alter the traditional understanding of *prayojana*, or did he act in fulfillment of Shri Chaitanya's mission by emphasizing proselytizing more than the practice of *raga*? Stated in another way, in a tradition that views *bhakti* as both its means and its end, to what extent are the words "back to godhead" (the title of ISKCON's monthly magazine) world affirming or world denying? Evolving theological constructs that replace this either/or dichotomy with a both/and synthesis would demonstrate that these seemingly competing moods are in fact outward and inward expressions of the same Krishna Consciousness, reflecting the esoteric and exoteric nature of Shri Chaitanya's own appearance.

One might begin by justifying Prabhupada's sacralization of a broad range of missionary endeavors as *sankirtana*—the celebratory glorification of the lord. Beyond the public chanting of the Hare Krishna mantra popularized by Shri Chaitanya, Prabhupada exploited diverse resources to publicize Krishna's glories, at the same time promising that all such efforts are a powerful, transformative force, purifying the consciousness and enabling one gradually to come face to face with God.

One might continue to theologize by suggesting that with the advance of *kali yuga*, the present age of degradation, a more contemplative mood now appears inadequate and difficult. Few are prepared to renounce the world, and those who are not lack the purity to stay in it. The solution? *Sankirtana*, taking part in Shri Chaitanya's mission, which compensates for all personal insufficiencies by attracting Krishna's special mercy. Does Krishna not state in the *Gita* 18:69 that those who preach his message are the most dear to him?

While such facile theologizing may be textually and pragmatically legitimized, it easily can spawn (and has spawned) disquieting modalities: e.g., "mission as warfare," and the no less savory, "mission as business." Devotees transform into soldiers, temples into arsenals, stockpiling caches of time bombs (cases of books), zealously deployed at airports amid unsuspecting souls—the result: "Hare Krishna Explosion!"[28] Similar mercantile metaphors can easily be derived.[29] Its leadership scandalized, its population decimated, and a whole generation of Krishna kids feeling forlorn as parents trooped off to fight battle after battle, ISKCON needs much fixing.

If within the realm of *prayojana*, mission is to retain the premier status Prabhupada assigned it, "compassion" will have to replace "warfare" as the appropriate modality as the members of both ISKCON and those of mainstream society increasingly integrate. Prabhupada writes:

> One who is interested in his own salvation is not as advanced in Krishna consciousness as one who feels compassion for others and who therefore propagates the Krishna consciousness movement. Such an advanced devotee will never fall down for Krishna will give him special protection.[30]

Brahmins are especially dear to Krishna. Will he not be pleased if ISKCON members exchange their past aggressive militancy and mercantile acquisitiveness for brahmanic compassion? For this to happen, proselytization will need to be balanced with more contemplative practices. Rupa Gosvamin emphasizes five items that are most potent: residence in Mathura-Vrindavan, divine image worship, recitation and hearing of the *Bhagavata*, chanting of the holy names, and service to exalted Vaishnavas. With the turn inward, attraction (*raga*) more than rules (*vidhi*) gradually will govern personal development.

These changes are taking place already. Seminars offered to devotees during the past decade have largely centered upon missionizing ethics, personal lifestyle, and individual realization, indicating an unquestionable shift from quantitative to qualitative evaluation.[31] Conferences on women, on youth, and on family are signs of social maturation, as the refreshingly honest and open *ISKCON Communications Journal*, now in its tenth year of publication, forecasts an increasingly healthy intellectual muscularity. And another sign of change: the transition from monastic *ashram* life to private households that has characterized ISKCON demographics since the founder's demise has not necessarily been a move away from contemplative life. Instead, sacred space is increasingly defined in terms of the individual/familial rather than the communal/collective. Unable to worship daily at the temple due to work, and consequently with less institutional pressures, individuals are free to pursue their own perfection, which they now do most often in the context of family life.[32] A profusion of newly published titles—many of them translations into English from the standard Chaitanya Vaishnava corpus—now support the cultivation of *raganuga-sadhana-bhakti*. Devotional biographies of recently deceased ISKCON Vaishnavas hint at their attainment of Krishna *prema*.[33] All these developments indicate the dichotomous questions noted earlier are being resolved naturally—even while a theology that endorses the solutions is yet to be articulated officially.

This essay, an attempt to suggest the directions such theologizing might take, lays the groundwork by organizing inquiry along the divisions of *sambandha*, *abhidheya*, and *prayojana*. Their usefulness here leads us to recommend them as investigative categories for other forms of Hinduism and beyond. The authors have explored as a possibility an open-ended, gender-equal, less culturally specific, and less hierarchical theological model that attempts to engage diverse theological communities and to serve as a comparative frame for other Hinduisms while retaining a Vaishnava *bhakti* outlook. In doing so, we have taken for granted a plurality of religious perspectives as a healthy, commonplace fact of life. ISKCON members clearly are obliged to recognize and interact with a field of ideas and worldviews much broader than premodern Chaitanya Vaishnavas ever encountered. If they continue to equate literalism with intellectual chastity, if they hesitate to contextualize and properly interpret the words of their founder, there will be little room for acknowledging and welcoming this multiplicity of voices in the pursuit of a wider spiritual community. We believe that the principle of balancing what we referred to as "lateral" and "vertical" coordinates can and must be extended beyond present devotional relationships if ISKCON members are to recognize their responsibility to themselves and to the tradition they hope to represent.

NOTES

1. See Rochford 1998.
2. For readers unfamiliar with the tradition: "Shri Chaitanya" would be pronounced "Shree Chaitanya." Apologies to Sanskritists and knowers of Bengali: diacritics have been dropped from this article to accommodate a wider readership.
3. For the rationale, see the essays, particularly those of Jackson, Cabezon, Gross, and Coreless, in Jackson and Makransky 2000.
4. For Prabhupada's use of the term, see his morning walk conversation with disciples, 26 June 1975, Los Angeles. *Bhaktivedanta Vedabase #1—Bhaktivedanta* (CD-ROM, Version 4.11) (Sandy Ridge, NC: Bhaktivedanta Archives, 1998).
5. *Pramana* and *prameya* are not specifically Gaudiya categories of investigation. "These are the three parts of all textual argument: What the matter of the discourse is (*sambandha*), what the argument will be, or the means of reaching the conclusion (*abhidheya*), and the resolution (*prayojana*)" (Dimock 1999:640*n*109). Though the term *abhidheya* normally conveys the meaning "what is signified," Stuart Elkman notes that Jiva Gosvamin "qualifies the term with the expression *vidheyasaparyaya*, i.e. 'in the sense of something to be performed'" (Jiva Gosvamin 1986b:73*n*2). According to Sir Monier Monier-Williams, *A Sanskrit-English Dictionary* (1899; reprint, Delhi: Motilal Banarsidass, 1995), *saparya* means "worship, homage, adoration"; specifically, *vidheya-saparyaya* is "worship, devotion, etc. that is to be performed."
6. *veda-shastra kahe—"sambandha," "abhidheya," "prayojana" "krishna"—prapya sambandha, "bhakti"—praptyera sadhana.*
7. For Jiva Gosvamin, see Elkman 1986, 73. For Prabhupada, see his commentary to *Chaitanya Charitamrita* 2.6:135.
8. See Matilal 1986, 1.
9. For the most authoritative work on Bhaktivinoda, see Shukavak 1999.
10. Few subjects seem to vex outside representations as Krishna does. Christian missionaries, Orientalists, Hindu reformers, the Krishna-Christ debaters, and figures such as Bankim Chandra Chatterjee—the varying agendas of nineteenth- and twentieth-century colonial discourse—all share a communal discomfort; see Haberman 1994.
11. For an overview of the history of women in ISKCON and their present status, see Visakha et al. 2000.
12. See *Shrimad Bhagavatam* 1.2:11: *vadanti tat tattva-vidas tattvam yaj jnanam advayam | brahmeti paramatmeti bhagavan iti sabdyate||*
13. *Brahmavadins* recognize *bhagavan* but prefer *brahman,* while *mayavadins* ultimately recognize only *brahman.* Examples of the former, before their meeting with

bhagavan Narayana, are the four sages Sanat-kumara, Sanatana, Sanandana, and Sanaka; see the *Bhagavata Purana* canto 3, chapter 15. The followers of Shankara typify the latter.

14. Prabhupada composed an invocational prayer to himself for ISKCON's liturgy: "You are kindly preaching the message of Lord Chaitanya and delivering the Western countries, which are filled with impersonalism and voidism [*nirvishesha-shunyavada*]"; see Bhaktivedanta Book Trust 1974, 15.

15. *ye yatha mam prapadyante tams tathaiva bhajamy aham.*

16. For instances where Prabhupada emphasizes commonalities shared by the *jnanin*, *yogin*, and *bhakta*, see for example his lecture on SB 1.2:10 in Bombay, 28 December 1972, or his Bombay press interview on 31 December 1976. See Vishakha et al. 2000.

17. For example, through a Christian, process hermeneutic, Sally McFague tests the notions of "God as mother, lover, and friend of the world as God's body"; see McFague 1988.

18. Paul Griffiths's discussion on "comprehensiveness," "insurpassability," and "centrality" as phenomenal characteristics of all religious accounts offers a useful framework for understanding the Vaishnava concern to establish *bhakti*'s preeminence within their system of practice; see Griffiths 1999, 3–13.

19. For Rupa Gosvamin's classic treatise on *bhakti*, see Bhakti Hridaya Bon (1965) and Prabhupada's summary study (1982).

20. The verse appears in a song from the collection entitled *Prema Bhakti-chandrika*; see translation of Bhumipati Das.

21. "Last" in order of mention, though not in order of importance, based on the Mimamsa rule that weights a later statement.

22. See *Chaitanya-Charitamrita* 1 chap. 1. For a discussion of the oneness and difference of the supreme and the guru as it relates specifically to ISKCON, see Hridayananda 2000.

23. *Bhagavad Gita* 11:41, 42.

24. *Chaitanya-Charitamrita* 2:chap. 8.

25. This ethos shaped ISKCON's official statement on its relationship with "people of faith in God"; see Saunaka Rishi 1999, 1–9.

26. Madhva's notion of the "inner witness," or arbiter of all experience, deserves investigation in this regard; see Lott 1980, 11, 91–92.

27. Shukavak Das raises the question whether an ISKCON more concerned with the exoteric mode embodied in *vaidhi-sadhana-bhakti* can in fact offer the esoteric depth of *raganuga-bhakti-sadhana* for which the tradition is principally known; see Shukavak 1998.

28. See the title of Hayagriva 1985.

29. For an analysis of ISKCON's changing missionary strategies in relation to its economy, see Rochford 1985.

30. See the commentary to *Shrimad Bhagavatam* 6.2:36.

31. Seminars are held occasionally at various ISKCON centers and annually in Mayapur and Vrindavan, India, Gita Nagari in Pennsylvania, and Radhadesh in Belgium.

32. See Rochford 1995 and 1998, as well as E. Burke Rochford Jr., letter to Tamal Krishna Goswami, 27 August 2001 (Tamal Krishna Goswami archive, ISKCON–Dallas, Dallas, TX).

33. See for example Bhakti Balabh Puri Goswami 2001.

REFERENCES

Bhakti Balabh Puri Goswami. *Simple for the Simple*. Hungary: Lal Kiado, 2001.

Bhakti Hridaya Bon, trans. *Shri Rupa Gosvami's* Bhakti-rasamrta-sindhuh, vol. 1. Vrindaban: Institute of Oriental Philosophy, 1965.

Bhaktivedanta Book Trust. *Songs of the Vaisnava Acharyas: Hymns and Mantras for the Glorification of Radha and Krishna*. Los Angeles: Bhaktivedanata Book Trust, 1996.

Bhumipati dasa, trans. *Shri Prema Bhakti-candrika: The Moonrays of Loving Devotion* by Shrila Narottama dasa Thakura Mahasaya, with commentary of Shrila Vishvanatha Chakravarti Thakur. Vrindavan: Touchstone Media, 1999.

Dimock, Edward C. Jr., trans. and commentary. *Chaitanya Charitamrita of Krsnadasa Kaviraja*. Introduction by Edward C. Dimock Jr. and Tony K. Stewart. Ed. Tony K. Stewart. Harvard Oriental Series, vol. 56. Cambridge: Department of Sanskrit and Indian Studies, Harvard University, 1999.

Elkman, Stuart Mark, trans. *Jiva Gosvamin's Tattvasandharbha: A Study on the Philosophical and Sectarian Development of the Gaudiya Vaisnava Movement*. Delhi: Motilal Banarsidass, 1986.

Griffiths, Paul J. *Religious Reading: The Place of Reading in the Practice of Religion*. New York/Oxford: Oxford University Press, 1999.

Haberman, David L. "Divine Betrayal: Krishna-Gopal of Braj in the Eyes of Outsiders." *Journal of Vaisnava Studies* 3 (1) (winter 1994): 83–111.

Hayagriva das. *The Hare Krishna Explosion: The Birth of Krishna Consciousness in America (1966–1969)*. N.p.: Palace Press, 1985.

Hrdayananda dasa Goswami. *Our Original Position: Shrila Prabhupada and the Vaisnava Siddhanta*. ISKCON GBC Press, 1996.

———. "The Role of the Guru in a Multi-guru Society." *ISKCON Communications Journal* 8 (1) (June 2000): 45–53.

Jackson, Roger and John Makransky, eds. *Critical Reflections by Contemporary Buddhist Scholars*. Surrey, UK: Curzon, 2000.

Knott, Kim. "The Debate about Women in the Hare Krishna Movement." *ISKCON Communications Journal* 3 (2) (Dec. 1995): 33–49.

Lott, Eric. *Vedantic Approaches to God*. London: Macmillan, 1980.

Matilal, Bimal Krishna. *Perception: An Essay on Classical Indian Theories of Knowledge*. New York: Oxford University Press, 1986.

McFague, Sallie. *Models of God: Theology for an Ecological, Nuclear Age*. Philadelphia: Fortress Press, 1988.

O'Connell, Joseph T. "Chaitanya Vaisnava Community as Devotional Symbolism." Unpublished paper.

Prabhupada, A.C. Bhaktivedanta Swami. *The Nectar of Devotion: A Summary Study of Shrila Rupa Gosvami's Bhaktirasamrta-Sindhu*. 1970; 2nd ed., Los Angeles: Bhaktivedanta Book Trust, 1982.

———, trans. and commentary. 1987. *Shrimad Bhagavatam*, 12 cantos. (Cantos 1–10 chapter 13 by Prabhupada; canto 10 chapter 14–canto 12 by his disciples.) Los Angeles: Bhaktivedanta Book Trust, 1987.

———, trans. and commentary. *Bhagavad-gita As It Is*, 2nd ed., revised and enlarged. Los Angeles: Bhaktivedanta Book Trust, 1989.

———, trans. and commentary. *Shri Chaitanya-Charitamrita*. 9 vols. Los Angeles: Bhaktivedanta Book Trust. 1996.

Prentiss, Karen Pechilis. *The Embodiment of Bhakti.* Oxford: Oxford University Press, 1999.

Rochford, E. Burke, Jr. *Hare Krishna in America.* New Brunswick: Rutgers University Press, 1985.

——. "Family Structure, Commitment and Involvement in the Hare Krishna Movement." *Sociology of Religion* 56 (2) (1995): 153–75.

——. "Prabhupada Centennial Survey Report." Submitted to ISKCON's Governing Body Commission. November 1998.

Saunaka Rsi dasa. "ISKCON in Relation to People of Faith in God." *ISKCON Communications Journal* 7 (1) (June 1999): 1–9.

Shukavak N. Dasa. "ISKCON's Link to Sadhana-Bhakti within the Chaitanya Vaishnava Tradition." *Journal of Vaisnava Studies* 6 (2) (spring 1998): 189–212.

——. *Hindu Encounter with Modernity: Kedarnath Datta Bhaktivinoda, Vaisnava Theologian.* Los Angeles: Shri (Sanskrit Religions Institute), 1999.

Smith, Frederick M. "Notes on the Development of Bhakti." *Journal of Vaisnava Studies* 6. (1) (winter 1998): 17–36.

Vishakha Dasi, Sudharma Dasi, et al. "Women in ISKCON: Presentations to the GBC 2000." *ISKCON Communications Journal* 8 (1) (June 2000): 1–22.

Waldman, Marilyn Robinson. "Tradition as a Modality of Change: Islamic Examples." *History of Religions* 25 (4) (1986): 318–40.

CONCLUDING REFLECTIONS

EDWIN F. BRYANT AND MARIA L. EKSTRAND

T HERE APPEAR TO BE A NUMBER of challenges facing ISKCON and
its offshoots if they are to establish relevancy for themselves on the religious landscape of the twenty-first century. Two areas of obvious
tension emerge from the pages of this volume with immediate urgency, one
intellectual, one sociological. Before discussing these, we must first note that,
from the perspective of the philosophy of religion, Chaitanya Vaishnavism is
an authentic expression of Hindu religiosity, as indicated by the first and second sections of this volume. By this we mean that it is one of an ongoing series of unique and distinctive religious traditions emerging from Puranic Hinduism since the late Vedic period that has made serious and extensive efforts
to establish its credentials by interpreting the gamut of Sanskrit literature from
the perspective of its own theological truth claims. Like other sectarian expressions of the post-Vedic period, it has attempted to resolve the plethora of
seemingly conflicting statements from the vast warehouse of Hindu scriptures
within its own particular hierarchical schema of coherence.

This is not to say that there are not significant problems with such enterprises—promoting Krishna as the absolute godhead of the (rather problematically defined) "Vedic culture" is no easy task when there is nary a mention of him in the entire corpus of Vedic literature—the four Vedas, Brahmanas, Aranyakas, and Upanishads[1] (there are even tensions in this regard in the quintessential Krishna scripture, the *Bhagavata Purana*[2]). But such is the lot of any Hindu sectarian tradition, and Chaitanya Vaishnavism has by now found its distinctive niche in the Hindu religious landscape and long carved out specific areas of influence in such places as Vrindavan and East India. Accordingly, as Schweig notes, the society's theological inheritance must be kept in mind, regardless of all the sociological problems it has generated.

The transplantation of the tradition to the modern West introduced conflicts that are far different from those experienced historically by the movement on its native soil, and these have been amplified by Bhaktivedanta Swami's repeated claim, cited in a number of essays in this volume, that "Krishna Consciousness is for the educated and intelligent class of men." Delmonico and Shukavak both draw attention to one obvious conflict that has so far been avoided by most Chaitanya followers in the West—that between scriptural literalism and the critical historical analysis of a tradition. As Delmonico points out, there is no easy way to bridge these two worlds of discourse, but "it is certain that modern members of the Chaitanya tradition, both within ISKCON and beyond it, must resolve the challenge somehow if they wish to engage today's intelligent and educated people in any kind of meaningful dialogue." Shukavak develops the same point: "If Chaitanya Vaishnavism is to have a lasting position in and a positive impact on the West, then it must move beyond the literalism by which it entered the region and begin to develop new forms of intellectual expression and perspectives that are a part of the western intellectual and academic traditions."

Shukavak presents Bhaktivinoda Thakur, the father of Bhaktivedanta Swami's guru, as a pivotal forerunner and role model in this regard from within the Chaitanya tradition itself. As Bhaktivinoda was fully aware, few in the post-Enlightenment West are likely to take the superhuman stories and fantastic time calculations of the Puranas and Epics at face value as historical events, and Bhaktivinoda's devotion to Krishna was not at all threatened by accounting for these aspects of the tradition as "fictional narratives." Needless to say, the opposition to such hermeneutics personally encountered by Shukavak from western devotees schooled within the parameters of literalist thought is likely to remain. But it is impossible to see how Chaitanya Vaishnavism will ever generate a significant educated following among its own stated target group, the intelligentsia, unless symbolic or other nonliteral modes of interpretation become acceptable options. One might point out, to those whose literalist sensitivities are bruised by such suggestions, that the process of *bhakti yoga* as promoted in the *Bhagavata Purana*, the primary source of authority for Gaudiya Vaishnavism, involves immersing the mind in Krishna by engaging in the various processes of *bhakti*, but it does not legislate how the narrative stories of the text need be interpreted.[3] Clearly, those influenced by the rational intellectual currents of the post-Enlightenment world—Bhaktivedanta Swami's target group of the "educated class of men"—will need nonliteralist interpretational modalities if they are to be attracted to the process of *bhakti yoga* on any significant scale (indeed, as an aside, William Deadwyler's paper acknowledges that Bhaktivedanta Swami himself was disappointed in the intellectual caliber of the people he was attracting).

One might also add that such "modern" or rational modes of relating to the tradition do not need to displace traditional ones but coexist with them, thus expanding the participatory possibilities of Gaudiya Vaishnavism. Every mainstream religion exhibits a tension between a literalist, fundamentalist element that is concerned that the essence of the tradition be preserved and not diluted away by the very values it opposes, and a liberal, intellectually revisionistic or progressive one that is concerned with ensuring that the tradition be relevant to the cultural context and that is prepared to prune the tradition of historical trimmings deemed incompatible with the modern world. One can argue that such dialectical tension is inherently healthy for the survival of any tradition as a religious entity that is both theologically distinctive and faithful to its essence, but also able to dialogue with the dominant intellectual and social currents of the times in a manner that is relevant and mutually productive. Western Gaudiya Vaishnavism has so far sprouted literalist and fundamentalist modes; it has yet to develop significant and visible "modern" or intellectually innovative ones.

The second area of tension evidenced in these pages is, of course, sociological, and most of the essays in this volume have touched upon the abusive ordeals experienced by significant numbers of ISKCON members. A variety of possible "root causes" for ISKCON's postcharismatic problems and failures have been outlined. The most immediate issue after Bhaktivedanta Swami's death was, of course, that of formulating how the role of guru was to be perpetuated. From the sheer number of times it surfaces in the different chapters in this volume, it is clear that the "zonal *acharya*" system was perhaps the single most devastating development in the postcharismatic period, triggering a massive exodus of Bhaktivedanta Swami's disciples from the parent organization. While ISKCON has since opened up the initiatory role to any member of whom the GBC has not disapproved, three of the essays outline two alternative systems whose followers are actively canvassing among the Chaitanya Vaishnava community in the West: the *ritvik* system, and submission to

Gaudiya authorities outside of ISKCON, such as Shridhara Maharaja and Narayana Maharaja. Given that the zonal *acharya* system was promoted by the entire GBC for over a decade as representing Bhaktivedanta Swami's intentions in the matter of disciplic succession, and that ISKCON's subsequent reformed position, as well as these ongoing alternative systems banned by the society, are held with just as equal assurance to be representative of the founder's wishes, it seems hard to avoid the conclusion that Bhaktivedanta Swami did not leave clear guidelines as to how the role of guru was to emerge in the organization after his death. Since this contrasts vividly with the ubiquitously clear and undisputed set of directives he left pertaining to the managerial structure of ISKCON, namely the GBC, we can only speculate as to his motives for this omission; but this void has produced enormous consequences in the postcharismatic period.

While the proponents of these individual systems would likely find such differences divisive to the overall mission, the increasing variety of options available within western Chaitanya Vaishnavism could be viewed as a positive development. By providing more outlets for new recruits, as well as creating alternatives within the greater lineage for existing members disenfranchised from the parent organization of ISKCON, such options can be seen as opportunities to stem the hemorrhaging from the overall Chaitanya tradition. But ultimately, how the tradition can expect to attract followers, expand, and flourish in the absence of charismatic leadership with moral integrity remains to be seen. As Gelberg notes, the failure to produce "pure devotees" can only mean that Chaitanya Vaishnavism has yet to attain its own criteria for success, and until then, it is certain to experience the kinds of conflicts described in Collins's paper between ISKCON and itinerant charismatic individuals from other branches of the lineage.

While problems of succession are almost inevitable upon the demise of a charismatic individual, including, as Brzezinski has outlined, following previous seminal junctures in the Chaitanya lineage itself, perhaps the more structural and endemic problem that clearly needs to be resolved by followers of Chaitanya Vaishnavism involves the social goals embedded in Bhaktivedanta Swami's vision. Many of the essays in this volume have been candid about the wide-ranging failures of the movement to approach anything approximating its own ideals, or to prevent the widespread exploitation of its most vulnerable members. A number have touched upon some of the human rights abuses inflicted on the women and children who took shelter in ISKCON, as well as the disillusionment undergone by so many sincere young people who dedicated the prime of their lives to an organization that proved capable of developing and perpetuating the types of social structures and attitudes revealed here. We would like to acknowledge the candidness of the authors still connected with the parent organization in acknowledging ISKCON's wide-ranging failures while nonetheless holding out hope for a reformed future. We would also like to recognize the courage of those no longer connected with ISKCON for pursuing their alternative visions, as well as the concern expressed by the nonparticipant scholars of the tradition over some of the directions it has taken in its short history in the West. These are all essential steps in the right direction, if the transplanted tradition is to survive, and we add our own observations to their analysis of the postcharismatic trauma undergone by the fledgling movement.

Many of the institutional problems outlined in these pages can be connected with the movement's attempts to organize and regulate itself along the lines of traditional *varnashram dharma*, the ancient Indian system of socio-religio-political organization. This volume has touched upon the treatment of women; the fate of the children in the *gurukula* schools; the crisis of faith in leadership, much of which ensued from the inability of members to maintain the vows incumbent on the hallowed *sannyasi* celibate order; the transmogrification of the chaste order of *brahmacharya*, hermitic studentship, into an activity of door-to-door salesmanship and street peddling—all by-products of this "*varnashram* experiment." The fact is that this experiment has failed in almost all of its stated goals—not the least of which is Bhaktivedanta Swami's vision of ISKCON communities providing ideal alternatives to a decadent western culture. Moreover, it is this very aspect of the society's goals that has greatly alienated not only the mainstream society, including many otherwise sympathetic to the theology and practices of Chaitanya Vaishnavism, but also large swathes of its own membership.

Lorenz's second essay reveals how undefined the *varnashram* experiment was in its inception. One need only consider that the pivot of the institution of traditional *varnashram* is that of monarchy to realize how at odds such a social order is with the modern world, and thus with Bhaktivedanta Swami's intention of appealing to the "intelligent class of men." With an elected Governing Board Commission as its ultimate legislative authority, ISKCON's kingless version of *varnashram* was a hybrid melange of modernity and tradition from its very genesis, and this structure has produced a number of further ambiguities. The tension between the absolute nature of the guru in an organization where the bureaucratic GBC is the ultimate institutional authority has been touched upon in this volume, but we can also point to the incompatibility between membership in the *sannyasa* order and membership in the GBC. *Sannyasis* are traditionally supposed to represent a total renunciation of all social structures and material resources, while a place in the GBC, a body historically comprised primarily of *sannyasis*, represents the most powerful social position in ISKCON with the most access to material resources and their accompanying temptations. Apart from such discordance between the institutional roles accepted by many ISKCON *sannyasis* and the expectations outlined in traditional sources for the *sannyasa ashram*, the blending of the functions of a religion's ultimate managerial body with those of significant numbers of its highest spiritual representatives results in the loss of credibility in the latter, when ineptitude and corruption is evidenced by the former; there are obvious advantages in separating these functions. Such problems are not unique to ISKCON, of course, but they do further underscore the contradictions inherent in the movement's attempts at implementing, or even articulating, a coherent schema of *varnashram*, where such distinctions between roles are prerequisite. And, of course, the massive 90 percent "fall-down" rate from the order of *sannyasa* suggested by W. Deadwyler speaks for itself.[4]

But perhaps the greatest confusion stems from grafting this hybrid temporal structure onto a soteriological religion whose goals are transcendent and almost all of whose primary authority figures (with a few exceptions like Bhaktivinoda Thakur) have been ascetic renunciates who abandoned the social orders of their day. As Knott and Lorenz note, the confusion is exacerbated by simultaneously maintaining theoretical allegiance to *varnashram* while expecting members to strive to be transcendent Vaishnavas dedicated to the exclusive pursuit of *bhagavata dharma* (the practices of mantra meditation, deity worship, study of scripture, etc.).[5] From the perspective of the former, the ideal devotees are Brahmin teachers who can provide spiritual direction to a misguided society, and from the perspective of the latter, they should aspire to shed identifications with their material bodies, occupational propensities, and social roles, and dedicate themselves exclusively to the worship and service of Krishna.

As Knott further points out, the already inherent ambiguities between *bhagavata dharma* and *varnashram dharma* are not likely to be resolved in an organization that holds both scripture and guru to be authoritative. Any attempt to reconcile the traditional injunctions of the *dharmashastra* texts, which outline codes of conduct and legislation relevant to the *varnashram* system of India in the late and post-Vedic age, with Bhaktivedanta Swami's direction to his disciples to attempt to implement a hybrid version of this in the modern West can hardly be expected to solve ISKCON's social problems. This is all the more so since, as Lorenz's essay reveals, he did not give anything approximating a comprehensive or coherent master plan as to how this was to be accomplished.

These contradictions in theory, coupled with the debacle of ISKCON's attempts at social organization in practice, call for a major reevaluation of this aspect of the Chaitanya tradition's goals in the West. Given the enormous gulf separating Bhaktivedanta Swami's perspectives on dictatorship, women, children, and *shudras*, etc., as outlined by Lorenz in his second essay, and the normative social and intellectual convictions of our day and age; given the failure of his disciples to prevent widespread human rights abuses on ISKCON's own membership in the name of *varnashram*; given that the spiritual practice of *bhagavata dharma* is the primary concern of all the authority figures of the Chaitanya lineage beginning with Chaitanya himself, and not *varnashram*; and given that new devotees are initially attracted to the former when recruited into the lineage and often alienated by the implications of the latter (particularly if they are women), it seems hard to avoid the conclusion that a good number of ISKCON's woes would be at least ameliorated by reconsidering its commitments to *varnashram*. If it is to achieve its stated purpose of appealing to "the intelligent class of men," the society might well reflect upon whether this class is truly likely to be convinced that an ideal world order involves reverting to monarchy and rolling back decades of hard-fought advances made by women and other disadvantaged social groups, particularly given the abysmal reality of ISKCON's experiment in this regard. Gaudiya Vaishnava devotees are far more likely to gain a place in the religious landscape of the modern world as morally virtuous exemplars of the distinctive theological beliefs and practices of *bhagavata dharma* than as heralds of a confused version of a pre-medieval social structure about which there is no consensus in ISKCON, and, indeed, upon the merits of which Bhaktivedanta Swami himself seemed to oscillate.[6]

As Rochford notes, in contrast to the 1960s and 1970s, the present demographics of ISKCON indicate that the vast majority of members now live outside the temples and communities, and thus participate in the social, economic, and legal structures of the greater society. Major temples such as New York, Berkeley, and Chicago, which had up to 200 resident members three decades ago, now find themselves with an in-house staff of less than a dozen. *Varnashram dharma*, in its idealized version represented in the *Bhagavata Purana*, may have been the natural recourse available to Bhaktivedanta Swami as a traditional *sannyasi* when confronted (against his own expectations) with the sudden and rapid expansion of his movement and the ensuing need to organize the material and social logistics of thousands of young men and women, but historical hindsight and present-day demographics call for a radical re-envisioning of ISKCON's social and economic goals. We note that Bhaktivedanta Swami himself did not hesitate to change his own plans on several occasions, when they proved to be ineffective or detrimental to his overall mission.[7]

The tradition's trajectory in the West points to discrete groups of devotees (including, by all means, male and female orders of celibacy) dedicated to the practices of *bhagavata dharma* situated harmoniously within a greater context both of its own lay membership and the normative economic, social, and legalistic structures of mainstream societies; ISKCON's attempt to set up an alternative infrastructure based on notions of a *varnashram* system in opposition to hegemonic society has failed. Such coexistence need not dilute the tradition's religious imperative to be morally mindful of the greater society and to work toward benevolent social change, but such efforts will likely be more successful when attempted in cooperation with existing social structures, rather than in competition with them. The essays in this volume suggest that a serious discussion on the merits of attempting to establish the so-called *varnashram dharma* as an objective of ISKCON, even for its own communities, rather than exclusively focusing on the cultivation of *bhagavata dharma*, is a priority for the western followers of Chaitanya Vaishnavism.

Such considerations will inevitably lead toward a further set of tensions that can already be glimpsed in the pages of this volume, namely that between fidelity to the perceived instructions of the guru, whose absoluteness, as Lorenz points out, was so stressed by Bhaktivedanta Swami, and the imperatives on the disciple of making the tradition relevant to modernity. As becomes clear from Swami Bhakti Bhavana Vishnu's paper, disobedience of the order of the guru is considered the most dangerous deviation a disciple can countenance. Thus, any proposals pertaining to adjustments, reconsiderations, or re-envisioning of the Chaitanya mission in the West risk potentially explosive repercussions from the "orthodoxy," if they remotely involve any conflict with the majority's understanding of Bhaktivedanta Swami's recorded statements. There are clear signs, pointed to in Conrad's and Collins's essays, that a new "Prabhupada lineage" seems to be emerging among certain areas of influence—not just in ISKCON, but (even more so) among *ritvik* supporters expelled or ostracized from the institution—a proxy "International Society for Prabhupada Consciousness," rather than for "Krishna Consciousness," wherein Bhaktivedanta Swami's status supersedes any other type of authority, including the scriptures of the lineage itself. Irrespective of any other issues raised by such absolutism, this move clearly has serious implications for the greater Chaitanya tradition's ability to move beyond nostalgic hankerings after ISKCON's quasi-mythic golden days of the 1960s and early 1970s, to adapt itself to the fluid requirements of time and place in the real world, as any religion must do if it is to endure.

We should also note opposite trends that have surfaced outside the jurisdiction of ISKCON, where voices have been raised by some of Bhaktivedanta Swami's seniormost but now disaffiliated disciples (e.g., the former Jagadish, quoted in Lorenz), inclined to trace ISKCON's problems back to policies enacted by Bhaktivedanta Swami himself. The most recent prominent voice in this regard has been that of one of the original 11 zonal *acharyas*, the former GBC for Russia and Eastern Europe, erstwhile chief financier of the ISKCON world headquarters city project in Mayapur, West Bengal, and most powerful man in ISKCON throughout the 1990s. Although such criticisms are not tolerated by the institution and thus can only surface among disenfranchised ex-members, it can hardly be an easy task for even the most stalwart disciple to ignore, for example, the relationship between Bhaktivedanta Swami's written statements about women and the sexist attitudes imbibed by many of his followers. While, as noted by both Knott and Muster, Bhaktivedanta Swami's female disciples often vouch for his affectionate dealings with them in person, it is his written statements that remain for posterity. Nor can it be a comfortable duty for his followers to justify the comments he made about *shudras* or "Negroes," as compiled by Lorenz, to anyone schooled in the egalitarian ethos of the modern day.

One can, of course, account for these statements by noting that such attitudes would not be untypical for Bhaktivedanta Swami as an orthodox Hindu *sannyasi* born in a traditional high-caste Bengali household at the turn of the twentieth century, where and when such views might have been more normative. However, such contextualization immediately problematizes simplistic notions of the absolute nature of the guru. Indeed, Herzig and Valpey implicitly suggest stirrings in this direction among elements of the intelligentsia of ISKCON itself. Their essay, all the more significant given the constraints within which such individuals operate, suggests that influential elements within the organization are willing to promote a rationalized, liberal, egalitarian ethic relevant to the real-life exigencies of this day and age. These authors' appeal to reinvent the tradition and adapt it to context and circumstance—as Bhaktivedanta Swami himself did in coming to western shores, and as he continued to do as his own perceptions changed and events dictated—evidences a significant development in attitude, although the extent to which ISKCON as a body will tolerate the development of a liberal progressive element within its own ranks, as opposed to outside the margins of its jurisdiction, remains to be seen. We can only lament the untimely demise of Herzig (Tamal Krishna Maharaja) shortly after his submission of his essay to this volume.

There are other developments that also bode well for ISKCON: the Center for Vaishnava and Hindu Studies affiliated with Oxford University provides devotees with unique opportunities for engaging in interreligious dialogue, submitting their own tradition to critical scrutiny and opening themselves to the academic and intellectual currents of the day. The *ISKCON Communications Journal* also willingly provides a widely distributed forum for insider intellectuals and outsider academics to voice their critiques and concerns over the tradition's trajectory. *The Journal of Vaishnava Studies*, founded by Steven Rosen, a contributor to this volume, although not an ISKCON product as such, shows that a believer may sponsor and sustain a truly nonpartisan enterprise that highlights contemporary research by major scholars not only of the Chaitanya tradition but also of Vaishnavism in general.

On a more humanistic level, Wolf's essay acknowledges the beneficial deterrents to human rights abuses that accrue when an institution opens itself up to scrutiny from mainstream legal and social structures. The establishment of the Office for the Protection of Vaishnava Children and the organization Children of Krishna, which provides grants to help second-generation youth, as well as the creation of an ombudsman system to mediate grievances are also positive developments (unfortunately, it may be a case of too little too late, as noted by Wolfe; at the time of writing, at least a dozen U.S. temples are filing chapter 11 bankruptcy to protect themselves from the multimillion-dollar lawsuits filed by alumni of ISKCON's *gurukula* boarding schools[8]). Outside of ISKCON, other significant offshoot developments now reconnected with different lineal branches of the Chaitanya tradition are taking root: the Jiva Institute in Vrindavan, for example, is emerging as a center of learning where Krishna devotees from all around the world can directly study the seminal works of Chaitanya's Goswami followers, as well as other classical bodies of Sanskritic learning—an enterprise historically deemed suspect in ISKCON.[9]

It is certainly premature to write ISKCON's epitaph, or that of other manifestations of Chaitanya Vaishnavism in the West, but the ability of the tradition's followers to identify and preserve the essence of their religion and discard the extraneous trappings that have proved detrimental to its development will do much to determine the relevance of the tradition to the modern world. Indeed, the very fact that there exists a growing spectrum of participatory possibilities outside the jurisdiction of ISKCON suggests that Chaitanya Vaishnavism has established some broader roots in the West, and this can be viewed as a positive development that maximizes the chances of survival for the overall tradition.

If Chaitanya Vaishnavism can emerge from its crises of transplantation and institutionalization, as well as from the trauma of its present postcharismatic turmoil, it has a unique role to play among the various Hindu religious expressions that have flourished in the West, since it is the only representative of the prominent monotheistic sects of India to have attracted converts on a wide scale (most other expressions of Hinduism that have attracted western interest are representatives of monistic sects). All in all, the trajectory of the Hare Krishna movement provides fascinating multidisciplinary material from the perspective of the study of religion, and offers a unique glimpse at the formative stages of a religious tradition struggling to establish roots in a foreign environment.

NOTES

1. With the exception of a much debated reference in the Chandogya Upanishad 3.17.
2. See the introduction of Edwin Bryant, *Krishna, the Beautiful Legend of God: The Srimad Bhagavata Purana Book X* (London: Penguin, 2003), for discussion and further references.
3. Indeed, the text makes a point of stressing that even Krishna's enemies attained liberation even though their minds were absorbed in him in enmity and hatred (e.g., X.66.24; X.87.23).

4. The ISKCON *sannyasa* ministry puts the figure at approximately 60 percent. Given this track record, it might be relevant to note that even in traditional Hindu sources, the taking of *sannyasa* is forbidden for this day and age (e.g., *Brahma Vaivarta Purana, Krishna Janma Khanda* 185.180).

5. The *Bhagavata Purana* (XI.29.21) gives a novel meaning to the traditional concept of *dharma*, normally understood as social and familial duty, by construing it in the context of *bhakti* as denoting unalloyed devotion and service to Krishna, hence *bhagavata dharma*.

6. See, in this regard, Ravindra Svarupa Dasa, "ISKCON and Varnashrama-Dharma: A Mission Unfulfilled," *ISKCON Communications Journal* 7 (1) (1999): 35–44.

7. Ibid.

8. Anuttama Das, ISKCON Communications International, press release, 6 February 2002.

9. Many of these original writings, in both Sanskrit and Bengali, are also available on a Web site created by Brzezinski and Delmonico (http://www.granthamandira.org/).

GLOSSARY OF SANSKRIT TERMS
(AS UNDERSTOOD IN ISKCON)

acharya—founder guru of a religious institution

achintya—inconceivable

adhikara—authority

advaita Vedanta—nondualist school of Vedanta philosophy

aishvarya—the opulence and power of God

arati—public worship of the deity in a temple

archanam—ritualistic worship of the deity

ashram—monastic community

avatara—incarnation of God

babaji—ascetic

bhadra loka—westernized, educated, urban class in nineteenth-century Bengal

Bhagavad Gita—Sanskrit text, Krishna's instruction to Arjuna

Bhagavan—term for God

Bhagavata Purana—Sanskrit text featuring the life of Krishna

bhakta—devotee

bhakti—the yoga path of devotion

Bhaktisiddhanta Maharaja—Bhaktivedanta Swami's guru

Bhaktivedanta Swami—founder of ISKCON

bheda—difference (between the soul and God in philosophical texts)

brahmacari—celibate student; first stage in life

brahman—name for the absolute truth in philosophical texts

brahmana—member of priestly and intellectual caste

Chaitanya Charitamrita—hagiography of Chaitanya

Chaitanya Mahaprabhu—sixteenth-century mystic, considered by his followers to be an incarnation of Krishna

Chaitanya Vaishnavism—the school of Vaishnavism stemming from Chaitanya Mahaprabhu, a.k.a. Gaudiya Vaishnavism

chaturvarnya—four castes or social occupations of the Vedic social system *chit*—consciousness

daivi varnashrama dharma—Vaishnava version of *caturvarnya*

darshana—beholding the deity in the temple

dasya—servitude, one of the five *rasa*s

devata—minor god, celestial being

Devi—the Goddess

dharma—socioreligious duty

diksha—initiation

dvaita—dualistic school of Vedanta philosophy

garbhadhana-samskara—life-cycle rites

Gaudiya *Math*—religious institution founded by Bhaktisiddhanta Swami

Gaudiya Vaishnavism—the school of Vaishnavism stemming from Chaitanya Mahaprabhu, a.k.a. Chaitanya Vaishnavism

GBC (Governing Board Commission)—ISKCON's ultimate managing authority

gopa—cowherd boy

gopi—cowherd maiden

grihastha—householder; the second stage in life

guna—one of the three modes or influences that underpin all reality

guru parampara—lineage of spiritual teachers

gurukula—the house of the guru; traditional religious school for young students

harinama—chanting devotional names publicly

hladini (shakti)—Krishna's pleasure potency

Ishvara—God

ISKCON—International Society for Krishna Consciousness; the Hare Krishna movement

japa—devotional repetition of mantras in a meditative mood

jivatma—the embodied soul

jnana—knowledge

kali yuga—present and fourth world age

kama—desire, lust

kanishtha adhikara—neophyte devotee

karmi—nondevotee who works for personal gain (in ISKCON parlance)

kirtana—chanting of devotional mantras, usually communal

Krishna—incarnation of God; supreme godhead for the Chaitanya sect

kshatriya—member of warrior caste

Lakshmi—Goddess of Fortune

lila—divine pastimes of the deity

madhurya—conjugal relationship between devotee and Krishna, in the Chaitanya sect

Madhya lila—section of the *Chaitanya Charitamrita*

Mahabharata—epic describing the saga of the Pandava brothers

mahamantra—the Hare Krishna mantra

mangala-arati—predawn morning worship in the temple

marga—spiritual path

math—monastic institution

moksha—liberation from the cycle of birth and death

murti—deity

namahatta—organized propagation of chanting the Krishna mantra

nirguna brahman—impersonal aspect of the absolute truth

pancha tattva—Chaitanya and his four principal associates

Pancharatra—texts outlining details of ritualistic worship

pandita—scholar

paramatman—personal manifestation of Krishna in the heart of all creatures (according to Vaishnava theology)

parampara—lineage of gurus

pramana—epistemology

prasadam—sanctified food offered to the deity and then distributed to the public

prema—love

puja—ritualistic worship of a deity

pujari—priest performing worship in a temple

purnavatara—full (as opposed to partial) incarnation of godhead

purusha—soul; also name of supreme being in certain texts

Purusha sukta—Rigvedic hymn to the supreme being

raganuga bhakti—yoga path of spontaneous (rather than rule-bound) devotion

rasa—one of five devotional modes of interacting with God in the Chaitanya tradition: conjugal, parental, friendship, servitude, neutral

rasalila—Krishna's circle dance with the *gopis*

rasika—one who relishes *rasa*

Rig-Veda—oldest Vedic text; consists of hymns of supplication to gods

ritvik—officiating priest initiating on behalf of the guru (in ISKCON parlance)

sadhana—spiritual practice

sadhu sanga—association of saintly people

sampradaya—lineage of gurus

samsara—cycle of birth and death

sanatana dharma—"eternal religion"; traditional Hinduism

Sandarbhas—group of six philosophical texts written in the sixteenth century by Jiva Goswami

sankirtana—public chanting of Krishna mantra in the Chaitanya tradition

sannyasa—renunciation; the fourth stage of life

sannyasi—one who has entered the order of *sannyasa*

sat—being; eternity

seva—service, usually to a deity or religious institution

shabda—revealed scripture; divine sound

shabda brahman—absolute truth in the form of sound

shakti—power of the deity

shaktyavesha—spiritual being invested with power

shastra—sacred scripture

shishya—disciple

shringara—conjugal *rasa*, a.k.a. *madhurya*

shruti—revealed scripture

shudra—member of the laborer or artisan caste

six Goswamis—scholarly followers of Chaitanya who established the canon for the Chaitanya sect

stri dharma—women's socioreligious duties

tridanda sannyasa—Vaishnava *sannyasa*

Upanishads—oldest Hindu philosophical texts

uttama adhikari—advanced Vaishnava devotee

Vaikuntha—divine realm; abode of Vishnu

Vaishnava—follower of Vishnu

vaishnava aparadha—offense against a Vaishnava

vaishya—member of the merchant caste

varnashrama/varnashramadharma—socioreligious division of labor in ancient India

vatsalya—parental relationship between the devotee and Krishna in the Chaitanya sect

vidhi marga—bhakti yoga path of rule-bound (rather than spontaneous) devotion

vishishtadvaita—monotheistic school of Vedanta philosophy

Vishnu—the supreme godhead in Vaishnavism; a manifestation of Krishna for the Chaitanya sect

vyasasana—seat of guru

yajna—sacrifice to the divine

yoga—any spiritual path leading to union with the divine

yuga—one of four world ages

yuga dharma—religious process for the age; in ISKCON, the chanting of the Hare Krishna mantra for the present age

yugavatara—incarnation according to each age

zonal *acarya* **(guru) system**—onetime system in ISKCON wherein prospective disciples were directed toward initiating gurus appointed according to geographical location

INDEX

DATE DUE

S